GLOBAL POLITICAL ECONOMY

GLOBAL POLITICAL ECONOMY: THEORY AND PRACTICE

Second Edition

Theodore H. Cohn
Simon Fraser University

Longman

New York   San Francisco   Boston
London   Toronto   Sydney   Tokyo   Singapore   Madrid
Mexico City   Munich   Paris   Cape Town   Hong Kong   Montreal

Vice President and Publisher: Priscilla McGeehon
Executive Editor: Eric Stano
Associate Editor: Anita Castro
Senior Marketing Manager: Megan Galvin-Fak
Media Supplements Editor: Patrick McCarthy
Production Manager: Joseph Vella
Project Coordination, Text Design, and Electronic Page Makeup: Shepherd, Inc.
Cover Design Manager: John Callahan
Cover Designer: Maria Illardi
Cover Illustration: Digital Imagery © 2002 PhotoDisc, Inc.
Manufacturing Buyer: Dennis J. Para
Printer and Binder: Maple-Vail Book Manufacturing Group
Cover Printer: Coral Graphics Services

Library of Congress Cataloging-in-Publication Data

Cohn, Theodore H., 1940–
    Global political economy : theory and practice / Theodore H. Cohn.—2nd ed.
      p. cm.
    Includes bibliographical references and index.
    ISBN 0-321-08873-5 (alk. paper)
    1. International economic relations. 2. International trade. 3. International finance.
  I. Title
  HF1359.C654 2002
  337—dc21

                            2002016066

Please visit our website at http://www.ablongman.com

ISBN 0-321-08873-5

1 2 3 4 5 6 7 8 9 10—MA—05 04 03 02

Contents

Preface

This book introduces undergraduate students and beginning graduate students to the complex and important issues of global political economy. I wrote the book because of a long-held conviction that it is only possible for students to understand the broader implications of international political economy (IPE) issues by examining them in a theoretical context. Without the organizing framework of theory, it is difficult to make sense of the growing body of IPE facts and statistics and to interpret events in the global political economy. Thus, the text takes a comprehensive approach to the study of IPE, focusing on both theory and practice. To help in drawing connections between the theory and the substantive issues, the book focuses on three major themes or challenges: globalization, North-North relations (among the developed countries), and North-South relations (among the developed countries of the North and the developing countries of the South). Considerable space is also devoted to the emerging centrally planned economies of the former Soviet bloc and Soviet Union, which are becoming increasingly integrated in the capitalist global political economy.

Although a major focus of the text is globalization, I do *not* claim that globalization is leading to some sort of a world society or world government. Indeed, considerable space is devoted to the increasing importance of regional blocs and organizations such as the European Union, the North American Free Trade Agreement, and Mercosur, and Chapter 9 is devoted to the subject of regionalism. Furthermore, there is discussion throughout the text of the interconnections between domestic and international issues both globally and regionally. These domestic-international interactions are generally more important in the study of IPE than in the study of security issues.

CHANGES IN THE SECOND EDITION

The second edition of this book is revised and updated throughout. Some of the most important changes including the following:

- The second edition contains an assessment of the role of civil society groups, and there is some discussion of the theoretical approaches (such as Gramscian analysis) to civil society. The substantive chapters discuss the response of civil society groups to the management of international trade, foreign debt, international development, and foreign investment issues.

- Chapter 2 contains a more detailed discussion of global economic relations before World War II to provide the student with more historical background.
- Chapter 6 on international monetary relations includes a substantially expanded and updated discussion of European monetary relations, dollarization and the changing role of the U.S. dollar, and monetary uncertainty in East Asia.
- Chapter 7 on foreign debt discusses a number of newer developments and policies, such as the Heavily-Indebted Poor Countries Initiative, and provides more analysis of debt problems in Eastern Europe and the former Soviet Union countries.
- Chapter 8 on global trade relations provides considerable detail on the first seven years of experience with the World Trade Organization and on the negotiations leading to the accession of China to the World Trade Organization.
- Some of the most extensive revisions in the book are in Chapter 9 on regionalism and the global trade regime. The section on North America in the first edition has been expanded and is now entitled the "Western Hemisphere." This section discusses the North American Free Trade Agreement, the Mercosur (or Southern Common Market Treaty), and the negotiations to form a Free Trade Area of the Americas. The sections on Europe and Japan/China/East Asia are also substantially expanded and updated.
- Chapter 10 on multinational corporations has been extensively revised. The section on attempts to develop a regime for foreign direct investment contains expanded discussions of bilateral investment treaties and regional approaches, and an extensive discussion of the attempt by the Organization for Economic Cooperation and Development to form a multilateral agreement on investment. The chapter also introduces a new section on the interaction of business firms with nongovernmental organizations.
- As with Chapter 9, Chapter 11 on international development is one of the most extensively revised chapters. The discussion of development strategies is substantially updated to include a discussion of the World Bank's attempts to alter its approach to development since 1995. Updated discussions are also provided on development experiences in East Asia, sub-Saharan Africa, and Latin America.

In addition to changes in the substantive chapters, the book contains revised and updated discussions of theory and of the relationship of theory to practice.

ACKNOWLEDGMENTS

I am grateful for the comments, advice, and support of a number of individuals in writing and revising this book. First, I want to thank Mark Zacher of the University of British Columbia and Michael Webb of the University of Victoria for providing helpful advice and comments on numerous occasions with regard to the organization and content of the first edition of the text. I would also like to thank Benjamin Cohen of the

University of California, Santa Barbara, for his advice on monetary issues for the second edition. I want to recognize the contribution the late Harold K. Jacobson of the University of Michigan has made to my studies. The emphasis of this IPE text on international institutions and governance owes a great deal to the interest I developed in the subject years ago when Professor Jacobson was my Ph.D. supervisor. I am indebted to the following external reviewers for providing useful comments that were extremely helpful in making revisions. Some of these reviewers provided comments for the first edition, and others for the second edition: Sherry L. Bennett, Rice University; Vicki Birchfield, Georgia Institute of Technology, Kurt Burch, University of Delaware; Jeffrey Cason, Middlebury College; Vincent Ferraro, Mount Holyoke College; David N. Gibbs, University of Arizona; Vicki L. Golich, California State University, San Marcos; Robert Griffiths, University of North Carolina at Greensboro; Beverly G. Hawk, University of Alabama at Birmingham; Michael J. Hiscox, University of California, San Diego; Matthias Kaelberer, University of Northern Iowa; Quan Li, Florida State University; Thomas Oatley, University of North Carolina at Chapel Hill; Howard Richards, Earlham College; David E. Spiro, University of Arizona; and Kenneth P. Thomas, University of Missouri, St. Louis. In addition, thanks are due to several colleagues at Simon Fraser University with whom I discussed various aspects of the text, including Stephen McBride, Michael Howlett, Tsuyoshi Kawasaki, James Busumtwi-Sam, and Anil Hira.

The competent editorial staff at Longman Publishers has given active support to this book. For the first edition, I especially want to thank Jennie Errickson and Ellen MacElree for the time and effort they put into the project. For the second edition, I greatly appreciate the careful attention Anita Castro and Jeff Stiles (of Shepherd, Inc.) have given to ensure that the revisions were included in a timely and careful manner. I also appreciate the assistance of others at Longman, and would especially like to thank Eric Stano and Megan Galvin-Fak. Finally, I would like to thank the copy editors for the careful work they did for both editions of the text.

My acknowledgments would not be complete without mentioning the important role my students have played over the years in asking insightful questions, raising important issues, and giving me feedback as to what aspects of IPE they found clear or confusing. My sons Daniel and Frank also gave me assistance in a variety of areas, and I want to thank them for their patience with my extended working hours. Finally, I am dedicating this book to my wife Shirley, for her caring advice, support, and encouragement.

P A R T   I

INTRODUCTION AND OVERVIEW

The field of international relations traditionally focused primarily on the study of security issues and largely ignored economic issues, but it has become increasingly evident that the political, economic, and social aspects of international relations are closely intertwined. As a result, *international political economy* (IPE) has emerged as an important area of study in international relations. Chapter 1 provides answers to some basic questions such as "What is IPE?" and "Why is IPE a relatively new area of study?" It then discusses the basic themes of this book and introduces the main theoretical perspectives in the field. Chapter 2 begins with a brief historical discussion of the development of the international economy from the fifteenth century to World War II. Most of the chapter then provides a general overview of the world economy since World War II, with particular emphasis on the institutions developed to manage international economic relations.

CHAPTER 1

Introduction

In July 1944, while World War II was still raging in Europe and the Pacific, delegates from 44 countries held a conference in the small resort town of Bretton Woods, New Hampshire, to reach a broad-ranging agreement for economic cooperation. The **Bretton Woods system** that emerged from the conference helped to shape international economic relations in the postwar era. After World War II, however, the emergence of the Cold War between the United States and the Soviet Union became the central concern of Western policymakers, and international economic issues often seemed to be of lesser priority. Thus, postwar international relations scholars placed primary emphasis in their research on security issues related to the Cold War, or "high politics." International economic issues, by contrast, were considered to be relatively nonpolitical and were relegated to the area of "low politics." As this book will discuss, by the late 1960s and early 1970s it became increasingly evident to both policymakers and academics that they had underestimated the political importance of international economic issues. Indeed, some of the most contentious international issues in the 1970s were both economic and political by nature. It was at about this time that IPE, which examines the interaction among the political, economic, and social aspects of international relations, emerged as an important field of study. A few examples of major issues and events clearly demonstrate how international politics and economics are often closely intertwined.

The Persian Gulf War   In August 1990, Iraq invaded its much smaller neighbor Kuwait and was in a position to control about one-fifth of the oil production of the Organization of Petroleum Exporting Countries (OPEC). The Western industrial states and Japan were concerned not only about the strategic implications of the Iraqi invasion, but also about the possible economic effects in view of their high degree of dependence on Middle East oil imports. When Iraq failed to withdraw from Kuwait by a specified date, the United Nations Security Council endorsed the use of force by a U.S.-led military coalition against Iraq. Because one Communist regime after another in Eastern Europe had disintegrated in 1989 and the Soviet Union itself was on the verge of dissolution, the United States was able to engage in military actions against Iraq without concerns about any counteraction from the Soviets. Nevertheless, the American *economic* position was no longer as predominant as it had been in the 1950s and 1960s. The United States therefore insisted that Japan, Germany, Saudi Arabia, and Kuwait provide a substantial amount of funding to help finance the Gulf War effort (Japan and Germany did not participate in the military operations). A close relationship exists between economic "wealth" and political "power" internationally, and the cost-sharing plan agreed to in the Gulf War could serve as a model for some future U.S.-led military operations.

European Integration   In 1951, six Western European countries (France, West Germany, Italy, Belgium, the Netherlands, and Luxembourg) joined together to form the European Coal and Steel Community (ECSC), which was designed to coordinate the policies of member states and reduce their trade barriers in coal and steel. Although the ECSC was designed to promote *economic* integration of the member countries' coal and steel resources, the reasons for its formation in 1951 were primarily *political*. The French foreign minister, Robert Schuman, had two major purposes in developing the plan for the ECSC: first, to meet U.S. demands that West Germany be rebuilt to help deter any aggression by the Soviet Union, and second, to allay French domestic fears of renewed aggression by a rearmed Germany. Over the centuries, Germany and France had repeatedly fought over access to coal and steel resources in border areas such as Alsace-Lorraine. It was therefore felt that a sharing of coal and steel resources in the ECSC would help rebuild Germany and also make future wars between France and Germany virtually impossible. Thus, the preamble to the ECSC treaty states that the member countries wish "to create, by establishing an economic community, the basis for a broader and deeper community among peoples long divided by bloody conflicts."[1]

The ECSC was successful in integrating the coal and steel resources of the six member states, and the members agreed to extend it to a full-scale regional integration agreement with the formation of the European Economic Community (EC) in 1957. Today, this community—which is now called the **European Union (EU)**—has 15 full members and a large number of associate member states. One of the original purposes of economic integration in Europe—to end armed hostilities and war between France and Germany—has certainly been achieved.

World Bank Loans to Third World Countries   This book will show that politics and economics often are inextricably linked in the decision making of the major international economic organizations. Such linkages are evident in the lending activities of the *World Bank*, which is the largest source of **multilateral** development finance for Third World countries (also called economically less developed countries or LDCs). The *Articles of Agreement* of the World Bank state that the bank "shall not interfere in the political affairs of any member" and that "only economic considerations shall be relevant" to its lending decisions.[2] Many analysts argue, however, that the bank's loans are inevitably based on political as well as economic considerations. For example, the World Bank has had a clear preference for lending to countries that emphasize private enterprise, and this preference became far more pronounced after the Third World foreign debt crisis in the 1980s (the debt crisis is discussed in Chapter 7). Although bank officials argue that those countries with a private market orientation are more likely to be economically efficient, the bank's preference for private enterprise is also based on the political and ideological leanings of its most powerful members—the advanced industrial states. In the 1950s to 1970s, the bank gave some support to a Third

World development strategy that combined state action with private entrepreneurship, and it provided finance for some **infrastructure** projects such as roads, railways, airports, water systems, and public utilities that involved state-owned corporations. Even in these early years, however, the bank showed a definite preference for private enterprise, and one noted observer of the global political economy has written that Eugene Black, World Bank president from 1949 to 1962, was "inclined to talk as if there were some kind of exclusive relationship between political freedom and private enterprise, and as if he believed that his main task is therefore to defend the only true economic faith throughout the world."[3]

In the 1980s the bank followed such national leaders as British Prime Minister Margaret Thatcher and U.S. President Ronald Reagan in a shift to the Right, and was far more inclined to view governments and public enterprise as hindrances to growth. Thus, World Bank structural adjustment loans (SALs) to indebted Third World countries in the 1980s and 1990s have been linked with the agreement of these countries to institute policies promoting privatization, deregulation, and trade liberalization. In sum, international politics and international economics have been so intertwined in the area of Third World development policy that the World Bank has been both unwilling and unable to fully follow the directive of its Articles of Agreements that its loans should be based solely on economic considerations.

The Boeing Company's Merger with McDonnell Douglas Corporation   This book demonstrates that the economic activities of private actors such as international banks and multinational corporations often have major political implications. A prime example of such political-economic linkages is evident in the decision of two American aircraft companies—Boeing and McDonnell Douglas—to merge their operations in early 1997. When the merger proposal was first announced, the EU swiftly raised objections and threatened to retaliate against Boeing, which was based in Seattle, Washington (a decision was later made to move Boeing headquarters to Chicago, Illinois). The EU's concerns stemmed largely from the fact that Boeing had a much larger market share for commercial aircraft than Europe's Airbus Consortium. The Europeans feared that spillovers as a result of the McDonnell Douglas Corporation's experience with defense production, and an increase in defense-related public funding for research and development would enable Boeing to increase its domination of the civil aircraft business. Furthermore, the Europeans objected to the 20-year contracts with exclusive-supplier provisions that Boeing signed with three U.S. airlines—Delta, American, and Continental. Although the merger was approved by the U.S. Federal Trade Commission and supported by the White House, Boeing had to be concerned about European retaliation. The Europeans could not block a merger between two U.S. companies, but they threatened to impose fines for violations of their competition rules that would make it difficult for Boeing to operate in Europe. They also threatened to withdraw from the 1992 U.S.-EU bilateral civil aircraft agreement, which was aimed at limiting direct and indirect subsidies in the aircraft sector. To avoid these actions, Boeing eventually agreed not to enforce the exclusive-supplier provisions of its agreements with the three U.S. airlines, to supply information to the EU about the indirect subsidies it gained from government-sponsored research, and to provide some benefits to European companies.

The United States has initiated similar clashes with Europe over civil airlines issues. Indeed, after years of bitter disputes over European government subsidies to
Airbus, which contributed to its growing sales vis-à-vis Boeing, the United States pressured the Europeans to sign an agreement in 1992 limiting the Airbus subsidies. Almost 10 years later in 2001, the United States was expressing strong concerns about
Airbus's increasing market share and about financing by EU governments for a new
Airbus superjumbo jet that would compete directly with Boeing's 747. The civil airline
industry has been described as being "the most politicized in the world—apart from
the defense industry," with which it is closely tied.[4] However, as global competition increases in a wide range of economic areas, disputes such as those involving Boeing and
Airbus will become more frequent. Because governments often feel a stake in the welfare of their domestically based multinational corporations (MNCs), disputes over
economic market share often become highly politicized.

The "Nixon Economic Shocks"   This book shows that economics and politics are
closely intertwined in foreign policymaking. On August 15, 1971, President Richard
Nixon responded to growing U.S. balance of payments deficits by suspending the convertibility of the U.S. dollar into gold, and imposing a ten percent surcharge on all dutiable imports. These "Nixon shocks" will be explained fully later in this book, in the
chapters on monetary and trade relations. What is of interest here is the reaction of
Henry Kissinger, who was President Nixon's national security adviser (and later secretary of state), to the crisis with Europe and Japan surrounding the "Nixon shocks."
Kissinger later wrote in his memoirs:

> My own participation in the economic deliberations during this period was peripheral.
> From the start I had not expected to play a major role in international economics,
> which—to put it mildly—had not been a central field of study for me. Only later did I
> learn that the key economic policy decisions are not technical but political. At first I
> thought that I had enough on my hands keeping watch on the State and Defense De-
> partments and the Central Intelligence Agency without also taking on Treasury, Com-
> merce, and Agriculture. I took a crash "tutorial" from Professor Richard N. Cooper of
> Yale University to learn the rudiments of the subject. I appointed the brilliant econo-
> mists Fred Bergsten and Robert Hormats to my staff.[5]

The foregoing examples demonstrate that politics and economics are often inextricably linked in the real world of international relations. Before discussing the purposes
and themes of this book, we need to address two important questions: What is IPE?
And why is IPE a relatively new area of study?

WHAT IS INTERNATIONAL POLITICAL ECONOMY?

As a field of study that bridges the disciplines of politics and economics, IPE is concerned with the interaction between "the state" and "the market." The state and the
market, in turn, are associated with the (political) pursuit of power and the (economic)
pursuit of wealth. As the political component of IPE, a *state* is a sovereign territorial
unit with a government and a population. As the economic component, the **market** is

"the co-ordinating mechanism where the forces of supply and demand in an economy determine prices, output and methods of production via the automatic adjustment of price movements."[6]

An inherent tension often exists between the state and the market. The state is concerned with preserving national sovereignty and unity while the market is associated with economic openness and the breaking down of state barriers.[7] For example, the 1988 Canada-U.S. Free Trade Agreement (CUSFTA) extended the "geographic space" to include an open market between the two countries, but many Canadians feared that this expanded market posed a threat to Canadian sovereignty in some areas such as energy, foreign investment, and cultural industries. When CUSFTA was extended to form the **North American Free Trade Agreement (NAFTA)** in 1994, many Mexicans were concerned that NAFTA might encroach on their sovereignty in areas such as energy and agriculture. Although the United States is a much larger economy than its two North American neighbors, many Americans feared that NAFTA would lead to a loss of national control over such issues as employment and the environment.

Despite the inherent tensions between states and markets, they also often have a complementary and even symbiotic relationship. Domestically, states establish rules to protect private property rights and to provide infrastructure such as transportation and communications facilities required for market transactions. Internationally, states join in agreements and form organizations to promote economic openness and stability. Furthermore, there is often a close relationship between a state's wealth and market size on the one hand and its military and political power on the other. As interdependence has increased, states have been drawn more closely into the competitive forces of the world economy. Thus, states today are sometimes called *competition states* because they are closely involved in supporting research and development in high-technology sectors, in restructuring industry, and in deregulating financial markets.[8] The impressive economic growth rates of some states seem to be closely related to their success in fostering a symbiotic relationship with the competitive marketplace. As we will discuss, Japan and the newly industrializing economies (NIEs) of East Asia (Hong Kong, Singapore, South Korea, and Taiwan) were especially successful in fostering such state-market relationships from the 1960s to the 1980s.

Although state-market interactions continue to be the core issue in the study of IPE, we are also concerned with other types of organizational relationships. Primary among these is the interaction between states and MNCs—also referred to as transnational corporations. The MNC is the main nonstate actor with which the state must contend today. Indeed, the 600 largest MNCs now each benefit from worldwide sales of more than $1 billion, and together they produce more than 25 percent of world gross domestic product; the 350 largest corporations account for about 40 percent of world trade. As is the case with states and markets, there is an inherent tension between the state and the MNC, but they can also have a complementary and cooperative relationship.

The traditional view of the MNC is that it is closely linked with the "home" state where its headquarters are located. Although the MNC opens foreign branch plants in "host" countries, its main financial, and research and development activities remain firmly planted in the home country. The directors and shareholders in the home country also retain primary responsibility for management of the MNC's foreign operations. From this perspective, the home state is in a more powerful position than its

MNCs, because it provides the basic environment and legal structure within which its MNCs must function. However, this traditional model has been supplemented by other models in which the host country gains more control over its MNC branch plant operations, and in which the MNC extricates itself from control by any single state. This latter type is sometimes referred to as a "geocentric" or "stateless" corporation, because its ownership and board of directors become internationalized. Some MNCs follow a deliberate strategy of internationalizing their operations to increase their freedom of operation. Although stateless corporations have to take different national markets into account in their production and marketing strategies, they are no longer beholden to any single country. As discussed in Chapter 10, IPE scholars differ over the importance they attach to these various models of the MNC-state relationship.[9]

Whether one focuses on state-market, state-MNC, or power-wealth interactions, there is general agreement that the field of IPE is interdisciplinary in nature. It draws on contributions from political scientists, economists, sociologists, anthropologists, historians, and geographers. IPE theorists also seek to overcome the limitations imposed by the current disciplinary boundaries. On the one hand, they criticize some economists for **economism**—that is, for overestimating the importance of the economic sphere and for underestimating the importance and autonomy of the political sphere. On the other hand, IPE theorists accuse some political scientists of "politicism"—that is, for devoting too much attention to politics and the exercise of power and too little attention to the impact of economic structures and processes on political relationships.[10]

The challenge of engaging in interdisciplinary study is obviously magnified when we examine political economy at the international level. How does one develop an IPE theory that examines international influences and that accounts for the multitude of social, cultural, economic, political, and developmental variations across nation-states? Furthermore, IPE scholars find it more essential than security specialists to focus on the linkages between international and domestic politics. Foreign policy and defense officials normally have considerable leeway in dealing with security matters because domestic groups and individuals are generally willing to leave decision making on these issues to the government experts. In contrast, domestic groups often see a close relationship between their own economic welfare and international economic issues such as trade and foreign investment, and they therefore demand a greater role in government decision making on these issues. Thus, "scholars and practitioners alike have begun to understand that effective international economic cooperation depends not only on the external interests and actions of states, but on their ability to manage, channel, or circumvent domestic political pressures as well."[11] IPE scholars have the daunting tasks of focusing on domestic as well as international interactions and of crossing the boundaries between a number of social science disciplines.

Why Is IPE a Relatively New Area of Study?

The relative newness of international political economy as an academic area of study is ironic, not only because of the close interaction between politics and economics, but also because awareness of these linkages extends back to ancient times. Indeed,

Thucydides (471–400 B.C.), who has often been described as the founder of international relations, demonstrated an acute awareness of the linkages between power and wealth. In his *History of the Peloponnesian War* dealing with conflict among the Greek city-states, Thucydides wrote that "war is a matter not so much of arms as of money, which makes arms of use."[12] Our earlier discussion of the cost-sharing arrangements in the 1990s Persian Gulf War demonstrates that Thucydides' work continues to be relevant. Aristotle (384–322 B.C.) also demonstrated a sensitivity to political-economic interconnections, and he in fact subsumed economics under the study of politics.[13]

Despite this early awareness of the linkages between politics and economics, several factors led to the tendency in modern times to view them as distinct areas of study: the influence of the liberal school of thought, the "hierarchy" of international concerns after World War II, and the organization of disciplines in universities. As discussed in Chapter 4, liberal-economic theorists such as Adam Smith (1723–90) considered economic and political matters to be largely separable. In Smith's view, economic activity operates under a naturally harmonious system of laws, whereas politics does not obey natural laws and is not harmonious. As a result, Smith is often associated with calls for "laissez-faire" capitalism, in which the economic system functions best with minimal interference from the government. The liberal tendency to view politics as separable from economics, and to believe that the state should have a minimal role in operation of the market, contributed to a turning away from the study of political economy.

In the post–World War II period, the most pressing international concerns were in the security area. The rapid emergence of the Cold War led scholars to view the questions of war and peace as the truly important ones, or "high politics." Postwar international economic relations, by contrast, were marked by a large degree of stability and cooperation under U.S. leadership, and scholars therefore viewed international economic matters as being outside the realm of high diplomacy, or as "low politics."[14] International relations specialists in the postwar period therefore accepted the liberal dictum that politics was separable from economics, but one could say that they "turned Adam Smith on his head," because they gave clear priority to political security over economic issues. A perusal of many international politics texts dating from the 1950s to the 1970s and even later clearly demonstrates the lack of attention given to political-economic interactions.[15]

Beginning in the late 1960s and early 1970s, several factors contributed to a reversal of these trends and to a new interest in IPE among both policymakers and academics. On the one hand, détente between the United States and the Soviet Union ushered in a period of decreased tension and concern about global security matters. On the other hand, the relative decline of U.S. economic power, combined with economic threats resulting from such events as the OPEC oil price increases in the 1970s and the Third World foreign debt crisis in the 1980s heightened concerns about international economic stability. Thus, it was evident that international economic issues had become high politics and required urgent attention.

Since the mid-1970s, the North American academic community has made great strides in developing the field of IPE. Nevertheless, the social sciences in most universities continue to be organized in separate disciplines, with political science, economics, sociology, anthropology, and geography in separate departments. These disciplinary divisions in universities have considerable influence over "rewards, interactions, and the flow of thought itself."[16] It is evident that despite the obstacles posed by the inflexibility of academia, world events will make the study of IPE increasingly relevant. With the end of the Cold War, the advanced industrial states in the North, the Third World countries in the South, and the emerging economies in Eastern Europe and the former Soviet Union (FSU) are all directing much of their attention to economic problems.

It is also important to note, however, that ethnic conflicts since the end of the Cold War in areas such as the former Yugoslavia, Somalia, Rwanda, and the Middle East have led to terrible human suffering. The horrific attack on the World Trade Center in New York has also raised the specter of terrorism as a major global threat. These events have economic as well as security components, and while IPE and international security are now each important areas of study, "we should expect scholarship that links economics and security to become increasingly prominent in the post-Cold War . . . [international relations] literature."[17]

THE PURPOSE AND THEMES OF THIS BOOK

This book provides a comprehensive approach to the study of international political economy. Part II introduces the student to the main theoretical perspectives in the field, and Part III examines current issues in IPE in historical perspective relating to monetary and financial relations, foreign debt, foreign trade, foreign investment, and international development. It is possible to understand the broader implications of current IPE issues only by examining them in a theoretical context. The substantive chapters in Part III, on trade, monetary relations, and so forth, therefore direct the reader to the interaction between theory and practice. To help draw connections between the theory and the substantive issues, this book focuses on three major themes or challenges: globalization, North-North relations, and North-South relations.

Globalization

Globalization is a process that has two major aspects: the broadening and the deepening of interactions and interdependence among societies and states throughout the world. In regard to broadening, globalization extends linkages geographically to encompass virtually all major societies and states. Thus, events and policies adopted in one part of the world are likely to have a major impact on distant locations. In regard to deepening, globalization involves a marked increase in the frequency and intensity of interactions and interdependence among societies and states. Globalization is contributing to fundamental changes in the relationship between markets, states, and multinational corporations—the subject of international political economy. Although states have often adopted policies that promote it, globalization is basically an economic process with political consequences.[18] The chapters in Part III point to indications of globalization in various aspects of the political economy. For example, the *daily* volume of foreign exchange trading in currencies rose from about $1 billion in the mid-1970s to $1.2 trillion in the mid-1990s; foreign direct investment (FDI) flows reached $315 billion in 1995, nearly a sixfold increase over the 1981–85 level; and global trade grew twelvefold in the postwar period, amounting to more than $4 trillion a year by 1995.[19]

This book is concerned with both the causes and the effects of globalization. In terms of effects, we are particularly interested in the impact of globalization on interactions among states, between the state and the market, and between the state and MNCs. For example, state policies that were traditionally considered to be domestic now often have a significant impact on other states and on international business. Pressures have therefore increased to subject "domestic" factors such as competition policies, trade-distorting subsidies, and financial market activity to international regulation. MNCs are also demanding nondiscriminatory trade and investment rules so that they can operate without restrictions internationally, and these new rules could impose additional restrictions on the policymaking autonomy of nation-states.

Globalization is a controversial term, especially because some extreme globalizers claim that we are entering a "borderless world" in which MNCs are losing their national identities and distinct national economies are being subsumed under the global marketplace.[20] This book adopts a less extreme version of globalization in four respects. First, globalization is not a uniform process throughout the world. The effects of globalization are far more evident, for example, in major urban centers than they are in rural areas, on remote islands, and in extremely underdeveloped areas of the Third World. Second, globalization is *not* causing the state to wither away. Although autonomy in regard to implementing economic policies is eroding in some important respects, the state is also adopting some new and more complex functions to deal with a highly interdependent world. Furthermore, governments continue to have choices in how they respond to the forces of globalization. When domestic groups have appealed for assistance in dealing with global competitive pressures, some states have resorted to trade protectionism, other states have adopted industrial policies to promote competitiveness, and still others have permitted the market to function without interference.[21]

Third, globalization is *not* leading to some sort of world society or world government. Indeed, the forces of globalization can lead to fragmentation and conflict as well as to unity and cooperation. For example, some writers argue that the increase in global **competitiveness** is contributing to the formation of three economic blocs in the world, centered in Europe, North America, and Japan/East Asia. Opinions differ widely as to whether the relationship among these three blocs will become more cooperative or conflictual in nature. And fourth, interdependence and globalization are not unique to the present-day period. A survey of history shows that the internationalization of finance, trade, and production has fluctuated over time, and it is possible that international events could eventually reverse the current moves toward globalization. For example, before World War I there was a high degree of interdependence in trade, foreign investment, and other areas. In 17 industrial countries for which there are comparative data, exports as a share of **gross domestic product (GDP)** or total output averaged 12.9 percent in 1913, which is comparable to the 1993 level of 14.5 percent, and the migration of people around the world was more extensive in some earlier periods than it is today. The interdependent linkages of the nineteenth and early twentieth centuries were subsequently eroded during World War I, and in the interwar period these linkages virtually collapsed as a result of increased nationalism and the Great Depression. Only after World War II did global economic ties begin to increase again.[22]

Despite the historical changes in interdependence over time, globalization is more encompassing today than it was at any time in the past. With advances in technology, communications, and transportation, the activities of states are being internationalized to a degree not previously experienced. In communications, for example, the cost of an international telephone call fell by more than 90 percent from 1970 to 1990, telecommunications traffic increased by about 20 percent a year in the 1980s, and more than 50 million people were using the Internet by the late 1990s. Indeed, the spread of ideas through the media, television, videos, and the Internet seems to be contributing to the emergence of a global culture. In transportation, shipping costs fell by more than two-thirds between 1920 and 1990, and the operating costs per mile for the world's airlines fell by 60 percent from 1960 to 1990.[23] Global interdependence today is also qualitatively different from what it was in the past. Although a number of corporations globalized their activities in the nineteenth century, the role of the MNC in generating foreign direct investment, trade, and technology is a modern-day phenomenon. By 1988, there were about 19,000 MNCs, which accounted for 25 to 30 percent of the gross domestic product of all market economies and for 80 percent of the trade in managerial and technology skills.[24]

The geographic reach of the capitalist economic system is for the first time also encompassing virtually the entire globe, with LDCs becoming more actively involved in the global economy and the "emerging" centrally planned economies (CPEs) of Eastern Europe and the former Soviet Union liberalizing their economies since the demise of communism. Thus, for the first time, membership in the major international economic organizations such as the **International Monetary Fund (IMF),** the World Bank, and the **World Trade Organization (WTO)** is becoming truly global in scope.[25] This book examines the implications of these changes as well as the differing attitudes of theorists, government officials, and the broader public as to whether globalization is a positive or negative phenomenon. Regarding the public reaction to globalization, we discuss the dramatic increase in activism by **civil society** in recent years. The term "civil society" was an old idea that emphasized civic responsibility and community service by voluntary associations or nongovernmental organizations (NGOs), including caring for the poor and sick, and filling gaps in social services. Today, the term civil society not only refers to these operational functions, but also to the political advocacy functions of NGOs. In this book we emphasize the political advocacy functions and define civil society as "a broad collectivity of non-governmental, non-commercial" organizations outside of official circles pursuing "objectives that relate explicitly to reinforcing or altering existing rules, norms and/or deeper social structures."[26] Of particular interest are environmental, labor, women's, development, and human rights groups, as well as other social movements.

North-North Relations

The second theme of this book concerns the relationship among the advanced industrial states in the North. As globalization has increased, countries have found it more difficult to manage their economic affairs individually, and they have been inclined to seek regional and global solutions. The Northern states in Western Europe, North America, and Japan are the only countries with the wealth and power to look after international management of the global economy. Thus, the international management issue is primarily a North-North issue involving the advanced industrial states. This book discusses two factors that IPE scholars have focused on as contributing to international economic management: hegemony and international institutions.

Because of its combined economic and military power, the United States was the undisputed leader or *hegemon* in the early postwar period. One important measure of a country's economic power is its GDP, the total value of the goods and services produced by the country over a specified period—usually a year. Alternatively, some economists measure a country's total output in terms of its **gross national product (GNP).** The GNP is similar to the GDP except that the GDP is used more widely because it provides a better measure of economic activity within a country's borders. While the GDP includes all of the interest and profits that foreign individuals and companies earn in a country, it does *not* include the income that residents of the country earn abroad. The GNP is derived by adding the income residents of a country earn from foreign activity to the GDP, and subtracting the income foreigners earn from activity in the country. For example, the income that a U.S. resident earns in France is part of the U.S. GNP but not the U.S. GDP. On the other hand, this income is included in the French GDP but not the French GNP. In keeping with common usage, this book usually uses the term *GDP.* However, movements in the GDP and GNP normally do not differ greatly, and sometimes data are given in terms of a country's GNP.

Regardless of whether GDP or GNP is used as a measure, the United States was clearly the economic hegemon after World War II. Indeed, during the war the GDP of the United States increased by about 50 percent, whereas Western European countries lost one-quarter of their GDPs on the average and the economies of the Soviet Union and Japan were severely damaged. Thus, in 1950 the U.S. economy was 3 times the size of the Soviet Union's, 5 times the size of Britain's, and 20 times the size of Japan's. The Western European countries and Japan at this time were also highly dependent on U.S. aid and foreign investment for postwar reconstruction.[27]

In the 1950s and 1960s, the *relative* economic position of the United States vis-à-vis other advanced industrial states inevitably began to decline as Western Europe and Japan gradually recovered from the war. The extent of the U.S. decline and the possibilities for a renewal of U.S. predominance are matters of intense debate among IPE theorists. However, almost all would agree that U.S. power resources relative to those of other advanced industrial states have fallen since the end of World War II. For example, the U.S. dollar continued to be the top currency for international economic transactions, but the Japanese yen and German mark gained in importance, and the Euro emerged as a new currency for the EU countries; in 1971 the United States shifted from having balance-of-trade surpluses every year to having balance-of-trade deficits (i.e., imports greater than exports); the United States increasingly became a recipient as well as a source of foreign direct investment; and in 1989 Japan surpassed the United States for the first time as the largest single donor of development assistance to the Third World. This book examines the effects of the relative decline of U.S. economic hegemony on the management of the global economy. We are particularly interested in whether economic management has become more difficult and in how the nature of management has changed over time.

The second factor in global management of interest to us is the role of international institutions. Under U.S. and British leadership, three international economic organizations were established to help manage the global economy at the end of World War II: the IMF, the International Bank for Reconstruction and Development (IBRD or the World Bank), and the **General Agreement on Tariffs and Trade (GATT).** Because the advanced industrial states have been the dominant powers influencing the policies of these organizations, the institutional management of the global economy has been largely a North-North issue. This book examines the role of these institutions in the management (or mismanagement) of the international political economy.

Although the rich Northern states have often acted in concert to look after global economic management, there are also significant differences and divisions among these states. For example, with the demise of the Cold War between the United States and the Soviet Union and the relative decline of U.S. economic hegemony, three major economic blocs have emerged: in Europe, North America (led by the United States), and East Asia (led by Japan). Because much of the world's economic, technological, scientific, and military power is encompassed in these three major blocs, the competitiveness among them has major consequences for the future of the global economy.[28] Thus, the second theme of this text relates to both the linkages and the divisions among the advanced industrial states of the North.

North-South Relations

Some analysts question whether it is meaningful today to speak of "the South" as a group of countries with common characteristics when there are major differences in the level of income and economic development among Southern countries. On the one hand, the East Asian NIEs—South Korea, Taiwan, Singapore, and Hong Kong—have relatively high per capita incomes and literacy rates, and they are quite competitive in some areas with the industrial states of the North. On the other hand, the United Nation's (UN) list of 48 least developed countries (LLDC)—mostly in sub-Saharan Africa and South Asia—have extremely low per capita incomes and literacy rates, and there are formidable problems to overcome before their populations can be elevated above the subsistence level.[29] Despite the disparities in wealth and economic development among Southern countries, it is meaningful to generalize about the problems of the South because countries such as the East Asian NIEs tend to be the exception rather than the rule. Indeed, two of the four East Asian NIEs—Singapore and Hong Kong—have a unique status in the Third World. Both are so small geographically that they are more akin to city-states, and Hong Kong was a British crown colony before it was incorporated into mainland China. Furthermore, even some East Asian NIEs such as South Korea have been vulnerable to financial and currency crises in recent years (see Chapter 11). Thus, a major characteristic of the global economy today is the marked inequality in wealth and power between the advanced industrial states of the North on the one hand and the *great majority* of LDCs in the South on the other.

This book uses the terms *less developed countries* or *LDCs* and *Third World* to refer to the countries in the South. These countries often have colonial histories and low levels of social and political as well as economic development. Economically, LDCs generally have low per capita incomes, inadequate infrastructure facilities (such as poor transportation and communications), and limited availability of modern technology. The poorer LDCs, which include many countries in sub-Saharan Africa and in Asia, have widespread poverty and malnutrition. The lack of economic resources in LDCs also limits their abilities to foster social development. Thus, many Third World countries have limited educational facilities, low literacy rates, and inadequate health and sanitary facilities. Assessing political development in a country is a more difficult and contentious issue. However, Third World countries are more likely than advanced industrial states to have unstable and authoritarian governments.[30] It is important to note that the term "LDCs" is sometimes not used because of concerns that it indicates third world countries are a homogeneous group, are inferior, and/or are expected to follow the same path to development as the industrial or developed countries. However, "LDCs" is used in this book simply as an abbreviation to indicate that these countries are economically less-developed. LDCs may have histories and cultures as rich or richer than those of developed countries. As this book shows, LDCs are also a very diverse group of countries that do not all follow the same path to development.

The Third World includes almost all the countries of Latin America and the Caribbean, Asia and Oceania, and Africa and the Middle East. In 1950, the Third World accounted for almost 65 percent of the total world population, and by 1996, the Third World population had climbed to almost 80 percent of the world total. A number of countries in the former Soviet Union and Eastern Europe that were previously part of the Communist Second World are now receiving foreign debt and development financing from the advanced industrial states and are in effect also a part of the Third World. When we speak of the world, we therefore must give a great deal of attention to the LDCs or the Third World.[31] Although our main concern when discussing international inequality is with the differences between the industrial states of the North and the LDCs of the South, it is important to note that the global economy is also marked by differences in the wealth and power of individuals *within* states. As noted in Chapter 11, some groups within Third World states, such as women and children, are often in especially disadvantageous positions. (Disparities in wealth of course are also prevalent within many Northern industrial states.) This book discusses the effects of changes in the global economy, such as globalization and the liberalization of trade and financial flows, on the inequalities between rich and poor both within states and among states.

Third World countries have relatively little influence in setting the agenda and making decisions regarding the international political economy. This is evident, for example, in important international economic organizations such as the WTO, the IMF, and the World Bank. Over the years, a variety of strategies have been followed to promote Third World economic development, and the LDCs have also sought to increase their power and influence over international economic issues. Although a relatively small number of LDCs—particularly in East and Southeast Asia and in Latin America—have improved their economic positions, the great majority of Third World countries have been frustrated in their efforts to promote development and exert more influence. Even among the more successful Third World countries in East Asia and Latin America, recent events indicate that their economic progress may be precarious.[32] Thus, the United Nations Development Program reported in 1996 that "the world has become more polarized, and the gulf between the poor and rich of the world has widened even further."[33] This book examines competing views as to why most Third World countries continue to be poor and why they continue to have little influence on IPE issues, and it explores the strategies Third World countries have employed to promote economic development and increase their influence.

Finally, considerable space is devoted to the former Second World, that is, the former CPEs that are liberalizing as a result of the breakup of the Soviet bloc and the Soviet Union itself. (Chapter 7, for example, discusses the fact that the foreign debt crisis has had a major impact on debtor countries in the former Eastern bloc as well as in the Third World.) Nevertheless, East-West relations is not a major theme of this book because the Cold War has virtually ended, and the former CPEs are becoming increasingly involved in the capitalist global political economy. The more developed emerging countries, such as the Czech Republic and Hungary, are approaching the level of development of some of the advanced industrial states in the North, and the poorer countries of the former Second World are essentially becoming members of the South.

THE IPE THEORETICAL PERSPECTIVES

Many students have a natural tendency to avoid studying "theory," and this seems to be particularly true in the case of IPE. Without theory, however, we are basically studying a series of facts, and we are unable to assess the broader implications of these facts for international political and economic relations in general. One might argue that the facts speak for themselves, but in reality a person will interpret "the facts" quite differently depending on whether he or she is viewing them "from a bank office in Zurich, a *maquiladora* [border factory] in Mexico, a shantytown in Peru, a rice paddy in Sri Lanka . . . [or] a trade office in Washington, D.C."[34] We all interpret "the facts" on the basis of our theoretical views of the world, and the only choice is whether our views remain implicit or whether we explicitly examine the theories we use to interpret issues and events.

A scholar's choice of theoretical perspective will also determine what "facts" he or she chooses to focus on or ignore. For example, theorists writing from the realist perspective place considerable emphasis on the struggle for power in international relations, and some realists claim that "power is the essence of politics."[35] Although realists provide us with many useful insights regarding relations among the most powerful industrial states, they normally have little interest in examining the conditions of the poorest and weakest Third World countries. Only when Third World entities such as OPEC or the NIEs challenge the predominant position of the North do realists usually take notice. Dependency theorists writing from the historical structuralist perspective, by contrast, devote most of their attention to examining the conditions of Third World countries in the periphery of the global economy. However, they are so concerned with examining external exploitation of the Third World by the advanced industrial states that they often fail to look at purely *domestic* factors in Third World countries that interfere with their development.

International political economy is a field of study in which scholars apply a wide range of theories and analytical methods. Three theoretical perspectives have been most prominent in the study of IPE: the realist, liberal, and historical structuralist perspectives. Realism is the oldest theoretical perspective in both international relations and IPE. According to realists, the state is the principal or dominant actor in international politics. Realists also view the international system as a "self-help" system without a centralized authority, in which each state must build up its own power to prevent being dominated by other states. International relations is often characterized by realists as a zero-sum game, in which one state's gain is another state's loss. "Relative gains," or the gains a state achieves in relation to the gains achieved by other states, are therefore extremely important to realists. Each state can be expected to manipulate the market to capture relative gains vis-à-vis other states.

Although realism is the most important perspective in international relations in general, liberalism is the most important school of thought in IPE. To avoid confusion, it is important to note that the use of the term *liberal* is different in IPE and American domestic politics. In the United States, "liberals" are viewed as supporting greater government involvement in the market to prevent inequalities and to stimulate growth. "Conservatives" in the United States, by contrast, are committed to free markets and minimal intervention by the government. Orthodox liberals in IPE are more akin to U.S. conservatives; they emphasize the importance of free markets and private property rights and prescribe only a limited government role in economic activities. However, Chapter 4 discusses the fact that some nonorthodox liberals are more accepting of government intervention. Liberals are more optimistic than realists about the prospects for cooperation among states, and they believe that international organizations and other institutions can help promote such cooperation. Thus, in the view of liberals, economic relationships are a positive-sum game in which all states benefit, even if they do not benefit equally.

This book uses the term *historical structuralism* for the third perspective because scholars in this group argue that history has been marked by structural means of exploitation, in which one class dominates another.[36] The main characteristic of the current system is the dominance of capitalist relations of production, with the capitalist class (the bourgeoisie) exploiting the workers (the proletariat). Some historical structuralists, such as dependency and world-system theorists, focus on the exploitation of Third World states in the periphery by the advanced capitalist states in the core of the global economy. Unlike liberals and realists, who are generally supportive of the capitalist system, historical structuralists typically advocate a transformation to socialism as the key to an end to exploitation.

Becoming familiar with realism, liberalism, and historical structuralism is an important starting point in developing alternative "lenses" for viewing the various substantive issue areas (such as trade and monetary relations) in IPE. However, the field of IPE is not neatly divided into these three perspectives. First, the margins separating these perspectives have often become blurred as these views have evolved and influenced each other over time. Second, some of the most important theoretical approaches in IPE, such as regime theory and hegemonic stability theory, are "hybrid" theories that draw on more than one of the three perspectives. Third, much of the recent literature examining the relationship between domestic institutions and IPE does not fit easily into any one of the three traditional perspectives. In addition to the three main theoretical perspectives, this book looks at the hybrid theories and at domestic-international interactions. For example, the chapters in Part III discuss the fact that major decisions and events in such areas as monetary relations, trade, foreign investment, and international development are affected by domestic as well as international interests and developments.

Three major perspectives and a growing range of theoretical approaches are used in the study of IPE. Some social scientists view this diversity as an indication of our failure to develop an all-embracing theory. However, the existence of different perspectives and theories should not be viewed as a weakness. Social science theory "is always *for* someone and *for* some purpose,"[37] and because the three IPE perspectives are based on differing sets of values, it is unlikely they will ever be entirely compatible. The three IPE perspectives have differing interpretations of the three main themes in this book relating to globalization, North-North relations, and North-South relations. In regard to the first theme, for example, realists, with their emphasis on the importance of the nation-state, question whether significant globalization is in fact occurring; liberals believe there is a significant level of globalization, and they view it in very positive terms; and historical structuralists also believe globalization is significant, but they feel it is having extremely negative consequences for lower classes and poorer nations in the periphery of the global economy. In regard to the second theme, liberals are far more inclined than realists or historical structuralists to argue that international institutions can play an important role in promoting international economic cooperation. In regard to the third theme, historical structuralists place far more emphasis than liberals or realists on the inequalities between the North and the South and on the North's exploitation of the South.

FOCUS OF THIS BOOK

This book introduces undergraduate students and beginning graduate students to the study of international political economy. Several distinguishing features of the book have already been discussed. First, it provides an in-depth background to IPE theory, a discussion of current IPE issues in historical perspective, and an examination of the interplay of theory and practice. Without the organizing framework of theory, discussions about trade, foreign investment, development, and other substantive IPE issues simply become a series of disparate facts. Second, Part III of the book focuses on three major themes relating to globalization, North-North relations, and North-South relations.

Third, this book emphasizes the role of international economic organizations such as the WTO, the International Monetary Fund, and the World Bank in the management of the global political economy. It also devotes considerable attention to important regional organizations such as the EU, NAFTA, the Southern Common Market Treaty (Mercosur), and the Asia-Pacific Economic Cooperation forum (APEC). Most IPE textbooks devote some space to international organizations (IOs), but the coverage is very limited and unsystematic. This is a reflection of the relative lack of emphasis on IOs in the field of international relations in general. Early scholarship on IOs had a strong idealistic and legal focus on the bodies, rules, and procedures in the League of Nations and then the UN. Post–World War II realists understandably felt that these legalistic studies provided us with little information about the real world of power politics, and they turned away from the study of IOs. In recent years, however, a number of scholars have recognized the importance of studying IOs as part of, rather than divorced from, the realities of international politics. It is especially important that we devote more attention to IOs in the case of IPE, where the WTO, EU, NAFTA, IMF, World Bank, and other organizations have significant roles.[38]

The book does *not* attempt to glorify IOs, and it discusses their limitations and problems as well as their possibilities. For example, IOs always remain to a considerable degree "creatures" of the nation-states that created them, even though the leaders of these bodies have some leeway in formulating objectives and conducting their operations. Furthermore, IOs are having great difficulty managing the international economy in an age of globalization. Indeed, the total resources of the UN, the World Bank, and the IMF are far smaller than the daily flows of foreign exchange on global markets. Developing mechanisms for global management is nevertheless a major challenge today. IOs often serve as important forums for negotiation of management issues, and they assist in upholding critical principles, norms, and rules of the global political economy.

A fourth emphasis of this book is on regional as well as global relations in the international political economy. Most IPE texts focus almost exclusively on the global political economy and contain no systematic discussion of trends toward regionalism. Yet these trends are inevitably affecting the management of the global political economy, and this book therefore devotes a full chapter to regionalism and globalism in trade. With the formation of NAFTA, "the trade and economic relations of the two largest markets in world trade—the European Community and the United States—are increasingly conditioned by regional agreements."[39] Third World countries have also been establishing their own regional trade agreements, and two of the largest South American countries, Brazil and Argentina, are members of the Mercosur. Two other major economies, Japan and China, are not yet members of regional trade agreements. However, APEC (which includes Japan and China as well as the United States) has a goal of establishing a free and open trade and investment area for developed country members by the year 2010 and for less developed members by 2020. Regionalism of course affects other areas in addition to trade, and Part III devotes some attention to regional trends in the chapters on monetary relations, foreign investment, and international development. It is impossible to devote a great deal of space to regionalism in an IPE text, and we are therefore mainly concerned with the *relationship between* regionalism and globalism in the international economy.

A fifth focus of this book relates to its coverage of North-South issues. Instead of discussing North-South issues in a separate section, the book integrates the North-North and North-South discussions as much as possible for several reasons. The three main IPE perspectives should be assessed in terms of their approach to global political economy issues, which relate to *all* countries, both rich and poor. Indeed, the historical structuralist perspective (discussed in Chapter 5) focuses almost exclusively on the weaker and exploited classes and countries, and an adequate examination of it necessarily includes a discussion of the Third World. Chapters 3 through 5 therefore discuss each perspective's approach to North-South as well as North-North issues. Part III also integrates the discussion of North-North and North-South relations because the process of globalization in trade, foreign investment, and monetary relations is by definition affecting all areas of the globe. Two chapters are largely devoted to the Third World. Chapter 7 on the foreign debt crisis deals with an issue that specifically has affected LDCs. Even this chapter, however, includes a discussion of Eastern Europe and the FSU. Chapter 11 is devoted to a detailed discussion of alternative strategies to promote Third World development.

Finally, this book provides substantial coverage of the issues surrounding the emerging states of Eastern Europe, the FSU, and China. These countries are undergoing a gradual (and often extremely difficult) transition from CPEs to more market-oriented economies. As part of this change, they are seeking to establish closer economic ties with the advanced industrial states and to become active members of the major international economic organizations. The emerging CPEs are discussed along with other countries in Part III.

Political leaders and international relations scholars have devoted much more attention to international economic issues in recent years, particularly since the decline of the Cold War. This book focuses on the major theoretical perspectives and substantive issues in IPE and on the interaction between theory and practice. To assess some of the changes occurring in the international economy, we focus on three major themes: globalization, North-North relations, and North-South relations. Chapter 2 provides an overview of the development of the international political economy in the post–World War II period, with an emphasis on the development of postwar institutions. Chapters 3 through 5 discuss the basic assumptions and historical evolution of the three main IPE theoretical perspectives and examine how each perspective approaches North-South relations. Chapters 6 to 11 cover monetary relations, foreign debt, global trade, trade regionalism, MNCs, and international development.

NOTES

1. Preamble to *Treaty Establishing the European Coal and Steel Community*, Paris, April 18, 1951 (London: Her Majesty's Stationery Office, 1972).
2. International Bank for Reconstruction and Development, *Articles of Agreement* as amended effective February 16, 1989 (Washington, DC: World Bank, August 1991), Article 4, section 10.

3. Andrew Shonfield, *The Attack on World Poverty* (New York: Random House, 1960), p. 147. On the World Bank's changing political and ideological leanings see David A. Baldwin, "The International Bank in Political Perspective," *World Politics* 18 (October 1965), pp. 68–81; Theodore H. Cohn, "Politics in the World Bank: The Question of Loans to the Asian Giants," *International Organization* 28-3 (Summer 1974), pp. 561–571; and Luiz Carlos Bresser Pereira, "Development Economics and the World Bank's Identity Crisis," *Review of International Political Economy* 2-2 (Spring 1995), pp. 211–247.

4. "Boeing v. Airbus," *The Economist,* July 26, 1997, pp. 59–61; Edmund L. Andrews, "Europeans Take Boeing to Brink," *New York Times,* July 24, 1997, pp. A1, C5. The Boeing-Airbus dispute highlights important differences between the United States and the EU over legal philosophies, enforcement priorities, and economic assumptions. See Eric J. Stock, "Explaining the Differing U.S. and EU Positions on the Boeing/McDonnell-Douglas Merger: Avoiding Another Near-Miss," *University of Pennsylvania Journal of International Economic Law* 20-4 (Winter 1999), pp. 825–909.

5. Henry Kissinger, *White House Years* (Boston: Little, Brown and Company, 1979), p. 950.

6. Robert Boyer and Daniel Drache, "Introduction," in Robert Boyer and Daniel Drache, eds., *States Against Markets: The Limits of Globalization* (London: Routledge, 1996), p. 3.

7. Robert Gilpin, with Jean M. Gilpin, *The Political Economy of International Relations* (Princeton, NJ: Princeton University Press, 1987), pp. 8–11. The tensions between the state and the market are reflected in the titles of some books on IPE, such as Boyer and Drache, eds., *States Against Markets;* and Herman M. Schwartz, *States Versus Markets: The Emergence of a Global Economy,* 2nd ed., (New York: St. Martin's Press, 2000).

8. Philip G. Cerny, *The Changing Architecture of Politics: Structure, Agency and the Future of the State* (London: Sage, 1990), pp. 228–229.

9. Lorraine Eden, "Bringing the Firm Back in: Multinationals in International Political Economy," in Lorraine Eden and Evan H. Potter, eds., *Multinationals in the Global Political Economy* (New York: St. Martin's Press, 1993), pp. 25–26; United Nations Development Programme, Human Development Report—1997 (New York: Oxford University Press, 1997), p. 92; Stephen D. Krasner, "Power Politics, Institutions, and Transnational Relations," in Thomas Risse-Kappen, ed., *Bringing Transnational Relations Back In: Non-State Actors, Domestic Structures and International Institutions* (Cambridge: Cambridge University Press, 1995), pp. 277–279; Wyn Grant, "Perspectives on Globalization and Economic Coordination," in J. Rogers Hollingsworth, ed., *Contemporary Capitalism: The Embeddedness of Institutions* (Cambridge: Cambridge University Press, 1997), pp. 322–325.

10. Richard K. Ashley, "Three Modes of Economism," *International Studies Quarterly* 27-4 (December 1983), p. 463; Colin Hay and David Marsh, "Introduction: Towards a New (International) Political Economy?," *New Political Economy* 4-1 (1999), pp. 9–10.

11. Michael Mastanduno, David A. Lake, and G. John Ikenberry, "Toward a Realist Theory of State Action," *International Studies Quarterly* 33-4 (December 1989), p. 458.

12. Thucydides, *The History of the Peloponnesian War,* translated by Richard Crawley (London: Dent & Sons, Everyman's Library, 1910), p. 41.

13. Martin Staniland, *What Is Political Economy? A Study of Social Theory and Underdevelopment* (New Haven, CT: Yale University Press, 1985), p. 11; Aristotle, *Politics,* translated by Benjamin Jowett (New York: Modern Library, 1943).

14. Postwar international relations scholars were more inclined than government officials to differentiate between high and low politics. See Richard N. Cooper, "Trade Policy Is Foreign Policy," *Foreign Policy* 9 (Winter 1972–73), p. 18.

15. Some scholars called for greater emphasis on the study of IPE from an early period. See, for example, Klaus Knorr, "Economics and International Relations: A Problem in Teaching," *Political Science Quarterly* 62-4 (December 1947), p. 560; Susan Strange, "International

Economics and International Relations: A Case of Mutual Neglect," *International Affairs* 46 (April 1970), p. 307; and Christopher Brown, "International Political Economy: Some Problems of an Interdisciplinary Enterprise," *International Affairs* 49-1 (January 1973), p. 52.

16. Michael Mastanduno, "Economics and Security in Statecraft and Scholarship," *International Organization* 52–4 (Autumn 1998), p. 853. See also James A. Caporaso, "False Divisions: Security Studies and Global Political Economy," *Mershon International Studies Review* 39–1 (April 1995), pp. 117–122.

17. James Caporaso, "International Political Economy: Fad or Field?" *International Studies Notes* 13 (Winter 1987), p. 2.

18. Anthony G. McGrew et al., *Global Politics: Globalization and the Nation-State* (Cambridge: Polity Press, 1992), p. 23; Claire Turenne Sjolander, "The Rhetoric of Globalization: What's in a Wor(l)d?" *International Journal* 51-4 (Autumn 1996), p. 605.

19. United Nations Development Programme, *Human Development Report 1997*, p. 83.

20. See Paul Hirst and Grahame Thompson, *Globalization in Question: The International Economy and the Possibilities of Governance* (Cambridge: Polity Press, 1996), ch. 1. The term *borderless world* is taken from Kenichi Ohmae, *The Borderless World: Power and Strategy in the Interlinked Economy* (New York: Harper Perennial, 1990).

21. Philip G. Cerny, "Globalization and Other Stories: The Search for a New Paradigm for International Relations," *International Journal* 51-4 (Autumn 1996), pp. 617–637; Ethan B. Kapstein, *Governing the Global Market: International Finance and the State* (Cambridge, MA: Harvard University Press, 1994), p. 7.

22. United Nations Development Programme, *Human Development Report 1997*, p. 83. For a historical discussion of globalization, see Paul Bairoch, "Globalization Myths and Realities: One Century of External Trade and Foreign Investment," in Boyer and Drache, eds., *States Against Markets*, pp. 173–192. For a study that questions how extensive globalization is today, see Hirst and Thompson, *Globalization in Question*.

23. United Nations Development Programme, *Human Development Report 1997*, p. 83.

24. John H. Dunning, *Multinational Enterprises and the Global Economy* (Wokingham, UK: Addison-Wesley, 1993), pp. 14–15.

25. Russia is not yet a member of the WTO, but it is an observer in the WTO and is actively seeking to join.

26. Jan Aart Scholte with Robert O'Brien and Marc Williams, "The WTO and Civil Society," *Journal of World Trade* 33-1 (February 1999), p. 109; David Robertson, "Civil Society and the WTO," *World Economy* 23-9 (September 2000), p. 1121–1123.

27. Joseph S. Nye, Jr., *Bound to Lead: The Changing Nature of American Power* (New York: Basic Books, 1990), p. 70.

28. For a dramatic portrayal of this competitiveness, see Lester Thurow, *Head to Head: The Coming Economic Battle Among Japan, Europe, and America* (New York: Morrow, 1992).

29. For information on the least developed countries, see United Nations Conference on Trade and Development, *The Least Developed Countries, Annual Reports* (New York: United Nations).

30. Howard Handelman, *The Challenge of Third World Development* (Upper Saddle River, NJ: Prentice-Hall, 1996), pp. 3–10.

31. Mike Mason, *Development and Disorder: A History of the Third World Since 1945* (Toronto: Between the Lines, 1997), p. 1.

32. For example, see "South-East Asia Loses Its Grip," *The Economist,* July 19, 1997, p. 15; and Edward A. Gargan, "Currency Assault Unnerves Asians," *New York Times,* July 29, 1997, pp. A1, C15.

33. United Nations Development Programme, *Human Development Report 1996* (New York: Oxford University Press, 1996), p. 2.

34. James A. Caporaso, "Global Political Economy," in Ada Finifter, ed., *Political Science: The State of the Discipline II* (Washington, DC: American Political Science Association, 1993), p. 451.

35. Hans J. Morgenthau, revised by Kenneth W. Thompson, *Politics Among Nations: The Struggle for Power and Peace*, 6th ed. (New York: Knopf, 1985), p. 10.

36. The term *historical structuralism* emerged in discussions with a colleague, Professor James Busumtwi-Sam, for which I am grateful.

37. Robert W. Cox, "Social Forces, States and World Orders: Beyond International Theory," *Millennium* 10-2 (1981), p. 128. See also Roger Tooze, "Perspectives and Theory: A Consumer's Guide," in Susan Strange, ed., *Paths to International Political Economy* (London: Allen & Unwin, 1984), pp. 3–4.

38. For a detailed discussion of the inadequate attention given to the study of international organizations, see J. Martin Rochester, "The Rise and Fall of International Organization as a Field of Study," *International Organization* 40-4 (Autumn 1986), pp. 777–813; Pierre de Senarclens, "Regime Theory and the Study of International Organizations," *International Social Science Journal* 45-138 (November 1993), pp. 453–462; and J. Martin Rochester, "The United Nations in a New World Order: Reviving the Theory and Practice of International Organization," in Charles W. Kegley, Jr., ed., *Controversies in International Relations Theory: Realism and the Neoliberal Challenge* (New York: St. Martin's Press, 1995), pp. 199–221.

39. World Trade Organization, *Regionalism and the World Trading System* (Geneva: World Trade Organization, April 1995), p. 27.

CHAPTER 2

Managing the Global Economy Since World War II: The Institutional Framework

After three years of preliminary negotiations, delegates from 44 countries met in July 1944 in Bretton Woods, New Hampshire, to convene the United Nations Monetary and Financial Conference, known as the Bretton Woods conference. Within 22 days, the delegates endorsed agreements to institute a framework for international economic cooperation after World War II. These Bretton Woods agreements were of historic significance because they marked "the first successful attempt consciously undertaken by a large group of nations to shape and control their economic relations."[1] The Bretton Woods conference led directly to the establishment of two new international economic organizations—the IMF and the IBRD or World Bank. Several years later, the GATT was to become the main global trade organization. These three organizations became part of a complex institutional framework that developed to help manage the global economy in the postwar period.

The critical negotiations preceding the Bretton Woods conference, and the conference itself, were in fact "very much an Anglo-American affair, with Canada playing a useful mediating role."[2] Some other major countries had less important roles in the conference or did not even attend the meetings: Although a French delegation under Pierre Mendès-France participated in the conference, France was still occupied by Germany at the time of Bretton Woods; Germany, Italy, and Japan, as enemy countries, were not represented; and the Soviet Union had only a limited role in the conference and did not sign the final agreements. Twenty-seven LDCs were present (19 of them Latin American), but their role was marginal. The chief planners for the conference were Harry Dexter White of the U.S. Treasury and John Maynard Keynes of Britain. Although the delegates had some fundamental differences of outlook, there was a large degree of consensus on the type of institutional order required for the postwar period. They were particularly concerned with avoiding a repetition of the disastrous events of the interwar period, when increased exchange controls and trade protectionism had contributed to the Great Depression of the 1930s and to World War II itself. Although this chapter focuses on global economic management in the post–World War II era, it is important to provide some historical background on the development of global economic relations in earlier periods.

GLOBAL ECONOMIC RELATIONS BEFORE WORLD WAR II

The substantive chapters in this text begin with some historical background on each issue area such as trade and monetary relations. This section is designed simply to identify important historical benchmarks, including the mercantilist period, the Industrial Revolution and British hegemony, the decline of British hegemony and World War I, and the interwar period. We also discuss the institutional framework that was established from 1815 to World War II to deal with international economic issues.

The Mercantilist Period

The origins of IPE are closely associated with the development of the modern European state system and its related global markets.[3] The modern European state gained official recognition at the 1648 Treaty of Westphalia, which marked the end of the Thirty Years' War in which mostly Protestant countries in Northern Europe defeated the Hapsburg countries, which were Catholic. The Peace of Westphalia institutionalized changes that had been occurring for at least 150 years by upholding the sovereignty and territorial integrity of states. The Westphalian view of each state as an equal and independent member of the international system legitimized the idea that external religious and secular authorities (e.g., the Pope, the Holy Roman Emperor, and other states) should not interfere in a state's internal affairs.

A major factor contributing to the establishment of central state authority vis-à-vis both internal and external forces was the development of **mercantilism.** The term "mercantilism" was first used by Adam Smith, an eighteenth-century economist and philosopher, in reference to much of the economic thought and practice in Europe from about 1500 to 1750.[4] (As we discuss later, Adam Smith as a liberal economist was highly critical of the mercantilists.) Mercantilists were acutely aware of the close linkage between politics and economics, because they believed that power and wealth were closely related and that both were legitimate goals of national policy. In the view of mercantilists, a state's power depended above all on the amount of gold and silver it could accumulate in the public treasury. With these precious metals, the state could build up its armed forces, hire mercenaries, and influence its allies as well as its enemies. Mercantilist states therefore took all necessary measures to increase their exports and decrease their imports as a means of accumulating gold and silver. While mercantilist states sought to increase exports of their manufactured goods, they restricted exports of raw materials and technology in efforts to limit the ability of others to develop their own manufacturing capabilities. They also limited imports of manufactured and luxury goods, and only imported raw materials that would reduce costs for their own manufacturers.

Colonialism was an integral part of mercantilism, because the colonies provided the metropole with revenues and raw materials for processing, and served as markets for manufactured products from the metropole. In accordance with the economic logic of mercantilism, the metropole prohibited manufacturing in the colonies. Because it is impossible for all states to have a balance-of-trade surplus (i.e., more exports than imports), liberals such as Smith strongly criticized mercantilists for following beggar-thy-neighbor policies that would inevitably lead to international conflict.[5] Nevertheless, mercantilism served an important *internal* function in building up state authority and territorial unification through its emphasis on national power. The establishment of the sovereign European state system in turn was a major factor contributing to the development of the international political economy.[6]

Although sovereignty at least in principle gives states supreme authority within their own territory, there is of course a "pecking order" in which some states are more powerful than others in the international system. A number of international relations scholars have examined the role of successive dominant or *hegemonic* powers in leading the international system, and in Chapter 3 we discuss and critique hegemonic stability theory that many scholars have applied to the study of IPE. Some international relations scholars have examined the role of world powers during the mercantilist period and have identified such countries as Portugal, Spain, the Netherlands, and Britain as world powers. However, there is considerable debate among scholars as to which countries were world powers during the mercantilist period and as to whether they were dominant enough to be considered "hegemonic."[7] It is important to note that most hegemonic stability theorists maintain that only two global hegemons have existed, both of them after the mercantilist period: Britain in the nineteenth century and the United States in the twentieth century.

The Industrial Revolution and British Hegemony

"Mercantilism" as we use the term in this book is a preindustrial doctrine, and the Industrial Revolution enhanced "the position of a country [Britain] already made supremely successful in the preindustrial, mercantilist struggles of the eighteenth century," and transformed "it into a different sort of power."[8] The Industrial Revolution was a gradual process that began around 1780, affected only some manufactures and means of production, and progressed from region to region rather than involving entire countries. Nevertheless, Britain was basically the first country to industrialize, and this helps to explain why it emerged as a hegemonic power in the nineteenth century. By 1860 Britain accounted for about 37 percent of total European industrial production and for 20 percent of world industrial production. Britain's lead was even greater in the newer technology industries, because 75 to 85 percent of these newer industries were located in the United Kingdom.[9]

The increase in Britain's competitive edge, combined with a series of domestic changes, caused Britain to slowly alter its mercantilist policies and shift toward freer trade. By the 1830s, Britain had removed most of its industrial tariffs and trade restrictions, but it continued to impose barriers to agricultural imports. In 1846 Britain finally abolished its *Corn Laws,* which had restricted agricultural imports, and this decision contributed to an extended period of free trade in the nineteenth century.[10] Both domestic and external factors account for the liberalization of Britain's agricultural trade policies. Domestically, legislative and demographic changes caused industrial groups to gain in representation vis-à-vis landed agricultural groups in the British Parliament. Because the agricultural elite's ability to promote protectionism in the Parliament declined, it was unable to prevent the repeal of the Corn Laws. Externally, Britain opened its markets to imports of agricultural goods and raw materials so that foreign countries would accept its manufactured goods in return. The resultant division of labor in which Britain increasingly specialized in industrial exports clearly served its hegemonic interests. Britain's hegemony resulted partly from the fact that it had an import market large enough to cause others to orient their production in line with British preferences. In addition to the repeal of the Corn Laws, another free-trade landmark was the 1860 *Cobden-Chevalier Treaty* between Britain and France, which resulted in a network of commercial treaties lowering tariff barriers throughout Europe.[11]

The Decline of British Hegemony and World War I

By the late nineteenth century, industrial protectionism on the European continent, depressed economic conditions, and a decline of British hegemony in some areas such as trade and industrial productivity slowed the growth of trade liberalization. The major Western European states abandoned free trade during the 1870s and 1880s, and after 1890 even Britain turned increasingly to its colonial markets. Britain's share of world trade fell from 24 percent in 1870 to 14.1 percent in 1913, whereas Germany's share rose from 9.7 to 12.2 percent and the U.S. share rose from 8.8 to 11.1 percent in the same period. In view of its declining export competitiveness, Britain's ability to serve as a market of last resort for other countries' exports also decreased.[12] A major factor explaining Britain's declining trade hegemony was the decline in its productive base relative to that of its two main competitors: the United States and Germany. The banks and the state (including U.S. state governments) played a significant role in promoting productivity in the United States and Germany through finance and investment in infrastructure such as railroads and canals, and in industrial production, and the two countries used trade protectionism to build up their infant industries so they could more effectively challenge British industry in global markets.[13] By 1913 on the eve of World War I, the United States had become the greatest industrial power, accounting for about 32 percent of total world industrial output.[14]

Despite Britain's decline in trade and industrial power, it continued to dominate in international finance until World War I. The City of London was the main center of the international financial system, the British pound was the international currency, and in 1913 the British had $19.5 billion invested overseas, which amounted to about 43 percent of the world's foreign investments.[15] World War I marked "the shift in financial preeminence from London to New York," and greatly hastened Britain's decline as a hegemonic power.[16] The war increased Britain's foreign liabilities, marked the emergence of the United States as a net creditor nation for the first time, and further disrupted the prewar trade and monetary regimes that Britain had helped to maintain.

The Interwar Period

The United States emerged from World War I as the world's largest industrial power and the only major net creditor nation. Although the United States lent as much as $10 billion to cash-short countries during the 1920s, some of its policies did not facilitate a return to an open, liberal economy. As the largest creditor nation in the interwar period, the United States initially insisted that European nations repay all of their war debts, even though this contributed to serious financial problems for its World War I allies. Indeed, Britain and France had the largest war debts to the United States, amounting to almost $5 billion and more than $4 billion, respectively (before interest multiplied the totals).[17] The United States also imposed trade barriers during this period, which made it extremely difficult for the Europeans to gain needed revenues from exports. The U.S. Congress responded to a recession with the Fordney-McCumber Act of 1922, which raised customs duties on agricultural and other products. When the U.S. economy moved into depression after the 1929 stock market crash, the Congress then passed the 1930 Smoot-Hawley Act, which increased American tariffs to their highest level in the twentieth century.[18] European countries rushed to retaliate with their own import restrictions, and world trade declined from $35 billion in 1929 to $12 billion in 1933.[19]

The disastrous experience of the interwar period resulted partly from a lack of economic leadership, and hegemonic stability theorists argue that a global hegemon increases the likelihood that there will be a more stable, open international economy. According to these theorists, Britain served as the global hegemon in the nineteenth century. However, in the interwar period Britain was no longer able, and the United States was not yet willing to assume the hegemonic duties of promoting freer trade and an open, stable economic system.[20] (Debates over the validity of hegemonic stability theory are discussed in Chapter 3.) Other theorists argue that domestic politics was a major factor explaining the economic disarray and conflict. For example, the domestic policy-making system in the United States contributed to the rise in U.S. tariffs despite the growing economic power of the United States. The American Constitution gives the Congress the authority to regulate commerce with foreign nations, but the Congress is a large, unwieldy body subject to special interests, and it was unable to resist the demands of its constituents for greater protection.[21]

In efforts to reverse the damage caused by the increase in trade restrictions the U.S. Congress passed the *Reciprocal Trade Agreements Act (RTAA)* in 1934. Most important, the RTAA delegated tariff-setting policy to the president, who could resist the pressures of special interests and negotiate a reduction in tariffs more effectively than the Congress. The RTAA, however, did *not* indicate that the United States was willing to "adopt the policies of a hegemonic leader," and "protection at home remained an important goal of American trade strategy."[22] In view of the widespread increase in global protectionism, the RTAA reflected a U.S. conviction that lower tariffs abroad and an ability to bargain bilaterally for these reductions would help restore U.S. export markets. The RTAA resulted in a number of bilateral trade agreements between the United States and other countries, but tariff rates were so high in the early 1930s that these agreements were not sufficient to stem the forces of trade protectionism.

The Institutional Framework Before World War II

European states established most of the IOs between 1815 and 1914, and the membership in these organizations was predominantly European. A majority of the IOs created during this period were economic in nature and were designed to promote economic regulation, take advantage of technological innovations, and facilitate commerce. The first permanent functional intergovernmental organization established in the modern era was the Central Commission for the Navigation of the Rhine, which was created at the Congress of Vienna in 1815 to maximize the use of the river for commerce. To gain commercial advantages from the technological innovation of the steamship, it was necessary to ensure that states did not interfere with the free flow of traffic on the Rhine. The invention of the telegraph led to the creation of the International Telegraph Union in 1865, and the Universal Postal Union was established in 1874 to promote speed and efficiency in postal deliveries among the original 22 member states.[23]

After World War I, the League of Nations Covenant (Article 23e) pledged that the member states "will make provision to secure and maintain freedom of communications and of transit and equitable treatment for the commerce of all Members of the League."[24] Thus, international economic organizations continued to take advantage of technological innovations and to facilitate transportation, communications, and commerce. The first financial IO was also established in the interwar period (in 1930): the **Bank for International Settlements** (**BIS**). Located in Basle, Switzerland, the BIS was formed to oversee the settlement of German reparations after World War I. The main purpose of the BIS, however, was to promote cooperation among central banks in developing their financial policies. (The BIS is discussed in greater detail in Chapter 6.)[25]

Other than the BIS, the economic IOs in the interwar period generally were designed almost solely to promote international *coordination,* or the standardization of basic facilities, equipment, and installations that were crucial for the functioning and growth of the global economy. These organizations were ill equipped to deal directly with major economic problems that arose, such as the Great Depression. As economic differences increased in the 1920s and 1930s, several conferences were convened in efforts to jointly confront the trade and financial problems. For example, in 1922 an international conference in Genoa, Italy, called on central banks to cooperate in managing exchange rates among currencies and to make greater use of currencies such as the pound sterling that were convertible into gold. However, these conferences failed to resolve the central problems related to war reparations and debt, disorderly exchange conditions among currencies, and a decline in world trade. When the gold exchange standard regime collapsed in the 1930s, the 1933 world economic and monetary conference in London failed to reach agreement on a dollar-sterling rate of exchange. (The gold exchange standard is discussed in Chapter 6.) It was not until 1936 that Britain, the United States, and France were able to reach a tripartite agreement to recognize international responsibility for exchange rates.[26] This experience demonstrated that permanent international economic organizations promoting active *collaboration* as well as coordination were needed to support open and stable economic relations after World War II. The IMF, the World Bank, and GATT were established to promote collaboration in the areas of monetary, financial, and trade relations.[27]

THE FUNCTIONS OF THE INTERNATIONAL MONETARY FUND, THE WORLD BANK, AND GENERAL AGREEMENT ON TARIFFS AND TRADE

In contrast to the interwar period, the United States emerged as a more mature power at the end of World War II, both willing and able to assume a leadership position. In addition, the major powers established an institutional framework to help prevent a recurrence of the interwar problems. Although some writers refer to the IMF, the World Bank, and GATT as the Bretton Woods institutions, GATT was in fact established several years after the Bretton Woods conference. In this book we refer to the three organizations as *keystone international economic organizations* (*KIEOs*) to indicate the central role they have played in international finance, trade, and monetary relations.[28]

The IMF was created to support international monetary stability and the elimination of currency exchange restrictions. To promote monetary stability, the IMF monitored a system of fixed or pegged exchange rates, in which currencies were given official exchange rates in relation to gold and the U.S. dollar. The pegged exchange rate system was designed in part to avoid the competitive devaluation of currencies, which had led to trade wars during the interwar period. **Devaluation** refers to a reduction in the official rate at which one currency is exchanged for another. When a country devalues its currency, the prices of its imported goods and services increase, and its exports become less expensive to foreigners. Countries with deficits in their **balance of payments** (that is, with more money leaving than entering the country) are inclined to devalue their currencies to increase their revenue from exports. The IMF was authorized to provide short-term loans to help countries deal with temporary balance-of-payments problems and maintain the **fixed exchange rates** of their currencies.

The *IBRD* or *World Bank* was created to provide long-term loans (unlike the IMF's short-term loans) for postwar reconstruction in Europe and for economic development in the Third World. As with the IMF, the World Bank's role was designed to prevent problems that had occurred in the interwar period. After World War I, numerous problems stemming from the cost of servicing war debts and bringing about economic recovery had contributed to economic tensions and conflicts. To prevent a recurrence of these problems after World War II, the World Bank had the role of providing long-term loans for postwar reconstruction and for development. The GATT was designed to lower countries' tariff rates in multilateral negotiations so that they would not resort to protectionist trade barriers as they had during the interwar period. In addition to providing a forum for trade negotiations, GATT established rules for the conduct of international trade relations and developed procedures for settling disputes among member states over trade issues.

Because the IMF, the World Bank, and GATT were established partly to avoid problems that had developed during an earlier period (the interwar years), the functions of these institutions inevitably had to evolve along with changes after World War II. For example, the task of European reconstruction proved to be larger than originally anticipated, and the United States therefore established the European Recovery Program (the Marshall Plan) in 1948 to give **bilateral aid** to the Western European countries. As a result, the World Bank played only a minor role in European reconstruction and shifted its attention almost completely to providing loans for economic development. As for the IMF, it lost one of its main functions when the fixed-exchange-rate system for currencies collapsed in the early 1970s and was replaced by a system of **floating exchange rates.** However, the IMF's profile increased again in the early 1980s when it became the lead international agency dealing with the foreign debt crisis, which began when Mexico threatened to default on its loans in 1982 (see Chapter 7). The World Bank also has provided financing to the foreign debtor countries, and recipients of IMF and World Bank loans now include countries in Eastern Europe and the FSU as well as the Third World.

GATT was created under special circumstances, and to understand its evolution as an organization it is necessary to be aware of its origins. Negotiations were held for several years after the Bretton Woods conference to create an international trade organization (ITO) comparable in strength to the IMF and the World Bank. However, trade is one of the most sensitive economic issues to countries, and the U.S. Congress was unwilling to support the formation of a strong trade organization such as the ITO. As a result, the "temporary" GATT, which was signed by 23 governments in 1947 to initiate postwar trade negotiations, became the main global trade organization by default. Because GATT was designed to be only a provisional treaty, it never became a fully developed IO. Indeed, countries that joined GATT became "contracting parties" rather than formal "members" of the agreement (this book uses the term *GATT membership* for the sake of brevity). Despite its humble origins, GATT proved quite effective for a number of years in liberalizing trade. However, members were able to circumvent a number of the GATT regulations, the GATT dispute settlement system was weak, and GATT was not well equipped to deal with many new areas of trade. In January 1995, the GATT was superseded by a new WTO, which is a full-fledged IO. Unlike GATT, the WTO deals not only with trade in goods, but also with trade in services, intellectual property rights, and trade-related investment measures.

THE INTERNATIONAL ECONOMIC ORGANIZATIONS AND THE UNITED NATIONS

Figure 2.1 shows that the IMF and World Bank are specialized agencies theoretically under the auspices of the Economic and Social Council, which is one of the six principal organs of the UN. When the WTO was established in 1995, the members decided that it should not be a UN specialized agency.[29] Thus, the WTO is listed as a "related organization" in Figure 2.1, and it does not report to the ECOSOC. As Figure 2.1

shows, the World Bank today is in fact a **World Bank group** of five institutions (see Chapter 11).

Although the IMF and World Bank are UN specialized agencies, the UN in fact has little authority or influence over them—and the same applies to the WTO. The UN signed an agreement with the World Bank when it was formed (and a similar agreement with the IMF), acknowledging that "it would be sound policy to refrain from making recommendations to the Bank with respect to particular loans or with respect to terms or conditions of financing."[30] A major reason for the lack of UN leverage is that the IMF and the World Bank are far more financially sound as institutions than the UN; in September 1995 the UN even indicated that it might try to borrow money from the World Bank to deal with its deficit problem. (This action was vetoed by some major UN member states.) Chapters 6 and 11 discuss the fact that the IMF and the World Bank have weighted voting systems in which the rich Northern states have the most votes. This contrasts with the one-nation, one-vote system of many UN bodies. Because the Northern states prefer weighted voting, they have directed most of their funding for multilateral economic management away from the UN and toward the KIEOs.[31]

Although the KIEOs generally act independently of the UN, UN bodies have sometimes induced them to revise their policies and adopt new programs. Examples include the UN's role in the World Bank's creation of a soft-loan agency (see Chapter 11), the IMF's establishment of a compensatory financing facility (see Chapter 6), and the decision of the IMF and the World Bank to introduce human and social dimensions to their lending programs. The World Bank has also cooperated with a number of UN bodies in providing development assistance to the Third World.[32]

POSTWAR ECONOMIC INSTITUTIONS AND THE ADVANCED INDUSTRIAL STATES

The role of the advanced industrial states in the international political economy is marked by three major characteristics, which are also evident in the management of the postwar economic institutions. First, the United States has been and continues to be the most powerful single state, but its hegemony is gradually giving way to a three-way predominance shared by a *triad* composed of North America, Western Europe, and Japan-East Asia. (The chapters in Part III demonstrate how influential the triad has become in each of the issue areas we examine.) Second, the triad led by the advanced industrial states is responsible for the largest share of international economic transactions today, such as foreign investment, trade in manufactures and services, and **capital** flows. For example, in 1995 the advanced industrial states were the largest source *and* the largest recipients of foreign direct investment (FDI), accounting for 92.1 percent of the outward stocks and 71.9 percent of the inward stocks of FDI. In 1995, North America, Western Europe, and Asia also accounted for almost 93 percent of the world exports of manufactures and for 89.3 percent of world exports of commercial services.[33]

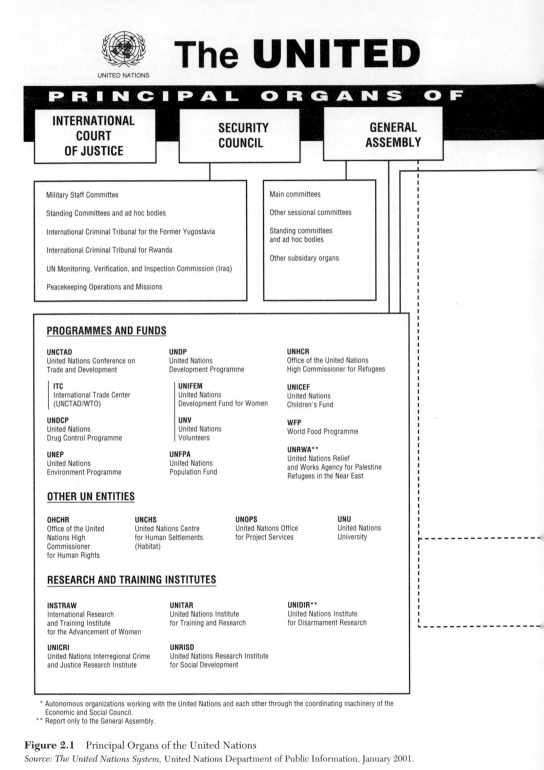

Figure 2.1   Principal Organs of the United Nations

Source: The United Nations System, United Nations Department of Public Information, January 2001.

NATIONS system

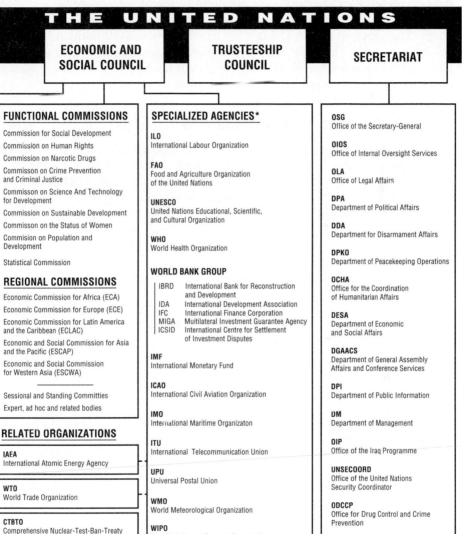

THE UNITED NATIONS

| ECONOMIC AND SOCIAL COUNCIL | TRUSTEESHIP COUNCIL | SECRETARIAT |

FUNCTIONAL COMMISSIONS

Commission for Social Development

Commission on Human Rights

Commission on Narcotic Drugs

Commisson on Crime Prevention and Criminal Justice

Commisson on Science And Technology for Development

Commission on Sustainable Development

Commisson on the Status of Women

Commision on Population and Development

Statistical Commission

REGIONAL COMMISSIONS

Economic Commission for Africa (ECA)

Economic Commission for Europe (ECE)

Economic Commission for Latin America and the Caribbean (ECLAC)

Economic and Social Commission for Asia and the Pacific (ESCAP)

Economic and Social Commission for Western Asia (ESCWA)

Sessional and Standing Committies

Expert, ad hoc and related bodies

RELATED ORGANIZATIONS

IAEA
International Atomic Energy Agency

WTO
World Trade Organization

CTBTO
Comprehensive Nuclear-Test-Ban-Treaty Organization

OPCW
Organization for the Prohibition of Chemical Weapons

WTO
World Tourism Organization

SPECIALIZED AGENCIES*

ILO
International Labour Organization

FAO
Food and Agriculture Organization of the United Nations

UNESCO
United Nations Educational, Scientific, and Cultural Organization

WHO
World Health Organization

WORLD BANK GROUP

IBRD	International Bank for Reconstruction and Development
IDA	International Development Association
IFC	International Finance Corporation
MIGA	Muitilateral Investment Guarantee Agency
ICSID	International Centre for Settlement of Investment Disputes

IMF
International Monetary Fund

ICAO
International Civil Aviation Organization

IMO
International Maritime Organizaton

ITU
International Telecommunication Union

UPU
Universal Postal Union

WMO
World Meteorological Organization

WIPO
World Intellectual Property Organization

IFAD
International Fund for Agricultural Development

UNIDO
United Nations Industrial Development Organization

SECRETARIAT

OSG
Office of the Secretary-General

OIOS
Office of Internal Oversight Services

OLA
Office of Legal Affairs

DPA
Department of Political Affairs

DDA
Department for Disarmament Affairs

DPKO
Department of Peacekeeping Operations

OCHA
Office for the Coordination of Humanitarian Affairs

DESA
Department of Economic and Social Affairs

DGAACS
Department of General Assembly Affairs and Conference Services

DPI
Department of Public Information

DM
Department of Management

OIP
Office of the Iraq Programme

UNSECOORD
Office of the United Nations Security Coordinator

ODCCP
Office for Drug Control and Crime Prevention

UNOG
UN Office at Geneva

UNOV
UN Office at Vienna

UNON
UN Office at Nairobi

Published by the United Nations
Department of Public Information
DPI/2079 — January 2001

The third characteristic is that countries within the triad conduct most of their international economic transactions with each other, and their trade and investment flows with other parts of the world are relatively small. U.S. MNCs have shown a strong preference for investing in Europe, intra-European investment has accelerated, and Japan and Western European countries have invested heavily in the United States. The advanced industrial states still occupy the dominant position in the global political economy. Although Third World countries and the emerging countries of Eastern Europe and the FSU are increasing their linkages with the industrial states, they continue to occupy peripheral economic positions.

The IMF, the World Bank, and the WTO

In view of their role in global economic transactions, the advanced industrial states have the most influence in determining the agenda and operations of the KIEOs. For example, the rich Northern states provide most of the funding for IMF and World Bank loans and have the most votes in these weighted-voting institutions. The five countries with the largest number of votes in the IMF and World Bank are the United States, Japan, Germany, France, and Britain. Although the WTO has a one-nation, one-vote system, the major trading nations, which are mainly Northern countries, have the largest role in setting the agenda in multilateral trade negotiations. Northern dominance in these institutions is also evident from the nationalities of their chief executive officers. By tacit agreement, the World Bank president has always been an American, and the managing director of the IMF has always been a European. All the directors-general of GATT and the WTO from 1948 to September 2002 were also from industrial states. On 1 September 2002, however, Dr. Supachai Panitchpakdi of Thailand will become the first WTO director-general from an LDC. Third World countries have been underrepresented on the professional staffs of all three KIEOs, and most Communist countries were not members of the KIEOs from the 1940s to the 1970s.[34]

The Bretton Woods system and its institutions are often credited with contributing "to almost unprecedented global economic growth and change over the past five decades."[35] However, the type of growth these institutions foster has closely followed the prescriptions of the United States and other advanced capitalist countries. The KIEOs therefore support a liberal-economic approach to growth, which holds that international prosperity and peace are most likely when there is a free flow of goods and capital around the world. As discussed in Chapter 5, historical structuralists argue that this liberal-economic approach to growth benefits the wealthy capitalist countries in the core of the global economy but disadvantages the lower classes and peripheral Third World countries.

Judged by liberal-economic criteria, the KIEOs were quite effective in the 1950s and 1960s in promoting economic liberalization, growth, and stability. A number of factors help to account for their effectiveness. First, the Cold War increased the incentive of the United States to cooperate economically with Western Europe and Japan; vigorous economic recovery was viewed as a prerequisite for a strong anti-Soviet alliance system. Second, the United States as the global hegemon was able and willing to provide leadership in establishing principles and rules for the conduct of postwar trade, financial, and monetary relations. Third, a relatively small number of politically and economically like-minded countries that accepted U.S. leadership were involved in developing the postwar economic system. Finally, the postwar international institutions were designed so that governments could pursue domestic policy objectives such as full employment and also abide by international rules and obligations.[36]

Despite the early effectiveness of the KIEOs, they encountered increasing problems in managing the global economy beginning in the late 1960s. With Europe and Japan growing much faster than the United States in the 1960s, the United States became less confident about its economic dominance and less inclined to support economic liberalism. For example, pressures for trade protectionism increased in the United States when its balance of trade shifted to a deficit position in 1971. Europe and Japan also began to question U.S. leadership, and the decline of the Cold War permitted the frictions among the advanced capitalist states to increase. A second factor posing a challenge to the KIEOs was the increased influence of the Third World. LDCs had long been dissatisfied with the policies of the KIEOs, and in the 1970s the LDCs were able to put some force behind their protests. A critical turning point was the first oil shock following the October 1973 Middle East War. At this time, the members of OPEC limited the supply of Persian Gulf oil, and its price increased by more than 400 percent. The subsequent disruption in the global economy challenged the management capabilities of advanced industrial states and the KIEOs.

A third challenge to the KIEOs resulted from the forces of globalization, such as increased capital flows. As discussed in Part III, increased capital mobility has made it difficult for the KIEOs to manage, and even to monitor, many activities in the global economy. The total economic resources of the KIEOs "pale in comparison to daily market-driven foreign exchange cash flows,"[37] and no IO effectively oversees the activities of MNCs and international banks, which are major contributors to these massive capital flows. As a result, a number of analysts today are skeptical about the ability of the KIEOs to oversee the effective management of the global economy.[38] Finally, the growing membership of the KIEOs with the influx of Third World and former Soviet bloc countries has also interfered with their management capabilities. By January 2002, there were 183 members of the IMF, 183 members of the World Bank, and 144 members of the WTO. Although some argue that the KIEOs must become more broadly representative, others point to the problems of decision making in such large, unwieldy institutions. The large, diverse memberships of these organizations can contribute to serious difficulties and frustrations in consultation, coordination, and the supervision of policies.

The IMF, the World Bank, and the WTO continue to have important functions in the global economy, but their large memberships have led some liberal analysts to argue that "they must be led by a much smaller core group whose weight confers on them the responsibility of leadership."[39] In the postwar period, the advanced industrial states have in fact often conferred among themselves in smaller groups before seeking endorsement of their policies by the larger KIEOs. As Figure 2.2 shows, these groups include the Organization for Economic Cooperation and Development (OECD), the **Group of Ten (G-10)**, the **Group of Five (G-5)**, and the **Group of Seven (G-7)**. These smaller groups are often more manageable for dealing with coordination of policies among the advanced industrial states in an age of globalization and

ORGANIZATION FOR ECONOMIC COOPERATION AND DEVELOPMENT
(YEAR OF ADMISSION)

Australia	1971	Hungary	1996	Poland	1996
Austria	1961	Iceland	1961	Portugal	1961
Belgium	1961	Ireland	1961	Slovak Republic	2000
Canada	1961	Italy	1961	South Korea	1996
Czech Republic	1995	Japan	1964	Spain	1961
Denmark	1961	Luxembourg	1961	Sweden	1961
Finland	1969	Mexico	1994	Switzerland	1961
France	1961	Netherlands	1961	Turkey	1961
Germany	1961	New Zealand	1973	United Kingdom	1961
Greece	1961	Norway	1961	United States	1961

Smaller Groups

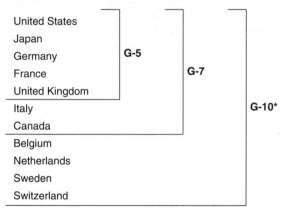

*Today the G-10 has 11 members.

Figure 2.2   Groups of Advanced Industrial States

power sharing among the United States, Europe, and Japan. Furthermore, the industrial states can meet in these groups without sharing information and decision-making power with the LDCs. Unlike liberal economists, who view these smaller groups as essential for promoting economic leadership and stability, historical structuralists argue that the groups permit the most powerful capitalist countries to exclude peripheral states from the decision-making process. Although the IMF and the World Bank have weighted voting, they are nevertheless preferable to the smaller groups from this perspective because the LDCs are at least present at the bargaining table.

The OECD

The Organization for Economic Cooperation and Development (OECD) is a group of mainly advanced industrial states that is based in Paris, France. As Figure 2.2 shows, the OECD had 30 members as of 2001. From the time of its creation in 1961, the OECD has been committed to liberalizing international transactions such as trade and capital flows. The OECD is well known for its policy studies of economic and social issues, but it also serves as a forum for the industrial states to discuss members' economic policies, review common problems, and promote cooperation and policy coordination. In an age of globalization, a country's domestic policies can often have international consequences, and OECD members seek to achieve a consensus on implementing domestic policies that will minimize conflict. Although the OECD has the authority to adopt binding as well as nonbinding agreements, it usually operates through a system of mutual persuasion, in which governments exert peer pressure on each other to meet their commitments.[10]

The advanced capitalist states use the OECD not only to promote cooperation but also to develop a more unified developed country position in setting the agenda and conducting negotiations in the IMF, the World Bank, and the WTO. For example, as early as 1963, an OECD report recommended that the World Bank establish an international agency to guarantee funds that private investors direct to LDCs. This report eventually served as the basis for the World Bank's decision to establish the Multilateral Investment Guarantee Agency (MIGA) in 1988. The OECD's work on liberalization of trade in services also led to the decision that the new WTO should be responsible for liberalizing trade in services as well as goods.[41]

Less frequently, the OECD has been *directly* involved in negotiating agreements in areas where the industrial states have a special interest. For example, the OECD has negotiated agreements on *export credit,* "an insurance, guarantee or financing arrangement which enables a foreign buyer of exported goods and/or services to defer payment over a period of time."[42] Almost all export credit is provided by the OECD countries, and the purpose of the OECD agreements is to prevent cut-throat competition among the export credit providers. In 1995 the OECD also began negotiations to conclude a Multilateral Agreement on Investment (MAI), which was designed primarily to protect foreign investors. Because many LDCs in the WTO were opposed to such an agreement, the industrial states decided to negotiate the MAI in the OECD. Nevertheless, the MAI negotiations were suspended in 1998 because of divisions among OECD members and strong opposition by Third World countries and civil society activists (see Chapter 10).

Although OECD membership was for years generally limited to the advanced capitalist states, a debate in the early 1990s resulted in a decision that the organization should be open to some enlargement. Thus, Figure 2.2 shows that six countries outside the industrial core group have become OECD members since the 1990s: Mexico in 1994; the Czech Republic in 1995; Hungary, Poland, and South Korea in 1996; and the Slovak Republic in 2000. Other countries are also seeking membership in the organization. Although some OECD countries are open to this enlargement, others warn that "transforming the OECD into a mini–United Nations could well jeopardize its ability to achieve high quality agreements among like-minded countries."[43]

Three smaller groupings that are limited to the most important countries in the OECD—the G-10, G-5, and G-7—have taken on significant functions in recent years. The G-10 was the first of these small groups to be formed, in 1962. As Figure 2.2 shows, the G-10 now actually includes 11 countries: the United States, Japan, Germany, France, Britain, Italy, Canada, Belgium, the Netherlands, Sweden, and Switzerland. As mentioned in Chapter 6, the IMF lacked sufficient funding in the early 1960s to meet the borrowing requirements of its member countries. The G-10 countries therefore established the General Arrangements to Borrow (GAB) in 1962, under which they agreed to provide loans to the IMF in their own currencies when it needed supplementary resources. After a financial crisis in Mexico in 1994, it was evident that substantially more resources might be needed to respond to future financial crises. In 1997, the G-10 therefore agreed to supplement the GAB with New Arrangements to Borrow. The New Arrangements to Borrow are credit arrangements between the IMF and 25 member states and institutions that are prepared to supply the IMF with supplementary resources.[44]

Although the OECD and G-10 coordinated the economic policies of the advanced industrial countries throughout the 1960s, the main focus of policy coordination shifted to two smaller groupings in the 1970s: the G-5 and G-7. With the increase in globalization, it was felt these groups would have special advantages in policy coordination: Their numbers are very small, they include the most powerful industrial states in the global economy, they are flexible groupings without formal constitutions, and top political leaders with the authority to implement agreements often attend their meetings.[45]

The G-5, G-7, and G-8

The G-5 includes the finance ministers and governors of the **central banks** of the five largest industrial economies: the United States, Japan, Germany, France, and Britain (see Figure 2.2). These five countries also have the most votes in the IMF and World Bank policymaking bodies. The G-5 first met in 1967 to informally discuss international monetary issues, and it was felt that such meetings were useful and should be continued.[46] In 1975, the G-5 agreed to hold more formal summit meetings at which their heads of government or state could discuss international economic issues. The interest in more formal meetings followed major changes in the global economy, including the need for more collective leadership with the decline of U.S. hegemony, the growing interdependence among the advanced industrial states, the OPEC oil crisis, and the world economic recession. Italy was invited along with the G-5 countries to attend the first summit in 1975, and Canada was invited to the second summit in 1976. Once invited, they continued attending the summits, and the G-7 was created. Although the G-7 summit is not a decision-making forum, summiteers seek to arrive at a consensus on key issues at the highest political level.[47]

From 1975 to 1986, the G-5 and G-7 met as two largely separate entities. While the G-5 finance ministers and central bank governors held informal and confidential meetings on monetary and financial issues, the G-7 heads of state and government held highly publicized meetings on political as well as economic matters. In 1986, the G-7 largely displaced the G-5, and today there are two different layers of the G-7: At the top are the heads of state or government, who meet in annual summits, and at the second level are the ministers of finance and central bank governors.

The G-5 and G-7 meetings performed some critical functions in the 1970s and 1980s, coordinating **macroeconomic,** currency, and monetary policies among the advanced industrial states. (Macroeconomic policies deal with problems such as employment income and prices in the economy as a whole, and microeconomic policies refer to the decisions of individual households and firms.) The meetings were also important in arranging financing and other measures to deal with East-West economic issues, global energy problems, and the 1980s Third World debt crisis. Furthermore, the G-7 summit agenda has expanded to include discussions of a wide range of "microeconomic, environmental, transnational and political-security subjects."[48] In 1991 the G-7 leaders invited the Russian president (Gorbachev at the time) for the first time to meet with them at their summit meeting in London. The invitation was designed to help the Russians come to terms with their loss of superpower status after the breakup of the Soviet Union, and to encourage them to continue with economic and political reform. The Russians became gradually more involved in each successive G-7 summit, and in 1997 U.S. President Clinton made the G-7 summit in Denver the first "Summit of the Eight," with Russia participating alongside the G-7 countries from the outset. The G-7 has therefore become a **Group of Eight (G-8)** with Russia participating. Nevertheless, Russia is far more involved in the political than in the economic discussions at the summits, and in some economic areas such as finance the main actors are still limited to the G-7 countries.[49]

Some analysts argue that the G-7 meetings of finance ministers and central bank governors have become far less effective in recent years, and they raise serious concerns about "the apparent inability of G-7 macroeconomic cooperation to ensure stability in the markets, or to sustain global economic growth."[50] Two major factors account for the decline of the G-7's effectiveness. First, with the demise of the Cold War, economic policy coordination among the capitalist states seems to have less urgency, and conflicts among the G-7 countries have increased. The lack of a common purpose has been exacerbated by the decline of the United States' ability and willingness to exert economic leadership. The second reason for the G-7 decline relates to its difficulties in coping with the increase in globalization. For example, the massive international flows of private capital today interfere with the ability of G-7 monetary authorities to influence currency markets.

In the view of some scholars and policymakers, continued G-7/G-8 leadership is essential for international economic stability and prosperity.[51] To regain its influence, the G-7/G-8 must make the necessary transition from unilateral U.S. leadership to effective collective leadership. This involves both U.S. willingness to share decision making and the willingness of countries such as Japan and Germany to assume more global responsibilities. The G-7/G-8 must also address the question of its legitimacy among countries outside its select group, especially because some of these countries are becoming important global economic actors. Indeed, it is striking that the G-7/G-8 has no LDC members, considering the size and economic importance of such countries as China, India, Brazil, and Indonesia. The G-7/G-8 also has no oil-exporting country among its members (e.g., Saudi Arabia), despite the effect of petroleum on economic developments since the 1970s. Although the G-7/G-8 is not likely to expand its membership in the near future, countries such as China, India, and Brazil cannot be ignored, and the G-7/G-8 must be willing to consult with nonmembers more seriously if it is to regain its influence.[52]

Divisions Among the Advanced Industrial States

To this point, we have focused mainly on groupings in which the advanced capitalist states cooperate and coordinate their policies on a global basis. Even in these groupings, divisions have increased among the industrial states as U.S. economic hegemony has declined and as the end of the Cold War has permitted differences to emerge. Globalization has also had the dual effect of creating pressures for cooperation and co-ordination of policymaking on the one hand and adding to sources of conflict on the other hand as states seek to preserve their autonomy. This book discusses numerous instances of divisions among the advanced industrial states. The following examples relate to the postwar economic institutions.

In recent years, some industrial states have expressed dissatisfaction with their level of representation in the KIEOs. A number of critics in Germany and Japan in particular have argued that their countries' influence in these organizations has not kept pace with their growing economic importance. Thus, a German representative at the 1988 annual meetings of the IMF-World Bank boards of governors asserted that "the Americans have the power, the French get the top jobs, and the Germans and the Japanese come up with the money."[53] None of the chief executive officers of the three KIEOs (the World Bank president, IMF managing director, and GATT/WTO director-general) was from Germany or Japan until March 2000, when the IMF executive board selected a German national (Horst Köhler) as its new managing director.[54] Even the United States has expressed dissatisfaction with the fact that all the GATT directors-general were European. When it came time to select the first WTO director-general in 1995, the United States therefore supported a Mexican for the post. As discussed in Chapter 8, the Mexican was not selected, but a New Zealander (Mike Moore) became the first non-European WTO director-general in September 1999.

The most important institutional sign of divisions among the advanced industrial states in recent years has been the development and growth of regional trade agreements (RTAs). Although some analysts view these regional groups as stepping-stones to global cooperation, others warn that they may promote divisiveness and interfere with globalism. Many factors account for this turn to regionalism, including impatience of countries with decision making in the large, heterogeneous global organizations; the growing interest of the United States in regionalism as its global hegemonic position has declined; and increased competitiveness among three major regional blocs in the world centered in the European Union, the United States, and Japan-East Asia. (Chapter 9 provides a detailed discussion of regionalism.) The EU has advanced to a further stage of integration than most other regional agreements, such as NAFTA, and to understand the phenomenon of regionalism it is necessary to briefly discuss the stages of regional economic integration.

The Stages of Regional Economic Integration   As Figure 2.3 shows, there are five levels of regional economic integration.

1. **Free trade area (FTA).** In an FTA, member countries progressively eliminate tariffs on substantially all their trade with each other. Every country in the FTA retains the right, however, to follow its own trade policies toward nonmember states. As a result, an FTA poses less of a threat to national sovereignty and tends to be more acceptable to countries with politically sensitive relationships. One of the most important FTAs established in recent years is NAFTA. Most economic integration agreements are FTAs.

	Free trade area (FTA)	Customs union (CU)	Common market	Economic union	Political union
Removal of all tariffs among members	X	X	X	X	X
Common external tariff		X	X	X	X
Free movement of factors (labor and capital)			X	X	X
Harmonization of economic policies				X	X
Political unification					X

Figure 2.3   Stages of Regional Economic Integration

2. **Customs union (CU).** A CU has the same characteristics as an FTA *plus* a common external tariff toward outside countries. Because a CU involves common trade barriers, member countries must surrender more of their ability to make independent decisions. Thus, Britain was originally unwilling to join the EC (a customs union) because it wanted to retain its Commonwealth preference system with countries such as India, Canada, and Australia. Britain's trade became increasingly Europe oriented, and it eventually joined the EC in 1973 and agreed to phase out its Commonwealth preferences. Compared to the number of FTAs, the number of customs unions is relatively small.

3. **Common market.** A common market has the same characteristics as a customs union *plus* the free mobility of factors of production (labor and capital) among the member countries. Because a common market leads to increased labor mobility, there is a tendency to establish similar health, safety, educational, and social security standards so that no country's workers have a competitive advantage. The EU has generally progressed to the common market stage.

4. **Economic union.** An economic union has the characteristics of a common market, but it also involves the harmonization of industrial, regional, transport, fiscal, monetary, and other economic and social policies. A full economic union also includes a monetary union, with the adoption of a common currency by the members. In January 1999, 11 members of the EU formed an economic and monetary union, and moved to adopt a new currency—"the Euro"—in place of their national currencies. Greece joined the EMU in January 2001. (The 12 members of the EMU have an * in Figure 2.4.)

5. **Political union.** A political union has all the characteristics of an economic union but extends from the economic area to such political areas as foreign and defense policy. A fully developed political union is more akin to a federal political system than to an agreement among sovereign states.

Year of membership	Members
1957	*France Germany (Federal Republic) *Italy *Belgium *Netherlands *Luxembourg
1973	Britain Denmark } First enlargement *Ireland
1979	*Greece
1986	*Spain } Second enlargement *Portugal
1990	*Germany unified
1995	*Austria *Finland } Third enlargement Sweden

*Members of the European Economic and Monetary Union.

Figure 2.4   Expanding Membership of the European Union

It is important to note that these stages of regional integration are pure models; they do not fully describe reality. NAFTA, for example, is primarily at stage 1 (an FTA). However, NAFTA contains some provisions requiring more openness toward foreign investment, normally identified with stage 3 (a common market).

The Growing Impact of Regionalism   In the postwar period, it is possible to identify two major phases in the growth of regionalism. The first phase began in 1957, when six countries formed the EC, now called the EU (see Figure 2.4). Following the example of the EC, a number of Third World countries sought to establish their own RTAs in the 1960s. However, this first phase of regionalism "had virtually died by the end of the [1960s] decade, except for the original European Community."[55] In the 1980s there was a revival of regionalism, and many analysts believe that this second phase of regionalism is likely to be far more successful. The United States had refused to join RTAs in the first phase but became more supportive of regionalism in the second phase. Thus, in the 1980s the United States concluded free trade agreements with Israel and Canada, and in the early 1990s it formed NAFTA with Canada and Mexico.

Several possible reasons can be given for the willingness of the United States to participate in RTAs in the 1980s. First, the United States was reacting to the broadening and deepening of integration in the EU, an expanding trade bloc from which it was excluded. As Figure 2.4 shows, membership in the EU grew from 6 states in 1957 to 15 in 1995, and a number of Eastern European countries would like to join in the future. A second factor in the U.S. conversion was dissatisfaction with the slow progress of multilateral trade negotiations. Indeed, it was during the protracted eighth round of GATT negotiations (the Uruguay round) that the United States established its free trade agreements with Israel, Canada, and Mexico. A third factor relates to the relative decline in U.S. economic hegemony. During the first phase of regionalism, the United States as global economic hegemon took the main responsibility for upholding the global trade regime as the best path to trade liberalization. However, frustration over its chronic trade deficits has pushed the United States to seek regionalism as another possible route to expanding its export markets.

As discussed in Chapter 9, some U.S. domestic groups strongly oppose NAFTA and any attempts to extend it to other countries such as Chile. Nevertheless, since the U.S. conversion to regionalism in the 1980s, all major advanced industrial states except Japan are now members of RTAs. Japan and the United States are both members of the *APEC* forum, which was formed in 1989. APEC has a goal of establishing a free and open trade and investment area for its developed country members by 2010, and if this goal is achieved, Japan will also be a member of an RTA.

What is the significance of the growth of regionalism for relations among the advanced industrial states? Some observers think this is a period of "open regionalism" that will serve as a stepping-stone to global cooperation, and they point out that APEC has a broad range of members from Asia, Australasia, and North and South America. Others argue, however, that regionalism is a divisive force that could eventually result in the splitting of the world into three major economic blocs based in Europe, the Western Hemisphere, and East Asia.

Despite the divisions among the advanced industrial states, they are normally able to cooperate when necessary to preserve their predominant influence vis-à-vis the Third World in the IMF, the World Bank, and the WTO. It is therefore important to examine why Third World countries have had so little influence in these institutions and what actions they have attempted to take to remedy this situation.

POSTWAR ECONOMIC INSTITUTIONS AND THE THIRD WORLD

The Bretton Woods system and its institutions are often credited with contributing "to almost unprecedented global economic growth and change over the past five decades."[56] This economic growth, however, has not been shared by all. Poverty and its attendant problems, such as disease and hunger, are prevalent in much of the world, and there is a major gulf between the rich nations of the North and the poor nations of the South. Third World countries are characterized not only by low levels of economic development, but also by low levels of social development. Economic development indicators include such factors as per capita income, infrastructure facilities (for example, transportation, communications, and electrical power and water facilities), and the availability of modern technology. Social development indicators include literacy rates, health and sanitary facilities, and infant mortality and life expectancy rates.

Table 2.1 includes figures on one of the main indicators of economic development, per capita income. The first column shows that Northern states have much higher per capita incomes than most Southern states. Thus, the average per capita in-

TABLE 2.1

AVERAGE PER CAPITA INCOME AND PER CAPITA INCOME OF THE POOREST 20%, 1993 (U.S. DOLLARS)

Country	Average Per Capita Income	Per Capita Income of the Poorest 20%
United States	$24,240	$5,814
Japan	20,850	9,070
Netherlands	17,330	7,105
United Kingdom	17,210	3,958
Korea, Republic of	9,630	3,563
Chile	8,400	1,386
Hungary	6,050	2,297
Brazil	5,370	564
Guatemala	3,350	352
Indonesia	3,150	1,370
Nigeria	1,400	357
India	1,220	537
Bangladesh	1,290	613
Nepal	1,020	464
Guinea-Bissau	840	88
Tanzania	580	70

Source: Human Development Report 1996, p. 13, table 1.1. © 1996 by the United Nations Development Programme. By permission of Oxford University Press.

come in the United States in 1993 ($24,240) was almost 8 times greater than the per capita income in Indonesia ($3,150), almost 20 times greater than the per capita income in India ($1,220), and more than 40 times greater than the per capita income in Tanzania ($580). The second column shows there is also a major gap between the rich and the poor within countries of the North as well as the South. Thus, the per capita income of the poorest 20 percent of people in Japan ($9,070) is less than one-half of the average per capita income in Japan ($20,850), the per capita income of the poorest 20 percent in the United States ($5,814) is less than one-fourth of the U.S. average ($24,240), and the per capita income of the poorest 20 percent in Guatemala ($352) is barely one-tenth of the Guatemalan average ($3,350).

The following examples show that the economic gap between the rich states in the North and the poor states in the South is not only great but is widening.

- In 1993, the global GDP amounted to about $23 trillion. (The global GDP refers to the total value of production of goods and services in the world.[57]) Of this $23 trillion, the LDCs, with almost 80 percent of the world's population, accounted for only $5 trillion, whereas the industrial countries accounted for $18 trillion.
- The share of global income of the poorest 20 percent of the world's people his declined from 2.3 to 1.4 percent in the last 30 years, whereas the share of the richest 20 percent has increased from 70 to 85 percent.
- The gap in per capita income between the industrial countries and the LDCs almost tripled from $5,700 in 1960 to $15,400 in 1993.[58]

TABLE 2.2

HUMAN DEVELOPMENT INDICATORS

Region	Real GDP Per Capita (US Dollars)		Infant Mortality Rate (per 1,000 Live Births)		Adult Literacy Rate (%)		Safe Water Access (Percent of the Population)	
	1960	1998	1960	1998	1970	1998	1975–80	1990–98
Sub-Saharan Africa	$990	$1,607	166	106	27	58.5	24	54
South Asia	698	2,112	163	72	32	54.3	30[a]	85[a]
East Asia	729	3,564	146	37	88	83.4	—	68
East Asia excluding China	869	13,635	84	10	88	96.3	70	92
Southeast Asia and Pacific	732	3,234	127	41	65	88.2	15	71
Latin America and Caribbean	2,137	6,510	107	32	72	87.7	60	78
Arab States	931	4,140	166	55	30	59.7	71	83
All LDCs	915	3,270	149	64	43	72.3	41	72

[a]Excluding India.

Source: United Nations Development Programme, *Human Development Report 1996,* p. 209; *Human Development Report 2000,* pp. 160, 171, and 189.

Although the economic gap between the Northern and Southern states has generally increased in recent years, there are also growing divisions *within* the South. Thus, Table 2.2 shows that the East Asian and Latin American countries generally score higher in terms of both economic and social indicators than the South Asian and sub-Saharan African countries. The sub-Saharan Africans and East Asians demonstrate some of the most striking differences in development levels. The per capita GDP in sub-Saharan Africa in 1960 ($990) was slightly higher than the per capita GDP in East Asia excluding China ($869). By 1998, however, the per capita GDP in East Asia excluding China ($13,635) was over eight times higher than the per capita GDP in sub-Saharan Africa ($1,607). Sub-Saharan Africa also registered lower levels of development than most other regions on such social measures as infant mortality, adult literacy rate, and access to safe water, whereas the development level for East Asia excluding China was well above the average in these areas. The infant mortality rate of 106 per 1,000 live births for sub-Saharan Africa in 1998 was particularly high, and in fact increased from a mortality rate of 97 per 1,000 live births in 1994.

Recognizing the major divisions among LDCs, the UN in 1971 compiled a list of 24 of the poorest countries that it identified as LLDCs, and the UN list of LLDCs has grown to 31 countries in 1980 and to 48 countries today. The UN has singled out the LLDCs for special attention because they generally have extremely low per capita GDPs, literacy rates, and shares of manufacturing. Table 2.3 shows that almost three-quarters of the 48 LLDCs are in Africa, and that there are also a substantial number in the Asia/Pacific. The third column in the table shows that 19 of the 43 LLDCs for which statistics are available had *negative* GDP per capita growth rates from 1990 to 1998.

TABLE 2.3

DEVELOPMENT INDICATORS OF THE LEAST DEVELOPED COUNTRIES (LLDCs)

LLDCs	1998 GDP Per Capita (U.S. dollars)	1998 Population (millions)	1990–1998 Real Growth Rate Percent (GDP per capita)
Afghanistan	—	21.4	—
Angola	523	12.1	–3.2
Bangladesh	350	124.8	3.1
Benin	405	5.8	1.8
Bhutan	623	0.6	4.2
Burkina Faso	249	11.3	0.7
Burundi	149	6.5	–5.3
Cambodia	299	10.7	2.3
Cape Verde	1380	0.4	3.0
Central African Republic	340	3.5	–0.7
Chad	231	7.3	–0.8
Comoros	325	0.7	–3.3
Dem. Rep. of the Congo	124	49.1	–8.3
Djibouti	757	0.6	–4.6[a]
Equatorial Guinea	1050	0.4	15.3
Eritrea	190	3.6	2.0[b]
Ethiopia	113	59.7	2.0
Gambia	349	1.2	–1.2
Guinea	573	7.3	0.9
Guinea-Bissau	173	1.2	–1.1
Haiti	356	8.0	–3.4
Kiribati	639	0.1	1.6
Lao People's Democratic Republic	406	5.2	3.7
Lesotho	485	2.1	4.8
Liberia	—	2.7	—
Madagascar	231	15.1	–2.0
Malawi	169	10.4	2.7
Maldives	1209	0.3	3.6
Mali	264	10.7	1.3
Mauritania	478	2.5	1.3
Mozambique	169	18.9	1.8
Myanmar	—	44.5	—
Nepal	218	22.9	2.4
Niger	216	10.1	–1.2
Rwanda	279	6.6	–1.7
Samoa	967	0.2	0.9
Sao Tome and Principe	339	0.1	–0.6
Sierra Leone	160	4.6	–6.1
Solomon Islands	751	0.4	0.3
Somalia	—	9.2	—

(*Continued*)

TABLE 2.3

(*CONTINUED*)

LLDCs	1998 GDP Per Capita (U.S. dollars)	1998 Population (millions)	1990–1998 Real Growth Rate Percent (GDP per capita)
Sudan	296	28.3	5.8
Togo	337	4.4	–0.5
Tuvalu	—	—	—
Uganda	338	20.6	4.3
United Republic of Tanzania	173	32.1	0.0
Vanuatu	1415	0.2	–0.5
Yemen	250	16.9	–1.0
Zambia	427	8.8	–1.4

[a]1992–98
[b]1986–90
Source: United Nations Conference on Trade and Development, *The Least Developed Countries 2000 Report,* Annex Table 1, p. 215.

Although a relatively small number of LDCs—particularly in East and Southeast Asia—have improved their economic positions, the great majority of Third World countries have been frustrated in their efforts to promote development and exert more influence. As discussed in Chapter 11, even some East and Southeast Asian countries, such as South Korea, Indonesia, Malaysia, and Thailand, which had been viewed as exemplars of economic development, confronted serious financial crises in the late 1990s. The most significant gap in economic and social development therefore continues to be the division between the advanced industrial states of the North on the one hand and the large majority of LDCs in the South on the other. Because most LDCs are in a very weak position individually, only collective action has provided some opportunity for extracting costly concessions from the North. Thus, the Third World has often attempted to present a unified front vis-à-vis the Northern industrial states in the UN and other institutional forums.

LDC Efforts to Alter the Institutional Framework

Many LDCs have been dissatisfied with the KIEOs because of their lack of influence in these organizations. From the perspective of many LDCs, the KIEOs also promote policies that either do not contribute to or pose major obstacles to LDC economic development.[59] This chapter briefly discusses LDC efforts to bring about changes in the postwar international institutions and to create new institutions that would increase their influence and development prospects. Subsequent chapters examine the position of LDCs on issues such as foreign debt and foreign investment, and Chapter 11 outlines alternative strategies the LDCs have followed for promoting development.

The 1950s   An early target of LDC dissatisfaction was the IBRD or World Bank, which was designed to provide long-term loans for economic development. As discussed in Chapter 11, the IBRD provides *hard loans,* with relatively high interest rates and shorter repayment periods; for example, the interest rate on IBRD loans in 1995 was about 7.1 percent. Because the poorest LDCs require **concessional** or **soft loans,** the IBRD funding is available mainly to middle-income LDCs. Third World countries were also dissatisfied with the weighted voting system of the IBRD, which favored—and continues to favor—the rich Northern states. In 1997, for example, the 26 developed countries had 61.6 percent of the votes in the World Bank board of governors, and the G-7 countries alone had 47.8 percent of the governors' votes. The 163 LDC members of the World Bank, by contrast, had only 38.4 percent of the votes.[60]

Throughout the 1950s, the LDCs repeatedly pressured the UN to establish a new agency that would have a more equitable voting system than the World Bank and would provide grants or soft loans (with low or no interest and long repayment periods) to Third World countries. These proposals repeatedly failed, however, because of opposition from the advanced industrial states. With decolonization increasing and LDC needs for capital becoming more evident, in 1960 the developed states finally agreed to establish a soft-loan aid agency, the *International Development Association (IDA).* As is often the case, however, the Northern states were *not* willing to accede to LDC demands for greater power over decision making, and they insisted that the IDA become a part of the World Bank group with its weighted voting system (see Figure 2.1). Furthermore, the largest share of World Bank group loans continues to be hard loans provided by the IBRD. The soft IDA loans (or IDA "credits") are more limited in amount and are available only to poorer LDCs. In fiscal year 2000, for example, IBRD loan disbursements totaled about $13.3 billion, whereas IDA credit disbursements amounted to $5.2 billion.[61]

The 1960s In the 1960s decolonization transformed North-South relations as many new African and Asian LDCs gained their political independence and joined the UN. (Most Latin American LDCs had become independent in the nineteenth century.) Thus, the number of new African and Asian states in the UN increased from 10 in 1955 to 55 in 1966, and by 1966 they accounted for about 45 percent of the countries in the UN.[62] In 1964, the 77 Third World countries in the UN from Africa, Asia, and Latin America met to express their dissatisfaction with the KIEOs and to prepare for a major conference on trade and development.[63] This caucus of LDCs now has well over 100 members, but it is still referred to as the **Group of 77 (G-77).**

The conference organized by the G-77 in Geneva in March 1964 was the first **United Nations Conference on Trade and Development (UNCTAD).** In view of the growing numbers of LDCs in the United Nations, the G-77 was able to convene UNCTAD I despite the initial opposition—and then the grudging acceptance—of the advanced industrial states. UNCTAD I was "the first institutional response in the economic sphere to the entry of the Third World on the international scene," and UNCTAD subsequently became a permanent organ of the UN General Assembly (see Figure 2.1).[64] Although all members of the UN are members of UNCTAD, the LDCs with their greater numbers have had the predominant role in setting UNCTAD's agenda and work program. In marked contrast to the KIEOs, the secretariat of the UNCTAD has openly supported LDC interests, and the UNCTAD secretary-general has always been from a Third World country.

UNCTAD experienced some success in espousing an alternative approach to trade and economic development, in inducing GATT to give more priority to Third World trade interests, and in overseeing certain areas of trade negotiation such as the establishment of international commodity agreements. However, GATT/WTO continues to be the unrivaled international organization monitoring the principles, norms, and rules of the global trade regime. Because UNCTAD's orientation posed a direct challenge to the liberal-economic order and to the power position of the North, the advanced industrial states simply refused to accept it as a major forum for negotiations on international economic relations. Thus, UNCTAD's main role has not been in international management but in serving as a pressure group for Third World interests.

The 1970s   Although Third World countries attempted to improve their position vis-à-vis the North in the 1960s, their stance became far more militant in the 1970s when OPEC drastically increased oil prices. A number of factors contributed to OPEC's success in raising prices, including the growing dependence of the advanced industrial states on Middle Eastern oil and the unifying effect on Arab OPEC members of the October 1973 Middle East War. LDC oil importers as well as industrial states were hurt by the OPEC price increases, but most LDCs nevertheless viewed OPEC as an example of what they might also do to increase their power and wealth vis-à-vis the North. Thus, the OPEC example, along with increases in the prices of a number of commodities that LDCs exported, led to LDC calls for a **New International Economic Order** (**NIEO**) in the 1970s. The NIEO was a multilateral strategy designed to gain major economic concessions from the North and to increase the economic and political power of the South.

The advanced industrial states were willing to join in NIEO negotiations with the Third World in the 1970s because of their concerns about the increased leverage of OPEC. Indeed, implicit linkages were drawn between guaranteed supplies of OPEC oil at lower prices on the one hand and Northern willingness to discuss the NIEO demands on the other. Third World demands in the NIEO negotiations were numerous, including an increase in **foreign aid,** LDC sovereignty over their economies and natural resources, increased LDC control over foreign direct investment, more access to Northern technology on easier terms, preferential treatment for LDC exports to Northern states, international commodity agreements, and increased LDC decision-making power in the IMF and the World Bank group.[65]

The Third World countries did register some gains in the NIEO negotiations. For example, the voting shares of OPEC countries increased somewhat in both the IMF and the World Bank, and the industrial states eventually agreed to a generalized system of preferences (GSP) for LDC exports (see Chapter 8). These gains, however, were clearly limited, and industrial states became less willing to make concessions to the Third World as bargaining power gradually shifted back in favor of the North. Indeed, oil proved to be a unique commodity; LDC producers of other commodities could not acquire similar marketing power. The industrial states also gradually gained access to other sources of oil and became less dependent on the OPEC producers. The most significant factor shifting the balance of power back toward the North, however, was the Third World foreign debt crisis that began in the 1980s.

The 1980s and 1990s   Chapter 7 focuses on the Third World foreign debt crisis, which began in 1982 when Mexico threatened to default on its loans. As discussed in Chapter 7, the debt crisis was closely related to the OPEC oil price increases of the 1970s. OPEC countries deposited a large share of their oil revenues in international banks, which recycled these "petrodollars" by extending massive loans to LDC oil importers. A combination of imprudent lending, imprudent borrowing, and unexpected international events contributed to overborrowing by many LDCs in the 1970s and to the LDCs' dependence on debt relief assistance in the 1980s and 1990s. In return for extending structural adjustment loans to the LDC debtors, the IMF and the World Bank, backed by the advanced industrial states, imposed conditions requiring that LDCs open their economies to trade, foreign investment, and other economic linkages with the North. Thus, Third World countries have generally taken a more conciliatory approach toward the North since the 1980s, and they have been more willing to accept Northern demands for such policies as liberalization, privatization, and deregulation.

This shift in the balance of power toward the North is evident in changes occurring in UNCTAD, which has been "the principal locus of Third World efforts to obtain changes in the trade and other economic relationships between developed and developing countries."[66] UNCTAD's pressures on behalf of the Third World had increased during the 1970s when the Third World was demanding an NIEO. By the late 1980s, however, UNCTAD began to shift its policy toward a more conciliatory approach because of threats that it could become totally irrelevant. This change was evident in UNCTAD's relationship with GATT, which shifted from an emphasis on conflicting to complementary interests between the two organizations. The change was also evident in the tone of discussion in UNCTAD conferences, which are normally held once every four years. The sixth UNCTAD conference (UNCTAD VI) in 1983 was marked by confrontation, but UNCTAD VII and VIII in 1987 and 1992 were notable for efforts to identify common North-South interests. Because it was the first UNCTAD conference since the breakup of the Soviet bloc, UNCTAD VIII "brought together a virtually universal view that economic policies based on market forces were the best basis for achieving development."[67] UNCTAD's reversal of policy was only one indication that most Third World countries in the 1990s saw little alternative to operating within the framework of the KIEOs and the liberal-economic system of the advanced industrial states. Nevertheless, this book will discuss indications that Third World conflict with the industrial states could increase in the new millennium if greater economic openness does not produce clearcut socioeconomic benefits for the LDCs.

POSTWAR ECONOMIC INSTITUTIONS AND THE CENTRALLY PLANNED ECONOMIES

International organization scholars generally consider the IMF, the World Bank, and GATT/WTO to be universal membership organizations, in which all states can become members.[68] For much of the history of these organizations, however, the CPEs of Eastern Europe, the Soviet Union, and China either were nonmembers or played a very limited role. At the end of World War II there was an institutional division of labor, with the UN concentrating primarily on political and military security matters and the Bretton Woods institutions taking responsibility for economic cooperation. Nevertheless, political security issues were inevitably a factor in the deliberations of the KIEOs.[69] The Western allies generally felt that universalism was the best approach to creating a more secure environment, and Harry Dexter White of the U.S. Treasury Department wrote in his April 1942 draft Bretton Woods plan that "to exclude a country such as Russia would be an egregious error. Russia, despite her socialist economy could both contribute and profit by participation."[70] The allied governments also expected that the Eastern European states, which previously had close economic ties with the West, would become full members of the Bretton Woods organizations.[71]

Although the Soviet Union was fearful of capitalist encirclement, it wanted to gain access to economic and financial aid to reconstruct its war-damaged economy. The Soviet Union therefore was actively involved in the deliberations leading up to and including the Bretton Woods conference. As the only Communist state at Bretton Woods (Poland and Czechoslovakia were not yet Communist), the Soviet Union expressed a number of concerns regarding such issues as special consideration for state-trading countries, the paid-in subscriptions and voting procedures of the IMF and World Bank, and the amount of information the IMF and World Bank would require of member states. The major Western countries made limited concessions to the USSR in the *IMF Articles of Agreement* concerning the payment of subscriptions and the provision of information to the IMF, and the Soviet Union signed the Bretton Woods agreements. However, it continued to oppose the method of allocating votes in the IMF and the World Bank, the transfer of gold to U.S. territory, and the conditions that the IMF would place on its loans. After the first IMF/World Bank board of governors meeting in March 1946, the Soviet Union stopped participating, and it did not become a member of these organizations. By this time, Cold War issues were intruding (e.g., disputes over the administration of Berlin and the Soviet occupation of Eastern Europe), and both the Soviet Union and the West backed away from the goal of universality. Thus, the Soviet Union did not even attend the conferences designed to develop a global trade organization.[72]

In 1947, the United States responded to the continuing economic problems in Western Europe—the near exhaustion of foreign exchange reserves for purchasing needed food, energy, and raw materials—with the European Recovery Program, or Marshall Plan. When U.S. Secretary of State George C. Marshall introduced the plan, he invited the Soviet Union and Eastern Europe to participate. However, the Soviets refused to join in and vetoed the idea of participation by the East Europeans. Particularly objectionable to the Soviets were U.S. requirements that the United States have some advisory authority over the internal budgets of Marshall Plan aid recipients, that the European countries cooperate with each other in the use of Marshall Plan aid, and that most of the aid be used to purchase U.S. exports. Only Western European states therefore joined with the United States in the Marshall Plan, and the Soviet Union established the *Council for Mutual Economic Assistance* (CMEA) in January 1949 as a counterweight. Composed of the Soviet Union and Eastern European states other than Yugoslavia, the CMEA solidified the economic and political divisions between Eastern and Western Europe.[73]

The Soviet-led CMEA was involved with a number of economic activities such as technical cooperation and joint planning, and its strategies for promoting cooperation among the CPEs sharply differentiated it from the market-oriented Bretton Woods system. For example, the CMEA emphasized central planning for almost all economic decisions, such as resource allocation; the nationalization of the factors of production, including capital, natural resources, and in most cases land; the collectivization of agriculture; and a rather rigid separation of the domestic economy from external economic influences. The main purpose of CMEA was to reorient Eastern European trade away from the West and to solidify the economic linkages between the Soviet Union and Eastern Europe. Thus, the CMEA established two institutions, the International Bank for Economic Cooperation (in 1964) and the International Investment Bank (in 1971), which were designed to assume functions similar to those of the IMF and the World Bank. These two CMEA banks were very inadequate substitutes, however, because they were associated with increased bilateralism, a currency (the ruble) with unrealistic conversion rates that limited trade, and inward-looking policies vis-à-vis the world economy.[74]

The growing economic rift between East and West resulted not only from actions of the Soviet Union but also from policies of the Western industrial states. For example, the United States restricted trade with Communist countries from 1948, and the 1949 U.S. Export Control Act authorized the president to establish a licensing system that would regulate exports to the Communist states. The United States also pressured its allies to join in the *Coordinating Committee (COCOM)*, which was established to coordinate Western embargoes of strategic goods to the Soviet bloc. COCOM was an effort to limit the Soviet Union's military advances, and it was designed to hurt the Soviet Union economically and isolate it politically. Furthermore, the U.S. Congress passed the Trade Agreements Extension Act in 1951, which withdrew trade concessions previously granted to all Communist countries other than Yugoslavia.

The liberal-economic orientation of the KIEOs was yet another factor contributing to the East-West split. Theoretically, the lending decisions of the IMF and World Bank are to be nonpolitical in nature, and the IBRD Articles of Agreement explicitly state that "only economic considerations shall be relevant" to the bank's decisions.[75] A number of analysts argue, however, that these institutions are committed to a capitalist world economy and that they make decisions on the basis of political and ideological as well as economic considerations.[76] Even when these organizations are not consciously promoting Western-style capitalism, the values of their professional staff members, who have received their education and training mainly in Western capitalist countries, affect the decision-making process.[77]

In view of the major East-West divisions, it is not surprising that most linkages between the Communist states and the KIEOs were severed during the 1950s. Although Czechoslovakia, Poland, Yugoslavia, China, and Cuba had been founding members of the IMF and the World Bank, their membership ended or their status changed after they became centrally planned socialist economies (the sole exception was Yugoslavia). As Table 2.4 shows, Poland withdrew from the IMF and the World Bank in 1950, charging that these institutions were largely controlled by the U.S. government, and Czechoslovakia was expelled from the World Bank and the IMF in 1954. The ostensible reasons for expulsion related to Czechoslovakia's failure to pay part of its capital subscription to the IBRD and its refusal to consult with the IMF and provide it with information.[78] Yugoslavia was the only Eastern European country to remain in the IMF and the World Bank in the 1950s, but it was a special case because of its independence from the Soviet Union. The Republic of China (Taiwan) occupied the China

TABLE 2.4

MEMBERSHIP OF THE EMERGING ECONOMIES IN THE KEYSTONE INTERNATIONAL ECONOMIC ORGANIZATIONS

	IMF	World Bank	GATT/WTO
1946	Poland, Czechoslovakia, Yugoslavia & China (founding members of IMF and World Bank)		
1948			Czechoslovakia and China (founding members)
1950	Poland withdraws from IMF and World Bank		Republic of China (Taiwan) withdraws from GATT
1954	Czechoslovakia ousted from the IMF and World Bank		
1966			Yugoslavia
1967			Poland
1971			Romania
1972	Romania	Romania	
1973			Hungary
1980	People's Republic of China (replaces Taiwan in the IMF and World Bank)		
1982	Hungary	Hungary	
1986	Poland	Poland	
1990	Bulgaria Czechoslovakia	Bulgaria	East Germany accedes to GATT by virtue of reunification
1991	Albania, Lithuania	Albania Czechoslovakia	
1992 to 1996	Russian Federation, other FSU[a] republics, Croatia, Slovenia, Macedonia, Bosnia and Herzegovina, Czech Republic, Slovak Republic (IMF & World Bank)		Bulgaria, Czech Republic, Slovak Republic, Slovenia
1998 to 2001	Federal Republic of Yugoslavia (IMF & World Bank)		Kyrgyz Republic, Estonia, Croatia, Albania, Georgia, Lithuania, Moldova, China
2002			Taiwan

[a]FSU = Former Soviet Union republics

Sources: International Monetary Fund, *Annual Report of the Executive Board* (Washington, D.C.: IMF, various years); *World Bank Annual Report* (Washington, D.C.: World Bank, various years); General Agreement on Tariffs and Trade, *GATT Activities* (Geneva, Switzerland: GATT, various years).

seat in these institutions after the People's Republic of China took over the mainland in October 1949, and Cuba under Fidel Castro withdrew from the World Bank in 1960 and from the IMF in 1964.

Table 2.4 shows that China and Czechoslovakia were founding members of GATT in 1948, but the Chiang Kai-shek government (which had fled from the mainland to

Taiwan) withdrew from the organization in 1950, purportedly on behalf of China. Czechoslovakia remained a member of GATT (but not of the IMF and the World Bank), even though its membership was basically inactive for a number of years. Czechoslovakia was able to retain membership because of GATT's status as a highly informal organization.

As nonmembers of the KIEOs, the Soviet bloc countries joined the Third World in supporting the formation of alternative organizations in which the advanced capitalist states would have less control. For example, the Soviet Union strongly endorsed the formation of the UNCTAD. By the late 1960s, however, the Soviet bloc countries became less interested in UNCTAD and other alternative organizations for a number of reasons. These included the emergence of East-West détente, the increase of tensions and economic problems within the Eastern bloc's CMEA, the growing dependence of Eastern European countries on Western markets for their exports, and the political desire of Eastern Europeans to gain more independence from the Soviet Union. Thus, Table 2.4 shows that some Eastern European countries (Poland, Romania, and Hungary) joined the KIEOs beginning in the late 1960s, and the People's Republic of China replaced Taiwan in the IMF and the World Bank in 1980. The most far-reaching change occurred in the early 1990s after the breakup of the Soviet Union, when Russia and other FSU republics joined the IMF and World Bank, and a number of countries from the former East bloc joined the GATT/WTO. Another momentuous change occurred in November 2001, when China and Taiwan became members of the WTO in December 2001 and January 2002, respectively. Some analysts predict that China could eventually join the United States and EU as the most important members of the WTO. Of the major emerging economics, only Russia has not yet become a WTO member. The emerging economies have had to accept more market reforms when joining the KIEOs, and the KIEOs in turn have had to become more open to some degree of central planning. Later chapters discuss in greater detail the gradual moves toward integration of the emerging economies with the IMF, the World Bank, and the GATT/WTO.

POSTWAR ECONOMIC INSTITUTIONS AND CIVIL SOCIETY

Although Third World countries have been the main disadvantaged group, a wide range of NGOs focusing on the environment, women, labor, development, and human rights have also been largely excluded from positions of power. These NGOs are extremely diverse, but have often been categorized together under the "civil society" label. Operational NGOs emphasize the provision of voluntary social services, whereas advocacy NGOs are politically active and seek to influence decision making in governments and international organizations. When we discuss civil society in this book, we are referring primarily to the advocacy functions of NGOs. Critics sometimes argue that advocacy NGOs like to describe themselves as civil society groups because the term connotes civic duty and responsibility, and therefore masks their political ambitions. Supporters counter that advocacy NGOs are compensating for a "democracy deficit" by expressing the views of disadvantaged and underrepresented groups, but critics maintain that these NGOs are self-appointed and not necessarily representative of broader public concerns.[79] Although a clear majority of these groups express their views primarily by peaceful means, demonstrations at gatherings such as the Third WTO ministerial conference in Seattle in November 1999 show that a rather small minority of these groups either engage in violent protest or condone such violence. We use the term civil society to refer to groups that are generally committed to peaceful discussion and protest. Among the major groups that often feel excluded from decision making in the KIEOs, women's, environmental, labor, and development groups are especially prominent.

Women's Groups

Women's groups have expressed concerns regarding the small proportion of women in influential positions in international organizations and the failure of these organizations to take sufficient account of gender issues in their deliberations and policy decisions. Article 8 of the United Nations Charter states that the UN "shall place no restrictions on the eligibility of men and women to participate in any capacity and under conditions of equality in its principle and subsidiary organs."[80] Although this article was included to give legitimacy to hiring women as permanent international organization staff members, it is phrased in prohibitive terms rather than as an affirmative obligation to hire women. Women have always constituted a majority of clerical workers but a minority of professional staff in the UN and its specialized agencies.

After decades of pressure by women's groups, the UN secretary-general appointed a Co-ordinator for the Improvement of the Status of Women in 1985 and set goals for increasing women's representation. As a result, women's representation on the UN professional staff increased from 19 percent in 1980 to 34 percent in 1995 and 39 percent in 1999. Women in the UN nevertheless have fewer positions at the higher levels. In 1999, 48 percent of junior professionals but only 21 percent of senior managers on the UN professional staff were women. Of 21 under-secretary-generals, two were women. Women's representation on the professional staff of the UN specialized agencies at the end of 1998 was 32 percent, and among senior managers 16 percent, both lower than in the UN secretariat. Women have been appointed to head some UN agencies, including the UN Children's Fund (UNICEF), the UN Development Fund for Women (UNIFEM), the office of the UN High Commissioner for Refugees (UNHCR), and the UN Fund for Population Activities (UNFPA), but these agencies deal primarily with social issues, which are often identified as women's areas. No head of the major international economic organizations—the IMF, the World Bank, GATT/WTO, or OECD—has been a woman.[81]

Some feminist theorists argue that the small number of women in high foreign policy and international organization positions is "symptomatic of a much deeper issue . . . the extent to which international politics is such a thoroughly masculinized sphere of activity that women's voices are considered inauthentic."[82] They also maintain that these institutions often make decisions that disadvantage women and merely reinforce the gendered divisions of labor and power in society. In Chapter 11, we discuss this critique as it applies to World Bank structural adjustment loans to Third World countries.

Environmental and Labor Groups

Environmental and labor groups also contend that they are excluded from positions of influence in major international economic institutions, and that these institutions largely ignore environmental and labor considerations in their decision-making processes. For example, a considerable amount of literature exists on the exclusion of environmental NGOs from a formal role at the WTO, and the WTO has been criticized for not taking sufficient account of environmental and labor issues in its dispute settlement and rule-making procedures. Furthermore, a wide array of literature exists that is critical of the World Bank's failure to give higher priority to the environment in its Third World development projects. Although the KIEOs have in varying degrees sought to address these concerns, many environmental and labor groups argue that the KIEO efforts have been insufficient.[83]

Development Groups

It is important to note that the concerns of labor and environmental groups sometimes run counter to the perceived interests of the Third World countries. For example, many LDCs argue that environmental and labor standards can be used by the industrial states as an excuse for imposing trade barriers against Third World exports. Furthermore, LDCs maintain that their economic development prospects will be severely jeopardized if they are expected to adhere to the same environmental and labor standards as the advanced industrial states. A number of civil society groups have been concerned specifically with promoting development in Third World countries. For example, some of these groups have called for more foreign debt relief for low-income LDCs through accelerating the relief process, broadening the eligibility criteria, and increasing the amount of assistance to eligible countries. Civil society groups have also called for drastic reform of IMF and World Bank SALs to LDCs. The role of these development groups is discussed in Chapters 7 and 11.

Conclusion

This chapter has examined the changing institutional framework for managing the global economy in the postwar era. The member states at the 1944 Bretton Woods conference had great faith in the establishment of international institutions to prevent a recurrence of the problems of the interwar years, and the three KIEOs have been important contributors to prosperity in the postwar period. Nevertheless, there is a hierarchy of states within the IMF, the World Bank, and GATT/WTO, and postwar prosperity has not been equally distributed among states and peoples. The United States and other advanced industrial countries have been at the top of the hierarchy, in a position to establish and uphold the principles and rules for the functioning of the global economic order. The Third World countries have sought to alter the KIEOs and to establish alternative organizations such as the UNCTAD. However, their gains have been limited, and events such as the foreign debt crisis of the 1980s have greatly weakened their position.

Unlike the Third World countries, the centrally planned economies for many years were nonparticipants in the KIEOs, and the Soviet Union established the Council for Mutual Economic Assistance as an alternative organization for the Eastern bloc. However, economic problems, political tensions, and growing economic dependence on advanced capitalist states gradually pushed the Eastern bloc countries to join the Western-dominated KIEOs. The breakup of the Soviet bloc and the Soviet Union has sped up this integration process. The Third World debt crisis has similarly forced many LDCs to become more dependent on the IMF and the World Bank for SALs and to become more closely integrated with the capitalist economic order. Thus, one student of globalization argues that "we can no longer identify three worlds or two superpowers but rather a singular system in which the critical basis for international relations is no longer the ownership of military hardware but both economic muscle and the ability to influence ideas and commitments."[84]

The globalization process has therefore contributed to the increase in membership of the IMF, the World Bank, and the WTO, and for the first time they are in fact becoming universal membership organizations. Although globalization has contributed to the increased size of the KIEOs, it has also made it more difficult for these international institutions to manage global economic relations. The rapid movement of capital around the world is simply one indication of the pervasive influence of private actors such as MNCs and international banks in an age of "cascading interdependence."[85] These changes are posing an increasing challenge not only to the management capabilities of the large IOs but also to the nation-states that undergird these IOs. In efforts to coordinate their activities, the advanced capitalist states have therefore often turned to smaller, more informal groupings such as the G-7.

Although globalization is challenging the management capabilities of states and international organizations, it is *not* leading to a "borderless world." In fact, states are seeking to survive and prosper in the new age of global competitiveness. With the demise of the Cold War, new economic power centers have been able to emerge in Europe and East Asia, posing a challenge to U.S. economic hegemony. These three regional blocs have extended competitiveness among the advanced industrial states to the global level. Despite these regional divisions, however, one can argue that the advanced capitalist states "are still committed through the G7, the IMF, the World Bank, and the World Trade Organisation to continue to manage the international system."[86]

Divisions have become more evident not only among the advanced industrial states but also among the LDCs. Indeed, some analysts argue that the so-called Third World has fragmented into a number of groups, with the largest gap developing between the LLDCs and the East Asian NIEs. The Third World has also been fragmenting on a regional basis, with some LDCs joining in regional groupings along with advanced industrial states. Notable examples include the associate membership of the African, Caribbean, and Pacific countries in the EU; Mexico's membership in NAFTA; and the joining of industrial and Third World countries in the APEC. In recent years, divisions have also become far more prominent between the major international economic institutions on the one hand and civil society groups representing women, the environment, labor, and development interests on the other. As globalization has increased, these groups have been concerned that the KIEOs are subordinating "issues such as environmental protection, gender equality, and labour rights to a liberalisation drive."[87] How this challenge from civil society groups plays out will have a major impact on global economic management in the twenty-first century.

NOTES

1. Armand Van Dormael, *Bretton Woods: Birth of a Monetary System* (London: Macmillan, 1978), p. ix.
2. Richard N. Gardner, "The Political Setting," in A. L. K. Acheson, J. F. Chant, and M. F. J. Prochowny, eds., *Bretton Woods Revisited* (Toronto: University of Toronto Press, 1972), p. 20; Margaret Garritsen de Vries, "The Bretton Woods Conferences and the Birth of the International Monetary Fund," in Orin Kirshner, ed., *The Bretton Woods-GATT System: Retrospect and Prospect After Fifty Years* (Armonk, NY: M. E. Sharpe, 1996), pp. 3–18.
3. Herman M. Schwartz, *States versus Markets: The Emergence of a Global Economy*, 2nd ed., (New York: St. Martin's Press, 2000), p. 11.
4. Adam Smith used the term mercantile system, and German writers in the 1860s used the term Merkantilismus to describe this doctrine. Only afterward did the term *mercantilism* become standard in the English language. See Jacob Viner, "Mercantilist Thought," in David L. Sills, ed., *International Encyclopedia of the Social Sciences*, (New York: Free Press, 1968), 4, p. 436; and David A. Baldwin, *Economic Statecraft* (Princeton, NJ: Princeton University Press, 1985), p. 72.
5. See Adam Smith, *The Wealth of Nations* (London: Dent, Everyman's Library no. 412, 1910), vol. 1, bk. 4, p. 436.
6. Classic studies of mercantilism include Eli F. Heckscher, *Mercantilism*, vols. 1 and 2, rev. 2nd ed. translated by Mendel Shapiro (London: George Allen & Unwin, 1955); and Jacob Viner, *Studies in the Theory of International Trade* (New York: Augustus M. Kelley, 1965), chs. 1 and 2.
7. For competing views on world powers during the mercantilist period, see George Modelski, "The Long Cycle of Global Politics and the Nation-State," *Comparative Studies in Society and History* 20-2 (April 1978), pp. 214–235; Immanuel Wallerstein, "The Three Instances of Hegemony in the History of the Capitalist World-Economy," in *The Politics of the World-Economy: The States, the Movements and the Civilizations* (London: Cambridge University Press, 1984), pp. 37–46; George Modelski, *Long Cycles in World Politics* (Seattle, WA: University of Washington Press, 1987), ch. 2; George Modelski and William R. Thompson, *Seapower and Global Politics, 1494–1993* (London: Macmillan, 1988), ch. 5; Joshua S. Goldstein, *Long Cycles: Prosperity and War in the Modern Age* (New Haven, CT: Yale University Press, 1988), pp. 99–147.
8. Paul Kennedy, *The Rise and Fall of the Great Powers: Economic Change and Military Conflict from 1500 to 2000* (New York: Random House, 1987), p. 151.
9. Paul Bairoch, "International Industrialization Levels from 1750 to 1980," *Journal of European Economic History* 11-2 (Fall 1982), pp. 291–292.
10. Some writers feel that the degree to which the British were able in promote freer trade in the nineteenth century is often overestimated. See Timothy J. McKeown, "Hegemonic Stability Theory and 19th Century Tariff Levels in Europe," *International Organization* 37-1 (Winter 1983), pp. 73–91.
11. See Edward John Ray, "Changing Patterns of Protectionism: The Fall in Tariffs and the Rise in Non-Tariff Barriers," *Northwestern Journal of International Law & Business*,

8 (1987), pp. 294–295; and Stephen D. Krasner, "State Power and the Structure of International Trade," *World Politics* 28-3 (April, 1976), pp. 330–335.

12. David A. Lake, *Power, Protection, and Free Trade: International Sources of U.S. Commercial Strategy, 1887–1939* (Ithaca, NY: Cornell University Press, 1988), p. 31.

13. On the role of banks and the state in promoting industrialization in late industrializers, see Alexander Gerschenkron, *Economic Backwardness in Historical Perspective* (Cambridge, MA: Harvard University Press, 1962). In the nineteenth century the United States and Germany were late industrializers relative to Britain.

14. Lake, *Power, Protection, and Free Trade,* pp. 30–32; Bairoch, "International Industrialization Levels from 1750 to 1980," pp. 292–293 and 297.

15. Kennedy, *The Rise and Fall of the Great Powers,* p. 230.

16. Albert Fishlow, "Lessons from the Past: Capital Markets during the 19th Century and the Interwar Period," *International Organization* 39-3 (Summer 1985), p. 390; David A. Lake, "British and American Hegemony Compared: Lessons for the Current Era of Decline," in Michael Fry, ed., *History, The White House and The Kremlin: Statesmen as Historians* (London: Pinter, 1991), p. 108.

17. Sally Marks, *The Illusion of Peace: International Relations in Europe 1918–1933* (New York: St. Martin's Press, 1976), p. 47; Charles P. Kindleberger, *The World in Depression 1929–1939,* rev. and enlarged ed. (Berkeley, CA: University of California Press, 1986), pp. 23–26.

18. Robert A. Pastor, *Congress and the Politics of U.S. Foreign Economic Policy, 1929–1976* (Berkeley, CA: University of California Press, 1980), p. 78; John M. Dobson, *Two Centuries of Tariffs: The Background and Emergence of the U.S. International Trade Commission* (Washington, DC: U.S. International Trade Commission, December 1976), p. 32.

19. For a discussion of the effects of the 1930 U.S. tariff see Joseph M. Jones, Jr., *Tariff Retaliation: Repercussions of the Hawley-Smoot Bill* (Philadelphia, PA: University of Pennsylvania Press, 1934).

20. See Kindleberger, *The World in Depression.*

21. The classic study of domestic pressures on the U.S. Congress during the interwar period is E. E. Schattschneider, *Politics, Pressures and the Tariff: A Study of Free Private Enterprise in Pressure Politics, as Shown in the 1929–1930 Revision of the Tariff* (Hamden, CT: Archon Books, 1963, unaltered from the 1935 edition). On the role of domestic forces in protectionism see Helen V. Milner, *Resisting Protectionism: Global Industries and the Politics of International Trade* (Princeton, NJ: Princeton University Press, 1988).

22. Lake, *Power, Protection, and Free Trade,* p. 204.

23. Harold K. Jacobson, *Networks of Interdependence: International Organizations and the Global Political System* (New York: Alfred A. Knopf, 1979), pp. 230–231; Javed A. Ansari, *The Political Economy of International Economic Organization* (Sussex, England: Wheatsheaf, 1986), pp. 6–7; Kelly-Kate S. Pease, *International Organizations: Perspectives on Governance in the Twenty-First Century* (Upper Saddle River, NJ: Prentice-Hall, 1999), pp. 18–19.

24. *Covenant of the League of Nations,* Article 23e.

25. For a discussion of the BIS see Age F. P. Bakker, *International Financial Institutions* (New York: Longman, 1996), ch. 6; and Hazel J. Johnson, *Global Financial Institutions and Markets* (Oxford: Blackwell, 2000), pp. 410–411.

26. de Vries, "The Bretton Woods Conference and the Birth of the International Monetary Fund," pp. 3–4.

27. On the difference between "coordination" and "collaboration," see Arthur Stein, "Coordination and Collaboration: Regimes in an Anarchic World," in David A. Baldwin, ed., *Neorealism and Neoliberalism: The Contemporary Debate* (New York: Columbia University Press, 1993), pp. 41–45.

28. The term *KIEOs* is used in Harold Jacobson and Michel Oksenberg, *China's Participation in the IMF, the World Bank, and GATT: Toward a GlobalEconomic Order* (Ann Arbor, MI: University of Michigan Press, 1990).
29. Communication from a Counsellor, External Relations Division, WTO, November 8, 2001.
30. Quoted in Sidney Dell, "Relations Between the United Nations and the Bretton Woods Institutions," *Development* 4 (1989), p. 28. The UN General Assembly has tried to influence the World Bank's loan-giving activities at various times, but these efforts have been largely unsuccessful. See Samuel A. Bleicher, "UN v. IBRD: A Dilemma of Functionalism," *International Organization* 24-1 (Winter 1970), pp. 31–47.
31. "United Nations-Bretton Woods Collaboration: How Much Is Enough?" *Report of the Twenty-sixth United Nations Issues Conference* (Muscatine, IA: Stanley Foundation, February 24–26, 1995), p. 18.
32. For a detailed discussion of the range of UN interactions with the Bretton Woods institutions, see Dell, "Relations Between the United Nations and the Bretton Woods Institutions," pp. 27–38; and Edward S. Mason and Robert E. Asher, *The World Bank Since Bretton Woods* (Washington, DC: Brookings Institution), pp. 566–576.
33. United Nations Conference on Trade and Development, *World Investment Report 1996* (New York: United Nations, 1996), pp. 239–247; World Trade Organization, *WTO Annual Report 1996* (Geneva: WTO, 1996), vol. 2, pp. 24, 67.
34. There are a number of reasons for the underrepresentation of LDCs on the KIEO professional staffs. See Theodore Cohn, "Developing Countries in the International Civil Service: The Case of the World Bank Group," *International Review of Administrative Sciences* 41-1 (1975), pp. 47–56.
35. Bretton Woods Commission, *Bretton Woods: Looking to the Future;* Commission Report, Staff Review, Background Papers (Washington, DC: Bretton Woods Committee, July 1994), p. B-3.
36. Barry Eichengreen and Peter B. Kenen, "Managing the World Economy under the Bretton Woods System: An Overview," in Peter B. Kenen, ed., *Managing the World Economy: Fifty Years After Bretton Woods* (Washington, DC: Institute for International Economics, 1944), pp. 5–6; John Gerard Ruggie, "International Regimes, Transactions, and Change: Embedded Liberalism in the Postwar Economic Order," in Stephen D. Krasner, ed., *International Regimes* (Ithaca, NY: Cornell University Press), pp. 195–231.
37. "United Nations-Bretton Woods Collaboration: How Much Is Enough?" p. 2.
38. Aaron Segal, "Managing the World Economy," *International Political Science Review* 11-3 (1990), p. 367.
39. C. Fred Bergsten and C. Randall Henning, *Global Economic Leadership and the Group of Seven* (Washington, DC: Institute for International Economics, June, 1996), p. 15.
40. Organization for Economic Co-operation and Development, *The OECD in the 1990s* (Paris: OECD, 1994), p. 9; David Henderson, "The Role of the OECD in Liberalising International Trade and Capital Flows," in Sven Arndt and Chris Miller, eds., Special issue of *The World Economy* on "Global Trade Policy" (1996), pp. 11–28.
41. Bernard Colas, "The OECD's Legal Influence in a Global Economy," *World Economic Affairs* 1–3 (Spring/Summer 1997), pp. 66–67; William J. Drake and Kalypso Nicolaïdis, "Ideas, Interests, and Institutionalization: 'Trade in Services' and The Uruguay Round," *International Organization* 46-1 (Winter 1992) pp. 37–100.
42. OECD, *Export Credit Financing Systems in OECD Member and Non-Member Countries—1999 Supplement* (Paris: OECD, 1999), p. 1. See also David J. Blair, *Trade Negotiations in the OECD: Structures, Institutions and States* (London: Kegan Paul, 1993); and Andrew M. Moravcsik, "Disciplining Trade Finance: The OECD Export Credit Arrangement," *International Organization* (Winter 1989), pp. 173–205.

43. Colas, "The OECD's Legal Influence in a Global Economy," p. 67; Henderson, "The Role of the OECD," pp. 21–22.
44. International Monetary Fund, "IMF Survey Supplement," vol. 29, September 2000, p. 22.
45. Michael C. Webb, *The Political Economy of Policy Coordination: International Adjustment Since 1945* (Ithaca, NY: Cornell University Press, 1995), pp. 176–177.
46. Michael P. Blackwell, "From G-5 to G-77: International Forums for Discussion of Economic Issues," *Finance & Development* 23-4 (December 1986), p. 40.
47. Segal, "Managing the World Economy," p. 362; Robert D. Putnam and Nicholas Bayne, *Hanging Together: Cooperation and Conflict in the Seven-Power Summits,* rev. ed. (London: Sage, 1987), pp. 150–154.
48. John Kirton, "The Diplomacy of Concert: Canada, the G7 and the Halifx Summit," *Canadian Foreign Policy* 3-1 (Spring 1995), p. 66. See also Nicholas Bayne, *Hanging in There: The G7 and G8 Summit in Maturity and Renewal* (Aldershot: Ashgate, 2000); and Peter I. Hajnal, *The G7/G8 System: Evolution, Role and Documentation* (Aldershot: Ashgate, 1999).
49. Bayne, *Hanging in There,* pp. 116–118.
50. Stephen Gill, "Global Finance, Monetary Policy and Cooperation Among the Group of Seven, 1944–92," in Philip G. Cerny, ed., *Finance and World Politics: Markets, Regimes and States in the Post-Hegemonic Era* (London: Elgar, 1993), p. 104; Paul Lewis, "An Eclipse for the Group of Seven," *New York Times,* May 1, 1995, p. C2; C. Fred Bergsten, "A Clinton Round or a Pacific Free Trade Area?" *New Perspectives Quarterly* 10-2 (Spring 1993), pp. 19–22.
51. Bergsten and Henning, *Global Economic Leadership and the Group of Seven,* pp. 6–7.
52. Bergsten and Henning, *Global Economic Leadership and the Group of Seven,* pp. 43–49.
53. Quoted in Klaus Engelen, "Comment," in Kenen, ed., *Managing the World Economy,* p. 79. See also Klaus C. Engelen, "Anger and Angst: Why the Germans Hate the World Bank and the IMF," *The International Economy* 2–5 (Sept./Oct. 1988), pp. 74–78.
54. Despite some opposition to the Köhler nomination from the United States, the Chancellor of Germany (Gerhard Schröder) was "determined to have a German succeed Michel Camdessus of France" as IMF Managing Director. (Edmund L. Andrews, "New Candidate Proposed for I.M.F.," *New York Times,* March 8, 2000, p. C4.)
55. Jagdish Bhagwati, "Regionalism and Multilateralism: An Overview," in Jaime de Melo and Arvind Panagariya, eds., *New Dimensions in Regional Integration* (Cambridge: Cambridge University Press, 1993), p. 29.
56. Bretton Woods Commission, *Bretton Woods,* p. B-3.
57. See the glossary for a more precise definition of the GDP.
58. United Nations Development Programme, *Human Development Report 1996* (New York: Oxford University Press, 1996), p. 2.
59. There are numerous studies of Third World dissatisfaction with the KIEOs, mainly from a historical structuralist perspective but also from a realist perspective. See, for example, Kevin Danaher, ed., *Fifty Years Is Enough: The Case Against the World Bank and the International Monetary Fund* (Boston: South End Press, 1994); John Cavanagh, Daphne Wysham, and Marcos Arruda, eds., *Beyond Bretton Woods: Alternatives to the Global Economic Order* (London: Pluto Press, 1994); and Stephen D. Krasner, *Structural Conflict: The Third World Against Global Liberalism* (Berkeley, CA: University of California Press, 1985).
60. *The World Bank Annual Report 1997* (Washington, DC: World Bank, 1997), pp. 227–230.
61. *The World Bank Annual Report 2000* (Washington, D.C.: World Bank, 2001), p. 1.
62. David A. Kay, *The New Nations in the United Nations, 1960–1967* (New York: Columbia University Press, 1970), pp. 2–3.
63. The term *Third World* was apparently first used by a French demographer, Alfred Sauvy, in 1952.

64. Michael Zammit Cutajar, ed., *UNCTAD and the North-South Dialogue: The First Twenty Years* (Oxford: Permagon Press, 1985), p. vii.
65. There are many books on the LDCs' call for a new international economic order. See, for example, Jeffrey A. Hart, *The New International Economic Order: Conflict and Cooperation in North-South Economic Relations, 1974–77* (London: Macmillan, 1983); and Ervin Laszlo, et al., *The Obstacles to the New International Economic Order* (New York: Pergamon Press, 1980).
66. Tyrone Ferguson, *The Third World and Decision Making in the International Monetary Fund: The Quest for Full and Effective Participation* (London: Pinter Publishers, 1988), p. 33.
67. Grant B. Taplin, "Revitalizing UNCTAD," *Finance & Development* 29-2 (June 1992), pp. 36–37; Marc Williams, *International Economic Organisations and the Third World* (New York: Harvester Wheatsheet, 1994), p. 192; Carlston B. Boucher and Wolfgang E. Siebeck, "UNCTAD VII: New Spirit in North-South Relations?" *Finance & Development* 24-4 (December 1987), p. 14.
68. Harold K. Jacobson, *Networks of Interdependence: International Organizations and the Global Political System* (New York: Knopf, 1979), p. 13.
69. Henry Morgenthau, Jr., "Bretton Woods and International Cooperation," *Foreign Affairs* 23-2 (January 1945), p. 186.
70. Quoted in Joseph Gold, *Membership and Nonmembership in the International Monetary Fund: A Study in International Law and Organization* (Washington, DC: IMF, 1974), p. 129.
71. Jozef M. van Brabant, *The Planned Economies and International Economic Organizations* (Cambridge: Cambridge University Press, 1991).
72. Valerie J. Assetto, *The Soviet Bloc in the IMF and the IBRD* (Boulder, CO: Westview Press, 1988), pp. 56–66, 185; Brabant, *The Planned Economies and International Economic Organizations,* pp. 45–48; Laszlo Lang, "International Regimes and the Political Economy of East-West Relations," *Occasional Paper Series* no. 13 (New York: Institute for East-West Security Studies, 1989), pp. 19–22.
73. For a discussion of the relationship between the Marshall Plan and the formation of the CMEA (also called COMECON), see William R. Keylor, *The Twentieth Century World— An International History* (New York: Oxford University Press, 1984), pp. 274–275, 359; and Michael Kaser, *Comecon: Integration Problems of the Planned Economies* (London: Oxford University Press, 1965), pp. 9–12.
74. Klaus Schröder, "The IMF and the Countries of the Council for Mutual Economic Assistance," *Intereconomics* 2 (March/April 1982), p. 87; Brabant, *The Planned Economies and International Economic Organizations,* p. 70.
75. *IBRD—Articles of Agreement,* as amended effective February 16, 1989 (Washington, DC: IBRD, August 1991), Article 4, section 10.
76. For a discussion of the involvement of politics in World Bank decision making, see David A. Baldwin, "The International Bank in Political Perspective," *World Politics* 18-1 (October 1965), pp. 68–81; and Theodore H. Cohn, "Politics in the World Bank Group: The Question of Loans to the Asian Giants," *International Organization* 28-3 (Summer 1974), pp. 561–571. For critiques of the IMF and World Bank's political/ideological orientation from a historical structuralist perspective, see Cheryl Payer, *The Debt Trap: The IMF and the Third World* (Middlesex, UK: Penguin, 1974); and Teresa Hayter, *Aid as Imperialism* (Middlesex, UK: Penguin, 1971).
77. Assetto, *The Soviet Bloc in the IMF and the IBRD,* pp. 53–54.
78. Gold, *Membership and Nonmembership in the International Monetary Fund,* pp. 342–379; Marie Lavigne, "Eastern European Countries and the IMF," in Béla Csikós-Nagy and David G. Young, eds., *East-West Economic Relations in the Changing Global Environment* (London: Macmillan, 1986), p. 298; and Assetto, *The Soviet Bloc in the IMF and the IBRD,* pp. 69–93.

79. David Robertson, "Civil Society and the WTO," *World Economy* 23-9 (September 2000), pp. 1119–1123.

80. *The Charter of the United Nations,* Chapter III, Article 8.

81. United Nations Department of Social and Economic Affairs, *The World's Women—2000* (New York: United Nations, 2000), pp. 167–168; Hilary Charlesworth, Christine Chinkin, and Shelley Wright, "Feminist Approaches to International Law," *American Journal of International Law* 85-4 (October 1991), pp. 621–626; V. Spike Peterson and Anne Sisson Runyan, *Global Gender Issues,* 2nd ed. (Boulder, CO: Westview Press, 1999), pp. 74–81.

82. J. Ann Tickner, *Gender in International Relations: Feminist Perspectives on Achieving Global Security* (New York: Columbia University Press, 1992), p. 4.

83. See, for example, Daniel C. Esty, "Non-Governmental Organizations at the World Trade Organization: Cooperation, Competition, or Exclusion," *Journal of International Economic Law* 1-1 (March 1998), pp. 123–147; Jim Rollo and J. Alan Winters, "Subsidiarity and Governance Challenges for the WTO: Environmental and Labour Standards," *World Economy* 23-4 (April 2000), pp. 561–576; Ibrahim F. I. Shihata, "Implementation, Enforcement and Compliance with International Environmental Agreements—Practical Suggesions in Light of the World Bank's Experience," *Georgetown International Environmental Law Review* 9-1 (1996), pp. 37–51; Robert O'Brien et al., *Contesting Global Governance: Multilateral Economic Institutions and Global Social Movements* (Cambridge: Cambridge University Press, 2000).

84. Malcolm Waters, *Globalization* (London: Routledge, 1995), p. 116.

85. See James N. Rosenau, "The State in an Era of Cascading Politics: Wavering Concept, Widening Competence, Withering Colossus, or Weathering Change?" *Comparative Political Studies* 21-1 (April 1988), pp. 13–44.

86. Andrew Gamble and Anthony Payne, "Conclusion: The New Regionalism," in Andrew Gamble and Anthony Payne, eds., *Regionalism and World Order* (London: Macmillan, 1996), p. 253.

87. O'Brien et al. *Contesting Global Governance,* p. 21.

THE THEORETICAL PERSPECTIVES

Part II of this book focuses on the three main theoretical perspectives in the study of IPE: realism, liberalism, and historical structuralism. Before discussing these perspectives, it is necessary to make some general points about them. First, the three main perspectives are not mutually exclusive ideologies. Although the perspectives remain distinctive, they have interacted and influenced one another over time, and the margins between them are sometimes blurred. Many IPE theories such as regime theory, hegemonic stability theory, and the business conflict model also are "hybrids" that draw on more than one of the three major perspectives. In addition, the research of an increasing number of scholars on the intersection of domestic and foreign policy variables in IPE cannot be neatly classified under one of the three traditional perspectives. Chapters 3 through 5 discuss some of these hybrid theories under the perspective with which they are *most* closely identified.

Second, it is somewhat simplistic to state that there are three main IPE perspectives; in fact, each perspective contains a wide diversity of writings. Liberalism is perhaps the most broad ranging of the perspectives, and historical structuralism encompasses writings ranging from classical Marxism to dependency theory and world-system theory. Nevertheless, a diversity of writings can be grouped within each school of thought because the authors generally agree on a core set of assumptions about IPE.*

And third, the three perspectives do not adequately address some of the "newer" issues in IPE relating to the environment, gender, technology, and migration. Nevertheless, no new theoretical approaches to this point have posed a major challenge to the three traditional IPE perspectives in terms of the scope and importance of their explanations.† Becoming familiar with these perspectives is an important starting point in the study of IPE.

---

*See Thomas J. Biersteker, "Evolving Perspectives on International Political Economy: Twentieth-Century Contexts and Discontinuities," *International Political Science Review* 14-1 (January 1993), pp. 7–33.
†See Stephen D. Krasner, "International Political Economy: Abiding Discord," *Review of International Political Economy* 1-1 (Spring 1994), pp. 13–14.

It is useful to provide a brief preview here of the organization of Chapters 3 through 5. To compare the main IPE perspectives, each chapter begins with a discussion of how the perspective deals with three key questions: (1) What is the role of domestic actors, particularly the individual, the state, and societal groups? (2) What are the nature and purpose of international economic relations? and (3) What is the relationship between politics and economics? Although these three questions provide a basis for comparing the IPE perspectives, they gloss over the differences among writers *within* each perspective. The second part of each chapter therefore examines the historical development of the perspective, with particular emphasis on the diversity of views contained within the perspective. Each chapter concludes with a discussion of the perspective's approach to North-South relations.

C H A P T E R   3

The Realist Perspective

Part II begins in this chapter with a discussion of the realist perspective, the oldest school of thought in international relations. Indeed, Thucydides (ca. 471–400 B.C.) is often credited with writing the first important work on international relations—*The History of the Peloponnesian War* on war between the Greek city-states—and also with being the first writer in the realist tradition.[1] In addition to being the oldest school of thought, realism was also the most influential school affecting the views and policies of American foreign policy leaders after World War II. Despite realism's prominence in international relations in general, it has been far less important than the liberal perspective in the subfield of IPE, for several reasons. First, realists have developed their theories by drawing mainly on politics and history rather than on economics, and second, the realists' emphasis on power has most often directed their attention to security issues rather than to economic issues. Nevertheless, the realist emphasis on the role of the state and power is of considerable importance in the study of IPE.

There are variations among writers in all three main IPE perspectives. Thus, we can identify two major strains of realism, one that has largely neglected economic matters and a second that has been far more attuned to economic-political interactions. The first strain stems from the views of Niccolò Machiavelli, an Italian philosopher and diplomat who lived from 1469 to 1527. Machiavelli is best known for his classic work *The Prince*, in which he provided advice to leaders on how to gain and maintain power. Machiavelli saw little connection between economics and politics, and he wrote, "Fortune has decreed that, as I do not know how to reason either about the art of silk or about the art of wool, either about profits or about losses, it befits me to reason about the state."[2] Machiavelli also considered military strength to be far more important than wealth in making war because "gold alone will not procure good soldiers, but good soldiers will always procure gold."[3] An important writer on the linkages between security and economics has argued that Machiavelli's work should be supplemented with economic advice for the modern prince "on the most efficient use of quotas, exchange controls, capital investment, and other instruments of economic warfare."[4] As discussed in this chapter, postwar American realists, like Machiavelli, relegated economics to a relatively low level of importance.

The other strain of realism, stemming from Thucydides and the mercantilists, has been associated with a distinctive realist approach to IPE. Theorists in this strain draw close linkages between traditional realist concerns with power and security on the one hand and economic relations on the other hand. In *The History of the Peloponnesian*

War, for example, Thucydides attributed war among the Greek city-states to a number of economic changes, including the growth of trade, the emergence of new commercial powers such as Athens and Corinth, and the use of money in traditional agrarian economies. Thucydides (unlike Machiavelli) also considered wealth to be a vitally important source of military strength, and he wrote that "war is a matter not so much of arms as of money, which makes arms of use."[5] Thucydides often referred to economic issues, but it was the classical mercantilists of the sixteenth to nineteenth centuries who first engaged in *systematic* theorizing on IPE from a realist perspective.[6] The explicit emphasis of the mercantilists on the linkages between wealth and power was a major factor in the establishment of a realist perspective on IPE.

BASIC TENETS OF THE REALIST PERSPECTIVE

The Role of the Individual, the State, and Societal Groups

Realists emphasize the fact that there is no central authority above nation-states in the international system. Unlike most domestic societies, international relations is a "self-help" system in which each state must look after its own interests.[7] Thus, realists consider the state to be the principal or dominant actor in international politics, and they place considerable emphasis on the preservation of national sovereignty and the pursuit of the national interest. A state has internal sovereignty when it has a monopoly on the legitimate use of force within its territory, and it has external sovereignty when it is free of control by any outside authority. To retain its sovereignty, a state must have sufficient power to defend its interests against outside forces. Realists therefore consider the pursuit of power to be a primary objective in furthering the national interest. Indeed, Hans Morgenthau, the foremost realist writer in the post–World War II period, wrote in *Politics Among Nations* that "international politics, like all politics, is a struggle for power."[8] Power is an essential requirement for the pursuit of state goals, whether they be security, wealth, or power itself, but in a ranking of objectives, realists give top priority to the survival and security of the state.

The state, according to realists, is not only the most important international actor but also a rational, unitary actor that seeks to maximize the benefits and minimize the costs involved in achieving national objectives. Realists studying foreign economic policymaking have recognized the need to focus on domestic as well as international variables in explaining a state's actions.[9] Nevertheless, most modern-day realists continue to emphasize the unitary nature of the state in foreign policy and to downgrade the political importance of subnational and nonstate actors such as interest groups and MNCs. In the realist view, nonstate actors generally operate within the rubric of state policies. Realists therefore argue that liberals overestimate the role of interest groups, international institutions, and MNCs in state policymaking and that historical structuralists overestimate the degree to which the state is beholden to major industrial and financial interests.[10]

The Nature and Purpose of International Economic Relations

According to realists, because international relations is a self-help system, each state must above all look after its own survival and security. Nevertheless, a "security dilemma" results when each state takes actions to bolster its own security because such actions increase the fear and insecurity of other states. For example, a state may build up its armaments solely for defensive purposes, but this action may raise the fears of other states and contribute to an arms race. In view of the security dilemma, realists argue that states are most concerned about *relative gains,* and each state tries to improve its position vis-à-vis other states. Thus, a number of realist writers contend that "even though two states may be gaining absolutely in wealth, in political terms it is the effect of these gains on relative power positions which is of primary importance."[11] Unlike realists, liberals concentrate more on *absolute gains,* in which each state seeks to maximize its own gains and is less concerned with the gains or losses of others.

The emphasis of realists on relative gains stems from their view that economic relations in an anarchical international system is often a zero-sum game in which one group's gain equals another group's loss. This contrasts with the liberal view of economic relations as a positive-sum game in which different groups may gain together. The liberal versus realist view of international institutions provides a prime example of this difference in outlook. Liberals assume that the major international economic organizations—the IMF, the World Bank, and the WTO—are politically neutral and benefit all states that adhere to their liberal-economic guidelines. Realists, by contrast, believe that the most powerful states shape the rules of these organizations to fit with their own particular national interests and that international organizations serve primarily as "arenas for acting out power relationships."[12]

Although in the realist view all states are concerned with relative gains, the objectives of states may be either offensive or defensive in nature. Aggressive states may use the international economy to promote imperialist expansion or to extend their national power over others, whereas defensive states may simply seek to maintain their economic positions in the system. Whether a state is more aggressive or defensive in nature, its interests and policies are determined by its power position in the international system. Thus, realists believe that a hegemonic state with dominant power is likely to have very different interests and policies from less powerful states.

Despite the realist attention to changes in the relative power among states, historical structuralists argue that realists are mainly concerned with redistribution of power *within* the capitalist system and that they share the commitment of the liberals to capitalism. Historical structuralists, by contrast, believe that a more equitable distribution of wealth and power is not possible under capitalism, and they therefore question the capitalist system itself. In the view of historical structuralists, there are only "two main modes of development in contemporary history: capitalist and redistributive," and they group realism along with liberalism in the capitalist mode.[13]

The Relationship Between Politics and Economics

Realists give priority to politics over economics, and they assume that the state has considerable capacity to structure economic relations at the international level. Thus, they are highly critical of liberal theorists who argue that increasing interdependence and globalization are eroding state control. Some realists question the very premise that interdependence and globalization are increasing.[14] Others acknowledge that globalization may be occurring, but they disagree with liberals about both the causes and the consequences of this phenomenon. Whereas liberal theorists attach considerable importance to technological change and advances in communications and transportation as factors behind globalization, realists believe that globalization (to the extent that it is occurring) increases only because states permit it to increase. Thus, the largest states have the capability of either opening or closing world markets, and they can use the globalization process to improve their power positions vis-à-vis smaller and weaker states.[15] Realists also place considerable emphasis on the ability of a hegemonic state to create an open and stable economic order that can further the globalization process. (The different versions of hegemonic stability theory are discussed later in this chapter.)

THE MERCANTILISTS

The term **mercantilism** was first used by Adam Smith, an eighteenth-century economist and philosopher, in reference to much of the economic thought and practice in Europe from about 1500 to 1750.[16] As discussed in Chapter 2, mercantilism played an important role in state building and territorial unification after the demise of feudalism through its emphasis on national power. Mercantilists believed that a state's power depended on the amount of gold and silver it could accumulate in the public treasury. With these precious metals, the state could build up its armed forces, hire mercenaries, and influence its allies as well as its enemies. Mercantilist states therefore took all necessary measures to increase their exports and decrease their imports as a means of accumulating gold. It is impossible for all states to have a balance-of-trade surplus, so mercantilists believed that conflict was central to international economic relations and that relative gains were more important than absolute gains. Thus, the mercantilists stood firmly within the realist school of thought.

A number of writers from different countries contributed to classical mercantilist thought over several centuries; thus, it is not surprising that there are disputes over the interpretation of their ideas. For example, some analysts argue that classical mercantilists considered national power to be the most important goal and that they viewed the acquisition of wealth as simply a means of gaining power—the ultimate objective. Others, by contrast, maintain that the mercantilists placed power and wealth on an equal footing, viewing them both as "proper ultimate ends of national policy."[17] Despite these differences of view, analysts generally agree that mercantilism focused on the national interest and on the pursuit of wealth as well as power by the state.

In the late eighteenth century, important thinkers began to develop comprehensive critiques of mercantilism on political and ethical as well as economic grounds. The mercantilists were criticized, for example, for not guaranteeing the freedom of the individual from intrusive regulation by the state and for contributing to the continuous cycle of wars and preparation for wars in Europe. Adam Smith launched a vigorous economic attack on mercantilism, arguing that it encouraged states to engage in "beggaring all their neighbours" and caused trade and commerce to become a "fertile source of discord and animosity."[18] The liberal criticisms of mercantilism were highly effective, and liberal views of free trade became dominant in England—the major power of the time—for much of the nineteenth century.

It is important to note that some authors use the term *mercantilism* in a more general sense in reference to realist thought and/or practice in IPE. Thus, they refer not only to the mercantilist period in the sixteenth to eighteenth centuries but also to "neomercantilist" states today, which rely on government involvement and various forms of protectionism to promote self-sufficiency and increase their power and wealth. To avoid confusion, this book uses the term *realism* in reference to the general school of thought in IPE; it uses the term *mercantilism* to refer only to the specific period when states sought to accumulate precious metals and increase their national power in the sixteenth to eighteenth centuries.

REALISM AND THE INDUSTRIAL REVOLUTION

Although the liberal critics of mercantilism were highly successful, some thinkers and policymakers continued to emphasize realist practices. Mercantilism was basically a preindustrial doctrine, and the advent of the Industrial Revolution gave a new impetus to realist thought. Industrialization in the realist view had become a central requirement for countries seeking to gain national security, military power, and economic self-sufficiency. Foremost among the realist thinkers at this time were the first U.S. Secretary of the Treasury, Alexander Hamilton (1755–1804), and a German civil servant, professor, and politician who was imprisoned and exiled because of his dissident political views, Friedrich List (1789–1846).

The classical mercantilists were the first to engage in systematic realist theorizing on IPE, but Hamilton's 1791 *Report on the Subject of Manufactures* "contains the intellectual origins of modern economic nationalism and the classic defense of economic protectionism."[19] Hamilton considered the strengthening of the American economy and the promotion of economic development to be essential for the preservation of national independence and security. His preferred policies to achieve economic growth were largely realist, including an emphasis on industry over agriculture, economic self-sufficiency, government intervention, and trade protectionism. Although Hamilton realized that agriculture was important, he believed that the growth of manufacturing was more essential for diversifying the U.S. economy and decreasing its vulnerability to external forces. In his *Report on Manufactures*, Hamilton therefore wrote:

> Not only the wealth; but the independence and security of a Country, appear to be materially connected with the prosperity of manufactures. . . . The extreme embarrassments of the United States during the late War, from an incapacity of supplying themselves, are still matter of keen recollection.[20]

Because the British government had discouraged manufacturing in the American colonies, Hamilton felt that U.S. government intervention was necessary to help establish an industrial base. To counter the advantages of British over American industries,

Hamilton argued that the U.S. government should encourage the introduction of foreign technology, capital, and skilled labor. The government should also adopt protectionist trade policies, including tariffs, quotas, and bounties, to bolster its fledgling industries. Hamilton's advocacy of protectionism differed from classical mercantilism, however; he did not consider the accumulation of gold and a positive balance of trade to be the primary objectives. Instead, he emphasized the development of a strong manufacturing economy.

List was strongly influenced by Hamilton's ideas, and like Hamilton, he placed considerable emphasis on the development of manufacturing industries for a country's economic development. Indeed, in his seminal work, *The National System of Political Economy* (1841), List wrote that "a nation which exchanges agricultural products for foreign manufactured goods is an individual with *one* arm, which is supported by a foreign arm."[21] List had lived in the United States as well as in Germany, and he argued that these two countries would never equal Britain's wealth and power if they did not develop their manufacturing industries. In regard to promoting the development of manufacturing, List placed particular emphasis on the imposition of trade barriers, the importance of national unity, and the development of "human capital."

If Germany and the United States were to catch up with the British, List argued, they would have to provide some degree of trade protection for their infant industries. Indeed, Britain itself had adopted a protective commercial policy that had enabled it to attain manufacturing supremacy, and only after it became the economic leader did it support free trade. By turning to a free trade policy in the nineteenth century, Britain was able to promote a division of labor that enabled it to retain its supremacy in industry and technology. Thus, in the first half of the nineteenth century, trade between Britain and the United States consisted mainly of the export of British manufactured products in exchange for U.S. wool and cotton. Although states can benefit from free trade in the long term, List argued, the economic development of Germany and the United States would be constrained in an open competitive economy as long as they lagged behind Britain. It was therefore necessary for the United States and Germany to impose some protective trade policies as a means of building up their productive potential.

List also emphasized the importance of national unity, which would enable the state to implement policies promoting economic development. List's preoccupation with national unification was understandable because of the prevalence of internal duties on trade within Germany at the time. A strong, unified state was necessary, List believed, not only to impose external trade barriers and engage in national projects such as the building of railroads but also to promote the development of human capital. List attributed British leadership in manufacturing and trade to the superiority of the British educational system, and he thought that governments had special responsibilities for the education of their citizens.[22]

As a realist, List strongly criticized the views of the liberal economist Adam Smith, who favored a division of labor in production and free trade. In List's view, liberals like Smith placed too much emphasis on the existence of natural harmony and peace and underestimated the extent to which the world is divided by national rivalries and conflict. It is important to note, however, that List recognized the importance of a division of labor and free trade *in the long term*. In the short term, he believed government involvement in developing human capital and protecting infant industries was necessary in countries such as Germany and the United States, which were lagging behind. Only when the less advanced nations could be "raised by artificial measure," as the British had been, wrote List, could "freedom of trade . . . operate naturally."[23]

REALISM IN THE INTERWAR PERIOD

As discussed in Chapter 2, Britain repealed its Corn Laws in 1846, opening its markets to agricultural imports and ushering in a period of free trade that continued until the latter part of the nineteenth century. However, changes occurring in the late nineteenth century caused liberal free trade ideas to lose some of their appeal. Under the pressures of World War I and the economic crises and conflicts of the interwar years, there was a virtual breakdown of cooperative relations based on liberalism. Realist ideas gained more influence as each country sought to protect its own national interest, and countries turned to policies of protectionism, competitive currency devaluations, and foreign exchange controls. The dire economic circumstances also encouraged extremists, especially on the right, who "took advantage of the economic dislocation to attack the entire liberal-capitalist system and to call for assertive 'national' policies, backed if necessary by the sword."[24]

The experience of extreme nationalism and trade protectionism in the interwar years, and its linkage with the Great Depression and the outbreak of World War II, provided an impetus for leaders at the Bretton Woods conference to establish a more liberal economic system. Thus, liberalism became the dominant school of thought in the postwar international economic system. In the postwar international *political* system, however, realist thought was to reign supreme. Unlike the earlier mercantilists, the postwar realist scholars were to be largely unconcerned with economic matters.

REALISM IN THE POST–WORLD WAR II PERIOD

Although realists such as Thucydides, the mercantilists, Hamilton, and List had been highly attuned to economic issues, U.S. realist scholars after World War II focused almost exclusively on security issues. With the rapid emergence of the Cold War between East and West, security matters were a major preoccupation, and international economic issues by contrast seemed to have little political importance. Under U.S. leadership, a consensus developed at Bretton Woods that seemed to usher in a period of economic stability and prosperity. Third World countries felt that their interests received too little attention at Bretton Woods, but they had little ability to influence the postwar economic policies. The Cold War was also largely excluded from the postwar economic system because most Soviet bloc countries were not members of the IMF, the World Bank, and GATT. Their nonparticipation did not interfere with the functioning of these organizations because the Eastern bloc accounted for only a small share of global economic interactions. These organizations were largely dominated by the Western industrial states and espoused liberal principles; realists therefore tended to view them as involved with "low politics" and therefore not worthy of much attention.[25]

Postwar realist scholars were also influenced by liberal views on the separability of economics and politics. However, unlike liberals such as Adam Smith, who supported the idea of a laissez-faire economy free of political constraints, the realists emphasized political forces and largely ignored economics. Traditional U.S. views that there *should be* a clear separation between the state and the economy were yet another source of influence on postwar realists. Government involvement in military and defense matters was fully accepted in the United States, but state involvement in the economy was viewed as somehow less legitimate. Finally, the superpower status of the United States led U.S. realists to fix their attention so firmly on the power struggle with the Soviet Union that they "overlooked the economic relations beneath the flux of political relations."[26] As a result, liberalism and Marxism clearly overshadowed realism as schools of thought in IPE in the 1950s and 1960s.

THE REVIVAL OF REALIST IPE

In the 1970s and 1980s, some realist writers began to return "to a realist conception of the relationship of economics and politics that had disappeared from postwar American writings."[27] For example, one of the leading scholars in the realist rediscovery of IPE was Robert Gilpin, who devoted an entire book to the study of U.S. power and the MNC in 1975.[28] Several major factors contributed to the reemergence of realism as a major perspective on IPE. First, the decline of the Cold War and the increasing disarray in the global economy forced many realists to broaden their focus beyond security issues, and second, realists were highly critical of the liberal and Marxist economic analyses of IPE.

Although Western monetary, trade, and aid relations had prospered under U.S. leadership in the 1950s and 1960s, major changes occurred in the 1970s and 1980s with destabilizing consequences for the global economy. These changes included the emergence of OPEC as a powerful new world actor; the relative decline of U.S. economic hegemony; the increase in economic frictions and competitiveness among the United States, the EC, and Japan; and the emergence of a foreign debt crisis in many LDCs. The new sources of instability in the postwar economic system forced realists to confront the fact that economic issues were of central importance and could no longer be relegated to the category of "low politics."

Realists also criticized liberal and Marxist students of IPE for being "economistic," that is, for exaggerating the importance of economics and underestimating the importance of politics.[29] A number of developments in the postwar period demonstrated the necessity for realist studies of IPE, with their emphasis on political issues and the role of the state. For example, the "Keynesian revolution" from the 1930s to the 1950s caused industrial states to become heavily involved in macroeconomic management and public social expenditures, the breakdown of colonialism led to the establishment of many newly independent states that developed forms of government quite different from the Western liberal democratic model, and the growing international competition facing the United States in the 1970s and 1980s led to protestations that the state should be doing more to promote U.S. industry. An updated realist perspective was therefore needed to "bring the state back in" to the study of IPE.[30]

In their approach to IPE, the newer realists posed a direct challenge to liberal interpretations of economic change. According to liberals, international economic relations had flourished after World War II because of the growth of interdependence. This inter dependence in turn was closely linked with advances in communications and transportation, and with the increased role of nongovernmental actors such as MNCs. Realists, by contrast, with their emphasis on the state and power, argued that *the distribution of power among states* (not advances in transportation and communications) is the most important factor determining whether international economic relations will flourish. A major factor to consider in power distribution is whether there is a global hegemonic state with predominant power willing and able to provide leadership. Thus, the newer realists have been strong advocates of hegemonic stability theory, which draws linkages between the existence of a hegemonic state and the nature of global economic relationships.[31]

Although hegemonic stability theory is closely tied with the realist school of thought, it is a "hybrid" theory that also draws on the liberal and historical structuralist perspectives. The discussion that follows therefore demonstrates that hegemonic stability theory cannot be neatly categorized. Nevertheless, the main aspects of hegemonic stability theory are discussed in this chapter because it forms such a central part of the realist approach to IPE.

HEGEMONIC STABILITY THEORY

Hegemonic stability theory asserts that a relatively open and stable international economic system is most likely when there is a single dominant or hegemonic state with two characteristics: it has a sufficiently large share of resources that it is *able* to provide leadership, and it is *willing* to pursue policies necessary to create and maintain a liberal economic order. In addition to being willing and able to lead, the hegemon must follow policies that other major actors believe are relatively beneficial. When a global hegemon is lacking or declining in power, economic openness and stability are more difficult—but not impossible—to maintain. It is generally agreed that hegemonic conditions have occurred at least twice—under Britain in the nineteenth century and under the United States after World War II. Some writers maintain that there were other world powers before the nineteenth century, including Portugal, Spain, the United Provinces or the present-day Netherlands, and (again) the British.[32] However, most believe that these countries did not have international influence comparable to British and American influence during the nineteenth and twentieth centuries.

Hegemonic stability theory has spawned a vast array of literature as well as lively discussion and debate in the field of IPE. Scholars have critiqued virtually all aspects of the theory, some simply calling for revisions and others questioning its basic assumptions. In response, hegemonic stability theorists have defended the theory and revised certain aspects of it. Many of the criticisms are based on empirical grounds. For example, critics question whether theorists can draw meaningful generalizations about hegemonic behavior based on the experiences of only a small number of global hegemons during limited historical periods. There is also considerable disagreement as to the definition and measurement of hegemony, with different authors focusing variously on the military, political, economic, and cultural aspects. In view of the differences over measurement, it is not surprising that analysts differ over when British hegemony declined and over whether U.S. hegemony is declining. Even those theorists who agree that the United States is a declining hegemon have different views about timing. Furthermore, some theorists question one of the basic premises of the theory: that a global hegemon in fact contributes to economic openness and stability. Rather than examining the numerous studies critiquing and defending hegemonic stability theory, we focus here on four questions that have been a major source of division among theorists:

1. What is hegemony?
2. What are the strategies and motives of hegemonic states?
3. Is hegemony necessary and/or sufficient for producing an open economic system?
4. Is U.S. hegemony declining?

What Is Hegemony?

The distribution of power among major states is rarely equal. Indeed, realists and some historical structuralists (such as world-system theorists, discussed in Chapter 5) believe that the international system is marked by unequal growth, with some states increasing and others declining in power. The term **hegemony** is used when the distribution of power is *extremely* unequal, and realists view hegemony in state-centric terms. For example, one important realist writer describes the international system as "imperial" or "hegemonic" when "a single powerful state controls or dominates the lesser states in the system."[33] A definition of this sort, however, does not provide us with answers as to how much control, and what types of control, are necessary for a state to be hegemonic. Can a state attain a hegemonic position based on military or economic power alone, or must it achieve a leadership position in both areas? Most theorists have rather stringent conditions for hegemonic status, and they therefore believe that hegemonic conditions have been fulfilled on only two or three occasions. Thus, one prominent definition limits hegemony to a relationship among states that is so unbalanced that "one power can largely impose its rules and wishes (at the very least by effective veto power) in the economic, political, military, diplomatic and even cultural arenas."[34]

Although most theorists define hegemony in state-centric terms, *Gramscian* theorists use the term *hegemony* in a cultural sense to connote the complex of *ideas* that social groups use to assert their legitimacy and authority. (Gramscian analysis, which stems from the writings of Antonio Gramsci, an Italian Marxist, is discussed in Chapter 5.[35]) Thus, Gramscians refer to the hegemony of ideas such as capitalism and to the global predominance of American culture. According to Gramscians, the capitalist class agreed to provide a wide range of concessions—such as welfare payments, unemployment insurance, and workers' rights to organize—to subordinate social classes. In return for these concessions, subordinate social classes viewed the hegemony of the capitalist class as being perfectly acceptable and legitimate. This hegemony is difficult to overcome, because opposing groups must first make the subordinate classes aware that they are being oppressed. As globalization has proceeded in such areas as trade, foreign investment, and finance, some Gramscians refer to the emergence of a "transnational capitalist class" that is establishing its hegemony at the global level. The transnational capitalist class is ensuring that all impediments to the free flow of capital around the world are being removed.[36]

The Gramscian views clearly enrich our understanding by focusing on aspects of hegemony that are not adequately covered in the state-centric definitions. Nevertheless, the state-centric definition is used by most writers involved in debates over hegemonic stability theory.

What Are the Strategies and Motives of Hegemonic States?

Although hegemonic stability theorists agree that a hegemon must be willing and able to lead, they have differing views regarding the hegemon's leadership methods and goals. Thus, authors refer to three models of hegemony, ranging from "benevolent" at one end of the spectrum to "coercive" at the other end.[37] In the first model, the hegemon is benevolent in methods as well as goals. It is more concerned about promoting generalized benefits than its self-interest, and it relies on rewards rather than threats to ensure compliance by other states. In the second, "mixed" model, the hegemon has an interest in general as well as personal benefits, but it relies on coercive methods when necessary to achieve its objectives. In the third model, the hegemon is exploitative because it exerts leadership out of self-interest, and it is more inclined than hegemons in the first two models to use coercion to enforce compliance. Benevolent hegemons are more concerned with the absolute gains of states, coercive hegemons are more concerned with relative gains, and hegemons with mixed motives and methods are interested in both absolute and relative gains.

Liberals view hegemony in the most benevolent terms, emphasizing the degree to which the hegemon is willing to "take on an undue share of the burdens of the system."[38] According to the liberal view, the hegemon is willing to provide public goods in order to create and maintain open, stable economic regimes. **Public goods** have two main characteristics: they are nonexcludable and nonrival. Nonexcludability means that others can benefit from the good, even if they do not contribute to its provision. A sidewalk can be considered a public good, for example, because even those individuals who have not helped pay for it through taxes are free to use it. Nonrivalness means that one state's (or individual's) use of the good does not seriously decrease the amount available to others. Again, a sidewalk is nonrival because many individuals can simultaneously benefit from using it.

In the liberal view, a benevolent hegemon is willing to provide a wide range of public goods to ensure there is economic openness and stability. For example, the United States as global hegemon permits its currency to be used as the principal reserve asset, supplies adequate U.S. dollars to permit the growth of international trade, provides financing for economic growth of Third World countries, and maintains a relatively open market for other countries' exports. There are very few pure public goods because a hegemon may be able to enforce at least partial exclusion of countries. In contrast to public goods, private goods are both excludable and rival.[39] States receive a public good even if they do not help to provide it, so they tend to become noncontributors or *free riders,* and public goods are underproduced in relation to private goods.

Realists are more inclined than liberals to portray the hegemon as assuming leadership to further its national self-interest rather than the general good. In the realist view, a rising hegemonic state prefers an open international system because such openness can contribute to the hegemon's rate of economic growth, national income, and political power.[40] Realists are also more likely than liberals to portray the hegemon as coercive, threatening to cut off trade, investment, and aid in efforts to force other states to share the costs of public goods. Nevertheless, many realists indicate that hegemonic states can have mixed motives and that the overall effects of hegemony can be beneficial. One important realist writer therefore argues that

> there is no question that the creation of a system of multilateral trade relations was in the interests of the United States. . . . It does not follow from this fact, however, that American efforts to achieve such a system were solely self-serving. . . . Nor does it follow that what is good for the United States is contrary to the general welfare of other nations.[41]

Among proponents of the three main IPE perspectives, historical structuralists are the least likely to view the hegemon as benevolent. Some historical structuralists argue that the hegemon coordinates the responses of the developed states in the core of the global economy, enabling them to solidify their dominance over the LDCs in the periphery. Only when the hegemonic power declines is there disarray among the leading capitalist states, which undermines their ability to continue extracting surplus from the periphery. Thus, Gramscian theorists advocate the development of a "counterhegemony" among disadvantaged groups in the periphery as a means of freeing themselves from their disadvantageous position vis-à-vis the hegemonic forces in the core.[42]

Is Hegemony Necessary and/or Sufficient for Producing an Open Economic System?

Hegemonic stability theorists believe that the existence of a hegemonic state increases the likelihood that there will be an open and stable international economy. One of the ways in which a hegemon promotes openness and stability is by helping to create and maintain liberal international regimes (discussed in detail in Chapter 4). International **regimes** can be defined as "sets of implicit or explicit principles, norms, rules, and decision-making procedures around which actors' expectations converge in a given area of international relations."[43] In other words, the regime concept addresses the fact that a degree of governance above the nation-state level exists in specific areas of international relations, even without a centralized world government. Member states of the WTO, for example, abide by certain trade regime principles such as nondiscrimination, reciprocity, and trade liberalization, and they follow trade regime rules that (with certain exceptions) ban the use of import quotas and export subsidies.

According to hegemonic stability theorists, the United States as global hegemon has played a major role in creating and maintaining open and stable monetary, trade, and aid regimes since the end of World War II. Through the provision of public goods and rewards and the use of coercion, the United States as global leader gives other states the incentive to abide by the regime principles, norms, and rules. Thus, hegemonic stability theorists assume that open, stable economic regimes are more difficult to maintain if a hegemonic state is declining or there is no hegemon. On the basis of these assumptions, hegemonic stability theorists have made a number of assertions about the liberalizing effects of British and American hegemony:

- British hegemony in the nineteenth century was a major factor contributing to trade liberalization.
- The decline of British hegemony after 1875 led to a decline in free trade.
- The lack of a hegemon willing and able to lead between World Wars I and II resulted in increased protectionism culminating in the Great Depression.
- The emergence of the United States as a global hegemon after World War II resulted in the reemergence of open and stable international economic regimes.

A number of empirical studies, however, have questioned the assumption that hegemony is necessary and/or sufficient for producing economic openness. For example, many writers agree that Britain was a declining hegemon after 1875. However, some empirical findings reveal that there was no widespread return to protectionism after 1875 and that it was World War I, *not* Britain's relative decline as a hegemon, "that sounded the death knell for liberalized international trade."[44] Some critics concede that a hegemonic state may play an important role in creating open international economic regimes but argue that these open regimes will not necessarily weaken after the hegemon declines. Open economic regimes can have beneficial effects on the major states, which may have sufficient incentive to maintain these regimes through cooperative efforts even after the hegemon declines. Thus, it is important to ask, not only whether a hegemon is available to *supply* open regimes, but also whether there is sufficient *demand* for such regimes in a posthegemonic period.[45]

Others point out that hegemonic powers were not uniformly committed to free trade and that domestic interest groups in a hegemonic state can cause it to be protectionist in some sectors. For example, as noted in Chapter 6, the United States generally supported an open international trade regime in the 1940s but did *not* endorse an open, liberal international financial order. Instead, the United States joined European countries in supporting the use of national controls on capital flows. Even in the trade area, the United States was not uniformly liberal in the postwar era. In response to domestic interests, the United States insisted that GATT provide several major exceptions for agriculture and supported the creation of a restrictive Multi-Fiber Agreement to limit textile imports.[46]

Some writers also maintain that factors other than hegemony can account for economic openness and stability. For example, general world prosperity can result in open economic regimes, whereas economic downturns can cause countries to adopt more closed, protectionist policies. Furthermore, industries are more inclined to pressure for trade protectionism when they produce surpluses and are more likely to support trade openness during periods of shortages.[47] Most critics therefore seem to agree that there may be *some* connection between hegemony and economic openness. However, they question whether hegemony is necessary and/or sufficient for creating and maintaining open, liberal economic regimes.

Is U.S. Hegemony Declining?

One of the most vigorous debates in the hegemony literature focuses on whether U.S. hegemony has declined. This debate stems from the fact that there is no clear consensus on criteria for determining when a state is hegemonic. Debate continues to this day over the timing of Britain's hegemon decline. Although some authors emphasize Britain's declining hegemony in trade and industrial competitiveness from about 1875, others note that Britain maintained its hegemonic position in finance until World War I (see a more detailed discussion of this issue in Chapter 2).[48] With regard to the United States, a number of theorists are "declinists" who argue that hegemony is inherently unstable and that "one of the most important features of American hegemony was its brevity."[49] Declinists often draw parallels between the United States and Britain, and note that Germany and Japan's erosion of U.S. dominance in the 1970s and 1980s had similarities with U.S. and German erosion of British dominance in the 1890s. There is often a sense of inevitability in the declinist literature, with one noted historian writing that "the only answer to the question increasingly debated by the public of whether the United States can preserve its existing position is 'no'—for it simply has not been given to any one society to remain *permanently* ahead of all the others."[50] Declinists cite a variety of reasons for U.S. hegemonic decline, including the hegemon's tendency to overextend itself in both military and economic terms (or "imperial overstretch"),[51] the tendency of free riders to gain more from economic openness than the hegemon does, and the emergence of more dynamic and competitive economies that challenge the hegemon's predominant position. Although declinists believe that U.S. hegemony will not persist over the longer term, they do sometimes predict that the United States will continue to be a highly significant power in a multipolar world.

Pitted against the declinists are a number of "renewalists" who challenge the assumption that the United States is a declining hegemon. Although most renewalists acknowledge that U.S. economic power has declined in a relative sense since 1945, they argue that this fact has not had a significant effect on U.S. hegemony. U.S. predominance at the end of the war was so great that the country's relative position was bound to decline as a result of economic reconstruction in Europe and Japan. Nevertheless, U.S. economic power today, even with some decline, is "quite enormous when compared to that of any other country, and has an international aspect which gives the US government a unique prerogative *vis-à-vis* the rest of the world."[52] Some renewalists also argue that most of the U.S. economic decline occurred before the mid–1970s and that the U.S. share of global economic output has been fairly constant since that time.

As evidence of its continued hegemony, renewalists maintain that the United States has a considerable amount of co-optive power (also referred to as "structural" or "soft" power): it is often successful in getting "other countries to *want* what it wants."[53] Thus, the United States continues to have a large degree of control over setting the global agenda and determining how issues are dealt with in international politics. In explaining the continued U.S. influence, renewalists criticize declinists for failing to consider noneconomic factors. Thus, U.S. television, movies, and magazines have an enormous effect on cultural tastes and habits around the world, despite the efforts of some countries to limit such influences, and U.S. supremacy in the military-security area also permits it to exercise power in the economic sphere. Although the decline of the Cold War has decreased the scope of security threats to Western Europe and Japan, new global security threats are likely to emerge, and the breakup of the Soviet bloc has solidified American military-security predominance.[54]

The financial crisis in East and Southeast Asia in the late 1990s, and Japan's inability to assume a leadership role and revive its own lackluster economy, also has led renewalists to argue that the United States is regaining its economic predominance. Compared with East Asia and Japan, the United States was experiencing high economic growth and low unemployment and inflation rates. Although the United States had lost market share to Japan in many industrial goods such as automobiles and in some high technology products, "the renovation of US manufacturing, the US services offensive, and the inherent limitations of the Japanese model created a complex situation by the end of the 1990s."[55] Thus, articles have appeared in such journals as *Foreign Affairs* projecting that the United States will continue to be the global hegemon in the twenty-first century. Declinists, however, reject the idea that the American economic revival in the 1990s is a long-term structural phenomenon, and they argue instead that it as a sign of short-term cyclical fluctuations. In the declinist view, the mid- to long-term trend is clearly operating against U.S. hegemony.[56]

Hegemonic stability theory has contributed to a wide range of literature and discussion among scholars of IPE. Indeed, some international relations theorists have described hegemonic stability theory as "the most prominent approach among American political scientists for explaining patterns of economic relations among the advanced capitalist countries since 1945."[57] However, this discussion has shown that the tenets of hegemonic stability theory are controversial and have contributed to vigorous debates among theorists. Although realists at first turned to hegemonic stability theory partly as a response to liberal interpretations of IPE, liberal versions of the theory have also been prominent, and historical structuralists (e.g., world-system and Gramscian theorists) have also focused on hegemony. It is not surprising that realists have been particularly interested in hegemonic stability because of their preoccupation with interactions among the most powerful states. In IPE, the most powerful countries are the advanced capitalist states of the North.

REALISM AND THE ROLE OF THE STATE IN IPE

The realist emphasis on the state, and the liberal emphasis on the market and MNCs are both essential for the study of IPE. For example, technological change is an extremely important source of economic growth, and to understand the role of technological innovation we must draw on both the liberal and realist perspectives. Most of the technological innovation occurs within business enterprises, but "the institutional environment is key to understanding whether firms will be successful or not in creating new products and processess."[58] Thus, to understand the sources of technological innovation it is important to examine the interaction among three institutional spheres: industry, government, and academia.[59] The substantive chapters in this book discuss a clash of perspectives regarding the role of the state versus the role of the market in such areas as trade competitiveness, economic development, and the phasing out of controls on capital flows. A major contribution of realism continues to be its role in bringing "the state back in" to the study of IPE.[60]

REALISM AND NORTH-SOUTH RELATIONS

Although realists are very concerned about relative gains, their preoccupation with power and influence usually leads them to examine distributional issues only among the most powerful states, that is, among the advanced industrial states of the North. In security studies, for example, realists during the Cold War were far less concerned about conflicts in most Third World areas (Korea, Vietnam, and the Middle East were exceptions) than they were about possible conflict "in Europe, where fear of the catastrophic escalation potential of any East-West confrontations prevented even the most minor form of warfare between the two power blocs."[61] Indeed, superpower intervention in Third World conflicts was often viewed as a permissible "safety valve" not available in a European context. In IPE, the realist tendency to ignore the interests of the poorer countries of the South extends back to the nineteenth century writings of Friedrich List. As discussed earlier in this chapter, List believed that Northern countries such as Germany and the United States should develop their manufacturing industries so that they could compete more effectively with Britain. However, List did not consider industrialization to be a legitimate objective for the colonial territories of the South, which served as a source of raw materials and agricultural goods for the North. In *The National System of Political Economy,* List therefore wrote that the Northern countries were "specially fitted by nature for manufacturing" and that the Southern countries should therefore provide the North with "colonial produce in exchange for their manufactured goods."[62]

As a result, realist international relations scholars have until recently only rarely focused on issues involving North-South relations.[63] Realists in IPE have written more studies on North-South relations in recent years, but this is primarily because some Southern countries have posed a challenge to the power position of the North. In the 1970s, for example, realists became interested in OPEC when it wrested control over oil prices and production levels from the international oil companies and launched "the most effective exercise of power by the South against the North since the conclusion of the Second World War."[64] (Membership in the OPEC cartel is limited to LDCs.) When OPEC supported the G-77's demands in the UN for an NIEO, which was designed to alter the imbalance of power between the North and the South, realists also wrote a number of studies on the NIEO's possible impact. In the 1980s and 1990s, realists became less interested in OPEC as its ability to control oil supplies and prices declined. They turned their attention instead to the newly industrializing economies in East Asia, which seemed to pose a new challenge to the power position of the North. Thus, realists became involved in a vigorous debate with liberals: Were the economic successes of the East Asian NIEs (South Korea, Taiwan, Singapore, and Hong Kong) due more to their market orientation (the liberal view) or to government-business cooperation and government involvement in the market (the realist view)? Even when realists study North-South relations, however, they generally do not have a sustained interest in Third World development as a legitimate area of inquiry. Thus, an author of one of the major realist studies on North-South relations written in the late 1970s warned that his book dealt with issues that do not normally fall within the domain of international relations.[65]

The realist and liberal perspectives on North-South relations differ in some important respects. Whereas liberals assert that LDCs are primarily interested in achieving economic growth and prosperity, realists argue that LDCs are seeking increased power as well as wealth in efforts to decrease their vulnerability to the North. In the realist view, most problems of the LDCs can be traced not only to their poverty but also to their position of weakness in the international system. Even when LDCs experience absolute economic gains, they continue to feel vulnerable because of their relatively weak position vis-à-vis the North.[66] The section that follows briefly discusses three strategies realists claim LDCs employ to decrease their vulnerability. (These strategies are discussed in more detail in Part III.)

First, realists note, LDCs employ collective action vis-à-vis the North based on their greater numbers, because they have little power individually. For example, the LDCs formed the G-77 in the early 1960s (see Chapter 2). This caucus, which now has well over 100 LDC member states, has served as a major vehicle for the expression of Third World interests. Other joint actions by LDCs to strengthen their position have included producer associations such as OPEC and regional trade agreements (discussed in Chapter 9). Second, realists argue, LDCs emphasize government involvement in the promotion of development. As discussed in later chapters, LDCs have often opted for economic development policies (both import substitution and export-led growth) in which the government has played a major role in supplementing the market. These policies draw on the assumptions of Hamilton and List, that is, that free trade is in the interest of early industrializers but that late industrializers will never be able to catch up if there is open competition. Thus, for late industrializers, the state often takes responsibility for actively promoting development and industrialization.[67]

A third strategy realists identify is the effort of Third World countries to alter international regimes and organizations governing economic relations. At the end of World War II, the United States used its hegemonic position to establish international regimes that upheld liberal principles, norms, rules, and decision-making procedures. LDCs, which are at a disadvantage in purely market-oriented transactions, often seek to alter the principles and rules of these liberal regimes. Third World countries would prefer more authoritative, less market-oriented regimes in which international organizations would make decisions redirecting both power and wealth from the advanced industrial states to the LDCs. The LDCs would also prefer to have international economic organizations (such as UNCTAD) based on the one-nation, one-vote principle rather than weighted-voting organizations such as the IMF and the World Bank. As discussed in Chapter 11, Third World efforts to alter market-oriented regimes was most evident in the demands for an NIEO in the 1970s.[68]

Although realists, unlike liberals, focus on the struggle for a redistribution of power and wealth between North and South, they assume that such a redistribution is fully possible within the capitalist system. In other words, both realists and liberals generally accept capitalism as the most desirable system for conducting economic relations. As discussed in Chapter 5, historical structuralists such as dependency and world-system theorists by contrast believe that a significant redistribution of power and wealth between the North and the South is impossible under capitalism and that such a redistribution can occur only under socialism.

CRITIQUE OF THE REALIST PERSPECTIVE

This discussion focuses on some of the more important general criticisms of the realist perspective. Realists often correctly criticize both the liberals and historical structuralists for "economism," that is, for exaggerating the importance of economics and underestimating the importance of politics. In seeking to remedy this deficiency, however, realists sometimes go to the other extreme and overemphasize the centrality of politics and the state in relation to economics. The preoccupation of U.S. realists in the early postwar period with international security issues, and their almost total neglect of economic issues, was a prime example of this mistake.

Since the 1970s and 1980s, some writers have revitalized the realist study of IPE and have contributed to important theorizing in this area, for example, with the realist approach to hegemonic stability theory and the role of the state in IPE. Nevertheless, these theorists often continue to downgrade the importance of economic issues that are not closely related to the realists' central concerns with power, security, and relative gains. This chapter noted, for example, that realists have not had a sustained interest in North-South relations and that liberal and historical structuralist analyses have therefore been far more important in this area.

Realists often pride themselves on being the most parsimonious of international relations theorists. Their simplifying assumptions regarding the rational, unitary state and other issues have enabled them to develop some elegant theories; nevertheless, the "state as unitary actor" view is probably the most controversial of the realist assumptions.[69] As interdependence and globalization increase, domestic processes and nongovernmental actors have a greater role in foreign policy, but the realist perspective is less attuned to this vision of the state. Transnational actors such as MNCs and international banks are particularly important in the economic arena; therefore, the parsimonious habits of realists sometimes limit their analyses of important economic issues. In recent years, some students of foreign economic policymaking have tried to develop a realist theory of state action that takes account of domestic as well as international factors.[70] However, liberal IPE theorists continue to be far more attuned to domestic-level variables than are realists.[71]

Realists also place more emphasis on relative than absolute gains, an attitude that is a direct result of their concern with state survival and security in an anarchic self-help system. Relative gains are clearly of primary concern in some interstate relationships, such as U.S.-Soviet relations during the Cold War and relations between India and Pakistan during periods of hostility. However, absolute gains are often of greater concern in interdependent relationships in which states cooperate and do not threaten each other with force.[72] Even when realists study international economic organizations, they are more attuned to concerns about relative than absolute gains in these institutions. For example, one realist study of the EU concludes that "the weaker but still influential partners will seek to ensure that the rules" established give them the opportunity "to voice their concerns and interests and thereby prevent their domination by stronger partners."[73] The preoccupation of realists with relative gains causes them to be highly skeptical about the possible influence of international institutions. If member states are always concerned that they may gain less than others, realists argue, they will be very reluctant to transfer significant authority to these international bodies. Nevertheless, international economic organizations at the global and regional levels—such as the IMF, the World Bank, the WTO, the EU, and the NAFTA—have had a significant effect on some areas of the international economy. To better understand the functioning of the global economy, theorists must study such institutions further.

Although the realist perspective has had remarkable longevity and success in international relations in general, its preoccupation with security issues has limited its influence in the study of international economic matters. We now turn to a discussion of liberalism, which has been the most important theoretical perspective in IPE.

NOTES

1. For a discussion of Thucydides and realism, see Michael W. Doyle, "Thucydidean Realism," *Review of International Studies* 16-3 (1990), pp. 223–237; and Laurie M. Johnson Bagby, "The Use and Abuse of Thucydides in International Relations," *International Organization* 48-1 (Winter 1994), pp. 131–153.
2. Quoted in Albert O. Hirschman, *National Power and the Structure of Foreign Trade,* exp. ed., (Berkeley, CA: University of California Press, 1980), p. xv.
3. Niccolò Machiavelli, *The Prince and the Discourses* (New York: Modern Library, 1940), pp. 308–310.
4. Hirschman, *National Power and the Structure of Foreign Trade,* p. xv.
5. Thucydides, *The History of the Peloponnesian War,* translated by Richard Crawley (London: Dent, Everyman's Library, 1910), p. 41; Robert G. Gilpin, "The Richness of the Tradition of Political Realism," *International Organization* 38-2 (Spring 1984), p. 293.
6. Thomas J. Biersteker, "Evolving Perspectives on International Political Economy: Twentieth-Century Contexts and Discontinuities," *International Political Science Review* 14-1 (1993), p. 25.
7. On a "self-help" system, see Kenneth N. Waltz, *Theory of International Politics* (Reading, MA: Addison-Wesley, 1979), pp. 105–107.
8. Hans J. Morgenthau, revised by Kenneth W. Thompson, *Politics Among Nations: The Struggle for Power and Peace,* 6th ed., (New York: Knopf, 1985), p. 31.
9. See, for example, Stephen D. Krasner, *Defending the National Interest: Raw Materials Investments and U.S. Foreign Policy* (Princeton, NJ: Princeton University Press, 1978); and Michael Mastanduno, David A. Lake, and G. John Ikenberry, "Toward a Realist Theory of State Action," *International Studies Quarterly* 33-4 (December 1989), pp. 457–474.

10. Robert O. Keohane, "Theory of World Politics: Structural Realism and Beyond," in Robert O. Keohane, ed., *Neorealism and Its Critics* (New York: Columbia University Press, 1986), pp. 164–165.

11. Robert Gilpin, *U.S. Power and the Multinational Corporation: The Political Economy of Foreign Direct Investment* (New York: Basic Books, 1975), p. 34. See also Waltz, *Theory of International Politics,* p. 126; and Joseph M. Grieco, "Anarchy and the Limits of Cooperation: A Realist Critique of the Newest Liberal Institutionalism," *International Organization* 42-3 (Summer 1988), p. 498.

12. Tony Evans and Peter Wilson, "Regime Theory and the English School of International Relations: A Comparison," *Millennium* 21-3 (Winter 1992), p. 330.

13. Robert W. Cox, *Production, Power, and World Order: Social Forces in the Making of History* (New York: Columbia University Press, 1987), p. 6.

14. See, for example, Kenneth N. Waltz, "The Myth of National Interdependence," in Charles P. Kindleberger, ed., *The International Corporation* (Cambridge, MA: MIT Press, 1970), pp. 222–223; Janice E. Thomson and Stephen D. Krasner, "Global Transactions and the Consolidation of Sovereignty," in Ernst-Otto Czempiel and James N. Rosenau, eds., *Global Changes and Theoretical Challenges: Approaches to World Politics for the 1990s* (Lexington, MA: Heath, 1989), p. 197.

15. Andrew Hurrell and Ngaire Woods, "Globalisation and Inequality," *Millennium* 24-3 (1995), p. 458.

16. Adam Smith used the term *mercantile system,* and German writers in the 1860s used the term *Merkantilismus* to describe this doctrine. Only afterward did the term *mercantilism* become standard in the English language. See Jacob Viner, "Mercantilist Thought," in David L. Sills, ed., *International Encyclopedia of the Social Sciences* (New York: Free Press, 1968), vol. 4, p. 436; and David A. Baldwin, *Economic Statecraft* (Princeton, NJ: Princeton University Press, 1985), p. 72.

17. Jacob Viner, "Power Versus Plenty as Objectives of Foreign Policy in the Seventeenth and Eighteenth Centuries," *World Politics* 1 (October 1948), pp. 10, 17; Eli F. Heckscher, *Mercantilism* (London: Allen and Unwin, 1934), vol. 2, p. 17.

18. Adam Smith, *The Wealth of Nations* (London: Dent & Sons, Everyman's Library no. 412, 1910), vol. 1, bk. 4, p. 436.

19. Robert Gilpin with Jean M. Gilpin, *The Political Economy of International Relations* (Princeton, NJ: Princeton University Press, 1987), p. 180.

20. Alexander Hamilton, *The Report on the Subject of Manufactures,* December 5, 1791, in Harold C. Syrett, ed., *The Papers of Alexander Hamilton,* Vol. 10 (New York: Columbia University Press, 1966), p. 291.

21. Friedrich List, *The National System of Political Economy,* translated by Sampson S. Lloyd (London: Longmans, Green 1916), p. 130.

22. List's emphasis on the importance of human capital is discussed in David Levi-Faur, "Friedrich List and the Political Economy of the Nation-State," *Review of International Political Economy* 4-1 (Spring 1997), pp. 154–178.

23. List, *The National System of Political Economy,* p. 107. On the greater role of government in late industrializers see Alexander Gerschenkron, *Economic Backwardness in Historical Perspective: A Book of Essays* (Cambridge, MA: Harvard University Press, 1962).

24. Paul Kennedy, *The Rise and Fall of the Great Powers: Economic Change and Military Conflict from 1500 to 2000* (New York: Random House, 1987), p. 283.

25. Michael Mastanduno differentiates realist government practitioners from scholars in the early postwar period. Although U.S. officials were highly active in international economic policy and provided leadership in creating the IMF, World Bank, and WTO, they linked and subordinated their economic initiatives to U.S. security objectives. American realist

scholars in the early postwar period, by contrast, devoted scant attention to economic issues, and "analyses of the interplay between economics and security . . . were conspicuous
by their absence." (Michael Mastanduno, "Economics and Security in Statecraft and Scholarship," *International Organization* 52–4 (Autumn 1998), p. 835.)

26. Gilpin, "The Richness of the Tradition of Political Realism," p. 294.

27. Gilpin, *The Political Economy of International Relations*, p. xii.

28. See Gilpin, *U. S. Power and the Multinational Corporation.*

29. Richard K. Ashley, "Three Modes of Economism," *International Studies Quarterly* 27-4
(December 1983), p. 463.

30. Theda Skocpol, "Bringing the State Back In: Strategies of Analysis in Current Research," in
Peter B. Evans, Dietrich Rueschemeyer, and Theda Skocpol, eds., *Bringing the State Back
In* (Cambridge: Cambridge University Press, 1985), pp. 6–7.

31. The first realists writing about hegemonic stability theory were Robert Gilpin and Stephen
Krasner.

32. See George Modelski, "The Long Cycle of Global Politics and the Nation-State," *Com-
parative Studies in Society and History* 20-2 (April 1978), pp. 214–235; Immanuel
Wallerstein, "The Three Instances of Hegemony in the History of the Capitalist World-
Economy," in *The Politics of the World-Economy: The States, the Movements and the
Civilizations* (London: Cambridge University Press, 1984), pp. 37–46; George Modelski,
Long Cycles in World Politics (Seattle, WA: University of Washington Press, 1987),
ch. 2; George Modelski and William R. Thompson, *Seapower and Global Politics,
1494–1993* (London: Macmillan, 1988), ch. 5; Joshua S. Goldstein, *Long Cycles: Prosperity and War in the Modern Age* (New Haven, CT: Yale University Press, 1988),
pp. 126–133.

33. Robert Gilpin, *War and Change in World Politics* (Cambridge: Cambridge University
Press, 1981), p. 29; Joseph S. Nye, Jr., *Bound to Lead: The Changing Nature of American
Power* (New York: Basic Books, 1990), pp. 37–40.

34. Wallerstein, "The Three Instances of Hegemony in the History of the Capitalist World-
Economy," p. 38.

35. See Antonio Gramsci, *Selections from the Prison Notebooks of Antonio Gramsci*, edited and
translated by Quintin Hoare and Geoffrey Nowell Smith (New York: International Publishers, 1971).

36. See Stephen Gill, ed., *Gramsci, Historical Materialism and International Relations* (Cambridge: Cambridge University Press, 1993).

37. See Duncan Snidal, "The Limits of Hegemonic Stability Theory," *International Organization* 39-4 (Autumn 1985), pp. 585–586.

38. Charles P. Kindleberger, *The World in Depression 1929–1939* (Berkeley, CA: University of
California Press, 1973), p. 28.

39. James A. Caporaso, "Global Political Economy," in Ada Finifer, ed., *Political Science: The
State of the Discipline II* (Washington, DC: American Political Science Association, 1993),
p. 453; Snidal, "The Limits of Hegemonic Stability Theory," pp. 590–592; Charles P.
Kindleberger, "Dominance and Leadership in the International Economy," *International
Studies Quarterly* 25-2 (June 1981), p. 244. See also the definition of public goods in Man-
cur Olson's classic study *The Logic of Collective Action: Public Goods and the Theory of
Groups* (Cambridge, MA: Harvard University Press, 1965), pp. 14–15.

40. Stephen D. Krasner, "State Power and the Structure of International Trade," *World Politics* 28 (April 1976), p. 322.

41. Robert Gilpin, "The Politics of Transnational Economic Relations," in Robert O. Keohane
and Joseph S. Nye, Jr., eds., *Transnational Relations and World Politics* (Cambridge, MA:
Harvard University Press, 1972), p. 58.

42. Wallerstein, "The Three Instances of Hegemony in the History of the Capitalist World-Economy," pp. 44–46; Robert W. Cox, "Gramsci, Hegemony and International Relations: An Essay in Method," in Stephen Gill, ed., *Gramsci, Historical Materialism and International Relations* (Cambridge: Cambridge University Press, 1993), pp. 64–65.

43. Stephen D. Krasner, "Structural Causes and Regime Consequences: Regimes as Intervening Variables," in Stephen D. Krasner, ed., *International Regimes* (Ithaca, NY: Cornell University Press, 1983), p. 2.

44. Arthur A. Stein, "The Hegemon's Dilemma: Great Britain, the United States and the International Economic Order," *International Organization* 38-2 (Spring 1984), p. 373.

45. See Robert O. Keohane, *After Hegemony: Cooperation and Discord in the World Political Economy* (Princeton, NJ: Princeton University Press, 1984); and Robert O. Keohane, "The Demand for International Regimes," in Stephen D. Krasner, ed., *International Regimes* (Ithaca, NY: Cornell University Press, 1983), pp. 141–171.

46. Eric Helleiner, *States and the Reemergence of Global Finance: From Bretton Woods to the 1990s* (Ithaca, NY: Cornell University Press), p. 4; Theodore H. Cohn, "The Changing Role of the United States in the Global Agricultural Trade Regime," in William P. Avery, ed., *World Agriculture and the GATT, International Political Economy Yearbook* (Boulder, CO: Rienner, 1993) vol. 7, pp. 20–24; Vinod K. Aggarwal, *Liberal Protectionism: The International Politics of Organized Textile Trade* (Berkeley, CA: University of California Press, 1985), pp. 77–81.

47. Timothy J. McKeown, "Hegemonic Stability Theory and Nineteenth Century Tariff Levels in Europe," *International Organization* 37-1 (Winter 1983), p. 89; Peter F. Cowhey and Edward Long, "Testing Theories of Regime Change: Hegemonic Decline or Surplus Capacity?" *International Organization* 37-2 (Spring 1983), pp. 157–188.

48. See, for example, David A. Lake, *Power, Protection, and Free Trade: International Sources of U.S. Commercial Strategy, 1887–1939* (Ithaca: Cornell University Press, 1988), pp. 30–32; Albert Fishlow, "Lessons from the Past: Capital Markets during the 19th Century and the Interwar Period," *International Organization* 39-3 (Summer 1985), p. 390.

49. Robert O. Keohane, *After Hegemony: Cooperation and Discord in the World Political Economy* (Princeton, NJ: Princeton University Press, 1984), p. 139. The IPE literature is replete with statements about the decline of U.S. hegemony. See, for example, Michael C. Webb and Stephen D. Krasner, "Hegemonic Stability Theory: An Empirical Assessment," *Review of International Studies* 15 (Spring 1989), p. 185; and Wallerstein, "The Three Instances of Hegemony in the History of the Capitalist World-Economy," p. 46.
    Other declinist literature includes Kennedy, *The Rise and Fall of the Great Powers;* David P. Calleo, *Beyond American Hegemony: The Future of the Western Alliance* (New York: Basic Books, 1987); and Walter Russel Mead, *Mortal Splendor: The American Empire in Transition* (Boston: Houghton Mifflin, 1987).

50. Kennedy, *The Rise and Fall of the Great Powers,* p. 533.

51. Kennedy, *The Rise and Fall of the Great Powers,* p. 515.

52. Stephen Gill, "American Hegemony: Its Limits and Prospects in the Reagan Era," *Millennium* 15-3 (Winter 1986), p. 331. See also Samuel Huntington, "The U.S.—Decline or Renewal?" *Foreign Affairs* 67-2 (Winter 1988–89), pp. 76–96.

53. Joseph S. Nye, Jr., "Soft Power," *Foreign Policy* 80 (Fall 1990), p. 166. See also Nye, *Bound to Lead;* and Susan Strange, "The Persistent Myth of Lost Hegemony," *International Organization* 41-4 (Autumn 1987), pp. 551–574.

54. Bruce Russett, "The Mysterious Case of Vanishing Hegemony; or, Is Mark Twain Really Dead?" *International Organization* 39-2 (Spring 1985), p. 230; Susan Strange, "The Future of the American Empire," *Journal of International Affairs* 42 (Fall 1988), pp. 1–17.

55. Herman M. Schwartz, *States versus Markets: The Emergence of a Global Economy,* 2nd ed., (New York: St. Martin's Press, 2000), p. 298.

56. For differing views of the 1990s U.S. economic revival, see Mortimer B. Zuckerman, "A Second American Century," *Foreign Affairs* 77-3 (May/June 1998), pp. 18–31; Paul Krugman, "America the Boastful," *Foreign Affairs* 77-3 (May/June 1998), pp. 32–45; and "United States: Too Triumphalist by Half," *The Economist,* April 25, 1998, pp. 29–30.

57. Webb and Krasner, "Hegemonic Stability Theory," p. 183.

58. Jorge Niosi, "Canada's National R&D System," in Robert Anderson, Theodore Cohn, Chad Day, Michael Howlett and Catherine Murray, eds., *Innovation Systems in a Global Context: The North American Experience* (Montreal: McGill-Queen's University Press, 1998), p. 91.

59. Henry Etzkowitz, "The Triple Helix of Academia-Industry-Government: The U.S. National Innovation System," in Anderson, et al., *Innovation Systems in a Global Context,* pp. 127–147.

60. Skocpol, "Bringing the State Back In," pp. 6–7.

61. Amitav Acharya, "Beyond Anarchy: Third World Instability and International Order after the Cold War," in Stephanie G. Neuman, ed., *International Relations Theory and the Third World* (New York: St. Martin's Press, 1998), p. 165.

62. List, *The National System of Political Economy,* p. 154.

63. David A. Lake, "Power and the Third World: Toward a Realist Political Economy of North-South Relations," *International Studies Quarterly* 31-2 (June 1987), p. 217.

64. Stephen D. Krasner, *Structural Conflict: The Third World Against Global Liberalism* (Berkeley, CA: University of California Press, 1985), pp. 108–109.

65. Robert L. Rothstein, *The Weak in the World of the Strong: The Developing Countries in the International System* (New York: Columbia University Press, 1977), p. ix.

66. Krasner, *Structural Conflict,* p. 3; Rothstein, *The Weak in the World of the Strong,* p. 8.

67. Chalmers Johnson, *MITI and the Japanese Miracle: The Growth of Industrial Policy, 1925–1975* (Stanford, CA: Stanford University Press, 1982), p. 19. On the role of government involvement for late industrializers, see Alexander Gerschenkron, *Economic Backwardness in Historical Perspective: A Book of Essays* (Cambridge, MA: Harvard University Press, 1962).

68. Krasner, *Structural Conflict,* p. 7.

69. Joseph M. Grieco, "Realist International Theory and the Study of World Politics," in Michael W. Doyle and G. John Ikenberry, eds., *New Thinking in International Relations Theory* (Boulder, CO: Westview Press, 1997), p. 168.

70. See Mastanduno, Lake, and Ikenberry, "Toward a Realist Theory of State Action," pp. 457–474.

71. For an alternative view, see Jennifer Sterling-Folker, "Realist Environment, Liberal Process, and Domestic-Level Variables," *International Studies Quarterly* 41-1 (March 1997), pp. 1–25.

72. Robert O. Keohane, "Neoliberal Institutionalism: A Perspective on World Politics," in Robert O. Keohane, *International Institutions and State Power: Essays in International Relations Theory* (Boulder, CO: Westview Press, 1989), pp. 10–11.

73. Joseph M. Grieco, "The Maastricht Treaty, Economic and Monetary Union and the Neorealist Research Programme," *Review of International Studies* 21 (January 1995), p. 34.

The Liberal Perspective

L iberalism is the most influential perspective in IPE. Most important international economic organizations, and the economic policies of most states today, are strongly influenced by liberal principles. The term *liberal,* however, is used differently in IPE and U.S. domestic politics. Liberalism in the United States is often contrasted with conservatism. Whereas U.S. conservatives are committed to free markets and minimal intervention by the government, U.S. liberals are inclined to support greater government involvement in the market to prevent inequalities and to stimulate growth. Liberal economists, by contrast, have many similarities with U.S. conservatives; they emphasize the importance of the free market and private property rights and call for only a limited government role in economic activities. However, there are also variations among economic liberals. Although some liberal economists believe there should be as little government involvement in the economy as possible, others consider a degree of government intervention to be necessary for the effective functioning of markets.

BASIC TENETS OF THE LIBERAL PERSPECTIVE

Liberal international theory is exceedingly diverse in nature, and it is extremely difficult to provide a single "core statement of the liberal credo."[1] Compared with the liberal perspective, the core statements in realism and Marxism are easier to identify. A major reason for this difference is that realists and Marxists place more emphasis than liberals on developing "parsimonious" theories, that is, on economy and simplicity in the assumptions they make. Whereas realists oversimplify by focusing on the rational, unitary state as their guiding principle, Marxists view the world in terms of class relations. Liberals are pluralist by nature, so they focus on a wider range of actors and levels of analysis. Although this broader outlook enables liberals to capture many of the complexities of international relations that realists and Marxists overlook, it also interferes with their development of a coherent and encompassing liberal international theory.

This chapter focuses primarily on three variants of liberalism that are directly relevant to the study of IPE: orthodox, interventionist, and institutional liberalism.[2] *Orthodox liberals* are mainly concerned with promoting "negative freedom," or the freedom of the private sector and the market to function with minimal interference from the state. The earliest economic liberals, such as Adam Smith and David Ricardo, adhered to liberal orthodoxy. *Interventionist liberals* believe that an exclusive focus on negative freedom is too narrow because we cannot always be certain that the private sector and the market will be progressive and produce widespread benefits. Interventionist liberals therefore see benefits from some government involvement to promote more equality, fairness, and justice in a free **market economy.** *Institutional liberals* also believe that some outside involvement is necessary to supplement the functioning of the market, and they favor the development of strong international institutions such as the WTO, the IMF, and the World Bank. Orthodox liberals often do not devote sufficient attention to institutions because of the emphasis they place on the market.

The Role of the Individual, the State, and Societal Groups

The liberal perspective takes a "bottom-up" approach to politics and gives primacy of place in society to the individual consumer, firm, or entrepreneur.[3] In the liberal view, individuals have inalienable natural rights that must be protected from both private and public collectivities such as labor unions, churches, and the state. If individuals are free to pursue their own political and economic interests, the welfare of society and its inhabitants is most likely to be achieved. Thus, Adam Smith, an orthodox liberal writing in the eighteenth century, discussed the "invisible hand," which converts the individual's selfish interest into advantage for society as a whole:

> Every individual is continually exerting himself to find out the most advantageous employment for whatever capital he can command. It is his own advantage, indeed, and not that of the society, which he has in view. But the study of his own advantage naturally, or rather necessarily, leads him to prefer that employment which is most advantageous to the society.[4]

Because the hidden hand of the market performs so efficiently, society can regulate itself best with minimal interference from the state. Some liberals even reject the idea that the state can be an important autonomous actor, with motivations and resources different from those of other societal institutions. Instead, they view the state as simply an aggregation of private interests, with public policy resulting from a struggle among interest groups.[5] The interventionist strain of liberalism, however, points to the limitations of markets in dealing with some economic problems, such as unemployment, and foresees some role for the government in these situations.

The Nature and Purpose of International Economic Relations

After World War II, three major international economic organizations were established: the IMF, the IBRD or the World Bank, and the GATT. These organizations are all based on liberal-economic principles, and it is therefore not surprising that liberals have a rather positive view of international economic relations as currently structured. They maintain that the formal rules of behavior of the KIEOs are politically neutral and that all states' growth and economic efficiency benefit when their economic interactions conform to the liberal principles of the KIEOs. If existing international relationships do not bring about growth and efficient allocation of resources, liberals often argue that the problem is not with the international economic system but with the unwillingness of governments to pursue rational liberal-economic policies.

Liberalism assumes that international economic interactions can be mutually beneficial, or a positive-sum game, if they are permitted to operate freely. All states and individuals are likely to gain from open economic relationships, even if they do not gain equally. In view of the overall positive effect of economic relations, liberals are often less concerned with *distributional* issues and are less likely to differentiate between rich versus poor or large versus small states. Certainly, liberalism encompasses a range of views on distributional issues, with interventionist liberals emphasizing equality and social democracy as well as liberty and efficiency. All liberals, however, believe that the international economic system will function most efficiently if it ultimately depends on the price mechanism and the market. This emphasis on the market generally causes liberals to be more preoccupied with such values as liberty and efficiency.

Many liberals believe that LDCs today face basically the same challenges that countries in Europe and North America did during the nineteenth century. Unlike the case in the earlier period, however, LDCs today can benefit from a diffusion of advanced technology and modern forms of organization from the advanced industrial states. Greater integration with the centers of modern economic and political activity therefore spurs modernization and rapid economic growth in LDCs, whereas relative isolation from these centers of activity results in LDC backwardness. In sum, liberals believe that all states, including LDCs, can benefit from the growth of interdependence and globalization if they follow open, liberal policies.

According to the liberals, the purpose of international economic activity is to achieve the optimum or most efficient use of the world's scarce resources and to maximize economic growth and efficiency. Liberals are therefore primarily concerned with *aggregate* measures of economic performance such as the growth of GDP, trade, foreign investment, and per capita income. If the overall level of foreign trade and investment is increasing, this is more important to liberals than any relative gains and losses in trade and foreign investment among states.

The Relationship Between Politics and Economics

Liberals tend to view politics and economics as basically separable and autonomous areas of activity. Many liberals also assume that international economic interests are in basic harmony with a state's national interest, and they therefore believe governments should not interfere with international economic transactions. To the extent that the government has a substantive role, it should be to create an open environment within which individuals and private firms can freely express their economic preferences. Thus, the state has a role in preventing restraints on competition and free trade and in providing public goods such as national defense and infrastructure, including roads and railways to facilitate production and the transport of goods and people. Everyone will benefit from the more efficient use of the world's scarce resources if government restrictions do not impede the free exchange of commodities and investment flows. If governments permit the market to operate freely, a natural division of labor develops in which each country specializes in producing those goods for which it has a comparative advantage. As we discuss later, interventionist liberals accept a greater degree of government involvement than orthodox liberals.

ORTHODOX LIBERALISM

The liberal tradition dates back to at least the seventeenth century with the writings of John Locke (1632–1704). Locke believed government should be able to take limited enforcement actions to extract taxes and require military service, but he argued that the primary role of the state was to ensure the *"Preservation of . . .* [peoples'] Lives, Liberties and Estates, which I call by the general Name, *Property."*[6] Although Locke predated Adam Smith (1723–1790) by almost a century, Smith is considered to be the central figure adopting the orthodox liberal approach to political economy. Unlike Locke, who based his support for the minimal state largely on political doctrines, Smith emphasized laissez-faire economics and led the way in opposing mercantilist economic thought (discussed in Chapter 3). Smith argued that freely operating markets based on a division of labor maximize efficiency and prosperity and that such productive gains are likely to be positive-sum in nature. (In a positive-sum game, all states can gain together, unlike a zero-sum game, in which one state's gain is equal to another state's loss.) The mercantilists believed a country could gain wealth and power only at the expense of other countries, but Smith cautioned against such views:

> By such maxims as these . . . nations have been taught that their interest consisted in beggaring all their neighbours. Each nation has been made to look with an invidious eye upon the prosperity of all the nations with which it trades, and to consider their gain as its own loss. Commerce, which ought naturally to be, among nations, as among individuals, a bond of union and friendship, has become the most fertile source of discord and animosity.[7]

As a strong advocate of free trade, Smith opposed the barriers that mercantilist states erected against the free exchange of goods and the enlargement of markets. Although Smith realized that merchants who benefited from protectionism would try to retain their advantages, he differentiated such specific groups from the populace in general, who would gain the most from freer trade. Smith's arguments for free trade were based on the principles of division of labor and economic interdependence. Each state in an unregulated international economy would find a productive niche based on **absolute advantage.** It would benefit by specializing in those goods it produced most efficiently and by trading with other states. David Ricardo (1772–1823) subsequently strengthened the free trade defense by explicitly arguing that two countries would benefit from trade based on **comparative advantage.** Even if one of the countries had no absolute advantage in the production of any good, it should specialize in and export those products for which it had a *relative* advantage (i.e., the least cost disadvantage). The concepts of absolute and comparative advantage are explained in detail in Chapter 8.

Although Smith was a strong supporter of free trade, he did not believe it should be a unilateral or unconditional policy. For example, he thought that a country should be able to impose limits on free trade to meet national security requirements and to retaliate against unfair trade restrictions imposed by foreign countries. Smith also believed that by implementing free trade gradually, a government could ensure that domestic industry and labor groups would have time to adjust to international competition. Furthermore, Smith tempered his arguments for limited government intervention with an awareness of political realities. Thus, he indicated that the state should perform three important but circumscribed functions: to provide for national defense, to protect members of society from injustice or oppression, and to provide public works and institutions (i e., public goods), which private individuals and groups would not provide on their own.[8]

It is important to note that despite their openness to some government involvement, Smith and other orthodox liberals believed this involvement should be extremely circumscribed and limited to actions that would promote the functioning of the market.

THE INFLUENCE OF JOHN MAYNARD KEYNES

John Maynard Keynes (1883–1946) once wrote that "the ideas of economists and political philosophers, both when they are right and when they are wrong, are more powerful than is commonly understood."[9] Certainly Keynes's ideas had a powerful influence on both the theory and practice of political economy, and some scholars argue that he was "the most influential economist of his generation."[10] Although Keynes was a liberal economist, he called for a much greater degree of government interventionism than did the orthodox liberals. Keynes strongly opposed the extreme level of nationalism and beggar-thy-neighbor policies of the interwar years associated with realism. However, he also viewed the Great Depression as an indication that the orthodox liberal belief in the convergence between self-interest and the public interest was overdrawn. Orthodox liberal theory provided virtually no guidance or remedies for dealing with the high levels of unemployment in the 1930s, which had devastating economic and social consequences.

In contrast to the orthodox liberal view that markets tend inherently toward a socially beneficial equilibrium, Keynes argued that market-generated equilibrium between production and consumption might occur at a point where labor and capital are underutilized. Producer organizations, the variability of business confidence, and other factors that introduce rigidities into markets, can contribute to instability in the private economy and to prolonged stagnation and unemployment. For example, Keynes noted that economic adjustment tended to result in unemployment rather than wage cuts because labor unions often resisted the downward movement of wages. This rise of unemployment in turn led to decreased demand and to a reduction in production and investment. Governments could remedy this situation, in Keynes's view, by becoming involved in the management of aggregate demand. Thus, Keynes placed new emphasis on the need for governments to implement fiscal policies (and to a lesser extent monetary policies) designed to increase demand, and he supported government investment when necessary in public projects. In his major work *The General*

Theory of Employment, Interest, and Money, Keynes wrote that "the central controls necessary to ensure full employment will, of course, involve a large extension of the traditional functions of government."[11] Keynes's view that the state had the responsibility to intervene regularly in the economy of course marked a divergence from the laissez-faire doctrine of orthodox liberals.

Keynes's support for government involvement resulted in a greater "willingness to accept public sector deficits in order to finance public works or other spending programs designed to lower unemployment."[12] Keynes's emphasis on full employment also caused him to place less priority than the orthodox liberals on specialization and international trade. Indeed, he argued that it was sometimes justifiable to limit imports in order to bolster domestic employment, even if the goods could be produced more cheaply abroad. When unemployment levels reached record highs in the 1930s, Keynes in fact wrote that goods should "be homespun whenever it is reasonably and conveniently possible."[13] After World War II, Keynes moved toward supporting more multilateral, internationalist solutions in the Bretton Woods negotiations, but this was largely because he foresaw the possibility of planning on a global scale (the United States basically overruled this objective). Keynes's concessions to multilateralism were also contingent on solutions to Britain's financial problems. As Britain's chief postwar negotiator, he pressured the Labour government to pursue open liberal policies, and in return the United States provided the British with $3.75 million in loans.[14]

Keynes's support of a greater role for economic management at both the national and international levels had a major impact on liberal-economic thought. Because markets often behave differently than the orthodox liberals predicted, Keynes explicitly called for the state to play a role in combating the problem of unemployment. Nevertheless, Keynes considered his techniques of macroeconomic management to be alternatives to more extreme forms of state intervention. Despite his divergence from liberal orthodoxy, Keynes remained firmly within the liberal-economic tradition, believing in the importance of individual initiative and in the inherent efficiency of the market. Greater management, in Keynes's view, would facilitate rather than impede the efficient functioning of world market forces. Thus, Keynes favored intervention by the government, not to replace capitalism but to rescue and revitalize it. Keynes's views, calling for greater government intervention in the economy, gave rise to the interventionist strand of liberalism.[15]

LIBERALISM IN THE POSTWAR PERIOD

Post-1945 liberal-economic theories developed in efforts to avoid the economic problems of the interwar years, including trade wars, financial crises, and the depression. The postwar economic planners were influenced not only by the ideas of Keynes, but also by those of Karl Polanyi. In his classic 1944 work *The Great Transformation,* Polanyi warned of the dangers of the orthodox liberals' commitment to the "self-regulating market," with little concern about the effects on society. In Polanyi's view, society would move to protect itself from unregulated market activities, because disasters such as the depression of the interwar years would result if society was unprotected.[16] Influenced by

Keynes's and Polanyi's ideas, the postwar planners designed the international economic order on the basis of an interventionist or embedded liberal compromise. The "embedded" term refers to the fact that postwar efforts to maintain an open liberal international economy were "embedded" in societal efforts to provide domestic security and stability for the populace.[17] Thus, movement toward greater openness in the international economy included measures to cushion domestic economies from external disruptions, and policies to provide domestic stability in turn were designed to minimize interference with the expansion of global economic relations. In trade policy, for example, Western leaders called for tariff reductions on a multilateral basis, but they also permitted countries to include safeguards and exemptions from the trading regulations to protect their balance of payments and to promote full employment.

Underlying the postwar interventionist liberal compromise was a domestic class compromise between business and labor. Thus, labor unions largely abandoned their demands that the economy be socialized, and in return they benefited from collective bargaining, the welfare state, and political acceptance. Business for its part accepted a greater role for the government, welfare, and collective bargaining, and in return it won broad societal acceptance of freer international trade, private ownership, private profit, and the market.[18]

The predominant strand of liberalism in the postwar period was interventionist in nature; it viewed government intervention as necessary to counteract the socially unacceptable aspects of the market. These interventionist liberals, however, opted for government measures that would reinforce rather than replace the market, and they looked to the market as the preferred means of determining production and distribution.

A RETURN TO ORTHODOX LIBERALISM

Although the liberalism of Western policymakers in the postwar period was highly accepting of government interventionism, orthodox liberal theorists retained considerable influence in some circles. In 1947 Friedrich Hayek organized the first meeting of what became known as the Mont Pelerin Society, a transnational private forum of scholars and political figures committed to orthodox liberal ideas. Proponents of a return to orthodox liberalism, such as Hayek, Ludwig von Mises, and Milton Friedman, placed the highest priority on competitive markets and the efficient allocation of resources, and they often viewed economics and politics as being even more separable than did Adam Smith and David Ricardo. Thus, Friedman (b. 1912) wrote in 1962 that "the kind of economic organization that provides economic freedom directly, namely, competitive capitalism, also promotes political freedom because it separates economic power from political power."[19] Hayek and Friedman also expressed extremely negative views of state interference with the market. For example, Milton Friedman and Rose Friedman argued:

> Wherever we find any large element of individual freedom, some measure of progress in the material comforts at the disposal of ordinary citizens, and widespread hope of further progress in the future, there we also find that economic activity is organized

mainly through the free market. Wherever the state undertakes to control in detail the economic activities of its citizens . . . there ordinary citizens are in political fetters, have a low standard of living, and have little power to control their own destiny.[20]

Proponents of orthodox liberalism also rejected the notion that free market policies contribute to inequality, and they were extremely critical of Keynes's emphasis on government involvement to combat unemployment. Private initiative and free enterprise rather than government intervention, in their view, were most likely to result in full employment, rising wages, and a higher standard of living for the average person.[21]

Despite the ongoing influence of orthodox views, the policies of interventionist liberalism maintained their centrality during the expansive years of the 1950s and 1960s. However, the OPEC oil price shock in 1973 and the prolonged global recession after 1974 made it more costly for governments to continue with welfare and full-employment policies, and the contradictions between capital accumulation and the re-distribution of wealth became more evident. Orthodox writings of economists such as Hayek and Friedman therefore experienced a revival in the late 1970s and 1980s and began to exert more influence over government policies. Foremost among political leaders pushing for this revival were Prime Minister Margaret Thatcher in Britain and President Ronald Reagan in the United States.

In the view of many critics, the Thatcher-Reagan policies concentrated on revitalizing the confidence of business in government, largely rejecting the attempt to ease the effects of liberalism on vulnerable groups. These policies therefore resulted in open conflict with government employees, trade unions, and welfare recipients. As the changes initiated under Reagan and Thatcher spread to other countries, there were growing pressures on governments to adopt orthodox liberal policies in the 1980s and 1990s, with an emphasis on privatization, deregulation, and the promotion of free trade and foreign investment. To legitimize their confrontational approach toward excluded groups, the newer orthodox leaders sometimes appealed to traditional values such as "the work ethic, family, neighborhood, and patriotism."[22]

This return to orthodox liberalism is very different from the liberalism of Adam Smith in some important respects. Most importantly, the pressures for liberal orthodoxy are now global in extent, for several reasons. First, advances in technology, communications, and transportation have enabled MNCs and international banks to shift their funds and their activities around the world. Second, the IMF, the World Bank, and the industrial countries have provided Third World debtors with financing since the foreign debt crisis erupted in 1982, but the conditions on this financing have included pressures for Third World countries to privatize, deregulate, and liberalize their economies. Third, with the breakup of the Soviet bloc and the Soviet Union, orthodox liberal pressures have also spread to the former CPEs. To differentiate this new liberal orthodoxy from the liberalism of Smith and Ricardo, some scholars use the term "neoliberalism."

LIBERALISM AND INSTITUTIONS

As discussed in Chapter 1, theorists point to "hegemony" and "institutions" as two important mechanisms for the management of the international political economy. Two types of institutions are of interest here: international regimes and IOs.[23]

Regime theory is the main theoretical approach of international relations scholars to the study of institutions. Although hegemonic stability theory draws on more than one IPE perspective, it was covered in Chapter 3 because of its close links with realism. Regime theory also draws on more than one IPE perspective. Although a liberal scholar first used the "regime" term in an IPE context, a realist scholar edited what is considered to be a definitive volume on regimes.[24] However, institutions and regimes are discussed in this chapter because liberals generally attach more importance to these concepts than do realists. Because international regimes help to promote cooperation in issue areas such as international trade and monetary relations, in which there is a high degree of interdependence among states, we begin with a discussion of interdependence theory.[25]

Interdependence Theory

Interdependence can be defined as "mutual dependence," in which "there are reciprocal (although not necessarily symmetrical) costly effects of transactions."[26] Interdependence is not a new phenomenon in international relations; a number of theorists wrote thoughtful studies on the subject in the early 1900s.[27] By the 1940s, scholars were publishing works on interdependence in international trade and monetary relations.[28] Despite these early studies, Richard Cooper's book *The Economics of Interdependence* (1968) is credited with being the first systematic study of the growing economic interdependence among states.[29] Cooper argues that growing economic interdependence as a result of advances in transportation, communications, and technology "negates the sharp distinction between internal and external policies that underlies the present political organization of the world," and increasingly circumscribes "the ability of nation-states to achieve their desired aims, regardless of their formal retention of sovereignty."[30] The response of states to their loss of autonomy, according to Cooper, may be passive, exploitative, defensive, aggressive, or constructive. The *constructive* response to the growth of interdependence in Cooper's view is the attempt by governments to develop and implement their policies jointly. This coordination of actions could include "a wide range of policies concerning taxation, the regulation of business structure and activity, the framing of monetary policy, and other 'domestic' policies."[31]

Although Cooper considers cooperation to be the best response to the challenge of interdependence, he does not explicitly consider how *political* conditions can promote or undermine international cooperation. In their seminal work *Power and Interdependence*, published almost a decade after Cooper's study, Robert Keohane and Joseph Nye go a step further and analyze how international politics is transformed by interdependence. Although Keohane and Nye agree with Cooper that interdependence offers new opportunities for cooperation, they argue against an overly optimistic view of global harmony. Thus, they maintain that economic changes do not negate politics but simply create a new type of politics:

> Asymmetrical interdependence [i.e., mutual dependence that is not evenly balanced] can be a source of power. . . . . A less dependent actor in a relationship often has a significant political resource, because changes in the relationship . . . will be less costly to that actor than to its partners.[32]

Nevertheless, Keohane and Nye as well as Cooper have a rather benign view of the effects of asymmetrical interdependence on smaller states. Indeed, they argue that interdependent relationships increase the opportunities for bargaining and permit smaller states to achieve their objectives in disputes with larger states more often than one might anticipate. In a study of asymmetrical interdependence between the United States and Canada, Keohane and Nye conclude that Canada's ability to successfully confront the United States in conflicts results largely from the highly interdependent relationship between the two countries. According to Keohane and Nye, Canada benefits from "complex interdependence" with the United States, in which multiple channels connect societies, there is an absence of hierarchy among issues (military security does not dominate the agenda), and military force is not used by one government (the United States) against another government (Canada).[33] Some Canadian foreign policy analysts, however, strongly disagree with these conclusions. The United States as the larger power, they argue, is not content to let market transactions dictate its interdependence with Canada and instead is inclined to demand a wide array of "side payments." For example, Canadian side payments in exchange for free trade with the United States include concessions to U.S. demands regarding sharing of energy resources and openness to foreign investment (see discussion in Chapter 9).[34] A small number of Canadian analysts go even further and are inclined to characterize Canada's relationship with the United States in terms of dependence rather than interdependence.[35]

Interdependence theorists explicitly question the realist assumptions that states are unitary rational actors, that states are the only important actors in international relations, and that military force is always useful for promoting a state's national interest. They also maintain that the scope of international relations has expanded dramatically beyond the areas that realists emphasize, encompassing "new" issues such as environmental pollution, human rights, immigration, monetary and trade instabilities, and **sustainable development.** These new issues are more *intermestic* in nature (domestic as well as international) than traditional security issues.[36] Thus, interdependence theorists often criticize realists for overemphasizing the divisions between international and domestic politics. Although interdependence theorists are critical of many realist assumptions, they view their model as supplementing rather than replacing realism. Indeed, they acknowledge that realism is still the best model for understanding many security situations, in which power and force are of prime importance. They maintain, however, that interdependence theory is often more applicable than realism in explaining international socioeconomic relations.

The Liberal Approach to Cooperation

Achieving cooperation in a world of nation-states is problematic because there is no centralized international authority to establish and enforce rules for state behavior. Game theory is useful for assessing the prospects for cooperation among states, and the **prisoners' dilemma** is the game most often used by international relations theorists. The prisoners' dilemma game examines situations in which cooperation provides mutual benefits to states if they can rely on each other to honor agreements, but each state has an incentive to cheat regardless of the actions taken by others.

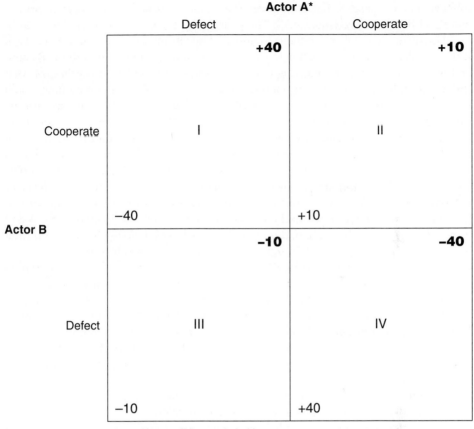

Figure 4.1   Prisoners' Dilemma

The term *prisoners' dilemma* derives from the story used to describe the game: The police arrest two individuals, actor A and actor B, for committing fraud. The police suspect that A and B have also committed robbery, but they cannot prove it without a confession. The police put A and B in different cells so they cannot communicate with each other, then question each prisoner separately. In Figure 4.1, prisoners A and B "cooperate" with each other if they do not confess to committing robbery, and they "defect" (or cheat on each other) if they confess to the crime. The prisoners receive "payoffs" (i.e., benefits or losses) depending on the decisions they make. The numbers at the top right-hand corner of the squares in Figure 4.1 are the payoff figures for A, and the numbers at the bottom left-hand corners are the payoffs for B. The police make a tempting offer to induce A to confess (i.e., to defect). First, the police tell A that conviction for fraud is certain and will result in a sentence of 1 year for both prisoners if they do not confess (square II in Figure 4.1). However, if A confesses to robbery (i.e., defects) and B does not (i.e., cooperates), A will go free and B will get 10 years' imprisonment (square I). If both A and B defect and confess to robbery, they will get a reduced sentence of 5 years (square III). Finally, if A does not confess to robbery (i.e., cooperates) but B confesses (i.e., defects), A will get 10 years' imprison-ment and B will go free (square IV). The police offer the same set of conditions to B.

The question is, what will the prisoners do? According to *individual* rationality, if B defects, A is better off defecting (a payoff of −10) than cooperating (−40). If B coop-erates, A is also better off defecting (+40) than cooperating (+10). Regardless of what B does, therefore, it would seem rational for A to defect! The same reasoning would apply to B's decisions. A fears B will defect, and A wants to avoid ending up with the worst possible penalty by cooperating (−40 in square IV); thus, A is almost certain to defect, and B, too, who similarly mistrusts A, is likely to defect. A and B are therefore both likely to defect and end up with the third-best outcome (square III), even though both would have been better off cooperating and ending up with the second-best out-come (square II). Square III is referred to as a *Pareto-suboptimal* or *Pareto-deficient* outcome because *all* actors (A and B) would prefer another outcome (II). Square II, by contrast, is the **Pareto-optimal** outcome or the best collective outcome for A and B; no single actor can be made better off without making someone else worse off (that is, if A's payoff increases to +40 in square I, B's payoff decreases to −40).[37]

The dilemma in this game results from the fact that individual rationality differs from collective rationality and therefore leads to an outcome (square III) that is Pareto-suboptimal for both prisoners.[38] In international relations, we ask how (and whether) states can move from a Pareto-suboptimal outcome (mutual defection or DD) to the Pareto-optimal outcome (mutual cooperation or CC). In the view of liber-als, "cheating" by states can inhibit cooperation, but the move to mutual cooperation is often possible if cheating can be controlled. The existence of a global hegemon, and the existence of international institutions, can limit cheating and facilitate movement toward mutual cooperation. A global hegemon prevents cheating by providing public goods and coercing other states to abide by agreed rules and principles. Institutions such as IOs prevent cheating simply by bringing states together on a regular basis. A state that interacts regularly with other states in IOs is less likely to cheat because the other states will have many opportunities to retaliate. International institutions also enforce principles and rules to ensure that cheaters will be punished, and they collect information on each member state's policies, increasing "transparency" or confidence that cheaters will be discovered. Finally, international institutions contribute to a mu-tual learning process in which states become aware of the mutual gains that result from cooperation.[39]

Realists are far more skeptical than liberals that international institutions can play a significant role in moving states to a Pareto-optimal (i.e., cooperative) outcome. In the realist view, institutions often serve the interests of the most powerful states rather than inducing the powerful to seek cooperative solutions with weaker states. Realists also place more emphasis than liberals on state concerns with *relative gains* as a major obstacle to cooperation, and they are highly skeptical of the liberal view that interna-tional institutions can refocus a state's interests toward absolute, mutual gains. Be-cause of their basic interests in survival and security, states will continue to be con-cerned about their capabilities *relative to* those of other states. Even when two states have common interests, they may be unwilling to cooperate because of each state's concern that the other will receive greater gains. Institutions can play a significant role in promoting cooperation, according to many realists, only if the institutions can ensure member states that their gains will be balanced and equitable. However, gains are rarely equal, so this will be an extremely difficult objective for international institutions to achieve.[40] As is the case with all three schools of thought, there are gradations of view, and some realists have been more willing to concede that institutions may have an important role in specific instances. Robert Gilpin, for example, maintains that international economic organizations can be of importance when they "do not infringe on the security interests of powerful states."[41] Nevertheless, realists as a group are clearly less inclined than liberals to attribute an important role to international institutions in managing the global economy.

It is important to note that prisoners' dilemma is not the only game used by theorists to explicate international behavior. Theorists also use other games such as "stag hunt," where cooperation is more likely than in prisoners' dilemma, and "deadlock," where cooperation is less likely.[42] In this book, we discuss only prisoners' dilemma because it is the most common game used by international relations theorists.

Regime Theory

Although realists simply assume that the international system is anarchic because a central authority above nation-states is lacking, regime theory first developed in efforts to explain why international interactions seem to be more orderly in some issue areas than in others.[43] With the growth of interdependence, states have established some principles, norms, and rules to regulate each others' behavior in such areas as trade, aid, and monetary relations. Thus, *regimes* can be defined as "sets of implicit or explicit principles, norms, rules, and decision-making procedures around which actors' expectations converge in a given area of international relations."[44] International regimes are normally associated with IOs. For example, the WTO is embedded in the global trade regime, and the IMF is embedded in the global monetary regime. Regime *principles* and *norms* refer to general beliefs and standards of behavior that determine how relations are conducted in a specific issue area. Important principles of the global trade regime, for example, include trade liberalization, reciprocity, and nondiscrimination.[45] Regime *rules*, which are more specific than principles and norms, refer to the types of behavior that are considered to be permissible and impermissible. Rules and decision-making procedures stem from principles and norms, which are the most central components of a regime. For example, "trade liberalization" is an important principle of the postwar trade regime. To promote this principle, the GATT/WTO has developed rules that outlaw import quotas and decrease tariff barriers, and decision-making procedures such as multilateral trade negotiations. The sections that follow briefly examine some of the research done on the formation and consequences of regimes.

The Formation of Regimes   Some theorists argue that the existence of a hegemonic state or group of states is necessary for both the formation and persistence of regimes. Others draw a distinction between the creation and maintenance of a regime. A hegemonic power plays a major role in the creation of regimes through providing public goods and coercing other states, but it is easier to maintain regimes than it is to establish them. Thus, countries that have benefited from a regime may be willing to cooperate with each other to maintain it, even after a hegemonic state has declined.[46] Some theorists go even further and argue that hegemony is not necessary for either the creation or the maintenance of regimes. For example, some regimes may arise through negotiations among willing states that are relatively equal in stature. In such cases, the common interests of these states is sufficient to form the regime even in the absence of a hegemon.[47]

Are Regimes Important?   Research on the formation of regimes is of interest, but a more central question to ask is whether regimes "make a difference" in international relations. In assessing the importance of regimes, some researchers examine whether member states regularly abide by regime principles, norms, and rules; whether regimes cause states to alter their perceptions of self-interest; whether regimes adequately manage the international problems they were formed to deal with; and whether regimes persist even when there is a deterioration in overall relations.

In the view of traditional realists the existence of regimes is uncertain, and even if they do exist they have little effect. The most powerful states, from this perspective, have the most influence in establishing regime principles, norms, and rules that fit with their national objectives. However, these states will not continue adhering to the regime principles, norms, and rules if they come into conflict with their changing national interests. As global interdependence increased, modified realists acknowledged that regimes may be of some importance, but only in certain areas (for example, in trade and monetary relations) and under rather restrictive conditions. In comparison with the modified realists, liberals are far more likely to view regimes as a pervasive and significant phenomenon in international relations.[48]

In this book we assume regimes do have a significant impact on the international behavior of states in certain issue areas.[49] Regime principles, norms, and rules can help to establish standards in specific areas by which member states can assess their own and others' actions. In setting standards, regimes can provide countries with reliable information, decrease the likelihood of misunderstandings, and increase the possibilities for cooperation. Regimes can also induce national governments to follow consistent policies, limit actions that adversely affect other states, and become less responsive to special interest groups. To say that regimes and their IOs can influence international behavior does not indicate that their effect is always as positive, as liberals imply. As both realists and historical structuralists point out, the principles, norms, and rules of a regime may simply reflect or further the interests of the most powerful states, and it is the least powerful states that are expected to abide by them.[50] The chapters in Part III examine the role of regimes and IOs in greater detail.

LIBERALISM AND DOMESTIC-INTERNATIONAL INTERACTIONS

Scholars of IPE are more likely than security specialists to focus on the linkages between international and domestic politics. A major reason is that domestic groups and individuals often see a close relationship between international economic interactions (such as trade and foreign investment) and their own welfare. Much of the literature on domestic structure and IPE cannot be neatly categorized under any one of the three IPE perspectives; however, the liberals most closely adhere to the view that domestic societal pressures affect state policy (as discussed in Chapter 5, one strand of Marxism also considers the state to be an "instrument" of the dominant capitalist class).

One IPE area in which international relations specialists have examined domestic-international interactions extensively is foreign economic policymaking. Foreign policy specialists are more inclined than other international relations theorists to recognize the need to examine domestic politics. A state's foreign economic policy results at least as much from domestic factors as it does from international factors.[51] For example, some analysts have argued that more centralized states such as Japan and France can often respond more decisively to external events than can more decentralized states such as the United States. It is argued that the separation of powers in the United States between the president and the Congress and the division of powers between the federal government and the states make the U.S. government more vulnerable to interest group pressures and less able to respond promptly to international crises. Thus, France promptly took actions to increase its autonomy and security of energy supplies after the 1973 OPEC oil price increases by supporting French oil companies, promoting special relations with former French colonies that had oil, and developing nuclear energy as an alternative source of supply. The decentralized U.S. government, by contrast, acted far more indecisively because it was subject to a variety of competing societal pressures from oil companies, environmentalists, and other groups.[52]

Although the strong state/weak state distinction may be helpful in comparing industrial state policies in a general sense, more recent studies have argued that states are not uniformly strong or uniformly weak across different issue areas and time periods.[53] Thus, the U.S. executive has been able to implement monetary policy far more easily than trade policy because societal groups see their economic fortunes as being far more affected by trade. Although societal groups exert pressures on Congress to express their interests on controversial trade issues such as NAFTA, they give government leaders considerable latitude in the formulation and implementation of monetary policy. States such as Japan, which are considered to be highly centralized, also do not necessarily act decisively in regard to every issue. Thus, when a financial crisis affected East and Southeast Asia in the late 1990s, Japan had great difficulty in adopting some of the bold policy measures required to alleviate the crisis (see Chapter 11).

As long as one takes account of variations over issue areas and time periods, domestic structure can be an important factor in explaining a country's foreign economic policies. For example, hegemonic stability theorists look at U.S. economic and political resources, but they largely ignore the *domestic* constraints confronting U.S. policymakers. The domestic divisions within both the U.S. polity (for example, between the president and Congress) and the U.S. society can make it difficult for the United States to provide international leadership *even if* the United States has the external strength one associates with a hegemon. Japan, by contrast, with fewer external power resources, may benefit from a greater unity of purpose in its polity and society under certain circumstances.

International relations specialists have also focused on domestic-international interactions when examining international economic negotiations. For example, theorists often view international negotiations as a "two-level game" involving a relationship between a state's international interests and obligations (level 1) on the one hand

and its domestic interactions (level 2) on the other.[54] At the international level of the two-level game, state representatives bargain with each other to reach an agreement. At the domestic level, these representatives must bargain with their own domestic constituencies, whose concurrence is often needed to arrive at legitimate and effective agreements. A certain degree of consistency must develop between the international and domestic interests if agreements are to be signed and implemented. The two-level game framework is especially useful in examining issues such as agricultural trade, in which a wide range of domestic interests come into conflict with the international interests and obligations of the state.[55]

In addition to examining foreign economic policymaking and international negotiations, IPE specialists have sought to explain international economic cooperation and conflict in terms of domestic variables.[56] Chapters 6 and 8, for example, refer to some writers who argue that domestic factors have been more important than the existence of a hegemon in explaining cooperation and conflict in the global monetary and trade regimes. There is a wealth of literature on domestic interactions in the field of IPE; this book can only begin to discuss the subject.

LIBERALISM AND NORTH-SOUTH RELATIONS

Liberals generally agree that the key factors in development are the efficient use of scarce resources and economic growth, which is often defined as an increase in the total per capita income of a country. Beyond these broad areas of agreement, however, the liberal development school "lacks a central unifying, theoretical argument."[57] When discussing liberal theory in general, we referred to orthodox liberals such as Adam Smith and Milton Friedman and to interventionist liberals such as John Maynard Keynes. The same division is evident among liberal development theorists.

Orthodox Liberals and North-South Relations

North-South distributional issues are not a major concern of the orthodox liberals. Because orthodox liberals consider international economic relations to be a positive-sum game, they believe that the growth of interdependence will have a mutually beneficial effect on states. Indeed, orthodox liberals often argue that North-South linkages provide even more benefits to the LDCs than to the advanced industrial states. The economic problems of LDCs, in the orthodox liberal view, stem from irrational or inefficient domestic policies and not from their unfavorable position in the global economy. The sections that follow outline the views of orthodox liberals regarding domestic and external determinants of development.

Domestic Development Factors   Orthodox liberals assume that development problems in the Third World stem largely from irrational or inefficient policies of LDCs. In the 1950s and 1960s, liberal *modernization theorists* compared traditional and modern societies and traced the development process from traditionalism to modernity. Although modernization theory was considered to be largely passé by the 1970s, its precepts continue to influence orthodox liberal thought. Modernization theory asserts that the Northern industrial states achieved economic development by abandoning traditional methods of organizing society and that the North's development experience serves as an indispensable guide to development for the South. From the modernization perspective, LDCs must replace their traditional values, institutions, and patterns of activity if they are to overcome the obstacles to development. The individual and societal changes required may produce considerable dislocation and hardship, but the rewards and opportunities in societies that successfully modernize are also great. To bring about modernization, society must develop a system of rewards for innovation. Innovation and other internal mechanisms for generating surpluses contribute to increased investment, which in turn leads to self-sustaining growth.[58]

It is generally conceded today that modernization theorists' concepts of "traditional" and "modern" were imprecise, that the two concepts are not mutually exclusive, and that modern values and practices are not always superior to traditional ones. Nevertheless, orthodox liberals continue to believe that the main factors hindering Third World development are domestic. For example, they argue that the countries of Western Europe that protected private property rights experienced early success in industrialization and development and that Third World governments that do not enforce these rights hinder foreign investment and the adoption of new technologies. In the orthodox liberal view, LDC governments should permit private producers to operate freely through the price mechanism and should limit their own involvement to providing public goods such as national security, education, and services designed to improve the functioning of markets.[59]

Paths to Development   A number of modernization theorists were quite deterministic, arguing that LDCs must follow the same path to development that was previously taken by Northern states. For example, one theorist wrote in the 1960s that the Western development model "reappears in virtually all modernizing societies of all continents of the world, regardless of variations of race, color or creed."[60] The best-known study prescribing a single development path is Walt Rostow's *The Stages of Economic Growth,* which received widespread attention from the time of its publication. Rostow takes a highly deterministic position, claiming that societies move through five specific stages on their way to modernity: traditional society, the preconditions for takeoff, the takeoff, the drive to maturity, and the age of high mass consumption.[61]

Although Rostow's model initially had considerable influence, his stages were extremely difficult to apply to specific Third World countries, and his predictions regarding LDC growth were unduly optimistic. Thus, Rostow argued that an LDC reaching the takeoff stage would be transformed in such a way that its growth would be self-sustaining thereafter. Such predictions raised false hopes that Third World economic development was a readily achievable and irreversible process. Although some modernization theorists were more open to the idea that LDCs could follow different routes to development, much modernization theory was—like Rostow's—marked by determinism.[62]

Critics of modernization theory have strongly challenged the view that all countries can or should follow similar paths to development, pointing out that the challenges facing LDCs today are very different from those that confronted early developers. The forces of globalization, the need to compete with advanced industrial states, and the proliferation of MNCs all indicate that development today cannot simply be a repetition of the earlier Western model.[63] Nevertheless, even after modernization theory was considered to be passé, orthodox liberals continued to view the Western model as the only legitimate path to development. In the 1970s, for example, orthodox liberals strongly opposed the OPEC cartel's strategy to raise oil prices because it interfered with market-oriented pricing, and they opposed the Third World prescription for an NIEO, objecting that it would redistribute wealth and power on the basis of political pressure rather than efficient economic performance.[64] With the breakup of the Soviet bloc, orthodox liberals became even more assertive. Thus, by the late 1980s and early 1990s, some theorists were writing that "third-world countries are much like those of the first world and will, with a modicum of external aid and internal stability, follow in the path of their predecessors" and that "what we may be witnessing is not just the end of the Cold War" but "the universalization of Western liberal democracy as the final form of human government."[65]

External Development Factors   Internationally, orthodox liberals view North-South relations as a positive-sum game that benefits the South, and they strongly reject the idea that the advanced industrial states are responsible for poverty in the Third World. On the contrary, orthodox liberals often argue that "the late-comers to modern economic growth tend to catch up with the early-comers."[66] In the liberal orthodox view, Third World countries are more likely to achieve development if they are closely integrated in the global economy through freer trade and capital flows. LDCs that have few trade and foreign investment linkages with the North are the poorest and least developed countries. Because LDCs have shortages of capital and technology, foreign investment and the diffusion of advanced technologies are of particular importance to them. Exports are also of critical importance to LDCs because of their small domestic markets, and international trade permits LDCs to specialize in the goods they can produce most efficiently. Thus, two well-known orthodox liberal economists have written in regard to the African country of Tanzania that "such economic development as has taken place is in large measure due to access to Western markets and to Western enterprise, capital, and ideas."[67]

Because orthodox liberals advocate free trade, they were extremely critical of the **import-substituting industrialization (ISI)** policies followed by a number of LDCs in the 1950s and 1960s. (Some Latin American LDCs continued to follow ISI policies in the 1970s and early 1980s.) These policies involved protection of local industry through a wide array of tariffs and **nontariff barriers (NTBs),** with an emphasis on production for the domestic market over production for export. In the orthodox liberal view, ISI causes economic distortions in LDC economies and fosters uncompetitive industries with high prices and low-quality products.[68]

Orthodox liberals, by contrast, attributed the economic success of the East Asian NIEs to their "export-led development" model, which these theorists viewed as clearly preferable to the import substitution model. As its name implies, **export-led growth** relies on deep involvement in international trade as a "motor" to development. Thus, the orthodox liberals Milton Friedman and Rose Friedman argued that "Malaysia, Singapore, Korea, Taiwan, Hong Kong and Japan—all relying extensively on private markets, are thriving" while "India, Indonesia, and Communist China, all relying heavily on central planning, have experienced economic stagnation and political repression."[69] As discussed in Chapter 3, realists disputed the liberal view that the East Asian NIEs' success in exporting depended mainly on market-oriented policies. Instead, the realists argue that government-business cooperation and selective government involvement was key to East Asian economic development. Chapter 11, on international development, examines this debate in greater detail.

Interventionist Liberals and North-South Relations

Interventionist liberals begin with the same basic assumptions as orthodox liberals that LDCs with efficient, market-oriented policies are most likely to achieve economic growth. In contrast to orthodox liberals, however, interventionists point to the pronounced inequalities between North and South, and they call on the advanced industrial states to give more consideration to the special needs of LDCs. The interventionists believe that "economic forces left entirely to themselves tend to produce growing inequality," especially when income distribution is highly distorted (as is the case between North and South).[70] They therefore recommend a variety of changes that involve some degree of intervention in the market, including the removal of Northern trade barriers to Southern states while permitting some degree of protectionism for LDC industries, the provision of increased financial resources to indebted LDCs through the IMF and the World Bank, and the assurance that MNCs will not take undue advantage of LDC needs for foreign investment and technology. Interventionists also argue that Northern assistance to the South is a matter of enlightened self-interest because "the countries of the North, given their increasing interdependence with the South, themselves need international economic reform to ensure their own future prosperity."[71]

Although interventionists argue that corrective devices are needed to provide for the special needs of the South, they believe that the necessary changes can occur within the international liberal order and that a radical redistribution of wealth and power between North and South is not necessary. They also share the faith of other liberals in private enterprise, believing that private sector interactions between North and South should be encouraged. Finally, interventionist and orthodox liberals agree that many Southern development problems are rooted in domestic inefficiencies and that LDCs therefore have the primary responsibility for confronting their development problems.[72]

CRITIQUE OF THE LIBERAL PERSPECTIVE

It is impossible to provide a detailed critique of the liberal perspective here. This section focuses mainly on some of the more important general criticisms that theorists from the two competing perspectives (realists and historical structuralists) level against the liberals. As this chapter notes, liberals tend to view international economic relations as occurring in a competitive market in which all countries benefit from trade, foreign investment, and other economic linkages. Because these exchange relations produce mutual benefits, orthodox liberals are not particularly concerned about the fact that all countries do not benefit equally. Although interventionist liberals point out that unemployment can occur under pure market conditions and that LDCs may require special and differential treatment, they feel that these problems can be resolved by supplementing the liberal-economic system rather than replacing it.

Both realists and historical structuralists criticize liberals for their inattention to power and distributional issues. In contrast to liberals, who emphasize the mutual gains from exchange, realists emphasize the relative distribution of gains across states, with the more powerful states capturing a larger share of the benefits. Realists argue that economic exchanges are in fact rarely free and equal and that bargaining power based on monopoly and coercion can have important political effects. Thus, the more powerful states can injure the weaker states simply by reducing or terminating their linkages in such areas as trade, aid, and foreign investment.[73] Historical structuralists often accuse liberals of seeking to legitimize inequalities and exploitation. Domestically, liberals mislead the working class into believing that it will reap the benefits of economic prosperity along with the capitalist class, and internationally, liberals disguise exploitation and imperialism under the cloak of "interdependence."

Critics also question the liberal view that technology, rather than global redistribution, can solve many of the world's most urgent economic and environmental problems. Even with technological advances, the liberal international order that seemed so positive-sum in the immediate postwar years is becoming more intensely competitive as we move away from a world of abundant resources. A world where resources are becoming scarce will inevitably become more zero-sum in nature. Furthermore, orthodox liberals underestimate the degree to which technological advances may contribute to greater inequalities between rich and poor countries. "Endogenous growth theory" posits that technological change is not simply the result of fortunate breakthroughs in the quest for new knowledge which are exogenous to the basic factors of production determining economic growth. Instead, technological knowledge is an important endogenous factor of production along with labor and capital that provides developed countries and their firms major advantages over LDCs. Thus, "increasing returns to knowledge make it possible for a large and rich economy to grow indefinitely at a faster pace than a small and poor economy."[74] Although some of the claims of endogenous growth theorists are controversial and not yet proven, they raise important questions about the orthodox liberal assumption that "the late-comers to modern economic growth tend to catch up with the early-comers."[75]

In regard to North-South relations, orthodox liberals also assume that open economic policies will improve LDC opportunities, without considering the political and power relationships between North and South. Aside from some aberrant cases such as OPEC and the East Asian NIEs, critics argue, North-South relationships are highly asymmetrical, with LDCs far more dependent on the advanced industrial states than vice versa. Thus, President Julius Nyerere of Tanzania remarked to the ministerial meeting of the G-77 Third World states in February 1979 that

> what we have in common is that we are all, in relation to the developed world, dependent—not interdependent—nations. Each of our economies has developed as a by-product and a subsidiary of development in the industrialized North, and is externally oriented.[76]

It is evident that this dependent relationship provides the North with a potent source of power over the South. The liberal perspective, however, tends to avoid the subject of power, discounting the effects of North-South asymmetries by arguing that North-South relations are a positive-sum game in which everyone benefits. One liberal assessment of NAFTA, for example, indicates that the United States, Canada, and Mexico agreed to "a partial surrender of autonomy in order to achieve the benefits that are available from mutual relaxation of protectionism."[77] However, orthodox liberals avoid asking whether the Southern states (i.e., Mexico in NAFTA) must surrender more autonomy than the Northern states (the United States and Canada).

Liberals are also criticized for putting too much faith in the market and for disregarding the role of the state. Although liberals such as Adam Smith recognized that the state had to perform certain essential functions, orthodox liberalism generally provides for a minimal role for the state. Interventionist liberals such as John Maynard Keynes have viewed states as performing various corrective functions, but even interventionists can be criticized for undertheorizing the role of the state. Liberal theory portrays the state as simply performing functions that the market does not perform, and it does not sufficiently explore either the capacities or constraints of the state. Thus, realists argue that we should "bring the state back in" to our research because of its central role in policymaking.[78]

Chapters 3 and 4 have demonstrated that realists and liberals have differing perceptions regarding a wide range of issues in IPE. However, these two schools of thought are much closer together than the third school—the historical structuralists—in one important respect. Whereas liberals and realists accept and basically approve of the capitalist system as a given, historical structuralists generally view capitalism as an exploitative system that should—and will—eventually be replaced by socialism. It is to the historical structuralists that we now turn.

NOTES

1. R. D. McKinlay and R. Little, *Global Problems and World Order* (London: Pinter, 1986), p. 41. Andrew Moravcsik attempts to identify the core analytical propositions of liberalism in "Taking Preferences Seriously: A Liberal Theory of International Politics," *International Organization* 51-4 (Autumn 1997), pp. 513–553.

2. For a discussion of the various strands of liberalism, see Mark W. Zacher and Richard A. Matthew, "Liberal International Theory: Common Threads, Divergent Strands," in Charles W. Kegley, Jr., ed., *Controversies in International Relations Theory: Realism and the Neoliberal Challenge* (New York: St. Martin's Press, 1995), pp. 107–150.

3. Moravcsik, "Taking Preferences Seriously," p. 517.

4. Adam Smith, *The Wealth of Nations* (London: Dent, Everyman's Library no. 412, 1910), vol. 1, bk. 4, p. 398.

5. See, for example, E. E. Schattschneider, *Politics, Pressures and the Tariff: A Study of Free Enterprise in Pressure Politics, as Shown in the 1929–1930 Revision of the Tariff* (Hamden, CT: Archon Books, 1963, reprint of the 1935 edition).

6. John Locke, *Two Treatises of Government* (Cambridge: Cambridge University Press, 1964), ch. 9 of the Second Treatise, p. 368.

7. Adam Smith, *The Wealth of Nations,* vol. 1, bk. 4, p. 436.

8. Smith, *The Wealth of Nations,* vol. 2, bk. 4, pp. 180–181; George T. Crane and Abla Amawi, *The Theoretical Evolution of International Political Economy: A Reader* 2nd ed. (New York: Oxford University Press, 1997), p. 56.

9. John Maynard Keynes, *The General Theory of Employment, Interest, and Money* (New York: Harcourt, Brace & World, 1936), p. 383.

10. Peter A. Hall, "Introduction," in Peter A. Hall, ed., *The Political Power of Economic Ideas: Keynesianism across Nations* (Princeton: Princeton University Press, 1989), p. 4.

11. Keynes, *The General Theory of Employment, Interest, and Money,* pp. 378–379.

12. Hall, "Introduction," p. 7.

13. John Maynard Keynes, "National Self-Sufficiency," *The Yale Review* 22 (1933), p. 758. For a discussion of Keynes's changing view of trade protection, see Barry Eichengreen, "Keynes and Protection," *Journal of Economic History* 44–2 (June 1984), pp. 363–373.

14. Fred L. Block, *The Origins of International Economic Disorder: A Study of United States International Monetary Policy from World War II to the Present* (Berkeley, CA: University of California Press, 1977), pp. 62–69; D. E. Moggridge, *Keynes* (London: Macmillan, 1976), p. 147.

15. Anthony Arblaster, *The Rise and Decline of Western Liberalism* (New York: Basil Blackwell, 1984), p. 292; B. Greenwald and J. E. Stiglits, "Keynesian, New Keynesian and New Classical Economics," *Oxford Economic Papers* 39-1 (1987), p. 119; Donald Winch, "Keynes, Keynesianism, and State Intervention," in Hall, ed., *The Political Power of Economic Ideas: Keynesianism across Nations,* pp. 109–110.

16. Karl Polanyi, *The Great Transformation* (Boston: Beacon Press, sixth printing, 1965).

17. The term "embedded liberalism compromise" was coined by John Gerard Ruggie in his important article "International Regimes, Transactions, and Change: Embedded Liberalism in the Postwar Economic Order," in Stephen D. Krasner, ed., *International Regimes* (Ithaca, NY: Cornell University Press, 1983), pp. 204–214.

18. Peter Gourevitch, *Politics in Hard Times: Comparative Responses to International Economic Crises* (Ithaca, NY: Cornell University Press, 1986), pp. 166–169; Adam Przeworski, *Capitalism and Social Democracy* (Cambridge: Cambridge University Press, 1985), pp. 205–211.

19. Milton Friedman, *Capitalism and Freedom* (Chicago: University of Chicago Press, 1962), p. 9.

20. Milton Friedman and Rose Friedman, *Free to Choose: A Personal Statement* (New York: Harcourt Brace Jovanovich, 1980), pp. 54–55.

21. See Friedman, *Capitalism and Freedom,* pp. 171–172; F. A. Hayek, *New Studies in Philosophy, Politics, Economics and the History of Ideas* (Chicago: University of Chicago Press,

1978), p. 209; and Ludwig von Mises, *Planning for Freedom* (South Holland, IL: Libertarian Press, 1974), p. 17.

22. Robert Cox, *Production, Power, and World Order: Social Forces in the Making of History* (New York: Columbia University Press, 1987), pp. 286–288. See also Alain Lipietz, *Towards a New Economic Order: Postfordism, Ecology and Democracy,* translated by Malcolm Slater (New York: Oxford University Press, 1992), pp. 30–31.

23. Robert Keohane identifies three types of international institutions: IOs, international regimes, and conventions. See his article "Neoliberal Institutionalism: A Perspective on World Politics," in Robert O. Keohane, *International Institutions and State Power: Essays in International Relations Theory* (Boulder, CO: Westview Press, 1989), pp. 3–4.

24. In the IPE field, John Gerard Ruggie first used the regime term in his article "International Responses to Technology: Concepts and Trends," *International Organization* 29–3 (Summer 1975), pp. 570–573. Stephen Krasner edited the definitive volume referred to entitled *International Regimes.*

25. Ernst B. Haas, "Words Can Hurt You; or, Who Said What to Whom About Regimes," in Krasner, ed., *International Regimes,* p. 27.

26. Robert O. Keohane and Joseph S. Nye, *Power and Interdependence,* 2nd ed. (Glenview, IL: Scott, Foresman, 1989), pp. 8–9.

27. See Sir Norman Angell, *The Foundations of International Polity* (London: Heinemann, 1914); Francis Delaisi, *Political Myths and Economic Realities* (London: Douglas, 1925); Ramsay Muir, *The Interdependent World and Its Problems* (Boston: Houghton Mifflin, 1933); and David A. Baldwin, "Interdependence and Power: A Conceptual Analysis," *International Organization* 34-4 (Autumn 1980), pp. 481–482.

28. See W. A. Brown, Jr., *The International Gold Standard Reinterpreted, 1914–1934,* 2 vols. (New York: National Bureau of Economic Research, 1940); and Albert O. Hirschman, *National Power and the Structure of Foreign Trade* (Berkeley, CA: University of California Press, 1945).

29. Richard N. Cooper, *The Economics of Interdependence: Economic Policy in the Atlantic Community* (New York: McGraw-Hill, 1968).

30. Richard N. Cooper, "Economic Interdependence and Foreign Policy in the Seventies," *World Politics* 24 (January 1972), p. 179.

31. Cooper, "Economic Interdependence and Foreign Policy in the Seventies," pp. 170–171.

32. Keohane and Nye, *Power and Interdependence,* p. 11. See also Crane and Amawi, *The Theoretical Evolution of International Political Economy,* pp. 14, 107–109.

33. See Keohane and Nye, *Power and Interdependence,* pp. 24–29 and ch. 7.

34. See, for example, Ricardo Grinspun and Maxwell A. Cameron, eds., *The Political Economy of North American Free Trade* (Montreal: McGill-Queen's University Press, 1993).

35. See, for example, Wallace Clement, *Continental Corporate Power: Economic Linkage Between Canada and the United States* (Toronto: McClelland and Stewart, 1976); Glen Williams, "On Determining Canada's Location Within the International Political Economy," *Studies in Political Economy* 25 (Spring 1988), pp. 107–140; and Duncan Cameron and Mel Watkins, eds., *Canada Under Free Trade* (Toronto: Lorimer, 1993).

36. Bayless Manning coined the term *intermestic* in "The Congress, The Executive and Intermestic Affairs: Three Proposals," *Foreign Affairs* 55 (June 1977), pp. 306–324.

37. The term *Pareto-optimal* is named after an Italian sociologist, Vilfredo Pareto (1848–1923).

38. Robert Axelrod, *The Evolution of Cooperation* (NY: Basic Books, 1984), p. 9.

39. See Keohane, "Neoliberal Institutionalism," pp. 1–20; and Robert Axelrod and Robert O. Keohane, "Achieving Cooperation Under Anarchy: Strategies and Institutions," in Kenneth

A. Oye, ed., *Cooperation Under Anarchy* (Princeton, NJ: Princeton University Press, 1986), pp. 226–254.

40. For the realist view of institutions, see John J. Mearsheimer, "The False Promise of International Institutions," *International Security* 19-3 (Winter 1994–95), pp. 5–49; and Joseph Grieco, *Cooperation Among Nations: Europe, America, and Non-Tariff Barriers to Trade* (Ithaca, NY: Cornell University Press, 1990).

41. Robert Gilpin with Jean M. Gilpin, *Global Political Economy: Understanding the International Economic Order* (Princeton, NJ: Princeton University Press, 2001), p. 83, fn. 13.

42. For a discussion of the various games used by international relations theorists, see the articles in Oye, ed., *Cooperation Under Anarchy*.

43. Mark W. Zacher with Brent A. Sutton, *Governing Global Networks: International Regimes for Transportation and Communications* (Cambridge: Cambridge University Press, 1996), p. 1.

44. Krasner, "Structural Causes and Regime Consequences: Regimes as Intervening Variables," in Krasner, ed., *International Regimes*, p. 2.

45. One criticism of regime theory is that a clear consensus among scholars on the difference between regime "principles" and "norms" is lacking. For example, in an important article on the global trade regime, Mark Zacher and Jock Finlayson describe trade liberalization, nondiscrimination, and reciprocity as regime "norms." In a subsequent article, Zacher decides it is better to refer to these as regime "principles." See Jock A. Finlayson and Mark W. Zacher, "The GATT and the Regulation of Trade Barriers: Regime Dynamics and Function," in Krasner, ed., *International Regimes*, pp. 273–314; Mark W. Zacher, "Trade Gaps, Analytical Gaps: Regime Analysis and International Commodity Trade Regulation," *International Organization* 41–2 (Spring 1987), p. 176, fn. 8.

46. Robert O. Keohane, *After Hegemony: Cooperation and Discord in the World Political Economy* (Princeton, NJ: Princeton University Press, 1984), pp. 49, 244–245.

47. Oran R. Young, "Regime Dynamics: The Rise and Fall of International Regimes," in Krasner, ed., *International Regimes*, pp. 98–101; and Mark A. Levy, Oran R. Young, and Michael Züm, "The Study of International Regimes," *European Journal of International Relations* 1–3 (1995), p. 286.

48. Stephen Krasner uses the terms "conventional structuralists" for the traditional realists, "modified structuralists" for the modified realists, and "Grotians" for the liberals who see regimes as a pervasive phenomenon. See Krasner, "Structural Causes and Regime Consequences," pp. 5–10. The most often cited traditional realist critique of international regime theory is Susan Strange, "Cave! Hic Dragones: A Critique of Regime Analysis," in Krasner, ed., *International Regimes*, pp. 337–354.

49. On the need for more studies of the effectiveness of regimes see Robert O. Keohane, "The Analysis of International Regimes: Towards a European-American Research Programme," in Volker Rittberger, ed., with Peter Mayer, *Regime Theory and International Relations* (Oxford: Clarendon Press, 1993), pp. 32–34; Volker Rittberger and Michael Züm, "Towards Regulated Anarchy in East-West Relations: Causes and Consequences of East-West Regimes," in Volker Rittberger, ed., *International Regimes in East-West Politics* (London: Pinter, 1990), pp. 20–22.

50. For a discussion of the historical structuralist perspective and regime theory see Fred Gale, "Cave 'Cave! Hic dragones': A Neo-Gramscian Deconstruction and Reconstruction of International Regime Theory," *Review of International Political Economy* 5-2 (Summer 1998), pp. 252–283.

51. Even realists who examine foreign economic policy must be more attuned to domestic issues. See Stephen D. Krasner, *Defending the National Interest: Raw Materials Investments and U. S. Foreign Policy* (Princeton, NJ: Princeton University Press, 1978), pp. 12–13; and

Michael Mastanduno, David A. Lake, and G. John Ikenberry, "Toward a Realist Theory of State Action," *International Studies Quarterly* 33-4 (December 1989), pp. 457–474.

52. See Peter J. Katzenstein, "International Relations and Domestic Structures: Foreign Economic Policies of the Advanced Industrial States," *International Organization* 30-1 (Winter 1976), pp. 41–42; Peter J. Katzenstein, ed., *Between Power and Plenty: Foreign Economic Policies of Advanced Industrial States,* special issue of *International Organization* 31-4 (Autumn 1977); Matthew Evangelista, "Domestic Structure and International Change," in Michael W. Doyle and G. John Ikenberry, eds., *New Thinking in International Relations Theory* (Boulder, CO: Westview Press, 1997), pp. 206–208.

53. See G. John Ikenberry, David A. Lake, and Michael Mastanduno, ed., *The State and American Foreign Economic Policy,* special issue of *International Organization* 42-1 (Winter 1988); and William D. Coleman and Grace Skogstad, *Policy Communities and Public Policy in Canada: A Structural Approach* (Mississauga, ONT: Copp Clark Pitman, 1990), p. ix.

54. The two-level game approach was developed by Robert Putnam. See Robert D. Putnam, "Diplomacy and Domestic Politics: The Logic of Two-Level Games," *International Organization* 42-3 (Summer 1988), pp. 427–460; and Peter B. Evans, Harold K. Jacobson, and Robert D. Putnam, eds., *Double-Edged Diplomacy: International Bargaining and Domestic Politics* (Berkeley, CA: University of California Press, 1993).

55. See William P. Avery, ed., *World Agriculture and the GATT* (Boulder, CO: Rienner, 1993); Theodore H. Cohn, "The Intersection of Domestic and Foreign Policy in the NAFTA Agricultural Negotiations," *Canadian-American Public Policy,* no. 14 (Orono, ME: University of Maine, September 1993); and William P. Avery, "American Agricultural and Trade Policymaking: Two-Level Bargaining in the North American Free Trade Agreement," *Policy Sciences* 29 (1996), pp. 113–136.

56. See, for example, Peter Alexis Gourevitch, "Squaring the Circle: The Domestic Sources of International Cooperation," *International Organization* 50-2 (Spring 1996), pp. 349–373.

57. David A. Lake, "Power and the Third World: Toward a Realist Political Economy of North-South Relations," *International Studies Quarterly* 31-2 (June 1987), p. 218.

58. C. E. Black, *The Dynamics of Modernization: A Study in Comparative History* (New York: Harper & Row, 1966), p. 27; Daniel Lerner, "Modernization: Social Aspects," in David Sills, ed., *International Encyclopedia of the Social Sciences* (New York: Macmillan, 1968) vol. 10, pp. 386–388.

59. Robert Wade, *Governing the Market: Economic Theory and the Role of Government in East Asian Industrialization* (Princeton, NJ: Princeton University Press, 1990), pp. 11–14.

60. Daniel Lerner, *The Passing of Traditional Society: Modernizing the Middle East* (New York: Free Press, 1964), pp. viii–ix. (This quotation appears in the preface to the paperback edition.)

61. See W. W. Rostow, *The Stages of Economic Growth: A Non-Communist Manifesto* (Cambridge: Cambridge University Press, 1960), pp. 4–92.

62. Studies that were less deterministic include Gabriel A. Almond and James S. Coleman, eds., *The Politics of the Developing Areas* (Princeton, NJ: Princeton University Press, 1960); Samuel P. Huntington, *Political Order in Changing Societies* (New Haven, CT: Yale University Press, 1968); and Alexander Gerschenkron, *Economic Backwardness in Historical Perspective: A Book of Essays* (Cambridge: Harvard University Press, 1962).

63. Alejandro Portes, "On the Sociology of National Development: Theories and Issues," *American Journal of Sociology* 82-1 (July 1976), p. 60.

64. McKinlay and Little, *Global Problems and World Order,* p. 96; Peter T. Bauer and Basil S. Yamey, "World Wealth Redistribution: Anatomy of the New Order," in Karl Brunner, ed., *The First World and the Third World: Essays on the New International Economic Order* (Rochester, NY: University of Rochester Policy Center Publications, 1978), p. 193.

65. Lloyd G. Reynolds, *Economic Growth in the Third World, 1850–1980* (New Haven, CT: Yale University Press, 1985), p. 6; Francis Fukuyama, "The End of History?" *The National Interest* 16 (Summer 1989), p. 4.

66. W. W. Rostow, *Why the Poor Get Richer and the Rich Slow Down* (Austin, TX: University of Texas Press, 1980), p. 259.

67. P. T. Bauer and B. S. Yamey, "Against the New Economic Order," *Commentary* 63-4 (April 1977), p. 27.

68. For a useful survey of literature criticizing LDC import substitution policies, see Carlos F. Díaz-Alejandro, "Trade Policies and Economic Development," in Peter B. Kenen, ed., *International Trade and Finance: Frontiers for Research* (London: Cambridge University Press, 1975), pp. 112–116.

69. Milton Friedman and Rose Friedman, *Free to Choose: A Personal Statement* (New York: Harcourt Brace Jovanovich, 1980), p. 57. See also Bela Balassa, "The Process of Industrial Development and Alternative Development Strategies," in Bela Balassa, ed., *The Newly Industrializing Countries in the World Economy* (New York: Pergamon Press), pp. 16–17.

70. Independent Commission on International Development Issues (henceforth, Brandt Commission I), North-South, *A Program for Survival* (Cambridge, MA: MIT Press, 1980), pp. 103–104.

71. Brandt Commission I, *North-South*, p. 33. See also Albert Fishlow, "A New International Economic Order: What Kind?" in Albert Fishlow, Carlos F. Díaz-Alejandro, Richard R. Fagen, and Roger D. Hansen, *Rich and Poor Nations in the World Economy* (New York: McGraw-Hill, 1978), pp. 51–76.

72. Stephen D. Krasner, *Structural Conflict: The Third World Against Global Liberalism* (Berkeley, CA: University of California Press, 1985), pp. 22–25.

73. Charles E. Lindblom, *Politics and Markets: The World's Political-Economic Systems* (New York: Basic Books, 1977), p. 48.

74. Michael Parkin and Robin Bade, *Modern Macroeconomics,* 4th edition (Scarborough: Prentice-Hall, 1995), p. 255. On endogenous growth theory, see Paul M. Romer, "Increasing Returns and Long-Run Growth," *Journal of Political Economy* 94-5 (October 1986), pp. 1002–1037; Paul M. Romer, "Endogenous Technological Change," *Journal of Political Economy* 98-5 (October 1990), pp. S71–S102; Philippe Aghion and Peter Howitt, *Endogenous Growth Theory* (Cambridge: MIT Press, 1998).

75. Rostow, *Why the Poor Get Richer and the Rich Slow Down,* p. 259.

76. "Address by His Excellency Mwalima Julius K Nyerere, President of the United Republic of Tanzania, to the Fourth Ministerial Meeting of the Group of 77," Arusha, 12–16 February 1979, in Karl P. Sauvant, *The Group of 77: Evolution, Structure, Organization* (New York: Oceana Publications, 1981), p. 133.

77. Steven Globerman and Michael Walker, "Overview," in Steven Globerman and Michael Walker, eds., *Assessing NAFTA: A Trinational Analysis* (Vancouver, BC: The Fraser Institute, 1993), p. ix.

78. Theda Skocpol, "Bringing the State Back In: Strategies of Analysis in Current Research," in Peter B. Evans, Dietrich Rueschemeyer, and Theda Skocpol, eds., *Bringing the State Back In* (Cambridge: Cambridge University Press, 1985), p. 6.

CHAPTER 5

The Historical Structuralist Perspective

The term *historical structuralism* encompasses a wide range of theoretical approaches, including Marxism, dependency theory, world-system theory, and Gramscian analysis. All the theoretical approaches in this perspective have some roots in Marxism, but some have diverged quite substantially from mainstream Marxist ideas. As we will discuss, some Marxists accuse dependency and world-system theorists of not being sufficiently Marxist and of being mistaken in their interpretation of Third World development.

There are several reasons why this book refers to the third IPE perspective as historical structuralism. The term *structuralist* reflects this perspective's focus on structural means of exploitation, in which one class dominates another, or rich Northern states in the center or core of the global economy dominate poorer Southern states in the periphery. However, some realists are also structuralists; they explain state behavior on the basis of the structure of the international system. To these realists, a state's power and position in the system are the critical factors affecting its behavior.[1] To differentiate this third perspective from structural realism, we add the word *historical* because theorists in the third perspective take a historical approach to the study of IPE.[2] According to this group of theorists, history has been marked by exploitation, and the main characteristic of the current system is the dominance of capitalism, with the capitalist class (the *bourgeoisie*) exploiting the workers (the *proletariat*). Thus, the term *historical structuralism* best describes this school of thought.

It is especially difficult to generalize about the basic tenets of the third IPE perspective because of the wide diversity of historical structuralist approaches. The discussion of theoretical developments is therefore particularly important in this chapter; it provides some indication of the wide differences among writers in this school of thought. There is no separate section on North-South relations in this chapter because some historical structuralist approaches—especially the dependency approach—focus almost exclusively on North-South issues.

BASIC TENETS OF THE HISTORICAL STRUCTURALIST PERSPECTIVE

The Role of the Individual, the State, and Societal Groups

Marxists identify the relationship among classes as the main factor affecting the economic and political order. Each mode of production (e.g., feudalism and capitalism) is associated with two opposing classes: an exploiting nonproducing class and an exploited class of producers. Classes are absent only in the simplest mode of production, the primitive-communal, and in the future Communist mode. Thus, Karl Marx and Friedrich Engels write in *The Communist Manifesto:*

> The history of all hitherto existing society is the history of class struggles. . . . The modern bourgeois society that has sprouted from the ruins of feudal society, has not done away with class antagonisms. It has but established new classes, new conditions of oppression, new forms of struggle in place of the old ones.[3]

In most of Marx and Engels's writings, they depict the state as being nothing more than an agent acting at the behest of the dominant class—in capitalism, the bourgeoisie. Indeed, the bourgeoisie uses the state as an instrument for the exploitation of wage labor. Marx and Engels suggest that under certain conditions, the state may have some autonomy from a dominant class. For example, the state's autonomy may increase temporarily during transition periods, when the power of warring classes is more equally balanced.[4] But in the long run, Marx and Engels argue, the state cannot escape from its dependence on the owners and controllers of capital. Only when the proletarian revolution eliminates private ownership and class distinctions will the state no longer be needed as an instrument of class oppression. A number of later writers— both within and outside the Marxist tradition—have been highly critical of the Marx and Engels position that state actions simply reflect the views of the dominant class (see the following discussion).

The Nature and Purpose of International Economic Relations

Whereas liberals consider economic relations to be a positive-sum game, historical structuralists as well as realists view economic relations as being basically conflictual and zero-sum in nature. Thus, Marx and Engels argue that "one fact is common to all past ages, *viz.*, the exploitation of one part of society by the other."[5] This exploitation takes the form of a class struggle, with capitalism being the most advanced stage. Under capitalism, a class of private owners of the means of production extracts surplus value from a class of free but propertyless wage laborers. The private owners then convert this surplus value into capital, which is invested in new means of production.

It is well known that the views of historical structuralists evolved along with changes in the international system. Thus, Marx and Engels initially predicted that the contradictions within the capitalist world would contribute to the absolute poverty of the working class, surplus production, economic downturns, and the eventual collapse of the capitalist system. When this dire prediction was not realized, Lenin and others maintained that *imperialism* explained the continued survival of capitalism.[6] Imperialism delayed the downfall of capitalism because colonies supplied the "metropole" states with a cheap source of agricultural and raw materials and provided an outlet and market for the metropoles' surplus of capital and manufactured goods.

When the process of decolonization marked an end to the age of imperialism, capitalism continued to demonstrate resilience, and some historical structuralists turned their attention from colonialism to *neocolonialism* as the explanation. Although the imperial powers had ceded direct political control over their former colonies, they continued to control the newly independent Third World states economically,[7] Others who have sought to explain the persistence of capitalism and Third World underdevelopment include dependency theorists and world-system theorists. *Dependency theorists* argue that the world is hierarchically organized, with the leading capitalist states in the *center* or *core* of the global economy dominating and exploiting poor states in the *periphery.* Only the core states can make autonomous choices about domestic and foreign economic policies, and market mechanisms simply reinforce socioeconomic and political inequalities. Some early dependency theorists asserted that the core states *underdeveloped* the peripheral states, but LDC success stories such as the emergence of the NIEs caused later theorists to acknowledge that development is possible in some Third World states. Nevertheless, these theorists argue that LDC economic growth takes the form of *dependent development,* which involves a close association between elites in the core and the periphery.

Historical structuralists focus on the exploitative nature of capitalism and are thus similar to realists in considering the purpose of economic and political activity to be the redistribution of wealth and power. Unlike realists, however, historical structuralists reject the idea that a meaningful redistribution of wealth and power can occur within the capitalist system. Actively taking the side of the poor and less powerful, historical structuralists argue that the inequalities under capitalism will disappear only after there is a transformation to socialism. The ultimate goal of exploited states and classes, according to historical structuralists, should be to break linkages with the capitalist states and/or to overthrow the capitalist system.

The Relationship Between Politics and Economics

History, according to Marx, is a dialectical process in which there is a contradiction between evolving economic modes of production (e.g., feudalism, capitalism, and socialism) on the one hand and the political system on the other. This contradiction is resolved when changes in the mode and relations of production eventually cause the political "superstructure" to undergo similar changes. Marx viewed politics as being subordinate to economics, and his writings provided the foundation for the instrumentalist tradition in Marxist thought.[8] **Instrumental Marxism,** like liberalism, perceives formal government institutions as responding in a rather passive manner to socioeconomic pressures. Liberals, however, believe that any societal interest group may have political influence, whereas instrumental Marxists believe the state's policies reflect the interests of the capitalist class. To support their position, instrumental Marxists point to the personal ties between leading capitalists and public officials and to the movement of individuals back and forth between business and government. One instrumental Marxist, for example, argues that the individuals in *"all* command positions in the state system have largely, and in many cases overwhelmingly, been drawn from the world of business and property, or from the professional middle classes."[9]

After World War II, many Marxist as well as non-Marxist scholars strongly criticized the instrumental Marxist views because industrial states were adopting a number of social policies such as welfare and unemployment insurance *despite* the opposition of important business groups. As a result, a second tradition of **structural Marxism** emerged. In contrast to the instrumentalists, structural Marxists argue that the state is relatively autonomous from direct political pressure by the capitalist class. Thus, the state may adopt some policies that provide benefits to all major groups in society, including the working class. Although in the short term, some capitalists oppose these state policies, they in fact serve the longer term interests of the bourgeoisie. The bourgeoisie, which has internal divisions, may be less well placed than the state to recognize what policies best serve its own long-term interests. Thus, by providing welfare and other benefits, the state often placates the workers and gains their support for the continuance of capitalism.[10]

Although they consider the state to be relatively autonomous, structural Marxists differ from realists in some important respects. The state is not under the direct control of the bourgeoisie in the structural Marxist view, but it shares with that class a commitment to the long-term maintenance of the capitalist system. Realists, by contrast, believe the state has genuine independence from the economic interests of any societal group. Thus, the state in the realist view is free to take those actions it deems necessary to further the "national interest."

KARL MARX AND IPE

Karl Marx (1818–83) did not write systematically on international relations, but his theory of capitalism and class struggle provided the basic framework for historical structuralist approaches to IPE. Although Marx wrote a number of articles about the effect of Western capitalism on non-European areas, his knowledge of economically less developed areas outside Europe was in fact quite limited. At the time Marx was writing, "relatively few sources of information" on non-European areas "were available to him."[11] Marx's specific references to the present-day Third World focused primarily on India and China.[12] It was no accident, in Marx's view, that capitalism first emerged in Europe, where the feudal mode of production was prevalent. Feudal landholdings were private, so these landholdings could be converted into private bourgeois property when the feudal mode of production was replaced by capitalism.

Marx argued that in contrast to the situation in Europe, an "Asiatic" mode of production that was outside the mainstream of Western development was prevalent in such countries as India and China. The state's presence was much greater in the Asiatic mode, because climate and geography made centralized irrigation important in agriculture. Thus, strong central governments in China and India developed large public work projects to provide water over extensive land areas. At the local level, Marx portrayed oriental society as characterized by small, self-sufficient village communities in which there was communal rather than individual ownership. Because communal property (locally) and public property (centrally) overshadowed private property in the Asiatic mode, Marx saw no basis for a transformation—as there was in feudalism—from private feudal landholdings to private capitalist holdings. As a result, Marx believed that "oriental societies" such as China and India had no internal mechanisms for change and that external pressure from Western imperialism was necessary if these countries were to progress to capitalism—and then to socialism.[13]

Marx certainly does not glorify British imperialism in India in his writings. Indeed, he harshly criticizes England's role in destroying the Indian handicraft textile industry, first by preventing India from exporting cotton to the European market and then by inundating India with British textiles. Nevertheless, Marx views the stagnant Asiatic society as being even worse than capitalism because it lacked capitalism's capacity for development. He therefore warns us that India's village communities "restrained the human mind within the smallest possible compass, making it the unresisting tool of superstition, enslaving it beneath traditional rule, depriving it of all grandeur and historical energies."[14]

In contrast to his view of stagnating Asiatic societies, Marx considered capitalism to be a dynamic, expansive system with a historical mission to move the development process forward throughout the world. Thus, Marx viewed England as performing a dual function in India—first, in destroying the old Asiatic society, and second, in providing the foundation for Western society in Asia. Without this introduction of Western capitalism, Marx reasoned, the conditions for a Communist revolution in Asia would not be met:

> Can mankind fulfill its destiny without a fundamental revolution in the social state of Asia? If not, whatever may have been the crimes of England, she was the unconscious tool of history in bringing about that revolution.[15]

Although Marx strongly criticized the exploitative nature of British imperialism, he nevertheless viewed it as enabling India to move from the stagnant Asiatic mode of production to the dynamic exploitative mode. The move to the capitalist mode, according to Marx, was a necessary evil because it was a prerequisite for subsequent moves to socialism and communism. It is important to note that there were some major defects in Marx's analysis of Asiatic societies, which are attributed to his lack of first-hand knowledge and his Eurocentric prejudices. Indeed, later in his life Marx repudiated some of his own ideas regarding the Asiatic mode of production and the role of imperialism in promoting capitalism in the East. Despite his apparent change of view, Marx never explained how capitalism could be developed in the Asiatic villages without Western imperialism.[16]

MARXIST STUDIES OF IMPERIALISM

Although Marx raised some important—and contentious—questions about the impact of Western capitalism on non-European societies, systematic studies of imperialism depended on later writers. In contrast to most liberal theories, which emphasize the mutual benefits of international interactions, theories of imperialism portray the world as hierarchically organized, with some societies engaging in conquest and control over others. Most non-Marxists have used the term *imperialism* in reference to a political rather than an economic relationship between advanced metropolitan countries and their colonies or dependencies. It is therefore ironic that a non-Marxist English economist, John A. Hobson (1858–1940), developed one of the most influential economic theories of imperialism. Hobson argued that three major problems plague capitalist societies: low wages and underconsumption by workers, oversaving by capitalists, and overproduction. Although capitalism is highly efficient and contributes to the production of growing surpluses, private owners increase their profits by paying extremely low wages to their workers. As a result, workers in the capitalist countries have very limited purchasing power, and the capitalists must look to countries abroad as an outlet for their excess goods and profits. Their forays into what is now termed the Third World give rise to imperialism.[17]

Despite the influence of Hobson's writings, the most important group of theories of imperialism are Marxist. Indeed, *Imperialism: The Highest Stage of Capitalism* by Vladimir Lenin (1870–1924) became the most widely cited work in this area, even though Lenin borrowed many of his ideas from earlier Marxist and non-Marxist writers.[18] Lenin was interested in the new, expanded form of imperialism of the late nineteenth century, "in which the dominance of monopolies and finance capital [had] established itself" and "the division of all territories of the globe among the great capitalist powers [had] been completed."[19] Lenin, writing in the Marxist tradition, took a far more doctrinaire approach than Hobson. Although Hobson and Lenin agreed that imperialism resulted from low wages and underconsumption by workers, their prescribed solutions were fundamentally different. As a liberal, Hobson believed that imperialism would become less essential if wages were increased and income was redistributed *within* the capitalist system. Lenin as a Marxist, by contrast, believed that exploitation of the workers and imperialism were *inevitable* outcomes of the highest stage of capitalism, and that imperialism could disappear only with the advent of universal socialism.

Like Marx, Lenin argued that capitalism contributes to overproduction and underconsumption, to lower wages and lower employment for the working class, and to falling rates of profit for the capitalists. However, Marx had predicted that the growing misery of the proletariat would lead to revolution in the advanced capitalist countries, and Lenin turned to imperialism to explain why such a revolution had not occurred. Under imperialism, the export of capital and goods to colonial areas provided new "superprofits" for capitalist firms, which helped them avert economic crises. By using a portion of these superprofits to bribe the working class (or "labor aristocracy") in their home countries with higher wages, the capitalists were able to delay the revolution. However, Lenin argued that imperialism did not mark an end to capitalism's underlying contradictions and that the revolution was still inevitable. Once the capitalist states had divided up the globe into colonial areas, competition among them would lead to interimperialist wars and the downfall of capitalism.

Lenin's position on the effects of colonialism on capitalist development in Third World countries was somewhat ambivalent. On the one hand, Lenin predicted that capitalist monopolies would oppose industrialization in the colonial territories and would use the colonies as sources of raw materials and markets for their manufactures.

On the other hand, Lenin agreed with Marx that colonialism was also a progressive force that was essential for Third World modernization. Indeed, Lenin maintained that capitalism has an inherent contradiction: it develops rather than underdevelops the Third World. As the Western capitalist states export capital and technology to their colonies, they help create foreign competitors with lower wages, which can out-compete them in world markets. The increase of economic competition between rising and declining capitalist powers eventually leads to economic conflict and imperial rivalries.

Although Marx and Lenin viewed colonialism as a necessary evil that would bring capitalist development to the colonial territories, industrialization and development did not occur as anticipated. For example, even after most Latin American colonies gained their independence from Spain and Portugal in the early nineteenth century, their production continued to be concentrated on primary products, their industrialization was limited, and they were highly dependent on capital and technology from the advanced industrial states. The failure to bring about capitalist development in the colonies and former colonies led to major rifts among the Marxists. Most notably, Otto Kuusinen, a Finnish member at the Sixth Congress of the Communist International (Comintern) in 1928, argued that imperialism was economically regressive rather than progressive as Lenin had maintained. The views of Marxists such as Kuusinen were particularly important: they provided a basis for the arguments of the Latin American dependency movement that emerged after World War II.[20] As the following discussion demonstrates, dependency theorists "turned classical Marxism on its head" and focused on capitalism's role in hindering rather than facilitating Third World development.

DEPENDENCY THEORY

Writers on dependency (or *dependencistas*) were originally Latin American and/or focused on Latin America, and **dependency theory** became the dominant approach to development among Latin American intellectuals in the 1960s. Some of the important early studies were published only in Spanish; it was not until a number of years later that they were translated and made available to most English-speaking scholars. Dependency theorists reject the optimism of liberal modernization theorists (discussed in Chapter 4) and maintain that the advanced capitalist countries either underdevelop the Third World or prevent Third World countries from achieving genuine autonomous development. The discussion here examines the origins, basic tenets, and critiques of dependency theory. However, it is important to note that there is in fact considerable diversity among the writers who are identified as dependency theorists.[21]

The Origins of Dependency Theory

Dependency theory is based on two major theoretical traditions: Marxism and Latin American structuralism. Some of the most prominent writers on dependency explicitly express their allegiance to Marxism.[22] Dependency theorists, like Marxists, limit their studies almost exclusively to capitalist development, and they adopt much of the language of Marxists, using terms such as *class, mode of production,* and *imperialism.* Dependency theorists and Marxists also have a common commitment to taking political action as well as conveying ideas, and both groups advocate the replacement of capitalism with socialism. However, Marxists take a more doctrinaire approach than many dependency theorists regarding the inevitability of socialism.[23]

A fundamental difference between Marxism and dependency theory is the fact that dependency theorists focus almost exclusively on North-South relations and on development problems in the Third World. As we discussed, dependency theorists also strongly reject Marxist views that Northern industrial countries are performing a service to Third World countries in the long term by contributing to the spread of capitalism. A key figure in the transition from classical Marxism to dependency theory was Paul Baran. Baran was the first important Marxist theorist to view the Third World as a major area of study, and he differed from his predecessors in arguing that capitalist development was a fundamentally different process in advanced and underdeveloped countries. Unlike Marx, who viewed colonialism as enabling countries such as India to advance from the Asiatic to the capitalist mode of production, Baran emphasized the contradictions between the objectives of the advanced capitalist states on the one hand and the development of "backward" nations on the other. Thus, Baran wrote that

> economic development in underdeveloped countries is profoundly inimical to the dominant interests in the advanced capitalist countries. Supplying many important raw materials to the industrialized countries, providing their corporations with vast profits and investment outlets, the backward world has always represented the indispensable hinterland of the highly developed capitalist West. Thus the ruling class in the United States (and elsewhere) is bitterly opposed to the industrialization of the so-called "source countries."[24]

Baran further maintained that foreign capitalists form alliances with elites in LDCs in their efforts to prevent Third World industrialization. These elites include feudal landed interests and a *comprador class* composed of merchants who import manufactured goods from the industrial states. Thus, Baran diverged from the Marxists, arguing that capitalist development in the industrial states occurs *at the expense of* autonomous development in the Third World. His view was to become a fundamental tenet of the dependency approach.

In addition to its beginnings in Marxism, dependency theory has origins from Latin American structuralism, particularly the ideas of the Argentinian economist Raúl Prebisch, who became director of the United Nations Economic Commission for Latin America (ECLA) in the late 1940s. Prebisch and his followers were called structuralists because they focused on the structural obstacles to Third World development. Prebisch particularly questioned the liberal assumptions that everyone benefits from freer trade, and he argued instead that Third World countries in the periphery of the global economy suffer from declining **terms of trade** with advanced industrial states in the center or core. (Prebisch began to use the terms "center" and "periphery" as early as the 1950s.) Third World countries, according to Prebisch, are at a marked disadvantage because they export mainly primary commodities and import finished goods from the core. Whereas demand for finished goods increases with rising incomes, demand for primary products remains relatively constant (for example, wealthy individuals drink only so much coffee or tea, regardless of their incomes). Furthermore, the industrial states can often develop substitute or synthetic products if Third World countries attempt to charge higher prices for their raw materials.

According to Prebisch and his followers, Third World countries could develop only through government involvement to promote industrialization and decrease dependence on trade with the advanced industrial states. Thus, they advised Third World states to follow ISI policies to protect their infant industries, imposing tariff and nontariff barriers and emphasizing domestic production of manufactures to satisfy demand previously met by imports.[25] A number of LDCs, especially in Latin America, were influenced by Prebisch's structuralist views, and they adopted ISI policies in the 1950s and 1960s. By the 1960s, however, there was growing disillusionment with ISI policies, which contributed to a wide range of problems for LDCs, including uncompetitive industries and growing balance-of-payments deficits. (ISI is discussed in more detail in Chapter 11.) Scholars challenged the Prebisch approach from both the right and the left, and many left-leaning scholars turned to dependency theory. Dependency theorists adopted many of Prebisch's ideas, but their views of both the problems and solutions for the Third World were generally more extreme than those of Prebisch. Unlike Prebisch, for example, dependency theorists did not believe the core would ever willingly transfer resources to the periphery. A number of dependency theorists therefore called for a domestic social revolution in Third World countries and/or a severing of contacts with the advanced industrial states.[26]

The Basic Tenets of Dependency Theory

A discussion of the basic tenets of dependency theory is complicated by the fact that there is considerable variation among writers in this tradition. Two major strains of dependency theory are of particular importance. The first strain, which is closely identified with the work of two Latin Americans—Fernando Henrique Cardoso and Enzo Faletto—took a less doctrinaire and more variegated position to North-South relations. Because Cardoso and Faletto's seminal book, *Dependency and Development in Latin America,* was not available in English translation until a number of years after it was published, much of the early North American "consumption" of dependency theory relied on a second strain.[27] The second strain, which drew its inspiration from André Gunder Frank, became influential in the United States at an early stage. This strain took a more radical, doctrinaire position regarding both the impact of dependency on the Third World and the proposed solutions. In efforts to organize the discussion and draw comparisons, the next sections examine dependency views regarding the source of Third World problems, possibilities for development in the periphery, and prescriptions for change. When relevant, we differentiate between the two main strains of dependency theory.

The Source of Third World Problems   Dependency theorists reject the views of liberal theorists that Third World economic problems result primarily from inefficient domestic policies and that greater North-South interdependence promotes Third

World development. In contrast, dependency theorists argue that external factors related to the global capitalist economy are primarily responsible for constraining development possibilities in the Third World. Although the core countries in the North benefit from their global capitalist linkages and experience dynamic development based on internal needs, development in the peripheral countries of the South is severely constrained as a result of their interaction with the core. Although dependency theorists attach primary importance to external constraints on development, there has been variation among authors. The Gunder Frank strain placed far more emphasis on the external forces, whereas the Cardoso-Faletto strain was highly sensitive "to local as well as international variations in dependency relations and to the independent significance of internal structures even in an approach that highlights external conditioning."[28]

Class struggle is one factor that links external and internal forces, and a number of dependency theorists have examined the class linkages between individuals within the peripheral and core states. Thus, they describe the development of a class alignment in the South, where elites in Third World countries (*compradores*) act as intermediaries between the capitalist international order on the one hand and the subjected local peoples on the other. Although this collaborating *comprador* class may have local concerns, it ultimately depends on the international economic order to ensure its survival as a class. Thus, the main political alliances of the *compradores* are with foreign capitalists in the North, and the elites in the South often take actions that reinforce the pattern of Third World dependency.[29]

LDC Possibilities for Development   Dependency theorists have had differing views regarding LDC possibilities for development. Those in the Gunder Frank strain argued that the development of the capitalist economies in the core *required* the underdevelopment of the periphery. These theorists were highly deterministic: they believed that LDCs could not escape from underdevelopment as long as they maintained linkages with the wealthy capitalist states. Although developed countries may have been *un*developed in the past, they were not *under*developed because they were not yet part of the periphery in the global capitalist economy. When these undeveloped countries became part of the periphery, they became underdeveloped *as a result of their involvement with the countries in the capitalist core.*[30]

Theorists in the Cardoso-Faletto strain took a more nuanced approach, arguing that in some cases development was possible in the periphery. This was, however, "associated dependent development" in which the links of dependency were maintained.[31] The Cardoso-Faletto view gained support over time, because theorists who viewed underdevelopment as the only possible fate for peripheral countries found it increasingly difficult to explain why industrialization *was* occurring in some LDCs. Liberals, realists, and some Marxists all pointed to the fact that the NIEs such as South Korea, Taiwan, Brazil, and Mexico were experiencing impressive economic growth rates. Furthermore, countries such as South Korea and Taiwan had close linkages with the global capitalist structure in the core. A number of dependency studies in the late 1970s and 1980s therefore followed the Cardoso-Faletto example and focused on the issue of "dependent development" rather than "underdevelopment."[32] Gunder Frank's writings evolved, and by the 1980s even he was writing about countries that were undergoing dependent development.[33]

Those who write about dependent development are more attuned to the wide variety of local conditions and dependency relations in the Third World. Certain LDCs can undergo development, according to this view, when a particularly favorable alliance forms between foreign capital, domestic capital, and the Third World state. This alliance enables the Third World country to benefit from capital accumulation and from some degree of industrialization. Despite recognizing the diversity of LDC situations, however, these authors maintain that even the more favored LDCs remain fundamentally dependent and cannot attain genuine autonomous development. In the final analysis, those LDCs experiencing dependent development cannot escape from their dependent linkages with the core countries, and their development is therefore conditioned by the requirements of the core. Dependency theorists argue that although the NIEs seem to be examples of success in the Third World, workers in these countries often receive low wages and produce less technologically sophisticated goods than those of the industrial states in the core. The production of capital goods in these countries is also limited, and ultimately they depend on imports of machinery, technology, and foreign investment from the core.[34]

Prescriptions for Change   Dependency theorists believe that LDCs cannot escape from their dependent position in the capitalist system; thus, they often prescribe a breaking of linkages with the core countries and/or a socialist revolution to bring about more social justice and equality. The goals of autonomy and socialism are not necessarily compatible, however, and theorists do not explicitly state which of these two goals is more important for decreasing dependency. Those who emphasize autonomy tend to call for highly nationalistic and antiforeign actions such as the cutting of linkages with the developed core states. Such actions do not ensure that the other goal of dependency theorists will be achieved; policies that increase a state's autonomy do not ensure that there will be more social justice or equality for the bulk of the population. Nevertheless, dependency theorists at least hope that an end to dependent linkages will lead a country to "emphasize distribution and participation rather than accumulation and exclusion."[35]

Critiques of Dependency Theory

Dependency theory became a favorite target of criticism in the 1970s and 1980s, and other theories have subsequently become more important in the historical structuralist school of IPE. One major criticism is that dependency theorists do not adequately define their basic concepts. For example, theorists tend to view countries in dichotomous terms as either dependent or not dependent, and it is unclear how one can measure lesser or greater *degrees* of dependence. There are also different *forms* of dependence, such as military, economic, and cultural dependence, but these different forms are not usually identified. Furthermore, "developed versus underdeveloped" or "core versus periphery" are extremely broad categories that include a wide range of countries. What does the term *periphery* signify when it includes countries as diverse as

Brazil, India, and Haiti? How does one justify including Portugal along with the United States, Japan, and Germany as a developed country in the core? Critics argue that these concepts are too vague to make the types of distinctions required for good theorizing.[36]

A second criticism relates to the preoccupation of dependency theorists with capitalism and their failure to consider other forms of exploitation. Some critics argue that the most important factor in dependency is not capitalism (as dependency theorists maintain) but unequal power among states. As long as power is unequal, larger and more powerful states are able to impose dependence on smaller states.[37] Thus, some scholars have done studies of the former Soviet bloc to demonstrate that dependency relations can also exist in noncapitalist systems. These studies show some marked differences between the Soviet and Western systems. For example, postwar Soviet dominance contributed to rapid industrialization with an emphasis on heavy industry in Eastern Europe, which was quite different from the Western model in the Third World; and political linkages were more important in the Soviet bloc, whereas economic linkages were central to the West's relations with the South. Despite the differences, however, both the Soviet and the capitalist systems were marked by "asymmetric and unequal linkages between a dominant center and its weaker dependencies."[38] Dependency theorists also did not usually examine the role socialist states played in the capitalist world economy, and since the collapse of the Soviet Union, they have not explored where countries such as North Korea and Cuba fit in a world of core and peripheral countries.[39]

A third criticism is that dependency theory attaches too much importance to the international system and too little to domestic policies and behavior as a source of LDC development problems. Although the dependency theorists in the Cardoso-Faletto strain do focus on domestic structures in Third World states, they continue to give primacy to the importance of external factors. Dependency theorists therefore have a tendency to portray LDCs as being virtually helpless vis-à-vis outside forces, and they cannot adequately explain why Third World countries sometimes respond in very different ways to similar external constraints. To explain such differences, critics charge, it is necessary to give more consideration to the importance of domestic economic and political factors.[40] A fourth criticism is that dependency theory's predictions regarding Third World development prospects are often simply incorrect. For example, China was initially held up as a model of agrarian self-reliance, but in 1976 it turned to a policy of openness rather than closure to promote national development. This change in policy contributed to rapid economic growth in China, and LDCs that are the most integrated in the world economy are sometimes the fastest growing countries.

A fifth criticism is that dependency theorists' prescriptions for change are rather vague and ill defined. Although dependency theorists call for socialism as one of their two main goals, they do not clearly indicate what they mean by the term, they do not explain how a socialist revolution will enable countries to escape dependency, and they do not describe how the revolution will occur. Dependency theorists also do not explain how peripheral countries can become more autonomous and "de-link" themselves from the core countries. The vagueness of prescriptions in dependency theory relates partly to the tension between the goals of autonomy and socialism and partly to the fact that Marxist-Leninist predictions regarding a socialist revolution in the advanced industrial states often proved to be inaccurate.

Finally, some of the strongest criticisms of dependency theory come from within the Marxist tradition. The American social scientist Bill Warren, for example, presented updated arguments to support Marx's thesis regarding the potential for Third World development. Although imperialism contributed to exploitation and inequality, Warren argued, it also provided the conditions for capitalist development in the Third World. In the postwar period, the LDCs could use the East-West conflict and the competition among Western industrial states and MNCs to promote their own capitalist national development (on the way to socialism). In contrast to dependency theorists, Warren maintained that the obstacles to this development "originate not in current imperialist-Third World relationships, but almost entirely from the internal contradictions of the Third World itself."[41] Some Marxist scholars also criticize dependency theorists for being overly nationalistic and not sufficiently Marxist. These scholars point to the problem dependency theorists have with focusing on both core-periphery and class divisions. The Marxist critics insist that the most fundamental problem is not *foreign* control or domination, as some dependency theorists maintain, but *private* control and domination of the means of production. Thus, they criticize dependency theorists for putting more emphasis on "relations of exchange" (i.e., between core and peripheral states) than on "relations of production" (i.e., between the proletariat and bourgeoisie).[42]

The numerous criticisms of dependency theory from both the right and the left have had a telling effect. Unfortunately, the criticisms were often aimed at the most extreme, doctrinaire versions of dependency theory and did not do justice to the less extreme forms in the Cardoso-Faletto strain. Thus, one noted dependency theorist predicted in 1985 that the dependency label would disappear because the term was "too closely associated with simplistic hypotheses of external determination" and "the impossibility of either capitalism or democracy on the periphery."[43] Although it is unusual for writers to identify themselves as "dependency theorists" today, development theorists in fact continue to draw on many aspects of dependency theory in their studies of Latin America, Africa, and Asia.[44] The case for continuing to use some of the basic ideas and concepts of dependency theory is strengthened by the further marginalization of some peripheral Third World countries as globalization pressures increase. Thus, one noted development economist considers it a serious misconception to believe "that the dependency debate is dead forever and that it has no relevance in the modern world. . . . There are indeed many issues and areas of development where dependency plays a major role."[45] The next section raises questions about the future of the historical structuralist perspective in IPE in view of the breakup of the Soviet bloc and the Soviet Union, and the final sections of the chapter discuss some historical structuralist approaches that seem to be particularly promising.

WHITHER THE HISTORICAL STRUCTURALIST SCHOOL OF IPE?

With the failed predictions of the Marxist-Leninists regarding the downfall of capitalism and the strong criticisms of historical structuralist approaches such as dependency theory, numerous questions were raised about the vitality of the historical structuralist perspective in general. Since the breakup of the Soviet bloc and the end of the Cold War in the late 1980s and early 1990s, some theorists have launched the harshest criticism of all: that the historical structuralist perspective has become irrelevant. For example, one liberal theorist argues that "the implosion of the Soviet Union, and domestic changes in Eastern Europe, have eliminated the significance of the socialist economic model," and another claims that the discrediting of Marxism-Leninism is leading to "an unabashed victory of economic and political liberalism."[46] Many observers are also referring to the "triumph" of liberalism in the Third World. LDCs in the 1960s and 1970s turned to economic nationalism, state socialism, and trade protectionism, but there has been a marked turnaround in their policies today. For a number of reasons discussed in this book, LDCs since the 1980s have been moving en masse toward liberal policies of reduced state intervention in the economy, increased reliance on the market, and liberalized trade and foreign investment policies.[47]

Despite these negative prognostications about the historical structuralist perspective, it continues to have major relevance today. Most important, historical structuralists devote considerable attention to the poorest and weakest individuals and states and to distributive justice issues, which are not dealt with adequately by either liberals or realists. Although liberals and realists accept the capitalist system largely as a given, the historical structuralists raise serious questions about inequality and exploitation under capitalism, and they discuss the possibilities of alternative systems. Historical structuralism continues to be an important perspective in IPE, and the following sections discuss three theoretical approaches with linkages to this school of thought that are currently of considerable interest: world-system theory, Gramscian theory, and the business conflict model.

World-System Theory

World-system theory has many similarities with dependency theory, and some former dependency theorists now identify themselves as world-system theorists. Like dependency theorists, world-system theorists view capitalism as basically exploitative, and they openly advocate major changes in global economic relations. Nevertheless, world-system theory is accepted as more relevant than dependency theory today because the world-system approach is more broad ranging and flexible. Instead of limiting their inquiry to the peripheral states as dependency theorists do, world-system theorists (as their name indicates) focus on the entire world system. Indeed, world-system theorists such as Immanuel Wallerstein consistently begin by focusing on the global system and only secondarily move on to analyses of individual countries. This ordering reflects the view of world-system theorists that a country's development prospects depend more on the nature of the global system than on its internal structures.

World-system theorists are concerned not only with the exploitation of states in the periphery but also with relationships among states in the core and with the rise and decline of hegemonic states. World-system theorists also delve more deeply than dependency theorists into the historical development of capitalism in their attempts to explain the core's exploitation of the periphery. Indeed, much world-system analysis extends back to at least the sixteenth century and examines not only world economic structure but also cyclical fluctuations ranging from economic depressions to recessions, upswings, and booms. Finally, as we will discuss, world-system analysts introduce the concept of the semiperiphery, and they question the dependency theorists' view that all Third World states must be permanently relegated to the periphery.[48]

Only a brief discussion of world-system theory is provided here; the student should refer to more detailed sources.[49] Although the fundamentals of the world-system approach derive largely from the voluminous works of Wallerstein, there are of course other important world-system theorists, such as Christopher Chase-Dunn. Some former dependency theorists such as Samir Amin and Gunder Frank have also incorporated some of Wallerstein's propositions in their analyses.[50] There are some major differences in view among world-system theorists; the discussion that follows refers primarily to the writings of Wallerstein.

The main unit of analysis in world-system theory is the world-system, which can be defined as "a unit with a single division of labor and multiple cultural systems."[51] World-systems can be of two major types: *world-empires,* which have a common political system, and *world-economies,* which do not have a common political system. Today there is only one world-system, a world-economy that is capitalist in form. This capitalist system became predominant with the emergence of the modern world-economy in Europe during the "long" sixteenth century (1450–1640). The essential feature of a capitalist world-economy is production for sale in a market with the goal of realizing the maximum profit. Capitalism is also characterized by unequal exchange relationships, which strong core states enforce on weak peripheral areas. Thus, Wallerstein argues that "capitalism involves not only appropriation of the surplus value by an owner from a laborer, but an appropriation of surplus of the whole world-economy by core areas."[52]

World-system theorists take the capitalist world-economy as their main unit of analysis; they do not consider states to be meaningful actors in their own right, apart from their position in the world-economy.[53] Thus, long before the breakup of the Soviet Union, Wallerstein always rejected the idea that truly socialist states could exist in a capitalist world-economy:

> There are today no socialist systems in the world-economy any more than there are feudal systems because there is *one* world-system. It is a world-economy and it is by definition capitalist in form.[54]

World-system theorists also believe that neither the internal nor the external strength of a state can be viewed separately from its position in the world-economy. Core states are therefore relatively strong states by definition, and peripheral states are relatively weak.

In response to the fact that some Third World states, such as the East Asian and Latin American NIEs, are industrializing, world-system theorists modify the classical dependency argument by asserting that a limited number of countries can ascend to a *semiperiphery,* which is situated somewhere between the periphery and the core. Semiperipheral states have more capital-intensive industry than peripheral states but less than core states, and they are stronger and more autonomous from the core than peripheral states.[55] Although some states in the semiperiphery seem to be models of economic success, they are in fact simply "the more advanced exemplars of dependent development" because they are still dependent on the core.[56] It is possible, according to world-system theorists, for states to ascend from the periphery to the semiperiphery and then from the semiperiphery to the core. It is also possible for some states to descend from the core to the semiperiphery. Nevertheless, world-system theorists are far more pessimistic than liberal theorists about the future prospects for today's Third World countries, and they believe that a country's ascent from the periphery is a relatively rare occurrence. Thus, world-system theorists consider the division of the world-economy into the core, periphery, and semiperiphery to be an enduring feature of the capitalist world-economy.[57]

In the world-system view, the existence of the semiperiphery contributes to the stability of the capitalist world-economy and to the continued predominance of the industrial states in the core. The distribution of wealth and power in the capitalist world-economy is highly unequal, and it would be natural for the peripheral countries to directly confront the core countries that acquire most of the benefits. The periphery includes the overwhelming majority of states, and a rebellion against the minority of states within the core would have a good chance of success if the periphery remained united. However, the semiperipheral states divide the majority in the periphery so that the core states are not faced with a unified opposition. Even though the semiperipheral states are disadvantaged by capitalism, they "tend to think of themselves primarily as better off than the lower sector rather than as worse off than the upper sector."[58] They therefore have a dual role as both exploiter and exploited, effectively dividing the periphery and stabilizing the capitalist world-economy.

The continued expansion of the core combined with some growth of the semiperiphery has contributed to a less polarized and more politically stable capitalist world-economy and to a further weakening of the periphery. Despite this apparent political stability, however, the capitalist world-economy continues to have contradictions that could threaten its long-term survival. World-system theorists therefore raise the prospect of the decline of the capitalist world-economy and its replacement by socialism, but their predictions regarding the timing of these changes are surprisingly vague and long term. For example, Wallerstein asserts that the internal contradictions in the capitalist world-economy should "bring it to an end in the twenty-first or twenty-second century."[59] Wallerstein believes that socialism could become a new type of world-system, but he is vague about when such a new world-system will develop.

Liberal, realist, and Marxist scholars express numerous criticisms of world-system theory, which in many cases are similar to the critiques of dependency theory. Some classical Marxists charge that world-system theorists (like dependency theorists) place more emphasis on "relations of exchange" among core, semiperipheral, and peripheral states than on "relations of production" between capitalists and workers. Writers from all three schools argue that world-system theorists place too much emphasis on external factors and too little emphasis on internal factors in explaining conditions in the periphery. Indeed, Wallerstein moved even further away from examining individual states, than did dependency theorists such as Gunder Frank. Wallerstein's interest in individual states "is limited to showing how they are incorporated into . . . [the world-economy] and the subsequent effect upon their social, political and economic systems."[60]

Realists are especially critical of world-system theorists for overemphasizing economic relationships and underemphasizing the role of the state. Thus, they accuse Wallerstein of rather simplistically assuming that "strong states" naturally exist in the core and that "weak states" are found in the periphery. Many authors have provided counterexamples that challenge such statements. First, they argue that some of the strongest states in the sixteenth century (e.g., Spain and Sweden) were in the periphery, whereas the core states of this period, Holland and England, had relatively weak state structures. Second, they note that "late industrializers" have often demonstrated successful development because of strong state leadership. This was true of Russia and Germany in the past, and it is true of the East Asian NIEs (the semiperiphery) today. Finally, some writers argue that the United States, which remains the leading economic and military power today, is a relatively weak state because of its separation of powers and its federal division of powers.[61]

Despite the numerous criticisms of world-system theory, it provides us with an important alternative approach to the study of IPE. As historical structuralists, world-system theorists offer a long-term historical view of social, economic, and political change going back to at least the sixteenth century. This contrasts with theorists in the other two IPE perspectives, who either have been ahistorical in their approach or have devoted too little attention to historical change. For example, the views of liberal modernization theorists that Third World countries could and should follow the development path of Western industrial states proved to be misguided, but many liberals still adhere to a (more sophisticated) variation of these views today. Critics understandably argue that liberals underestimate the importance of historical differences between the industrializing countries in the past and the Third World countries today. In view of historical and other changes, Third World countries today may not choose to, or be able to, follow the development path Western industrial countries have taken in the past.

World-system theory also avoids some of the pitfalls of dependency theory by asserting that countries can sometimes ascend from the periphery to the semiperiphery and the core. However, world-system theorists avoid the overoptimism of liberal theorists regarding the prospects for ascent from the periphery. Unlike realists and liberals, world-system theorists focus on the poorest and weakest in the periphery of society and on the exploitation of the periphery by the core. Although world-system theorists may be accused of overestimating the degree to which external exploitation causes Third World problems, realists and liberals err in the opposite direction by largely ignoring the role of external exploitation of the poor and weak in the capitalist world-economy. Even those realists and liberals who are critical of some aspects of capitalism accept it largely as a given.

World-system theorists have proved to be dynamic as a group, able to adjust their theoretical views in response to criticism. This brief description of the world-system approach does not convey the degree to which there is a wide variation of views among world-system theorists or the degree to which world-system theory is evolving.

Gramscian Analysis

Antonio Gramsci, a former leader of the Italian Communist party, drew many of his ideas from Marxism. Gramsci argued, however, that Marxism was overly economistic; that is, it exaggerated the importance of economics relative to political, social, and cultural factors. Thus, classical Marxists were unable to explain crucial aspects of political and social reality during Gramsci's time, such as the role of Catholicism and the rise of Mussolini in Italy. The domination of capitalism, Gramsci asserted, depends only partly on economic factors such as the private ownership of the means of production. To understand capitalist domination, the student must also be familiar with the political, ideological, and cultural aspects of class struggle. Similarly, we must consider politics and culture as well as economics when discussing the reorganization of society under socialism. Thus, Gramsci placed much more emphasis than classical Marxists on the role of culture, ideas, and institutions in explaining societal organization and change.[62]

As noted in Chapter 3, the Gramscian view of hegemony is quite different from that of the realists. Unlike the realists, who identify hegemony solely with the predominant power of a nation-state (or a group of core states), Gramscians also view hegemony in terms of class relationships. If the dominant class rules almost exclusively by coercion, this is *not* the Gramscian idea of hegemony. In such societies the overthrow of the dominant class is possible simply by using physical force, because the roots of its power do not penetrate into all aspects of social life. A dominant class has hegemony, by contrast, when it legitimates its power through institutions and makes concessions to encourage subordinate groups to support the existing social structure. Thus, the hegemonic rule of a particular class is based not only on coercion, but, even more important, on social-moral leadership. The ruling class gains the active consent of the subordinate class on the basis of shared values, ideas, and material interests. The bourgeoisie often achieve such a consensus by providing the subordinate classes with a range of concessions, such as social and economic benefits and support for workers' efforts to organize labor unions. In return, the subordinate classes are accepting or even supportive of continued leadership by the bourgeoisie.

Gramscian theorists use the term *historic bloc* to refer to the congruence between state power on the one hand and the prevailing ideas guiding the society and the economy on the other. The historic bloc established under bourgeois hegemony is difficult for subordinate groups to replace because it is supported not only by physical power but also by the power of ideas. Like the classical Marxists, Gramsci was committed to political action as well as theory, and he wrote about the importance of building a *counterhegemony* among subordinate groups. A counterhegemony is an alternative ethical view of society that poses a challenge to the dominant bourgeois-led view. If subordinate groups become sufficiently dissatisfied, a counterhegemony organized around socialist ideas could pose a challenge to the hegemony organized around capitalism. For example, the propensity of governments to decrease socioeconomic benefits to subordinate classes in this age of global competitiveness might eventually cause disadvantaged groups to pose such a counterhegemonic challenge. If the proletariat succeeded in supplanting bourgeois hegemony with their own counterhegemony, they would create a new historic bloc based on socialism.[63]

Gramsci's analysis was limited primarily to the national level. Writers such as Robert Cox and Stephen Gill have extended his ideas and applied them to international relations. For example, Cox refers to the 1945–65 period as a hegemonic world order under the United States. U.S.-dominated institutions such as the UN Security Council, the IMF, the World Bank, and the GATT helped uphold the system's norms and values of political and economic liberalism, which legitimized U.S. hegemony and minimized the need for force.[64] Cox and Gill also argue that in this age of globalized production and exchange, a *transnational historic bloc* may be developing. The main institutions in this bloc are the largest MNCs, international banks, IOs such as the IMF and the World Bank, and international business groups in the most powerful capitalist states. With the development of a transnational bloc, class relations can now be viewed on a global scale. As discussed in Chapter 4, the predominant strand of liberalism in the post–World War II period was interventionist in nature; it drew on Keynesianism and viewed government intervention as necessary to counteract the socially unacceptable aspects of the market. Thus, countries balanced movement toward greater openness in the international economy with measures to cushion the effects on vulnerable groups in society through such measures as welfare and unemployment insurance. According to Gramscian theorists, the developing transnational historic bloc is threatening the interventionist liberal compromise of the postwar period.

A crucial element of the transnational historic bloc today is the power and mobility of transnational capital, which is putting both national labor unions and national business groups on the defensive. As discussed in Chapter 6 on monetary relations, the advanced industrial states imposed controls on capital flows in the 1950s and 1960s, but these controls were gradually removed beginning in the 1970s. The increased ability of transnational capital and MNCs to shift location from one country to another enables them to play off national labor groups—which are relatively immobile—against one another. Those workers who are employed by MNCs in both the core and the periphery also tend to identify their own interests with those of transnational capital, and this attitude divides the working class and further limits its ability to build a counterhegemony. The transnational historic bloc is also posing a threat to the ability of elected governments to make autonomous policy decisions. The recessionary conditions in the 1980s, for example, induced states to engage in "competitive deregulation" of their national **capital markets** in efforts to attract more capital and foreign investment, accelerating the reduction of barriers to capital mobility. Further solidifying this transnational historic bloc is a hegemonic ideology, which portrays capital mobility as contributing to economic efficiency, consumer welfare, and economic growth.[65]

Despite the solid foundations of the transnational historic bloc, there are indications that dissatisfaction with the transnational liberal forces could eventually stimulate a counterhegemonic response. For example, IMF and World Bank structural adjustment loans or SALs (discussed in Chapters 7 and 11), which are linked to pressures for privatization, deregulation, and trade liberalization, are creating resentment in some Third World recipient countries, and there is disillusionment with moves toward a market economy in Eastern European and FSU countries. Gramscian theorists therefore argue that although the forces of transnational capital are currently in the ascendancy, this situation may not continue indefinitely.

In discussing a possible reaction to the current transnational historic bloc, Gramscians often refer to *civil society*. Gramsci's analysis of civil society, like his study of hegemony, has long been viewed as one of his most important theoretical contributions. Civil society in his *Prison Notebooks* has different meanings, including both "the realm in which the existing social order is grounded," and "the realm in which a new social order can be founded."[66] In other words, civil society can help to sustain the hegemony of the bourgeoisie, but can also be the source of a counterhegemony. In supporting bourgeois hegemony, civil society is part of a "top-down" process in which the dominant capitalist class gains acquiescence from most of the population. As part of a counterhegemony, civil society is part of a "bottom-up" process in which disadvantaged elements of the population try to displace the hegemonic capitalist order. Gramsci's analysis has considerable relevance for discussions of civil society protests today at meetings of the IMF, World Bank, WTO, and other international groupings. Although the civil society protests have "certainly not attained the status of a counterhegemonic alliance of forces on the world scale," they do demonstrate considerable concern about the effects of orthodox liberalism and globalization on people's lives today.[67]

Gramscian analysis, like world-system theory, has been criticized on a number of grounds. For example, critics charge that Gramscians (like Marxists, dependency theorists, and world-system theorists) are so preoccupied with examining the problems of capitalism and the hegemony of transnational capital that they do not explore the potential problems of dominance and subordination in other possible global systems (e.g., socialism). Gramscians may have avoided some of the pitfalls of classical Marxists, who often made unrealized predictions regarding the downfall of capitalism. However, Gramscians also provide little guidance as to when a counterhegemony might develop and what form it might take. As a result, Gramscians, like world-system theorists, are better at pointing to the problems with the capitalist system than they are at offering solutions.

Despite these criticisms, Gramscian analysis has many important strengths. For example, the Gramscian view of hegemony has advantages over the realist and liberal views. As we discussed, realists and liberals define hegemony in state-centric terms, and they can identify only two or three times when there was a hegemonic state (Britain, the United States, and perhaps the Netherlands). Their ability to examine the effects of hegemony on IPE is therefore limited to only two or three relatively brief historical periods. *Gramscian* theorists, by contrast, use the term *hegemony* in a cultural sense to connote the complex of *ideas* that social groups use to assert their legitimacy and authority, and they extend the concept of hegemony to include nonstate actors such as MNCs and international banks as well as nation-states. Thus, the Gramscian concept of hegemony is far less restrictive, and we can use it to examine a far wider range of events in the global economy. The Gramscian concept of *counterhegemony* is also useful for examining the diverse range of groups in civil society today that are protesting globalization pressures on behalf of the environment, labor, human rights, women, and other interests. Gramscians ask whether these diverse groups are likely to coalesce sufficiently to form a counterhegemony that would challenge the current hegemonic ideology.[68]

The Business Conflict Model

The business conflict model, like hegemonic stability theory and regime theory, is a hybrid approach that draws on more than one theoretical perspective (in this case, historical structuralism and liberalism).[69] According to business conflict theorists, business groups—especially large corporations—are the most important societal groups affecting government policymaking, but there are major cleavages within the business community over policy issues. The cleavages include "divisions among corporations of different nationalities, among corporations of the same nationality, and among internationally owned corporations."[70] These divisions lead to conflicts within and among states with regard to policy, and they have a major impact on government policy processes and output. Business conflict theorists examine conflicts that occur within as well as across state borders, providing another example of the growing trend in IPE toward studying domestic-international interactions.

The business conflict model is discussed with historical structuralism because it emphasizes class (that is, business) as a major factor in foreign policymaking and views business firms as being motivated primarily by profit. Nevertheless, there are significant differences between business conflict theorists and instrumental Marxists, who argue that "the state serves the interests of the capitalist class because it is controlled by this class."[71] Instrumental Marxists simply assume that the capitalist class is united in furthering its interests, whereas business conflict theorists maintain that divisions among capitalists are pervasive. Business conflict theorists are also highly critical of structural Marxists, who believe that the state (though committed to ensuring the long-term survival of capitalism) is relatively autonomous from direct political pressure of the capitalist class. In the view of business conflict theorists, the state does not have relative autonomy from the pressure of business groups, even in the short term.[72] The business conflict model has some similarity to liberal pluralism. Both are society-centered theories that emphasize the role of interest groups in government policymaking. In the view of pluralists, however, no single interest group or class dominates society and the state. Business conflict theorists, by contrast, believe that "business groups have often been able to shape and direct . . . foreign investment and trade strategy independent of other pressure groups."[73]

In the view of business conflict theorists, the most significant division in the business community is between internationalist and nationalist business groups.[74] Nationalist firms are smaller and oriented primarily to the domestic market; internationalist firms are larger, more competitive, and heavily involved with foreign trade and investment. The diverse positions of the nationalist and internationalist firms give them different vested interests in policymaking. For example, nationalist firms often feel threatened by imports and favor trade protectionism, whereas internationalist firms with integrated multinational operations and substantial dependence on exports resist protectionism and favor open international markets.[75]

In pressuring for more open foreign trade and investment policies, internationalist business firms usually benefit from a close working relationship with the executive branch in the United States. Business internationalists also form organizations to influence and work with U.S. foreign policy officials, who are more likely to listen to the internationalists than to other groups. Smaller domestic business groups, which are more inclined to favor economic closure and protectionism, do not benefit from such connections with the U.S. foreign policy establishment. As a result, business nationalists often concentrate their efforts on influencing congressional committees that affect foreign policy outcomes. Although domestic businesses lack the wealth, connections, and expertise of the business internationalists, the diverse membership of Congress permits domestic business to gain influence by targeting individual representatives. Thus, protectionist pressures from domestic business in Congress often collide with business internationalist pressures for liberalization in the executive branch of government.

Even internationalist business groups are sometimes divided among themselves over foreign economic strategies, and this situation can affect their ability to influence policymaking. For example, internationalist firms that depend extensively on labor-intensive production in Third World countries often favor military force to quell leftist insurgencies, and they support military governments that discipline the domestic labor force and ensure that wages are low. Internationalist firms that are less labor intensive, by contrast, are less likely to support military action.[76] The business conflict model postulates that divisions between business nationalists and internationalists and divisions among internationalists are reflected in foreign policy outcomes. The model is a promising new approach to foreign economic policymaking that draws on both historical structuralism and liberal pluralism.

CONCLUSION

The relative influence of the three major perspectives on IPE as a discipline varies over time. The historical structuralist perspective may have faltered in recent years, but there are a number of promising new theoretical approaches in this school of thought. It is also certainly possible that the historical structuralist perspective could gain more influence in the future. Current pressures to replace postwar interventionist liberalism with a return to liberal orthodoxy is causing considerable dissatisfaction among many "have-nots" in society, providing a stimulus to a possible revival of historical structuralism. Furthermore, although some historical structuralist approaches, such as dependency theory, have been discredited in recent years, many of the concerns of dependency theorists continue to be relevant. Recent advances in world-system, Gramscian, business conflict, and other theories in this school clearly indicate that historical structuralism provides an important alternative perspective to the liberal and realist views.

NOTES

1. The seminal structural realist (or neorealist) study is Kenneth N. Waltz, *Theory of International Politics* (Reading, MA: Addison-Wesley, 1979). See also Robert O. Keohane, "Theory of World Politics: Structural Realism and Beyond," in Robert O. Keohane, ed., *Neorealism and Its Critics* (New York: Columbia University Press, 1986), pp. 158–203.
2. The term *historical structuralism* emerged in discussions with a colleague, Professor James Busumtwi-Sam, for which I am grateful.

3. Karl Marx and Friedrich Engels, *The Communist Manifesto* (New York: International Publishers, 1948), p. 9.
4. For a discussion of the two strands of Marxist writing on the state, see Bob Jessop, *The Capitalist State: Marxist Theories and Methods* (Oxford, UK: Martin Robertson, 1982), pp. 1–31; and David Held, *Models of Democracy* (Cambridge, UK: Polity Press, 1987), pp. 113–121.
5. Marx and Engels, *The Communist Manifesto*, p. 29.
6. See V. I. Lenin, *Imperialism: The Highest Stage of Capitalism,* rev. trans. (New York: International Publishers, 1939).
7. See, for example, Jack Woddis, *An Introduction to Neo-Colonialism* (London: Lawrence & Wishart, 1967); and Harry Magdoff, "Imperialism Without Colonies," in Roger Owen and Bob Sutcliffe, eds., *Studies in the Theory of Imperialism* (London: Longman, 1981), pp. 144–169.
8. Some authors argue that Marx was not a strict economic determinist. See, for example, David McLellan, *Marx,* (7th ed. London: Fontana/Collins, 1980), p. 41; and Gabriel Palma, "Dependency: A Formal Theory of Underdevelopment or a Methodology for the Analysis of Concrete Situations of Underdevelopment?" *World Development* 6-7/8 (July/August 1978), pp. 883–884.
9. Ralph Miliband, *The State in Capitalist Society* (New York: Basic Books, 1969), p. 66. On instrumental Marxism, see David A. Gold, Clarence Y. H. Lo, and Erik Olin Wright, "Recent Developments in Marxist Theories of the Capitalist State," *Monthly Review* 27-5 (October 1975), pp. 32–35.
10. For a discussion of structural Marxism, see Gold, Lo, and Wright, "Recent Developments in Marxist Theories of the Capitalist State," pp. 35–40; and Pat McGowan and Stephen G. Walker, "Radical and Conventional Models of U.S. Foreign Economic Policy Making," *World Politics* 33-3 (April 1981), pp. 357–360.
11. James H. Mittelman and Mustapha Kamal Pasha, *Out from Underdevelopment Revisited: Changing Global Structures and the Remaking of the Third World* (London: Macmillan, 1997), pp. 90–91.
12. Marx's writings on the non-European world are contained in Shlomo Avineri, ed., *Karl Marx on Colonialism and Modernization: His Despatches and Other Writings on China, India, Mexico, the Middle East and North Africa* (Garden City, NY: Doubleday, 1968). For conflicting interpretations of Marx's views of the Third World, see Carlos Johnson, "Ideologies in Theories of Imperialism and Dependency," in Ronald H. Chilcote and Dale L. Johnson, eds., *Theories of Development: Mode of Production or Dependency?* (Beverly Hills, CA: Sage, 1983), pp. 75–104.
13. Brendan O'Leary, *The Asiatic Mode of Production: Oriental Despotism, Historical Materialism and Indian History* (Oxford, UK: Basil Blackwell, 1989), p. 263. See also Anthony Giddens, *Capitalism and Modern Social Theory: An Analysis of the Writings of Marx, Durkheim and Max Weber* (Cambridge: Cambridge University Press, 1971), pp. 24–27; Lawrence Krader, *The Asiatic Mode of Production: Sources, Development and Critique in the Writings of Karl Marx* (Assen, The Netherlands: Van Grocum & Comp., 1975); and Timothy Brook, ed., *The Asiatic Mode of Production in China* (Armonk, NY: M.E. Sharpe, 1989).
14. Karl Marx, "The British Rule in India," in Avineri, ed., *Karl Marx on Colonialism and Modernization,* pp. 86–88.
15. Marx, "The British Rule in India," p. 481.
16. B. N. Ghosh, *Dependency Theory Revisited* (Aldershot, UK: Ashgate, 2001), p. 19.
17. J. A. Hobson, *Imperialism: A Study* (Ann Arbor, MI: University of Michigan Press, 1965), p. 81.

18. For differing views of Lenin's contribution to the study of imperialism, see Anthony Brewer, *Marxist Theories of Imperialism: A Critical Survey,* (2nd ed. London: Routledge, 1990), p. 116; and Tom Kemp, "The Marxist Theory of Imperialism," in Roger Owen and Bob Sutcliffe, eds., *Studies in the Theory of Imperialism* (London: Longman, 1972), pp. 26–30.

19. Lenin, *Imperialism: The Highest Stage of Capitalism,* p. 89.

20. Thomas Biersteker, "Evolving Perspectives on International Political Economy: Twentieth-Century Discontinuities," *International Political Science Review* 14-1 (January 1993), p. 12; Palma, "Dependency," pp. 896–897.

21. Thomas B. Gold, *State and Society in the Taiwan Miracle* (Armonk, NY: M.E. Sharpe, 1986), pp. 13–17.

22. See, for example, Peter Evans, "After Dependency: Recent Studies of Class, State, and Industrialization," *Latin American Research Review* 20-2 (1985), p. 159; and Fernando Henrique Cardoso and Enzo Faletto, *Dependency and Development in Latin America,* translated by Marjory Mattingly Urquidi (Berkeley, CA: University of California Press, 1979), p. ix.

23. Aidan Foster-Carter, "From Rostow to Gunder Frank: Conflicting Paradigms in the Analysis of Underdevelopment," *World Development* 4-3 (March 1976), p. 175.

24. Paul A. Baran, *The Political Economy of Growth* (New York: Monthly Review Press, 1962), pp. 11–12.

25. See Raúl Prebisch, "The Economic Development of Latin America and Its Principal Problems," *Economic Bulletin for Latin America* 7-1 (February 1962), pp. 1–22 (First published in Spanish in May 1950).

26. Joseph L. Love, "The Origins of Dependency Analysis," *Journal of Latin American Studies* 22 (February 1990), pp. 143–60.

27. See Fernando Henrique Cardoso, "The Consumption of Dependency Theory in the United States," *Latin American Research Review* 12–3 (1977), pp. 7–24. Cardoso and Faletto's *Dependencia y desarrollo en América Latina* was published in 1971, but it was not available in an English edition until eight years later. See Cardoso and Faletto, *Dependency and Development in Latin America.*

28. Gary Gereffi, *The Pharmaceutical Industry and Dependency in the Third World* (Princeton, NJ: Princeton University Press, 1983), p. 18; Gold, *State and Society in the Taiwan Miracle,* pp. 14–15. Despite his far greater emphasis on external forces, even Gunder Frank recognized the need to examine external-internal interactions.

29. Tony Smith, "Requiem or New Agenda for Third World Studies?" *World Politics* 37-4 (July 1985), pp. 546–547.

30. See, for example, André Gunder Frank's "The Development of Underdevelopment," *Monthly Review* 18-4 (September 1966), pp. 17–31.

31. Cardoso and Faletto, *Dependency and Development in Latin America,* p. 174.

32. See, for example, Peter Evans, *Dependent Development: The Alliance of Multinational, State, and Local Capital in Brazil* (Princeton, NJ: Princeton University Press, 1979); Gereffi, *The Pharmaceutical Industry and Dependency in the Third World;* and Gold, *State and Society in the Taiwan Miracle.*

33. See, for example, André Gunder Frank, "Asia's Exclusive Models," *Far Eastern Economic Review* 116-26 (June 25, 1982), pp. 22–23.

34. Gunder Frank, "Asia's Exclusive Models," *Far Eastern Economic Review* p. 23.

35. Evans, *Dependent Development,* p. 329. See also Gereffi, *The Pharmaceutical Industry and Dependency in the Third World,* p. 24; Cardoso and Faletto, *Dependency and Development in Latin America.*

36. See Colin Leys, "Underdevelopment and Dependency: Critical Notes," *Journal of Contemporary Asia* 7-1 (1977), pp. 92–107.

37. David Ray, "The Dependency Model of Latin American Underdevelopment: Three Basic Fallacies," *Journal of Interamerican Studies and World Affairs* 15-1 (February 1973), pp. 7–8. Although some dependency theorists acknowledge that dependent relationships can exist between socialist countries, they generally limit their analyses to the capitalist system.

38. Cal Clark and Donna Bahry, "Dependent Development: A Socialist Variant," *International Studies Quarterly* 27-3 (September 1983), p. 286.

39. Mittelman and Pasha, *Out from Underdevelopment Revisited,* p. 46.

40. Tony Smith, "The Underdevelopment of Development Literature: The Case of Dependency Theory," *World Politics* 31-2 (January 1979), pp. 257–258; Stephan Haggard, "The Newly Industrializing Countries in the International System," *World Politics* 38-2 (January 1986), p. 346.

41. Bill Warren, "Imperialism and Capitalist Industrialization," *New Left Review* 81 (September–October 1973), p. 4. See also Bill Warren, *Imperialism: Pioneer of Capitalism* (London: New Left Books and Verso, 1980). This book was edited by John Sender after Warren's death in 1978.

42. Ernesto Laclau, "Feudalism and Capitalism in Latin America," *New Left Review* 67 (May–June, 1971), p. 25.

43. Evans, "After Dependency," p. 158.

44. See, for example, many of the articles in the journal *Latin American Perspectives;* recent books and articles by authors such as James Petras and Ronald Chilcote; David L. Blaney, "Reconceptualizing Autonomy: The Difference Dependency Theory Makes," *Review of International Political Economy* 3-3 (Autumn 1996), pp. 457–497; Jill Hills, "Dependency Theory and Its Relevance Today: International Institutions in Telecommunications and Structural Power," *Review of International Studies* 20-2 (April, 1994), pp. 169–186; and Ghosh, *Dependency Theory Revisited.*

45. Ghosh, *Dependency Theory Revisited,* p. 133.

46. John Gerard Ruggie, "Multilateralism: The Anatomy of an Institution," in John Gerard Ruggie, ed., *Multilateralism Matters: The Theory and Praxis of an Institutional Form* (New York: Columbia University Press, 1993), p. 33; Francis Fukuyama, "The End of History?" *The National Interest* 16 (Summer 1989), pp. 3, 11.

47. Thomas J. Biersteker, "The 'Triumph' of Neoclassical Economics in the Developing World: Policy Convergence and Bases of Governance in the International Economic Order," in James N. Rosenau and Ernst-Otto Czempiel, eds., *Governance Without Government: Order and Change in World Politics* (Cambridge: Cambridge University Press, 1992), pp. 102–131.

48. For a discussion of the differences between dependency and world-system theory, see Peter Evans, "Beyond Center and Periphery: A Comment on the Contribution of the World System Approach to the Study of Development," *Sociological Inquiry* 49-4 (1979), pp. 15–20.

49. A very useful beginning source on world-system theory is Thomas R. Shannon, *An Introduction to the World-System Perspective,* 2nd ed. (Boulder, CO: Westview Press, 1996).

50. See Samir Amin, *Empire of Chaos,* translated by W. H. Locke Anderson, (New York: Monthly Review Press, 1992).

51. Immanuel Wallerstein, "The Rise and Future Demise of the World Capitalist System: Concepts for Comparative Analysis," in Immanuel Wallerstein, *The Capitalist World-Economy* (New York: Cambridge University Press, 1979), p. 5.

52. Wallerstein, "The Rise and Future Demise of the World Capitalist System," pp. 18–19.

53. Immanuel Wallerstein, "Class Formation in the Capitalist World-Economy," in Wallerstein, *The Capitalist World-Economy,* p. 230.

54. Wallerstein, "The Rise and Future Demise of the World Capitalist System," p. 35.

55. Wallerstein was not the first to refer to a middle "class" between the center and the periphery. Ruy Mauro Marini referred to "subimperial states," and Johan Galtung described "go-between" nations. See Ruy Mauro Marini *Subdesarollo y Revolución* 9th ed. (Mexico: Siglo Veintiuno, 1978); and Johan Galtung, "A Structural Theory of Imperialism," *Journal of Peace Research* 8-2 (1971), p. 104.

56. Evans, *Dependent Development,* p. 33.

57. Shannon, *An Introduction to the World-System Perspective,* pp. 146–149.

58. Immanuel Wallerstein, "Dependence in an Interdependent World: The Limited Possibilities of Transformation Within the Capitalist World-Economy," in Wallerstein, *The Capitalist World-Economy,* p. 69.

59. Wallerstein, "Dependence in an Interdependent World," p. 67; Wallerstein, "The Rise and Future Demise of the World Capitalist System," p. 35.

60. Gold, *State and Society in the Taiwan Miracle.,* pp. 13–14.

61. Theda Skocpol, "Wallerstein's World Capitalist System: A Theoretical and Historical Critique," *American Journal of Sociology* 82-5 (March 1977), pp. 1084–1088; Alexander Gerschenkron, "Economic Backwardness in Historical Perspective," in Alexander Gerschenkron, *Economic Backwardness in Historical Perspective: A Book of Essays* (Cambridge, MA: Belknap Press of Harvard University Press, 1962), pp. 16–21; Peter J. Katzenstein, ed., "Between Power and Plenty: Foreign Economic Policies of Advanced Industrial States," special issue of *International Organization* 31-4 (Autumn 1977).

62. For an exposition of Gramsci's ideas, see Antonio Gramsci, *Selections from the Prison Notebooks of Antonio Gramsci,* edited and translated by Quintin Hoare and Geoffrey Nowell Smith (New York: International Publishers, 1971). See also John Merrington, "Theory and Practice in Gramsci's Marxism," in New Left Review, ed., *Western Marxism: A Critical Reader* (London: New Left Review, 1977), pp. 142–150.

63. See Robert W. Cox, "Gramsci, Hegemony and International Relations: An Essay in Method," *Millennium* 12-2 (1983), pp. 162–175; and Mark Rupert, *Producing Hegemony: The Politics of Mass Production and American Global Power* (Cambridge: Cambridge University Press, 1995), p. 29.

64. Robert W. Cox, "Social Forces, States and World Orders: Beyond International Relations Theory," in Robert O. Keohane, ed., *Neorealism and Its Critics* (New York: Columbia University Press, 1986), pp. 204–254; Fred Gale, "Cave 'Cave! Hic Dragones': A Neo-Gramscian Deconstruction and Reconstruction of International Regime Theory," *Review of International Political Economy* 5-2 (Summer 1998), pp. 269–277.

65. See Stephen Gill and David Law, "Global Hegemony and the Structural Power of Capital," in Stephen Gill, ed., *Gramsci, Historical Materialism and International Relations* (Cambridge: Cambridge University Press, 1993), pp. 93–124.

66. Robert W. Cox, "Civil Society at the Turn of the Millennium: Prospects for an Alternative World Order," *Review of International Studies* 25 (1999), p. 4.

67. Cox, "Civil Society at the Turn of the Millennium," p. 13. See also Joseph A. Buttigieg, "Gramsci on Civil Society," *Boundary 2* 22–3 (Fall 1995), pp. 1–32.

68. See, for example, Mark E. Rupert, "(Re) Politicizing the Global Economy: Liberal Common Sense and Ideological Struggle in the US NAFTA Debate," *Review of International Political Economy* 2-4 (Autumn 1995), pp. 658–692.

69. This discussion of the business conflict school relies on David N. Gibbs, *The Political Economy of Third World Intervention: Mines, Money, and U.S. Policy in the Congo Crisis* (Chicago: University of Chicago Press, 1991); Ronald W. Cox, *Power and Profits: U.S. Policy in Central America* (Lexington KY: University Press of Kentucky, 1994); and David Skidmore, "The Business of International Politics," *Mershon International Studies Review* 39, suppl. 2 (October 1995), pp. 246–254. See also Gregory P. Nowell, *Mercantile States*

and the World Oil Cartel, 1900–1939 (Ithaca, NY: Cornell University Press, 1994); and Robert Vitalis, *When Capitalists Collide: Business Conflict and the End of Empire in Egypt* (Berkeley, CA: University of California Press, 1995).

70. Gibbs, *The Political Economy of Third World Intervention*, p. 30.
71. McGowan and Walker, "Radical and Conventional Models of U.S. Foreign Economic Policy Making," p. 352.
72. Gibbs, *The Political Economy of Third World Intervention*, pp. 13–19.
73. Cox, *Power and Profits*, p. 4.
74. Skidmore, "The Business of International Politics," p. 246.
75. Helen Milner, *Resisting Protectionism: Global Industries and the Politics of International Trade* (Princeton, NJ: Princeton University Press, 1988), pp. 24–25.
76. Cox, *Power and Profits*, p. 15.

PART III

THE ISSUE AREAS

Part III focuses on the main substantive issue areas in IPE. Chapter 6 begins by examining international monetary relations because the most significant types of transactions in the international economy—including trade, investment, and finance—all depend on the availability of money and credit. The chapter is devoted mainly to monetary relations but also discusses some of the crucial connections between monetary and financial issues. Next, Chapter 7 covers the issue of foreign debt, which is closely linked with international monetary and financial relations. Thus, the IMF has been the lead IO dealing with both monetary and foreign debt issues.

Chapters 8 and 9 deal with trade relations at both the global and regional levels. Regionalism is a major issue affecting all the substantive issue areas we examine. For example, Chapter 6 on monetary relations devotes some attention to the establishment of an economic and monetary union in Europe. Chapter 9 is devoted to regionalism and globalism in trade because trade liberalization has been so central to regional integration agreements such as the EU, the NAFTA, and the Southern Common Market Treaty (Mercosur). Chapter 10 deals with the most important private actor in the international economy, the MNC. With the increase of globalization and international competitiveness, the relationship between the MNC and the state is a matter of great concern to policymakers. Chapter 11 deals with the issue of international development. Most of the chapters in Part III devote some attention to Third World issues; Chapter 11 focuses specifically on alternative strategies and approaches to promoting economic development. The final section of each chapter in Part III draws linkages between the issue area on the one hand and the main themes and theoretical perspectives in IPE on the other.

C H A P T E R 6

International Monetary Relations

nternational monetary relations, the first substantive area addressed in this book, is the most central issue area in IPE. The most important types of transactions in the international economy—including trade, investment, and finance—all depend on the availability of money and credit. Thus, one long-term analyst of global monetary issues states that the most critical issue to hegemonic stability theorists should "not [be] what the hegemon does or does not do in trade . . . but what it does or fails to do to maintain peace and what it does or fails to do to keep the monetary system stable and credit flowing in a steady fashion."[1] Although international monetary relations is one of the most difficult issues for students to master, some background in this area can provide a sound basis for understanding other major issues in IPE.

The sheer volume of international monetary and financial transactions is playing a major role in reshaping the global political economy. Indeed, the amount of money handled *daily* by foreign exchange markets increased from negligible amounts in the late 1950s, to $590 billion in 1989, and to $1.5 trillion in 1998. About 25 to 33 percent of the world's circulating currency is now located outside the country issuing it, and in the mid-1990s at least $300 billion of the three top currencies (U.S. dollar, German deutsch mark, and Japanese yen) were circulating outside the country of origin.[2] Liberal interdependence theorists assert that this marked increase in international financial transactions has resulted largely from advances in communications, technology, and transportation and that nation-states are therefore finding it increasingly difficult to regulate economic activities. Realist scholars, by contrast, argue that financial transactions have increased with the permission (and sometimes the encouragement) of the most powerful states and that these states continue to dictate the terms for such transactions.[3]

Realists can also point to the fact that international monetary transactions still rely primarily on the existence of separate national currencies. As discussed later in this chapter, some assets, such as special drawing rights, are more international in scope, and the establishment of a new "euro" currency for the countries in the European Economic and Monetary Union (EMU) may pose a major challenge to the predominance of the nationally based U.S. dollar in the future. Nevertheless, the global monetary regime continues to function primarily in a world of separate national currencies, where states must inevitably be concerned about their balance of payments—the total flow of money into and out of the state.[4] A country's balance of payments tells us not only about its overall financial position but also about its position in other areas such as trade and foreign investment. It is therefore necessary to provide some background on the balance-of-payments issue.

THE BALANCE OF PAYMENTS

The **balance of payments,** which records the debit and credit transactions by residents, firms, and governments of one country with foreign countries and international institutions, is composed of two broad categories: the **current account,** which includes all transactions related to a country's current expenditures and national income, and the **capital account,** which includes all transactions related to movements of financial capital into and out of a country. As Table 6.1 shows, the current account comprises four types of transactions:

1. *Merchandise trade,* or the export and import of tangible goods. The difference between the value of merchandise exports and imports is the *merchandise trade balance.*
2. *Services trade,* or intangible items such as insurance, information, transportation, banking, and consulting, provided to or by foreigners. A country's merchandise and services exports minus its merchandise and services imports (items 1 and 2 in the table) are equal to its *balance of trade.*
3. *Investment income and payments,* which measure interest and dividend payments on investments by citizens of the home country to foreigners and by foreigners to citizens of the home country.
4. *Remittances and official transactions,* which include income that migrant workers or foreign companies send out of a country, military and foreign aid, and salaries and pensions paid to government employees abroad.

Table 6.1 shows that Japan had a current account *surplus* of $117.64 billion (U.S.) in 1992, whereas the United States had a current account *deficit* of $66.30 billion. The critical item for both countries was the merchandise trade balance, with Japan having a merchandise trade *surplus* of $132.40 billion and the United States having a merchandise trade *deficit* of $96.14 billion. As noted in Chapter 8, the United States has had annual merchandise trade deficits since 1971, whereas Japan has had substantial trade surpluses. The largest U.S. trade deficits are often with Japan; this fact has been a constant source of friction between the two countries. Table 6.1 shows that in contrast to its merchandise trade deficit, the United States had a positive balance in its *services* trade in 1992 (+$42.32 billion). For many years the United States has been a net exporter of services, because of its many skilled consultants and its highly developed markets in insurance and banking. This helps to explain why the United States exerted strong pressure to include services trade in the CUSFTA and in the last round of GATT negotiations (the Uruguay round in 1986–93). The United States also had a

TABLE 6.1

BALANCE-OF-PAYMENTS DATA, 1992 (BILLIONS OF DOLLARS)

	United States	Japan
Current account		
1. Merchandise trade		
Exports	+440.14	+330.81
Imports	–536.28	–198.47
Merchandise trade balance	–96.14	+132.40
2. Services trade		
Credit	+159.40	+48.31
Debit	–117.08	–89.73
Services trade balance	+42.32	–41.42
Balance of trade (1 + 2)	–53.82	+90.98
3. Investment income and payments		
Credit	+130.95	+145.75
Debit	–110.55	–114.47
Balance	+20.40	+31.28
4. Remittances and official transactions	–32.88	–4.62
Current account balance	**–66.30**	**+117.64**
Capital account		
5. Direct investment and other long-term capital	–17.61	–30.78
6. Short-term capital	+54.19	–75.77
Capital account balance	**+36.58**	**–106.55**
Statistical discrepancy	**–12.34**	**–10.46**
Total	**–42.06**	**+0.63**
Change in reserves°	**+42.06**	**–0.63**

°Increase in reserves: –; decrease in reserves: +.

Source: International Monetary Fund, *Balance of Payments Statistics Yearbook,* vol. 44, part 1, 1993 (Washington, DC: IMF, 1993), pp. 366, 742.

positive balance in the investment income and payments item of the current account in 1992 (+$20.40 billion) because of interest and dividend payments received on past investments, but the positive balances on services and investment income were not sufficient to overcome the large U.S. negative balance on merchandise trade. Thus, the overall U.S. current account balance in 1992 was negative (–$66.30 billion).

The second major item in the balance of payments is the *capital account,* which measures long-term and short-term flows of investment (items 5 and 6 in Table 6.1). A country's capital exports are *debit* items because they involve payments to foreigners and use foreign exchange; its capital imports are *credit* items because they involve payments from foreigners and earn foreign exchange. (This is the opposite of merchandise trade, in which exports are credits and imports are debits.) Short-term investments normally have a maturity of less than one year, whereas long-term investments extend beyond this period. Long-term capital flows are further subdivided into FDI and portfolio investment. FDI is capital investment in a branch plant or subsidiary of an MNC in which the investor has voting control. **Portfolio investment,** by contrast, is investment in bonds or a minority holding of shares that does not involve legal control.

Governments tend to offset imbalances in their current accounts with changes in their capital accounts. Thus, a country with a current account deficit often seeks to offset this deficit by seeking foreign investment or an inflow of funds into its capital account. A current account surplus, on the other hand, permits a country to have a capital account deficit through investment abroad or the accumulation of foreign assets. Accordingly, Table 6.1 reveals that Japan (which had a current account *surplus*) had a capital account *deficit* of $106.55 billion in 1992 and that the United States (which had a current account *deficit*) had a capital account *surplus* of $36.58 billion.

In addition to the current and capital accounts, the balance of payments includes two items of lesser importance. The first is referred to as the *statistical discrepancy*. This item results partly from errors in collecting and computing data, but, more importantly, it stems from a government's failure to include all the goods, services, and capital flows that cross its borders. The final item in the balance of payments is the *change in official reserves*. Each country has a **central bank** (for example, the U.S. Federal Reserve or the Bank of Canada) that holds reserves of foreign exchange and gold. When a country has a deficit in its current *and* capital accounts (the "Total" item in Table 6.1), this amount must be matched by an equivalent reduction in reserves. When a state has a surplus in its current and capital accounts, it accumulates the surplus money in its reserves. The total of a country's current account, capital account, statistical discrepancy, and change in reserves always equals zero, hence the term *balance of payments*. Note in Table 6.1 that, by standard balance-of-payments accounting, a *minus* figure equals an *increase* in reserves and a *plus* figure equals a *decrease* in reserves. (This is merely a bookkeeping exercise so that the balance of payments will equal zero, and it should not be of concern to the student.) Thus, in 1992 U.S. reserves *decreased* by $42.06 billion, and Japanese reserves *increased* by $0.63 billion.

Although all international payments in the balance-of-payments account always balance (i.e., equal zero) in a bookkeeping sense, this fact does not indicate that a country never has payments difficulties. On the contrary, analysts commonly speak of a country as having a *balance-of-payments surplus* or a *balance-of-payments deficit*. These terms refer only to the current and capital account parts of the balance of payments; they exclude any changes in official financing. A government with a balance-of-payments surplus reduces its liabilities to foreign governments and/or adds to its holdings of official reserves, and a government with a balance-of-payments deficit increases its liabilities and/or reduces its official reserves. The main body of the balance of payments therefore informs us about a state's overall position in terms of financial assets and liabilities.[5]

GOVERNMENT RESPONSE
TO A BALANCE-OF-PAYMENTS DEFICIT

Countries with balance-of-payments deficits normally feel far more pressure to correct the imbalances than countries with balance-of-payments surpluses. A deficit country's reserves can eventually be depleted, but a surplus country can continue to increase its reserves indefinitely. Furthermore, realists believe that a balance-of-payments surplus, even if it is maintained with the help of government policy, is an indication of "superior competitive performance."[6] Surplus countries can in fact feel both economic and political pressures to correct their surpluses in the longer term. For example, excessive official reserves can lead to rising prices and inflationary pressures at home, and large balance-of-payments surpluses can force up the value of a country's currency, in turn making the country's exports more expensive for foreigners. Nevertheless, surplus countries normally view their payments disequilibrium as an economic as set rather than a liability, and we therefore focus here on a country's response to a payments deficit When governments have a balance-of-payments deficit, they have two basic policy choices: They can either *finance* the disequilibrium or *adjust* to it. Governments often prefer financing measures because they can defer the costs to the future, when foreign debts must be repaid. Adjustment measures, by contrast, can have major political risks because some societal groups must bear the costs of adjustment in the present.[7]

Adjustment Measures

Governments opting for adjustment measures rely on three types of policy instruments to affect the balance of payments: monetary policy, fiscal policy, and commercial policy. Whereas monetary and fiscal policy affect the level of economic activity, commercial policy directly influences a country's trade flows. **Monetary policy** influences the economy through changes in the money supply. When a government uses monetary policy to deal with a balance-of-payments deficit, its central bank limits public access to funds for spending purposes and makes such funds more expensive. For example, the central bank raises interest rates to make borrowing more costly, it decreases the amount of money available for loans by requiring commercial banks to hold larger reserves, and it sells government bonds so that money is withdrawn from the economy. These policies are designed to produce a contraction of the economy, less spending on goods and services, and hence a lowering of the payments deficit. **Fiscal policy** affects the economy through changes in government spending and/or taxes. When a government uses fiscal policy to deal with a balance-of-payments deficit, it lowers government expenditures and/or raises taxes to withdraw purchasing power from the public. Economies with balance-of-payments surpluses often follow the opposite policies; for example, they may adopt measures to expand the money supply, increase the budget deficit, and inflate the economy.

Governments using various combinations of monetary, fiscal, and commercial policy may opt for adjustment measures that are *external* or *internal* in nature. *External adjustment methods,* which cause foreigners to pay more of the adjustment costs, include such measures as tariffs, import quotas, export subsidies, tax incentives, and currency devaluation. External measures are designed to reduce payments to foreigners (by decreasing imports and outflows of foreign investment) and to increase payments from foreigners (by increasing exports and foreign investment inflows). Because external adjustment measures are aimed at foreign countries, a major pitfall of this approach is that others often retaliate and everyone loses in the long run. The competitive devaluation of currencies, with each country attempting to lower the value of its currency—and thus the relative price of its exports—is a prime example of the results of such retaliation. Although a government may adopt external measures to avoid making politically unpopular decisions at home, even external measures impose costs on some domestic groups. For example, a reduction in imports may promote domestic production and employment, but it also has adverse effects on importing businesses and on the choice of products available to consumers.

Internal adjustment methods cause individuals and groups at home to pay more of the adjustment costs. These are usually deflationary monetary and fiscal measures designed to slow down business activity in efforts to decrease the deficit. Examples of such measures include higher taxes and higher interest rates to reduce spending levels by individuals, businesses, and the government. The costs of internal adjustment methods are most evident domestically; they can contribute to unemployment, a reduction in living standards, business bankruptcies, and a phasing out of publicly financed programs. However, internal adjustment measures can also affect foreigners by deflating the economy and lowering the demand for foreign imports.

Financing

Instead of using adjustment methods, a country may seek *financing* to deal with its balance-of-payments deficit. Governments that choose financing must borrow from external credit sources and/or decrease their foreign exchange reserves. Governments often prefer to postpone difficult political decisions and to opt for future over current costs, so they tend to shift from adjustment to financing when reserves and access to credit are available. However, financing is difficult to arrange over a lengthy period; a country's reserves can be depleted, and foreigners are reluctant to invest in a country with chronic foreign debt problems.

In recent years the United States has normally depended on financing through its capital account (+$36.58 billion in 1992, as shown in Table 6.1) to counter its current account deficit (–$66.30 billion in 1992), which has resulted primarily from its merchandise trade deficit. In 1999, the U.S. trade deficit and current account deficit reached record levels of $268 billion and $339 billion, respectively. In the year 2000, the U.S. current account deficit reached a record 4.4 percent of U.S. GDP. One result of this long-term deficit is that the United States has changed from being a net creditor nation of $300 billion in 1980 to a net debtor of $1.5 trillion in 1998, with debt projections up to $3 trillion to $4 trillion by 2005.[8]

Some analysts argue that U.S. preoccupation with its merchandise trade deficit is a "dangerous obsession," which could initiate a new round of trade protectionism. The U.S. negative trade balance from this perspective is no longer a valid measure of U.S. global sales competitiveness, because corporate America in fact "has never been better positioned to compete in the global marketplace."[9] U.S. firms often prefer to sell goods abroad through their foreign subsidiaries rather than exporting them from the United States. Thus, U.S. foreign affiliate sales of $2.4 trillion in 1998 were far greater than U.S. global exports, which amounted to $933 billion.[10] The merchandise trade deficit is not a concern from this perspective, because U.S. firms today are highly competitive.

Certainly it is true that the balance of trade is not the only measure of "economic health," as the current economic problems of Japan clearly demonstrate. (Japan's economic problems are discussed later in this chapter and in Chapter 11.) Nevertheless, as we discuss in Chapter 10, there is considerable debate among scholars as to whether the competitiveness of a nation-state is synonymous with the competitiveness of its MNCs. A number of economists in fact argue that the chronic U.S. balance of trade and payments deficits are a cause for some concern. The United States has been able to rely on financing rather than adjustment measures because its large economy and its political stability attract foreign investors. Nevertheless, if a country depends on large capital inflows over time, it begins to pay out more in interest and dividends to foreigners than it receives (the investment income and payments item under the current account). Canada is a prime example of a country that has a long history as a net international borrower, and its investment income and payments have therefore been a high-debit item. Unlike the United States, Canada had a positive merchandise trade balance of +$8.18 U.S. billion in 1992. However, Canada had a services trade balance of –$11.45 billion and, most important, it had a balance on investment income and payments of –$27.42 billion, contributing to a negative current account balance of –$23.02 billion in 1992. Like the United States, Canada had to turn to the capital account to help counter its current account deficit (the Canadian capital account balance in 1992 was +$13.79 billion).[11] As a result of regular U.S. borrowing on its capital account to deal with its merchandise trade deficit, the United States' investment income and payments item under its current account also became a negative item in 1998 (–$6.21 billion) and 1999 (–$18.48 billion).[12] Other possible problems that could result from the long-term U.S. deficits and foreign debt could include a protectionist backlash against U.S. liberal trade policy, a loss of U.S. disposable income, increased leverage vis-à-vis the United States by foreign governments that have substantial official U.S. dollar holdings, and disruptive market volatility against the U.S. dollar. Thus, one noted economist warns that "the longer the large U.S. external deficit continues and the foreign debt increases, the more likely will be a hard landing for the dollar and the U.S. economy."[13]

Adjustment, Financing, and the Theoretical Perspectives

In reality, states usually employ a combination of external adjustment, internal adjustment, and financing measures to deal with their payments deficits. Although economic factors may have some effect on the country's choice of methods, political factors also have a major influence.[14] Liberals, realists, and historical structuralists have differing preferences regarding these policy instruments. Orthodox liberals generally believe that payments deficits result from domestic inefficiencies and that governments should adopt internal adjustment measures as a necessary form of discipline. Liberals oppose external adjustment measures, which contribute to trade barriers and the distortion of economic exchange, and they oppose external financing because it permits countries to delay instituting necessary internal reforms.

Realists and historical structuralists, by contrast, often oppose internal adjustment methods that interfere with domestic autonomy in policymaking. Dependency theorists believe that the international system serves the interests of the rich Northern states, so they view the situation as doubly unjust if LDCs must bear the costs of adjustment internally. External adjustment measures are far more acceptable to both realists and historical structuralists. Realists view such external measures as "fair game" in a state's efforts to improve its competitive position vis-à-vis other states, and historical structuralists believe Third World countries may have to impose import controls because of their unfavorable terms of trade with industrial states. Some historical structuralists also argue that the North, which benefits most from the international system, should provide Southern states with liberal financing to help alleviate their balance-of-payments problems.

INTERNATIONAL MONETARY RELATIONS BEFORE BRETTON WOODS

The literature on the modern period of international monetary relations commonly refers to the existence of four successive monetary regimes.[15] The first regime, from the 1870s to the outbreak of World War I in 1914, is identified with the international gold standard; the second regime, during the first part of the interwar period, is identified with a gold exchange standard; the third regime, from 1944 to 1973, is identified with the Bretton Woods system; and the fourth regime, from 1973 to the present, is identified with a system of floating exchange rates. This chapter focuses primarily on the third and fourth regimes, which developed after World War II. However, to understand the Bretton Woods regime it is necessary to provide some background discussion of the first two regimes.

The International Gold Standard (1870s to 1914)

The international **gold standard** was a *fixed exchange rate* regime in which each country's currency was given an official exchange rate in relation to gold. By making the real values of national currencies more stable, the gold standard was designed to facilitate transactions between economies. For example, if the U.S. dollar was pegged at $35 per ounce of gold and the British pound was pegged at £14.5 per ounce of gold, the exchange rate between the dollar and the pound would remain constant at $2.41 per £1 (35 divided by 14.5). Although all countries had to undergo adjustments to maintain their exchange rates, the gold standard functioned reasonably well because it was backed by British hegemony and by cooperation among the core countries at the time (especially Britain, France, and Germany).[16] By providing public goods to other countries, such as investment capital, loans, and an open market for imports, Britain assumed a leadership role in stabilizing the gold standard. Thus, Western Europe and the United States generally maintained their official gold parities for about 35 years.[17]

The gold standard regime was based on orthodox liberal ideas in some important respects. The primary objective was to promote monetary openness and stability through the maintenance of stable exchange rates. This was a period before John Maynard Keynes introduced his interventionist liberal ideas to combat unemployment, and countries were expected to sacrifice domestic social objectives for the sake of monetary stability. Orthodox liberals have sometimes referred to the gold standard in highly idealized terms, and in 1981 President Ronald Reagan even created a special commission to determine whether the United States should return to the gold standard (the commission's recommendation was negative).[18] However, critics maintain that the poorest countries, and the poorest classes within countries, often assumed the largest burden of adjustment under the gold standard through sacrifices in both welfare and employment.

The Interwar Period (1914 to 1944)

World War I completely disrupted international monetary relations, but after the war Great Britain attempted to establish a *gold exchange standard* regime. A gold exchange standard, like a gold standard, is based on fixed exchange rates among currencies. The international reserves of a country under the nineteenth-century gold standard, however, were officially held in gold, whereas official reserves under a gold exchange standard consist of both gold and reserve currencies (such as the British pound or U.S. dollar). Although many central banks had in fact held reserve currencies as well as gold in earlier years, the gold exchange standard institutionalized this practice.[19] Because gold itself is in scarce supply and depends on new discoveries, a gold *exchange* standard permits more flexibility in increasing international reserves. (Furthermore, the largest gold producers are South Africa and Russia, which were not always the most favored countries.)

British efforts to reestablish monetary stability with the gold exchange standard continued for several years, but these efforts eventually failed. As a result, monetary relations for much of the interwar period were marked by competitive devaluations, a shift to floating rather than fixed exchange rates, destabilizing speculative capital movements, and increased trade protectionism, which culminated in the Great Depression. Some theorists maintain that the failure to reestablish monetary stability in the interwar period resulted from the decline of British hegemony and Britain's inability to pursue effective stabilizing policies as it had before World War I. Others, however, argue that the main factor in the breakdown of monetary stability was the growing reluctance of countries to sacrifice domestic goals such as full employment for the sake of currency stability.

Those who argue that domestic factors were mainly responsible for the breakdown of monetary stability point to major differences in domestic politics before World War I and in the interwar period. In most countries before World War I, voting was limited, labor unions were weak, farmers were not organized, and left-leaning parties were restricted. Thus, governments generally felt free to raise interest rates, decrease government expenditures, and raise taxes if necessary to bolster the value of their currencies in relation to gold, even if these policies contributed to unemployment and other domestic hardships. By the end of World War I, however, domestic groups had gained more influence through the extension of suffrage, the legalization of labor unions, the organization of farmers, and the development of mass political parties. It was no accident that Keynes introduced his interventionist liberal ideas at this time, positing that some government intervention is necessary to deal with domestic economic problems such as unemployment. Thus, governments could no longer easily sacrifice the domestic welfare of their citizens to maintain external balance in support of the gold exchange standard, and one government after another responded to economic difficulties in the interwar period by turning away from international openness.[20]

THE FORMATION OF THE BRETTON WOODS MONETARY REGIME

World War II was marked by a breakdown of monetary cooperation and a period of exchange controls, and planning for a postwar monetary regime culminated in the 1944 Bretton Woods conference. The Bretton Woods monetary regime was a gold exchange system in which the value of each country's currency was pegged to gold or the U.S. dollar. Unlike the previous two regimes, however, the Bretton Woods system was based on the postwar interventionist liberal compromise (see Chapter 4).[21] On the one hand, postwar planners assumed that the pegged exchange rates would provide sufficient monetary stability to permit a resumption of normal international trade. On the other hand, the planners ensured that there was some flexibility and assistance so that countries could pursue domestic objectives related to employment and inflation. This marked a contrast with the classical gold standard, in which long-term exchange rate stability took precedence over domestic socioeconomic requirements.[22]

The interventionist liberal compromise had three major elements. First, the postwar gold exchange standard was in fact an adjustable-peg exchange rate system rather than a fixed exchange rate system. Although countries were to maintain the par value of their currencies in the short term, all countries other than the United States (as we discuss later) could devalue or revalue their currencies under IMF guidance to correct *chronic* problems in their balance of payments. (Devaluation lowers the value and revaluation raises the value of a currency.) The Bretton Woods negotiators hoped that a cooperative IMF framework for changing the value of currencies would provide flexibility that was lacking with the classical gold standard and avoid the competitive devaluations that had occurred during the Great Depression. The second element of the interventionist liberal compromise was the creation of the IMF, which would provide short-term loans to countries with temporary balance-of-payments problems and thus alleviate domestic problems resulting from the need to maintain exchange rate stability. The third element of the compromise was the support for national controls over capital flows. Speculative capital flows had contributed to great instability during the interwar period, and the postwar negotiators feared that such speculation could similarly undermine efforts to maintain pegged exchange rates and promote freer trade under the Bretton Woods regime. The chief negotiators also believed that unrestricted capital flows would interfere with the functioning of the welfare state. If corporations and citizens could freely move their funds abroad to evade taxes, funding that the state required for social welfare expenditures would be jeopardized.[23]

THE INTERNATIONAL MONETARY FUND

The most important IO embedded in the Bretton Woods monetary regime was the IMF. The IMF, which is located in Washington, D.C., was created to promote stable and orderly exchange rates and to provide member states with short-term loans for temporary balance-of-payments problems. Under the IMF Articles of Agreement, members had to peg their currencies to gold or the U.S. dollar, which was valued at $35 per ounce of gold. Member countries were also to contribute to a "pool" of national currencies; those funds would be available for the IMF loans to deficit countries.[24] Each IMF member was given a *quota* based on its relative economic importance, and this quota determined the size of its *subscription*, or contribution to the IMF resource pool. The IMF has a weighted voting system in which the most economically powerful countries have the largest quotas and subscriptions and the most votes. At regular intervals of not more than five years, the IMF reviews member countries' quotas in view of changes in members' relative economic positions and decides whether to propose adjusting them.

The IMF approves loans to members in a series of stages, or *tranches*. In the 1980s, the IMF developed a number of new programs to deal with the foreign debt crisis, and member countries can now borrow amounts far above the level of their IMF quotas. IMF **conditionality** has become a major factor in its loan giving: members agree to adopt specific economic policies in return for IMF funding.[25] The more a member country borrows from the IMF (in relation to its quota), the more stringent are the IMF's conditionality requirements. Third World countries feel strong pressures to abide by IMF conditionality, not only because of the loans the IMF can provide but because the advanced industrial countries and private international banks often make the acceptance of IMF conditions a requirement for their own granting of loans and development assistance. The IMF usually requires the borrowing country to adopt contractionary monetary and fiscal policies that are liberal-economic in nature. In the view of IMF officials, these requirements are designed to ensure that the borrower addresses its balance-of-payments problems so that it can repay the IMF loan. From the perspective of many LDC loan recipients, however, the IMF's conditionality requirements often infringe on their sovereignty and do not address the basic structural problems hindering their economic development (see Chapter 7 for further discussion of this issue).

The two main policymaking bodies of the IMF are the *board of governors* and the *board of executive directors*. As is the case for the UN General Assembly, each IMF member appoints one representative (usually the finance minister or central bank governor) to the board of governors, but in the IMF, the voting power of each governor depends on the weighted voting system. The IMF board of governors meets only once a year in conjunction with the board of governors of the World Bank, and most of its powers are delegated to the board of executive directors (or executive board), which is in continuous session. The executive board, which also has weighted voting, is responsible for the IMF's daily business, including requests for financial assistance, economic consultations with member countries, and the development of policies. It consists of the IMF managing director as chair and 24 executive directors. In addition to the boards of governors and executive directors, the IMF has an *International Monetary and Financial Committee of the Board of Governors* (formerly the Interim Committee). Formed in the 1970s, this committee meets twice a year to make policy recommendations at higher political levels in a forum smaller than the annual meetings of the board of governors.

The countries with the largest subscriptions and the most votes in the IMF governing bodies are the G-5—the United States, Japan, Germany, France, and Britain. In April 2001, the G-5 countries had 39.28 percent of the votes in the board of governors. The United States had 17.16 percent, followed by Japan with 6.16 percent, Germany with 6.02 percent, and France and Britain with 4.97 percent each.[26] The G-5 countries all have a sufficient number of votes to appoint their own executive directors. Coalitions of member countries elect the other executive directors every two years. The advanced industrial states not only have the most voting power in the IMF governing bodies, they also have considerable influence in the operating staff. Thus, by tacit agreement, the top executive officer of the IMF, the managing director, has always been European, and the World Bank president has always been American.

In practice, the board of governors and the executive board arrive at most decisions through consensus rather than formal votes, but the weighted voting procedure gives the advanced industrial states the most influence in both bodies. The Third World countries nevertheless are able to influence IMF decision making through bloc voting under certain circumstances. Most IMF decisions are made with a simple majority vote, but majorities of 70 and 85 percent are required for some important decisions. The provision for these special majorities gives an effective veto to the United States, the EU, and the Third World countries *if* they act as a group. Although the Third World has on rare occasions blocked some initiatives requiring special majorities, it is not able to alter the existing structure of the IMF, which clearly favors the advanced industrial states. Because it includes such a large, amorphous group of countries, the Third World also has difficulty acting as a monolithic group to block IMF decisions.[27]

Not surprisingly, the LDCs have expressed dissatisfaction with the industrial states' dominance in the IMF, and the non-oil LDCs joined with OPEC after the 1973–74 oil price increases to demand greater voting power.[28] As a result of these demands, the OPEC countries benefited from the readjustment of IMF quotas and voting allocations, and Third World countries were included in more of the IMF's deliberations. Nevertheless, the IMF's weighted voting system continues to favor the interests and objectives of the advanced industrial states.

Chapter 2 noted that all the CPEs except Yugoslavia withdrew or were ousted from the IMF and the World Bank in the 1950s and 1960s. Membership issues in the two institutions are closely related; a country cannot join the World Bank without also becoming a member of the IMF. This requirement deterred most Communist countries from joining the World Bank for a number of years, even though they were interested in receiving World Bank financing, because they would have been subject to IMF conditionality. Although Romania joined the IMF and the World Bank in 1972, most former Soviet bloc countries did not join these institutions until the 1980s and 1990s. A number of the emerging economies of Eastern Europe and the FSU have experienced foreign debt problems; Chapter 7 discusses their membership in the Bretton Woods institutions.

THE FUNCTIONING OF THE BRETTON WOODS MONETARY REGIME

The Bretton Woods monetary regime was a gold exchange regime in which the main reserves were gold and the U.S. dollar. Economists generally ask three questions about the adequacy of reserve assets in upholding a monetary regime. First, is there a sufficient amount of reserves (that is, gold and the U.S. dollar) for **liquidity**, or financing purposes? As interdependence increases, more liquidity is necessary to cover the growing number of economic transactions among states, but if there is a surplus of liquidity, inflation and other problems can result. Second, is there a *confidence* problem with the existing reserve currencies? When countries lack confidence that a currency's value will remain stable, they are reluctant to hold that currency in its reserves. Confidence problems have led to periodic efforts to sell off British pounds and U.S. dollars. And third, what *adjustment* options do reserve-currency countries have in dealing with their balance-of-payments deficits? An effective regime should provide all deficit countries (including the top-currency country, the United States) with a sufficient range of adjustment options. The discussion that follows examines the problems with liquidity, confidence, and adjustment that developed in the Bretton Woods monetary regime.[29]

The Central Role of the U.S. Dollar

Events in the early postwar years dictated that the United States rather than the IMF take initial responsibility for managing the international monetary regime. Monetary relations immediately after the war were more unstable than expected, with balance-of-payments deficits and lack of foreign exchange seriously hindering recovery in Europe. Because the IMF's available funds were inadequate to meet the needs, the United States as global hegemon assumed much of the responsibility for providing finance. Thus, the United States opened its market to imports from foreign countries, provided long-term loans and grants to Europe through the European Recovery Program or Marshall Plan, and supplied the U.S. dollar as the main source of international liquidity. In opting for the Marshall Plan and other bilateral aid for postwar reconstruction, the United States effectively sidelined the IMF as a financing institution for Europe, and the IMF's main clients soon became the LDCs. However, LDCs were often deterred by the conditionality requirements that the IMF imposed on its loans; total drawings from the IMF fell to zero in 1950 and did not exceed 1947 levels again until 1956.[30]

Because the Bretton Woods monetary regime was based on a gold exchange standard, central banks could hold their international reserves in two forms—gold and foreign exchange—in any proportion they chose.[31] It is ironic, however, that the original attraction of gold as a reserve asset—its scarcity—became a liability as increased trade and foreign investment led to growing demand for international reserves. Gold-mining sources were limited, so only the U.S. dollar could meet this need for increased liquidity. Although it was vital that there be a sufficient number of dollars available for global liquidity purposes, large U.S. balance-of-trade surpluses in the late 1940s contributed to a dollar shortage. To remedy this problem, the United States distributed dollars around the world through economic aid and military expenditures from 1947 to 1958, providing liquidity for the international economy.

Under IMF guidance other countries at times changed the par value of their currencies relative to gold and the U.S. dollar, but the dollar's value was to remain fixed at the 1934 rate of $35 per ounce of gold. The fixed rate of the dollar was designed to ensure that it would be "as good as gold." Under the gold exchange standard, other currencies were not directly convertible into gold, but were convertible into U.S. dollars, which were in turn convertible into gold. Thus, the United States agreed to exchange all dollars held by foreign central banks and treasuries for gold at the official rate. This commitment seemed to be perfectly reasonable because the United States held a much larger share of the world's gold reserves after the war than any other country. Most other countries in fact preferred U.S. dollars to gold for their reserves and international transactions; dollars (unlike gold) earned interest, and they did not have to be shipped and stored. Although the IMF Articles of Agreement stated that "the par value of the currency of each member shall be expressed in terms of gold . . . or in terms of the United States dollar," IMF members usually related their par values to the dollar.[32]

Although the United States as global hegemon was providing its currency as a public good to meet international liquidity needs, it was also receiving the private benefit of seignorage. **Seignorage** is "the profit that comes to the seigneur, or sovereign power, from the issuance of money."[33] As the supplier of the key world currency, the United States gained financial power and influence, and it was largely exempt from the discipline that the international financial system imposed on other states. The United States was also able to trade and borrow in domestic currency and thus avoid exchange rate risks and transaction costs, and the dollar's leading role enabled New York City to retain its position as the world's financial capital. U.S. policy from 1947 to the late 1950s was therefore based on a mixture of altruism and self-interest, and other major countries acquiesced in U.S. monetary leadership because of the benefits they received.[34]

Despite the early emergence of the United States as hegemon in the global monetary regime, several changes in the late 1950s led to concerns about its continued leadership. The United States regularly had a substantial balance-of-trade surplus in the postwar period, but it had even larger debits because of the economic and military financing it was providing through the Marshall Plan and other assistance programs. As a result, the United States had an overall balance-of-payments deficit beginning in 1950. U.S. payments deficits averaged about $1.5 billion per year for most of the decade, but they increased rapidly in the late 1950s, and observers began to speak of a dollar "glut" rather than a dollar shortage. In 1960, the U.S. payments deficit was $3.7 billion, and foreign dollar holdings exceeded U.S. gold reserves for the first time.[35] Thus, European governments, which had eagerly sought to obtain dollars, were now reluctant to accumulate excessive dollar reserves.

To some economists, the dollar's declining fortunes demonstrated that there were fundamental problems with a monetary regime that relied on a single key currency. On the one hand, the need for sufficient liquidity caused the United States to spread dollars around the world by running balance-of-payments deficits. On the other hand, these payments deficits would eventually make it impossible for the United States to continue exchanging dollars for gold at $35 per ounce, and this would lead to the collapse of confidence in the dollar as the top currency. Any U.S. actions to drastically reduce its balance-of-payments deficit in order to restore confidence in the dollar would contribute to a shortage of global liquidity. The **Triffin dilemma** (named after economist Robert Triffin) refers to the problem confronting a monetary regime that depends on a single key currency: The liquidity and confidence functions of the currency eventually come into conflict.[36]

A second major change that raised questions about U.S. control over monetary relations was the growth of the *Eurocurrency market* (or *Euromarket*). **Eurocurrencies** are national currencies traded and deposited in banks outside the home country. As the name connotes, Eurocurrencies originally developed in Europe, with London the most important location. However, Eurocurrency activity gravitates toward areas with less regulation, and in recent years it has expanded to a number of Asian countries. About two-thirds of the Eurocurrencies are *Eurodollars* held in banks outside the United States. Other currencies often held abroad include pounds sterling, deutsche marks, and French and Swiss francs. The origins of the Eurocurrency market extend back to 1917, when the Communist government in Russia deposited its U.S. dollars in European banks to prevent the United States from seizing them. After World War II, the Soviet Union and Eastern European countries had to deal in dollars as part of their efforts to develop and modernize their economies. However, they preferred to hold their dollars in Europe rather than in the United States because of concerns that the Americans would freeze their holdings in the event of Cold War hostilities.

The Eurocurrency market as we know it developed in the 1960s when President Lyndon Johnson responded to the U.S. balance-of-payments deficits by imposing restrictions on foreign lending by American banks. To avoid these restrictions, U.S. companies began to finance their foreign operations from offshore banks, which were not subject to U.S. banking legislation. The Eurodollar market also grew because European banks involved with foreign transactions found it easier to use U.S. dollars than to constantly exchange their currencies. The main appeal of Eurodollars to depositors is that they are not subject to domestic government regulations. For example, the U.S. Federal Reserve requires banks to hold a certain percentage of their deposits as reserves, but the United States does not have this control over Eurodollar deposits. U.S. banks are not permitted to pay interest on deposits held less than 30 days, but European banks can pay interest on very short-term deposits.[37]

Liberal interdependence theorists point to the role that private actors such as international bankers played in the expansion of the Euromarket, and they view this as a natural development reflecting the increase in capital mobility, and global lending and borrowing. Some realists note that the leading states also contributed to the growth of the Euromarket because of perceived advantages it offered to them. For example, the British government allowed the Euromarket to operate without regulation in efforts to promote London as a leading financial center, and the American government permitted U.S. bankers to retain their dominant position in international finance by avoiding the U.S. capital control program and moving their international dollar business to London. In view of the declining confidence in its currency, the U.S. government also felt that the Euromarket would enhance the appeal of U.S. dollars to foreigners.[38]

Nevertheless, realists warn that the central role the British and American governments played in supporting the expansion of the Euromarket could have some unintended consequences: "It may prove to have been the most important single development of the century undermining national monetary sovereignty."[39] Persistent U.S. balance-of-payments deficits, combined with the growth of the Eurodollar market in the 1960s, posed questions about the United States' ability to manage international monetary relations, and this in turn contributed to a shift toward multilateralism.

A Shift toward Multilateralism

As U.S. balance-of-payments deficits continued to increase, the dollar slipped from top-currency to negotiated-currency status in the 1960s. A *top currency* is favored for international monetary transactions because others have confidence in the strong economic position of the issuing state. A *negotiated currency* does not benefit from this high degree of confidence, and the issuing state must offer inducements so that others will continue to accept its leadership.[40] A negotiated-currency state must also be open to multilateral management, and this was in fact the response to the U.S. problems. In 1962, 10 advanced industrial countries (the G-10) agreed to establish the GAB, in which they would lend the IMF up to $6 billion in their own currencies when there was a need for supplementary resources to cope with international monetary problems. As discussed in Chapter 2, the G-10 actually consists of 11 countries today: the G-7 countries (the United States, Japan, Germany, France, Britain, Italy, and Canada) plus Belgium, the Netherlands, Sweden, and Switzerland. The G-10 had to approve each request for supplementary support; this represented a shift from unilateral U.S. management to more collective management of international monetary issues.[41]

Another indication of the shift from unilateral to multilateral management was the increased role accorded to the *Bank for International Settlements (BIS)* in the 1960s. Located in Basle, Switzerland, the BIS is in fact the oldest of the international financial institutions. Although the BIS was formed in 1930 to help oversee the settlement of German reparations after World War I, its main purpose was to promote cooperation among central banks. The BIS became a controversial institution in the 1930s because of allegations regarding its pro-Nazi sentiments and its acceptance of looted gold from countries occupied by Germany. As a result, the United States wanted to disband the BIS and transfer its functions to the IMF when the Bretton Woods institutions were established, but the European countries would not agree to this proposal. Although the BIS resumed operations after it made the gold available to the countries from which it had been seized, the stigma of the earlier BIS activities "prevented it from being accepted as a dominant international financial institution."[42] Today the BIS is the main forum for cooperation and consultation among central bankers of the advanced industrial states. BIS meetings, which are held 10 times a year, permit the central bankers to freely discuss international monetary conditions and their countries' problems on a confidential basis. Central banks deposit part of their official currency reserves with the BIS, which can use them to deal with exchange rate problems and to provide credit to central banks that lack liquidity. When the U.S. dollar came under downward pressure in the 1960s, the BIS organized mutual lines of credit among the central banks to help stabilize exchange rates and the price of gold. The United States had refused to attend the monthly meetings of the BIS in the 1940s and 1950s, but it began to accept the need for multilateral management of international financial issues in the 1960s and has attended the BIS meetings since that time.[43]

Although Western European countries viewed the establishment of the G-10 and the upgraded role of the BIS as something of a victory, Third World countries were highly dissatisfied with the propensity of the G-10 and BIS to hold discussions about monetary issues outside the framework of the IMF, where the LDCs were represented.[44] The LDCs were not content with pressing their demands for greater participation only within the confines of the IMF, and they responded to the G-10 by setting up their own group in 1972. The **Group of 24 (G-24),** which is composed of eight finance ministers or central bank governors from each of the three main LDC regions (Africa, Asia, and Latin America), regularly reviews international monetary relations and tries to coordinate LDC monetary policies. It also has responded to G-10 reports on international monetary reform by presenting its own "counterreports." The G-24's ideas on monetary issues have received some recognition, but its influence (like the influence of UNCTAD and the G-77) is clearly circumscribed because it consists of the borrowers rather than the lenders in the IMF.[45]

Although the G-10 could jointly supply a substantial amount of financial resources, there were concerns that G-10 resources were not sufficient to defend the dollar if it came under attack. A rush to change dollars into gold became more likely as the U.S. balance-of-payments deficit continued to increase. A series of measures were therefore adopted to bolster the dollar, and the United States sought to improve its balance of payments by reducing capital outflows. In 1965, for example, the United States imposed limits on foreign investments and loans by U.S. firms and banks. Despite these efforts, U.S. gold stocks fell from $22.7 billion in 1950 to $10.7 billion in 1970, while dollar claims against the U.S. gold supply rose from about $5 billion to $70 billion. Thus, by 1968 the dollar had in effect become inconvertible into gold.[46]

Disagreement continues today about the basic causes of the U.S. balance-of-payments deficit. Some observers attribute the U.S. payments deficit to the public goods the United States as the hegemonic state provided to others, such as the Marshall Plan, the U.S. dollar as the key currency, and an open market for other countries' exports. However, critics argue that Americans and their governments have been unwilling to achieve a balance between revenues and expenditures. During the Vietnam War, for example, the U.S. Congress refused to raise taxes to pay for the war effort, and President Lyndon Johnson refused to cut domestic social programs. The United States also has a lower personal savings rate than the other G-5 countries. In 1980, for example, the personal savings ratio as a percentage of disposable income was 19.2 percent for Japan, 12.3 percent for Britain, 11.0 percent for France, 10.9 percent for West Germany, and only 6.0 percent for the United States. The difference in personal savings habits of Japan and the United States results both from cultural factors and from Japanese monetary and fiscal policies such as increasing interest rates on bank deposits. Thus, high-saving Japan has been the source of large-scale capital flows to the low-saving United States in recent years.[47]

Yet another possible reason for the U.S. balance-of-payments problem relates to the decline of U.S. competitiveness after the postwar recovery in Western Europe and Japan. Under the gold exchange standard, the United States was the only country that could not devalue its currency to become more competitive. Thus, the Bretton Woods regime did not provide the United States with sufficient adjustment options to deal with its decreased competitiveness. To confront the problem of declining confidence in the U.S. dollar, proposals were developed in the 1960s to create a new artificial reserve asset. The United States initially opposed this idea because it wanted to maintain the dollar's reserve role, but it eventually changed its position to take pressure off the dollar in international money markets.[48] France, however, resented U.S. privileges as the top-currency state, and it wanted the United States to deal with its balance-of-payments problems before a new reserve was created. After several years of negotiation, IMF members finally agreed in 1969 to create a new international reserve termed special drawing rights.[49]

Special drawing rights (SDRs) are artificial international reserves, created and managed by the IMF with the approval of the G-10, which may be used only by monetary authorities and other official agencies. Decisions to allocate SDRs require an 85 percent majority of the IMF board of governors, because the EC insisted that it should have a veto over SDR creation. This European veto power represented a marked decline in U.S. financial power.[50] All IMF members are allocated SDRs in proportion to their quotas, so that those with the highest quotas (the G-5 countries) receive the most SDRs. The first distribution of SDRs was an allocation of $9.5 billion over three years beginning in 1970, and a second allocation of $12 billion occurred in the 1977–81 period. In September 1997 the IMF board of governors adopted a resolution proposing an amendment to the Articles of Agreement, which would provide for a third allocation of SDRs. However, creating new SDRs has been a contentious issue, and by mid-2001 the amendment had still not been ratified by the required three-fifths of the IMF members having 85 percent of the total voting power.[51] At first, 35 SDRs were equal to $35 (U.S.) or to an ounce of gold, but from 1974 to 1980, after the move to floating currencies, the SDR value was determined by a *basket*, or weighted average of 16 currencies. In 1981, the basket was changed to a weighted average of the G-5 currencies. With the introduction of the euro, the basket was changed again in 2001 to a weighted average of only four currencies: the U.S. dollar, the euro, the Japanese yen, and the British pound sterling.[52]

Because movements in the exchange rates of the G-5 countries' currencies tend to offset one another (that is, some currencies rise while others drop in value), the value of the SDR is more stable than that of any single currency in the basket. This stability makes the SDR attractive as a unit of account to the IMF and other international and regional organizations. The SDR, however, has *not* met the original expectations IMF members had for it as a reserve asset. At its 1976 annual meeting, the IMF had set itself the objective of establishing the SDR as the principal reserve asset in the international monetary regime, and this decision was formalized in 1978 in the second amendment to the IMF's Articles of Agreement. Nevertheless, SDR holdings have steadily *declined* as a share of global foreign exchange reserves, from 6 percent in 1970, to 4.25 percent in 1987, and to 1.75 percent in 1998.[53] There are a number of reasons why the plans to develop the SDR as important international reserve were not realized. Although SDRs may have provided a possible solution to lack of confidence in the U.S. dollar during a period of pegged exchange rates, they seem far less necessary in today's world of flexible exchange rates (discussed later) and large private capital markets that lend reserves. Major conflict between industrial states and Third World countries over the issuance of additional SDRs has also limited their role (this issue is discussed later). Furthermore, SDRs can serve as a unit of account, but not as a medium of exchange. Finally, in a world of nation-states, a truly international reserve unconnected with an economically powerful state, or group of states such as the EU, may simply be ahead of its time. Indeed, "no money has ever risen to a position of international preeminence that was not initially backed by a leading economy."[54] Thus, despite current efforts to create new SDRs, it is likely that "the SDR will have no significant long-term future as an international reserve asset."[55]

The U.S. balance-of-payments deficit was not the only problem confronting the Bretton Woods system in the 1960s and 1970s. Despite the continuance of national controls on capital flows, investors lacked confidence in the existing exchange rates of currencies, and speculative capital flows increased significantly.[56] Speculative activity in the Euromarket was especially difficult to regulate, and MNCs were able to evade controls through transactions among their affiliates in different countries. Thus, MNCs became adept at moving their capital from one country to another to take advantage of interest rate spreads and expected exchange rate adjustments, and this increased capital mobility put growing pressures on states to realign their currency exchange rates. In efforts to prevent a run on their currencies, leaders often committed themselves to the established parities, severely limiting their policy options. Powerful domestic interest groups also often prevented governments from instituting needed realignment of their currencies. As a result, modest changes in parities were difficult to institute, and the monetary regime became overly rigid despite the need for flexibility.[57]

The Demise of the Bretton Woods Monetary Regime

By the late 1960s, the Bretton Woods monetary regime had become untenable. France's Charles de Gaulle was deliberately converting dollars into gold to bring about an end to the United States' hegemonic privilege as the key currency state, and the United States was increasingly making it awkward for foreign central banks to change their dollars into gold. Although U.S. balance-of-payments deficits extended back to 1950, these deficits had resulted from the huge amount of foreign investment and loans the United States was extending around the world. In 1971, however, the United States had its first balance-of-*trade* deficit since 1893, indicating that its trade competitiveness was seriously declining. President Richard M. Nixon therefore decided to suspend the official convertibility of the dollar into gold on August 15, 1971. This action sent shock waves throughout the world. The Nixon administration also imposed a 10 percent tariff surcharge on all dutiable imports, promising to remove it when other countries such as West Germany and Japan altered their "unfair" exchange rates. At the time of the Nixon shocks, the U.S. share of international reserves had fallen from a postwar level of 50 to 16 percent, and the EC's share had risen from 6.1 to 32.5 percent. In December 1971, the G-10 countries therefore agreed to lower the dollar's value by 10 to 20 percent vis-à-vis other major currencies in the first Smithsonian Agreement (negotiated at the Smithsonian Institute in Washington, D.C.). The U.S. balance-of-payments problem continued, and a second Smithsonian Agreement devaluing the dollar further was negotiated in February 1973.[58]

After announcing the first Smithsonian Agreement, the industrial states decided that monetary reform was urgently needed and that a **Committee of Twenty (C-20)** should be established to decide on the reforms. The industrial states occupied 11 seats in the C-20, and the LDCs (which had been angered by their exclusion from the G-10's Smithsonian Agreement) occupied the other 9 seats. Following two years of discussion, the C-20 reached an agreement for international monetary reform in June 1974. The agreement recommended that the system of stable but adjustable exchange rates be continued and that the SDR become the principal reserve asset, with a reduced role for gold and the U.S. dollar. The C-20 proposals ultimately failed, however, because of differences among the Europeans, the Americans, and the LDCs; destabilizing global changes such as the 1973–74 increases in OPEC oil prices; and the growing preoccupation in Germany and France with establishing a European monetary system. With the failure of the C-20 efforts, it was evident that the Bretton Woods regime of fixed exchange rates would collapse and would be replaced by a regime based on floating rates.[59]

It is impossible to detail all the differences among C-20 members; we refer here to only one conflict over the creation of SDRs to illustrate the difficulties the committee had in reaching a consensus on monetary issues. In the C-20 meetings, the Third World countries proposed that a "link" be established between the creation of new SDRs and the transfer of resources to LDCs for development purposes. If LDCs received most of the new SDRs, they reasoned, this would benefit the Third World while providing an increase in liquidity.[60] When the industrial states had first decided to create SDRs in 1969, they had initially planned to limit the allocation to the G-10 countries, but the IMF managing director insisted that SDRs should be allocated to all IMF members. The decision to distribute SDRs in accordance with IMF quotas was therefore a compromise agreement, and the developed states would not agree to further concessions. Thus, the 11 industrial states on the C-20 argued that the LDCs' link proposal would undermine the monetary integrity of the SDR, because it would blur the necessary division between monetary policy and development assistance. The industrial countries were particularly concerned that LDC needs for development assistance were almost limitless and might lead to the creation of an excessive amount of SDRs from a monetary standpoint. The LDCs tried to allay this fear by agreeing that new SDRs should be created only to satisfy international liquidity requirements and *not* to meet LDC needs. Furthermore, the G-10 and not the LDCs would retain decision-making power over when to create new SDRs. The developed states, however, were unmoved; they decided that any new SDRs should be allocated (as in the past) only according to a country's quota in the IMF.[61] In view of such major differences as the North-South split over SDR allocations, it is not surprising that the C-20 reached no agreement on altering the global monetary regime.

A multitude of problems confronted the Bretton Woods monetary regime by the early 1970s. First, although the U.S. role as the top-currency state was premised on the idea that it was an unrivaled economic hegemon, this no longer seemed to be the case. Second, as capital flows around the world increased, the Bretton Woods system of pegged exchange rates became increasingly untenable. And third, the three characteristics of reserves—liquidity, confidence, and adjustment—all presented serious problems. Thus, countries were reluctant to hold large supplies of U.S. dollars for liquidity purposes; the persistent U.S. balance-of-payments deficit contributed to a crisis of confidence in the dollar; and the dollar could not be adjusted through devaluation, even when the United States became less competitive. The Bretton Woods regime collapsed when the C-20 could not agree on a viable plan for saving it.

THE REGIME OF FLOATING (OR FLEXIBLE) EXCHANGE RATES

The Bretton Woods agreement had outlawed freely floating exchange rates, so all the major trading nations were "living in sin" by 1973.[62] The IMF meeting in Jamaica in January 1976 finally legalized the existing situation by permitting each government to decide whether to establish a par value for its currency or to shift to floating rates. In a *free-floating* regime, member countries do not intervene in currency markets, and the market alone determines currency valuations. IMF members have in fact relied extensively on *managed floating* in recent years, in which central banks intervene to deal with disruptive conditions such as excessive fluctuations in exchange rates. Although managed floating is considered to be legitimate, the IMF calls on central banks to avoid *dirty floating*, or "manipulating exchange rates . . . in order to prevent effective balance of payments adjustment or to gain an unfair competitive advantage."[63] Today the monetary regime is "mixed" in nature: Major industrial countries such as the United States, Japan, and Canada (and a number of LDCs) independently float their currencies; the EU countries seek increased regional coordination of their policies; and many Third World countries peg the value of their currencies to a key currency or basket of currencies. It is not surprising that some observers refer to the current system of monetary relations as a "nonsystem."[64]

Liberal economists were generally supportive of the move to floating rates, for a variety of reasons. First, a system of flexible rates had intellectual appeal for many liberals because adjustment of international exchange rates would depend on market pressures rather than government involvement. Thus, as early as 1953 the orthodox liberal economist Milton Friedman wrote a classic article strongly favoring the establishment of "a system of exchange rates freely determined in open markets, primarily by private transactions, and the simultaneous abandonment of direct controls over exchange transactions."[65] Although some liberals feared that floating rates could lead to instability because of speculative capital flows, as had occurred in the 1930s, Friedman argued that the instability in the 1930s had resulted more from fundamental economic and financial problems than from the floating of currencies. By the 1970s, there were additional reasons for liberal economists to favor a shift to floating rates. Liberals argued that with the marked increase in capital flows and speculative pressures, governments could no longer defend fixed exchange rates for currencies and that floating rates would contribute to rapid adjustments of international payments imbalances in response to market pressures.[66]

The results of the change to floating exchange rates, however, have not been as positive as expected. Most economists in the early 1970s underestimated the extent to which capital mobility would increase and thus disrupt exchange rates. Partly as a response to the return of orthodox liberalism, the United States and Britain rejected the postwar imposition of national controls on capital flows under Bretton Woods, shifting to policies of allowing capital to move more freely. Countries were competing for the inflow of foreign investment in the 1980s, and others followed the U.S. and British example. Thus, the United States and Britain removed their capital controls in the 1970s; Australia, New Zealand, Japan, and members of the EC removed most of their capital controls in the 1980s. The removal of capital controls, combined with technological advances in such areas as telecommunications, contributed to a massive growth in speculative capital flows, which had far-reaching effects on the world's financial markets.[67] In the face of these changes, two problems developed with the floating exchange rate regime: volatility and misalignment of exchange rates. *Volatility* refers to short-term instability in the exchange rate, and *misalignment* refers to the long-term departure of an exchange rate from its competitive level.[68]

The Bretton Woods pegged rate regime had limited the variability in exchange rates, but exchange rates are much more volatile under the floating system. Highly volatile exchange rates can create uncertainty, inhibit productive investments, and possibly interfere with international trade. Misalignment, however, is a more serious problem than volatility: misalignment can lead to prolonged changes in international competitiveness. Although some economists believed that misalignments would be eliminated with floating currencies, this has not been the case. Indeed, exchange rate misalignment under the floating regime has been as high as 20 to 30 percent for both the U.S. dollar and the Japanese yen.[69] Depending on whether a currency is under- or overvalued, misalignment can give a country substantial price advantages or disadvantages vis-à-vis its competitors.

When the industrial states abandoned the Bretton Woods regime, the IMF's original role in stabilizing the pegged exchange rates largely disappeared, and the IMF faced a crisis of purpose. The industrial states often held policy discussions regarding problems with the floating regime in the G-5 and G-7, outside IMF auspices. At the G-7 summits, member governments engaged in a limited degree of policy coordination to stabilize monetary relations. For example, at the 1978 Bonn Summit, the United States agreed to adopt policies to deal with its balance-of-payments deficits, and Germany and Japan agreed to adopt expansionary economic policies that would increase their demand for American goods.[70] This limited degree of policy coordination ended, however, with the Reagan administration in January 1981. When Ronald Reagan became president, he lowered taxes and raised spending for military-defense purposes. These policies contributed to a huge U.S. government deficit, which exceeded $200 billion annually by the mid-1980s. The United States required foreign investment to service its debt, so it raised interest rates to attract foreign capital. However, the increase in capital imports simply strengthened the U.S. dollar, and the American balance-of-trade and payments deficits began to spiral out of control.

The Plaza-Louvre Accords

With the U.S. dollar continuing to appreciate in value and U.S. deficits climbing, the United States became far more concerned with foreign exchange rates. In efforts to lower the value of the dollar, Secretary of the Treasury James Baker III assembled the finance ministers and central bank heads of the G-5 in New York City's Plaza Hotel in

September 1985. Here the G-5 agreed on joint intervention to raise the value of the major nondollar currencies through coordinated market intervention (that is, the buying and selling of currencies), and the United States in return promised to reduce government spending. The dollar depreciated significantly after the Plaza Agreement, so the G-5 met at the Louvre in Paris in February 1987 to prevent the dollar's value from slipping even further. The major countries involved at this point were the *Group of Three*—the United States, Japan, and Germany.[71]

The Plaza and Louvre accords marked a shift to managed floating, in which the major governments intervened to correct serious volatility and misalignment of currency rates. However, the major economies have not coordinated their interventions on a consistent basis since the Louvre accord. Although policy coordination is important for the maintenance of international currency stability today, it is difficult to achieve because of the high degree of mobility of international capital flows.[72] The unwillingness of governments to accept constraints on adopting fiscal and monetary policies as they see fit also limits the degree to which policy coordination is likely to occur. Thus, the floating monetary regime is far more unstable today than liberal economists had predicted, and it is uncertain that the major industrial states will coordinate their policies sufficiently to prevent future misalignment of currency rates.

ALTERNATIVES TO THE CURRENT MONETARY REGIME

With unstable global monetary relations under the flexible exchange rate regime and the U.S. dollar as the key international currency, there has been considerable discussion about the need for monetary reform. Two interrelated questions about alternatives to the current arrangements arise: Are there alternatives to the flexible exchange rate regime? Are there alternatives to the dominance of the U.S. dollar under the current regime?

Regarding the first question, some economists point to the problems of volatility and misalignment of exchange rates under the floating regime and argue in favor of returning to some sort of pegged or fixed exchange rate regime.[73] However, a more commonly held view is that efforts "to reestablish a system of pegged but adjustable rates will . . . prove futile."[74] With the rise in international financial transactions, it has become increasingly difficult for states to defend pegged exchange rates. The only possible way to enforce capital controls at a tolerable cost today would be through policy coordination among the major states, and such coordination has proved to be unfeasible. Thus, the current global monetary regime is likely to retain its "mixed" characteristics, with industrial countries such as the United States, Japan, and Canada (and some LDCs) independently floating their currencies, and with many LDCs pegging their currencies to a key currency such as the U.S. dollar or to a basket of currencies. The only major alternative to the current flexible exchange rate regime is regional monetary unification, and the most significant example of this today is the EMU.[75] The Western Hemisphere has no formal monetary arrangements comparable with those in Europe, but the supremacy of the U.S. dollar in the hemisphere is not in doubt. When a Latin American country decides to peg its currency, it normally pegs it to the U.S. dollar. The yen's position in the Asia-Pacific region is somewhat less certain. Japan's economic strength and its role as an exporter of goods and capital have contributed to the importance of the yen as an international currency. Unlike in Europe and North America, however, economic integration is not a clearly defined regional objective in East Asia. Furthermore, the Japanese economy has experienced serious economic problems in recent years that have decreased the prospects for the yen as the key currency for the Asia-Pacific region.[76]

Regarding the second question, the German deutsche mark and Japanese yen have been used most widely as international currencies after the U.S. dollar, and the new currency of the EMU, the *euro*, is expected to pose a major challenge to the supremacy of the dollar in the longer term. To this point, however, the dollar continues to be "the most-favored vehicle for currency exchange worldwide, appearing on one side or the other of some 87 percent of all transactions in 1998 . . . the deutsche mark appeared in 30 percent of transactions and the yen in 21 percent."[77] The dollar is also the dominant international currency for invoicing of international trade and for financial claims, including stocks, bonds, bank deposits, and loans.

In the sections that follow we examine monetary relations in the three major regions of Europe, East Asia, and the Western Hemisphere, and the likelihood of competition among the U.S. dollar, the euro, and the Japanese yen as international currencies. (Predictions about the future role of these currencies are discussed in more detail in Chapter 12).

EUROPEAN MONETARY RELATIONS

With the future of global monetary relations uncertain, "the only initiative that might be held out as a serious experiment" in international monetary reform today is taking place in Europe.[78] It is therefore important to examine the European approach to monetary relations. The Treaty of Rome creating the EC in 1957 provided specific details on eliminating trade barriers, but other than describing exchange rate policies as an issue of "common concern," it did not identify monetary integration as one of the treaty's goals. Nevertheless, a number of practitioners and scholars have long considered monetary union in Europe to be worthy of consideration. Since the 1960s, a series of events have given concrete form to the idea of European monetary integration, and in early May 1998, 11 members of the EU formally committed to replacing their national currencies with the euro as a single European currency.[79] The discussion that follows examines the reasons why the EU has established an EMU, the problems and tensions surrounding the formation of the EMU, and the implications of the EMU for European countries and the global monetary regime.

From 1958 to the late 1960s, the Bretton Woods monetary regime provided the EC with a framework for coordinating monetary policies and with some degree of stability under the system of fixed exchange rates. Several major changes in the 1960s, however, caused the EC countries to consider proposals for regional monetary integration more seriously. First, growing U.S. balance-of-payments deficits resulted in decreased confidence in the U.S. dollar and a threat to exchange rate stability. This threat rose dramatically in the 1960s when President Lyndon Johnson continued to pursue the Vietnam War at great expense to the United States and also launched ambitious domestic social programs. Second, rapid European progress in establishing a customs union and the development of the EC's Common Agricultural Policy increased the need for exchange rate stability among EC members.[80]

At their December 1969 summit meeting in The Hague, the original six members of the EC responded to these changes by proposing the establishment of a European monetary union. Pierre Werner, the Luxembourg prime minister, was appointed as chair of a group to develop the details of the proposal. The 1970 Werner Report subsequently recommended the gradual completion of a monetary union by 1980 through a phased approach, including the coordination and convergence of fiscal and monetary policies and the reduction of exchange rate fluctuations between EC countries. The vagueness of the Werner Report on policy details combined with turmoil on currency markets resulting from President Nixon's decision to suspend the convertibility of the dollar into gold in August 1971 interfered with the implementation of the report. One of the few elements of the Werner plan to survive was a "snake in the tunnel" arrangement that limited exchange rates among EC member currencies to a narrow band of +2.25 or –2.25 percent. However, the 1973–74 oil price hike and the 1975 global recession, combined with different inflation rates among EC countries, made it impossible for countries with weaker currencies to adhere to the narrow fluctuation band, and France, Ireland, Italy, and Britain soon left the snake agreement.[81]

By the late 1970s major fluctuations in the value of the U.S. dollar and variability in EC exchange rates made it evident that the "snake" would require major changes if European currencies were to have some degree of stability. A successor to the snake—the *European Monetary System (EMS)*—was therefore launched in March 1979. The EMS had two main features; an *exchange rate mechanism (ERM)* and a *European currency unit (ECU)*. The ERM was a form of adjustable peg system, similar to the original Bretton Woods regime. Participating countries decided on exchange rates for their currencies, setting bands beyond which the rates could not fluctuate (+2.25 to –2.25 percent for most EC countries). When the limits of a band were reached, central banks intervened to keep the exchange rates within the required levels. After consultation with other EMS members, countries could decide to realign their currencies. The second feature, the ECU, was a new currency based on a weighted basket or average of the EMS countries' currencies. Although the ECU served as a common unit of account and was used in cross-border banking activity, it was not generally used for commercial transactions in goods and services.[82]

The EMS experienced a reasonable degree of success, contributing to European habits of cooperation on monetary issues from 1979 to the early 1990s. However, the EMS had some major drawbacks because it was only a partial monetary union. For example, the EMS was subjected to frequent speculative attacks, and EC countries that could not keep their currency exchange rates within the narrow ERM band of +2.25 to –2.25 percent were permitted to move into a broader band of +6 to –6 percent. Some countries' currencies fluctuated within the broader band for most of 1979 to 1993. Britain also joined the EMS late, and some EC countries realigned their currencies more frequently than others. Furthermore, because the EMS depended largely on self-enforced rules, its credibility depended on the policy leadership of the German central bank, which created political tensions with some other EC members.[83]

The EC's economic problems were not limited to monetary issues, and economic recession, declining competitiveness, and continuing barriers to intra-EC trade resulted in major efforts to increase the level of European integration in the 1980s and 1990s. (The European trade issues are discussed in detail in Chapter 9.) In 1986, EC members signed the *Single European Act (SEA)* calling for completion of the internal market, or the removal of all barriers on the movement of goods, people, and capital within the EC by January 1, 1993. The SEA included a commitment to EMU, and in June 1988 the European Council decided to establish a committee to propose concrete steps toward this goal. The Delors Committee (chaired by Jacques Delors, the president of the European Commission) proposed a three-stage process toward EMU: first, the coordination of monetary policies; second, the realignment of exchange rates of currencies; and third, the creation of a single currency under a new central bank's authority. Subsequently, negotiations resulted in the *Treaty on European Union* or *Maastricht Treaty* in December 1991, an agreement to establish an EMU in 1999. The EMU was to include the creation of a central bank and a single currency, central control over the money supply, and wide-ranging influence over national tax and financial policies.[84]

When EU member states signed the Maastricht Treaty, many economists predicted that monetary integration would progress smoothly.[85] However, the steps toward monetary union have been difficult for a number of reasons. A major obstacle stemmed from the fact that the Maastricht agreement had rather rigid requirements for developing a single currency. These requirements were included mainly at the insistence of Germany. To join the EMU, countries were to have (or be showing substantial progress toward) budget deficits that did not exceed 3 percent of their GDPs, public debt that was no greater than 60 percent of their GDPs, and relatively low inflation rates. Only some of the EU countries were likely to meet these targets, and the required cuts in domestic welfare and social expenditures caused considerable discontent. For example, in December 1995 French workers staged massive strikes in Paris to protest planned cutbacks in social security programs.

Another related problem was that many Germans were fearful of sacrificing the deutsche mark, which reflected the country's economic strength, for what could be a much weaker euro. Germany accounts for about 25 percent of the EU's total economic output, and the deutsche mark has been the second largest currency (after the U.S. dollar) held in official reserves of countries throughout the world. As a result, there was considerable concern among Germans that weaker countries such as Italy could detract from the strength of the euro. Nevertheless, Chancellor Helmut Kohl of Germany strongly supported the EMU and staked his reputation on monetary integration. Although many Germans were fearful of the euro, other countries had different concerns. Thus, Britain, Denmark, and Sweden did not seek membership in the EMU in the "first wave" for political as well as economic reasons. In Britain in particular, the issue of preserving national sovereignty is extremely sensitive, and the fact that the new European central bank (ECB) was to be located in Frankfurt, Germany, delighted neither the British nor the French.

Despite the obstacles to implementing the goals of the Maastricht Treaty, the European commitment to monetary union remained very much alive. Thus, in January

1999, 11 members of the EU formed an EMU, and moved to adopt a new currency—"the euro"—in place of their national currencies. The 11 founding members of the EMU were Austria, Belgium, Finland, France, Germany, Ireland, Italy, Luxembourg, the Netherlands, Portugal, and Spain. Only 4 EU members did not participate in the agreement: Britain, Sweden, and Denmark chose not to join initially, and Greece was too weak economically. However, in January 2001 Greece was admitted to the EMU. Under the EMU, the euro was to be introduced in wholesale financial markets first, and at the retail-consumer level several years later. Although the euro became the legal currency of the EMU as of January 1, 1999, EMU members countries would not be required to withdraw all national currencies until June 30, 2002.[86]

Since the EMU was formed, intense debates have continued over the benefits and costs of a common currency in Europe, and over the possible future role of the euro as an international currency. Benefits of a monetary union include reduced exchange rate volatility and uncertainty, lower transaction costs, greater price transparency, and a better functioning internal market. The costs of a monetary union result mainly from the loss of the exchange rate as an available policy instrument; that is, a country in the monetary union can no longer pursue independent monetary policies by altering the exchange rate of its own currency vis-à-vis other currencies.[87]

A good deal of the economic debate on costs versus benefits has been framed by the work of Nobel laureate Robert Mundell many years earlier. In a 1961 article entitled "A Theory of Optimum Currency Areas," Mundell had posed a question that seemed radical at the time: When is it advantageous for regions to relinquish their monetary sovereignty in favor of a common currency?[88] An *optimum currency area* is an area that maximizes the benefits minus the costs of using a common currency. Regions that are optimum currency areas have certain characteristics; for example, they are subject to common economic shocks, have a high degree of labor mobility, and have a tax-transfer system that transfers resources from economically strong to weak areas. The policy implications of Mundell's optimum currency area framework have been controversial, with economists differing on the policy implications for regions such as Europe. Nevertheless, the framework is highly influential because it has been used ever since Mundell propounded it "to analyze the choice of currency regimes."[89] Mundell himself has been a strong supporter of a European common currency and he has been called the "Father of the Euro."[90] Although optimum currency area studies provide a framework for the economic debate on costs and benefits of monetary integration, it is important to note that political factors such as the existence of a regional hegemon and a regional sense of community also play a major role in determining whether countries will join in a monetary union. Indeed, one noted monetary specialist argues that "political conditions are most instrumental in determining the sustainability of monetary cooperation among sovereign governments."[91]

As for the issue of the euro as an international currency, the important questions are how soon will the euro emerge as a rival for the U.S. dollar, and how great a rival will it be? Despite the early decline in the value of the euro relative to the U.S. dollar, "euro-enthusiasts" argue that the euro will soon emerge as a strong and stable currency that will challenge the dollar's dominant position. The euro area is one of the largest economies in the world, accounting for about 15 percent of world GNP, and the euro area's share of world exports is almost 16 percent, which is well above the

U.S. and Japanese shares. Investors will therefore want to diversify their portfolios from dollars into euros, and "in the long term, the emergence of a European pole may lead to the creation of a new international monetary architecture."[92] "Euro-skeptics," on the other hand, believe that risk-averse investors may be reluctant to substantially increase their euro holdings for a number of reasons. For example, Europe's financial markets are fragmented, and other than the city of London, they do not pose a major challenge to U.S. financial markets in terms of size, openness, and operational efficiency. It will be a long time before the European financial markets benefit from the EMU through economies of scale and lowering of costs.[93] In Chapter 12 we discuss the future prospects of the euro vis-à-vis the U.S. dollar as part of a general discussion of hegemony.

THE ROLE OF THE JAPANESE YEN

In contrast to Europe, formal currency links are lacking in East Asia. For a number of years, however, some analysts have predicted that a powerful "yen bloc" will emerge in East Asia because of Japan's position as the world's top international creditor, the second largest national economy, and a major exporter. There were in fact a number of indications of the yen's increasing influence as Japan experienced a period of rapid economic expansion in the 1980s. For example, the yen's share of the Eurobond market grew from about 5 percent in 1980 to 13 percent in 1993. Although the yen accounted for only 9 percent of global foreign exchange reserves, its share of reserves in Indonesia, the Philippines, Singapore, and Taiwan was at least 30 percent. Nevertheless, no country pegged its exchange rate specifically to the yen, and in East Asia most countries maintained currency links with the U.S. dollar (often with a basket of currencies in which the U.S. dollar carried the most weight). Furthermore, the use of the yen as a medium for trade and investment continued to be limited. Japan's traditional lack of openness in trade and finance produced economic obstacles to the development of the yen as a major reserve for both regional and global trade and financial transactions. There were also political obstacles to overcome, because Asian countries with harsh memories of Japanese occupation during World War II were reluctant to give Japan a more prominent role in the region than it already had.[94]

Two interrelated changes in the 1990s resulted in a divergence of views regarding prospects for the development of a yen bloc. First, there was a rather abrupt halt to Japan's rapid economic growth largely as a result of problems with its domestic laws, customs, and institutions such as its fragile banking system. Since Japan's economic turnaround, it has experienced a lengthy period of economic stagnation. Second, in July 1997 a financial crisis began in Thailand and then spread to much of Southeast and East Asia. Foreign investors lost confidence in the currencies of these countries, and eventually the crisis spread to Japan. The baht currency in Thailand, where the financial crisis began, was pegged to a basket of currencies with the U.S. dollar having the dominant weight, and some analysts argued that the crisis "illustrated that the traditional exchange rate policy of pegging to the U.S. dollar can be incompatible with macroeconomic stability in the Asian countries."[95] Instead, they recommended that the East Asian countries peg their currencies more closely to the Japanese yen. (The East Asian financial crisis is discussed in detail in Chapter 11.)

Despite the view of some commentators that the possibility of forming a yen bloc should be "revisited," the reality is that the use of the yen internationally has *declined* since the mid-1990s in response to Japan's declining economic fortunes. The decrease in the yen's use has been most evident regionally in other Asian countries, where Japanese investment and bank loans have fallen dramatically. Although some analysts believe the yen's standing as an international currency could recover in the future, others believe the gradual decline of the yen's position is likely to continue. Japan has taken actions designed partly to revive the prospects for a yen bloc. Most prominently, in September 1997 the Japanese government proposed that an Asian Monetary Fund (AMF) be formed to provide emergency balance-of-payments support for the economies affected by the East Asian financial crisis. The United States strongly opposed the formation of the AMF on the basis that it would pose a threat to the effectiveness of the IMF, but U.S. Treasury officials were in fact "even more concerned about a possible threat to the dollar in the region."[96]

Although the U.S. blocked the formation of the AMF, the idea of such a fund continues to be discussed. If the AMF is ever established, it is likely that it will develop not from a Japanese government initiative, but as a result of "the increasing preference for the yen over the dollar by Asian governments and their economic agents, based on their own cost-and-benefit calculations."[97] The prospects for the yen in the future will depend on whether Japan can reform its banking sector and its domestic economic laws and institutions, and can shift to more open, liberal policies in international trade and finance. Although Japan has instituted some policies to liberalize its financial sector, these changes are far from complete. To further reform its economy and society, Japan will have to confront the vested interests of a number of powerful domestic private and public actors.[98]

THE ROLE OF THE U.S. DOLLAR

As we have discussed, the U.S. dollar continues to serve as the top, albeit negotiated, international currency. The formation of the EMU has also contributed to considerable discussion of the issue of *dollarization,* or the likelihood that a country will replace its own currency with the currency of another country—usually within the same region. (The terminology is somewhat misleading, because the currency adopted may be not only the U.S. dollar but also the euro, the yen, or some other currency.) For example, Ecuador and El Salvador recently adopted the U.S. dollar as legal tender. The dollarization issue has become a matter of considerable debate in Latin America, and even in Canada some liberal economists have argued that the government should adopt the U.S. dollar as legal tender. In Eastern and Central Europe and the Mediterranean, a number of countries hoping to eventually join the EU are similarly considering adopting the euro. It is important to note, however, that dollarization is a highly asymmetrical process. Unlike the EMU, in which *all* members sacrificed their own currency for a new common currency with collective managment of monetary policy, in dollarization one country relinquishes its own currency and control over monetary policy to another country (e.g., the United States) or a group of countries (eg., the EMU). For example, when a Latin American country adopts the U.S. dollar as legal tender, the U.S. "Federal Reserve has no responsibilities toward that country whatsoever."[99] As realists would point out, this is still an era of mainly "national currencies and national identities."[100] Even in the case of the EMU, Britain did not join as a founding member partly because of nationalist concerns that Germany would dominate the union by virtue of its larger economy. Thus, the much more asymmetrical process of dollarization is likely to be a highly contentious issue.[101]

CONCLUSION

At the end of World War II, the Bretton Woods negotiators opted for a monetary regime based on Keynes's ideas of interventionist liberalism, in which exchange rates were pegged to the U.S. dollar and gold, and the IMF provided short-term loans for balance-of-payments problems. To maintain exchange rate stability, the negotiators agreed that IMF member states should be able to impose controls on capital flows. However, persistent U.S. balance-of-payments problems, combined with pressures for a return to orthodox liberalism, contributed to a shift from pegged to floating exchange rates in 1973 and to a gradual freeing of capital controls throughout the 1970s and 1980s.

Liberal interdependence theorists believe that advances in technology and communications have made these changes irrevocable and that to return to the pegged rates of Bretton Woods in "today's world of globalizing capital markets, capital controls would have to be fierce."[102] In 1973, only $10 to $20 billion of currency was traded on world markets each day, and in 1983, the figure was still a modest $60 billion per day. Since 1983, however, trading of currencies has increased 20-fold, aided by new financial instruments and advanced-technology computers and telecommunications. Central bank reserves, by contrast, have grown far more slowly. Thus, the ability of central banks to cope with currency traders has greatly decreased.[103] In the view of orthodox liberals, the shift to floating currencies and to a freeing of capital flows is a positive development enabling markets to function more freely, with little interference from the state.

Historical structuralists, by contrast, view the increased mobility of capital as a highly negative development because the fear of capital outflows can force governments to adopt policies that adversely affect the poorest and weakest in society. If governments do not adopt "capital-friendly" policies, MNCs and international banks today can readily shift their funds to more welcoming locations. Thus, governments are inclined to lower their tax rates on corporate income even if this means a sacrifice in social programs.[104] The mobility of capital flows, according to historical structuralists, also increases the vulnerability of the working class. Unlike capital, labor is still largely immobile between countries, and countries with weaker labor unions will often draw investment away from countries where labor unions are stronger and more independent.[105]

Many realists, by contrast, argue that the degree to which globalization has occurred in monetary and financial relations is greatly exaggerated. Indeed, they often present evidence to show that there was more openness to capital flows before World War I than there is today.[106] To the extent that global financial flows have increased in recent years, realists believe that this has occurred with the permission and sometimes the encouragement of the most powerful states, and that these states continue to dictate the terms for such transactions. Some writers take a position that combines realism with liberalism, arguing that powerful states initially adopted policies that contributed to the globalization of finance but that this globalization "has had unintended consequences for those who promoted it."[107] Thus, it may no longer be possible for states to regain control over the global market forces they unleashed. Realists also argue that states have a more important role in the current regime of floating exchange rates than many liberals would lead us to believe. Indeed, the Plaza and Louvre accords show that the industrial states can manage exchange rates by intervening collectively in the market when they so choose. When this does not occur, it is because the most powerful states cannot agree on the need for, or type of, intervention, not because exchange rates are uncontrollable.

Realists also remind us that this is primarily a world of *national* currencies, in which the U.S. dollar continues to be the top—albeit negotiated—currency. Efforts to increase the role of SDRs as an alternative to the dollar have been largely unsuccessful, and in 1998 SDRs accounted for only 1.75 percent of global foreign exchange reserves. The dollar continues to account for more than 60 percent of reserves and more than half of global private financial wealth, and about 67 percent of world trade and 75 percent of international bank lending is invoiced in U.S. dollars.

Despite the dollar's continued importance, confidence in the U.S. currency is problematic because of general U.S. economic decline. For example, the United States now accounts for only 20 percent of global output and 14 percent of global exports, and the United States is now the world's largest debtor, even though countries with the world's key currencies have traditionally been international creditors.[108] There are also indications of U.S. hegemonic decline in global monetary relations. For example, the United States' percentage of votes in the IMF decision-making bodies has steadily fallen from about 40 percent in the 1940s to 17.16 percent in 2001, and collective leadership has replaced unilateral U.S. leadership in some important areas of monetary and financial policy.

With the relative decline in U.S. economic hegemony, the possibility has arisen that countries wishing to insulate themselves from the instabilities in the current global monetary regime of flexible exchange rates might seek regional alternatives. Of particular importance in this regard was the decision of a number of EU countries to form the EMU and replace their own currencies with a new regional currency—the euro. There is a difference of views as to how much of a challenge the euro will pose to the U.S. dollar as the key international currency, and as to how long it will take the EMU to establish the euro as a viable alternative to the dollar. Nevertheless, the creation of the euro has clearly shifted the "playing field" away from the realist world of exclusively national currencies. A number of analysts are looking not only to Europe but also to Asia and the Americas as possible future regional currency blocs. In this context, "dollarization" is a widely discussed issue today, but it is highly contentious, as realists point out, because it is an asymmetric process that could threaten national sovereignty.

Despite the relative decline of U.S. economic hegemony, it is important to note that Japan and Germany do not have economies as large as that of the United States and do not have financial markets with the same degree of depth and liquidity. Thus, it is likely the U.S. dollar will continue to be the top currency in at least the short- to medium-term future. Although realists and liberals are concerned with the status of U.S. hegemony in the international monetary regime, many historical structuralists believe this question will have little significance for LDCs in the periphery of the global economy. The rich Northern states have dominated the South in global monetary relations, from this perspective, and they will continue to do so even if U.S. hegemony declines.

NOTES

1. Susan Strange, "Protectionism and World Politics," *International Organization* 39-2 (Spring 1985), p. 257.
2. Benjamin J. Cohen, "Life at the Top: International Currencies in the Twenty-First Century," *Essays in International Economics,* no. 221 (Princeton, NJ: Princeton University, International Economics Section, December 2000), pp. 2–4; Eric Helleiner, *States and the Reemergence of Global Finance: From Bretton Woods to the 1990s* (Ithaca, NY: Cornell University Press, 1994), p. 1; Joseph S. Nye, Jr., "Soft Power," *Foreign Policy* 80 (Fall 1990), pp. 153–171.
3. Susan Strange, *Casino Capitalism* (Oxford: Basil Blackwell, 1986), p. 29.
4. Benjamin J. Cohen, "Introduction," in Benjamin J. Cohen, ed., *The International Political Economy of Monetary Relations* (Aldershot, UK: Elgar, 1993), pp. xi–xiv.
5. Richard G. Lipsey, Douglas D. Purvis, and Peter O. Steiner, *Economics,* 5th ed. (New York: Harper & Row, 1985), pp. 765–772; Benjamin J. Cohen, *Organizing the World's Money: The Political Economy of International Monetary Relations* (New York: Basic Books, 1977), pp. 20–24.
6. David Calleo and Susan Strange, "Money and World Politics," in Susan Strange, ed., *Paths to International Political Economy* (London: Allen & Unwin, 1984), p. 97.
7. This section on adjustment and financing relies partly on Mordechai E. Kreinin, *International Economics: A Policy Approach,* 6th ed. (San Diego, CA: Harcourt Brace Jovanovich, 1991), pp. 123–124; and Richard N. Cooper, *The Economics of Interdependence: Economic Policy in the Atlantic Community* (New York: McGraw-Hill, 1968), pp. 13–23, chs. 7–9.
8. Ernest H. Preeg, *The Trade Deficit, the Dollar, and the U.S. National Interest* (Indianapolis, IN: Hudson Institute, 2000), p. 1; Joseph Quinlan and Marc Chandler, "The U.S. Trade Deficit: A Dangerous Obsession," *Foreign Affairs* (May/June 2001), p. 87.
9. Quinlan and Chandler, "The U.S. Trade Deficit: A Dangerous Obsession," p. 97.
10. Quinlan and Chandler, "The U.S. Trade Deficit: A Dangerous Obsession," p. 88.
11. International Monetary Fund, *Balance of Payments Statistics Yearbook,* (Washington, DC: IMF, 1993), vol. 44, pt. 1, p. 118. It is important to note that changes in government policy resulted in a substantial decrease in Canada's foreign debt by 2000. See Bruce Little, "Debt Cut Puts Canada in Best Financial Shape in Half a Century," *Toronto Globe and Mail,* March 28, 2001, p. B1.
12. International Monetary Fund, *Balance of Payments Statistics Yearbook,* (Washington, DC: IMF, 2000), vol. 51, pt. 1, p. 917.

13. Preeg, *The Trade Deficit, the Dollar, and the U.S. National Interest*, p. 8. The Preeg book contains a detailed discussion of these issues.

14. Cooper, *The Economics of Interdependence*, p. 22.

15. See Kenneth W. Dam, *The Rules of the Game: Reform and Evolution in the International Monetary System* (Chicago: University of Chicago Press, 1982), p. 6; and Cohen, *Organizing the World's Money*, ch. 3.

16. Barry Eichengreen argues that cooperation among the major powers, and the willingness of these powers to undergo domestic adjustments when necessary, were more important than British hegemony in maintaining the pre–World War I gold standard. See Barry Eichengreen, *Golden Fetters: The Gold Standard and the Great Depression, 1919–1939* (New York: Oxford University Press, 1992), ch. 2.

17. John Gerard Ruggie, "International Regimes, Transactions, and Change: Embedded Liberalism in the Postwar Economic Order," in Stephen D. Krasner, ed., *International Regimes* (Ithaca, NY: Cornell University Press, 1983), pp. 204–207; Ronald I. McKinnon, "The Rules of the Game: International Money in Historical Perspective," *Journal of Economic Literature* 31-1 (March 1993), pp. 3–11.

18. Paul R. Krugman and Maurice Obstfeld, *International Economics: Theory and Policy*, 3rd ed. (New York: HarperCollins, 1994), p. 507.

19. Charles P. Kindleberger, *The World in Depression 1929–1939*, rev. and enl. ed. (Berkeley, CA: University of California Press, 1986), pp. 46–49.

20. Peter Alexis Gourevitch, "Squaring the Circle: The Domestic Sources of International Cooperation," *International Organization* 50-2 (Spring 1996), pp. 349–373. Two books that argue convincingly that domestic factors played a major role in the breakdown of monetary stability in the interwar period are Eichengreen, *Golden Fetters;* and Beth A. Simmons, *Who Adjusts? Domestic Sources of Foreign Economic Policy During the Interwar Years* (Princeton, NJ: Princeton University Press, 1994).

21. John Gerard Ruggie calls this the "embedded liberal compromise." See Ruggie, "International Regimes, Transactions, and Change," pp. 209–214.

22. Dam, *The Rules of the Game*, p. 38; Edward M. Bernstein, "The Search for Exchange Stability: Before and After Bretton Woods," in Omar F. Hamouda, Robin Rowley, and Bernard M. Wolf, eds., *The Future of the International Monetary System: Change, Coordination or Instability?* (Aldershot, UK: Elgar, 1989), p. 29.

23. Eric Helleiner, "From Bretton Woods to Global Finance: A World Turned Upside Down," in Richard Stubbs and Geoffrey R. D. Underhill, eds., *Political Economy and the Changing Global Order* (Toronto: McClelland & Stewart, 1994), p. 164; J. Keith Horsefield, ed., *The International Monetary Fund 1945–1965: Twenty Years of International Monetary Cooperation, Vol. 3: Documents* (Washington, DC: IMF, 1969), p. 67.

24. *Articles of Agreement of the International Monetary Fund*, adopted July 22, 1944 (Washington, DC: IMF, April 1993).

25. See Sidney Dell, "On Being Grandmotherly: The Evolution of IMF Conditionality," *Essays in International Finance*, no. 144 (Princeton, NJ: Princeton University, October 1981); and "Conditionality: Ensuring Effective Use of Revolving Resources," *IMF Survey—Supplement on the IMF*, 24 (September 1995), p. 9.

26. *Annual Report of the International Monetary Fund—2001* (Washington, DC: IMF, 2001) p. 176.

27. Marc Williams, *International Economic Organisations and the Third World* (New York: Harvester Wheatsheaf, 1994), pp. 67–68; Stephen D. Krasner, *Structural Conflict: The Third World Against Global Liberalism* (Berkeley, CA: University of California Press, 1985), pp. 138–140.

28. See Tyrone Ferguson, *The Third World and Decision Making in the International Monetary Fund: The Quest for Full and Effective Participation* (London: Pinter Publishers, 1988), pp. 90–91.

29. The three problems of liquidity, confidence, and adjustment were first identified by a group of 32 economists. See Fritz Machlup and Burton G. Malkiel, eds., *International Monetary Arrangements: The Problem of Choice: Report on the Deliberations of an International Study Group of 32 Economists* (Princeton, NJ: Princeton University, International Finance Section, 1964), p. 24.

30. Ruggie, "International Regimes," p. 223; Cohen, *Organizing the World's Money*, pp. 94–97.

31. See Dam, *The Rules of the Game*, pp. 64–69.

32. *Articles of Agreement of the IMF*, Article 4, section 1; John Charles Pool, Stephen C. Stamos, and Patrice Franko Jones, *The ABCs of International Finance*, 2nd ed. (Lexington, MA: Heath, 1991), pp. 67–68; Beth V. Yarbrough and Robert M. Yarbrough, *The World Economy: Trade and Finance*, 3rd ed. (Fort Worth, TX: Harcourt Brace, 1994), p. 640.

33. Charles P. Kindleberger, "Dominance and Leadership in the International Economy: Exploitation, Public Goods and Free Rides," *International Studies Quarterly* 25-2 (June 1981), p. 248.

34. Marina V. N. Whitman, "Leadership Without Hegemony," *Foreign Policy* 20 (Fall 1975), p. 140; "Will the Buck Stop Here?" *The Economist*, November 12–18, 1994, p. 88.

35. Robert A. Isaak, *Managing World Economic Change: International Political Economy*, 2nd ed. (Englewood Cliffs, NJ: Prentice-Hall, 1995), pp. 84–85.

36. See Robert Triffin, *Gold and the Dollar Crisis: The Future of Convertibility*, rev. ed. (New Haven, CT: Yale University Press, 1961).

37. Harold James, *International Monetary Cooperation Since Bretton Woods* (Washington, DC, and New York: IMF and Oxford University Press, 1996), pp. 179–181; Stuart Corbridge, *Debt and Development* (Oxford: Blackwell, 1993), pp. 30–31.

38. Helleiner, *States and the Reemergence of Global Finance*, pp. 81–100; Michael C. Webb, *The Political Economy of Policy Coordination: International Adjustment Since 1945* (Ithaca, NY: Cornell University Press, 1995), p. 16.

39. Susan Strange, *Sterling and British Policy: A Political Study of an International Currency in Decline* (London: Oxford University Press, 1971), p. 209.

40. Strange, *Sterling and British Policy*, pp. 5, 17.

41. C. Fred Bergsten and C. Randall Henning, *Global Economic Leadership and the Group of Seven* (Washington, DC: Institute for International Economic, June 1996), pp. 22–23.

42. Hazel J. Johnson, *Global Financial Institutions and Markets* (Oxford: Blackwell, 2000), p. 411.

43. Although the United States attended meetings, it was not until September 1994 that Alan Greenspan, governor of the U.S. Federal Reserve System, occupied the seat that had been reserved for him in the BIS. For a detailed discussion of the BIS, see Age F. P. Bakker, *International Financial Institutions* (New York: Longman, 1996), ch. 6; and Johnson, *Global Financial Institutions and Markets*, pp. 410–411.

44. Keith J. Horsefield, *The International Monetary Fund, 1945–65: Twenty Years of Monetary Cooperation* (Washington, DC: 1969), vol. 1, p. 514.

45. Ngaire Woods, "A Third World Voice within the IMF?" *The Round Table* 314 (April 1990), p. 196. See also C. Randall Henning, "The Group of Twenty-four: Two Decades of Monetary and Financial Co-operation Among Developing Countries," in United Nations Conference on Trade and Development, *International Monetary and Financial Issues for the 1990s—Vol. 1* (New York: United Nations, 1992), pp. 137–154.

46. Barry Eichengreen and Peter B. Kenen, "Managing the World Economy Under the Bretton Woods System: An Overview," in Peter B. Kenen, ed., *Managing the World Economy:*

Fifty Years After Bretton Woods (Washington, DC: Institute for International Economics, September 1994), pp. 26–34.

47. Krugman and Obstfeld, *International Economics,* pp. 311–313; Marin Bronfenbrenner and Yasukichi Yasuba, "Economic Welfare," in Kozo Yamamura and Yasukichi Yasuba, eds., *The Political Economy of Japan: The Domestic Transformation, Vol. 1* (Stanford, CA: Stanford University Press, 1987), p. 100.

48. For a discussion of the reasons for the shift in U.S. Policy, see John S. Odell, *U.S. International Monetary Policy: Markets, Power, and Ideas as Sources of Change* (Princeton, NJ: Princeton University Press, 1982), pp. 79–164.

49. For a discussion of the lengthy negotiations leading to the decision to create SDRs, see Susan Strange, *International Monetary Relations* (London: Oxford University Press, 1976), pp. 229–262.

50. Pierre-Paul Schweitzer, "Political Aspects of Managing the International Monetary System," *International Affairs* 52-2 (April 1976), p. 214; Graham Bird, "The Political Economy of the SDR: The Rise and Fall of an International Reserve Asset," *Global Governance* 4-3 (July 1998), p. 378, fn. 10. Long before the creation of SDRs, Keynes had proposed introducing a new international reserve asset, which he called "bancor." However, this proposal was rejected at the 1944 Bretton Woods conference.

51. For a discussion of the disagreements over a third allocation of SDRs see Bird, "The Political Economy of the SDR," pp. 363–377.

52. "SDR Supplements Existing Reserves and Constitutes IMF's Unit of Account," *IMF Survey Supplement* 29 (September 2000), pp. 26–27; "IMF Determines New Currency Amounts for SDR Valuation Basket," *IMF Survey* 30-1 (January 8, 2001), p. 15.

53. "IMF under the Leadership of Michel Camdessus," *IMF Survey Special Supplement* (February 2000), p. 7.

54. Cohen, "Life at the Top," pp. 5–6.

55. Bird, "The Political Economy of the SDR," p. 374. For competing views on the SDR's future see "Seminar on the Future of the SDR," entire issue of *IMF Survey,* (April 1, 1996).

56. Helleiner, *States and the Reemergence of Global Finance,* p. 102.

57. John Williamson and C. Randall Henning, "Managing the Monetary System," in Kenen, ed., *Managing the World Economy,* p. 89.

58. For a discussion of President Nixon's August 1971 decision and the Smithsonian agreements, see Robert Solomon, *The International Monetary System, 1945–1981,* 2nd ed. (New York: Harper & Row, 1982), pp. 176–234.

59. When the C-20's efforts failed, the Interim Committee of the IMF board of governors was established to carry on its work of monetary reform. For a discussion of the C-20's failed negotiations, see John Williamson, *The Failure of World Monetary Reform, 1971–74* (Sunbury-on-Thames, UK: Nelson, 1977).

60. The idea of linking development assistance to international liquidity creation was not new. Maxwell Stamp is credited with making the first linkage proposal in 1958. See Hon. Maxwell Stamp, "The Fund and the Future," *Lloyds Bank Review* (October 1958), pp. 14–20.

61. Graham Bird, *The International Monetary System and the Less Developed Countries,* 2nd ed. (London: Macmillan, 1982), p. 254. For a discussion of the link debate in the C-20, see Williamson, *The Failure of World Monetary Reform,* pp. 143–147.

62. Cohen, *Organizing the World's Money,* p. 115. Canada was an exception in the Bretton Woods regime, because it had floated its currency from 1950 to 1962. The United States (and the IMF) had agreed to this exception partly because of its "special relationship" with Canada. See A. F. W. Plumptre, *Three Decades of Decision: Canada and the World Monetary System, 1944–75* (Toronto: McClelland and Stewart, 1977).

63. *Articles of Agreement of the IMF,* Article 4, section 1-iii.
64. Yusuke Kashiwagi, "Future of the International Monetary System and the Role of the IMF," in Bretton Woods Commission, *Bretton Woods: Looking to the Future, Background Papers* (Washington, DC: Bretton Woods Committee, July, 1994), p. C-1.
65. See Milton Friedman, "The Case for Flexible Exchange Rates," *Essays in Positive Economics* (Chicago: University of Chicago Press, 1953), p. 203.
66. John Williamson, *The Exchange Rate System,* rev. ed. (Washington, DC: Institute for International Economics, June 1985), p. 9; Michael Devereux and Thomas A. Wilson, "International Co-ordination of Macroeconomic Policies: A Review," *Canadian Public Policy* 15, special issue (February 1989), pp. S22–S23; Kashiwagi, "Future of the International Monetary System and the Role of the IMF," p. C-1.
67. Helleiner, *States and the Reemergence of Global Finance,* pp. 115–116; Gordon G. Thiessen, "Foreign Exchange Markets Viewed from a Macro-Policy Perspective," *Canadian Public Policy* 15, special issue (February 1989), p. S68.
68. Williamson, *The Exchange Rate System,* pp. 9–10.
69. Williamson, *The Exchange Rate System,* p. 39.
70. Devereux and Wilson, "International Co-ordination of Macroeconomic Policies," pp. S23–S24.
71. Williamson and Henning, "Managing the Monetary System," p. 100.
72. For a discussion of the difficulties in bringing about policy coordination, see Webb, *The Political Economy of Policy Coordination.*
73. The Nobel laureate economist Robert Mundell has been controversial as a strong defender of the value of fixed exchange rates and the gold standard as an anchor for price stability.
74. Barry Eichengreen, *International Monetary Arrangements for the 21st Century* (Washington, DC: Brookings Institution, 1994), p. 5.
75. Examples of regional monetary integration in addition to the EMU include the Eastern Caribbean Currency Union and the CFA Franc Zone in Africa. (Benjamin J. Cohen, "Monetary Turbulence: Are National Currencies Becoming Obsolete?," Remarks for a conference on Global Turbulence: Instability in National and International Political Economy, Vancouver, Canada, July 19–20, 2001.)
76. Eichengreen, *International Monetary Arrangements for the 21st Century,* p. 5; Kashiwagi, "Future of the International Monetary System and the Role of the IMF," p. C-3.
77. Cohen, "Life at the Top," pp. 2–3.
78. Barry Eichengreen, "Prerequisites for International Monetary Stability," in Bretton Woods Commission, *Bretton Woods: Looking to the Future,* p. C-50.
79. See "Fanfare for the Euro," *The Economist,* May 2, 1998, pp. 45–46.
80. Michele Fratianni and Jürgen von Hagen, *The European Monetary System and European Monetary Union* (Boulder, CO: Westview Press, 1992), pp. 11–12.
81. David R. Cameron, "Transnational Relations and the Development of European Economic and Monetary Union," in Thomas Risse-Kappen, ed., *Bringing Transnational Relations Back In: Non-State Actors, Domestic Structures and International Institutions* (Cambridge: Cambridge University Press, 1995), pp. 39–41; Andrew Britton and David Mayes, *Achieving Monetary Union in Europe* (London: Sage Publications, 1992), pp. 6–9; A. J. Kondonassis and A. G. Malliaris, "Toward Monetary Union of the European Community: History and Experiences of the European Monetary System," *American Journal of Economics and Sociology* 53-3 (July 1994), pp. 292–294; Helmut Schlesinger, "On the Way to a New Monetary Union: The European Monetary Union," *Federal Reserve Bank of St. Louis Review* 76-3 (May/June 1994), p. 4; Malcolm Levitt and Christopher Lord, *The Political Economy of Monetary Union* (London: Macmillan, 2000), pp. 29–31.

82. A common unit of account was not a new idea in Europe and dated back to the 1950s when the six EC members formed a European Payments Union and used a European unit of account. Paul De Grauwe, *The Economics of Monetary Union,* 2nd rev. ed. (Oxford: Oxford University Press, 1994), pp. 98–102; Levitt and Lord, *The Political Economy of Monetary Union,* pp. 31–35.

83. Levitt and Lord, *The Political Economy of Monetary Union,* pp. 31–42.

84. Sylvester C. W. Eijffinger and Jakob de Haan, *European Monetary and Fiscal Policy* (Oxford: Oxford University Press, 2000), pp. 4–7; Michael H. Abbey and Nicholas Bromfield, "A Practitioner's Guide to the Maastricht Treaty," *Michigan Journal of International Law* 15-4 (Summer 1994), pp. 1329–1357.

85. Brian K. Kruzmann, "Challenges to Monetary Unification in the European Union: Sovereignty Reigning Supreme?" *Denver Journal of International Law and Policy* 23-1 (Fall 1994), p. 158.

86. "Fanfare for the Euro," p. 45.

87. A good discussion comparing the costs and benefits of a monetary union is found in Eijffinger and de Haan, *European Monetary and Fiscal Policy,* pp. 16–26.

88. Robert A. Mundell, "A Theory of Optimum Currency Areas," *American Economic Review* 51-4 (September 1961), pp. 657–665. Other contributors to the theory of optimum currency areas in the 1960s and early 1970s were Ronald I. McKinnon, Peter B. Kenen, and W. Max Corden.

89. James W. Dean, "Robert A. Mundell," in Abu Wahid, ed., *The Frontiers of Economics: Nobel Laureates 1969–99* (Westport, CT: Greenwood Publishing), forthcoming.

90. See Robert A. Mundell, "Uncommon Arguments for Common Currencies," in Harry G. Johnson and Alexander K. Swoboda, eds., *The Economics of Common Currencies* (London: Allen & Unwin, 1973), pp. 114–132; C. Randall Henning and Pier Carlo Padoan, *Transatlantic Perspectives on the Euro* (Washington, DC: Brookings Institution, 2000), pp. 6–12.

91. Benjamin J. Cohen, "Beyond EMU: The Problem of Sustainability," in Barry Eichengreen and Jeffry Frieden, eds., *The Political Economy of European Monetary Unification* (Boulder, CO: Westview Press, 1994), p. 152.

92. A. Bénassy, A. Italianer, and Jean Pisani-Ferry, "The External Implications of the Single Currency," *Économie et Statistique,* special issue (1993), p. 9.

93. Benjamin J. Cohen, *The Geography of Money* (Ithaca, NY: Cornell University Press, 1998), pp. 156–161; Eijffinger and de Haan, *European Monetary and Fiscal Policy,* pp. 165–174.

94. David D. Hale, "Is It a Yen or a Dollar Crisis in the Currency Market?" in Brad Roberts, ed., *New Forces in the World Economy* (Cambridge, MA: MIT Press, 1996), pp. 304–320; Jeffrey A. Frankel and Shang-Jun Wei, "Is a Yen Bloc Emerging?" in symposium on "Economic Cooperation and Challenges in the Pacific," *Joint U.S.-Korea Academic Studies* 5 (1995), pp. 145–175.

95. Chi Hung Kwan, "The Possibility of a Yen Bloc Revisited," *ASEAN Economic Bulletin* 17-2 (August 2000), p. 218.

96. Cohen, "Life at the Top," p. 18.

97. Kwan, "The Possibility of a Yen Bloc Revisited," pp. 227–230. For a detailed discussion of the AMF proposal, see Chang Li Lin, "The Economics and Politics of Monetary Regionalism in Asia," *ASEAN Economic Bulletin* 18-1 (April 2001), pp. 103–118.

98. Hale, "Is It a Yen or a Dollar Crisis in the Currency Market?" pp. 308–310; Cohen, *The Geography of Money,* pp. 161–164; Cohen, "Life at the Top," pp. 8–9.

99. Zanny Minton Beddoes, "From EMU to AMU? The Case for Regional Currencies," *Foreign Affairs* 78-4 (1999), p. 12. Even in the case of the EMU, some would argue that Germany by virtue of the size of its economy will dominate the monetary union.

100. See Eric Helleiner, "National Currencies and National Identities," *American Behavioral Scientist* 41-10 (August 1998), pp. 1409–1436.

101. On the dollarization issue, see Benjamin J. Cohen, "Monetary Turbulence: Are National Currencies Becoming Obsolete?," Remarks for a conference on Global Turbulence: Instability in National and International Political Economy, Vancouver, Canada, July 19–20, 2001; and Willem H. Butler, "The EMU and the NAMU: What is the Case for North American Monetary Union?" *Canadian Public Policy* 25-3 (1999), pp. 285–305.

102. Richard G. Lipsey, "Agendas for the 1988 and Future Summits," *Canadian Public Policy* 15, special issue (February 1989), p. S90.

103. "Big: The Foreign-exchange Market," *The Economist,* September 23, 1995, pp. 63–64.

104. The standard rate of corporate income tax in OECD countries did in fact fall from 43 percent in 1986 to 33 percent in 1995, while the average tax rate for workers increased. See "Survey: World Economy," *The Economist,* September 20, 1997, p. 33.

105. Stephen Gill and David Law, "Global Hegemony and the Structural Power of Capital," in Stephen Gill, ed., *Gramsci, Historical Materialism and International Relations* (Cambridge: Cambridge University Press, 1993), p. 108.

106. Paul Hirst and Grahame Thompson, *Globalization in Question: The International Economy and the Possibilities of Governance* (Cambridge, UK: Polity Press, 1996), p. 27.

107. Ethan B. Kapstein, *Governing the Global Economy: International Finance and the State* (Cambridge, MA: Harvard University Press, 1994), p. 6. This is also one of the themes in Helleiner, *States and the Reemergence of Global Finance.*

108. "Will the Buck Stop Here?" *The Economist,* November 12, 1994, p. 88.

C H A P T E R 7

Foreign Debt

The international debt crisis that erupted in the early 1980s was "one of the most traumatic international financial disturbances" of the twentieth century.[1] Debt crises had occurred frequently in the nineteenth century, and widespread defaults on loans in the 1930s had severely disrupted capital flows to Latin America and to Southern and Eastern Europe. Nevertheless, the world seemed unprepared for the 1980s debt crisis, which threatened the international banking system as well as some of the largest Third World countries. A number of authors have examined the similarities and differences between the 1980s debt crisis and earlier crises.[2] One significant difference relates to changes in lending mechanisms. In the 1920s, most lending to Latin America occurred through the bond markets, so country debt was held by numerous individual bondholders located in many different countries. When LDCs defaulted on their debts in the 1930s, the losses were fragmented among the many individual bondholders.

In the 1970s, by contrast, private bank lending to middle-income LDCs greatly increased. When the debtor countries threatened to default on their loans in the 1980s, the possible losses were therefore much more concentrated in the largest commercial banks, which occupied a central position in international finance. Indeed, the nine largest U.S. banks had loans outstanding to 17 highly indebted countries, amounting to 194 percent of the banks' capital and reserves in 1982; a major debt default could have affected the core of the banking system. Because the 1980s debt crisis posed a major threat to international financial stability, creditor governments felt more pressure to intervene in the debt-settlement process during this period.[3] Thus, another historical difference relates to the role of IOs and advanced industrial states.

In earlier periods of default, international institutions designed to deal with debt problems were almost nonexistent, and governments generally were less willing to intervene. In the 1980s, by contrast, the International Monetary Fund cajoled private banks to continue lending to LDC debtors on the one hand and pressured debtor countries to alter their economic policies on the other. There was also no hegemonic power to deal with the debt crisis in the 1930s, but the United States filled this position in the 1980s. Together, the United States and the IMF orchestrated the response to the 1980s debt crisis, with other actors such as the World Bank, the Paris and London Clubs, and the Bank for International Settlements (discussed later) playing supporting positions.[4]

WHAT IS A DEBT CRISIS?

As discussed in Chapter 6, a country has a current account deficit when its payments abroad are greater than those it receives. Countries must either finance their deficits or adjust to them, and those governments that choose financing must borrow from external credit sources and/or decrease their foreign exchange reserves. As governments continue to borrow to finance their budget deficits, they are burdened with growing foreign debt problems. However, the level of a borrower's outstanding debt is *not* the main factor determining whether it is facing a debt crisis. The United States today is the world's largest debtor country, and in 1991 the U.S. debt amounted to about $370 billion. The total foreign debt owed by all the LDCs in the Western Hemisphere in 1991, by comparison, was about $434 billion. Nevertheless, the U.S. GNP is also the world's largest, and there is no danger the United States will be unable to service the repayments on its outstanding debt. Whereas the U.S. net foreign debt amounted to only about 6.4 percent of its GNP in 1991, the net foreign debt of the LDCs in the Western Hemisphere amounted to more than 40 percent of their collective GNP.[5]

In determining the severity of a country's debt problem, therefore, we need to know not only the size of the debt, but also whether the country has the ability and commitment to service its debt repayments. A "debt crisis" results when countries lack sufficient foreign exchange to make the principal and/or interest payments on their debt obligations. Debt crises vary both in terms of severity and in terms of the length of time and types of measures required to bring about a resolution.[6] Although we have provided a standard definition of a debt crisis, it is important to note that there are also more subjective definitions of the term. For example, the Northern industrial states tended to define the 1980s debt crisis as the threat to "the stability of the international financial system" resulting from "the onset of widespread difficulties in servicing the mountain of developing country debt." The Southern LDCs, by contrast, defined the 1980s debt crisis as "a crisis of development, one element of the deepest economic downturn since the Great Depression, which had begun for some developing countries after the first oil shock."[7]

This chapter focuses on the debt crisis of the 1980s and 1990s, particularly on the origins of the debt crisis, the strategies adopted to deal with it, and the effects of the crisis on the debtor countries, the creditor countries, and the international banks.

THE ORIGINS OF THE 1980S DEBT CRISIS

According to most observers, the debt crisis began in August 1982, when Mexico announced it could no longer service its public sector debt obligations. The announcement produced shock waves because of the magnitude of the Mexican external debt, which was estimated at $78 billion by the end of 1981.[8] However, earlier warning signs of a possible crisis had been largely ignored. From 1976 to 1980, a number of LDCs, including Zaïre, Argentina, Peru, Sierra Leone, Sudan, and Togo, had been involved in debt rescheduling negotiations, and the external debt of LDCs in general had increased six-fold to $500 billion between 1972 and 1981. Foreign debt was also a growing problem in Eastern Europe, and Poland's indebtedness had reached serious proportions by 1981.[9] After Mexico's 1982 announcement, the debt crisis therefore spread rapidly as private creditor banks moved to decrease their loan exposure to other LDC borrowers. Thus, 25 LDCs requested debt restructuring on their commercial bank debt by the end of 1982, and in 1983 the World Bank reported that "almost as many developing countries have had to reschedule loans in the last two years as in the previous twenty-five years."[10]

Analysts have differing views regarding the causes of the 1980s debt crisis, stemming partly from their divergent ideological perspectives. Most commonly, the crisis is explained in terms of unexpected changes in the global economy, irresponsible behavior of the lenders, irresponsible behavior of the debtor countries, and dependence of the Third World countries on the advanced capitalist states.

Unexpected Changes in the Global Economy

Some observers attribute the debt crisis primarily to external shocks, as a result of unexpected global economic changes.[11] The first external shocks occurred in the early 1970s, when there was a sharp rise in the prices of foodgrains and oil. In the late 1960s, major surpluses of wheat and grain had accumulated, leading to a decline in international food prices and production cutback programs in the United States, Canada, and some other grain-exporting countries. As a result of these cutback programs, the world was especially vulnerable to unanticipated events such as inclement weather and crop shortfalls in the Soviet Union, which resulted in massive Soviet grain purchases and serious foodgrain shortages. In 1972–73, global food stocks fell to their lowest level in 20 years, the volume of food aid was drastically reduced, and there were substantial increases in foodgrain prices.[12] After the October 1973 Middle East war, the Arab countries in OPEC also managed to limit the supply of oil and drastically raise its price. Thus, those LDCs that imported oil as well as food were doubly hit by the food and oil crises.

Whereas many importing states were severely hurt by the increased oil prices, the OPEC countries accumulated unprecedented amounts of excess reserves—or "petrodollars"—which they deposited in the largest commercial banks. These banks played a major role in recycling the petrodollars through loans to middle-income LDCs, which were considered to be creditworthy for receiving commercial bank loans. Thus, about 60 percent of external financing for non-OPEC LDCs came from commercial bank credits between 1974 and 1979.[13] A second oil shock occurred in 1979, when OPEC more than doubled its prices. The private banks provided additional loans to help the LDCs pay for the new round of oil price increases, and they offered loans to oil-exporting LDCs to help develop their industries and diversify their economies.

The second oil shock contributed to a severe contraction in the industrial economies and thus to the worst global recession since the 1930s. As a result, LDCs faced a sharp decline in demand for their commodity exports, and they found it increasingly difficult to earn foreign exchange to service their debts. The 1979 oil price increases also produced inflationary pressures, which the industrial states sought to control by raising interest rates. In the United States, the Reagan administration's need to borrow abroad to cover its huge federal budget deficits was yet another source of upward pressure on interest rates. The creditor banks were providing short-term loans at variable interest rates, and the impact of the higher rates on LDC debt levels was rapid and severe.[14] It may seem ironic that the debt crisis began with Mexico—an oil exporter. Oil-exporting LDCs, however, had also borrowed private funds to launch ambitious development projects and other programs, without anticipating that oil prices—and thus their oil revenues—would fall sharply after 1979. Thus, the unexpected global economic changes in the 1970s and 1980s contributed to the external debt problems of Third World oil exporters as well as importers.

Unanticipated global changes certainly were a factor in the debt crisis, but critics point out that these changes were not the only cause. Although the external shocks affected a large number of LDCs, the East Asian NIEs fared far better than the Latin American LDCs. Both commercial banks and debtor countries often favor the "external shocks" explanation for the debt crisis because it awards "primary responsibility to economic policy shifts beyond their control."[15] Nevertheless, the policies of both the lenders and the borrowers must also be considered as explanations for the crisis.

Irresponsible Behavior of the Lenders

Historical structuralists and some interventionist liberals often consider irresponsible behavior by the creditor banks to be a major cause of the debt crisis. The commercial banks, according to this perspective, engaged in overlending, without being sufficiently concerned about the creditworthiness of borrowers or the nature of the activities they were financing. When the OPEC countries deposited a large amount of petrodollars in private commercial banks (mainly in New York and London), the banks aggressively sought to increase their loan activity in the Third World. The competition to lend funds, combined with inflationary conditions, meant that the large commercial banks charged extremely low interest rates, which did not give LDCs adequate signals as to when to stop borrowing. By the time the interest rates rose sharply in the early 1980s, LDC debtors had become overly dependent on commercial bank loans, and this factor heightened the severity of the crisis.[16] Thus, the commercial banks were often accused of "loan pushing" and of "urging the debtor countries to increase their liabilities."[17]

Some critics of the lenders' policies argue that the banks could not have engaged in overlending completely on their own, and that governments of the industrial countries shared responsibility for this development. After the first oil shock in 1973, the industrial states collectively and individually adopted a number of policies that encouraged the flow of private bank funds to the Third World. For example, in 1974 the central bankers in the G-10 countries provided assurances that they would assist banks recycling petrodollars if they encountered financial difficulties. The IMF also introduced new lending programs for LDC oil importers such as the 1974 oil facility and the 1974 Extended Fund Facility, which in turn encouraged private banks to upgrade their own lending activities. Furthermore, the gradual lifting of capital controls in the industrial states (discussed in Chapter 6) eased the process by which banks in the United States and Western Europe could recycle surplus petrodollars to the Third World. From this perspective, both the creditor international banks and the advanced industrial states in which they were located shared responsibility for overlending, which was a major cause of the debt crisis.[18]

Irresponsible Behavior of the Borrowing States

Many liberal theorists, especially orthodox liberals, attribute primary responsibility for the debt crisis to the imprudent behavior of the borrowing states. These critics often argue that the LDCs sought the easy route to borrowing from private banks in the 1970s in efforts to avoid the conditionality requirements of IMF loans. Unlike the IMF, private banking institutions were not inclined (and did not have the legal authority) to make loans to sovereign governments subject to policy conditions. Basic principles of the IMF financing regime—that governments should not have unlimited access to balance-of-payments financing and that countries with financing problems should undergo adjustment measures—were jeopardized because of the accessibility of private funds. As a liberal-economic institution, the IMF itself seemed to endorse this view in its 1977 *Annual Report:*

> Access to private sources of balance of payments finance may . . . in some cases permit countries to postpone the adoption of adequate domestic stabilization measures. This can exacerbate the problem of correcting payments imbalances, and can lead to adjustments that are politically and socially disruptive when the introduction of stabilization measures becomes unavoidable.[19]

In addition to citing imprudent borrowing behavior, liberals attribute the debt crisis at least in part to the domestic policies of borrowing states. Although some LDCs used the commercial bank loans wisely to finance productive investments and economic growth, a goodly number, according to this view, used the funds to make poor investments, increase public expenditures, import consumer goods, and pay off corrupt officials. Some LDCs reacted to the debt crisis in a timely manner with readjustment policies, but many others demonstrated unwillingness —or inability—to change. Liberal economists often contrast the strong economic performance of the East Asian debtor countries such as South Korea and Indonesia in the 1980s with the generally weak performance of the Latin American debtors. (The most notable exception to this comparison was the weak performance of the Philippines.)

The differential economic performance of the East Asians and Latin Americans, from this perspective, cannot be explained by differences in external shocks or even by the amount of external borrowing. Instead, the most important differences relate to these countries' policies on foreign trade and exchange rates. Whereas Latin American LDCs employed import substitution policies, the East and Southeast Asian LDCs placed far more emphasis on export-led growth. Exports are a critical source of foreign exchange for servicing a country's debts, so the East and Southeast Asians' outward-oriented policies placed them in a much stronger position to deal with their debt problems. Overvalued exchange rates also encouraged capital flight in Latin American countries such as Mexico and Argentina because residents feared precipitous declines in the value of their countries' currencies. The East and Southeast Asian LDCs, by contrast, had realistic exchange rates and generally avoided the Latin American problem of capital flight.[20]

TABLE 7.1

TOTAL DEBT AND DEBT INDICATORS, 1982 (MILLIONS OF DOLLARS)

	Total Debt	Debt/Exports (%)	Debt Service Ratio[a](%)
Latin America			
Argentina	43,634	447.3	50.0
Brazil	92,990	396.1	81.3
Chile	17,315	335.9	71.3
Colombia	10,306	204.3	29.5
Mexico	86,019	311.5	56.8
Peru	10,712	255.9	48.7
Venezuela	32,153	159.8	29.5
East and Southeast Asia			
Indonesia	24,734	116.3	18.1
Republic of Korea	37,330	131.6	22.4
Malaysia	13,354	93.4	10.7
Philippines	24,551	297.8	42.6
Thailand	12,238	130.0	20.6

[a]Debt service ratio: the ratio of a country's interest and principal payments to its export income.
Source: World Bank, *World Debt Tables 1992–93, Vol. 2: Country Tables* (Washington, DC: IBRD, 1992).

Table 7.1 illustrates the more favorable position of the East and Southeast Asians vis-à-vis the Latin Americans in 1982. The largest debtors in Table 7.1 are Latin American (the debts of Brazil, Mexico, and Argentina exceeded $92, $86, and $43 billion, respectively); some East and Southeast Asian countries such as South Korea, Indonesia, and the Philippines also had substantial debt levels (exceeding $37, $24, and $24 billion, respectively). However, the stronger export position of the East and Southeast Asians (except the Philippines) demonstrates they were in a much better position than the Latin Americans to service their debts. Economists often use the **debt service ratio,** which measures the ratio of a country's interest and principal payments on its debt to its export income, as a measure to assess the ability of a country to service its debt. The lower the debt service ratio (and the debt-to-export ratio), the more favorable are the prospects that a country will meet its debt obligations. Thus, Table 7.1 shows that the debt service ratios of Malaysia and Indonesia were as low as 10.7 and 18.1 percent in 1982, while the debt service ratios of Brazil and Chile had reached the very unfavorable levels of 81.3 and 71.3 percent.

The view that irresponsible LDC behavior was the major factor explaining the debt crisis, like the other perspectives, has been subjected to some severe criticism. Some political scientists point out that some LDC governments with good intentions simply lacked the *political* capacity and support to institute necessary economic reforms.[21] Other critics charge that the attribution of LDC responsibility ignores the fact that the debt crisis was *systemic* in nature. Indeed, "the simultaneous onset of the crisis in more than forty developing countries" indicates that some of the major contributing factors were external to the LDCs and largely beyond their control.[22] Furthermore, East and Southeast Asian LDCs such as Thailand, Malaysia, Indonesia, and

South Korea, which liberals identified as following responsible policies during the 1980s debt crisis, were the first to be hit by a severe financial crisis in the late 1990s (this issue is discussed in Chapter 11).

LDC Dependence on the Advanced Capitalist States

Some historical structuralists argue that the 1980s debt crisis cannot be traced simply to proximate actors and events but that it resulted from the long-term structural nature of the capitalist system. Thus, dependency and world-system theorists view LDC debt crises as simply extreme instances of a "debt trap," which exploits LDCs in the periphery and binds them to rich Northern states in the core.[23] Some writers draw linkages between Third World debt crises and the legacy of colonialism. The colonial powers established a division of labor in which the colonies provided agricultural products and raw materials to the metropole and served in turn as markets for the metropole's manufacturers. This pattern still characterizes the export and import structures of many LDCs today, preventing them from earning the foreign exchange necessary for development. Although some LDCs are industrializing, they remain dependent on MNCs and other institutions in the core for technology and finance, and they therefore find it impossible to escape from their indebtedness.[24]

Other historical structuralists point to foreign aid as a source of LDC debt crises because more than half of all official development assistance is disbursed as loans. A substantial share of World Bank financing is also disbursed to the Third World as *hard loans* with high interest rates and relatively short repayment periods (see Chapter 11). A large percentage of multilateral and bilateral foreign aid today is required simply to cover the LDCs' repayments of past aid disbursements. Thus, development assistance loans become simply another mechanism by which surpluses are transferred from the peripheral to the core states. Many historical structuralists also view IMF and World Bank conditionality requirements as infringing on LDC sovereignty and as incorrect prescriptions for reducing LDC debt problems. Thus, official IMF and World Bank loans, like commercial bank loans, serve to perpetuate rather than alleviate LDC dependency:

> If they seek official help on softer than commercial terms, they have to accept outside scrutiny . . . and accept conditions which doom their efforts at industrial, diversified development. If they accept suppliers' credits on commercial terms in order to go through with their cherished projects, they are caught anyway when the payments come due before they are able to meet them.[25]

Like the other interpretations of the debt crisis, the dependency interpretation has been subject to considerable criticism. Liberals in particular argue that dependency theorists attribute the LDCs' debt problems solely to external causes beyond their control and thereby avoid looking at the *domestic* sources of LDC problems—traditional attitudes, domestic inefficiencies, corrupt political leaders, and a reluctance to follow policies of economic openness.

We can safely conclude that all the preceding views regarding the origins of the foreign debt crisis have some validity. The unexpected food and oil price increases in the 1970s encouraged countries to increase their borrowing, and the monetary policy changes and world recession after the 1979 oil price increases added to the debt load of many LDC borrowers. Although these unexpected global changes made a debt crisis more likely, the behavior of the commercial banks, some industrial states, and some debtor governments certainly exacerbated the debt situation. Furthermore, the long-term structural dependency of Third World countries on the industrial states increased the vulnerability of LDCs to protracted debt problems. Mexico's minister of finance and public credit from 1982 to 1986 clearly identified the multiple causes of the debt crisis, and the failure of the world community to foresee it, when he stated that

> the origin of the debt itself is clearly traceable to a decision by both developing and developed countries that . . . resulted in the channeling of tens of billions of dollars to the debtor community of today. . . . The whole world congratulated itself on the success, smoothness, and efficiency with which the recycling process was achieved. *We all were responsible.*[26]

THE FOREIGN DEBT REGIME

Before discussing the world's reaction to the 1980s debt crisis, it is important to describe the elements of a foreign debt regime that developed to monitor and manage the crisis. A debt regime was more evident in the 1980s than it had been in the 1930s because a global hegemon (the United States) and a more developed institutional framework (including the IMF and the World Bank) existed to deal with the 1980s crisis. Before World War II, the mechanisms for coping with a debt crisis were largely limited either to unilateral actions by the creditors or debtors or to two-party solutions in which the debtors and creditors reached a compromise at the bargaining table. International debt settlements in the postwar period, by contrast, have often been three-party affairs involving international organizations such as the IMF and the World Bank and less formal groupings such as the Paris and London Clubs (discussed later). The United States has also acted as a third party in the postwar period, using its hegemonic position to pressure for debt settlements and to coordinate settlement efforts.[27]

Some regimes encompass only one sector or issue whereas others are broader in scope, and specific regimes may be nested within more diffuse regimes. For example, some authors have described textile and agricultural trade regimes as being nested within the more diffuse global trade regime.[28] Although the global trade regime principles, norms, and rules provide a general framework for the textile and agricultural trade regimes, textile and agricultural trade relations have their own unique characteristics and have often been treated as "exceptions" by the GATT/WTO. This chapter views the 1980s foreign debt regime as a specific regime nested within a more diffuse balance-of-payments financing regime, because foreign debt crises are a specific, more extreme type of balance-of-payments problem. Although there have been continuous efforts to negotiate agreements with individual debtor countries throughout the postwar period, the pressures resulting from the 1980s debt crisis produced more coordinated, longer term efforts to establish rules and decision-making procedures that we normally associate with an international regime.

A basic principle underlying the balance-of-payments financing regime is that an adequate but not unlimited amount of supplementary financing should be available to states for dealing with their balance-of-payments deficits. A second principle is that those providing this financing may attach conditions to the funding that they believe will correct the recipient states' balance-of-payments problems. The rules of the balance-of-payments financing regime include the explicit conditions that the IMF places on its borrowers.[29] In the 1970s, the balance-of-payments regime's basic principle of conditional lending was threatened because private banks with petrodollars to recycle provided debtor countries loans with extremely low interest rates and minimal conditions. Although these private bank loans were readily available to many middle-income countries (MICs) and (NIEs) in the 1970s, low-income LDCs (LICs) generally lacked creditworthiness to receive private bank loans, so they remained highly dependent on lending from the IMF and donor governments. Thus, Table 7.2 shows that in 1980 private bank loans accounted for only 6 percent of the debt of LICs but for 38 percent of middle-income country (MIC) debt and for 65 percent of the debt of the NIEs. **Official development assistance (ODA),** by contrast, accounted for 67 percent of LIC debt in 1980, but for only 25 percent of MIC debt and 4 percent of NIE debt. The willingness of private banks to provide for much of the financing needs of the more creditworthy LDCs greatly limited the IMF's ability to set conditions for these borrowers.

With the emergence of the debt crisis in 1982, however, private banks moved quickly to limit their loan exposure to LDCs, and the MICs and NIEs therefore had to look to the IMF, the World Bank, and official government aid agencies for assistance with their growing debt problems. This dependence on official financing provided the international organizations and the U.S. government with considerable leverage in establishing what we call the foreign debt regime. As with the pre-1970s balance-of-payments regime, the basic principle of the debt regime revolved around conditionality—that the provision of new loans and debt rescheduling were contingent on the debtor countries' commitment to market-oriented reforms. However, the 1980s debt regime was also different from the pre-1970s regime in some important respects.

First, the IMF (with U.S. backing) adopted a new role when it imposed pressures on the private commercial banks in the 1980s to continue providing loans to the debtor LDCs. Second, creditor clubs such as the Paris and London Clubs were used much more frequently during the 1980s and 1990s than in earlier periods. Third, both the IMF and the World Bank became involved in providing structural adjustment loans to indebted LDCs and to the emerging countries of Eastern Europe and the former Soviet Union. These SALs were conditioned on far more demanding requirements than previously—that the recipient LDCs adopt orthodox liberal reforms such as deregulation, privatization, and greater openness to trade and foreign investment. The changing roles of the IMF and the World Bank in the foreign debt regime are examined later in this chapter. We discuss here two sets of actors whose roles were also important: the emerging economies of Eastern Europe and the FSU, which became major debtor countries along with the LDCs, and the Paris Club and private creditor committees, which had a significant role in rescheduling loans.

TABLE 7.2
TOTAL DEBT, AND SHARE OF DEBT BASED ON ODA AND PRIVATE BANK LOANS FOR NONOIL LDCs

INCOME GROUP	1971			1975			1980			1982		
	Total Debt[a]	Percentage ODA	Percentage Private Banks	Total Debt	Percentage ODA	Percentage Private Banks	Total Debt	Percentage ODA	Percentage Private Banks	Total Debt	Percentage ODA	Percentage Private Banks
LICs	$18	74	2	$40	73	7	$86	67	6	$110	69	6
MICs	$25	45	14	$40	33	29	$107	25	38	$144	24	39
NIEs	$32	16	38	$72	9	60	$192	4	65	$266	3	67

[a]Total debt figures in billions.

Abbreviations: ODA = official development assistance
  LICs = low-income countries
  MICs = middle-income countries
  NIEs = newly industrializing economies

Source: External Debt of Developing Countries—1982 Survey, p. 34. Copyright © OECD, 1982. By permission of the Organisation for Economic Co-operation and Development.

TABLE 7.3
MEMBERSHIP OF THE EMERGING ECONOMIES IN THE IMF AND WORLD BANK

	IMF	World Bank
1946	Poland, Czechoslovakia, Yugoslavia, and China (founding members of IMF & World Bank)	
1950	Poland withdraws from IMF and World Bank	
1954	Czechoslovakia ousted from the IMF and World Bank	
1972	Romania	Romania
1980	People's Republic of China (PRC) replaces Taiwan in the IMF and World Bank	
1982	Hungary	Hungary
1986	Poland	Poland
1990	Czech and Slovak Republic, Bulgaria	
1991	Albania	Albania, Bulgaria, Czech and Slovak Federal Republic
1992 to 1996	Russian Federation, and other FSU[a] Republics, Croatia, Slovenia, Macedonia, Czech Republic, Slovak Republic, Bosnia and Herzegovina (IMF and World Bank)	
2000	Federal Republic of Yugoslavia (IMF and World Bank)	

[a]FSU = former Soviet Union

Sources: International Monetary Fund, *Annual Report of the Executive Board* (Washington, DC: IMF, various years); World Bank, *Annual Report* (Washington, DC: World Bank, various years).

The IMF, the World Bank, and the Emerging Economies

Chapter 2 noted that the Soviet bloc countries were nonmembers of the IMF and the World Bank for most of the early postwar period. Before examining the role of these countries in the foreign debt regime, we need to understand how they came to join the IMF and the World Bank. Membership issues in the two institutions are closely related: a country cannot join the World Bank without first becoming a member of the IMF. As Table 7.3 shows, Yugoslavia remained a member of the IMF and the World Bank from the time they were established. This was not surprising in view of Yugoslavia's defection from the Soviet Bloc in 1948 and its moves to develop an independent, nonaligned foreign policy. The Yugloslavs were also adopting policies such as workers' self-management and market socialism, which were more compatible with the liberal-economic orientation of the Bretton Woods institutions. In contrast to Yugoslavia, Poland and Czechoslovakia left the IMF and the World Bank in 1950 and 1954 (Czechoslovakia was expelled for not paying its dues), because during the height of the Cold War membership in these institutions was considered incompatible with their status as satellite countries in the Soviet bloc.

Table 7.3 shows that Romania was the first centrally planned economy (CPE) to join these institutions after the withdrawals or expulsions of the 1950s. Romania, like Yugoslavia, was atypical. It had distanced itself politically from the Soviet Union (but unlike Yugoslavia, Romania was still a member of the Soviet bloc). From Romania's perspective, the integration policies of the Soviet-led Council for Mutual Economic Assistance (CMEA) were hindering its industrialization, and membership in the IMF and the World Bank would enable Romania to benefit from their loans, upgrade its economic relations with the West, and further its political objectives. Remarkably, Romania became an IMF and World Bank member in 1972 without having to pass through a transition phase, even though its moves toward economic reform and decentralization were halting and it was building up a sizable foreign debt. Western countries downgraded the importance of these economic issues, largely because Romania's membership contributed to significant divisions within the Soviet bloc. Although Romania provided sensitive economic information to the IMF and the World Bank, the two institutions abided by a special agreement not to disclose this information in their statistical reports.[30]

The People's Republic of China (PRC) was the next CPE to participate in IMF and World Bank meetings, and its case, too, was atypical. The IMF and the World Bank both permitted the PRC to take over the China seat from Taiwan and thus treated the issue as one of representation rather than new membership. The PRC's decision to "return" to the Bretton Woods institutions in 1980 followed a radical change in its policies. The Sino-Soviet dispute of the late 1950s and early 1960s had caused Mao Zedong's PRC to turn inward with a policy of "self-reliance," and this inward-looking policy became far more extreme and autarkic from 1966 to 1969 during the PRC's Cultural Revolution. The political and economic problems wrought by the Cultural Revolution, however, caused China to become somewhat more open to the outside world. In response, the UN General Assembly voted to seat the PRC delegation in October 1971, and China's commercial contacts with the advanced industrial states increased.[31]

Although China's foreign policy was changing, there was little change in its domestic economic policy. It was not until Mao's death in 1976 and the subsequent arrest of cultural revolutionaries that the PRC launched the Four Modernizations program to increase economic productivity and efficiency and to develop a more active role for China in the global economy. Thus, China wanted to renew its membership in the IMF and the World Bank as a means of gaining access to capital finance for infrastructure projects that were essential for its economic modernization. In the negotiations that followed, several factors facilitated China's reentry application, including the active support of the United States and a compromise worked out regarding Taiwan's subscription.[32]

After the PRC's takeover of the China seat in 1980, both Hungary and Poland requested accession in late 1981. Unlike Romania, Hungary came much closer to meeting the IMF's normal economic requirements. In 1968, Hungary had introduced its New Economic Mechanism (NEM), designed to increase the country's economic decentralization, outward economic orientation, and competitiveness in international markets, and in the 1970s and 1980s, Hungary introduced other economic reforms. Hungary sought IMF membership to safeguard these reforms and to obtain assistance with its foreign debt, which was partly an outgrowth of its development plans. The debt situation was far more urgent for Poland, which had borrowed in international financial markets in the early 1970s as a substitute for introducing meaningful economic reform. Poland needed to reassure the financial community that it was committed to servicing its debt in the early 1980s, and IMF membership would be a part of this reassurance process. Although Hungary was admitted to the IMF and the World Bank in 1982, Poland's application was stalled by its imposition of martial law in December 1981. Thus, it was not until 1986 that Poland was admitted to the Bretton Woods institutions (see Table 7.3).[33]

Poland was the last Eastern European country to become a member of the IMF and World Bank before the cataclysmic changes in the Soviet bloc transformed East-West relations. After Mikhail Gorbachev took office, he attempted to revive the Soviet economy through a combination of economic restructuring (*perestroika*) and a turn to political openness (*glasnost*). Although Gorbachev's economic efforts failed, his policies contributed to a series of revolutionary changes. Thus, the disintegration of one Communist regime after another in Eastern Europe in 1989 and the unification of Germany in June 1990 led to the decision to dissolve the CMEA in June 1991. This was followed by the Moscow coup in August 1991, which led to the independence of the Baltic states and the formal dissolution of the Soviet Union itself in December 1991. Czechoslovakia and Bulgaria joined the Bretton Woods institutions in 1990 and 1991, but the most significant change was the accession of Russia and other FSU republics in 1992–93. Because Russia was facing an economic crisis, the IMF and Western donors offered it a $24 billion assistance package in return for Russia's commitment to decrease its budget deficit and inflation rate.[34]

The Bretton Woods institutions have worked closely together to assist the emerging economies of Eastern Europe and the FSU to make the transition to market orientation. The IMF has taken the lead in this process, estimating financing needs, providing policy advice, and setting conditions for economic reform. The World Bank has provided its usual financing for infrastructure and has offered technical assistance and funding to promote the development of market incentives, privatization of state monopolies, and a legal framework for the emerging private sector.[35] Tensions have of course existed between the emerging economies and the Bretton Woods institutions in view of their different economic outlooks. Nevertheless, the addition of so many new countries has put new pressures on IMF and World Bank resources, and Third World countries sometimes charge that the emerging economies are receiving favored treatment.

There does in fact seem to be some truth to these LDC charges. For example, the findings of one study revealed that Romania, Poland, and Hungary have received more IMF loans than one would expect on the basis of economic criteria.[36] Charges have also been made that Russia received a "sweetheart deal" when it joined the IMF in 1992: it was permitted to borrow more funds in relation to its IMF quota than other countries. These charges of favored treatment, however, do not seem to apply to all emerging economies. For example, a study in 1990 concluded that China has not received any special treatment in funding from the Bretton Woods institutions.[37] There may be disagreements over the extent to which the emerging economies have received favorable treatment, but there is no doubt that their membership has enhanced the universality of the Bretton Woods organizations. As noted later in this chapter, the foreign debt crisis in the 1980s affected the emerging as well as the Third

World economies. The expanding membership in the IMF and World Bank has inevitably meant that more debtor countries are competing for the limited funds of these two institutions.

The Paris Club and the Private Creditor Committees

Three major types of negotiations have occurred between creditors and debtors to deal with the 1980s debt crisis. In the first type of negotiation, the IMF and the World Bank agree to provide SALS to Third World debtor governments in exchange for the debtors' commitment to follow prescribed economic policies to eliminate their balance-of-payments problems. The other two types of negotiations involve meetings between the debtors and less formal creditor groupings than the IMF and World Bank: the Paris and London Clubs. The **Paris Club** is a quasi-institutional grouping of creditor governments, which in most cases are members of the OECD. The **London Club** is the term informally used for private creditor committees, which are composed of the largest commercial banks. The Paris and London Clubs have no charters or formal institutional structures, and their memberships vary with each rescheduling negotiation. The ad hoc nature of these clubs stems partly from the creditors' view that debt reschedulings should be unusual rather than common occurrences, and partly from the desire to avoid high-profile negotiations. Thus, the Paris Club has no legal status or written rules, no voting procedure (decision making occurs on the basis of consensus), and no regular office (meetings are usually held in the French Ministry of Finance).[38]

The Paris Club's first meeting was held in 1956 to negotiate a rescheduling of Argentina's foreign debt. Argentina was in arrears to several European governments, and this meeting was designed to provide a multilateral rescheduling forum as an alternative to a series of uncoordinated bilateral reschedulings. Paris Club meetings were originally limited in number, but they became much more frequent as debt problems increased. Indeed, the Paris Club concluded over twice as many agreements in the 7-year period from 1978 to 1984 as it did in the previous 22 years; these agreements from 1978 to 1984 resulted in the deferment of about $27 billion of debt service obligations. Participants in Paris Club debt reschedulings usually include the debtor country government, the governments of the main official creditors, and representatives of the IMF, the World Bank, the UNCTAD, and sometimes the regional development banks. In its deliberations, the Paris Club emphasizes three basic principles: imminent default, conditionality, and burden sharing.[39]

The first principle of imminent default is designed to limit requests for relief to those with a serious, justifiable need. To avoid unnecessary negotiations, the Paris Club will not even consider a debtor's request for relief unless the debtor has substantial external payments arrears and is likely to default on its payments. The second principle of conditionality stems from the creditor governments' concerns that the debtor will be able to service its external debts on schedule. Thus, the debtor country must first conclude a standby arrangement with the IMF, based on the IMF's conditionality requirements, before the Paris Club will agree to hold its own negotiations with the debtor.[40] In the small number of cases in which the debtor country was not an IMF member at the time of rescheduling (e.g., Poland, Cuba, and Mozambique), the Paris Club established its own conditionality program of stabilization measures. As for the third principle of burden sharing, all creditor governments must provide relief in proportion to their loan exposure to the debtor country. The burden-sharing principle is designed to avoid the problem of free riding among creditors, and it also extends to the private creditor banks; thus, the Paris and London Clubs cooperate and communicate with each other regularly.

Private debt reschedulings have a number of similarities with Paris Club agreements. In both cases, rescheduling is done on a case-by-case basis by mutual agreement between a single debtor and its creditors, and the debtor must normally commit to adjustment policies as agreed with the IMF. A fundamental difference, however, is that commercial banks are of course far more numerous than nation-states. A relatively small number of states can agree on rescheduling loans at Paris Club meetings, but the coordination problems for private creditors are more complicated. The most common method private creditors use to coordinate their activities is to establish "creditor committees" for the various debtor countries, with the largest international banks (those holding the most loans outstanding) representing the smaller creditor banks. The international banks on a creditor committee bargain with each other and with the debtor country to establish the terms for debt rescheduling, then present the agreement to the smaller creditor banks for ratification. Although the largest creditors would like to limit their loan exposure to a troubled debtor, they realize that the debtor country could default if all individual creditors withheld loans. Because the major international banks have high loan exposure and a long-term interest in the stability of international capital markets, they have a common interest in successful debt restructuring.

Smaller creditor banks, by contrast, have fewer loans at risk and less of a vested interest in maintaining the international credit system. Thus, they are reluctant to ratify restructuring agreements that require them to provide additional loans. Because smaller creditor banks are more inclined to think on the basis of individual rationality, in line with prisoners' dilemma (discussed in Chapter 4), there is a danger that all banks could defect and that massive debtor default could disrupt the international banking system. To prevent a Pareto-suboptimal outcome of this nature, the large international banks put considerable pressure on the smaller banks to avoid free riding and to participate in the debt restructuring agreements.[41] As discussed in the next section, this system of private creditor committees worked quite effectively in earlier years but was insufficient to deal with the 1980s debt crisis.

Historical structuralists, and many Third World debtors, have been highly critical of the Paris and London Club meetings. When a single debtor meets with all its major creditors at the bargaining table, the creditors are in a position to exert unusually strong pressures on the debtor government. The case-by-case approach of the Paris and London Clubs also prevents the debtors from developing a united front, and it ignores the systemic nature of the 1980s debt crisis by operating on the assumption that each debtor's situation can be treated individually. Finally, historical structuralists criticize the two clubs for the strong emphasis they place on IMF conditionality as a prerequisite for their negotiations.[42] At the UNCTAD V conference in 1979, the Third World's G-77 sought to replace the Paris and London Clubs with an international debt commission that would be more favorable to LDC interests. Although the creditor governments agreed to invite an observer from the UNCTAD secretariat to future Paris Club negotiations, it did not accede to LDC demands for an international debt commission. Thus, the creditors continue to set the rules and procedures for Paris and London Club negotiations.

STRATEGIES TO DEAL WITH THE 1980S DEBT CRISIS

The debt crisis was more prolonged than many observers had anticipated, and the major creditor states and international institutions gradually adopted more activist policies as it became evident that milder measures were insufficient. Two of the main actors involved in devising and implementing strategies were the United States and the International Monetary Fund. Although the IMF had lost some importance with the collapse of the pegged exchange rate system and the increase in private bank lending in the 1970s, the debt crisis of the 1980s placed it "back at the center of the international financial system, first as a coordinator in a crisis, and then . . . as a source of information, advice, and warning on the mutual consistency of national policies."[43] The IMF owed its more central role largely to the support of U.S. administration officials, who believed that U.S. (and Western) policies on debt issues could best be implemented through the multilateral institutions. The IMF could exert pressure on both the private banks and the Third World debtors, avoiding major protests over U.S. government interference with private sector lending and LDC sovereignty. International debt issues came onto the agenda of the G-7 summit meetings in the 1980s, and U.S. hegemony has been replaced to some extent by collective responsibility for Third World debt problems among the major economic powers (see the following discussion).[44]

The international debt strategies had three major objectives: to prevent the collapse of the international banking and financial systems, to restore capital market access for the debtor countries, and to minimize economic dislocation and restore economic growth in the debtor countries. The strategies employed to achieve these objectives can be divided into three successive phases: (1) from 1982 to 1985, the provision of emergency loans and private "involuntary" loans to debtor countries; (2) from 1986 to 1988, the introduction of the Baker Plan, which continued with private involuntary lending and placed new emphasis on official lending; and (3) from 1989 to 1994, the implementation of the Brady Plan, which emphasized debt reduction agreements.

Emergency Measures and Involuntary Lending: 1982 to 1985

The first phase in dealing with the debt crisis was a "firefighting" strategy in which the United States, the IMF, and other creditors provided short-term emergency financing to Mexico, Brazil, Venezuela, and other LDCs to avert a 1930s-style financial collapse. As part of this firefighting strategy, the BIS (see Chapter 6) provided some "bridging" finance to Third World debtor countries until IMF loans were approved.[45] This emergency lending was followed by a medium-term strategy in which the private banks engaged in "involuntary" lending. Involuntary lending, which is referred to more politely in official circles as *concerted lending,* can be defined as "the increase in a bank's exposure to a borrowing nation that is in debt-servicing difficulty and that, because of a loss of creditworthiness, would be unable to attract new lending from banks not already exposed in the country."[46]

In the late 1970s and early 1980s, the private creditor committees were quite successful in managing the debt situation; the largest international creditor banks induced the smaller banks to engage in involuntary lending when necessary in debt restructuring agreements. Only nine countries had to restructure their commercial debts from the mid-1970s to 1982, so interbank coordination was sufficient to manage the debt situation. Although the IMF had a role in supervising the debtors' economic policies, its involvement during this period was quite limited. The Mexican debt crisis in August 1982, however, drastically altered the system of debt management. The large international banks in this case were simply unable to cope with the debt crisis because of its massive scope, and many small banks in the U.S. Southwest with loans outstanding to Mexico were unwilling to increase their loan exposure. It was therefore necessary for the IMF to intervene with an activist policy:

> In November 1982, the Fund's Managing Director . . . took the unprecedented step of establishing mandatory levels of forced private lending before the I.M.F. would sign a stabilization agreement with Mexico. This bold action, repeated in the Brazilian case, was a turning point in the treatment of sovereign debt. It staked out a new leadership role for the Fund, and a new relationship between the Fund and private banks.[47]

In addition to pressuring the creditor banks, the IMF insisted that the debtor nations develop adjustment programs as the price for debt rescheduling and the provision of new lending. Thus, realists point out that it was creditor *states* operating through the IMF that managed the debt crisis, and not private banks and the market. The debt crisis posed such a major threat to the international financial system that only states were able to mobilize sufficient resources to deal with the crisis. Furthermore, only official pressures were sufficient to induce banks to continue lending to the debtors on the one hand and to force debtor governments to meet conditionality requirements on the other.[48] Liberals, by contrast, emphasize the role that the IMF played as an international institution in managing the debt crisis, and they disagree with the realist view that the IMF was simply doing the bidding of the major creditor states.

The general assumption of the IMF and creditor states in these early years was that the debt crisis was only a short-term problem stemming from the temporary inability of LDCs to service their debts. However, it soon became evident that the debt crisis posed an insolvency problem for many Third World states, which were unable to stem their growing debt problems even after significantly adjusting their policies.[49] Although the early firefighting tactics dealt with the immediate crisis, it was evident by 1985 that many LDC debtors had longer term economic and financial problems. Economic activity and investment in most debtor countries were declining, and international pressures for continued adjustment programs in the LDCs were interfering with their economic growth objectives. Furthermore, the private commercial banks were resisting IMF pressures and reducing their loan exposure in the debtor countries. Thus, official creditors such as the IMF rather than the private banks were assuming an increasing share of the lending risk. When James A. Baker III became the U.S. Secretary of the Treasury in 1985, he therefore moved to adopt a more structured approach to the debt crisis.

TABLE 7.4

GROSS EXTERNAL DEBT AND EXTERNAL DEBT AS A PERCENT OF GNP FOR THE BAKER-17 COUNTRIES, 1985 AND 1994 (US$ MILLIONS)

	1985		1994	
	Debt	**EDT/GNP%**	**Debt**	**EDT/GNP%**
°Brazil	106,148	50.3	151,104	27.9
°Mexico	96,867	55.2	128,302	35.2
°Argentina	50,946	84.2	77,388	27.8
°Venezuela	35,334	—	36,850	64.0
Philippines	26,622	89.1	39,302	59.3
Former Yugoslavia	22,251	48.2	13,557	—
°Chile	20,384	143.3	22,939	45.5
Nigeria	19,550	25.1	33,485	102.5
Morocco	16,529	136.6	22,512	76.3
°Peru	12,884	85.3	22,624	45.8
°Colombia	14,245	42.6	19,416	30.9
Cote d'Ivoire	9,745	154.2	18,452	338.9
°Ecuador	8,703	77.4	14,955	94.6
°Bolivia	4,805	176.6	4,749	89.4
°Costa Rica	4,401	120.8	3,843	47.8
°Jamaica	4,068	234.9	4,318	110.1
°Uruguay	3,919	89.7	5,099	33.2

EDT/GNP % = Total external debt to GNP. °indicates Latin American and Caribbean countries.
Source: World Bank, *World Debt Tables, 1992–93 and 1996, Vol. 2: Country Tables* (Washington, DC: IBRD, 1992 and 1996).

The Baker Plan: 1986 to 1988

In late 1985, Secretary Baker introduced a plan that provided a more concrete formula for dealing with the debt crisis and extended debt repayments over a longer period, but did not change the basic assumptions about the best strategy to follow. As was the case in the 1982–85 period, those who devised the **Baker Plan** underestimated the insolvency problem confronting many LDCs, and they therefore rejected the idea that major portions of the Third World debt should be forgiven. Thus, the Baker Plan emphasized the postponement of some debt payments, the provision of new loans, and changes in the debtor countries' policies. This strategy rested on the assumption "that principal debtor countries could grow their way out of debt and could expand their exports enough to reduce their relative debt burdens to levels compatible with a return to normal credit market access."[50]

The Baker Plan also focused primarily on Latin American debtors. When Secretary Baker referred to the heavily indebted countries, he identified 15 middle-income LDCs (later increased to 17) as the main target group for his international debt measures. As the asterisks in Table 7.4 show, 12 of the 17 countries targeted were Latin American and Caribbean, and the "Baker-17" list did not include the low-income

LDCs that were heavily indebted to official (rather than private) creditors.[51] Table 7.4 lists these 17 highly indebted countries in order of their total gross external debt from highest to lowest in 1985, shortly before the Baker Plan was instituted (the order of countries changed somewhat in 1994). As the table shows, the 4 countries with the highest debts among the 17 in 1985 (Brazil, Mexico, Argentina, and Venezuela) were all Latin American. However, we require more than figures on gross external debt level to assess a country's debt servicing abilities. We must also examine *debt indicators* such as a country's debt-to-export ratio and debt service ratio (shown in Table 7.1) and its debt as a percentage of total output or GNP. Table 7.4 shows that the countries with the highest gross external debts ranked well below some of the poorer and/or smaller LDCs in terms of debt as a percentage of GNP. Thus, the external debts as a percentage of GNP for the three largest debtor countries in 1987, Brazil, Mexico, and Argentina, were 50.3, 55.2, and 84.2 percent, respectively. Six of the other debtors on the list had much higher debt-to-GNP ratios in 1987, exceeding 100 percent. The countries on the Baker-17 list with the highest external-debt-to-GNP ratios were Jamaica (234.9 percent), Bolivia (176.6 percent), and Cote d'Ivoire (154.2 percent).

Although the Baker Plan focused only on a select group of indebted LDCs and did not recognize the severity of the debt problem, it did mark a turning point in one important respect. Recognizing that the debt crisis was becoming a longer term problem, the Baker Plan shifted emphasis from short-term balance-of-payments adjustment to long-term structural change and the resumption of economic growth in the LDC debtor states. In view of the new emphasis on long-term change, the World Bank and the Inter-American Development Bank (IDB)—with their longer term loans—assumed a more central role in the debt strategy. Thus, the Baker Plan proposed that the multilateral development banks increase their total lending by $10 billion to a gross level of $20 billion over three years and that the private banks also lend $20 billion to the major debtors. In return, the debtor countries were to institute significant liberal-economic reforms, including the liberalization of their trade and foreign investment policies and the privatization of state firms. These reforms had particular significance for many Latin American LDCs, which had previously followed protectionist import substitution policies.

Any possibilities that the Baker Plan could succeed were upset by unexpected changes in the global economy. For example, international oil prices collapsed shortly after the Baker Plan was announced, upsetting the recovery plans of oil-exporting debtor countries such as Mexico. The decline of oil prices also gave some oil-importing LDCs less incentive to adopt economic policy reforms that were necessary for their recovery. Thus, the Baker initiative lost much of its momentum by mid-1986. The Baker Plan also did not achieve adequate results in terms of economic growth in the debtor countries, and many LDC debtors refused to comply with IMF conditionality requirements (for example, Brazil declared a moratorium on paying its debts in 1987). Furthermore, commercial banks sought to reduce their loan exposure in the LDCs, and the lending risks continued to shift from the private banks to governments and multilateral agencies. The multilateral development banks also disbursed less funding than the Baker Plan had anticipated. As a result, the debt repayments of LDCs began to exceed the funding they were receiving in new loans. The net transfer of financial resources to LDCs shifted from a *positive* $29 billion in 1982 to a *negative* $34 billion by

1987, and the net resource transfer to the Baker-17 list of highly indebted countries shifted from +$11 billion to –$17 billion during the same period.[52]

Because the debtor countries' repayment requirements greatly exceeded their access to new financing, they experienced their deepest economic problems during the Baker Plan period. From 1981 to 1988, real per capita income in almost every South American country declined in absolute terms, and living standards in many LDCs fell to levels comparable with the 1950s and 1960s. Indeed, many analysts referred to the 1980s as a "lost development decade." Although the Baker Plan's failure resulted partly from unforeseen external events such as the collapse of international oil prices, historical structuralists viewed the plan as an "attempt to maintain the fiction that the debt crisis was only temporary and could be surmounted if all parties cooperated."[53] A number of the debtor countries seemed to be caught in a "vicious circle," in which their debt burdens interfered with their plans for economic growth, and their slow growth in turn prevented them from overcoming their debt problems.[54]

The Brady Plan: 1989 to 1994

The failure of the Baker Plan to promote economic recovery and growth in the Latin American LDCs posed a serious threat to U.S. exports in Latin American markets. Concerns were also voiced in the U.S. Congress about the possible negative effects of the continued debt problems on the revival of democratic governments in Latin America. Serious riots in Caracas, Venezuela, in February 1989 were associated with government austerity measures, providing further evidence that the Baker measures were insufficient. In 1987 and 1988 Mexico, Brazil, and Argentina negotiated agreements that provided for a reduction, and not merely a rescheduling, of some of their debts. In early 1989, Nicholas Brady, the new U.S. Treasury Secretary, sanctioned this approach of forgiving some debts by launching the "Brady Plan." The idea of *debt reduction*—that some debts would not be repaid in full—was still highly contentious, but differences among the major economic powers on this issue were resolved at the G-7 summit meeting in Paris in July 1989. As a result of the G-7 approval, the IMF adopted the Brady Plan at its Fall 1989 meeting.[55]

The Brady Plan was similar to the Baker Plan in several respects. For example, the Brady Plan opted for handling the debt problem on a case-by-case basis, in which each debtor LDC negotiated separately with its creditors, and it linked the easing of credit terms with the debtors' acceptance of IMF and World Bank requirements for liberal economic reform. However, the Brady Plan differed from the Baker Plan with its new emphasis on debt reduction, or partial forgiveness of debt. The Baker Plan had rejected the idea of debt reduction on the grounds that banks would not lend to countries that had failed to repay their debts, and that LDCs would be able to repay their debts and return to prosperity if the debt repayment period was simply extended. The Brady Plan, by contrast, recognized that LDCs could not regain their creditworthiness if their debt burden was too onerous, and that extending the debt repayment period without debt reduction had not led to a return of economic growth for some LDCs. The Brady Plan therefore encouraged U.S. private banks to accept a certain amount of debt reduction. Those creditor banks that agreed to reduce the value of the principal or interest on the debt owed to them would receive guarantees of repayment on the remaining portion of the debt. The IMF and World Bank would help finance these guarantees, and Japan committed funds for this purpose.[56]

In some respects the Brady Plan was quite successful, even though it took longer than expected to achieve results. For the 17 highly indebted countries on the Baker Plan list, the ratio of net external debt to exports of goods and services fell from 384 percent in 1986 to 225 percent in 1993. Furthermore, as Table 7.4 shows, the external-debt-to-GNP ratio was lower in 1994 than in 1985 for all the Baker-17 countries other than Nigeria, Cote d'Ivoire, and Ecuador.[57] However, the Brady Plan also had some definite shortcomings. Table 7.4 shows that overall foreign debt for most of the Baker-17 countries increased from 1985 to 1994. As mentioned, most of the Baker-17 countries were Latin American, and the combined foreign debt owed by Latin American states increased from $425 billion in 1987 to more than $600 billion in 1997. In 1997, Latin America was paying about 30 percent of its export earnings to service those debts, and it owed about 45 percent of its combined GDP to foreign creditors. The most serious shortcoming of the Brady Plan was that it dealt only with debt to commercial banks. It offered little to low-income LDC debtor states, because most of these countries' debts were to official creditors that included other governments and international financial institutions. Although the majority of these low-income debtors were in sub-Saharan Africa, they also included low-income LDCs in Asia and Latin America. In the 1990s, the debt situation was far worse for these low-income LDCs than it was for the middle-income LDCs on the Baker Plan's list of 17 countries.[58] Thus, it was necessary to develop a new debt relief plan, this time for the low-income LDCs.

The Heavily Indebted Poor Countries Initiative

From 1980 to 1990, the total external debt of sub-Saharan African countries increased from $56.2 billion (U.S.) to $147 billion, and their total external debt service payments (interest and principal) on long-term loans for this period rose from $4.5 billion to $11.1 billion. Thus, it was evident by the early 1990s that debt relief mechanisms were insufficient for the poorest, most heavily indebted LDCs, especially those in Africa. As mentioned, debt relief programs such as the Brady Plan did not deal with multilateral debt owed to the IMF, World Bank, and regional development banks. The 1996 G-7 summit meeting in Lyon, France, directly addressed this problem by agreeing to establish a plan aimed specifically at the debts of the poorest LDCs to the multilateral institutions, the **Heavily Indebted Poor Countries (HIPC) initiative.** The IMF and World Bank had previously refused to permit debt rescheduling of their loans, because of fears that this would damage their high credit ratings as international institutions. However, the presence of the IMF director-general and World Bank president at the Lyon G-7 meeting facilitated agreement on the HIPC initiative.[59]

The purpose of the HIPC program was to reduce the debts of eligible countries to a sustainable level, so they could service their debts without incurring loan arrears or requiring debt rescheduling, and without adversely affecting their economic development. The HIPC countries were those with low enough incomes to be eligible for soft loans from the World Bank group's IDA, and with external debts that were more than twice their annual export earnings. (See Chapter 11 for a discussion of the IDA). Forty-one countries initially met these criteria; 33 of them were in sub-Saharan Africa and the other 8 were in the Americas and Asia.[60] The HIPC program involved a demanding two-stage process, with each stage lasting up to three years. During the first stage, a country had to implement an IMF- and World Bank-supported economic reform program. If the IMF and World Bank then determined the existing debt relief mechanisms were insufficient, the country would enter the second stage, where it would receive some debt relief and financial support from bilateral and commercial creditors, and the multilateral institutions.[61]

The implemention of the HIPC initiative was therefore a slow process, and by May 1998 only 8 countries had made reasonable progress. Thirteen of the eligible countries had not even started the process. There were also indications that the debt situation of many of the poorest LDCs was not improving. For example, Honduras and Nicaragua were the only 2 Central American countries sufficiently poor to be on the list of 41 eligible for the HIPC program. Despite the HIPC program, economic growth was stagnant in Honduras and Nicaragua from 1990 to 1998, and in 1998 they had the largest external debt burdens of the Central American countries. In Africa, Zambia was devoting 40 percent of its national budget to foreign debt payments in 1997 and only 7 percent to basic education and health, sanitation, nutrition, clean water, and family planning. The costs of the debt crisis were also not spread evenly *within* debtor states, and there was considerable evidence that the poorest and most vulnerable people were the most adversely affected.[62] In response to the protracted debt problems of the low-income LDCs, a London-based "civil society" organization with worldwide connections called *Jubilee 2000* launched a debt forgiveness campaign in 1998.

Jubilee 2000 is composed of a large number of predominantly religious but also some secular civil society groups from around the world. Beginning in 1998, Jubilee 2000 called for full debt relief for low-income LDCs by the year 2000 and provided detailed proposals to accelerate the HIPC process, broaden its eligibility criteria, and increase the amount of assistance to the eligible countries. The rapid economic relief provided to more prosperous LDCs affected by the 1997 financial crisis in East and Southeast Asia demonstrated that the industrial states could move swiftly when foreign investment and the stock market were affected, and Jubilee 2000 supporters demanded a similar rapid response to the problems of the HIPCs. (The East Asian financial crisis is discussed in Chapter 11.) Jubilee 2000 also engaged in mass demonstrations; for example, it formed a human chain of 50,000 people around the convention center where the 1998 G-7 summit meeting was being held in Birmingham, England. The feeling was that an endorsement by the G-7 countries would ensure that the IMF, World Bank, and Paris Club would institute the desired changes in the HIPC initiative.

After some delays because of divisions among the G-7 countries, agreement was finally reached at the 1999 G-7 meeting in Cologne, Germany, to establish an *enhanced HIPC initiative,* and in September 1999, the IMF and World Bank governors adopted the major elements of the G-7 proposal. It appears that Jubilee 2000 had some influence in pressuring the industrial states to reach this decision. The enhanced initiative more than doubled the estimated amount of debt relief and added the central goal of reducing poverty in the poorest LDCs. In more specific terms, the enhanced initiative was designed to make the existing HIPC initiative faster (permitting LDCs to receive debt relief more quickly), broader (applying to more countries), and deeper (permitting a higher amount of debt write-off). Although these changes marked a significant improvement in the HIPC initiative, critics argue that the debt relief measures are still not sufficient and that IMF and World Bank SALs are not in the best interests of debtor LDCs (SALs are discussed later in this chapter and in Chapter 11). Even supporters of the enhanced HIPC initiative concede that "given the continued fragility of these countries, the initiative is not likely to provide recipients with a last exit from their debt problems, unless they achieve, strong, sustained economic growth."[63]

Assessing the Effectiveness of Debt Strategies

The international debt strategies had three main objectives: to prevent the collapse of the international banking and financial systems, to restore capital market access for the debtors, and to restore economic growth in the debtor countries. The Baker and Brady Plans were most successful in achieving the first two objectives. In regard to the first objective, by the late 1980s "the banks were no longer in the serious jeopardy that they faced at the outset of the debt crisis."[64] From 1982 to 1992, the loan exposure of all U.S. banks to the Baker list of 17 highly indebted countries fell from 130 percent of the banks' capital and reserves to only 27 percent; the loan exposure of British banks fell from 85 percent of capital to 12 percent; the loan exposure of German banks fell from 31 to 19 percent; and the loan exposure of French banks fell from 135 to 23 percent. In 1988, the BIS also oversaw an agreement that commercial banks in the OECD countries must have equity and reserves amounting to at least 8 percent of their outstanding loans, and this measure helped to restore some confidence in the international banking system.[65] In regard to the second objective, the Latin American debtor countries were able to return to the international financial markets far more rapidly after the 1980s debt crisis than they had after the 1930s crisis. Academics and policymakers with a liberal-economic orientation view these first two criteria as the most important for assessing the effectiveness of international debt strategies, and they therefore generally considered the Baker and Brady debt strategies to be successful.[66]

In marked contrast, historical structuralists and some interventionist liberals believe that the third objective of debt strategies—restoring economic growth in the Third World debtor countries—should be the most important, and they considered the Baker and Brady Plans to be largely ineffective. For example, one critic argued that the major creditor states and the IMF were primarily concerned with increasing "the immediate payment capacity of the debtor nations and not their development."[67] Historical structuralists also believed that the strategies for dealing with the debt crisis required far more sacrifice from the Third World than from the international bankers and the industrial states. These critics therefore concluded that "the debt crisis is by no means over yet; a banking crisis may have been tidied up, but a development crisis is in full swing."[68]

There is in fact considerable evidence that the Baker and Brady Plans had serious shortcomings in regard to the third objective of restoring LDC economic growth. This was true for the Baker-17 highly indebted countries, and was even more the case for the poorest LDC debtors, most of whom were not on the Baker-17 list. As discussed, the Baker and Brady Plans were concerned mainly with debt to commercial banks, and they did not provide relief for debt to the IMF and World Bank. Because the poorest LDCs were highly dependent on loans from the international institutions, the

Baker and Brady Plans were of little use to them. In 1996, the industrial states there-fore instituted the HIPC initiative for the poorest highly indebted states, most of them in sub-Saharan Africa, and in 1998 the enhanced HIPC initiative was introduced. The industrial states should be credited for gradually developing more assertive debt strategies, shifting from debt rescheduling under the Baker Plan to debt reduction un-der the Brady Plan to debt relief for the poorest LDCs under the HIPC initiative. However, one could argue that it always took a new crisis before the IMF, the World Bank, and industrial states upgraded their debt relief efforts, and it remains to be seen whether the latest HIPC initiative is sufficient to deal with the debt problems of the poorest LDCs.

The IMF and the World Bank have been special targets of criticism for historical structuralists, who argue that the Bretton Woods institutions have given highest priority to ensuring that LDC debtors adopt liberal-economic policies and repay their loans. Ac-cording to these critics, a radical restructuring of LDC debtor economies is required to promote their economic development, but IMF conditionality precludes such possibili-ties. Although some liberal economists concede that IMF and World Bank conditional-ity has contributed to economic dislocation in LDC debtor countries, they nevertheless argue that, in liberalizing their policies, the debtor countries have "laid the foundations for subsequent sustainable growth." However, critics of the debt strategies believe that

> there is some reason to be sceptical about the view that the Third World economies are now "leaner and fitter" to face the world ahead beyond the debt crisis. They are certainly leaner but whether they are fitter remains to be seen.[69]

It is important to note that the policies of the advanced industrial states in other areas such as trade sometimes counteract their efforts to assist the LDCs through debt relief strategies. For LDCs to both succeed in development and repay their debts, they require access to developed country markets for their exports. LDCs have a com-parative advantage in the production of agricultural goods, textiles, apparel, and other products that do not require large amounts of sophisticated machinery and technol-ogy. However, the industrial states currently impose some of their highest tariffs on these products because of domestic pressures from their workers. Although the indus-trial states give preferential treatment to some LDC exports, this treatment often does not extend to exports where LDCs have a comparative advantage (see Chapter 8). The foreign debt strategies would be far more effective if the industrial states were more willing to open their markets to LDC exports.[70]

To this point in the chapter, we have discussed the effects of the debt crisis only on the Third World countries. However, many emerging states in Eastern Europe and the FSU were also major foreign debtors in the 1980s and 1990s.

THE EMERGING ECONOMIES AND FOREIGN DEBT

The Soviet bloc countries contended with many of the same economic problems as the Third World during the 1980s debt crisis, including growing balance-of-payments deficits, declining terms of trade, and stagnating economic growth. The increased need for financing was also causing Soviet bloc countries to look toward the IMF and the World Bank. Thus, Hungary and Poland joined these institutions in the 1980s, partly in efforts to deal with their growing debt problems.[71]

Eastern Europe

During the 1970s, the Eastern Europeans borrowed heavily on international financial markets to finance industrial investment. However, the oil price shocks, poor investment decisions, economic inefficiency, lack of export competitiveness, and high interest rates on their foreign debt created severe economic problems. Indeed, "Eastern Europe experienced a debt crisis similar and prior to that of Latin America."[72] As early as 1981 an acute foreign exchange shortage forced Poland to negotiate a rescheduling of its debt with official and private creditors. Poland had financed an ambitious program of industrial investment with external funding, but its economic performance and export levels were insufficient to service its debt. Like the Third World, the Eastern European countries have followed alternative development strategies with major implications for their foreign debt. The two basic strategies for dealing with debt were often referred to as the Polish and Czech-Hungarian models.

The Polish model involved large debt buildup followed by repeated debt reschedulings and eventually official debt reduction, partly based on political considerations. Poland's net debt to the Western developed market economies increased from $7.6 billion in 1975 to $22.1 billion in 1980, and the country's debt and debt service ratio were the highest in the Soviet bloc in 1981. Because the Soviet Union seemed unwilling to assist Poland, and the Soviet bloc countries were not implementing effective adjustment measures, Western creditors responded by sharply reducing further credits to all Eastern European states, which exacerbated the crisis. The growing economic problems in Poland resulted in severe economic austerity measures and the formation of the Solidarity Movement. When the Polish government responded by imposing martial law in December 1981, the West in turn imposed trade sanctions and suspended debt repayment talks. Although private banks agreed to refinance some Polish debt, Western governments did not resume rescheduling negotiations on official debts until Poland ended martial law in August 1983.

Poland had seven reschedulings of its commercial bank debt and five reschedulings of its official debt from 1981 to 1990. When a democratically elected government took over from the communist military government in late 1989 and the new government adopted a program to promote macroeconomic stabilization and structural change in early 1990, the West became far more willing to provide further assistance under the Brady Plan. Indeed, Western governments, which held two-thirds of Poland's debt, offered a 50 percent forgiveness of its official bilateral debt in 1991 as a result of Paris Club negotiations. Although Poland had requested 80 percent forgiveness, the Paris Club's 50 percent offer was exceptionally high; the Club had previously offered a maximum forgiveness of 33 percent to low-income countries. Under pressure from the G-7 governments, the commercial banks also reached an agreement with Poland in March 1994 to reduce its private debt by 45 percent. Bulgaria, in many respects, followed the Polish model, and the private banks agreed in principle to a substantial reduction of Bulgaria's debt in late 1993 (most of Bulgaria's debt was private). The former Czechoslovakia and Hungary were also deeply affected by the 1980s debt crisis, but unlike the Polish-Bulgarian model they followed more restrained and prudent economic policies in efforts to achieve a favorable creditworthiness record. For example, in 1981 Hungary had the highest per capita debt in the Soviet bloc, and its debt service ratio was second highest after Poland. Nevertheless, Hungary joined the IMF and World Bank in 1982 and instituted a series of major economic reforms. As a result of their more prudent policies, both Hungary and the former Czechoslovakia did not require the debt relief measures that were offered to Poland and Bulgaria.[73]

As with the Third World countries, the differences in debt strategies of the emerging countries stemmed partly from domestic economic and political factors. For example, the Polish model of large debt buildup resulted partly from political events in the 1970s, which prevented the Polish government from taking decisive action to deal with its looming debt problems. After Wladyslaw Gomulka was removed as first secretary of the Communist party in Poland in 1970, policies were adopted that eventually led to decentralization of the party and divisions within the top political leadership. When high oil prices and difficulty in exporting goods contributed to serious economic problems in the late 1970s, the fractured political leadership in Poland enabled societal groups such as workers to resist austerity moves (which would have been made at the workers' expense). For example, when the leaders attempted to raise prices and hold down wages as part of an economic austerity program, several hundred strikes by workers forced them to reverse these moves. It was not until December 1981, when the military took control in Poland and dominated strong societal groups such as Solidarity, that an austerity program was introduced (which contributed to domestic hardship and eventually to further protests).[74]

In contrast to the case in Poland, in Hungary domestic political developments contributed to the implementation of more prudent economic policies. Although Hungary instituted some austerity measures, it also adopted a series of reforms to make the economy more efficient and to give profits and prices a larger role in resource allocation. The national trauma resulting from the suppression of the 1956 revolt in Hungary had led to a number of developments that contributed to these economic reforms. For example, Hungary turned to collective instead of one-person leadership, and these leaders supported the introduction of a limited market mechanism and a more balanced development strategy based on specific Hungarian conditions. Unlike reformers elsewhere, Hungarian supporters of economic reform also "sought not to weaken the [Communist] party but to use it to pursue their particular economic goals."[75] When Hungary was confronted with debt problems, its earlier reforms and its political ability to institute changes enabled it to meet its debt service obligations far more effectively than Poland.

Despite the different development strategies followed by Eastern European countries, their debt problems (as was the case for LDC debtors) also resulted from external events that were largely beyond their control. All Eastern European countries, for example, suffered economically from their increased dependence on imports from nonsocialist countries to promote economic growth and investment after 1985, from the collapse of the Soviet bloc's CMEA in 1991, and from deterioration in their terms of trade as the Soviet Union ended subsidized oil exports. External disruptions had a particularly severe effect on some Eastern European countries such as Bulgaria. Thus, the Gulf War adversely affected Bulgaria's exports to

Iraq, the breakup of the CMEA had major consequences for Bulgaria because of its high share of exports to the Soviet Union, and the war in Yugoslavia seriously disrupted Bulgarian export routes to Western Europe. The structural transition to market-oriented economies produced further instability, and domestic output in Eastern Europe fell by almost 25 percent in 1990–91. This combination of internal and external factors contributed to the foreign debt problems of the Eastern European states.

The FSU Countries

The Soviet Union also had external debt problems, which were greatly exacerbated by the breakup of the country. In mid-1992, Russia began negotiations with the other states of the FSU on "zero-option" agreements, in which Russia assumed responsibility for the entire debt of the FSU while taking control of all the FSU's foreign assets. Russia was willing to assume the entire FSU debt for several reasons: it had the strongest resource base with which to service the debt, the division of assets such as embassies seemed to make little sense, and the assumption of the debt could help preserve Russia's hegemonic role in the region. Assets that Russia received by assuming the external debt of the FSU included gold and foreign exchange, embassies abroad, and a portfolio of loans to countries such as India, Cuba, Libya, and Vietnam.[76]

However, the collapse of the Russian economy severely undercut the country's debt-servicing capacity, and Russia had to seek IMF loans and negotiate Paris Club reschedulings. In late 1997, Russia's foreign debt totalled $123.5 billion; $91.4 billion of this total was debt of the FSU, and $32.1 billion was the intrinsic debt of the Russian Federation. In the view of two Russian economists, "the future of Russia in the next ten to fifteen years will be defined by the terms on which the country is able to achieve the settlement of foreign debt."[77] The payments on Russia's foreign debt in 1999 amounted to about 10 percent of its GDP, which was comparable to the entire federal budget's share of GDP and about 30 percent of national savings. Thus, Russia will continue to require debt relief from the IMF and the Paris Club to meet its debt obligations. In the longer term, Russia will only be able to resolve its debt problems when it attains a higher economic growth rate. This will require accelerating economic reforms, restructuring enterprises, improving the investment climate by protecting the rights of investors and lenders, improving the tax system, ensuring reliable operation of the banking system, encouraging transparency in financial reporting by business, countering crime and corruption, and instituting social and political reforms.[78]

THE DEBT CRISIS AND THE CHANGING ROLES OF THE IMF AND THE WORLD BANK

A major new element in the 1980s debt crisis was the central role played by the international financial institutions—the IMF and the World Bank. The debt crisis also altered the relationship between the IMF and the World Bank as the two institutions adopted new functions that overlap in some significant respects. The problem of overlap was recognized when these two institutions were created, and the Bretton Woods negotiators deliberately excluded references to Third World development in the IMF Articles of Agreement because the "development" function was assigned to the World Bank.[79] Thus, the IMF was to provide short-term loans to *any* country with balance-of-payments problems, whereas the World Bank was to provide long-term loans specifically for reconstruction and development (see Chapter 11). The only direct linkage between the two organizations was that membership in the IMF was made a prerequisite for membership in the World Bank.[80]

Despite the initial separation of these two institutions, in the 1960s the World Bank began to infringe directly on the IMF's territory. Diverging from its practice of providing loans for specific development projects, the World Bank provided large-scale *program lending* to India for general balance-of-payments support. The bank also attempted to link this support with general conditions for policy reform by the Indian government.[81] The World Bank justified its actions by arguing that India's balance-of-payments deficit resulted from development problems that were long term rather than transitory in nature. However, IMF officials argued that the World Bank's balance-of-payments funding with conditionality attached was a direct infringement on the IMF's functions. In 1966 the two organizations signed an agreement in efforts to avoid further overlap problems, but the agreement did not fully clarify the differences in their responsibilities.[82]

Several changes in the 1970s contributed to a marked increase in overlap between IMF and World Bank functions. First, the IMF became less involved with promoting exchange rate stabilization when the Bretton Woods system of pegged exchange rates collapsed. The IMF's other major function of providing loans to countries, in which there are possibilities of overlap with the World Bank, therefore became more prominent. Second, the IMF initially provided loans to all countries, but by the late 1970s it was lending almost exclusively to LDCs—the same group of countries receiving World Bank loans. Third, although the World Bank Articles of Agreement (Article 3, Section 4) state that the bank should provide loans for specific projects "except in special circumstances," bank officials became increasingly aware of situations in which LDCs could not obtain needed funding for their development programs by borrowing only for specific projects. In 1971, the bank's executive directors therefore decided that program lending of the type they had provided to India in the mid-1960s was appropriate under certain circumstances. World Bank program lending to finance commodity imports has distinct similarities with IMF lending for balance-of-payments purposes.[83]

The most important reason for increased overlap related to the oil shocks in the 1970s and the foreign debt crisis in the 1980s. In reacting to the debt crisis, the IMF and the World Bank developed some remarkably similar new lending programs for indebted LDCs. The IMF found that its traditional short-term loans for balance-of-payments problems with 3- to 5-year repayment periods were not adequate for a number of LDCs that had protracted payments problems. To deal with the debt crisis, the IMF therefore also provided *medium-term* SALs with repayment periods ranging from 5.5 to 10 years. As for the World Bank, it found that its long-term loans for development projects with repayment periods of 15 to 20 years (and in some cases 40 years) were also not the type of funding Third World debtors required to deal with their more immediate balance-of-payments problems. Like the IMF, the World Bank therefore developed medium-term SALs for Third World debtors. Although the IMF still provided short-term balance-of-payments loans and the World Bank still provided long-term development loans, they *both* were now providing medium-term SALs to deal with the debt crisis.[84]

The greater overlap of functions between the IMF and the World Bank has increased both the potential for conflict and the need for collaboration between the two organizations. The overlapping of functions also raises questions as to whether both should continue to exist as separate institutions. Indeed, *The Economist* predicted in 1991 that a merger between the two Bretton Woods institutions "makes sense, and in time it will happen."[85] Despite this prediction, several reasons are given for maintaining the two as distinctive bodies. First, the World Bank group is composed of five institutions, and it is already too large by itself for efficient management (see Chapter 11). Joining the World Bank and the IMF would simply compound the problems related to size. Second, development issues are exceedingly complex, and it is important that a range of institutions provide advice and establish conditions for loans. Although historical structuralists argue that IMF and World Bank policies are virtually identical, liberal economists can point to IMF–World Bank disputes as an indication of competing perspectives. Third, the IMF's responsibilities extend well beyond providing loans to LDCs. Although the IMF's monetary role declined when the pegged exchange rate regime collapsed in the early 1970s, the IMF continues to provide advice to states on monetary issues, and it could play a more important role in global monetary and financial issues in the future.[86]

A final reason for maintaining a separate IMF and World Bank is that the disintegration of the Soviet bloc and the dire economic circumstances in much of sub-Saharan Africa provide sufficient economic challenges for both institutions, helping to restore a differentiation of their functions.[87] Although the IMF has been given the lead role in dealing with debt problems of the emerging states in Eastern Europe and the FSU, the World Bank as the main multilateral development institution has been coordinating aid efforts in sub-Saharan Africa.

THE IMF, THE WORLD BANK, AND THE DEBTOR COUNTRIES

Although new efforts at IMF–World Bank collaboration are partly designed to avert institutional conflict, Third World countries are highly suspicious of these moves. Historical structuralists and LDC debtors often criticize IMF conditionality as an unwarranted infringement on LDC sovereignty, and they argue that the liberal-economic conditions placed on IMF and World Bank loans hinder rather than facilitate development.[88] With moves toward IMF–World Bank collaboration, LDCs are concerned about the increased likelihood of *cross-conditionality,* in which the IMF's determination that a loan applicant is uncreditworthy prevents the applicant from receiving World Bank as well as IMF funding. Thus, Third World countries fear that the conditions placed on official loans will become even more onerous. Although the IMF and World Bank have ruled out cross-conditionality in a formal, legal sense, there is no doubt that they sometimes engage in this practice on an informal basis.[89]

Critics also charge that the IMF and World Bank's SALs put the onus of adjustment on the LDC debtors—and on the most vulnerable groups within LDCs—even though responsibility for the debt crisis was shared between North and South. SALs pressure LDC debtors to reduce the role of the state and increase the role of the market, with little concern for the distributional and social welfare effects of these policies. Because SALs are intended to improve LDCs' balance of payments by reducing spending for social services, lowering wages, emphasizing production for export over local consumption, and ending subsidies for local industries, it is the poorer, more vulnerable individuals in LDCs who are often the most severely affected. Thus, a large body of literature exists on the effects of IMF and World Bank SALs on poorer women and children in LDCs.

Historical structuralists argue that it is necessary to be aware of the negative distributional effects of IMF and World Bank SALs. Poorer women in LDCs, who have the responsibility for the unpaid work of managing the household, are the most severely affected by IMF and World Bank pressures for a reduction in LDC funding for public services. Women have primary responsibility in the household for cooking, cleaning, and health care, so public sector services such as clean water supplies, waste disposal, public transport, and health facilities lighten women's household work and enable them to gain education and skills so they can enter the paid work force. Thus, the burden on poorer women increases as IMF and World Bank structural adjustment programs require cutbacks in social expenditures on health and nutrition. As the government provides less of these services, women must make up the difference by providing them through the home. The school dropout rate of young girls is also likely to increase as a result of SALs because girls must help with the household labor and often work in sweatshops to supplement the family's income. Children, and pregnant and lactating mothers, are also the groups most seriously affected by IMF and World Bank pressures to remove food subsidies and increase food prices for consumers in LDCs. In other words, the informal sector in LDCs grows because of structural adjustment programs, and poorer women often pay the price through increased unpaid work and a deterioration of health and nutrition.[90]

In response to these criticisms, the World Bank has taken some measures to ameliorate the effects of LDC structural adjustment programs on the poor while retaining its concerns for promoting efficiency and liberal-economic growth. For example, the Bank continues to view cuts in food subsidies as desirable in terms of efficiency, but it has attempted to ameliorate the negative effects on the poor through school lunches, food stamps, and the provision of food aid.[91] IMF and World Bank officials would argue that structural adjustment programs aimed at market efficiency and decreased public sector involvement can be compatible with distributional and social welfare goals, but they have not convinced many of their critics.

CONCLUSION

What is the relevance of the three IPE theoretical perspectives and the three major themes of the text—globalization, North-North relations, and North-South relations—for the issue of foreign debt? The 1980s foreign debt crisis provides a prime example of the effects of growing interdependence and globalization on the policies of indebted Third World and emerging states. The origins of the debt crisis stemmed back to the

1970s, when commercial banks extended a large volume of loans to Third World countries after the OPEC price increases. These private loans were particularly attractive to the borrowing LDCs because of their low interest rates and lack of conditionality. Although orthodox liberals emphasize the imprudent borrowing behavior and inefficient domestic policies of LDCs as major causes of the debt crisis, historical structuralists focus instead on the long-term dependency of LDCs and the irresponsible behavior of the commercial banks and creditor governments. Despite these differences of view regarding the culpability of debtors versus creditors, most would agree that unexpected changes resulting from global interdependence, such as the oil and food crises of the 1970s, should be included among the major factors causing the debt crisis.

There is also broad agreement that the IMF and the World Bank have used SALs to induce debtor countries to adopt liberal-economic policies, thus opening their economies to the forces of globalization. For example, ever since Mexico declared in 1982 that it could no longer service its foreign debt, Mexican governments have steadily moved toward policies of economic liberalization. These moves include Mexico's shift from ISI to export-led growth policies, the massive withdrawal of public subsidies in most economic sectors, domestic economic changes to attract foreign investment, and the opening of the economy to international trade. In the trade area, Mexico joined GATT in 1986 and engaged in further liberalization of its trade and foreign investment policies before joining NAFTA in 1993. Mexico is of course not alone in making such changes, and one can see them throughout the Third World. Thus, the average import tariffs in Latin America as a whole declined from 56 percent in 1985 to 16 percent in mid-1992, largely as a result of unilateral trade liberalization, and Latin American states signed at least 31 agreements to liberalize trade from 1990 to 1996.[92]

Although these Third World policy changes resulted partly from evidence that some previous policies such as import substitution had been unsuccessful, there is no doubt that pressure from the major industrial states and the IMF and World Bank were also critical factors in the decision of indebted countries to open their economies. Sharp differences of view exist, however, regarding the effects of these liberal-economic policies on the indebted states. Liberal economists often argue that the strategies to deal with debt have been quite successful, preventing the collapse of the international banking system and restoring access to the capital market for many of the indebted states. Liberals assume that though the changes in policy required of debtor states have caused hardship for some groups and individuals, the long-term effects of the shift to economic openness will be beneficial for Third World and emerging countries.

Realists and historical structuralists, by contrast, argue that liberals largely ignore the effect of political and economic inequality among states on the debt issue. Although globalization has facilitated the *transmission* of liberal values and policies to the advanced industrial states, these values and policies have been *imposed on* the Third World debtor states. Liberals also consider the IMF and the World Bank to be politically neutral institutions, whereas realists and historical structuralists view them as conduits for the imposition of policies favored by the most powerful industrial states and private actors on the least powerful. Although IMF and World Bank SALs require borrowing countries to adopt prescribed liberal-economic policies, these conditions are ultimately set not by the IOs but by their most powerful member states.[93] Historical structuralists also argue that the debt strategies required far more sacrifice from the Third World debtors than from the international banks and that IMF and World Bank conditionality requirements have been designed to meet the needs of international capital rather than those of the indebted states. Indeed, IMF requirements that debtor countries reduce their social service expenditures, increase their exports, remove their restrictions on capital flows, and devalue their currencies have often had the most negative impact on the poorest and weakest groups in society.

This chapter on the debt crisis tells us a good deal not only about the themes of globalization and North-South inequality but also about the theme of North-North relations. Although the United States has declined as a hegemon in some economic areas, it clearly took a leadership position in helping to manage the debt crisis. U.S. leadership during the debt crisis was a reflection of the dominant position it maintained with regard to financial and monetary issues "well into the 1980s because of the relative attractiveness of U.S. financial markets, the preeminence of U.S. financial institutions and the dollar in global markets, and the relative size of the U.S. economy."[94] Even in this area, however, there were indications of a gradual shift from U.S. to more collective Northern leadership. Thus, a range of formal and informal institutions in which the industrial states dominated played a major role in LDC debt management. These institutions included the IMF, the World Bank, the BIS, the Paris Club, the London Club, and the G-7. Although the Paris and London Clubs had dealt with debt issues over a long period, the G-7 began to assume an important role on debt issues in the 1980s and 1990s. Consensus among the G-7 leaders ensured that the IMF would support adoption of the Brady Plan involving debt reduction in 1989, and the HIPC initiative for the highly indebted poor countries in 1996.

The largest international banks played an important role in managing LDC debt problems through private creditor committees (the London Club) until the Mexican debt crisis in 1982. Thereafter, realists can point out that it was the most powerful industrial states, and the international institutions such as the IMF and the World Bank that they supported, that managed the debt crisis, not the private banks and the market. Only states were able to mobilize sufficient resources to deal with the crisis, and only official pressures were sufficient to induce banks to continue lending to the debtors on the one hand and to force debtor governments to meet conditionality requirements on the other. However, liberal interdependence theorists and historical structuralists can point out that there were definitive limitations to the industrial state capacities for adequate economic management. The prolongation of the debt crisis despite successive strategies such as the Baker Plan, the Brady Plan and the HIPC initiative support the liberal contention that states today have only limited control over market transactions, capital flows, and the behavior of private institutions such as the international banks. Historical structuralists, on the other hand, have pointed to the fact that the debt management strategies were far more successful in protecting the major international banks and in restoring capital market access than they were in ensuring a return to economic growth in the debtor LDCs. Finally, it is important to note that civil society groups such as Jubilee 2000 had some role in pressuring the industrial states and international institutions to alleviate the debt problems of the poorest LDCs. Although these civil society groups were opposing the impact of globalization on the Third World debtors, they were also using the accoutrements of globalization such as the World Wide Web to communicate their ideas and exert some influence.

NOTES

1. William R. Cline, *International Debt Reexamined* (Washington, DC: Institute for International Economics, 1995), p. 1.
2. See Albert Fishlow, "Lessons from the Past: Capital Markets During the 19th Century and the Interwar Period," *International Organization* 39-3 (Summer 1985), pp. 383–439; Barbara Stallings, *Banker to the Third World: U.S. Portfolio Investment in Latin America, 1900–1986* (Berkeley, CA: University of California Press, 1987); Barry Eichengreen and Richard Portes, "Dealing with Debt: The 1930s and the 1980s," in Ishrat Husain and Ishac Diwan, eds., *Dealing with the Debt Crisis: A World Bank Symposium* (Washington, DC: World Bank, 1989), pp. 69–86; and Barry Eichengreen and Peter H. Lindert, eds., *The International Debt Crisis in Historical Perspective* (Cambridge, MA: MIT Press, 1989).
3. Stuart Corbridge, *Debt and Development* (Oxford: Blackwell Publishers, 1993), p. 25; Cline, *International Debt Reexamined*, p. 6.
4. Stallings, *Banker to the Third World*, pp. 313–314.
5. Paul R. Krugman and Maurice Obstfeld, *International Economics: Theory and Policy*, 3rd ed. (New York: HarperCollins, 1994), p. 327.
6. Rudiger Dornbusch and Stanley Fischer, "Third World Debt," *Science* 234, November 14, 1986, p. 836; Corbridge, *Debt and Development*, p. 15.
7. Miles Kahler, "Politics and International Debt: Explaining the Crisis," *International Organization* 39-3 (Summer 1985), p. 357.
8. John T. Cuddington, "The Extent and Causes of the Debt Crisis of the 1980s," in Husain and Diwan, eds., *Dealing with the Debt Crisis*, p. 15.
9. World Bank, *World Debt Tables 1992–93, Vol. 1* (Washington, DC: IBRD, 1992), pp. 41–45. For a historical structuralist perspective on early warning signs of a debt crisis, see Cheryl Payer, *Lent and Lost: Foreign Credit and Third World Development* (London: Zed Books, 1991), pp. 83–89.
10. The World Bank, *Annual Report—1983* (Washington, DC: IBRD, 1983), p. 34.
11. William R. Cline, "International Debt: Analysis, Experience and Prospects," *Journal of Development Planning* 16 (1985), p. 26.
12. Theodore H. Cohn, *Canadian Food Aid: Domestic and Foreign Policy Implications*, Monograph Series in World Affairs (Denver, CO: University of Denver, Graduate School of International Studies, 1979), pp. 25–26.
13. Charles Lipson, "The International Organization of Third World Debt," *International Organization* 35-4 (Autumn 1981), p. 611; Benjamin J. Cohen, "Balance-of-Payments Financing: Evolution of a Regime," in Stephen D. Krasner, ed., *International Regimes* (Ithaca, NY: Cornell University Press, 1983), p. 329.
14. Albert Fishlow, "Lessons from the Past," p. 433.
15. Kahler, "Politics and International Debt," pp. 358–359.
16. John Loxley, "International Capital Markets, the Debt Crisis and Development," in Roy Culpeper, Albert Berry, and Frances Stewart, eds., *Global Development Fifty Years After Bretton Woods: Essays in Honour of Gerald K. Helleiner* (New York: St. Martin's Press, 1997), pp. 138–142.

    Some analysts argue that the share of the OPEC surplus that was recycled through the banking system was actually quite small and that the low interest rates were the main reason for the increase in commercial bank loans to LDCs. See Edwin M. Truman, "U.S. Policy on the Problems of International Debt," *Federal Reserve Bulletin* 75-11 (November 1989), p. 728.

17. Stallings, *Banker to the Third World,* pp. 184–186; Ricardo Ffrench-Davis, "External Debt, Adjustment, and Development in Latin America," in Richard E. Feinberg and Ricardo Ffrench-Davis, eds., *Development and External Debt in Latin America: Bases for a New Consensus* (Notre Dame, IN: University of Notre Dame Press, 1988), p. 40.

18. Ethan B. Kapstein, *Governing the Global Economy: International Finance and the State* (Cambridge, MA: Harvard University Press, 1994), pp. 60–69.

19. International Monetary Fund, *Annual Report of the Executive Directors for the Fiscal Year ended April 30, 1977* (Washington, DC: IMF, 1977), pp. 40–41.

20. Cline, *International Debt Reexamined,* pp. 2–3; Jeffrey Sachs, "External Debt and Macroeconomic Performance in Latin America and East Asia," in William C. Brainard and George L. Perry, eds., *Brookings Papers on Economic Activity* 2 (Washington, DC: Brookings Institution, 1985), pp. 523–535.

21. Lewis W. Snider, "The Political Performance of Third World Governments and the Debt Crisis," *American Political Science Review* 84-1 (December 1990), pp. 1263–1280.

22. Sachs, "External Debt and Macroeconomic Performance in Latin America and East Asia," p. 526.

23. Cheryl Payer, *The Debt Trap: The IMF and the Third World* (Middlesex, UK: Penguin, 1974), pp. 45–49.

24. Peter Körner, Gero Maass, Thomas Siebold, and Ranier Tetzlaff, *The IMF and the Debt Crisis: A Guide to the Third World's Dilemma,* translated by Paul Knight (London: Zed Books, 1986), pp. 30–31; Peter Evans, *Dependent Development: The Alliance of Multinational, State, and Local Capital in Brazil* (Princeton, NJ: Princeton University Press, 1979).

25. Payer, *The Debt Trap,* p. 48. See also Robert E. Wood, *From Marshall Plan to Debt Crisis: Foreign Aid and Development Choices in the World Economy* (Berkeley, CA: University of California Press, 1986), pp. 233–241.

26. Jesús Silva-Herzog, "The Costs for Latin America's Development," in Robert A. Pastor, ed., *Latin America's Debt Crisis: Adjusting to the Past or Planning for the Future?* (Boulder, CO: Rienner, 1987), p. 33.

27. Peter H. Lindert and Peter J. Morton, "How Sovereign Debt Has Worked," in Jeffrey D. Sachs, ed., *Developing Country Debt and Economic Performance, Vol. 1: The International Financial System* (Chicago: University of Chicago Press, 1989), pp. 66–77. The concept of an international debt regime is discussed in Thomas J. Biersteker, "International Financial Negotiations and Adjustment Bargaining: An Overview," in Thomas J. Biersteker, ed., *Dealing with Debt: International Financial Negotiations and Adjustment Bargaining* (Boulder, CO: Westview Press, 1993), pp. 1–15.

28. The "nesting" terminology was first used by Vinod Aggarwal. For a discussion of the textile and agricultural trade regimes, see V. K. Aggarwal, *Liberal Protectionism: The International Politics of Organized Textile Trade* (Berkeley, CA: University of California Press, 1985); and Theodore H. Cohn, "The Changing Role of the United States in the Global Agricultural Trade Regime," in William P. Avery, ed., *World Agriculture and the GATT, International Political Economy Yearbook, Vol. 7* (Boulder, CO: Rienner, 1993), pp. 17–38.

29. Cohen, "Balance-of-Payments Financing: Evolution of a Regime," pp. 319–323.

30. Valerie J. Assetto, *The Soviet Bloc in the IMF and the IBRD* (Boulder, CO: Westview Press, 1988), pp. 186–187; Jozef M. van Brabant, *The Planned Economies and International Economic Organizations* (Cambridge: Cambridge University Press, 1991), p. 126.

31. Harold K. Jacobson and Michel Oksenberg, *China's Participation in the IMF, the World Bank, and GATT: Toward a Global Economic Order* (Ann Arbor, MI: University of Michigan Press, 1990), pp. 46–52.

32. William Feeney, "Chinese Policy in Multilateral Financial Institutions," in Samuel S. Kim, ed., *China and the World: Chinese Foreign Policy in the Post-Mao Era* (Boulder, CO:

Westview Press, 1984), pp. 266–271; Samuel S. Kim, "Whither Post-Mao Chinese Global Policy?" *International Organization* 35-3 (Summer 1981), pp. 455–457.

33. Klaus Schröder, "The IMF and the Countries of the Council for Mutual Economic Assistance," *Intereconomics* 2 (March/April 1982), pp. 88–90; Marie Lavigne, "Eastern European Countries and the IMF," in Béla Csikós-Nagy and David G. Young, eds., *East-West Economic Relations in the Changing Global Environment* (London: Macmillan, 1986), pp. 300–304.

34. Leah A. Haus, *Globalizing the GATT: The Soviet Union's Successor States, Eastern Europe, and the International Trading System* (Washington, DC: Brookings Institution, 1992), p. 104; "Sorting Out Russia," *The Economist*, September 26, 1992, pp. 97–98.

35. Aziz Ali Mohammed, "The Role of International Financial Institutions," in John P. Hardt and Richard F. Kaufman, eds., *East-Central European Economies in Transition* (Armonk, NY: Sharpe, for the Joint Economic Committee, U.S. Congress, 1995), pp. 192–195.

36. Assetto, *The Soviet Bloc in the IMF and the IBRD*, p. 50.

37. Jacobson and Oksenberg, *China's Participation in the IMF, the World Bank, and GATT*, p. 128; Feeney, "Chinese Policy in Multilateral Financial Institutions," p. 274; Richard W. Stevenson, "In Borrowing from the I.M.F., Did Yeltsin Get a Sweetheart Deal?" *New York Times*, March 3, 1996, p. A5.

38. Sources on the Paris and London Clubs include Alexis Rieffel, *The Role of the Paris Club in Managing Debt Problems* (Princeton, NJ: Princeton University, Essays in International Finance, no. 161, December 1985); Alexis Rieffel, "The Paris Club, 1978–1983," *Columbia Journal of Transnational Law* 23-1 (1984), pp. 83–110; and Christine A. Kearney, "The Creditor Clubs: Paris and London," in Biersteker, ed., *Dealing with Debt*, pp. 61–76.

39. Rieffel, *The Role of the Paris Club in Managing Debt Problems*, pp. 4–14.

40. Michael G. Kuhn with Jorge P. Guzman, *Multilateral Official Debt Rescheduling: Recent Experience, World Economic and Financial Surveys* (Washington, DC: IMF, November 1990), p. 7.

41. Charles Lipson, "International Debt and International Institutions," in Miles Kahler, ed., *The Politics of International Debt* (Ithaca, NY: Cornell University Press, 1986), pp. 222–226; and Charles Lipson, "Bankers' Dilemmas: Private Cooperation in Rescheduling Sovereign Debts," in Kenneth A. Oye, ed., *Cooperation Under Anarchy* (Princeton, NJ: Princeton University Press, 1986), pp. 200–225.

42. See Payer, *Lent and Lost*, pp. 52–56.

43. James, *International Monetary Cooperation Since Bretton Woods*, p. 347.

44. Benjamin J. Cohen, "International Debt and Linkage Strategies: Some Foreign-policy Implications for the United States," *International Organization* 39-4 (Autumn 1985), p. 722; Nicholas Bayne, *Hanging in There: The G7 and G8 Summit in Maturity and Renewal* (Aldershot, UK: Ashgate, 2000), p. 64.

45. Paul Krugman, "LDC Debt Policy," in Martin Feldstein, ed., *American Economic Policy in the 1980s* (Chicago: University of Chicago Press, 1994), pp. 692–694; Age F. P. Bakker, *International Financial Institutions* (New York: Longman, 1996), pp. 95–96.

46. William R. Cline, *International Debt and the Stability of the World Economy*, Policy Analyses in International Economics 4 (Washington, DC: Institute for International Economics, September 1983), p. 74.

47. Lipson, "Bankers' Dilemmas: Private Cooperation in Rescheduling Sovereign Debts," p. 223; Lipson, "International Debt and International Institutions," pp. 220–227.

48. Kapstein, *Governing the Global Economy*, p. 82.

49. Dornbusch and Fischer, "Third World Debt," p. 838.

50. William R. Cline, "The Baker Plan and Brady Reformulation: An Evaluation," in Husain and Diwan, eds., *Dealing with the Debt Crisis: A World Bank Symposium*, p. 177.

51. Corbridge, *Debt and Development*, p. 65.

52. Edwin M. Truman, "U.S. Policy on the Problems of International Debt," *Federal Reserve Bulletin* 75-11 (November 1989), p. 730; Richard E. Feinberg and Delia M. Boylan, "Modular Multilateralism: North-South Economic Relations in the 1990s," in Brad Roberts, ed., *New Forces in the World Economy* (Cambridge, MA: MIT Press, 1996), p. 45.

53. Payer, *Lent and Lost,* p. 97.

54. Paul R. Krugman, "Debt Relief is Cheap," *Foreign Policy* 80 (Fall 1990), pp. 141–152. Some economists considered the debt problem to be a symptom rather than a cause of slow economic growth. See, for example, Jeremy Bulow and Kenneth Rogoff, "Cleaning Up Third World Debt Without Getting Taken to the Cleaners," *Journal of Economic Perspectives* 4-1 (Winter 1990), pp. 31–42.

55. "Debtor's Prison" in a Survey of Third-World Finance, *The Economist,* September 25, 1993, pp. 11–12; Bayne, *Hanging in There,* p. 64.

56. Jeffrey Sachs, "Making the Brady Plan Work," *Foreign Affairs* 68-3 (Summer 1989), pp. 87–92.

57. The IMF statistics were not available for Venezuela and the former Yugoslavia.

58. Fred Rosen, "Back on the Agenda: Ten Years After the Debt Crisis," *NACLA Report on the Americas* 31-3 (1997), p. 22; William Cline, "Managing International Debt," *The Economist,* February 18, 1995, pp. 17–19; Ross P. Buckley, "The Facilitation of the Brady Plan: Emerging Markets Debt Trading from 1989 to 1993," *Fordham International Law Journal* 21-5 (1998), p. 1805.

59. Bichaka Fayissa, "Foreign Debt, Capital Inflows, and Growth: The Case of the Sub-Sahara African Countries (SSACs)," *Scandinavian Journal of Development Alternatives and Area Studies* 16-3&4 (September & December 1997), p. 253; Bayne, *Hanging in There,* p. 123; Paul Lewis, "I.M.F. and World Bank Clear Debt Relief," *New York Times,* September 30, 1996, p. C2.

60. Nigeria was included in the list of 41 HIPCs in 1996, but in 1998 it no longer met the criteria. Malawi was added to list in 1998 so there were still 41 HIPCs. In 1999 the number was reduced to 40 when Equatorial Guinea no longer met the criteria (U.S. General Accounting Office, "Debt Relief Initiative for Poor Countries Faces Challenges," GAO/NSIAD-00-161, June 2000, p. 11, fn. 6.).

61. U.S. General Accounting Office, "Status of the Heavily Indebted Poor Countries Debt Relief Initiative," GAO/NSIAD-98-229, September 1998, pp. 5–8 and 27.

62. Gerardo Esquivel, Felipe Larraín, and Jeffrey D. Sachs, "Central America's Foreign Debt Burden and the HIPC Initiative," *Bulletin of Latin American Research* 20-1 (January 2001), p. 2.; David Malin Roodman, "Ending the Debt Crisis," in Lester R. Brown et al., eds., *State of the World 2001* (New York: Norton, 2001), pp. 144–146.

63. U.S. GAO, "Debt Relief Initiative for Poor Countries Faces Challenges," p. 9. See also Martin Dent and Bill Peters, *The Crisis of Poverty and Debt in the Third World* (Aldershot, UK: Ashgate, 1999); Iain Guest, "Debt—The Next Cause Celebre?" *Christian Science Monitor,* May 27, 1998, p. 20; Bayne, *Hanging in There,* pp. 169–187; John Davies and Mariette Maillet, "The Debt Crisis: Perspectives of a Bilateral Donor," *International Journal* 55-2 (Spring 2000), pp. 270–280.

64. Cline, *International Debt Reexamined,* p. 70.

65. Cline, *International Debt Reexamined,* pp. 70–76; Bakker, *International Financial Institutions,* p. 94.

66. For example, see "Summary of Discussion on LDC Debt Policy," in Feldstein, ed., *American Economic Policy in the 1980s,* p. 737; Stallings, *Banker to the Third World,* pp. 313–315. See also Theodore H. Cohn, "The United States and Latin America: Ambivalent Ties," *The Canadian Review of American Studies* 20-2 (Fall 1989), pp. 255–263.

67. Ffrench-Davis, "External Debt, Adjustment, and Development in Latin America," p. 31.

68. Richard E. Feinberg, "Latin American Debt: Renegotiating the Adjustment Burden," in Feinberg and Ffrench-Davis, eds., *Development and External Debt in Latin America,* pp. 57–58; Corbridge, *Debt and Development,* p. 85.

William Cline provides some strong arguments from a liberal-economic perspective against the view that the debt strategies favored the banks over the debtor countries. See Cline, *International Debt Reexamined,* pp. 255–262.

69. H. W. Singer, "Beyond the Debt Crisis," *Development* 1 (1992), p. 36.

70. Denise Froning, "Will Debt Relief Really Help?" *Washington Quarterly* (Summer 2000), pp. 202–204.

71. Valerie J. Assetto, *The Soviet Bloc in the IMF and the IBRD* (Boulder, CO: Westview Press, 1988), pp. 189–190.

72. Cline, *International Debt Reexamined,* p. 360.

73. Cline, *International Debt Reexamined,* pp. 360–367; Assetto, *The Soviet Bloc in the IMF and the IBRD,* pp. 163–179.

74. Matthew Evangelista, "Domestic Structure and International Change," in Michael W. Doyle and G. John Ikenberry, eds., *New Thinking in International Relations Theory* (Boulder, CO: Westview Press, 1997), pp. 212–214; Kazimierz Poznanski, "Economic Adjustment and Political Forces: Poland Since 1970," *International Organization* 40-2 (Spring 1986), pp. 455–488.

75. Ellen Comisso and Paul Marer, "The Economics and Politics of Reform in Hungary," *International Organization* 40-2 (Spring 1986), p. 422. See also Laura D'Andrea Tyson, "The Debt Crisis and Adjustment Responses in Eastern Europe: A Comparative Perspective," *International Organization* 40-2 (Spring 1986), pp. 239–285.

76. Cline, *International Debt Reexamined,* pp. 346–360.

77. E. Iasin and E. Gavrilenkov, "The Problem of Settling Russia's Foreign Debt," *Problems of Economic Transition* 43-5 (September 2000), p. 88.

78. Iasin and E. Gavrilenkov, "The Problem of Settling Russia's Foreign Debt," pp. 86–95.

79. References to developing countries were later included in the second amendment to the IMF Articles of Agreement, when LDC members were more numerous. See Joseph Gold, "The Relationship Between the International Monetary Fund and the World Bank," *Creighton Law Review* 15 (1982), pp. 509–510.

80. Richard E. Feinberg, "The Changing Relationship Between the World Bank and the International Monetary Fund," *International Organization* 42-3 (Summer 1988), p. 547.

81. For a discussion of the bank's 1960s program lending to India, see Michael Lipton and John Toye, *Does Aid Work in India? A Country Study of the Impact of Official Development Assistance* (London: Routledge, 1990), ch. 3.

82. Jacques Polak, "The World Bank and the IMF: The Future of Their Coexistence," in *Bretton Woods: Looking to the Future* (Washington, DC: Bretton Woods Commission, July 1994), p. C-149; Edward S. Mason and Robert E. Asher, *The World Bank Since Bretton Woods* (Washington, DC: Brookings Institution, 1973), pp. 551–554.

83. Hiroyuki Hino, "IMF–World Bank Collaboration," *Finance & Development* 23-3 (September 1986), p. 11.

84. There is a wide range of literature on IMF and World Bank SALs. See, for example, Jacques J. Polak, *The World Bank and the International Monetary Fund: A Changing Relationship,* Brookings Occasional Papers (Washington, DC: Brookings Institution, 1994); Paul Mosley, Jane Harrigan, and John Toye, *Aid and Power: The World Bank and Policy-based Lending, Vol. 1* (London: Routledge, 1991); and Stanley Please, "The World Bank: Lending for Structural Adjustment," in Richard E. Feinberg and Valeriana Kallab, eds., *Adjustment Crisis in the Third World* (New Brunswick, NJ: Transaction Books, 1984), pp. 83–98.

85. "Survey: The IMF and the World Bank," *The Economist,* October 12, 1991, p. 48.
86. James, *International Monetary Cooperation,* p. 326; Polak, *The World Bank and the IMF: A Changing Relationship,* pp. 44–45.
87. Jeffrey Sachs, "Beyond Bretton Woods: A New Blueprint," *The Economist,* October 1, 1994, p. 23.
88. There are numerous critiques of IMF conditionality and the debt crisis. For example, see Kevin Danaher, ed., *Fifty Years Is Enough: The Case Against the World Bank and the International Monetary Fund* (Boston: South End Press, 1994); Payer, *Lent and Lost;* Martin Honeywell, ed., *The Poverty Brokers: The IMF and Latin America* (London: Latin America Bureau, 1983); and Körner, et al., *The IMF and the Debt Crisis.*
89. Feinberg, "The Changing Relationship Between the World Bank and the International Monetary Fund," pp. 552–556; Polak, *The World Bank and the IMF: A Changing Relationship,* pp. 16–17.
90. Diane Elson, "From Survival Strategies to Transformation Strategies: Women's Needs and Structural Adjustment," in Lourdes Benería and Shelley Feldman, eds., *Unequal Burden: Economic Crises, Persistent Poverty, and Women's Work* (Boulder, CO: Westview Press, 1992), pp. 26–48; Gita Sen and Caren Grown, *Development, Crises, and Alternative Visions: Third World Women's Perspectives* (New York: Monthly Review, 1987), pp. 62–63.
91. Marc Williams, *International Economic Organisations and the Third World* (New York: Harvester Wheatsheaf, 1994), p. 127.
92. Gerardo Otero, "Neoliberal Reform and Politics in Mexico: An Overview," in Gerardo Otero, ed., *Neoliberalism Revisited: Economic Restructuring and Mexico's Political Future* (Boulder, CO: Westview Press, 1996), pp. 6–7; Sebastian Edwards, "Latin American Economic Integration: A New Perspective on an Old Dream," *The World Economy* 16-3 (May 1993), p. 325; "Mercosur: The End of the Beginning," *The Economist,* October 12, 1996, pp. 3–4.
93. See Anthony Hurrell and Ngaire Woods, "Globalisation and Inequality," *Millennium* 24-3 (1995), pp. 447–470.
94. Eric Helleiner, *States and the Reemergence of Global Finance: From Bretton Woods to the 1990s* (Ithaca, NY: Cornell University Press, 1994), p. 13.

C H A P T E R   8

Global Trade Relations

From the earliest times, trade relations have aroused strong positive and negative emotions among societies and peoples. On the one hand, some early Christian philosophers argued that trade was divinely ordained and a part of the natural order, and proposals for world peace stemming from at least the seventeenth century drew strong linkages between free trade and the achievement of peaceful conditions.[1] On the other hand, trade conflicts have been common since the latter part of the Middle Ages, when the number of sovereign entities was increasing. Although these conflicts are often limited in scope, they sometimes escalate to the point of becoming major trade wars.[2] The high degree of controversy surrounding trade issues stems largely from the fact that interest groups and the broader public within states view their own welfare as being more affected by trade policy than by monetary, investment, or financial policy. Thus, business, labor, agricultural, consumer, environmental, and cultural groups have strongly vested interests in policies promoting trade liberalization or protectionism, and they regularly attempt to influence government trade policies.

Trading relations, like monetary and financial relations, have been strongly affected by the forces of globalization. From 1948 to 1997, real economic output grew at an average annual rate of 3.7 percent while trade increased at an annual rate of 6 percent. From 1985 to 1997, the ratio of trade to GDP rose from 16.6 to 24.1 percent in the industrial states, and from 22.8 to 38 percent in the LDCs.[3] Although foreign investment flows have increased even faster than trade flows, the two are closely related. A growing share of trade is taking place within MNCs and their affiliates. Indeed, *intrafirm trade* within MNCs or related partners now accounts for about one-third of total world trade. As a former director-general of the WTO has stated, "businesses now trade to invest and invest to trade—to the point where both activities are increasingly part of a single strategy to deliver products across borders."[4]

As global interdependence has increased and has had growing domestic effects, major societal groups have expressed strongly held views regarding trade liberalization agreements. On the one hand, internationalist firms and industries, which have become dependent on exports, imports, and multinational production, strongly favor global and regional trade liberalization agreements because protectionism is very costly to them. On the other hand, domestically oriented firms, threatened by surging import competition, may strongly oppose freer trade agreements.[5] A number of labor, environmental, cultural, and human rights groups have also opposed regional free trade agreements such as NAFTA and the efforts to expand the authority of the WTO. To many of these groups the WTO and NAFTA represent what they view as the dangers of globalization, and they fear that these trade organizations will force states to lower their environmental and labor standards to the "lowest common denominator." (Competing perspectives on this issue are discussed in this chapter and in Chapter 9.)

This chapter discusses the characteristics of the postwar global trade regime and the changing role of the advanced industrial states, the LDCs, and the emerging economies in the regime. A major theme relates to the competing pressures for the liberalization of trade on the one hand and for various forms of protectionism on the other.

TRADE THEORY

The promotion of freer trade is a central tenet of liberal theorists, who argue that trade is a positive-sum game that provides mutual benefits to states. Realists, by contrast, view trade in more competitive terms, with each state striving to increase its exports (especially of high-value-added goods) and decrease its imports. Historical structuralists view trade as a form of unequal exchange in which the advanced capitalist states in the core export manufactured and high-technology goods and import raw materials and lower technology goods from the periphery. Of the three main IPE perspectives, liberal theories of trade have clearly been the most influential among economists in the industrial states.

Although liberal trade theory has evolved considerably over time, the views of Adam Smith and David Ricardo still form a central part of the justification for freer trade. Smith argued that the gains from free trade result from *absolute advantage,* in which all states benefit if they specialize in the goods they produce best, and trade with each other. For example, if France can produce wine more cheaply than England and England can produce cloth more cheaply than France, both countries can benefit from specialization and trade. Ricardo's theory of *comparative advantage* is less intuitive—and a more powerful theory—because it indicates trade is beneficial even if absolute advantage does not exist. In his 1817 study *Principles of Political Economy and Taxation,* Ricardo argued that England and Portugal could gain from trading wine for cloth even if Portugal produced *both* goods more cheaply than England.[6] The following tables use arbitrary figures to demonstrate Ricardo's theory of comparative advantage. Table 8.1 gives the amount of labor required (for example, worker-days) in Portugal and England to produce one bottle of wine and one bolt of cloth.

TABLE 8.1
LABOR REQUIRED TO PRODUCE ONE BOTTLE OF WINE AND ONE BOLT OF CLOTH

	Wine	Cloth
England	6	5
Portugal	2	4

As Table 8.1 shows, Portugal can produce *both* wine and cloth with fewer labor inputs than England. Nevertheless, the two countries can gain from specialization and trade because England has less of a cost disadvantage in cloth than in wine production. In other words, England has a *comparative* advantage in cloth, and Portugal has a *comparative* advantage in wine. To demonstrate these gains, we assume that England shifts 30 units of labor from wine to cloth production and that Portugal shifts 12 units of labor from cloth to wine production. The total amount of labor used in the two countries remains constant, but this reallocation of labor causes the production changes given in Table 8.2.

As Table 8.2 shows, the shift of 30 units of labor from the wine to the cloth industry in England raises cloth production by 6 bolts (30 divided by 5) and reduces wine production by 5 bottles (–30 divided by 6). The shift of 12 units of labor from the cloth to the wine industry in Portugal raises wine production by 6 bottles (12 divided by 2) and reduces cloth production by 3 bolts (–12 divided by 4). Table 8.2 shows that with England specializing more in cloth and Portugal specializing in wine, the two countries together produce one more bottle of wine and three more bolts of cloth. Liberals therefore argue that two countries can enjoy mutual (but not necessarily equal) benefits from specialization and trade *even if* one of the two countries has an absolute advantage in producing all of the products traded.

Although Ricardo's theory provided a powerful liberal argument in favor of free trade, his assumption that comparative advantage results only from differences in labor productivity is far too limiting. In reality, comparative advantage also results from other factors of production such as capital and natural resources. In the 1920s and 1930s, liberal economists therefore turned to a more elaborate theory to explain a country's comparative advantage: the **Heckscher-Ohlin theorem,** which was developed by two Swedish economists, Eli Heckscher and Bertil Ohlin. According to this theory, a country's comparative advantage is determined by its relative abundance and scarcity of capital and labor. A country will have a comparative advantage in producing goods that involve intensive use of the factor it has in abundance. Thus, the more advanced economies, which are capital-rich states, will specialize in the production and export of capital-intensive goods, whereas the LDCs, which have an abundant supply of cheap labor, will specialize in labor-intensive goods. As was the case for Ricardo, the Heckscher-Ohlin theorem makes certain simplifying assumptions; for example, the theory assumes that technology and tastes do not differ among countries.[7]

Building on the Heckscher-Ohlin theorem, in the 1940s two economists in the United States (Wolfgang Stolper and Paul Samuelson) developed the *Stolper-Samuelson theory,* which helps to explain why some domestic groups in a state are

TABLE 8.2
CHANGES IN PRODUCTION OF WINE AND CLOTH

	Bottles of Wine	Bolts of Cloth
England	–5	+6
Portugal	+6	–3
Total	+1	+3

free trade oriented and other groups are protectionist. According to the Stolper-Samuelson theory, trade liberalization benefits abundantly endowed factors of production and hurts poorly endowed factors of production in a state. For example, if a state is rich in labor and productive land but poor in capital, freer trade would be beneficial to workers and farmers but detrimental to the owners of capital. Freer trade is therefore supported by owners of abundant factors and opposed by owners of scarce factors of production. The Stolper-Samuelson theory has been used to explain why blue-collar labor in the United States and Canada has opposed NAFTA (Mexico is more abundantly endowed with less skilled workers) and why wheat farmers in France have opposed moves to liberalize agricultural trade in the GATT/WTO (the United States, Canada, Australia, and Argentina are more abundantly endowed with land for wheat production).[8]

The Heckscher-Ohlin and Stolper-Samuelson models are controversial. Some empirical studies contradict their assumption that countries are always more successful in exporting goods produced with their abundantly endowed factors.[9] Nevertheless, these models continue to occupy a central place in international trade theory. The Stolper-Samuelson theory is also of considerable interest to us here because it points to the fact that there are inevitably both winners and losers as a result of freer trade. Although liberals concede that freer trade may produce job losses in some sectors, they argue that trade liberalization is nevertheless desirable because the gains in *overall* efficiency are greater than any losses. Thus, the winners (the owners of abundant factors) can compensate the losers (the owners of scarce factors) and still be better off as a result of freer trade. Realists and historical structuralists, by contrast, believe the losers will not be adequately compensated and will suffer as a result of their disadvantageous position.

Although liberal theories extending from Ricardo's comparative advantage to the Heckscher-Ohlin theorem are still considered important for explaining interindustry trade, they do not adequately explain the rapid increase in intraindustry and intrafirm trade. Traditional trade theory assumes that goods are homogeneous, but in *intraindustry trade* differentiated products are traded within the same industry group. For example, the United States, Japan, and Germany all produce automobiles and trade with one another. Product differentiation is important to most consumers, who do not consider the various types of automobiles to be perfectly interchangeable. The Heckscher-Ohlin assumption that trade is most beneficial between countries with different factor endowments does not provide an adequate explanation for intraindustry trade, which most often occurs among advanced industrial states with similar factor endowments. Thus, liberals have developed new theories that postulate that intraindustry trade provides benefits such as economies of scale, the satisfaction of consumer tastes for variety, and the production of more specialized and sophisticated manufactured products. For example, because of economies of scale countries can benefit more from producing large quantities of a smaller number of goods and engaging in trade than from producing small quantities of a larger number of goods.[10]

The Stolper-Samuelson theory explaining why some groups oppose or favor freer trade is also not as applicable to intraindustry trade. Because most intraindustry trade involves trade among advanced industrial states with similar factor endowments and trade in products that use similar factor intensities, it is less common to find owners of scarce factors opposing such trade. Thus, trade liberalization negotiations have been most successful for manufactured products in which advanced industrial countries are engaging in intraindustry trade. Trade barriers are more persistent for agricultural and other primary products, often traded between industrial states and LDCs, where factor endowments still play a major role. Much trade today is also *intrafirm* trade between parent companies of MNCs and their subsidiaries. Chapter 10 discusses the fact that theories of the firm best explain why trade occurs between an MNC's affiliates in different countries.

Realists have often argued that liberal assumptions about comparative advantage are overly static, underestimating the ability of a state to upgrade its advantages in trade. The growing amount of intraindustry and intrafirm trade among countries with similar factor endowments has added force to the realist arguments. Thus, realists question whether Ricardo's advice to Portugal in fact served its long-range interests. By following Ricardo's prescriptions and specializing in wine, Portugal might have gained some short-term advantages. However, it would have been less competitive than England over the long term because cloth production was a high-growth, high-technology industry at the time. According to realists, Portugal would have been better off *creating* a comparative advantage for itself in cloth through government assistance to the cloth industry, even if it had a "natural" comparative advantage in wine.[11]

Strategic trade theory emphasizes the creation of comparative advantage through industrial targeting. Strategic trade theorists justify and even promote the idea of government intervention in the economy, and they often prefer the terms *arbitrary comparative advantage* or *competitive advantage* to comparative advantage. Although efforts to gain competitive advantage in trade are not really new, the growing emphasis on high-technology industries provides "a fertile breeding ground for interventionist policies."[12] Strategic trade theorists have produced a wide range of studies to demonstrate that interventionist policies can improve a country's position in manufacturing and technology, and they often point to Japan and the East Asian NIEs as examples of states that have mobilized a limited amount of resources to create competitive advantage. However, liberal theorists argue that the benefits of strategic trade policy are likely to be small and the risks, great. According to strategic trade theory, each country wants its firms to capture a larger share of international export markets. However, it is more difficult to identify the nationalities of firms today because of the proliferation of joint ventures, strategic partnerships, and foreign stock ownership (see Chapter 10). If a government wants to target particular firms for assistance in exporting, how is it to determine exactly which are its firms? Strategic trade theorists also do not devote sufficient attention to the possible reaction of foreign governments to strategic trade policies. Although individual rationality might lead a country to attempt to increase its competitive advantage at the expense of others, other countries are likely to retaliate, and everyone will be worse off as a result (see the discussion of the prisoners' dilemma in Chapter 4).[13] Despite these liberal warnings, the temptations remain strong in an age of global competition for countries to gain a competitive advantage by targeting particular industrial and high-technology sectors.

GLOBAL TRADE RELATIONS BEFORE WORLD WAR II

Throughout modern history, countries have alternated between periods of trade liberalization and protectionism. Thus, mercantilist trade restrictions gave way to a period of freer trade in 1815, when Britain first lowered its import duties and then repealed its Corn Laws and opened its borders to food imports in 1846. Following the British lead, Latin America's newly independent republics adopted liberal trade policies; Prussia moved Germany to lower its trade barriers; and France joined with Britain in the Cobden-Chevalier Treaty of 1860, which resulted in a network of commercial treaties lowering tariff barriers between Britain and France and throughout Europe. After 1875, however, the enthusiasm for free trade waned somewhat because of the decline of British hegemony, the defeat of France in the 1870 Franco-Prussian War, and the depression of 1873–96. With the outbreak of World War I the network of European trade and commercial treaties was completely disrupted.[14]

After World War I, renewed efforts to remove trade restrictions were largely unsuccessful as countries reacted to harsh economic conditions by increasing their tariffs. Tariffs were rising not only in European nations recovering from the war but also in the United States, which had emerged from the war as a net creditor nation and the world's largest industrial power. Thus, the U.S. Congress enacted the Fordney-McCumber Tariff in 1922, which increased import duties to an average of 38 percent, well above the duty levels in the 1913 Underwood Tariff. After the 1929 stock market crash, Congress passed the 1930 Smoot-Hawley Tariff Act, which increased average U.S. ad valorem rates on dutiable imports to 52.8 percent, "the highest American tariffs in the twentieth century."[15]

The question arises as to why the United States as the top economic power in the interwar period did not act more forthrightly to limit the rise of trade protectionism. Hegemonic stability theorists often argue that the United States was able but unwilling to become the hegemonic leader until its position became more firmly established after World War II.[16] However, some analysts question whether the United States in fact had the ability to establish an open economic system during the interwar period. Although the United States was the top economic state at the time, its share of world trade and investment was well below that of Britain during the latter part of the nineteenth century.[17]

Others look to domestic politics rather than to the U.S. global position in explaining American protectionism. Although the United States emerged as the largest industrial power in the interwar period, a number of U.S. industries were fearful of renewed European competition, and U.S. agricultural groups were dismayed by a rapid decrease in agricultural prices. In their efforts to pressure for trade protectionism, these domestic groups benefited from the fact that the U.S. Constitution gives Congress the sole power to regulate commerce and impose tariffs. The members of Congress do not have national constituencies, so they are far more susceptible than the president to protectionist pressures. Producers and workers who wanted to limit imports were also politically organized and concentrated in specific industries, and by joining together they were able to convince Congress to enact the Smoot-Hawley tariff. Those groups benefiting from freer trade, such as consumers, by contrast, were far more diffuse in nature and had little influence. Party politics also played a role in the Smoot-Hawley tariff; the Republicans—who were more protectionist than the Democrats—held a majority in the Senate at the time.[18]

Regardless of the reasons for the U.S. Smoot-Hawley tariff, it had disastrous consequences as other countries rushed to retaliate with their own import restrictions.[19] Between 1929 and 1933, world trade therefore declined from $35 billion to $12 billion, and U.S. exports fell from $488 million to $120 million. In efforts to reverse this damage, the U.S. Congress passed the Reciprocal Trade Agreements Act (RTAA) in 1934. The RTAA in effect transferred tariff-setting authority from Congress to the president, who could lower tariffs by up to 50 percent from Smoot-Hawley levels in trade negotiations with other countries.[20] Although Congress authorized the president to conduct only bilateral (not multilateral) tariff negotiations, the RTAA marked a significant turning point because it directly linked the setting of tariffs to international negotiations. Instead of having Congress set tariffs on a unilateral, statutory basis, the president was now authorized to establish "bargaining tariffs" as a result of bilateral agreements.

The introduction of bargaining tariffs indicated a recognition that the United States would gain greater access to foreign markets only by opening its own market to imports.[21] From 1934, when the RTAA was approved, until 1945, the United States concluded bilateral trade agreements with 27 countries and lowered its tariff rates by an average of 44 percent. Tariff rates were so high in the early 1930s, however, that these agreements mainly served to correct earlier excesses. The decision of the Roosevelt administration to lower tariffs only in exchange for similar concessions by other countries (hence the name *Reciprocal* Trade Agreements Act) also limited the scope of the agreements. Furthermore, many countries were unwilling to lower their tariffs, and the RTAA agreements did not stimulate a worldwide movement toward trade liberalization. Thus, protectionism continued to affect trade relations during the rest of the interwar period.[22]

GATT and the Postwar Global Trade Regime

The United States and Britain wanted to ensure that the devastating effects of protectionism in the interwar period were not repeated, and they began to hold bilateral discussions in 1943 to lay the groundwork for postwar trade negotiations. In fall 1945 the U.S. State Department issued a document on trade and employment, which formed the basis for multilateral negotiations resulting in the Havana Charter or Charter for an international trade organization (ITO) in March 1948. The charter was unusually broad in scope, dealing not only with commercial policy but also with economic development, full employment, international investment, international commodity arrangements, restrictive business practices, and the administration and functions of an ITO.[23] In view of the protracted nature of the Havana Charter negotiations, the participating governments decided to begin negotiating a lowering of tariffs before the charter was actually approved and ratified. These negotiations were concluded in October 1947 when 23 governments signed the final act of the GATT.

It was assumed that GATT would simply be folded into a new ITO, but the U.S. Congress never ratified the Havana Charter, and GATT therefore became permanent by default. The reasons for the U.S. failure to ratify the charter are complex and ironic, especially because the United States had originally proposed the creation of an ITO.[24] In drafting the ITO charter, the trade negotiators were sensitive to the problems of different countries, such as the Europeans recovering from the war. However, in trying to meet everyone's demands, the negotiators satisfied neither the protectionists nor the free traders. Whereas U.S. protectionists argued that the ITO would lead to the import of low-cost goods and threaten the U.S. ability to form its own trade policy, free traders felt that the numerous escape clauses and exceptions in the charter would interfere with trade liberalization. Because the charter had little support within the United States, President Harry Truman agreed not to submit it to Congress for ratification, and the ITO was never formed.[25]

With the failure to establish the ITO, GATT became the permanent global trade organization by default. GATT did not even require ratification by the U.S. Congress because it was simply a trade agreement. Thus, countries that signed GATT were referred to as *contracting parties* rather than members as was the case for other international organizations. (This chapter uses the less accurate term *GATT members* for the sake of brevity.) Unlike the ITO, which would have become a UN specialized agency on a par with the IMF and the World Bank, GATT never attained specialized agency status. GATT continued to be primarily a written code of behavior on international trade, and it had more limited legal obligations and more primitive dispute settlement procedures than the planned ITO. GATT also lacked the Havana Charter's provisions relating to investment, employment, commodity agreements, and restrictive business practices.

Despite its informal origins, GATT gradually developed some of the characteristics of an IO; for example, it had a small secretariat and a number of committees and working parties, and it made decisions that were binding on its member states.[26] Some analysts even argue that GATT's informality enabled it to become a more effective organization than the IMF and the World Bank:

> Many observers would now conclude that the GATT was the more effective arrangement. The strength of a formal arrangement such as the IMF is its rigidity; that of an informal, ideas-based institution such as the GATT is its adaptability. The greater success of the GATT thus illustrates the importance for postwar economic performance of an adaptable institutional framework.[27]

Indications of GATT's strengths included its success in reducing tariffs, its negotiation of disciplines for nontariff barriers, and its steadily increasing membership. However, GATT's informality and flexibility also proved to be a source of weakness in several respects. First, some trade sectors such as agriculture and textiles were largely exempted from GATT regulations. From the time GATT was formed, agriculture was treated as an exception to the trade organization's restrictions on import quotas and export subsidies. Industrial states also imposed textile import quotas that contravened the spirit and rules of GATT, first through bilateral export restraints beginning in the 1950s and then through the multilateral Multi-Fiber Arrangement.

Second, GATT was more of a club than a formal organization, and its members could easily waive its regulations and avoid noticing violations. For example, some countries circumvented the GATT ban on import quotas by imposing **voluntary export restraints,** in which they pressured others to "voluntarily" decrease their exports. Third, when conflicts developed between countries over trade-distorting practices, GATT's rather weak dispute settlement procedures were often inadequate to deal with them. Fourth, burgeoning U.S. balance-of-trade deficits in the 1980s caused the United States to charge others with being unfair traders and to turn more often to trade unilateralism. Only by enhancing the trade regime's authority could the United States be assured that unilateral measures to ensure fair trade were unnecessary. And fifth, GATT's inadequacies became more evident as globalization increased, and the United States in particular demanded that the scope of GATT's activities be extended beyond trade in goods to such areas as trade in services, intellectual property, and investment.

By the mid-1980s, a number of trade experts therefore warned that GATT would become irrelevant if it did not tighten its regulations, improve its dispute settlement procedures, and extend its discipline to "older" areas such as agriculture and textiles and to "newer" areas such as services, intellectual property, and investment.[28] Although the GATT Uruguay round began with plans to simply upgrade the agreement, the decision was made during the round to replace GATT with a new WTO. (GATT continues to exist as the largest trade agreement under the WTO.)

PRINCIPLES OF THE GLOBAL TRADE REGIME

In some respects the GATT-based trade regime was not really new; its principles and rules codified past commercial practices, and its basic approach—that trade policy should be made through international negotiation—was established earlier by the 1934 U.S. RTAA. The GATT regime marked a turning point in one critical respect, however: it relied on *multilateral* negotiation. The postwar trading arrangements also reflected the interventionist-liberal compromise. Although the major trading nations approved of measures to liberalize trade, they also agreed to accept safeguards and exemptions to protect countries' balance of payments and domestic social policies.[29] Despite GATT's informal origins, the global trade regime became one of the most established regimes in terms of principles, norms, rules, and decision-making procedures. The sections that follow discuss the main trade regime principles and some of the threats posed to them.

Trade Liberalization

Liberalization is a central trade regime principle that GATT tried to enforce, first by lowering tariffs and then by regulating NTBs. Tariffs, or taxes levied on products that pass through a customs border, are usually imposed on imports but may also be applied to exports. GATT has always preferred tariffs to import quotas because tariffs (at reasonable levels) permit efficient producers to continue increasing their sales,

TABLE 8.3

THE ROUNDS OF GATT NEGOTIATIONS

Name	Years	Subjects Covered	Countries Participating
Geneva	1947	Tariffs	23
Annecy	1949	Tariffs	13
Torquay	1951	Tariffs	38
Geneva	1956	Tariffs	26
Dillon	1960–61	Tariffs	26
Kennedy	1964–67	Tariffs and antidumping measures	62
Tokyo	1973–79	Tariffs, nontariff measures, plurilateral agreements	102
Uruguay	1986–93	Tariffs, nontariff measures, rules, services, intellectual property, dispute settlement, trade-related investment, textiles, agriculture, creation of World Trade Organization	123

Source: WTO Focus Newsletter, No. 30, May 1998, p. 2. By permission of the World Trade Organization.

whereas quotas set an arbitrary limit on the amount imported and provide no reward for efficiency. Thus, GATT Article 11 called for the "general elimination of quantitative restrictions" or import quotas. A number of exceptions were permitted to Article 11, however, relating to balance-of-payments problems, infant industry protection for LDCs, enforcement of health standards, and national security. Countries could also impose import quotas on agricultural products when such regulations were needed to enforce domestic supply management measures.[30]

GATT explicitly permitted tariffs, not import quotas, but it sought to lower tariffs through successive rounds of multilateral trade negotiations (MTNs). As Table 8.3 shows, eight rounds of MTNs were held under GATT auspices. In the first five rounds, countries negotiated tariff reductions on a product-by-product basis. However, product-by-product negotiations became more complex and time consuming as GATT membership increased, and the sixth round (the Kennedy round) therefore shifted to "linear cuts" or across-the-board tariff reductions on industrial products. These linear tariff cuts resulted in an average tariff reduction of 35 percent in the Kennedy round for the OECD countries.[31]

The first five rounds of trade negotiations dealt only with the reduction of tariffs. However, GATT soon became a victim of its own success in reducing tariffs as member countries turned increasingly to NTBs as an alternative means of protecting their producers. NTBs include an incredibly large array of measures that restrict imports, assist domestic production, and promote exports, and they are often more restrictive, ill defined, and inequitable than tariffs. Negotiations to reduce NTBs are also more problematic than those for tariffs because it is difficult to quantify and measure the impact of NTBs, and countries tend to view NTBs as adjuncts of their domestic policies (and therefore as not subject to international regulation).[32]

The Kennedy round was the first round to go beyond tariff negotiations and begin the process of negotiating NTBs. The Tokyo round of negotiations on NTBs was far more extensive and resulted in a number of NTB codes dealing with technical barriers to trade, government procurement, subsidies and countervailing duties, customs valuation, and import licensing procedures. The use of codes resulted partly from the fact that LDCs opposed the extension of GATT discipline to NTBs. Thus, the NTB codes were *plurilateral trade agreements* that were not multilateralized in the GATT. They bound only the signatories, and most LDCs did not participate in them. The Uruguay round was the most complicated set of GATT negotiations because it widened the agenda to include not only trade in goods but also trade in services, intellectual property, and trade-related investment measures, and it began the process of applying global trade rules to sensitive areas such as agriculture and textiles.

Both the broadening of issues covered and the increased number of participants in the Uruguay round reflected the degree to which trade was increasingly affected by the forces of globalization. Thus, Table 8.3 shows that the number of participating countries rose from 23 in the first round (Geneva) to 123 in the eighth (Uruguay). Table 8.3 also shows that beginning with the Dillon round, each successive GATT negotiating round was more lengthy and complicated than the previous one. The Uruguay round involved seven years of difficult negotiations, and there were often concerns that the negotiators would never reach a final agreement. Nevertheless, the Uruguay round *was* completed, and it resulted in the establishment of a new WTO with jurisdiction over a much wider array of trade and related areas (such as investment and intellectual property) than the GATT.

One question asked by IPE scholars is *why* the trade liberalization principle has not only endured but been expanded, despite periodic threats to it and despite the decline in U.S. trade hegemony. In 1953 the United States was clearly the trade hegemon, accounting for almost 30 percent of all manufactured exports. By the late 1970s, however, the United States had fallen to second place as an exporter of manufactures, accounting for only 13 percent of the world total. West Germany had moved into first place with 16 percent, and Japan was close behind the United States with 11 percent. Although there was an increase in the "new protectionism" of NTBs in the late 1970s, the trade liberalization principle was *not* as seriously threatened in the late 1970s as it had been in the 1920s when Britain's trade hegemony was declining. Indeed, the GATT Tokyo round (1973–79) reduced weighted-average industrial tariffs to extremely low levels (5 percent in the EC, 4 percent in the United States, and 3 percent in Japan) and resulted in the regulation of NTBs through a series of codes.[33]

Some scholars believe that the difference between the 1920s and 1970s demonstrates the importance of regimes in upholding principles and norms that are eventually internalized by states. In contrast to the 1920s, a major global trade organization—GATT—existed in the 1970s, and the GATT-centered global trade regime maintained the trade liberalization principle even as U.S. trade hegemony was declining. Other scholars point to domestic politics to explain the different outcomes in the 1920s and the 1970s. As noted previously, the U.S. Congress alone has the power to regulate commerce and impose tariffs under the Constitution, and in the 1920s Congress responded to domestic interest group pressures and dramatically increased tariffs. By the 1970s, however, Congress was regularly transferring its tariff-making authority to the president, who was more insulated from interest group pressures (this transfer to the president had begun with the RTAA in 1934). Thus, a major change in the domestic structure of trade policymaking in the United States helps to account for the post-war vitality of the trade liberalization principle.

Another domestic factor of importance stems from the forces of globalization. Many industries in the United States and other countries in the 1920s had few international ties, and they were therefore domestically oriented and supported trade protectionism to limit external competition. By the 1970s, however, "the increased economic integration of advanced industrial states into the world economy . . . altered the domestic politics of trade."[34] Now there were many more internationalist firms than there had been in the 1920s, and these firms were highly dependent on multinational production, exports, imports, and intrafirm trade. Thus, despite the decline in the U.S. trade position, the resistance of industries and firms to the forces of protectionism was much greater in the 1970s than it had been in the 1920s. Domestic as well as international factors account for the resilience of the trade liberalization principle in the post–World War II era.

Nondiscrimination

Nondiscrimination is another basic principle of the global trade regime. Indeed, the first GATT director-general referred to nondiscrimination as "the fundamental cornerstone" of the global trade organization.[35] The nondiscrimination principle has two dimensions, one external (most-favored-nation treatment) and the other internal (national treatment). The unconditional **most-favored-nation (MFN)** principle in Article 1 of the General Agreement stipulates that every trade advantage or privilege that a GATT member gives to any country must be extended, immediately and unconditionally, to all other GATT members. By requiring equal treatment of imports from different origins, the MFN principle helps to ensure that imports come from the lowest cost foreign suppliers and that comparative advantage determines trading patterns. Unconditional MFN treatment can be traced back to fifteenth-century Europe and to the Cobden-Chevalier Treaty of 1860. However, unlike these earlier models, the GATT-centered MFN principle was based on *multilateral* commitments and regular multilateral consultations and negotiations.[36]

Despite the importance the GATT negotiators gave to MFN treatment, the GATT permitted exceptions to MFN on the basis of colonial preferences, regional integration agreements, balance of payments, and national security, and allowed exceptions as a response to "unfair" trade actions. Of these exceptions, the proliferation of free trade agreements and customs unions such as the NAFTA and the EU has posed the greatest threat to the MFN principle in recent years. The member states of these RTAs abolish tariff barriers among themselves, giving each other more favorable treatment than they give to other members of GATT/WTO. (Chapter 9 discusses the relationship between RTAs and GATT/WTO in more detail.)

Whereas MFN treatment is designed to prevent discrimination at a country's border, **national treatment** seeks to prevent internal discrimination. The national treatment provisions in GATT Article 3 require member countries to treat foreign products—once they have been imported—at least as favorably as domestic products with regard to internal taxes and regulations. This provision is designed to prevent countries from using domestic measures to limit foreign competition as their tariffs and other external trade barriers decline. The importance of the national treatment provision is seen by the frequency with which it has been tested in GATT dispute settlement cases. In a 1988 case, for example, a GATT panel found that pricing and listing practices of Canadian provincial liquor boards, which discriminated against foreign wines, were inconsistent with Canada's national treatment obligations.[37]

Reciprocity

Reciprocity, the concept that a country benefiting from another country's trade concessions should provide roughly equal benefits in return, is a fundamental principle in MTNs and in the admission of new members to the GATT/WTO. By ensuring that agreements are reached through a balanced exchange of concessions, the reciprocity principle limits free riding under the unconditional MFN principle. Liberal economists often argue that a country gains by liberalizing its trade unilaterally as well as through negotiation. However, unilateral trade liberalization is often not politically acceptable because protectionist forces in specific industries are usually well organized and able to mobilize domestic opposition to such policies. In reaching agreement on *reciprocal* trade concessions, by contrast, governments can depend on support from export-oriented domestic industries that will clearly gain from the agreement. New members in the WTO obtain all the benefits of market access resulting from earlier negotiating rounds, and they are expected to provide reciprocal benefits. Thus, joining the WTO involves negotiations in which an applicant must agree to liberalize access to its market.

In practice, the reciprocity principle ensures that tariff negotiations reflect the interests of the major trading nations. States benefiting from other countries' tariff reductions must be able to offer reciprocal concessions, and those states with large domestic markets and high trade volumes have the greatest concessions to offer and thus the most leverage.[38] The states with the largest reciprocal concessions to offer are the Big Three in the GATT/WTO: the United States, the EU, and Japan. Of these three, the United States and the EU have been the most important. Thus, the four years of negotiations in the Kennedy round culminated in marathon talks to resolve differences between the United States and the EC. When the Americans and Europeans reached a compromise on various sectoral issues, the Kennedy round was successfully completed.[39] The Tokyo round negotiations were also a pyramidal process, in which the principal actors—the United States and European Community—usually initiated agreements and other states were then involved in discussions to reach a consensus. Even among the LDCs there was a pecking order, with more important states such as Brazil, Mexico, and India taking priority. Although pyramidal negotiations realistically give priority to those with the power to veto an agreement, such negotiations limit the ability of smaller states to affect the outcome or protect their interests.[40] The LDCs had more influence in the Uruguay round than in previous rounds, but even in this case U.S. agreements with the European Community and Japan on agriculture were critical to ultimate success.[41]

As is the case for the global monetary regime, an informal institutional structure has developed to reflect the "pecking order" in the global trade regime. As discussed, both the G-10 and the G-7 have dealt with monetary issues. Although the G-7 devotes some attention to trade policy, its primary economic focus has been on monetary, financial, and macroeconomic policies. The G-7/G-8 heads of state and government also deal with a number of political-security issues. In 1982 the trade ministers of the United States, the European Community, Japan, and Canada therefore established the **Quadrilateral Group** or **Quad** to act as an informal grouping providing leadership in the global trade regime. (The EU trade minister is only one of four in the Quad because the European Commission is responsible for the EU's trade and commercial policy.) Although the trade ministers of the United States, the EC, and Japan (the Big 3) and sometimes Canada (the Big 4) had met informally in earlier years, the formation of the Quad represented a move toward collective consultation on trade issues in view of declining U.S. economic hegemony. Discussions at the Quads have focused on managing international trade disputes, promoting trade liberalization, and strengthening the multilateral trade regime. The Quad played an important role in all stages of the GATT Uruguay round.[42]

Reciprocity may be either specific or diffuse in nature. *Specific reciprocity* refers to "situations in which specified partners exchange items of equivalent value in a strictly delimited sequence"; *diffuse reciprocity* has a less precise definition of equivalence because "one's partners may be viewed as a group rather than as particular actors, and the sequence of events is less narrowly bound."[43] Whereas diffuse reciprocity can coexist with *unconditional* MFN treatment, specific (or aggressive) reciprocity is more akin to *conditional* MFN treatment. In conditional MFN, two countries granting concessions to each other extend these concessions to a third country *only if* it offers equivalent concessions.

Liberal economists argue that diffuse reciprocity is more conducive to interstate cooperation than is specific reciprocity because of the difficulty in determining whether concessions are exactly equivalent. If countries always demanded specific reciprocity from each other, it would be virtually impossible to conduct multilateral negotiations. Nevertheless, the United States responded to its declining trade hegemony and its balance-of-trade deficits since 1971 with claims that specific reciprocity is sometimes necessary to prevent other countries from acting as free riders. The United States has been particularly inclined to demand specific reciprocity from countries such as Japan with which it has large trade deficits. From the U.S. perspective, Japan has numerous hidden trade barriers and does not genuinely provide reciprocal access to its market. Thus, the United States has often demanded "results-oriented" agreements, in which it gains access to a certain share of the Japanese market for specific products in return for Japan's access to the U.S. market. Japan argues, by contrast, that its trade surpluses with the United States are due to its competitive advantages and not to unfair trading practices.[44]

Safeguards

Safeguards refer to government actions to limit imports that may cause harm to the importing country's industry or economy. The safeguard principle is an essential part of most trade liberalization agreements; countries would not agree to commitments if rigid adherence was necessary in all situations. Safeguard actions are usually tempo-

TABLE 8.4

SAFEGUARDS AND CONTINGENT TRADE MEASURES

SAFEGUARDS	
Temporary	**Permanent**
Import surges	General exceptions
Balance-of-payments problems	National security
Infant industries	Tariff renegotiations
General waivers	

Contingent Trade Measures

Antidumping duties (ADDs)
Countervailing duties (CVDs)

Sources: Bernard M. Hoekman and Michel Kostecki, *The Political Economy of the World Trading System: From GATT to WTO* (2nd edition Oxford: Oxford University Press, 2001); pp. 303–345; John H. Jackson, *The World Trading System: Law and Policy of International Economic Relations* (Cambridge, MA: MIT Press, 1989), pp. 149–187.

rary, but Table 8.4 shows that a government may also impose permanent trade barriers under certain circumstances. The most prominent temporary safeguard mechanism is the *general escape clause* (GATT Article 19), which permits a country to counter unforeseen "import surges" that cause, or are likely to cause, *serious* injury to a domestic industry. Such safeguard actions must be applied to all WTO members, and affected countries can request compensation. In view of these stringent requirements, countries do not often use the escape clause.[45] Table 8.4 shows that in addition to escape clause actions, a country may impose temporary import restrictions to safeguard its balance of payments and infant industries, and it may seek a general waiver from a specific obligation. Furthermore, a country may apply permanent safeguard measures under GATT clauses relating to general exceptions (e.g., to safeguard public morals, health, and natural resources), national security, and tariff renegotiations.

Safeguard provisions, permissible even when other countries engage in "fair" trade, are usually distinguished from *contingent trade measures* taken to counter allegedly unfair trade activities. The two main types of contingent trade measures are antidumping and countervailing duties (see Table 8.4). **Dumping** occurs when a firm sells a product in an export market at a lower price than it charges in the home market or below the cost of production. The WTO permits a country to impose **antidumping duties (ADDs)** if foreign goods are being dumped and the dumping is causing or threatening material injury to its domestic producers. A country may also impose **countervailing duties (CVDs)** against imports benefiting from *trade-distorting subsidies* in an exporting country that produce or threaten material injury to domestic producers.[46] Unlike safeguard actions, contingent trade measures may be imposed in response to *material* injury (which is less than *serious* injury), and the measures are targeted at specific countries charged with engaging in unfair trade.

Contingent trade measures may be legitimate responses to unfair trade, but they can also be used as a justification for trade protectionism. Thus, ADD and CVD actions are highly controversial, and dispute settlement panels in GATT/WTO and

NAFTA have often examined complaints about such actions. The United States was the first country to use CVDs, and it has been the largest user of CVDs in the post–World War II period. With the U.S. balance-of-trade deficits since 1971 and the decline of tariffs resulting from GATT negotiations, the U.S. Congress responded to domestic pressures by changing the rules and procedures so that CVDs could be imposed more easily. Thus, the United States was responsible for about 58 percent of all the countervail investigations launched from 1980 to 1992, and the United States initiated the largest number of antidumping investigations during this period. Other frequent initiators of antidumping investigations include Australia, the EU, Canada, and Mexico.[47]

Development

The failed Havana Charter contained a number of provisions on economic development that did not become part of the 1947 General Agreement, and development issues played only a minor role in the global trade regime in the 1940s and 1950s.[48] As the number of Third World GATT members increased, however, a "development principle" began to emerge. Several GATT provisions were added that gave LDCs special treatment and thus diverged from the nondiscrimination and reciprocity principles. However, development remains a less central trade regime principle because the major trading nations have agreed to only limited concessions to promote the interests of LDCs.[49] Later in this chapter we examine the changing role of development issues in the global trade regime.

FORMATION OF THE WORLD TRADE ORGANIZATION

By the early 1980s, the trade regime principles discussed previously were all in a state of flux, and many of the earlier GATT achievements in promoting freer trade seemed to be in jeopardy. In terms of the liberalization principle, previous GATT rounds had lowered tariffs, but countries were resorting to NTBs such as voluntary export restraints that were not even covered by GATT rules. Furthermore, liberalization did not extend to major areas such as textiles and agriculture, and the GATT procedures for dealing with trade disputes were inadequate. The nondiscrimination principle was also increasingly threatened by RTAs that did not adhere to MFN treatment. As for the reciprocity and safeguard principles, the United States and European Community were demanding specific rather than diffuse reciprocity from some of their trading partners, and countries dissatisfied with the GATT safeguards were sometimes resorting to unilateral protectionist actions. Finally, in regard to the development principle, Third World countries were only marginally involved in the GATT; most of them refused to sign the Tokyo round NTB codes.

In view of GATT's evident shortcomings, the United States in particular pressured for a new round of trade negotiations. With its balance-of-trade deficits increasing rapidly in the 1980s, the United States was especially interested in extending the trade regime rules to areas such as services and agriculture, where it continued to have a comparative advantage.[50] The trade regime inadequacies were also evident to other GATT members, and agreement was reached to begin the Uruguay round negotiations in 1986. The negotiators at first focused on extending GATT's jurisdiction, but in April 1990 Canada's trade minister proposed that a more formal WTO should replace the GATT.[51] The EC also supported the idea of creating a new multilateral trade organization, but the United States had several reservations about this proposal. American negotiators believed that the U.S. Congress would have concerns over loss of sovereignty as it had with the ITO in the 1940s, and the negotiators felt that plans to create a new trade organization would take time away from substantive negotiations in the Uruguay Round. In the end, a compromise was reached and the WTO replaced the GATT in January 1995 as the main global trading organization.[52]

In contrast to GATT, the WTO is a formal, legally constituted organization like the IMF and the World Bank. GATT has not disappeared but has reverted to its original status as an agreement for trade in goods. The trade rules that the WTO oversees are contained in various treaties, including GATT and several new treaties negotiated in the Uruguay round: the *General Agreement on Trade in Services (GATS)*, the *Agreement on Trade-Related Intellectual Property Rights (TRIPs)*, and the *Agreement on Trade-Related Investment Measures (TRIMs)*. Trade in goods is the largest aspect of international trade; thus, GATT is the most important trade agreement under WTO auspices.[53] The *Ministerial Conference*, which includes all member countries and meets every two years, is the highest authority in the WTO; it can take decisions on all matters under the multilateral trade agreements (see Figure 8.1). However, a number of subsidiary bodies are responsible for the day-to-day work of the WTO. The most important of these bodies is the *General Council*, which is composed of all WTO members and oversees the activities of the *Councils for Trade in Goods, Trade-Related Aspects of Intellectual Property Rights*, and *Trade in Services* (relating to the GATT, TRIPs, and GATS agreements).

The General Council also convenes in two particular forms when necessary—as the *trade policy review body* and the *dispute settlement body*. The trade policy review body conducts regular reviews of the trade policies of individual WTO members and ensures that others are promptly notified of policies that may interfere with trade. By increasing the transparency of members' policies, the review body helps to promote trust that agreements are being enforced. The dispute settlement body establishes panels to investigate complaints and adjudicate trade disputes. A member country may invoke the dispute settlement procedures if another member has broken a WTO regulation or has reneged on previously negotiated concessions. Dispute settlement procedures are more binding and timely under the WTO than they were under the GATT. A single GATT member (including one of the parties to a dispute) could block the adoption of a GATT panel report, but a consensus of member states is required to block WTO panel reports, a highly unlikely possibility. A WTO member may appeal a dispute settlement decision against it to the *appellate body* (see Figure 8.1), but if the appellate body agrees with the panel report, the member must implement the panel's recommendations or pay compensation. If a country refuses to implement a panel report or provide adequate compensation, the dispute settlement body can authorize the complainant to take retaliatory action.[54]

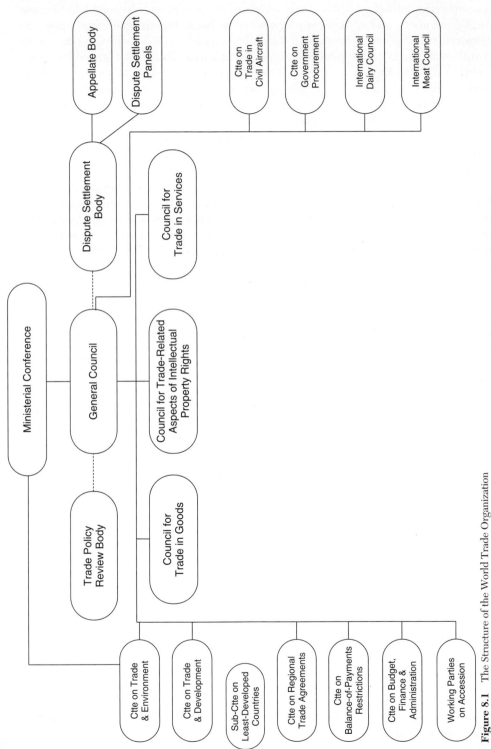

Figure 8.1 The Structure of the World Trade Organization

Source: From *WTO Focus Newsletter*, No. 1, January–February 1995, p. 5. By permission of the World Trade Organization.

In contrast to the voting systems in the IMF and the World Bank, the WTO's voting system (like GATT's before it) is based on the one-nation, one-vote principle. Depending on the issue, WTO votes require a simple majority, a special majority of two-thirds or three-fourths, or unanimity. The one-nation, one-vote system has given Third World countries less influence than one might expect, because consensus decision making is far more common than formal vote taking.[55] Furthermore, in MTNs, groups dominated by the industrial states such as the OECD, the G-7, and the Quad play a major role in setting the agenda.

The chief administrative officer of the WTO (and of the GATT in earlier years) is the director-general. Although a tacit agreement in the 1940s provided that the World Bank president would always be an American and the IMF managing director would always be a European, there was no similar agreement for GATT. For years the selection of GATT directors-general generated little controversy, but more recently the appointment of the director-general has become a contentious issue. Recent conflict over the selection process reflected the greater assertiveness of the United States in response to its declining hegemony in trade; the growing trade rivalry among Europe, the United States, and Japan; and the more assertive attitude of the LDCs. As Table 8.5 shows, all GATT directors-general from 1948 to 1995 were Europeans. When it came time to select the first WTO director-general, the United States supported a former Mexican president, Japan and most Asian countries supported the South Korean trade minister, and the EU supported the former Italian minister of foreign trade Renato Ruggiero. Although Ruggiero of Italy was the clear favorite in the one-nation, one-vote GATT, the major trading nations sought a consensus to avoid a divisive vote on the issue. The United States finally agreed to the selection of Ruggiero as director-general, partly because its own candidate was indirectly linked to several political scandals. However, the United States insisted that Ruggiero should serve only one four-year term and that the next WTO head should be non-European. When it came time to select the next WTO director-general, the conflict was renewed. This time most Northern countries other than Japan supported Mike Moore of New Zealand, and most Southern countries supported Supachai Panitchpakdi of Thailand. After a protracted dispute, the WTO General Council finally reached a compromise agreement that Moore should be director-general for a three-year term beginning in

TABLE 8.5
DIRECTORS-GENERAL OF GATT[a] AND WTO

	Years in Office	Nationality-Country
Sir Eric Wyndham-White	1948–68	Britain
Olivier Long	1968–80	Switzerland
Arthur Dunkel	1980–93	Switzerland
Peter Sutherland	1993–95	Ireland
Renato Ruggiero	1995–99	Italy
Mike Moore	1999–Present	New Zealand

[a]The name of the GATT's chief administrative officer was changed from *secretary-general* to *director-general* in 1965.

September 1999, and that Supachai should succeed him for a three-year term beginning in September 2002.[56]

THE WTO AND THE GLOBAL TRADE REGIME

The WTO was designed to be a more effective and authoritative organization than the GATT, and in some respects it has succeeded. Unlike the GATT, the WTO is a formal IO with a status comparable to the IMF and the World Bank. The WTO's binding dispute settlement system is also being used far more frequently by member states than was the case for the less authoritative dispute settlement procedures of the GATT. Furthermore, the WTO is becoming a more genuinely global trade organization, with 144 members as of January 2002, and with the approval of China's and Taiwan's admission to the organization during the WTO Ministerial conference in Doha, Qatar in November 2001. (Major countries that have still not joined the WTO include Russia, Ukraine, and Saudi Arabia.) In addition, the WTO not only oversees trade in goods, but also trade in services and trade-related intellectual property rights and investment measures. Finally, the WTO has made greater efforts to integrate the LDCs and emerging countries into the global trade regime and has begun a dialogue with a number of nongovernmental organizations.

Nevertheless, the WTO has also demonstrated some serious shortcomings, and the organization faces a number of obstacles in maintaining the momentum of global trade liberalization. Many of the problems that plagued the GATT have continued to have an adverse effect on the WTO, and it was unrealistic to assume that a new, more formal international organization would easily resolve the underlying sources of conflict. Liberal economists have argued that a new round of trade negotiations is essential to the vitality of the WTO and the global trade regime for several reasons. First, liberal economists believe that "*the bicycle must keep moving.* Forward momentum is essential to avoid backsliding into protectionism and mercantilism."[57] Second, negotiators at the GATT Uruguay round agreed to conduct further negotiations for trade in services and agriculture after the round was concluded. Nevertheless, self-standing negotiations on specific issue areas rarely succeed, because tradeoffs across issues are needed to satisfy the large number of participants in MTNs. This was another reason why a new round is viewed as necessary. Third, despite the improvement of dispute settlement procedures under the WTO, further negotiations are required to deal with lingering problems. For example, conflicts between the United States and EU over bananas, beef hormones, and the U.S. Foreign Sales Corporation program have demonstrated the need to improve the compliance provisions of the Dispute Settlement Understanding. Fourth, further negotiations are considered necessary to ensure that the growing number of RTAs are compatible with multilateral trade liberalization. In sum, further negotiations are required to strengthen the WTO-based trade regime.[58]

Initially, the plans were to launch a new round of trade negotiations at the WTO's Third Ministerial meeting in Seattle, Washington in November 1999. However, the pressures of globalization, combined with the broader scope and reach of the WTO's activities, elicited a strong negative reaction from civil society groups (the civil society issue is discussed later in this chapter). Prenegotiations in preparation for the Seattle Ministerial were also inadequate, and the WTO negotiators came to the meeting with widely divergent views on some critical issues. These underlying tensions became starkly evident at the Seattle meeting. Although anti-WTO protestors in the streets caused some disruptions, policy differences among WTO delegates themselves were the decisive factor contributing to the failure of the meeting. The major industrial states in the Quad all wanted a new multilateral trade negotiation, but they had strong disagreements over what issues should be negotiated. For example, the United States favored deep cuts in agricultural subsidies, but it opposed efforts of other states to re-form antidumping rules (which the United States used most frequently). Europe and Japan by contrast opposed further agricultural reforms, but sought new talks on com-petition and investment policy; and Canada wanted special exemptions for its cultural industries. Since the Quad members differed among themselves, they could not pro-vide leadership in forging a consensus among the WTO members. There were also major North-South differences, with the LDCs arguing that the industrial states should fulfill earlier promises in such areas as textiles and agricultural trade before they agreed to further negotiations in services trade and to new negotiations in such areas as investment and competition policy. The LDCs also wanted additional time to fulfill some of the commitments they had agreed to in the GATT Uruguay round.

The advanced industrial states were determined to hold a new WTO negotiating round, and after the failure in Seattle they planned to launch the round at the fourth WTO Ministerial meeting in Doha, Qatar in November 2001. A major factor in the de-cision to hold the meeting in Doha related to the ability to insulate the meeting from disruptive demonstrations of the type that occurred in Seattle. In view of serious divi-sions among the delegates, agreement was reached at Doha to launch a new round only after major compromises were made on all sides. For example, the EU accepted a stronger commitment to discuss phasing out farm export subsidies, the United States agreed to negotiations to improve rules on the use of countervailing and antidumping duties, the industrial states agreed to a (nonbinding) declaration that intellectual prop-erty rules should not prevent LDCs from gaining access to cheaper medicines for ill-nesses such as AIDs, and LDCs consented reluctantly to a commitment to future ne-gotiations on foreign investment, competition, and environmental issues. Although the agreement at Doha was a major achievement, there were indications that "this first step . . . [was] in fact the smallest one."[59] Shortly after the Doha Ministerial meeting was concluded, the United States and India were giving conflicting interpretations as to what exactly the delegates had agreed to in the final declaration.[60]

If the U.S. Congress fails to grant the president fast-track authority, this would prevent the United States from completing the new negotiating round. *Fast-track au-thority* requires Congress to vote yes or no on the implementing legislation for a trade agreement within 90 legislative days, without adding any amendments to the agree-ment. This serves as a confidence-building measure with U.S. trading partners, who know that under fast-track authority the U.S. Congress will not vote to amend trade agreements after they have been concluded. Fast-track authority contributed to the success of the GATT Tokyo and Uruguay rounds, and it was also used to enact the im-plementing bills for the U.S. free trade agreements with Israel, Canada, and Mexico.

However, the last Congressional grant of fast-track authority expired in 1994, and President Bill Clinton was unable to renew this authority during his administration. Although the U.S. president has been able to negotiate with other types of authority, the lack of fast-track authority limits the offers he is able to make. The failure to renew fast-track authority is partly symptomatic of protectionist sentiment in the United States, particularly from labor and environmental groups. The Doha agenda may make it more difficult to secure Congressional approval for fast-track authority, because legislators do not want to consider altering U.S. countervailing and antidumping procedures, and labor is dissatisfied with the lack of commitment to discuss trade and labor issues in the new round. Thus, there are numerous obstacles to a successful conclusion of the first round of trade negotiations under the WTO.[61]

THE THIRD WORLD AND GLOBAL TRADE ISSUES

The main participants in the GATT negotiations after World War II were advanced industrial states; the LDCs were largely uninvolved. This lack of involvement related partly to the nature of GATT and partly to LDC policies. The Havana Charter gave some attention to Third World issues in areas such as finance for economic development, preferential agreements among LDCs, and commodity agreements. When the charter was not approved, very few of these provisions were incorporated into GATT. Third World countries were also wary of participating in GATT because they felt that it did not take account of LDC needs for special and differential treatment.[62] For many years the LDCs therefore sought exemptions from some of the trade regime's principles and rules, and they wanted special access to developed country markets. In the 1980s, however, the LDCs became more accepting of the regime's liberal-economic values and more interested in participating in the global trade regime. Liberals and historical structuralists have very different views regarding the needs of LDCs for special treatment, the reasons why LDC policies changed in the 1980s, and the effects of the trade regime on LDC interests. The discussion that follows identifies four general stages of LDC participation in the postwar trade regime:

1. *The 1940s to early 1960s.* LDCs had only limited involvement in the GATT.
2. *The early 1960s to early 1970s.* LDCs increased their GATT membership and sought special and differential treatment.
3. *The early 1970s to 1980.* North-South confrontation increased, along with LDC demands for an NIEO.
4. *1980 to 1995.* LDCs became more willing to accept the liberal-economic principles of the global trade regime.
5. *1995 to the present.* Although most LDCs remain committed to liberal-economic principles, the nature and degree of their involvement in the WTO remain uncertain.

The 1940s to Early 1960s: A Period of Limited LDC Involvement

Third World countries had only limited involvement in the global trade regime in the early postwar years because of their relatively small numbers (many were still colonial territories), their protectionist trade policies, and GATT's inattention to their development problems. Most LDCs in the 1950s adopted protectionist ISI policies, which were designed to replace industrial imports with domestic production. Raúl Prebisch, an Argentinian economist, was the most influential figure supporting ISI policies in the postwar period. Prebisch argued that structural inequality between the industrial states in the core and the LDCs in the periphery was a major characteristic of the capitalist world economy. As long as LDCs were dependent on exports of primary products, they could not achieve high economic growth rates. Prebisch therefore advised LDCs to pursue ISI policies to increase their production of manufactures.[63]

Latin American LDCs in particular, influenced by Prebisch's arguments, adopted policies that emphasized industrial over agricultural development, production for the domestic market over production for export, and protection of local industry through import barriers. With this focus on inward-looking policies, most LDCs did not seek to actively participate in GATT. Thus, only 10 of the original 23 GATT members were LDCs. Although 20 LDCs had joined GATT by 1960, only 7 participated in the fifth (Dillon) round of GATT negotiations.[64] The only major provision in the General Agreement dealing directly with the trade problems of LDCs was GATT Article 28, which gave Third World countries some flexibility in imposing import quotas to protect their infant industries and alleviate their balance-of-payments problems. The LDCs insisted that GATT should be doing more to give them special and differential treatment, but their influence in the 1950s was extremely limited.[65]

The Early 1960s to Early 1970s: Growing Pressures for Special Treatment

Two major changes occurred in the 1960s and 1970s, contributing to growing LDC pressures for special treatment. First, some LDCs began to modify their ISI strategies or shift to export-oriented growth strategies, and second, the bargaining power of LDCs increased. By the 1960s, many LDCs following ISI policies were experiencing serious economic problems, including a slowdown in the growth of exports, dependence on intermediate imports for the production of industrial goods, and growing balance-of-payments problems. (See Chapter 11 for further discussion of LDC development strategies.) As Third World countries turned from inward- to outward-looking policies, they demanded special treatment to promote their exports. The LDCs also became better able to press their demands as the North-South balance shifted because of decolonization. Thus, in 1961 the UN General Assembly declared the 1960s to be the UN Development Decade, and UNCTAD I, the first major North-South conference on development issues, convened in 1964. Third World countries also established the G-77 at this time, which became the main vehicle for expressing their economic interests vis-à-vis the advanced industrial states.[66]

UNCTAD never posed a serious challenge to GATT as the main global trading organization, but it did have some influence in directing attention to Third World issues. Thus, GATT members added a new Part IV to the General Agreement in February 1965, calling for special treatment for LDCs. Although Part IV called on the developed countries to reduce their import barriers to LDC goods, this was not a legally binding obligation, and Part IV was in fact largely symbolic in nature. Indeed, the industrial states were actually raising their trade barriers in the 1960s for some products in which LDCs had a comparative advantage. A prime example of developed country protectionism vis-à-vis LDCs was the case of textiles and clothing. To protect their domestic producers in the 1950s, some industrial states (for example, the United States and Britain) violated GATT Article 11, which outlaws import quotas, and imposed "voluntary" restraints on textile/clothing exports from Japan, Hong Kong, India, and Pakistan. The industrial states then sought to legalize these restrictions through multilateral agreements. In 1961, a Short-Term Arrangement on Cotton Textiles was negotiated, and this was succeeded by several Long-Term Arrangements and four successive Multi-Fiber Arrangements (MFAs). In marked contrast to GATT, these multilateral textile agreements endorsed industrial state protectionism and restricted the exports of LDCs.[67]

GATT Part IV was largely a symbolic gesture. The LDCs received a more concrete concession in 1971 when GATT permitted industrial states to establish a GSP for LDCs through a 10-year renewable waiver from the MFN clause.[68] The United States and some other industrial states had at first strongly opposed the GSP idea, but their position on the issue gradually softened. The GSP lowers tariff rates in industrial states for certain imports from LDCs. Although some LDCs have benefited from these special preferences, the benefits have been limited. Thus, the industrial states refused to accept any legal obligation to provide preferences or to bind themselves to an internationally agreed GSP scheme. Instead, each state established its own GSP scheme, often limited the amount of imports that could enter at lower duties, and excluded sensitive products such as textiles and apparel from preferential status. In view of the complexities of the different GSP schemes, the more competitive LDCs such as the East Asian NIEs have benefited most from the GSP, and it has offered very few benefits to poorer LDCs. One study, for example, found that only three economies—Hong Kong, South Korea, and Taiwan—accounted for 44 percent of the total gains from GSP tariff reductions. Finally, industrial states often reduced or eliminated their GSP for LDCs that were especially successful in increasing their exports.[69]

The Early 1970s to 1980: Increased North-South Confrontation

The success of OPEC in increasing oil prices in 1973–74 was a major factor encouraging the LDCs to issue calls for a NIEO in the UN General Assembly.[70] To bring about the NIEO, the LDCs sought a wide range of concessions from the North relating to LDC sovereignty over their natural resources, increased control over foreign investment, greater assistance for LDC debt and development problems, greater LDC influence in the international economic organizations, improved LDC access to industrial state markets, and increased prices for LDC commodity exports.[71] We focus here on a central trade-related demand of the LDCs—the negotiation of an *Integrated Program for Commodities (IPC)*.

For a number of years, the first secretary-general of UNCTAD, Prebisch, had insisted that commodity agreements were necessary to redress the problems of unstable earnings and declining terms of trade for LDC commodity exports. A resolution to establish the IPC was finally approved in 1976 at the UNCTAD IV conference, with the goal of establishing agreements for 18 commodities that accounted for a substantial share of LDC primary product exports. The two most important elements of the IPC were to be the creation of international buffer stocks and the creation of a common fund that would be used to acquire the stocks. By enlarging the stockpiles of those commodities with declining prices and selling stockpiles of those commodities with increasing prices, the IPC was designed to avoid excessive price fluctuations and to ensure producers of remunerative returns.

Despite UNCTAD's passage of the IPC resolution, implementation of the program proved to be difficult for several reasons. First, some major developed countries opposed the IPC proposal on liberal-economic grounds because of its strong emphasis on market intervention to stabilize prices. Industrial states were to be the largest contributors to the common fund, so their opposition did not bode well for implementation. Second, the LDCs' ability to influence the industrial states declined abruptly in the 1980s with the emergence of the foreign debt crisis. Third, some of the assumptions of the IPC were defective, and doubts were raised about the actual effect of raising commodity export prices. LDCs and developed countries are not neatly divided into commodity exporters and importers, and the raising of commodity prices would benefit some industrial state exporters and hurt some LDC importers.

In view of the opposition of the industrial states, the agreement to establish a common fund was not ratified until 1989; since 1989, the industrial states have contributed only limited amounts to the common fund. Furthermore, only one new international agreement, the International Natural Rubber Agreement, was instituted under the IPC, and the International Tin Agreement collapsed in 1985. The IPC gave UNCTAD an opportunity to raise its profile as a negotiating forum, and the willingness of industrial states to negotiate (albeit reluctantly) represented something of a success for the LDCs. Nevertheless, the failure of the IPC to meet LDCs' expectations demonstrates the aversion most industrial states have to nonmarket solutions and points out their ability to prevent successful implementation of such North-South agreements.[72]

Although the LDCs were confronting the industrial states in the UN in the 1970s, they were also participating in the GATT Tokyo round from 1973 to 1979. One result of the Tokyo round was the approval of the *enabling clause* in 1979, which "established for the first time in trade relations . . . a permanent legal basis for preferences in favour of developing countries."[73] The clause gave permanent legal authorization for the GSP and for preferential trading agreements among LDCs. To gain approval of the enabling clause, LDCs had to support the principle of "graduation" for those countries that demonstrated notable progress in development. Because some exports from more advanced LDCs were threatening American producers, the U.S. government demanded that these LDCs (e.g., South Korea, Taiwan, and Brazil) give up special treatment and accept greater GATT discipline.[74]

Another significant development in the GATT Tokyo round was the creation of codes to decrease NTBs in areas such as government procurement, subsidies, technical barriers to trade, import licensing, and antidumping duties. Most LDCs were unwilling to limit their use of NTBs, so the industrial states negotiated the codes among themselves. Only a small number of LDCs signed the codes, and some of the major industrial states threatened to deny the benefits of the codes to GATT members that were nonsignatories. However, the attitude of LDCs toward participation in the global trade regime was to change markedly in the 1980s and 1990s.

1980s to 1995: More Active and Cooperative
LDC Participation in GATT

Initially, Third World countries opposed the idea of a new round of trade negotiations in the 1980s. They pointed to continued inequities in the international trade regime, and they were suspicious of efforts to include new areas in GATT, such as services, intellectual property, and investment, in which the developed countries had a competitive advantage. The opposition of LDCs gradually softened, however, partly because the industrial states agreed to include issues of interest to the LDCs such as trade in textiles and tropical agriculture. In contrast to previous rounds, the LDCs accepted the reciprocity principle and participated actively in the Uruguay round negotiations. Most significant, the LDCs agreed to treat the many different Uruguay round agreements as a *single undertaking:* acceptance of the Uruguay round accord meant acceptance of *all* its agreements. The single undertaking was a marked contrast to the Tokyo round's NTB codes, in which most LDCs did not participate.[75] The LDCs continued receiving special and differential treatment in the Uruguay round, but in contrast to previous rounds the single undertaking principle demonstrated that they were willing to accept "a dilution of special and differential treatment in exchange for better market access and strengthened rules."[76] The types of special treatment LDCs received in the Uruguay round included greater flexibility in fulfilling their commitments, longer transition times for implementing agreements, and technical assistance from the advanced industrial states.

The more active LDC role in the Uruguay round was directly related to the decision of many of these countries to liberalize their trade policies in the 1980s. Liberal economists and historical structuralists cite different reasons for this dramatic shift in Third World policies. According to liberals, LDCs became increasingly aware of the advantages of adopting liberal-economic policies, for several reasons. First, the tariff preferences LDCs received through the GSP were eroding as tariffs on trade among the industrial states were falling with each round of trade negotiations. Thus, LDCs were gaining fewer advantages from special and differential treatment. Second, the industrial states viewed LDCs as free riders receiving special treatment, and the LDCs were therefore marginalized in trade negotiations. Many products of interest to the LDCs, such as textiles and tropical agriculture, were either excluded from the GATT negotiations or subjected to special protectionist rules. And third, liberals attributed the shift in LDC policies to the failure of inward-looking ISI policies and to the notable success of the East Asians' export-led growth strategies.[77]

Historical structuralists strongly disagree with liberals as to the reasons why LDCs shifted their trade policies in the 1980s. According to historical structuralists, LDCs were *forced* to alter their policies. In response to the foreign debt crisis in the 1980s, the IMF and the World Bank provided SALs to LDCs only on the condition that they decrease government spending, liberalize their trade, and privatize their economies. Because industrial states and private lenders are unlikely to extend loans to LDC debtors that do not first receive the IMF's stamp of approval, the debtor countries had no choice but to liberalize their trade policies. Thus, one writer argues that "the current rush toward free trade follows on the heels of 10 years of structural adjustment, a logical 'next step' in the overhaul of the global economy."[78]

1995 to the Present: Uncertainty over LDC Participation in the WTO

Liberals and historical structuralists also disagree in their assessment of the effects of the GATT Uruguay round on Third World countries. Liberals concede that the LDCs had to make concessions to the industrial states in such areas as intellectual property, services trade, and investment. However, they argue that these were short-term concessions and that LDCs will benefit in the long term from liberalizing their policies. Liberals also point to the advantages LDCs gained from participating in the Uruguay round in such areas as textiles and tropical agriculture. Finally, liberals note that LDCs still benefit from special and differential treatment in some areas; for example, LDCs have a lower level of obligations and more flexible implementation timetables, and they will benefit from special provisions for the LLDCs and from technical assistance and training. Many liberals acknowledge that industrial states should be doing more to open their markets to LDC exports, but on balance they would argue that the Uruguay round was beneficial to the LDCs.[79]

Historical structuralists, by contrast, argue that LDCs gave up far more than they received in the Uruguay round. The inclusion of trade in services and intellectual property ensures that income will be transferred from the poor to the rich countries because the LDCs cannot yet compete effectively in these areas. As for the "concessions" to LDCs, the agreement to phase out the protectionist MFA on textiles was "backloaded" so that almost one-half of the industrial states' import quotas are to be removed only at the end of a 10-year transition period. Historical structuralists are highly skeptical that the industrial states will comply with an agreement that is extended so far into the future.[80] Liberals and historical structuralists agree that LDCs are becoming more closely involved in the global trade regime but have very different views of the possible consequences for these countries.

Both the liberals and the historical structuralists have a point. Although the LDCs received some "fairly significant benefits from the Uruguay round," they also realized belatedly "that they had accepted fairly weak commitments in agriculture and textiles while making substantially stronger ones, especially in new areas such as intellectual property."[81] The LDCs generally remain committed to the path of more open participation in MTNs that they adopted in the GATT Uruguay round, but they are disillusioned with the results of the round and this could have a dampening effect on their active participation in future WTO negotiations. For example, LDCs were encouraged by the Uruguay round Agreement on Textiles and Clothing, which provided a 10-year transition period for phasing out quantitative restrictions on imports. Nevertheless, "the difficulty of industrialized importing countries, especially the United States and the European Union, in meeting their commitments under this agreement to liberalize textiles and clothing trade has been one of the greatest challenges facing the international economic system since 1995."[82] The LDCs have also been dissatisfied with lack of progress in dealing with other areas such as agricultural trade protectionism and ADDs, which industrial states often impose on Third World exports.[83]

The disillusionment of LDCs with the results of the GATT Uruguay round were evident at the third and fourth WTO Ministerial meetings in Seattle and Doha. Indeed, India almost blocked the decision to launch a new MTN round at Doha, and

LDCs "remain deeply suspicious of the rich world's commitment to truly freer trade."[84] Although liberal economists strongly support the new WTO round, they maintain that industrial states must do more to remove their barriers to LDC exports if the trade talks are to succeed:

> Europe and America must quickly open up their markets for farm products and tex-tiles. They must show that environmental concerns are not going to become a back-door excuse for renewed protectionism. They must reform their oft-abused system of anti-dumping rules. And they must deliver on promises to beef up poorer countries' capacity to deal with the intricate procedures in the world trading system.[85]

The nature and degree of LDC involvement in future WTO-based MTNs will de-pend largely on whether or not they feel the industrial states are taking their interests and concerns seriously.

THE EMERGING ECONOMIES AND GLOBAL TRADE RELATIONS

The Third World countries only gradually increased their involvement in the GATT trade regime, but most CPEs were not even members of GATT for many years after World War II. As was the case for LDCs, the General Agreement also largely ignored the issues of concern to CPEs.[86] The lack of attention to state trading and central plan-ning was not surprising; the Soviet Union had turned down an invitation to attend the Havana Charter negotiations (see Chapter 2), and it was simply assumed that GATT members would be free market economies. Indeed, one of the major functions of GATT was to limit government actions that interfered with market forces.

As Table 8.6 shows, Czechoslovakia was a founding member of GATT and re-mained a member even after it became Communist (for many years its membership was largely inactive). Other Eastern European countries (Yugoslavia, Poland, Roma-nia, and Hungary) joined GATT in the 1960s and 1970s. CPEs exclude foreign prod-ucts through administrative control over pricing and purchasing; thus, a lowering of tariffs does not necessarily increase access to CPE markets. GATT therefore admitted these Eastern European countries under special provisions (see the following discus-sion). In the late 1980s and 1990s, however, the requirements for membership be-came more rigorous, and nonmarket economies were expected to institute specific re-forms as a condition for admission. The more stringent requirements resulted from concerns about the possible admission of China and the Soviet Union (later Russia), the revival of orthodox liberalism in the 1980s, and the more formal characteristics of the WTO compared with its predecessor, GATT.

Although relations between GATT and its Eastern European members were of-ten difficult, the problems were limited because these countries had a relatively small effect on the global trade regime. This would not necessarily be the case if China or Russia joined the GATT/WTO, where their membership could have significant eco-

TABLE 8.6

MEMBERSHIP OF THE EMERGING ECONOMIES IN GATT/WTO

	GATT/WTO
1948	Czechoslovakia and China (founding members)
1950	Republic of China (Taiwan) withdraws from GATT
1966	Yugoslavia
1967	Poland
1971	Romania
1973	Hungary
1990	East Germany accedes to GATT by virtue of German reunification
1993	Czech Republic, Slovak Republic
1994	Slovenia
1996	Bulgaria
1998	Kyrgyz Republic
1999	Latvia, Estonia
2000	Albania, Croatia, Georgia
2001	Lithuania, Moldova, China
2002	Taiwan

Sources: General Agreement on Tariffs and Trade, *GATT Activities* (Geneva, Switz.: GATT, various years).

nomic and political consequences. China and Russia were readily admitted to the IMF and the World Bank because they are loan recipients and have little influence in these weighted-voting institutions.[87] The GATT/WTO, by contrast, does not have weighted voting, and the major trading nations were concerned that these two countries could shift the political and economic balance of power in the organization. Furthermore, if economies as large as China and Russia were admitted to the GATT/WTO before they evolved sufficiently toward developing market economies, there were fears that trade protectionism in the WTO could increase.[88] The sections that follow examine GATT/WTO relations with Eastern Europe, China, and the FSU countries.

The Eastern European Countries and GATT/WTO

Czechoslovakia was a founding member of GATT as well as the IMF and the World Bank. Although Czechoslovakia was ousted from the IMF and the World Bank shortly after it became a nonmarket economy, it was able to remain as a largely inactive member of the GATT for many years because of the informality of the General Agreement. Table 8.6 shows that four other Eastern European countries (Yugoslavia, Poland, Romania, and Hungary) joined GATT in the 1960s and early 1970s. Although some of these countries were becoming more market oriented, the decision to admit them also resulted from the Western policy of *differentiation*. Designed to contain the Soviet Union, the differentiation strategy rewarded Eastern European countries for adopting more independent foreign or domestic policies. The strong U.S. support for Romanian accession to GATT, for example, stemmed mainly from that country's collision with the Soviet

Union on foreign policy issues. The GATT secretariat also exerted pressure for the admission of Eastern European states because it aspired to the goal of universal membership.[89]

In accordance with the West's differentiation policy, GATT imposed a diverse range of conditions for admission of the Eastern European states. After its break with the Soviet bloc in 1948, Yugoslavia sought to redirect its trade to the West. When Yugoslavia first explored GATT affiliation in 1950, it was a full CPE, but it began efforts to engage in economic decentralization in 1952. Yugoslavia did not become a full member of GATT until 1966 because major reforms were required to move it from CPE protection toward the GATT model. This experience showed that a CPE that adopted an economic decentralization policy could participate in the GATT under conditions very similar to those for a market economy.

Unlike Yugoslavia, Poland and Romania applied for accession to GATT when they were not yet moving toward market reform. Tariffs have little influence over the import decisions of CPEs, so Poland and Romania had to commit to increasing their imports from GATT members in return for the benefits of GATT membership. When Poland became a GATT member in 1967, it agreed to increase its total value of imports from GATT members by 7 percent per year, and in return Poland received limited MFN treatment. The agreement with Poland had some major shortcomings. First, Poland's 7 percent import commitment was based on an estimate that its exports to GATT members would increase by the same amount. Because Poland did not meet the 7 percent import requirement, as a quid pro quo it had to decrease its exports to other GATT countries. Some analysts therefore argue that the 7 percent requirement served as a *disincentive* to Polish trade in GATT.[90]

When Romania applied for membership, GATT agreed to classify it as an LDC, and it was therefore subject to less rigid requirements than Poland. Instead of providing a specific commitment, Romania expressed a "firm intention" to increase its imports from GATT members by at least as much as its total imports from all countries were increasing. Although this approach avoided the problems of specific commitments encountered with Poland, the Romanian undertakings were so vague that they were unenforceable.[91] The conditions for Hungary's admission to GATT (in 1973) were somewhere in between those for Yugoslavia on the one hand and Poland and Romania on the other. Because Hungary had been instituting some liberal economic reforms under its New Economic Mechanism, GATT members permitted it to provide tariff concessions as an alternative to firm commitments to increase its imports. In contrast to other Eastern European countries, Bulgaria was rebuffed for many years in its attempts to join GATT. Bulgaria's efforts failed because it was a close Soviet ally during the Cold War and because of fears that its admission would create a precedent for admission of the Soviet Union. With the decline of the Cold War, the strategic rationale for denying Bulgaria WTO membership became less important, but the Bulgarian case continued to be enmeshed with the issue of WTO membership for Russia and China. It was not until 1996 that the WTO finally approved the entry of Bulgaria.[92]

Despite the openness of GATT to the admission of Eastern European countries, the acceptance of these countries was clearly conditional. For example, the accession agreements for Poland, Romania, and Hungary permitted the EC to continue imposing discriminatory quantitative restrictions on imports from these countries. Trade between the CPEs and the United States was also subject to special restrictions under

U.S. law. Thus, in some respects the Eastern Europeans were second-class citizens in GATT. With the breakup of the Soviet bloc, there were growing pressures to normalize the terms of participation for Eastern European countries. The EU agreed to dispense with its quantitative restrictions on Eastern European exports, and the WTO extended virtually the same treatment to Poland and Hungary as it does to market economies. However, Eastern European countries have still not been fully integrated into the global trade regime.[93]

China

China's decision to seek membership in GATT/WTO marked a significant departure from its policies in earlier years. In the early 1960s, China had followed a policy of "self-reliance," which emphasized import substitution, and its policies became even more autarkic in 1966 to 1969 during the Cultural Revolution. In the early 1970s, however, China occupied the "China seat" in the UN General Assembly (which had been held by Taiwan) and moved to expand its commercial contacts with the West. After Mao Zedong's death in 1976 and the imprisonment of Cultural Revolution leaders, China began to gradually liberalize its economy in 1978 and it sought to establish contacts with the GATT. In 1982, China was given observer status in GATT, permitting it to attend the annual meetings of the Contracting Parties, and in 1984 China was given special observer status allowing it to attend meetings of the GATT Council. In 1986 China indicated that it wanted to "rejoin" GATT as a full member, and it renewed its application in 1995 when the WTO was established.[94]

Compared with the relative ease with which it took over the China seat in the IMF and the World Bank (in 1980), China's accession to GATT/WTO was a protracted affair. The delay in reconciliation stemmed partly from conflicting views in China. Although China wanted to increase its linkages with the KIEOs in the late 1970s, it had a more restrained attitude toward GATT than toward the IMF and the World Bank. To participate in the IMF and the World Bank, China would have to provide economic data on itself and pay its subscription, but the benefits of receiving external financing and economic advice from these organizations greatly outweighed the drawbacks. As a full participant of GATT, by contrast, the requirements of China would be greater (e.g., submitting to the GATT rules and opening its market) and the benefits more uncertain. Furthermore, China received *de facto* MFN treatment from most countries even without being a member of GATT. The only major exception was the United States, where Congress held an annual vote on the issue, but even in this case Congress had always voted to renew MFN status for China.[95]

Despite its reticence about GATT membership, China decided to seek full participation in the GATT beginning in 1986. Overall, the Chinese leadership decided that the benefits of membership outweighed the costs. Membership would consolidate Chinese's past liberalization measures and provide motivation for further reforms, give China a legal right of access to its export markets, give China access to the GATT dispute settlement system to protect its trading rights, and permit it to participate in the GATT's rule-making process. China also became increasingly committed to joining the GATT/WTO as the ratio of imports and exports to its GDP rose from below 10 percent in 1978 to 30 percent in 1996.[96]

For a number of years China argued that its accession to the GATT should be easily achieved because it would be a resumption of membership rather than a new membership. China was a founding member of GATT when it came into force in 1948. However, it was in the midst of a civil war during the early years of GATT, and in 1950 the government of Chiang Kai-shek (which had fled to Taiwan) sent a cable withdrawing China from GATT membership. China maintained that the 1950 cable had no legal effect because Chiang Kai-shek was no longer leading the legally constituted government of China. China also argued that it had reoccupied "the China seat" without having to apply as a new member in the UN, the Food and Agriculture Organization, and the IMF and World Bank. Thus, China's desire to join GATT/WTO should be regarded as a resumption of membership rather than a new membership issue. A number of GATT members pointed out, however, that China did not participate in GATT negotiations or abide by GATT obligations for 35 years. Because China still had many characteristics of a CPE, conditions had to be placed on its membership. Thus, China had to eventually accept the fact that detailed negotiations would precede its accession to the GATT/WTO, and that procedures to be followed would be similar to those for other new members.[97] The procedures for admission to the WTO today (and the GATT before it) involve four stages:

1. A fact-finding stage, in which a WTO working party collects information on the applicant's trade policies.
2. A negotiations stage, in which the applicant holds bilateral talks with WTO members and multilateral talks with a WTO working party.
3. A decision stage, in which the WTO General Council decides whether to admit the applicant. Although the General Council normally decides by consensus, it could approve a draft decision to admit the applicant by a two-thirds majority.
4. An implementation stage, in which the applicant must make internal policy adjustments in accordance with the accession package.[98]

The discussion that follows outlines three issues that played a major role in China's negotiations for admission to the GATT/WTO.

Requirements That China Should Liberalize Its Economy   As discussed, China has introduced a wide range of market reforms to liberalize its CPE since 1978. Nevertheless, China's trade policies lack transparency, and government intervention in the economy continues to produce major trade distortions. For example, China limits imports with high tariffs for specific sectors, import quotas, import licenses and other barriers. The United States has reacted strongly to these trade distortions, because the U.S. trade deficit with China increased from $17.8 billion in 1989 to $68.7 billion in 1999. U.S. labor groups argue that many jobs have been lost because of the trade deficit with China, and they exerted strong pressure on the U.S. government to insist that China commit to much more economic liberalization, and to enforceable labor rights as a price for WTO membership.[99] Thus, there has been considerable pressure on China to offer specific commitments to liberalize its trade policies and to make its policies more transparent.[100]

The Question of China's Status in the WTO   Another major issue in the accession negotiations was China's status within the WTO. Should China be categorized as an industrial country or an LDC, and should it be viewed as a CPE? The answers to these questions had major implications for the conditions and terms of Chinese membership.

China regularly indicated that it expected "the same differential and more favourable treatment" in the WTO that was "accorded to developing countries at similar stages of economic development."[101] Romania was given developing country status when it was admitted to the GATT, and China wanted similar conditions. With developing country status, China would be eligible for the special treatment granted to other LDCs, such as protection for infant industries, the generalized system of preferences, and longer transition periods in implementing WTO agreements. Many industrial countries and LDCs in the WTO, however, argued that China should be treated as a developed country because of its size and status as a world exporter. From this perspective, China should be expected to meet the same reciprocity conditions as those expected of developed states. Even IOs present conflicting views regarding China's level of development. For example, although the World Bank predicts that China will be the second largest economy after the United States by the year 2020, it continues to categorize China's economy as "developing."[102]

A second issue related to whether China should be viewed as a CPE. China argued that the imposition of special conditions for its accession to the WTO was unnecessary because it had become much more market oriented. Thus, a Chinese member of the UNCTAD secretariat stated that "China expects unconditional most favoured-nation treatment equivalent to that accorded to all other Contracting Parties."[103] Major trading countries in the WTO, by contrast, maintained that the Chinese government continued to depend on strategic trade rather than comparative advantage as a basis for its policies. Although some Eastern European countries joined GATT as CPEs, China's sheer size and huge trading capacity made the imbalance in market access a much greater concern. The terms for admitting China to the WTO were therefore of considerable importance and in some respects the major trading powers would not accord China the same terms in the WTO that they gave to market economies. For example, the United States and China concluded their bilateral negotiations for China's accession to the WTO in November 1999. In the bilateral agreement the United States reserves the right to treat China as a nonmarket economy in some respects, and to use safeguard mechanisms that would unilaterally restrict Chinese exports. On the other hand, the WTO is permitting China to adopt a phase-in approach for many areas of its trade policy in recognition of the fact that China is a transitional economy.[104]

The Question of China's Implementation of Agreements   A third issue in the accession negotiations related to China's past record in implementing agreements. For example, in 1992 the U.S. Bush administration reached an agreement with China to improve protection of intellectual property. Despite the agreement, piracy of computer programs and music recordings became a thriving industry in southern China, and Chinese-made copies of pirated U.S. films, computer programs, and recordings were sent to Eastern Europe, Canada, and elsewhere. Although some argue that China's protection for intellectual property has improved, pirated intellectual property continues to be readily available in major Chinese cities.[105] Concerns about China's commitment and ability to implement agreements on market access and other areas therefore became an issue of concern in the accession negotiations.

Despite these contentious issues, China reached bilateral agreements on market access with the United States and the EU in late 1999 and early 2000 as a prelude to its accession to the WTO. The United States also had to address the issue of providing permanent MFN status to China, which WTO members normally grant to one another. The United States had provided China MFN status on an annual basis since 1980, and extension of MFN to China was not a major issue until the Tiananmen Square massacre in 1989. Each year after Tiananmen, the U.S. Congress used the annual MFN review to raise a number of concerns with China, ranging from human rights to arms sales and trading practices. Despite opposition from a number of labor and human rights groups, the U.S. Congress voted to grant permanent MFN status or "permanent normal trade relations" to China, and in October 2000 President Clinton signed the legislation. (In June 1999 the term "normal trade relations" replaced the term "most favored nation" in U.S. law, but the MFN term continues to be used in WTO and other trade agreements.)[106]

On November 10, 2001, the delegates at the Doha Ministerial meeting finally agreed to admit China to the WTO. One day later, they agreed to admit Taiwan ("Chinese Taipei"). China became a WTO member in December 2001, and Taiwan became a WTO member in January 2002. There is a wide range of views regarding the possible impact of China's membership in the WTO on China, the WTO, and other trading partners. Some analysts warn that "China's complex and opaque system of bureaucrats, provincial governments, and state-run enterprises, combined with its lack of a rule of law, could prove too much for the WTO."[107] Membership in the WTO is also likely to have some painful effects on the Chinese people and economy; for example, China's auto industry, agricultural sector, and financial services could all suffer as a result of freer trade in the WTO. Other analysts, however, take a more positive view, arguing that "China's accession to the WTO is in the interests of both China and its major trading partners" because it will result in the liberalization of China's economy and eventually its society and polity.[108] Thus, China's chief negotiator at the WTO negotiations argued that "if China wants to develop from a large economic country to an economic power, it must become part of the mainstream of the world economy, otherwise, it will . . . face the danger of marginalization."[109] In the view of many liberal theorists, China's accession to the WTO is more likely to be a positive experience if the Chinese government can begin to bridge the gap between an increasingly open economy and a closed political system.[110]

Russia and Other FSU Countries

After avoiding participation in GATT for more than three decades, the Soviet Union sought observer status in GATT and quietly explored the possibility of membership in the early 1980s. However, some important GATT members strongly opposed these efforts. Undeterred, the Soviets in August 1986 asked for observer status at the Punta del Este meetings to launch the GATT Uruguay round negotiations. This request came along with the announcement of Soviet plans to introduce extensive domestic economic and trade reforms.

The Soviet Union's change in policy should not have been surprising; a sharp drop in oil prices was posing a serious threat to Mikhail Gorbachev's five-year plan to restructure and modernize the economy. However, the major trading countries limited invitations to the GATT Uruguay round to contracting parties or to countries that had given formal notification of their intention to join GATT. This decision was designed to permit China's participation in the round, but to exclude the Soviet Union and Bulgaria. American officials in particular expressed strong opposition to Soviet participation, arguing that the Soviet economic system was incompatible with the trade regime's principles, norms, and rules. The major trading nations were also concerned that the Soviet Union would benefit more than the West from accession to the GATT and that the Soviets would politicize GATT activity, making it difficult to conduct trade negotiations.[111]

The United States and other Western countries were far more open to the accession issue after the breakup of the Soviet Union in December 1991, and WTO membership negotiations are ongoing with states of the FSU. Serious economic problems in the FSU countries and their halting steps toward establishing market economies pose obstacles to their accession to the WTO. However, as Table 8.6 shows, from 1998 to 2001 six FSU countries were admitted to the WTO (the Kyrgyz Republic, Latvia, Estonia, Georgia, Lithuania and Moldova), and others were certain to follow. Russia entered negotiations for accession to the WTO in July 1995, and successive WTO directors-general have expressed great interest in having Russia join the organization. Despite its economic problems, Russia has a large market capacity for goods, services, and investment, and Russian exports can significantly influence world commodity markets.[112]

As was the case for China, Russia has conducted bilateral and multilateral negotiations under WTO auspices with a view to eventual accession to the organization. Nevertheless, Russia is far less prepared than China for membership in the WTO. The breakup of the Soviet Union severed economic linkages that had been formed over decades, resulting in serious economic problems for Russia. A major obstacle to Russian negotiations for WTO accession is that its "internal systems require staggering reforms, a wholesale recreation of legal, taxing, banking systems."[113] Thus, some informed sources believe that Russia's accession negotiations will not be completed before 2005. Although Russia has not yet joined the WTO, a number of factors favor its eventual inclusion. As long as countries as important as Russia, Ukraine, and Saudi Arabia are not included, the WTO cannot claim to be a truly global trade organization. Furthermore, these countries are more likely to liberalize their economies from within than outside the WTO, and they are more likely to follow disruptive economic policies as long as they remain outsiders.[114]

CIVIL SOCIETY AND GLOBAL TRADE RELATIONS

The WTO was a target for protest by civil society groups even before it began operations in January 1995, but the Third WTO Ministerial meeting in Seattle in late 1999 marked a turning point in which the protests reached new levels. A major reason the WTO has become a target relates to the fact that it is the most important of the KIEOs. Unlike the GATT, which dealt only with trade in goods, the WTO has expanded to include trade in services, intellectual property, and trade-related investment measures. The WTO dispute settlement system is also considerably stronger than the GATT's, because parties to a dispute can no longer veto panel decisions against them. In view of the importance of the WTO today, many civil society groups have demanded a role in WTO decision making and have expressed strongly held views about what the WTO should or should not be doing.[115]

WTO agreements establish formal rights and obligations only for member governments, and WTO dispute settlement is formally open only to state actors. This limitation has rested on the realist assumption that sovereign states are the primary actors in the international system. According to this perspective, the WTO functions best "when governments can speak clearly to each other without a cacophony of other voices."[116] All sessions of the WTO General Council, committees, dispute settlement panels, and appellate body panels are closed to the public, and minutes of these meetings are not released. Although private parties have limited formal roles in some WTO dispute settlement cases, they have no *legal right* to these roles—it is always at the discretion of others. For example, WTO dispute settlement panels have the authority to consider submissions or advice from any private individual or group, but panels can choose whether or not to accept private party submissions.[117] Today, many NGOs are demanding that they should have a role in dispute settlement cases commensurate with their interests; for example, environmental NGOs argue that they should be involved in dispute settlement cases involving trade and the environment.

Civil society groups also have strongly held views regarding the role of the WTO. In view of the wide array of these groups, however, the views expressed are sometimes inconsistent. On the one hand, NGOs often portray the WTO as a major vehicle of globalization that has too much power to override the will of governments. On the other hand, a number of NGOs argue that the WTO should contribute to fair trade by exerting pressure on delinquent governments to upgrade their labor, environmental, and human rights standards. In this area, NGO views often diverge from the position of LDCs, which argue that such standards would infringe on their sovereignty, and would also provide industrial states with an excuse to impose protectionist trade barriers on LDC exports. It is impossible to devote space in this text to assessing the competing views regarding the proper role for NGOs in the WTO, and for the WTO on issues such as labor and the environment. Interested students should refer to the wide and growing amount of literature on the subject.[118]

CONCLUSION

This chapter demonstrates that international trade has been strongly affected by the forces of globalization. The changes are evident in the growing importance of international trade to national economies and to domestic groups within those economies, in the closer linkages between trade and other international issues, and in the increased membership of countries in GATT/WTO. Trade as a share of global output increased from 7 percent in 1950 to more than 22 percent in 1997, and trade grew 2.8 times faster than global output from 1984 to 1994. Internationalist firms have a major stake in an open trading system today because of their reliance on multinational operations, exports, imports, and intrafirm trade. GATT was designed to deal almost exclusively

TABLE 8.7

NEW LDC ACCESSIONS TO THE GATT, 1982–94
(DATES OF ACCESSION)

Angola	1994	Maldives	1983
Antigua and Barbuda	1987	Mali	1993
Bahrain	1993	Mexico	1986
Belize	1983	Morocco	1987
Bolivia	1990	Mozambique	1992
Botswana	1987	Namibia	1992
Brunei	1993	Papua New Guinea	1994
Costa Rica	1990	Paraguay	1993
Djibouti	1994	Qatar	1994
Dominica	1993	St. Kitts and Nevis	1994
El Salvador	1991	St. Lucia	1993
Fiji	1993	St. Vincent and Grenadines	1993
Grenada	1994	Solomon Islands	1994
Guatemala	1991	Swaziland	1993
Guinea, Republic of	1994	Thailand	1982
Guinea-Bissau	1994	Tunisia	1990
Honduras	1994	United Arab Emirates	1994
Hong Kong	1986	Venezuela	1990
Lesotho	1988	Zambia	1982
Macao	1991		

Source: Bernard Hoekman and Michel Kostecki, *The Political Economy of the World Trading System: From GATT to WTO* (Oxford: Oxford University Press, 1995) pp. 275–276.

with trade in tangible goods, but this coverage proved to be too narrow as trade in services increased. Furthermore, the WTO today is addressing a wide range of nontrade issues such as foreign investment, intellectual property, labor standards, and the environment, which have become closely intertwined with trade issues.[119] Foreign direct investment and trade, for example, are highly complementary because about one-third of trade today is conducted among affiliates of international firms. (Although some accords such as TRIPS extend beyond the trade area, internationalist firms are pleased to have them included in the WTO.)

Finally, membership and participation in GATT/WTO is for the first time becoming truly global in scope. For many years Third World countries in GATT did not fully participate in the negotiations, and a number of LDCs did not even join the organization. The foreign debt crisis that began in 1982 marked a turning point in LDC participation in the global economy in general and in the global trade regime in particular. Thus, Table 8.7 shows that 39 LDCs joined GATT from 1982 to 1994 (the year before the WTO was formed). Another major turning point was the breakup of the Soviet Union in the early 1990s, which led to a new wave of emerging countries seeking membership in GATT/WTO. As of January 2002 there were 144 member states in the WTO, and a number observer governments waiting to join the organization.

Liberals, realists, and historical structuralists have very different reactions to these changes in the global trade regime. Liberal economists believe that industrial, Third

World, and emerging countries are all benefiting from trade liberalization. Thus, one liberal researcher argues that "in one country after another, farsighted leaders have recognized that they themselves have the means to invigorating their economies by opening their borders."[120] Orthodox liberals also applaud the moves by many LDCs in recent years to liberalize their trade barriers unilaterally, arguing that the primary benefits go to those who liberalize. As for the services, investment, and intellectual property agreements that resulted from the GATT Uruguay round, liberals feel that they should and do "mark only the beginning, not the completion, of new liberalization."[121]

Many realists question whether there is genuine globalization of trading activity, and they point to the fact that countries today are not uniformly moving in the direction of trade liberalization. Today's "globalization," from this perspective, is actually a form of "triadization," in which the three most powerful and developed regions of the world—Western Europe, North America, and East Asia—have the most interactions. By far the largest amount of trade occurs between and within these three major regions, and trade flows involving other regions are relatively small. The Quad composed of the United States, the EU, Japan, and Canada also plays an important role in setting the agenda for global trade negotiations. Triadization is evident not only from facts and figures but also from general attitudes. Thus, Western Europeans, Japanese, and North Americans believe that the "world that counts is their world in which is located the scientific power, technological potentials and supremacy, military hegemony, economic wealth, cultural power and, therefore, mastery of conditions and ability to govern the world economy."[122] Realists also point out that the decline of U.S. trade hegemony has led to growing competition among the three major trading blocs. In this increasingly competitive world, strategic trade policies involving selective intervention by governments can greatly improve a country's trade position. Thus, realists often emphasize that states can create their own "competitive advantage" as an alternative to relying solely on static views of comparative advantage.

Historical structuralists, like realists, point to a hierarchy among states, in which the industrial states clearly dominate the global trade regime. However, historical structuralists are more concerned than realists with the consequences for Third World states. In the view of historical structuralists, LDCs have become more active participants in the global trade regime not by choice but by necessity. IMF and World Bank SALs since the 1980s have been linked with LDC commitments to engage in trade liberalization, privatization, and deregulation, and Third World debtors have had to comply with these conditions to receive international financing. The GATT Uruguay round agreement, from this perspective, was an unequal agreement in which industrial states received concrete gains in areas such as intellectual property and services trade while LDCs had to settle for the promise of possible future gains in areas such as textile trade.

The TRIPs agreement on intellectual property is a prime example of the differing views of liberals and historical structuralists. The Uruguay round agreement requires all signatories to provide intellectual property rights protection in a number of areas; for example, WTO members must develop legislation that provides patent protection for at least 20 years. Liberals argue that most innovation occurs privately, and groups and individuals will have little incentive to engage in research and development if they are not rewarded with sufficient patent protection. Thus, intellectual property rights are essential for the development of new inventions and innovations. Historical structuralists, by contrast, maintain that many of the TRIPs measures "are not explicitly related to trade—except in the name of the agreement."[123] Although Third World countries in the GATT Uruguay round had wanted the TRIPs discussions to be limited to trade-related measures, the industrial states used these discussions to develop measures they wanted that were outside the competence of GATT. More than 80 percent of the patents in the Third World are owned by foreigners, mainly MNCs with headquarters in the North. Thus, the TRIPs agreement, according to historical structuralists, will limit and distort trade, hinder the transfer of technology to the Third World, and lead to a net transfer of resources in rents from the LDCs to the advanced industrial states.[124]

Liberals, realists and historical structuralists in fact all point to important trends in the global trade regime. On the one hand, trade interdependence has been increasing, and there are strong pressures for further trade liberalization. If one considers the role of transnational actors today, it would seem that the forces for trade liberalization are inexorable. Nevertheless, realists point out that this growing interdependence and the decline of U.S. trade hegemony have led to increased competitiveness and greater temptations to resort to strategic trade policy. Historical structuralists argue that the main beneficiaries of trade liberalization have been the advanced industrial states, with the Third World countries occupying a peripheral position. Both realists and historical structuralists can also point to the wide range of civil society groups that have reacted against WTO policies that they associate with globalization. In sum, the pressures for trade liberalization have increased in recent years, but opposing forces have also gained strength and should not be underestimated.

NOTES

1. Jacob Viner, *Studies in the Theory of International Trade* (New York: Augustus M. Kelly, Reprint of Economic Classics, 1965), p. 100; David A. Baldwin, *Economic Statecraft* (Princeton, NJ: Princeton University Press, 1985), pp. 75–76.
2. A trade war is "a category of intense international conflict where states interact, bargain, and retaliate primarily over economic objectives directly related to the traded goods or service sectors of their economies, and where the means used are restrictions on the free flow of goods or services"; see John A. C. Conybeare, *Trade Wars: The Theory and Practice of International Commercial Rivalry* (New York: Columbia University Press, 1987), p. 3.
3. World Trade Organization, *Annual Report—1998* (Geneva, Switz.: WTO, 1998), p. 5.
4. Renato Ruggiero (director-general of the World Trade Organization), "Charting the Trade Routes of the Future: Towards a Borderless Economy," address delivered to the International Industrial Conference, San Francisco, September 29, 1997, *World Trade Organization Press Release*, Geneva, Press/77, p. 4.
5. Helen V. Milner, *Resisting Protectionism: Global Industries and the Politics of International Trade* (Princeton, NJ: Princeton University Press, 1988), pp. 290–291.

   Business conflict theory is directly relevant to disputes between internationalist and nationalist business groups over international trade. See the discussion of business conflict theory in Chapter 5 of this book.

6. David Ricardo, *The Principles of Political Economy and Taxation* (Homewood, IL: Irwin, 1963). See also Cletus C. Coughlin, K. Alec Chrystal, and Geoffrey E. Wood, "Protectionist Trade Policies: A Survey of Theory, Evidence, and Rationale," *Federal Reserve Bank of St. Louis Review* 70-1 (January–February, 1988), pp. 12–13.

7. Beth V. Yarbrough and Robert M. Yarbrough, *The World Economy: Trade and Finance*, 3rd ed. (Fort Worth, TX: Harcourt Brace, 1994), pp. 78–82.

8. Wolfgang F. Stolper and Paul A. Samuelson, "Protection and Real Wages," *Review of Economic Studies* 9-1 (November 1941), pp. 58–73; Ronald Rogowski, *Commerce and Coalitions: How Trade Affects Domestic Political Alignments* (Princeton, NJ: Princeton University Press, 1989).

9. For example, Wassily Leontief found that the United States was highly successful in exporting labor-intensive goods in the 1950s, a period in which it was the most capital-rich country. See Leontief's article "Domestic Production and Foreign Trade: The American Capital Position Re-examined," *Proceedings of the American Philosophical Society* 97-4 (September 1953), pp. 332–349. See also Harry P. Bowen, Edward E. Leamer, and Leo Sveikauskas, "Multicountry, Multifactor Tests of the Factor Abundance Theory," *American Economic Review* 77-5 (December 1987), pp. 791–809.

10. Elhanan Helpman and Paul R. Krugman, *Market Structure and Foreign Trade: Increasing Returns, Imperfect Competition, and the International Economy* (Cambridge, MA: MIT Press, 1985), p. 3; Robert Gilpin with Jean M. Gilpin, *The Political Economy of International Relations* (Princeton, NJ: Princeton University Press, 1987), pp. 175–178.

11. Bruce R. Scott, "National Strategies: Key to International Competition," in Bruce R. Scott and George C. Lodge, eds., *U.S. Competitiveness in the World Economy* (Boston: Harvard Business School Press, 1985), pp. 93–95.

12. Laura D'Andrea Tyson, *Who's Bashing Whom? Trade Conflict in High-Technology Industries* (Washington, DC: Institute for International Economics, November 1992), p. 4; F. M. Scherer and Richard S. Belous, *Unfinished Tasks: The New International Trade Theory and the Post–Uruguay Round Challenges*, Issues Paper no. 3 (Washington, DC: British–North American Committee, May 1994), p. 42.

13. Klaus Stegemann, "Policy Rivalry Among Industrial States: What Can We Learn from Models of Strategic Trade Policy?" *International Organization* 43-1 (Winter 1989), p. 99; Yarbrough and Yarbrough, *The World Economy*, pp. 271–274.

14. See Edward John Ray, "Changing Patterns of Protectionism: The Fall in Tariffs and the Rise in Non-Tariff Barriers," *Northwestern Journal of International Law & Business*, 8 (1987), pp. 294–295; and Rogowski, *Commerce and Coalitions*, pp. 168–169.

15. Robert A. Pastor, *Congress and the Politics of U.S. Foreign Economic Policy, 1929–1976* (Berkeley, CA: University of California Press, 1980), p. 78.

16. The classic statement of this position is found in Charles P. Kindleberger, *The World in Depression 1929–1939* (Berkeley, CA: University of California Press, 1973), pp. 291–307.

17. Stephen D. Krasner, "State Power and the Structure of International Trade," *World Politics* 28-3 (April 1976), p. 338.

18. See E. E. Schattschneider, *Politics, Pressures and the Tariff: A Study of Free Private Enterprise in Pressure Politics, as Shown in the 1929–1930 Revision of the Tariff* (Hamden, CT: Archon Books, 1963, unaltered from the 1935 edition); and Pastor, *Congress and the Politics of U.S. Foreign Economic Policy*, pp. 80–84.

19. For a discussion of the effects of the U.S. 1930 tariff, see Joseph M. Jones, Jr., *Tariff Retaliation: Repercussions of the Hawley-Smoot Bill* (Philadelphia, PA: University of Pennsylvania Press, 1934).

20. For a discussion of the reasons for Congressional passage of the RTAA, see I. M. Destler, *American Trade Politics,* 2nd ed. (Washington, DC: Institute for International Economics and The Twentieth Century Fund, June 1992), pp. 14–15.

21. Jones, *Tariff Retaliation,* pp. 303–305; Gilbert R. Winham, *The Evolution of International Trade Agreements* (Toronto: University of Toronto Press, 1992), p. 19; Henry J. Tasca, *The Reciprocal Trade Policy of the United States: A Study in Trade Philosophy* (New York: Russell & Russell, 1938), chs. 2–4.

22. John W. Evans, *The Kennedy Round in American Trade Policy: The Twilight of the GATT?* (Cambridge, MA: Harvard University Press, 1971), pp. 5–7.

23. Robert E. Hudec, *The GATT Legal System and World Trade Diplomacy* (New York: Praeger, 1075), pp. 7–18; Simon Reisman, "The Birth of a World Trading System: ITO and GATT," in Orin Kirshner, ed., *The Bretton Woods–GATT System: Retrospect and Prospect After Fifty Years.* (Armonk, NY: Sharpe, 1996), pp. 83–85. For detail on the early U.S.-U.K. bilateral discussions on trade, see E. F. Penrose, *Economic Planning for Peace* (Princeton, NJ: Princeton University Press, 1953), pp. 87–115.

24. William Diebold, Jr., *The End of the I.T.O.,* Essays in International Finance no. 16 (Princeton, NJ: International Finance Section, Department of Economics and Social Institutions, Princeton University, October, 1952), p. 2. See also Richard N. Gardner, *Sterling-Dollar Diplomacy in Current Perspective: The Origins and Prospects of Our International Economic Order* (New York: Columbia University Press, new expanded edition, 1980), pp. 348–380.

25. For studies favoring the ITO charter at the time, see Clair Wilcox, *A Charter for World Trade* (New York: Macmillan, 1949); and William Adams Brown, Jr., *The United States and the Restoration of World Trade: An Analysis and Appraisal of the ITO Charter and the General Agreement on Tariffs and Trade* (Washington, DC: Brookings Institution, 1950). For a study highly critical of the charter, see Philip Cortney, *The Economic Munich: The I.T.O. Charter, Inflation or Liberty, The 1929 Lesson* (New York: Philosophical Library, 1949).

26. John H. Jackson, *World Trade and the Law of GATT* (Indianapolis, IN: Bobbs-Merrill, 1969), pp. 120–121.

27. Barry Eichengreen and Peter B. Kenen, "Managing the World Economy Under the Bretton Woods System: An Overview," in Peter B. Kenen, ed., *Managing the World Economy: Fifty Years After Bretton Woods* (Washington, DC: Institute for International Economics, September 1994), p. 7.

28. Bernard M Hoekman and Michel M. Kostecki, *The Political Economy of the World Trading System: From GATT to WTO* 2nd edition (Oxford: Oxford University Press, 2001), pp. 1–3; Richard N. Gardner, "The Bretton Woods–GATT System After Fifty Years: A Balance Sheet of Success and Failure," in Kirshner, ed., *The Bretton Woods–GATT System: Retrospect and Prospect After Fifty Years,* p. 199.

29. John Gerard Ruggie, "International Regimes, Transactions, and Change: Embedded Liberalism in the Postwar Economic Order," in Stephen D. Krasner, ed., *International Regimes* (Ithaca, NY: Cornell University Press, 1983), p. 212.

30. Jock A. Finlayson and Mark W. Zacher, "The GATT and the Regulation of Trade Barriers: Regime Dynamics and Functions," in Krasner, ed., *International Regimes,* pp. 282–286; Hoekman and Kostecki, *The Political Economy of the World Trading System,* pp. 31–33.

31. Item-by-item negotiations continued in the Kennedy round for agricultural goods and some other sensitive products. See Hoekman and Kostecki, *The Political Economy of the World Trading System,* pp. 127–129; Robert E. Hudec, *Enforcing International Trade Law: The Evolution of the Modern GATT Legal System* (Salem, NH: Butterworth Legal Publishers, 1993), pp. 12–13.

32. Theodore H. Cohn, *The International Politics of Agricultural Trade: Canadian-American Relations in a Global Agricultural Context* (Vancouver: University of British Columbia Press, 1990), pp. 141–42.

33. Milner, *Resisting Protectionism,* p. 8; Marc L. Busch and Helen V. Milner, "The Future of the International Trading System: International Firms, Regionalism, and Domestic Politics," in Richard Stubbs and Geoffrey R. D. Underhill, eds., *Political Economy and the Changing Global Order* (Toronto: McClelland & Stewart, 1994), p. 264.

34. Milner, *Resisting Protectionism,* p. 290. The Milner volume focuses on a number of case studies to demonstrate the difference in domestic firms' trade preferences in the 1920s and the 1970s.

35. Eric Wyndham-White, "Negotiations in Prospect," in C. Fred Bergsten, ed., *Toward a New World Trade Policy: The Maidenhead Papers* (Lexington, MA: Heath, 1975), p. 322.

36. Charles Lipson, "The Transformation of Trade: The Sources and Effects of Regime Change," in Krasner, ed., *International Regimes,* p. 242.

37. Winham, *The Evolution of International Trade Agreements,* pp. 46–48; Hoekman and Kostecki, *The Political Economy of the World Trading System,* pp. 29–31.

38. Finlayson and Zacher, "The GATT and the Regulation of Trade Barriers," pp. 286–290.

39. Ernest Preeg, *Traders and Diplomats: An Analysis of the Kennedy Round of Negotiations Under the General Agreement on Tariffs and Trade* (Washington, DC: Brookings Institution, 1970), p. 195.

40. Gilbert Winham, *International Trade and the Tokyo Round Negotiations* (Princeton, NJ: Princeton University Press, 1986), pp. 172–175.

41. Theodore H. Cohn, "NAFTA, GATT and Canadian-U.S. Agricultural Trade Relations," *The North-South Agenda Papers,* no. 10 (Coral Gables, FL: North-South Center, University of Miami, November 1994), pp. 5–8.

42. Robert Wolfe, *Farm Wars: The Political Economy of Agriculture and the International Trade Regime* (London: Macmillan, 1998), p. 89; General Agreement on Tariffs and Trade, "The QUAD's Initial Market-Access Package," *GATT Focus Newsletter* no. 101, August–September 1993, p. 3; Fred Bergsten and Randall Henning, *Global Economic Leadership and the Group of Seven* (Washington, DC: Institute for International Economics, 1996), pp. 17–18; Communiqué of G-7 Summit, Tokyo, Japan, July 6–9, 1993, paragraph 7.

43. Robert O. Keohane, "Reciprocity in International Relations," *International Organization* 40-1 (Winter 1986), p. 4.

44. Carolyn Rhodes, "Reciprocity in Trade: The Utility of a Bargaining Strategy," *International Organization* 43-2 (Spring 1989), p. 276; Keohane, "Reciprocity in International Relations," p. 24; Tyson, *Who's Bashing Whom?*.

45. John Whalley and Colleen Hamilton, *The Trading System After the Uruguay Round* (Washington, DC: Institute for International Economics, July 1996), pp. 49–50; John H. Jackson, *The World Trading System: Law and Policy of International Economic Relations* (Cambridge, MA: MIT Press, 1989), p. 149.

46. Hoekman and Kostecki, *The Political Economy of the World Trading System,* pp. 303–304; Winham, *The Evolution of International Trade Agreements,* pp. 50–51; Finlayson and Zacher, "The GATT and the Regulation of Trade Barriers," pp. 290–293.

47. J. Michael Finger and Julio Nogues, "International Control of Subsidies and Countervailing Duties," *The World Bank Economic Review* 1 (1987), pp. 713–714; Hoekman and Kostecki, *The Political Economy of the World Trading System,* p. 307. For a comparison of American and Canadian contingent trade measures, see Theodore H. Cohn, "Emerging Issues in Canada-U.S. Agricultural Trade Under the GATT and FTA," *Canadian-American Public Policy,* no. 10 (Orono, ME: University of Maine, June 1992), pp. 18–22.

48. For a discussion of economic development issues addressed in the Havana Charter and ITO, see Wilcox, *A Charter for World Trade*, pp. 140–152.
49. Finlayson and Zacher, "The GATT and the Regulation of Trade Barriers," pp. 293–296.
50. Jeffrey J. Schott with Johanna W. Buurman, *The Uruguay Round: An Assessment* (Washington, DC: Institute for International Economics, November 1994), pp. 4–5.
51. Minister for International Trade, "Canada Proposes Strategy for Creation of a World Trade Organization," *News Release* no. 077, External Affairs and International Trade Canada, April 11, 1990.
52. John Croome, *Reshaping the World Trading System: A History of the Uruguay Round* (Geneva, Switz.: World Trade Organization, 1995), pp. 271–274 and 358–361; Ernest H. Preeg, *Traders in a Brave New World: The Uruguay Round and the Future of the International Trading System* (Chicago: University of Chicago Press, 1995), pp. 113–114 and 124–126.
53. Hoekman and Kostecki, *The Political Economy of the World Trading System*, p. 1.
54. Hoekman and Kostecki, *The Political Economy of the World Trading System*, pp. 74–98; Preeg, *Traders in a Brave New World*, p. 42.
55. Gardner Patterson and Eliza Patterson, "The Road from GATT to MTO," *Minnesota Journal of Global Trade* 3-1 (Spring 1994), p. 37.
56. Nathaniel C. Nash, "U.S. Backed Candidate for Trade Post Is Trailing," *New York Times*, December 3, 1994, p. 3; Madelaine Drohan, "Americans, Europeans at Odds Over Who Should Lead WTO," *Globe and Mail*, March 15, 1995, p. B6; David E. Sanger, "Yielding, U.S. Bows to Europe on Trade Chief," *New York Times*, March 21, 1995, p. C1; "New Zealand's Moore Heads WTO," *WTO Focus Newsletter*, no. 41, July–August 1999, pp. 1–2.
57. C. Fred Bergsten, "Fifty Years of Trade Policy: The Policy Lessons," *World Economy* 24-1 (January 2001), p. 1.
58. Jeffrey J. Schott, "The WTO after Seattle," in Jeffrey J. Schott, ed., *The WTO After Seattle* (Washington, DC: Institute for International Economics, July 2000), pp. 8–17; Bergsten, Fifty Years of Trade Policy," pp. 1–12.
59. "Beyond Doha," *The Economist*, November 17, 2001, p. 11.
60. World Trade Organization, "Ministerial Declaration," Ministerial Conference in Doha, Fourth Session, WT/MIN(01)/DEC/W/1, November 14, 2001; "The Doha Round: Seeds Sown for Future Growth," *The Economist*, November 17, 2001, pp. 65–67; "Chairman's Statement Casts Doubt on Final WTO Declaration," *Inside U.S. Trade*, November 15, 2001, pp. 1 and 15–16.
61. Schott, "The WTO after Seattle," pp. 3–8; Craig VanGrasstek, "US Plans for a New WTO Round: Negotiating More Agreements with Less Authority," *World Economy* 23-5 (May 2000), pp. 673–677. For a detailed discussion of U.S. fast-track authority see Craig Van-Grasstek, "Is the Fast Track Really Necessary?," *Journal of World Trade* 31-2 (April 1997), pp. 97–123.
62. Martin Wolf, "Two-Edged Sword: Demands of Developing Countries and the Trading System," in Jagdish N. Bhagwati and John Gerard Ruggie, eds., *Power, Passions, and Purpose: Prospects for North-South Negotiations* (Cambridge, MA: MIT Press, 1984), p. 202.
63. See Raúl Prebisch, "The Economic Development of Latin America and Its Principal Problems," *Economic Bulletin for Latin America* 7-1 (February 1962), pp. 1–59. Albert O. Hirschman, "The Political Economy of Import-Substituting Industrialization in Latin America," *Quarterly Journal of Economics* 82-1 (February 1968), pp. 1–32; Hollis Chenery, "The Structuralist Approach to Development Policy," *American Economic Review* 65-2 (May 1975), pp. 310–316.
64. Marc Williams, *Third World Cooperation: The Group of 77 in UNCTAD* (London: Pinter Publishers, 1991), p. 23.

65. Kenneth W. Dam, *The GATT: Law and International Economic Organization* (Chicago: University of Chicago Press, 1970), pp. 227–228; Robert E. Hudec, *Developing Countries in the GATT Legal System* (Aldershot, UK: Gower, for the Trade Policy Research Centre, 1987), pp. 23–24.

66. Karl P. Sauvant, *The Group of 77: Evolution, Structure, Organization* (New York: Oceana Publications, 1981), p. 3; Williams, *Third World Cooperation,* pp. 89–90.

67. Vinod K. Aggarwal, *Liberal Protectionism: The International Politics of Organized Textile Trade* (Berkeley, CA: University of California Press, 1985), p. 8.

68. For a discussion of UNCTAD's role in pressuring GATT to develop the GSP, see Anindya K. Bhattacharya, "The Influence of the International Secretariat: UNCTAD and Generalized Tariff Preferences," *International Organization* 30-1 (Winter 1976), pp. 75–90.

69. Anne O. Krueger, *Trade Policies and Developing Nations* (Washington, DC: Brookings Institution, 1995), pp. 40–42. See also Rolf J. Langhammer and André Sapir, *Economic Impact of Generalized Tariff Preferences,* Thames Essay no. 49 (Aldershot, UK: Gower, for the Trade Policy Research Centre, 1987).

70. The LDC demands were contained in several documents submitted to the General Assembly in 1974: the *Declaration on the Establishment of a New International Economic Order (NIEO),* the *Program of Action on the Establishment of a NIEO,* and the *Charter of Economic Rights and Duties of States.*

71. Jeffrey A. Hart, *The New International Economic Order: Conflict and Cooperation in North-South Economic Relations, 1974–77* (New York: St. Martin's Press, 1983), ch. 2.

72. Hart, *The New International Economic Order,* pp. 36–40; Williams, *Third World Cooperation,* pp. 133–159; Alfred Maizels, "Reforming the World Commodity Economy," in Michael Zammit Cutajar, ed., *UNCTAD and the South-North Dialogue: The First Twenty Years* (Oxford: Pergamon Press, 1985), pp. 101–121; Jock A. Finlayson and Mark W. Zacher, *Managing International Markets: Developing Countries and the Commodity Trade Regime* (New York: Columbia University Press, 1988).

73. Olivier Long, *Law and Its Limitations in the GATT Multilateral Trade System* (Dordrecht, Neths: Nijhoff, 1985), p. 101.

74. Hudec, *Developing Countries in the GATT Legal System,* pp. 70–91.

75. See Robert Wolfe, "Global Trade as a Single Undertaking: The Role of Ministers in the WTO," *International Journal* 51-4 (Autumn 1996), pp. 690–709; and Wolfe, *Farm Wars,* pp. 91–97.

76. Quoted in Mari Pangestu, "Special and Differential Treatment in the Millennium: Special for Whom and How Different?" *World Economy* 23-9 (September 2000), p. 1291. See also Edwini Kwame Kessie, "Developing Countries and the World Trade Organization: What Has Changed?" *World Competition* 22-2 (June 1999), pp. 98–110; and John Whalley, "Special and Differential Treatment in the Millennium Round," *World Economy* 22-8 (August 1999), pp. 1065–1093.

77. John Whalley, "Recent Trade Liberalisation in the Developing World: What Is Behind it and Where Is it Headed?" in David Greenaway, Robert C. Hine, Anthony P. O'Brien, and Robert J. Thornton, eds., *Global Protectionism* (London: Macmillan, 1991), pp. 225–253; Krueger, *Trade Policies and Developing Nations,* pp. 48–50.

78. John Gershman, "The Free Trade Connection," in Kevin Danaher, ed., *Fifty Years Is Enough: The Case Against the World Bank and the International Monetary Fund* (Boston: South End Press, 1994), p. 24.

79. See Bernard R. Hoekman, "Developing Countries and the Multilateral Trading System After the Uruguay Round," in Roy Culpeper, Albert Berry, and Frances Stewart, eds., *Global Development Fifty Years After Bretton Woods: Essays in Honour of Gerald K. Helleiner* (New York: St. Martin's Press, 1997), pp. 252–279.

80. For more detail on historical structuralist arguments, see Chakravarthi Raghavan, *Recolonization: GATT, the Uruguay Round and The Third World* (London: Zed Books, 1990); and Chakravarthi Raghavan, "A New Trade Order in a World of Disorder?" in Jo Marie Griesgraber and Bernhard G. Gunter, eds., *World Trade: Toward Fair and Free Trade in the Twenty-first Century* (London: Pluto Press, 1997), pp. 1–31.

81. Jayashree Watal, "Developing Countries' Interests in a 'Development Round,' " in Schott, ed., *The WTO after Seattle*, pp. 71–72.

82. Asoke Mukerji, "Developing Countries and the WTO," *Journal of World Trade* 34-6 (December 2000), p. 41.

83. Joseph E. Stiglitz, "Two Principles for the next Round or, How to Bring Developing Countries in from the Cold," *World Economy* 23-4 (April 2000), pp. 437–454.

84. "Beyond Doha," p. 11.

85. "Beyond Doha," p. 11.

86. See M. M. Kostecki, *East-West Trade and the GATT System* (London: Macmillan, for the Trade Policy Research Centre, 1979), p. 2; Zdenek Augenthaler, "The Socialist Countries and GATT," in Frans A. M. Alting von Geusau, ed., *Economic Relations After the Kennedy Round* (Leyden, Neths: Sijthoff-Leyden, 1969), p. 81.

87. In 1999, China and Russia together accounted for only 5.04 percent of the votes in the IMF and only 5.62 percent of the votes in the World Bank. (*IMF Annual Report—1999* (Washington, DC: IMF, 1999), pp. 194–197; *World Bank Annual Report—1999* (Washington, DC: World Bank, 1999), pp. 275–278.

88. Jackson, *The World Trading System*, pp. 283–286.

89. Leah A. Haus, *Globalizing the GATT: The Soviet Union's Successor States, Eastern Europe, and the International Trading System* (Washington, DC: Brookings Institution, 1992), pp. 15, 28; Bohdan Laczkowski, "Poland's Participation in the Kennedy Round," in Geusau, ed., *Economic Relations After the Kennedy Round*, pp. 83–93.

90. Eliza R. Patterson, "Improving GATT Rules for Nonmarket Economies," *Journal of World Trade Law* 20-2 (March/April 1986), p. 188; Jozef M. van Brabant, *The Planned Economies and International Economic Organizations* (Cambridge: Cambridge University Press, 1991), pp. 199–201.

91. Patterson, "Improving GATT Rules for Nonmarket Economies," p. 189; Paul D. McKenzie, "China's Application to the GATT: State Trading and the Problem of Market Access," *Journal of World Trade* 24-5 (October 1990), pp. 141–143.

92. "Preparations Intensify for Singapore; Membership of Bulgaria and Panama Approved," World Trade Organization, *WTO Focus Newsletter* no. 12, August–September, 1996, pp. 1–2.

93. Laszlo Lang, "International Regimes and the Political Economy of East-West Relations," *Occasional Paper Series 13* (New York: Institute for East-West Security Studies, 1989), pp. 35–36; Haus, *Globalizing the GATT*, ch. 3.

94. McKenzie, "China's Application to the GATT," pp. 144–145; Robert E. Herzstein, "China and the GATT: Legal and Policy Issues Raised by China's Participation in the General Agreement on Tariffs and Trade," *Law and Policy in International Business* 18-2 (1986), pp. 373–374.

95. Harold K. Jacobson and Michel Oksenberg, *China's Participation in the IMF, the World Bank, and GATT: Toward a Global Economic Order* (Ann Arbor, MI: University of Michigan Press, 1990), pp. 83–92.

96. Hiddo Houben, "China's Economic Reforms and Integration into the World Trading System," *Journal of World Trade* 33-3 (June 1999), pp. 4–5.

97. Chung-chou Li, "Resumption of China's GATT Membership," *Journal of World Trade Law* 21-4 (1987), p. 26; Herzstein, "China and the GATT," pp. 404–405; Jackson, *The World Trading System*, pp. 287–288.

98. U.S. General Accounting Office, "China Trade: WTO Membership and Most-Favored-Nation Status," Statement by JayEtta Z. Hecker before the Subcommittee on Trade, Committee on Ways and Means, U.S. House of Representatives, GAO/T-NSIAD-98-209, June 17, 1998, pp. 4–8.

99. For example, Robert E. Scott argues that "in 1996, the U.S. trade deficit with China eliminated over 600,000 jobs, most of them in high-paying manufacturing industries." See his article "WTO Accession: China Can Wait," *WorkingUSA* (September/October 1999), p. 82.

100. U.S. General Accounting Office, "China Trade," pp. 2–3; "The Storm after the Storm: China's WTO Accession and the US-China Trade Relationship," *Stanley Foundation Policy Bulletin*, October 26–28, 2000, p. 2.

101. Li, "Resumption of China's GATT Membership," p. 30.

102. "China and World Markets: The Debate over Trade Status," *Congressional Digest* 79 (June–July 2000), p. 161; U.S. General Accounting Office, "China Trade," p. 3.

103. Li, "Resumption of China's GATT Membership," p. 30.

104. McKenzie, "China's Application to the GATT," pp. 144–145; Herzstein, "China and the GATT," pp. 375–377; Yongzheng Yang, "China's WTO Accession: The Economics and Politics," *Journal of World Trade* 34-4 (2000), p. 80.

105. Greg Mastel, "China and the World Trade Organization: Moving Forward without Sliding Back," *Law and Policy in International Business* 31-3 (Spring 2000), pp. 988–991.

106. U.S. General Accounting Office, "China's Membership Status and Normal Trade Relations Issues," GAO/NSIAD-00-94, March 2000, p. 4, fn 1. For a good discussion of the arguments in the United States for and against granting permanent normal trade relations status to China, see "China and World Markets: The Debate over Trade Status," pp. 161–192.

107. Master, "China and the World Trade Organization," p. 997.

108. Yang, "China's WTO Accession," p. 92.

109. Statement by Long Yongtu quoted in Steven Chase and Miro Cernetig, "WTO Opens Door to China," *Globe and Mail*, November 12, 2001, pp. B1 and B5.

110. See Minxin Pei, "Future Shock: The WTO and Political Change in China," *Carnegie Endowment Policy Brief* 1-3 (February 2001), pp. 1–7.

111. Jacobson and Oksenberg, *China's Participation in the IMF, the World Bank, and GATT*, p. 94; Brabant, *The Planned Economies and International Economic Organizations*, pp. 1–6; Lang, "International Regimes and the Political Economy of East-West Relations," pp. 53–60.

112. Leonid Sabelnikov, "Russia on the Way to the World Trade Organization," *International Affairs* 72-2 (1996), pp. 345–355.

113. Quoted in "Working Party on Russia WTO Accession Gearing up for Next Session," *Inside U.S. Trade*, November 3, 2000.

114. McKenzie, "China's Application to the GATT," p. 150; "Russia and the WTO: Shaping Up for the Club," *The Economist*, November 24, 2001, p. 68.

115. Jan Aart Scholte with Robert O'Brien and Marc Williams, "The WTO and Civil Society," *Journal of World Trade* 33-1 (February 1999), pp. 107–123; David Robertson, "Civil Society and the WTO," *World Economy* 23-9 (September 2000), pp. 1119–1134.

116. Daniel C. Esty, "Non-Governmental Organizations at the World Trade Organization: Cooperation, Competition, or Exclusion," *Journal of International Economic Law* 1-1 (March 1998), p. 140.

117. "Understanding on Rules and Procedures Governing the Settlement of Disputes," Article 13-1 in World Trade Organization, *The Results of the Uruguay Round of Multilateral Trade Negotiations—The Legal Texts* (Geneva, Switz.: WTO, 1995), p. 416; Gabrielle Marceau and Peter N. Pedersen, "Is the WTO Open and Transparent?" *Journal of World Trade* 33-1 (February 1999), pp. 32–36.

118. For example, in addition to the sources listed in footnotes 109 to 111, see Robert O'Brien, Anne Marie Goetz, Jan Aart Scholte, and Marc Williams, *Contesting Global Governance: Multilateral Economic Institutions and Global Social Movements* (Cambridge: Cambridge University Press, 2000); Jeffrey L. Dunoff, "The Misguided Debate over NGO Participation at the WTO," *Journal of International Economic Law* 1-3 (September 1998), pp. 433–456; and G. Richard Shell, "The Trade Stakeholders Model and Participation by Nonstate Parties in the World Trade Organization," *University of Pennsylvania Journal of International Economic Law* 17-1 (1996), pp. 359–381.

119. John Whalley and Colleen Hamilton, *The Trading System After the Uruguay Round* (Washington, DC: Institute for International Economics, July 1996), pp. 2–3.

120. Jim Powell, "Self-Determination Through Unilateral Free Trade," in Doug Bandow and Ian Vásquez, eds., *Perpetuating Poverty: The World Bank, the IMF, and the Developing World* (Washington, DC: CATO Institute, 1994), p. 345.

121. Whalley and Hamilton, *The Trading System After the Uruguay Round*, p. 2; Hoekman and Kostecki, *The Political Economy of the World Trading System*, pp. 268–271.

122. Riccardo Petrella, "Globalization and Internationalization: The Dynamics of the Emerging World Order," in Robert Boyer and Daniel Drache, eds., *States Against Markets: The Limits of Globalization* (London: Routledge, 1996), p. 77.

123. Whalley and Hamilton, *The Trading System After the Uruguay Round*, p. 52.

124. For contending views on this issue, see Krueger, *Trade Policies and Developing Countries*, pp. 52–54; Raghavan, *Recolonization: GATT, the Uruguay Round and the Third World*, pp. 114–141; and Croome, *Reshaping the World Trading System*, pp. 130–138.

CHAPTER 9

Regionalism and the Global Trade Regime

The major trading nations gave strong support to multilateral trade liberalization with the formation of the GATT after World War II. However, regionalism also emerged as a significant force in postwar international trade with the formation of a number of regional trade agreements. As noted in Chapter 2, an RTA may exist at various stages of economic integration, ranging from a free trade area to a customs union, a common market, and an economic union (see Figure 2.3). There have been two major waves of regionalism in the postwar period, the first in the 1950s and 1960s and the second since the mid-1980s. The second wave has been especially significant, with the EU increasing its membership and deepening the integration process, and the United States reversing its long-standing policy of refusing to join RTAs. Of the 109 regional agreements reported to the GATT from 1947 to 1994, 33 were concluded from 1990 to 1994, and RTAs "have proliferated at an astonishing pace since the WTO Agreement took effect in 1995."[1] From 1995 to 2000, 69 new RTAs were notified to the WTO.[2] Table 9.1 shows that a wide range of reciprocal and nonreciprocal RTAs were in force as of January 1995 (the nonreciprocal RTAs are between developed countries and LDCs).

Under some circumstances, multilateralism and regionalism are competing approaches to trade and foreign investment policy. Whereas multilateralism contributes to worldwide liberalization of foreign trade and investment flows, regionalism may act as a balkanizing force that divides the world into competing trade blocs. However, "open" regionalism can be an important force in breaking down national trade barriers and thus in serving as a stepping-stone rather than an obstacle to global free trade. RTAs following open regionalism permit market forces to work, abolish trade barriers and discrimination within the RTA, and lower trade barriers to outsiders. States and MNCs today generally consider open regionalism and multilateralism to be complementary strategies, which they can use simultaneously to promote market forces and increase their competitiveness in the global economy.

Theorists from the three IPE perspectives have very different views of RTAs. Liberal economists consider GATT/WTO multilateralism to be the best possible route to trade liberalization because it breaks down regional as well as national barriers to trade. However liberals support open RTAs as a second-best route to trade liberalization

TABLE 9.1
REGIONAL TRADE AGREEMENT (RTAs) NOTIFIED TO GENERAL AGREEMENT ON TARIFFS AND TRADE (GATT) AND IN FORCE AS OF JANUARY 1995

Reciprocal RTAs

Europe

European Community (EC)

Austria	Germany	Netherlands
Belgium	Greece	Portugal
Denmark	Ireland	Spain
Finland	Italy	Sweden
France	Luxembourg	United Kingdom

EC Free Trade Agreements with

Estonia	Latvia	Norway
Iceland	Liechtenstein	Switzerland
Israel	Lithuania	

EC Association Agreements with

Bulgaria	Hungary	Romania
Cyprus	Malta	Slovak Rep.
Czech Rep.	Poland	Turkey

European Free Trade Association (EFTA)

Iceland	Norway	Switzerland
Liechtenstein		

EFTA Agreements with

Bulgaria	Israel	Slovak Rep.
Czech Rep.	Poland	Turkey
Hungary	Romania	

Norway Free Trade Agreements with

Estonia	Latvia	Lithuania

Switzerland Free Trade Agreements with

Estonia	Latvia	Lithuania

Czech Republic and Slovak Republic Customs Union

Central European Free Trade Area

Czech Rep.	Poland	Slovak Rep.
Hungary		

Czech Republic and Slovenia Free Trade Agreement

Slovak Republic and Slovenia Free Trade Agreement

North America

Canada–United States Free Trade Agreement (CUSFTA)

North American Free Trade Agreement (NAFTA)

Latin America and the Caribbean

Caribbean Community and Common Market (CARICOM)

Central American Common Market (CACM)

Latin American Integration Association (LAIA)

Andean Pact

Southern Common Market (Mercosur)

Middle East

Economic Cooperation Organization (ECO)

Gulf Cooperation Council (GCC)

Asia

Australia–New Zealand Closer Economic Relations Trade Agreement (CER)

Bangkok Agreement

ASEAN Preferential Trade Arrangement

Lao People's Dem. Rep. and Thailand Trade Agreement

Other

Israel–United States Free Trade Agreement

Nonreciprocal RTAs

Europe

EEC-Association of Certain Non-European Countries and Territories (EEC-PTOM II)

EEC Cooperation Agreements with

Algeria	Lebanon	Syria
Egypt	Morocco	Tunisia
Jordan		

ACP-EEC Fourth Lomé Convention

Asia

Australia–Papua New Guinea Agreement

South Pacific Regional Trade and Economic Cooperation Agreement (SPARTECA)

Source: Regionalism and the World Trading System, April 1995, p. 26, Table 1. By permission of the World Trade Organization.

when negotiating difficulties in the GATT/WTO pose obstacles to freer multilateral trade. Although most liberals acknowledge that some groups such as displaced workers may lose as a result of RTAs, they nevertheless argue that the gains in efficiency from open regionalism outweigh any costs incurred. Furthermore, liberals generally assume that all member states will benefit in the long term from open RTAs, even if they do not benefit equally. Power disparities are not a major problem for smaller states in RTAs, according to liberals. Indeed, they argue that RTAs provide more benefits to a small country than to a large country in terms of economies of scale and increased market demand for its exports.[3]

In contrast to liberals, realists and historical structuralists believe that RTAs have important distributional effects and that some member states and groups within states will benefit *at the expense of* others. Of particular concern to these theorists are RTAs with major asymmetries of power, levels of economic development among the member states, or both. Realists, for example, argue that the larger partner in an RTA either will not permit the smaller partner to receive disproportionate benefits or will expect some "side payments" in return. These side payments will be greater than any economic benefits the smaller partner receives from gains in market access and economies of scale. As noted in this chapter, Canada and Mexico sought free trade with the United States partly to gain more assured access to the large U.S. market. The United States, however, expected side payments in such areas as foreign investment, trade in services, and access to natural resources (especially energy).[4] In the long term, realists expect the distribution of benefits in regional agreements to reflect the asymmetries of power, wealth, and technology among the member states.

In the view of historical structuralists, MNCs and other sources of transnational capital are the main beneficiaries of RTAs such as the EU and NAFTA. The main losers are the working class and the poorest people within industrial and Third World states. From this perspective, RTAs permit MNCs to locate their production facilities in member states with the lowest wages, environmental standards, and taxes, and then to export freely to other states within the region. Historical structuralists also view some RTAs as means by which states in the core (often in association with transnational capital) exploit states in the periphery. For example, they argue that the institutional linkage of the EU with 71 African, Caribbean, and Pacific (ACP) "associate members" simply consolidates "the vertical economic relationship of the colonial period."[5] (See the discussion of EU associate membership later in this chapter.)

This chapter begins with a discussion of regionalism and how it relates to the process of globalization. It then provides some brief historical background on the development of RTAs, presents competing views as to why states form such agreements, examines the institutional relationship between the GATT/WTO and RTAs, and describes regionalism in three major trading areas—Europe, the Western Hemisphere, and East Asia.

REGIONALISM AND GLOBALIZATION

Regionalism is a difficult term to define because it usually connotes not only geographic proximity but also a sense of cultural, economic, political, or organizational cohesiveness. Efforts by international relations specialists to precisely define and identify regions have therefore usually resulted in frustration.[6] In this chapter the term *region-alism* is used primarily in reference to interactions among states in a particular geographic area, where there is a certain degree of economic and often organizational cohesiveness. A large portion of the chapter is devoted to a discussion of RTAs, which usually limit their membership to countries within a particular region.[7] However, Japan and the East Asian countries have close regional economic ties even though they are not joined together in an RTA. This discussion of trade regionalism is therefore not limited to RTAs.

Globalization and regionalism are both increasing today, and the relationship between these two processes is quite complex. In some respects, globalization limits the growth of regionalism. As global interdependence increases, many problems such as financial crises, trade wars, and environmental degradation take on worldwide dimensions and require multilateral management at the global level. Thus, multilateral institutions such as GATT/WTO, the IMF, and the World Bank are better equipped than regional organizations to deal with many of the problems resulting from globalization. Globalization also promotes growing linkages among regions as well as states, and in this sense it can undermine both national and regional cohesiveness.

Despite some inherent contradictions between global and regional processes, globalization may also act to stimulate the rise of regionalism. States must often rely on institutions above the national level to deal with problems arising from the increase in global interdependence. However, as an organization's membership increases, higher transaction and information costs interfere with the ability to identify common interests, and it becomes more difficult to identify and sanction defectors.[8] Thus, globalization pressures sometimes lead to shifts from national to regional institutions composed of like-minded states that are normally better at problem solving than larger, more diverse universal membership institutions at the multilateral level. Globalization also contributes to an increase in the intensity and scope of competition, and states and MNCs often are able to improve their global competitiveness by organizing regionally. Finally, globalization has been closely associated with the revival of classical liberalism, which favors a shift in authority from the state to the market. The heightened market pressures weaken state barriers and contribute to the growth of institutions at both the regional and global levels. Thus, the revival of regionalism since the 1980s has generally complemented rather than conflicted with the globalization process.[9]

A Historical Overview of Regional Trade Agreements

Regional integration is not a new phenomenon. From the seventeenth century to World War II there were many integration proposals involving colonies, provinces, and states, and some of the more successful agreements resulted in political as well as commercial union. Examples of early integration efforts in Europe and North America include a proposal for commercial union among Austria, Bavaria, Spain, and some German principalities in 1665; a CU between England and Ireland in 1826; a customs treaty establishing a single German *Zollverein* among German splinter states in 1833; and a Reciprocity Treaty removing all import tariffs on natural products between the United States and Canada in 1854. In the Southern Hemisphere, early agreements included a South African Customs Union among the Union of South Africa, Bechuanaland, Basutoland, and Swaziland in 1910, and a customs union between the British colonies of Kenya and Uganda in 1917, which was extended to include Tanganyika in 1927.[10]

Despite these early attempts to establish RTAs, regional integration in its modern form did not develop until after World War II, with the creation of the European Economic Community. This chapter is primarily concerned with the two major waves of regionalism in the postwar period, the first wave in the 1950s and early 1960s, and the second since the mid-1980s.

The First Wave of Regionalism

In 1949, the Soviet Union signed a treaty with Bulgaria, Czechoslovakia, Hungary, Poland, and Romania, establishing the CMEA. Although CMEA members engaged in technical cooperation and joint planning, the state-centered orientation of these CPEs precluded any genuine moves toward regional economic integration.[11] As a result, most writers view the first wave of regionalism as beginning with the formation of the EC in 1957 and the European Free Trade Association in 1960.[12] These European agreements provided a stimulus for the spread of regionalism throughout Latin America and Africa in the early 1960s. However, the RTAs in the Third World were formed for very different reasons from those in Western Europe. Because the small domestic markets of LDCs interfered with their efforts to pursue ISI policies, these LDCs looked to RTAs as a means of providing larger markets—and economies of scale—for their production of industrial goods. Thus, Third World regional agreements in the 1950s to 1960s were quite inward looking and were designed to pursue import substitution at the regional level.

By the early 1970s the first wave of regionalism had proved to be largely unsuccessful outside Europe, for several reasons. First, numerous problems arose with the Third World RTAs because there was a fundamental "contradiction between the idea of giving impetus to integration via trade liberalization and the protectionist logic of . . . import substitution" to promote industrialization.[13] Only a limited number of industries were willing to locate in Third World regions, so competition among LDC members of RTAs for these industries was fierce, and most of these industries located in the larger and more advanced LDCs. In the East African Common Services Union, for example, Tanzania and Uganda were resentful that the major industries were concentrated in Kenya. Thus, the benefits of RTAs among LDCs were often distributed very unequally, leading to numerous disputes among member states. To counter such inequities, some Third World RTAs tried to allocate industries among the member countries by bureaucratic means rather than relying on the market, but this practice led to economic inefficiencies and political conflicts. A second reason for the failure of the first wave of regionalism outside Europe was that the United States as the global hegemon was a firm supporter of multilateralism and generally did not endorse RTAs. Although the United States made an exception in supporting the EC largely for political-security reasons, it made vigorous efforts to open up the European integration process in the GATT Dillon and Kennedy rounds. In the second wave of regionalism, by contrast, the United States was to become an active participant in RTAs.[14]

The Second Wave of Regionalism

The second wave of regionalism started in the mid-1980s, and this time regionalism seems to be more durable, in non-European as well as European areas. The EC moved to widen and deepen its integration in the second wave. Widening occurred with the accession of Spain and Portugal in 1986 and Austria, Finland, and Sweden in 1995, and deepening occurred with the adoption of a single market in "Europe 1992" and the signing of the Maastricht Treaty (see the following discussion). The most significant change in the second wave was the dramatic turnaround in the United States. Shifting from its position as the key defender of the multilateral trade order in the postwar years, the United States has been willing to participate in RTAs since the mid-1980s. Finally, there has been a revival of RTAs among LDCs, and unlike the 1960s, these agreements are generally associated with the opening of the Third World to liberalism and global market forces.[15]

WHAT ARE THE REASONS FOR THE RISE OF REGIONALISM?

Although there is widespread agreement on some of the reasons for the rise of regionalism, realists, liberals, and historical structuralists emphasize different factors in their theoretical explanations. Whereas realists usually look to security issues and changing power relationships as explanations, liberals focus on the growth of interdependence, and historical structuralists emphasize the influence and demands of transnational capital.

Realist Explanations

Realists explain the development of Western European regional integration in the first wave (the 1950s to 1960s) as a response to changing security and power relationships. As the realist writer Kenneth Waltz has noted, "The emergence of the Russian and American superpowers created a situation that permitted wider ranging and more effective cooperation among the states of Western Europe."[16] After World War II the Western Europeans could focus more on promoting economic integration, because the United States and Soviet Union had assumed the main responsibilities in the political security sphere. Changing global power relationships also provided a positive incentive for Europeans to form the EC. With the European countries facing the eventual loss of their colonies and the United States and the Soviet Union emerging as the world's two superpowers, the Europeans realized that integration was necessary if they were to have continuing influence on the global scene.

Although the United States generally opposed RTAs in the 1950s and 1960s, it viewed a speedy economic recovery in Western Europe as essential to meet the strategic threat of the Soviet Union, and it therefore was generally supportive of Western European integration. Indeed, the United States's insistence that the Europeans develop a common recovery program in which they would jointly administer U.S. Marshall Plan aid resulted in the formation of the *Organization for European Economic*

Cooperation (OEEC) in 1948. In addition to developing a program for economic re-construction and organizing a fair distribution of Marshall Plan funds, the OEEC over-saw the moves toward convertibility of European currencies and the liberalization of trade in Western Europe. Furthermore, the OEEC contributed to the rapid integra-tion of West Germany in Europe, laying the foundations for the eventual formation of the EC.[17] Realists point out that another forerunner of the EC, the *ECSC*, was also created for security reasons. In 1951, six countries (Belgium, France, West Germany, Italy, Luxembourg, and the Netherlands) formed the ECSC primarily to prevent France and Germany from renewing their age-old rivalries. Seven years later, the six ECSC member countries expanded the integration process by forming the EC.

Realists also attribute the second wave of regionalism in the 1980s to shifting bal-ances in strategic and economic power. For example, they view the change from a bipolar to a multipolar international system as highly significant. In the postwar bipolar system, the Western Europeans and Japanese were willing to accept American leader-ship because of their dependence on U.S. nuclear deterrence and economic assistance. With the demise of the Soviet Union and the breakdown of bipolarity, U.S. allies have been more inclined to act independently of the United States, and a multi-lateral system has emerged centered in three major regional economic blocs in Eu-rope, North America, and Japan/East Asia.[18] Another important factor in the second wave, according to realists, has been the relative decline of U.S. economic hegemony. After World War II, the United States as global hegemon used its power and resources to help develop an open and integrated world economy. As its economic hegemony declined, the United States was less willing to provide the public goods to maintain an open multilateral trade regime, and it sought to regain some of its economic leverage and power by joining RTAs.[19]

It is important to note that theorists' predictions regarding the rise and fall of re-gionalism are of course not always accurate. For example, some realists predicted in the early 1990s that the removal of a major external threat to Western Europe with the breakup of the Soviet Union would increase concerns about relative gains among EU member states and place a significant check on the future progress of European inte-gration. Recent changes such as the formation of the EMU in January 1999 have shown this prediction to be incorrect.[20]

Liberal Explanations

Liberals focus on the growth of interdependence as a major factor in the revival of re-gionalism in the 1980s. As economic interdependence increased, states turned to eco-nomic liberalization to promote their exports, attract foreign investment, and upgrade their technological capabilities. However, the multilateral GATT-based trade regime had numerous problems in the 1980s (see Chapter 8), and regionalism therefore served as a second-best route for establishing trade linkages.[21] Regional trade negotia-tions, which involved small groups of like-minded states in geographically focused ar-eas, were easier to conduct than multilateral negotiations. RTA members also had a number of objective similarities, such as comparable levels of income and develop-ment, which often made negotiations easier. (Mexico's membership as an LDC in NAFTA was a notable exception.) Trade negotiations in the larger, more diverse

GATT were by contrast more complicated and difficult. Thus, liberals note approvingly that Canada and the United States negotiated issues in their 1988 free trade agreement (such as trade in services and agriculture) that had not yet been dealt with globally.[22]

The growth of interdependence, according to liberals, also led to increased demands by societal groups such as industries and firms for RTAs, and states in the 1980s were willing to supply these domestic groups with agreements. Along with the trend toward globalization, a growing number of firms became highly dependent on exports and imports, and they shifted their operations from the national to the multinational level. These internationalist firms pressured for a freeing of economic relationships at *both* the global and the regional levels. Regionalism in particular often improves the competitiveness of international firms, which can benefit from "the larger regional markets as their base rather than just the home market."[23]

As GATT/WTO trade negotations have reduced tariffs on a multilateral basis, one might expect that RTAs would provide fewer relative advantages to states. However, liberals point to the reasons WTO members continue to establish new RTAs at a rapid rate. In sectors where tariffs remain high or where a small tariff advantage is competitively significant, the elimination of tariffs in an RTA continues to provide advantages to members. Furthermore, the members of some RTAs benefit from the phasing out of nontariff barriers, and from exemptions from their regional partners' use of safeguards such as ADDs and CVDs. Some RTAs also contribute to deeper integration such as the harmonization of legal regulations governing commerce among the member states.[24]

Historical Structuralist Explanations

Historical structuralists, like liberals, believe that MNCs and other sources of transnational capital played a central role in the revival of regionalism in the 1980s. Unlike liberals, however, historical structuralists view this as a highly negative development. RTAs such as NAFTA, from this perspective, permit MNCs to become more competitive by locating their production facilities in states and regions with the lowest taxes, wages, and environmental standards. Whereas the capitalist class has benefited from this growth of regionalism, domestic labor has suffered because capital can move more easily to lower wage regions and countries. Historical structuralists also explain the revival of regionalism in terms of the desire of powerful states to seek regional hegemony over others. As its economic hegemony declined globally, the United States sought to recoup its losses by establishing its hegemony more firmly on a regional basis. Thus, some critics charge that NAFTA was "designed to fit Canada and Mexico into the American model of development, on terms amenable to American corporations." [25]

GATT/WTO and RTAs

The United States as global hegemon at the end of World War II strongly opposed preferential agreements and any other type of discrimination in international trade that would interfere with an open multilateral trade regime. The British, however, wanted to preserve their discriminatory imperial preferences, and a number of countries wanted to have the prerogative to establish RTAs. Thus, John Maynard Keynes expressed strong opposition to U.S. pressures for an end to imperial preferences, referring to "all the old lumber, most-favored-nation clause and the rest which was a notorious failure and made such a hash of the old world."[26] U.S. views on this issue prevailed to a large extent, and Article 1 of GATT called for unconditional MFN treatment. Nevertheless, GATT also permitted regional exceptions to the unconditional MFN clause: GATT Article 24 permits member countries to form CUs and FTAs that discriminate against other members, as long as these regional agreements meet specific conditions.[27] An examination of the reasoning behind Article 24 is crucial to understanding the relationship between the WTO and regional agreements.

Liberal economists consider global free trade to be the best possible route to maximizing welfare, and this was the approach taken by GATT as a liberal-economic institution. RTAs, which discriminate against outsiders, are clearly inferior to multilateral agreements, which liberalize trade without discrimination. Nevertheless, liberals believe that RTAs may offer a second-best route to trade liberalization when there are obstacles to freeing trade at the global level.[28] GATT Article 24 therefore sanctions the formation of CUs and FTAs, but it seeks to ensure that they are more trade creating than trade diverting.[29] Before discussing the GATT Article 24 provisions, it is necessary to describe the different ways RTAs may be trade creating and trade diverting.

Trade Diversion

RTAs inevitably result in some trade diversion because the reduction or elimination of trade barriers on intraregional trade produces some shifting of imports from more efficient outside suppliers to less efficient regional suppliers. Furthermore, competition increases within member countries' markets as trade within an RTA is liberalized. This competition can lead to greater adjustment pressures for inefficient industries, which try to shift some of the adjustment burden onto third countries by pressuring for increased external barriers. Thus, trade diversion can result when RTAs raise protectionist barriers against outsiders. Outside countries may also be harmed by investment diversion when an MNC sets up a branch plant inside an RTA to produce locally instead of producing in the least-cost location and shipping goods to the region.

A CU may be more trade diverting in some respects than an FTA. (As Figure 2.3 shows, a CU, unlike an FTA, has a common external tariff.) Even if external tariffs do not increase on the average when a CU is formed, protectionism may increase because of contingent trade actions; that is, the CU may impose ADDs and CVDs in response to pressures from import-competing industries. The EU's experience shows that such duties can pose a formidable trade barrier to outsiders because they limit exports to the entire CU area. ADDs and CVDs pose less of a problem for outsiders in an FTA because FTAs have no common external tariff and industries cannot pressure for areawide protection; in an FTA each member country levies its own duties.[30] Whereas contingent trade actions can have trade-diverting effects in CUs, **rules of origin** may have serious trade-diverting effects in FTAs. Because each FTA member retains its own external tariffs, FTAs must have rules of origin to prevent importers from bringing goods in through the lowest-duty member and then shipping them to partner countries whose duties are higher. The rules of origin are designed to determine whether goods crossing borders within the FTA should qualify for duty-free treatment. These rules are difficult to develop, because so many goods today are manufactured with numerous components originating in a number of countries. The rules of origin determine whether the products have undergone sufficient processing within the FTA to qualify for the FTA's trade preferences. Domestic firms in an FTA often pressure successfully for stiffer rules of origin, which become a form of trade protectionism against outside countries. Some CUs apply rules of origin, but they are generally a less significant issue for CUs because of the common external tariff.[31]

Trade diversion depends not only on internal political dynamics but also on the reaction of nonmember countries to RTAs. When one RTA is formed, nonmembers may have the incentive to establish their own RTAs in response, and regionalism proliferates. Thus, some countries establish RTAs in efforts to "better defend themselves against the discriminatory effects of *other* regional groups."[32] This proliferation of regionalism can increase trade conflicts and lead to fragmentation of the global trade regime. From this perspective, regionalism by its very nature causes trade diversion.

Trade Creation

The main source of trade creation in RTAs is the increased trade among member countries, which shifts demand from less efficient domestic country production to more efficient partner country production. Furthermore, RTAs often achieve a deeper level of integration than multilateral agreements because negotiations are occurring among a smaller number of like-minded partners. RTAs may therefore provide a positive demonstration effect and contribute to more effective MTNs. For example, the deepening of EC integration to include services trade was followed by the decision to also include services trade in the GATT Uruguay round, and the inclusion of agriculture, services, intellectual property, and investment provisions in the CUSFTA and NAFTA agreements provided a stimulus for negotiating these issues in the Uruguay round.

GATT Article 24 and RTAs

GATT Article 24 was designed to ensure that RTAs result in as much trade creation and as little trade diversion as possible. To ensure that RTAs are trade creating, Article 24 stipulates that FTAs and CUs are to eliminate tariffs and other trade restrictions on "substantially all" trade among the member states within a "reasonable" period. (GATT occasionally granted waivers from the "substantially all trade" requirement for sectoral FTAs; notable examples were waivers for the ECSC in 1952 and the Canada-U.S. Auto Pact in 1965.) This condition may seem ironic because maximum preferential liberalization diverges more from MFN treatment and therefore can be more injurious to nonmembers than partial liberalization, but it is included for several reasons. First, the GATT founders believed that a rigorous requirement to remove all tariff barriers in RTAs would prevent the proliferation of preferential agreements, which involve only partial trade liberalization among members. Preferential arrangements of this nature had contributed to trade discrimination and protectionism in the 1930s. Second, genuine FTAs or CUs are more likely to facilitate trade liberalization at the global level. When RTAs involve deeper integration than has occurred multilaterally (i.e., the removal of all tariffs), they can serve as stepping-stones to multilateral free trade. Preferential agreements with only partial trade liberalization do not have this positive demonstration effect.[33]

To ensure that an RTA minimizes the amount of trade diversion, Article 24 stipulates that trade barriers should not rise on the average to countries outside the agreement when the RTA is formed. Whereas individual member states in an FTA are not to raise their average level of duties, the common external tariff of a CU may not "on the whole" be higher than the member countries' separate duties were before the CU was established. These trade-diversion provisions are designed to limit reductions in imports from nonmembers as a result of the RTA.[34]

Although GATT Article 24 seems to provide a mechanism for regulating RTAs, in reality GATT/WTO has often had only limited influence in this area. It is therefore necessary to examine how effective GATT/WTO has been in monitoring and regulating RTAs.

The Effectiveness of GATT Article 24

When countries form an RTA, GATT/WTO establishes a working party to determine whether the RTA meets the requisite conditions. Although Article 24 has permitted GATT/WTO to exert some influence over RTAs, its influence in practice has been quite limited. GATT's regulations for RTAs were drafted with smaller agreements in mind, such as the Benelux CU negotiated by Belgium, the Netherlands, and Luxembourg in 1944. This situation changed dramatically in 1957, when the Treaty of Rome establishing the EC was notified to the GATT. In view of its size and importance, the EC was simply not willing to wait for GATT's approval under Article 24 before proceeding with economic integration. Negotiating the Treaty of Rome had been a difficult and sensitive process, and EC members indicated that they would not readjust the treaty to satisfy GATT.[35]

In the end, GATT acceded to the EC's demands and never completed its examination of the Treaty of Rome, even though GATT members had reached no consensus regarding the treaty's consistency with Article 24. GATT's acquiescence in this case had a detrimental effect on its ability to exert authority over subsequent RTAs. Thus, GATT working parties had little success in bringing about changes in the terms of RTAs after the member states in the region negotiated them. Whereas early agreements such as the EC and the Latin American Free Trade Association (LAFTA) were notified to the GATT before they entered into force, later RTAs were sometimes notified to the GATT belatedly. For example, two agreements that entered into force *before* working parties were even established to examine them were NAFTA in January 1994 and the agreement in which Austria, Finland, and Sweden acceded to the EU in January 1995.[36]

It is not surprising that GATT working parties had little influence over RTAs after they were negotiated. Governments had already engaged in extensive bargaining and were reluctant to reopen their negotiations in response to outside criticism. The most GATT working parties could accomplish was to embarrass RTA members over allegations of noncompliance and thus encourage countries to comply with GATT guidelines in the future. Nevertheless, the GATT rules had some influence on national decision making at earlier stages in the process. One authority on international trade issues points out that GATT Article 24 influenced the EC and CUSFTA at an early stage by setting broad parameters for the conduct of the regional negotiations:

> The diplomats negotiating each of these agreements were operating under instructions to make maximum efforts to comply with GATT rules, and the actual results of

these negotiations testify that a quite important degree of GATT compliance was achieved. Except for agriculture . . . and except for the EC's relationship with former colonies, the . . . developed-country agreements . . . were essentially GATT-conforming. To be sure, GATT was unable to do anything further once the agreements were signed and deposited in Geneva for review.[37]

Some analysts point out that GATT was less effective because the conditions it required of RTAs were not clearly specified. Legitimate differences exist over the interpretation of Article 24 requirements that RTAs cover "substantially all" trade, do not become more restrictive "on average," and be fully implemented in a "reasonable length of time." In addition to its imprecise wording, Article 24 does not adequately address such issues as contingent trade measures (ADDs and CVDs) and rules of origin, which may significantly increase the protectionism of RTAs vis-à-vis outside countries.[38] In view of the ambiguous Article 24 requirements, working parties were reluctant to give RTAs their unqualified approval. By the end of 1994, only 6 of 69 working parties had reached a consensus that particular RTAs conformed with the Article 24 conditions, and only 2 of the 6 "approved" RTAs are still operative.[39] In the great majority of cases, working parties simply noted that members had divergent views regarding the conformity of the RTA with GATT. However, GATT never explicitly concluded that an RTA had *not* met the legal requirements![40]

In efforts to improve the monitoring and regulation of RTAs, the Uruguay round negotiators reached a 1994 Understanding on the Interpretation of Article 24 (UR Understanding).[41] Furthermore, the GATS includes an article on regional integration in services trade (Article 5), which is similar to GATT Article 24. To address continuing concerns about RTAs, the WTO General Council established a *Committee on Regional Trade Agreements (CRTA)*, with a mandate to develop procedures for improving the RTA examination process. The Uruguay round agreements and the CRTA have dealt with some of the shortcomings of GATT Article 24, but a number of problems remain.

On the positive side, the UR Understanding strengthens the working party review process for RTAs and makes the stronger WTO dispute-settlement procedures applicable to RTAs. Dispute-settlement cases may help to resolve some of the issues that continue to be unclear in GATT Article 24. The UR Understanding also improves the methodology for determining whether the level of duties in a CU are higher "on the whole" as a result of the common external tariff. On the negative side, divisions among members persist on the interpretation of key concepts and on the admissibility of various RTAs. For example, working parties have repeatedly debated whether the "substantially all trade" requirement permits the exclusion of certain sectors (most often agriculture) from liberalization under an RTA. The UR Understanding makes very little progress in defining the "substantially all trade requirement." Furthermore, the Uruguay round negotiators reached no agreement on how to deal with restrictive rules of origin in RTAs. As discussed, rules of origin are among the most trade-restrictive aspects of many FTAs. In sum, it remains to be seen whether the WTO will be more successful than the GATT in monitoring and regulating RTAs, and whether the CRTA will help develop more effective WTO regulations in this area.[42]

Special Treatment for LDCs

Although GATT Article 24 was designed to apply to all RTAs, LDCs over time were given special and differential treatment in this area. Two types of RTAs involving

LDCs have been especially prominent: RTAs among LDCs and the EU's association agreements with LDCs.

RTAs Among LDCs   GATT's examination of RTAs among LDCs was even less stringent than its examination of RTAs among developed countries. For example, GATT did not openly object to the formation of the LAFTA in 1960, even though it was quite protectionist and "did not even approach the requirements of total integration."[43] After Part IV on trade and development was added to GATT in 1965, the LDCs sometimes invoked it to justify forming preferential RTAs that did not meet the "substantially all trade" requirement of GATT Article 24. When the 1979 enabling clause "established for the first time in trade relations . . . a permanent legal basis for preferences in favour of developing countries," it became the main legal cover for LDCs forming questionable regional agreements.[44] The enabling clause basically removes the requirement that RTAs among LDCs must cover substantially all trade, and it permits LDCs to lower rather than eliminate tariff barriers within their RTAs. Mercosur, a Third World/CU discussed later in this chapter, was notified to GATT under the enabling clause, not under Article 24.[45]

Despite the GATT/WTO's permissiveness with RTAs among LDCs, recent LDC moves toward trade liberalization have inevitably affected their RTAs. The negative experiences of LDCs with inward-looking import substitution policies, combined with IMF and World Bank pressures on LDC debtors to liberalize their policies, have increased the likelihood of LDCs forming more outward-looking RTAs since the 1980s.

The EU's Association Agreements with LDCs   Developed countries have often agreed to provide LDCs with nonreciprocal trade preferences. In Chapter 8, for example, we examined the GSP, which developed countries have provided to LDCs since 1971. As discussed, the developed countries unilaterally establish their GSP provisions without a formal role for LDCs in the decision making. Developed countries have also unilaterally established nonreciprocal trade schemes on a regional basis. For example, these plans include the *Caribbean Basin Initiative* (or *Caribbean Basin Economic Recovery Act*), which the United States created for 24 Central American and Caribbean countries, and the *Canadian Trade, Investment, and Industrial Cooperation program (CARIBCAN)*, which Canada enacted for 18 Commonwealth Caribbean countries and territories. In contrast to these unilaterally established programs, developed countries and LDCs have *jointly* negotiated several nonreciprocal regional preference programs; these have included the *Lomé Conventions* between the 15 EU countries and 71 associate LDCs, and the *South Pacific Regional Trade and Economic Cooperation Agreement (SPARTECA)* between Australia, New Zealand, and 13 island countries (see the nonreciprocal RTAs in Table 9.1).[46] Of all these RTAs, the EU agreements with associate LDCs are the most far-reaching and important.

When the EC was formed in 1957, France insisted that the trade preferences it was giving to its African Overseas Territories be continued. The French wanted to ensure that exports from its former colonies would have free access to the EC and that other EC members would eventually share the costs of providing economic assistance to its former colonies. Despite the opposition of some EC members, the French were adamant, and Part 4 of the Treaty of Rome provided for an extension of France's preferential arrangements under EC auspices. Initially, there were 18 LDCs with associate status, known as the Associated African States and Madagascar (AASM). Although Part 4 called for the gradual removal of tariffs between EC members and the associates, the associates could protect their infant industries and retain some tariffs for revenue purposes, and the EC was to provide financial aid to the associates through a European Development Fund.[47]

A number of countries in GATT argued that the EC was providing discriminatory trade preferences to the African associates because the associate system did not constitute a genuine FTA; that is, the African associates did not provide reciprocal free trade to EC members. As a result, the association agreements were in direct conflict with GATT's nondiscrimination principle.[48] The EC insisted, however, that the association agreements were fully coordinate with UN proposals that the North should promote economic and social development in the South. At a 1966 GATT working party examining the association agreements, for example, EC members

> expressed the view that in a free-trade area consisting of industrialized and less-developed countries the industrialized countries should not require reciprocal advantages from their less-developed partners. . . . In their view, Article XXIV had never been meant to apply to free-trade areas between developed and less-developed countries.[49]

Despite the controversy over the association agreements, the EC renewed them in the *Yaoundé Conventions,* signed at Yaoundé, Cameroon, in 1963 and 1969. After Britain joined the EC in 1973, the Yaoundé conventions were replaced by the first *Lomé Convention* at Lomé, Togo, in 1975, and the former British colonies gained associate status. The fourth Lomé Convention (Lomé IV) covered a 10-year period from 1990 to 2000 and included agreements with 71 ACP countries. The principle of nonreciprocity was central to the Lomé Conventions, because the EC offered duty-free access (with some exceptions) to its market while the ACP states maintained tariff barriers against European goods. The formation of the WTO in 1995 both "reflected and reinforced" strong orthodox liberal pressures for the liberalization of world trade, and this has "posed problems for trading arrangements such as the Lomé Conventions."[50] As mentioned, GATT Article 24 provides an exception to MFN treatment only for RTAs that follow the reciprocity principle. Furthermore, the 1979 enabling clause permits developed countries to provide trade preferences to LDCs, as long as *all* LDCs can gain access to these preferences. The enabling clause therefore does *not* sanction EU discrimination in favor of its ex-colonies at the expense of other LDCs. Unlike the EU's nonreciprocal agreements with associate LDCs, Mexico accepted almost the same reciprocal free trade obligations as the two developed countries (the United States and Canada) in the NAFTA in 1994. Thus, there have been strong external pressures on the EU to convert its LDC association agreements into *reciprocal* FTAs.[51]

Interestingly, historical structuralists as well as orthodox liberals have criticized the EU's association agreements. Historical structuralists have described the EU's system of nonreciprocal preferences "as a form of neocolonialism that perpetuates the production of and trade in products not compatible" with the long-term interests of the associate ACP countries. For example, the Lomé Conventions' trade preferences for bananas from the Windward Islands "have perpetuated the one-product economy of these islands and discouraged them from taking necessary measures to diversify production."[52] Historical structuralists have portrayed the EU's nonreciprocal agreements more generally as perpetuating a continuation of dependency by former LDC colonies on the European states.

Primarily because of the orthodox liberal criticisms emanating from the WTO, the EU is developing measures to make its association agreements with the ACP countries more WTO compatible. Official negotiations for a new EU-ACP agreement began in September 1998, with the ACP group arguing against rapid changes in the system of nonreciprocal preferences. After intensive negotiations, the EU signed a *New Partnership Agreement* (or Cotonou Agreement) with its associate ACP states in Cotonou, Gabon, in June 2000. It is only possible to discuss the EU's expressed intentions regarding a final agreement, because the New Partnership Agreement commits the EU and ACP countries to continue negotiations for a new WTO-compliant arrangement until 2008. On the one hand, the EU has indicated that the LLDCs among the ACP economies will retain some nonreciprocal trade privileges in accordance with special and differential treatment. On the other hand, LDCs that are not LLDCs will eventually have to grant reciprocity for EU preferences by reducing their own tariffs on imports from the EU. Although supporters of this change argue that the EU's LDC associates will benefit in the long term by liberalizing their trade policies, critics argue that EU-ACP nonreciprocal relations must continue because of the lower level of development of ACP economies. A major issue will be how much time associate LDCs are given to reduce their tariffs on EU exports.[53]

EUROPE

Postwar regional integration has been centered mainly in Europe. European countries were parties to 76 of the 109 RTAs notified to GATT from 1948 to 1994 (62 of these RTAs were still in force in December 1994). In 2000 the EU in particular was a party to 28 of the 91 RTAs in goods notified under GATT Article 24 and still in force, and the EU was a party to 8 of the 11 RTAs in services notified under GATS Article 5. The EU is the largest trading bloc in the world, with about 374 million inhabitants (compared with 268 million in the United States) and a GDP of $8.5 trillion in 1997 (compared with a GDP of $7.7 trillion in the United States).[54]

Postwar European integration can be traced to a French proposal in the interwar period that a European CU be formed to resolve the continent's political and economic problems. After World War II these plans for European integration were realized with U.S. support and encouragement, but only Western European countries were involved because of the Cold War. In 1951, six countries (Belgium, France, West Germany, Italy, Luxembourg, and the Netherlands) formed the ECSC, and these countries extended their integration under the Treaty of Rome to establish the EC and the European Atomic Energy Community (Euratom) in 1957. In 1960, seven European countries (Austria, Britain, Denmark, Norway, Portugal, Sweden, and Switzerland) responded to the EC by forming the EFTA. Although these "outer seven" countries wanted to be included in an FTA, they were not prepared to join the "inner six" EC countries. As a CU, the EC required a common external tariff and a degree of policy coordination that threatened Britain's Commonwealth preference system and the nonaligned policies of countries such as Sweden and Switzerland. The EFTA did not pose the same threat to these countries' autonomy because it did not require a common external tariff (see Figure 2.3). Since the formation of the EC and the EFTA, there has been a gradual deepening and widening of European integration. In the discussion that follows we use the term "EC" when discussing events from 1957 to 1992, and the term "EU" when discussing events from 1993 to the present. In 1993 there was a formal name change after the Maastricht Treaty to symbolize the extension of the community from trade and economic matters to a much broader range of activities.[55]

The Deepening of European Integration

Under vigorous leadership the European integration process began with considerable enthusiasm, and the EC accelerated its timetable for creating a CU among the original six member states. However, two events in the 1960s marked a setback for the integration process. In 1963, French President Charles de Gaulle unilaterally vetoed Britain's application for EC membership, and in 1965, de Gaulle withdrew France from the work of the Council of Ministers to protest against a commission proposal for financing the EC budget. The eventual compromise with France over the budgetary issue limited the EC Commission's power and undermined prospects for further integration in the 1960s. (The European Commission is the permanent executive of the EU, and the Council of Ministers is composed of the foreign ministers of the member states. Whereas the commission supports the EU's growing supranational authority, the Council of Ministers represents the continuing influence of the member nation-states.)

The outlook for integration became considerably dimmer in the 1970s because the EC was buffeted by turbulence in the global economy. The collapse of the Bretton Woods monetary regime, the OPEC oil crisis, and the onset of recession all contributed to a marked slowdown of the integration process. Although three countries joined the EC in 1973 (Britain, Denmark, and Ireland), Britain and Denmark opposed the development of strong EC supranational institutions. The EC did experience some successes such as the launching of the EMS in March 1979 (see Chapter 6). Nevertheless, the 1970s to early 1980s were generally marked by "Eurosclerosis" and a loss of faith in the EC's vitality.[56]

In the early 1980s, EC members became acutely aware of their lack of competitiveness in world markets vis-à-vis the United States and Japan. A major source of this problem was the persistence of differential taxation, border inspections, domestic subsidies, and internal impediments to market access within the EC. A more unified European market would produce more competitive European firms as a result of increased specialization and economies of scale. Thus, EC members launched a major effort to increase the level of integration in the 1980s and 1990s. A significant force for change was the new EC Commission President, Jacques Delor, who instituted a push for deeper integration. As a result of Delor's efforts, EC members signed the SEA in 1986, which was designed to complete the process of freeing the internal market by the end of 1992. The goals of the SEA included ending nontariff barriers to trade in industrial goods, liberalizing trade in services, and facilitating the free movement of capital and labor throughout the EC.[57]

In addition to its trade-related objectives, the SEA also included a commitment to EMU, and the European Council established the Delors Committee in June 1988 to propose a plan to achieve an EMU. This committee proposed a three-stage process toward EMU, and negotiations subsequently resulted in the Treaty on European Union or Maastricht Treaty in December 1991. The "centerpiece" of the Maastricht Treaty was the objective of establishing an EMU.[58] However, the treaty also had the noneconomic goals of establishing a European federal political system with common social, foreign, and security policies. The Maastricht Treaty initially met with a hostile reaction among a large segment of European public opinion, and this forced European governments to confront a problem they had often neglected—legitimizing an integration process in which European bureaucrats largely removed from the populace have played a major role. Because the EMU is discussed in Chapter 6, we briefly focus here on the two other aspects of the Maastricht Treaty that were designed to deepen European integation: cooperation on foreign and security policy, and on social policy.

The goal of establishing a common foreign and security policy was designed to move the EU much closer to *political* union. EU countries had been badly divided over issues such as the Gulf War, and European leaders believed that closer political union was necessary to increase the EU's international influence. However, the goals regarding foreign and security policy were highly sensitive and ambitious, and conflicting interests among the European powers interfered with progress in this area. The air war against Serbia resulted in an agreement among EU members to establish an autonomous military arm to decrease dependence on the United States. Nevertheless, the EU and United States would remain partners in defending Europe, and it remains to be seen how significant this military arm will be. The other major Maastricht Treaty area involves social policy, including policy toward organized labor, a welfare state, and migration into the EU. For example, the EU Council of Ministers was given broader authority to make decisions regarding such issues as working conditions and worker health and safety by qualified majority vote. These social issues are highly sensitive because of political divisions in Europe between conservatives and social democrats, and management to this point has occurred more through informal agreements than formal policy decisions. Of the Maastricht Treaty's broad goals for deepening integration, the objective of forming an EMU has been the most successful. As discussed in Chapter 6, 12 of the 15 EU members had joined an EMU, and the euro was circulating as a new common currency by early 2002.[59]

The Widening of European Integration

As discussed in Chapter 2, the EC expanded from 6 to 15 full members in three successive enlargements (see Figure 2.4). In the first enlargement, Britain, Denmark, and Ireland joined the EC in 1973; in the second enlargement, Greece joined in 1979 and Spain and Portugal joined in 1986; and in the third enlargement, Austria, Finland, and Sweden joined in 1995. While expanding its membership, the EC was also extending its associate linkages with the ACP and other Third World countries (discussed previously). The question arose as to whether the EC should be widening the integration process by accepting new members at the same time it was facing many challenges in deepening integration. Whereas deepening of integration has often been a response to "rapidly changing economic conditions," widening today is being "thrust on the EU by the failure of communism in Europe."[60] This section focuses on the issues confronting the EU regarding the possible accession of a large number of Central and Eastern European states.

The Soviet Union was extremely hostile to the EC when it was established in 1957, and the relationship continued to be strained throughout the 1960s and 1970s. The EC in turn did not want to give legitimacy to the Soviet-led CMEA, and it preferred to negotiate bilateral trade agreements with individual Eastern European countries outside CMEA auspices. Although the Soviet Union insisted that CMEA be the vehicle for EC economic contacts with Eastern Europe, the EC successfully encouraged some Eastern European states to break ranks with the Soviet position. For example, the EC granted the GSP to Romania in 1972, and in 1980 Romania and the EC signed a trade and cooperation agreement.

As economic conditions in Eastern Europe worsened in the 1980s and the Eastern bloc became more dependent on economic linkages with the West, the Soviet Union softened its position. In 1988 (under Premier Mikhail Gorbachev), an EC-CMEA agreement sanctioned the negotiation of trade agreements between the EC and individual Eastern European states. From 1988 to 1990, the EC therefore negotiated trade and cooperation agreements with the Soviet Union and most Eastern European countries. In addition to liberalizing trade, these agreements promoted economic cooperation and assistance from the EC.[61] A major landmark was the breakup of the Soviet bloc and Soviet Union, which led to CMEA's dissolution and the development of closer EU ties with Eastern Europe. In the early 1990s the EU negotiated "Europe agreements" with a number of Central and Eastern European countries (CEECs). However, the EU offered the CEECs fewer trade concessions than they had given to the associate ACP states, and one after another the CEECs applied for full membership in the EU. In July 1997, the EU Commission produced a report entitled *Agenda 2000*, which identified several issues that enlargement negotiations would have to address, including the relocation of firms, the migration of workers, and the financial burden on the EU.

The first issue relates to EU fears that firms might want to move eastward after enlargement, because of lower labor costs in Eastern Europe; relocation could be most marked in coal mining, agriculture, and traditional industries such as textiles. The second issue relates to EU concerns about migration pressures from the CEECs because of substantial wage differentials with the Western European states. The third issue relates to EU Commission concerns that enlargement would sharply increase the population eligible for assistance from EU social and economic development funds.[62] All of these issues relate to economic development disparities between the CEECs and most current EU members. Ten CEECs that signed Europe agreements with the EU had only one-fourth of the purchasing power of the present EU average, and about 20 percent of their workers had agricultural jobs compared with only 6 percent of EU workers.[63] These countries would add greatly to pressures on the EU's structural funds directed to poorer EU regions and on funds for agricultural subsidies. The Common Agricultural Policy (CAP) already absorbs about half the EU budget, and structural funds another 30 percent, so countries that contribute most to these funds (e.g., Germany, France, Britain, and the Netherlands) are concerned. The less developed southern European countries in the EU, such as Spain, Portugal, and Greece, also feel threatened by possible EU expansion because they share with CEECs such as

Poland and Hungary a comparative advantage in agriculture, traditional manufactures, and resource-intensive products.[64]

Despite these concerns, official EU statements have generally been supportive of enlargement. For example, at their December 1995 summit in Madrid, EU leaders concluded that "enlargement is both a political necessity and a historic opportunity."[65] Both the CEECs and the EU see a number of possible advantages from enlargement. The CEECs want to join with the EU and NATO to gain security vis-à-vis Russia, and they want access to EU capital, technology, and markets as a means of closing the economic gap with the West. As for the EU members, they want stable countries on the East as a buffer against political instability in the post-Soviet era. Economically, the EU's Northern more developed states such as Germany, Britain, and France have a comparative advantage in higher technology manufactures and service exports. The CEECs would provide these states with cheaper workers and more investment opportunities.[66]

About six months after the publication of the 1997 *Agenda 2000,* the EU officially launched the enlargement process. In November 2001 the European Commission issued a report suggesting that 10 CEECs could complete negotiations for joining the EU by the end of 2002. However, previous history indicates that the final steps toward full membership will be difficult. Spain and Portugal's accession negotiations, for example, took seven years, and they are still not fully assimilated in the EU. There are also dangers that a two-tiered system will develop, in which the more economically advanced CEECs such as Hungary and the Czech Republic are more likely to become full EU members than the less advanced CEECs such as Romania and Bulgaria.[67] Finally, as the negotiations enter their final year, some commentators are predicting that France might emerge as a "deal breaker." The driving force behind the EC/EU has traditionally been a Franco-German partnership, and France worries that Germany will look East as much as West in a larger EU. As a result, France could fall into the rank of second-tier powers in Europe. Other French concerns relate to the importance of agriculture in the CEECs, the propensity of Central Europeans to speak English rather than French, and the likelihood that the CEECs will make EU foreign policy more pro-American. Thus, obstacles still remain to full membership of the CEECs in the EU.[68]

The Theoretical Perspectives and the EU

Realists often focus on European integration as a means of increasing Europe's power vis-à-vis other major actors. Thus, the post—World War II bipolar system dominated by the United States and the Soviet Union was a major factor in the decision of Western European states to embark on economic integration to increase their influence. The United States was willing to support the formation of the EC because it viewed a strong Western Europe as an important component of the Western alliance vis-à-vis the Soviet Union. In the late 1960s, Jean-Jacque Servan-Schreiber's book *The American Challenge* focusing on the increased penetration of American capital in Europe also had a major impact on European thinking. Individual European states lacked the resources to develop firms that could rival U.S. MNCs, Servan-Schreiber argued, and only a united Europe could preserve European autonomy and influence.[69] In the 1980s and 1990s, European concerns about American and Japanese technological leadership were similarly a major factor in the signing of the SEA and the Maastricht Treaty.

Liberal economists are primarily concerned with ensuring that the EU is an "open" rather than a "closed" integration movement. However, liberals do *not* necessarily agree on whether the EU is more open or closed in nature. Some liberals express concerns about EU protectionism, and their concerns have increased during the moves toward consolidation in the SEA and the EU struggles with the United States in the GATT/WTO. In discussions of the EU's inward orientation, liberals point to the reorientation of trade away from third countries to other EU members following the creation of the community and the accession of new members. They also focus on specific EU policies, such as the CAP, as examples of extreme protectionism. Liberals often point to the detrimental effects of inward-looking EU policies on member states as well as outsiders. For example, one European specialist argues that "the use of protection to avoid industrial restructuring has almost certainly contributed to Europe's falling behind the United States and Japan in hi-tech goods."[70]

Other liberals disagree with these concerns and maintain that the EU is responding to globalization forces with outward-looking policies. For example, they note that the largest industrial firms in Europe were a major force behind the single-market program in the late 1980s and 1990s. These firms are global competitors that oppose regional protectionism because of fears of retaliation. The deepening and widening of integration also promises to add considerably to trade creation among EU members and is furthering the process of integrating the CEECs in the global economy. Some analysts predict that the EU could eventually expand from its current membership of 15 to more than 25 members, which would account for about 30 percent of world trade and production. Although this has the risk of contributing to trade diversion vis-à-vis outsiders, there would also be a substantial amount of trade creation within such a large regional bloc. As for global trade relations, these liberals point out that the EU eventually approved the Uruguay round agreement despite dire predictions that European intransigence over agriculture would lead to the failure of the round. Although some liberals are more optimistic than others about the openness of the EU, they all agree that RTAs should promote trade liberalization.[71]

Interventionist liberals praise the EU for directing more attention to social policy than some other RTAs, such as NAFTA. For example, the EC created a European Social Fund as early as the 1960s, with the goal of decreasing socioeconomic disparities among member states. Furthermore, Ireland and the poorer Southern European EC states were willing to support the SEA in the 1980s partly because they were promised increased structural funds. Historical structuralists are more inclined to view the European social programs as inadequate solutions to inequality and poverty, and they note that some European states oppose an increase in funding for social purposes. Thus, major disparities in wealth continue to exist between Northern and Southern European states and between different regions within European countries.[72]

Interventionist liberals and historical structuralists also differ in their views of the EU's relations with the ACP countries. In the liberal view, the EU has been willing to absorb the short-term economic costs of providing aid and trade preferences to the ACP countries in the interests of long-term economic and political security. Historical structuralists, by contrast, argue that the EU associate agreements are designed to perpetuate the dependence of ACP countries on their former colonial masters. Thus, the EU maintains the colonial pattern of trade, with European countries exporting industrial goods and the ACP countries exporting primary products. Historical structuralists therefore believe that "prospects for symmetrical EurAfrica relations remain . . . dim despite all the rhetoric to the contrary."[73] Historical structuralists are also highly skeptical that the CEECs will ever become full and equal members of the EU. From this perspective, "the present EU, plus perhaps some new central European members [such as Hungary and the Czech Republic], will be flanked to the east by a tier of excluded states available as sites for low-cost assembly by firms headquartered in the EU."[74]

THE WESTERN HEMISPHERE

The institutional architecture of the Western Hemisphere today is characterized by three overlapping regional integration processes: the first is centered in the United States and NAFTA; the second consists of a number of Latin American RTAs, the most prominent of which is Mercosur; and the third is the attempt to negotiate hemispheric integration in a Free Trade Area of the Americas (FTAA). As discussed, the United States was unwilling to participate in RTAs from the 1940s to the early 1970s because of concerns that they detracted from efforts to develop a strong GATT-based multilateral trade regime. However, a reversal of U.S. policies combined with greater openness to free trade in Canada and Mexico resulted in the creation of CUSFTA in the 1980s and NAFTA in the 1990s. Unlike the United States, Latin American and Caribbean countries had established several RTAs in the 1960s and 1970s, including the LAFTA, the Central American Common Market (CACM), the Andean Community, and the Caribbean Community and Common Market (CARICOM). However, these RTAs were generally inward looking and did not expose the member states to much international competition. Since the mid-1980s there has been a revival of Latin American regionalism, this time on a more open basis. Important RTAs in Latin America and the Caribbean today include CACM, CARICOM, the Andean Group, the Southern Cone Common Market (Mercosur), and the Group of Three (Colombia, Mexico, and Venezuela). NAFTA and Mercosur are the two dynamic poles in current efforts to negotiate an FTAA, and the two most important countries in the FTAA negotiation process are the United States (in NAFTA) and Brazil (in Mercosur).[75] This section focuses primarily on CUSFTA, NAFTA, Mercosur, and the proposed FTAA.

The Formation of CUSFTA and NAFTA

Although the United States and Canada did not establish a generalized FTA until the 1980s, moves toward free trade between the two countries have a remarkably long history. Indeed, a noted historian has observed that there is one economic issue in Canada that "comes close to rivalling the linguistic and race question for both longevity and vehemence, and this is, of course, the question of free trade with the United States."[76] In 1854, the United States and Canada concluded a Reciprocity Treaty providing for free trade in natural products such as grains, meat, dairy products, and fish. However, the United States abrogated the treaty in 1866, in reaction to an unfavorable trade balance with Canada, increased Canadian duties on U.S. manu-factures, and the British role in the American Civil War. The two countries tried to revive free trade in 1911 and 1948, without success. In 1965 they concluded the Canada-U.S. Automotive Agreement, which provided for free trade in automobiles and parts; a GATT waiver was necessary in this case because the automotive agree-ment did not meet the Article 24 requirement that an FTA should cover "substantially all trade." However, it was not until 1988 that the United States and Canada estab-lished a more generalized FTA, the CUSFTA. In December 1992, Mexico joined the United States and Canada in signing NAFTA, which superseded CUSFTA.

The question arises as to why these FTAs were formed after so many years. The U.S. policy reversal regarding participation in RTAs was essential before such agree-ments could be negotiated. This reversal came with the 1974 U.S. Trade Act, which permitted the president to "initiate negotiations for a trade agreement with Canada to establish a free trade area."[77] However, it was a Canadian and then a Mexican request for free trade negotiations that resulted in the CUSFTA and NAFTA. Protectionism increased in the United States in the mid-1980s because of massive balance-of-payments deficits during the Reagan administration. Canada decided an FTA was es-sential to gain more assured access to the U.S. market, because more than 75 percent of its exports were going to the United States. Of particular concern to Canada were U.S. CVDs and trade unilateralism. Another motivation for free trade with the United States was the perceived need to alter *Canadian* domestic economic policies. Business leaders in Canada (as in many other countries) were critical of the government's cen-tral role in the economy in the 1980s, and they felt that an FTA would force Canadians to place more reliance on market forces.[78]

Starting from high levels of protection, Mexico instituted unilateral measures to ease trade restrictions *before* it sought free trade negotiations with the United States. These unilateral moves were impelled by the conditions attached to IMF and World Bank SALs to deal with Mexican debt and by the realization that liberalization was necessary if Mexico was to attract foreign investment. Mexico, like Canada, depended on the United States for more than 70 percent of its exports, and it therefore shared Canada's concerns about gaining more assured access to the U.S. market. The foreign investment issue, however, was even more important to Mexico as a reason for seeking free trade. Despite Mexico's unilateral liberalization, potential foreign investors were skeptical that this change was permanent because of Mexico's long history of govern-ment intervention. An FTA with the United States would give Mexico's liberalization policies more credibility and permanence.[79]

The United States as a major economic power was more concerned about global than regional trade linkages; its decision to conclude the CUSFTA and NAFTA was motivated largely by frustration with the slow pace of negotiations in the GATT Uruguay round. Negotiating regional agreements, in the U.S. view, would induce other major economic powers—especially the EU and Japan—to offer concessions in the MTNs. Regionalism also has a tendency to breed more regionalism, and the EU's enlargement and consolidation in the SEA provided an additional U.S. incentive to es-tablish FTAs as a counterweight. Because its trade hegemony was declining, the United States was less committed to multilateralism as the sole option and more will-ing to participate in RTAs. Regional trade is of course less important to the United

States than it is to Canada and Mexico, but it is noteworthy that Canada and Mexico today are the United States's largest and second-largest single-country trading partners. Finally, the United States wanted Canada and Mexico to ease their regulations on foreign direct investment and natural resources, and it was willing to open its market more widely to Canadian and Mexican goods in return.[80]

The IPE Theoretical Perspectives and NAFTA

CUSFTA was a highly controversial treaty in Canada, and controversy continues to surround NAFTA in all three member countries. U.S. individuals and groups critical of NAFTA stretch across the political spectrum, ranging from liberals to nationalists and historical structuralists. Whereas nationalist critics maintain that NAFTA's environmental and labor side agreements do not provide genuine protection for U.S. jobs and the environment, historical structuralists argue that NAFTA facilitates the ascendancy of the transnational capitalist class over labor. Even U.S., Canadian, and Mexican critics viewing NAFTA from the same theoretical perspective often point to different shortcomings in the agreement. For example, U.S. liberals criticized Canada's failure to include culture and Mexico's unwillingness to include energy-sharing provisions in NAFTA, Canadian liberals criticized the United States for refusing to agree to agricultural export subsidy reductions, and Canadian and Mexican liberals have criticized U.S. persistence in using CVDs and ADDs.[81] Despite this controversy, many supporters maintain that all three countries have benefited from NAFTA. Because such a wide array of groups have strong views on NAFTA, this discussion of the theoretical perspectives is illustrative rather than all-inclusive.

The Orthodox Liberal Perspective   Liberal economists want to ensure that NAFTA contributes to trade openness and serves as a stepping-stone rather than an obstacle to multilateral free trade. Although open RTAs are a second-best option for liberals after global free trade, they have generally praised NAFTA for contributing to freer trade. The CUSFTA and NAFTA negotiations demonstrated that the United States might opt for regionalism as an alternative to multilateralism if the GATT Uruguay round was unsuccessful, and the EU and Japan were therefore more willing to compromise in the MTNs. NAFTA also had a positive "demonstration effect" on the WTO in services trade, investment, and intellectual property rights, and it goes beyond the WTO in coverage of these areas. For example, NAFTA follows a "negative list" approach to national treatment for trade in services; that is, all services not itemized on a country's list are automatically included. This approach puts the onus on each NAFTA member to identify services it wants to exclude from national treatment. The GATS, by contrast, takes a "positive list" approach to services trade; that is, national treatment applies only to sectors specifically included in a member's list of commitments. Thus, NAFTA's services trade provisions are more trade creating than those of GATS.[82] Liberal economists also point positively to NAFTA as the first FTA between an LDC and developed countries that does not give S&D treatment to the LDC (Mexico).

Although liberals generally have a positive view of NAFTA, they have also pointed to the agreement's shortcomings. The United States was the first country to use CVDs, and it has been the largest user of CVDs in the postwar period. With the U.S. balance-of-trade deficits since 1971 and the decline of tariffs resulting from GATT negotiations, the U.S. Congress responded to domestic pressures by changing the rules so that CVDs could be imposed more easily. Because of their asymmetrical relationships, U.S. CVDs "can have a severe impact" on Canada and Mexico whereas Canadian and Mexican CVDs are normally "little more than another irritant to the United States."[83] Canada in particular wanted CUSFTA and NAFTA to deal with contingent trade actions, and NAFTA (like CUSFTA before it) forms binational panels to assess disputes over each country's CVD and ADD decisions.[84] Unlike the previous system, in which domestic courts provided final review of CVD and ADD decisions, the binational panels ensure that both disputing countries' interpretations of trade law are considered in dispute-settlement cases. However, liberal critics in Canada note that each country retains the right to implement its own contingent trade legislation, and the binational panels can judge only whether a U.S. (or Canadian or Mexican) CVD or ADD decision is made in accordance with U.S. (or Canadian or Mexican) law; that is, the panels cannot assess the fairness of each country's laws.

Another liberal criticism of NAFTA relates to its complex rules of origin. Liberals often argue that rules of origin are a common protectionist device in FTAs, and in some respects NAFTA's rules of origin are more restrictive than those of CUSFTA. Examples of highly restrictive rules of origin in NAFTA include the requirements for automobiles, textiles and apparel, and color televisions.[85] A third criticism of NAFTA by orthodox liberals relates to the environment and labor side agreements. Liberals view these as nontrade issues that can be used by NAFTA members as an excuse to impose protectionist trade barriers.

Despite these reservations, orthodox liberals are generally favorable to NAFTA and believe that "on balance . . . the trade created by growth in the NAFTA region should more than offset the trade diverted."[86]

The Realist and Historical Structuralist Perspectives   Realists and historical structuralists believe that CUSFTA and NAFTA have significant distributional effects, which are determined by major asymmetries in power, levels of economic development, or both. Thus, realists reject the liberal view that smaller countries often benefit from FTAs more than larger countries because of economies of scale and increased exports. From the realist perspective, the United States as the larger partner naturally expected its benefits from free trade to outweigh those received by Canada and Mexico. For example, Canada sought free trade with the United States to gain more assured access to the U.S. market at a time when U.S. protectionism was increasing. In return for granting free trade, the United States expected a number of side payments, including an easing of Canadian regulations on U.S. foreign investment, greater U.S. access to Canadian energy supplies, and an agreement on trade in services. The United States also agreed to free trade with Mexico, but in return Mexico gave up claims to receive S&D treatment as an LDC in NAFTA.[87] Realists also object to NAFTA provisions that they believe have a detrimental effect on national sovereignty. For example, NAFTA's Chapter 11 permits investors to resort to binding international arbitration if they believe that a host government is violating NAFTA investment provisions related to national treatment. Whereas liberals view Chapter 11 as an innovative mechanism that permits foreign enterprises to prevent states from discriminating against them, realists warn that it provides "a vehicle for investors to harass governments whose policies they dislike."[88] Canadian nationalists have argued that Chapter 11 is being used by foreign (i.e., U.S.) firms to force changes in Canadian environmental and cultural policies.

In contrast to realists, historical structuralists focus on transnational capital and class relationships. From their perspective, NAFTA represents a shift in power in favor of the capitalist class and against labor groups. For example, NAFTA enables MNCs to avoid more rigorous labor and environmental standards in Canada and the United States by relocating production in Mexico. As capital leaves the United States and Canada, wages and opportunities for employment in these countries decline. Some historical structuralists use the terms *core* and *periphery* to designate social position and class rather than geographic location, arguing that NAFTA has relegated many impoverished American and Canadian workers to peripheral status.[89]

The losses for American and Canadian workers, according to historical structuralists, do not result in comparable gains for Mexican workers. For example, they argue that NAFTA is destroying the livelihoods of Mexican peasants because U.S. corn, which benefits from a range of government subsidies, will eventually be freely exported to Mexico.[90] Historical structuralists thus argue that NAFTA is increasing poverty and inequality between the rich and poor in all three member countries. Some Gramscian theorists discuss the possibility that progressive groups opposing NAFTA could form a counterhegemonic bloc based on opposition to the domination of corporate capital in North America. This broad-based coalition would consist of labor, environmental, consumer, and women's groups. A counterhegemonic bloc of this nature would seek to replace the current corporate view of liberalization in North America with a more democratic, participatory model.[91]

Mercosur

In March 1991 the presidents of Argentina, Brazil, Paraguay and Uruguay signed the Treaty of Asunción (TOA) with the objective of establishing Mercosur, or the Common Market of the South.[92] The TOA set out a timetable in three stages, including the formation of an FTA from 1991 to 1994, a CU in 1995, and eventually a common market. This was a surprisingly rapid schedule, and the specificity of the commitments were highly unusual in Latin America, where most previous RTA plans included only vague promises. The significance of Mercosur also stemmed from the importance of its two largest members: Brazil and Argentina. In 1999 Mercosur encompassed a population of 213 million and a GDP of almost $1.1 trillion.[93] However, many observers were skeptical that Mercosur would succeed for several reasons. First, efforts to form RTAs in Latin America since the early 1960s had encountered problems because of member countries' inward-looking development strategies, national security concerns, and unpredictable macroeconomic policies. Second, the relationship between the two major Mercosur countries, Brazil and Argentina, was marked by a 150-year history of suspicion and economic and military rivalry. However, much had changed by the time Mercosur was formed.

At the time the TOA was signed, most Latin American LDCs were already changing from import-substitution to export-oriented development strategies, unilaterally reducing their tariffs and NTBs, and becoming more active participants in the GATT

Uruguay round. Whereas earlier failed efforts to form RTAs tried to apply an interventionist and inward-looking national model to the regional level, Mercosur's approach placed more emphasis on open regionalism. Furthermore, elected civilian regimes replaced military dictatorships in the Mercosur region in the late 1980s and 1990s. Old antagonisms receded, and new types of relationships began to develop, because the political leadership in Brazil and Argentina felt that regional integration would bolster their fledgling democratic governments. The Argentine and Brazilian presidents in the early 1990s also supported integration as a component of their orthodox liberal economic strategies. Gradually a growing number of business and political groups came to depend on integration, and many of them continue to support Mercosur even when periodic crises occur. The end of the Cold War was an important international change giving momentum to Mercosur, because Latin Americans were concerned that the industrial states would devote little attention to their concerns. Whereas the EC was developing its single-market program and moving toward monetary integration, Mexico was joining with the United States and Canada in NAFTA negotiations. RTAs were beginning to play a more important role in global trade relations, and Argentina and Brazil viewed economic integration as a means of strengthening their position vis-à-vis the world's major trading blocs. Finally, some officials in Brazil's Foreign Ministry and armed forces viewed Mercosur as a means of gaining greater political and economic independence from the United States.[94]

Mercosur integration demonstrated considerable dynamism from 1991 to 1995, but integration has slowed down considerably since that time. When the Mercosur CU was formed in 1995, tariffs on about 90 percent of goods traded among the member states had been eliminated, and 88 percent of dutiable goods were included in the common external tariff. From 1991 to 1995 the share of intraregional trade in the exports of Mercosur countries rose from 8.9 percent to 20.3 percent, and the share of intraregional trade in the imports of these countries rose from 14.1 percent to 18.1 percent. Furthermore, increasing numbers of business firms in the Mercosur countries began to organize their production and sales activities on a regional basis. In addition, Chile and Bolivia became associate members by entering into FTAs with Mercosur in 1996 and 1997, respectively. Finally, Mercosur began to emerge as an important regional actor in the global economy. New initiatives to create an FTAA and an intercontinental FTA between the EU and Mercosur were an indication of the increasing interest of the United States and Europe in Latin America.[95]

However, it was evident by late 1995 that Mercosur integration was encountering problems. Beginning in 1995, Brazil and then Argentina introduced new import tariffs and NTBs, and such actions have limited intraregional trade. Although trade among members has quadrupled since the creation of Mercosur, it has fallen since 1998 and amounts to only about one-fifth of their total trade. Almost all trade in goods within Mercosur is now duty-free, but Mercosur discipline does not extend to services trade and government purchases, and a number of NTBs and administrative barriers remain. Furthermore, almost none of the deepening of integration associated with a CU has occurred. Mercosur has not agreed on common policies on customs codes, investment subsidies, and competition policy, and most disputes continue to be settled by presidential intervention rather than agreed rules. In some cases, Mercosur countries have not respected treaties they had ratified. For example, both Brazil and Argentina have held trade talks with the Andean countries and Mexico separately from their Mercosur partners, which violates their commitment to the CU. The automotive sector has a critical role, because it accounts for about 25 percent of intra-Mercosur trade. This sector continues to operate according to managed trade in which a Mercosur country is entitled to export as much as it imports from a partner country; such an approach runs counter to a free market philosophy and open regionalism. Tariffs and minimum content regulations for automobile imports into the Mercosur region are quite protectionist and reflect Brazil's regional goals.[96]

A number of international, regional, and national factors account for the problems confronting Mercosur. First, the disruption caused by international developments such as the Mexican and East Asian financial crises in the 1990s created highly adverse conditions on international financial markets (see Chapter 11). Financial turbulence during these crises contributed to the loss of important markets for Latin American exports in East Asia and a marked decrease in the prices of primary commodities. A second related problem stems from the fact that Mercosur members are LDCs, which are highly vulnerable to international developments. As discussed in Chapter 7, the Latin American LDCs had the highest debts during the 1980s foreign debt crisis, and indebtedness continues to plague these economies. In 1997, the combined debt of the four Mercosur countries amounted to 29 percent of their $1,134 million GNP. The total external debt as a percent of exports of goods and services for Argentina, Brazil, Uruguay, and Paraguay was 362.4, 291.6, 138.5, and 49.8 percent, respectively. Thus, the Mercosur countries continue to be highly dependent on external finance, and highly vulnerable to changes in global financial flows.[97]

A third problem is that Mercosur, unlike NAFTA, does not have a formal dispute-settlement process. Political negotiation is the means of handling all disagreements and conflicts. Brazil has always opposed creating a Mercosur dispute-settlement body, viewing this as a loss of sovereignty. Fourth, as is the case for NAFTA, the highly asymmetrical nature of Mercosur raises questions about the prospects for deepening integration. Brazil accounts for about 70 percent of Mercosur's GDP and accounts for 33 percent of Argentina's, 35 percent of Uruguay's, and 40 percent of Paraguay's exports. Thus, the Mercosur "integration process has been driven largely by the strategy and needs of Brazil."[98] Brazil has always viewed Mercosur as a means of gaining more influence vis-à-vis the outside world. Although other Mercosur members complain about Brazil's tendency to disregard their concerns, they often can do little to prevent Brazil from acting unilaterally and disregarding their concerns.

A fifth major obstacle to integration has been the disparity in macroeconomic and monetary policies between the two main Mercosur countries, Brazil and Argentina. In 1991 Argentina decided to peg its peso to the U.S. dollar, a policy that contrasted sharply with Brazil's policy of adjusting the exchange rate to account for inflation. After Brazil devalued its currency in 1999, Argentina's balance of trade with Brazil sharply deteriorated, and a number of companies moved operations from Argentina to Brazil.[99] By December 2001, Argentina had accumulated a massive foreign debt and had to default on its loans, because of a wide range of economic problems that were partly related to its policy of pegging the peso to the dollar. Although devaluation of the peso was essential, it threatened to greatly add to Argentina's debt burden, which was denominated in dollars. However, Argentina's decision to devalue the peso could eventually restore a competitive balance to Argentine manufacturing operations and repair relations with Brazil.

Despite the problems confronting Mercosur, it is clearly the most important Third World RTA. Some analysts believe that Mercosur's "trial by adversity" will increase the determination of the member countries to improve their relations and revitalize the integration process.[100] Certainly one of the main reasons the member states value Mercosur is that it "can maximize the political weight of each of its members in all external negotiations, whether conducted individually or en bloc."[101] As the following discussion shows, Mercosur has served as an important regional actor in negotiations for an FTAA.

Free Trade Area of the Americas

In June 1990, President George Bush responded to Latin America's economic problems by announcing a new framework for U.S.–Latin American relations: the Enterprise for the Americas Initiative (EAI). The EAI called for investment promotion, U.S. aid in debt reduction, and the elimination of trade barriers. Whereas the investment and debt-reduction provisions were quite modest, the trade provisions were the centerpiece of the EAI. Bush assumed the United States would sign separate FTAs with different regional groupings, which would serve as stepping-stones to a larger hemispheric FTA. Although this vision was superseded by NAFTA, which the U.S. came to view as the best route to hemispheric integration, the EAI had an important role in stimulating moves toward hemispheric free trade.

In December 1993 U.S. Vice President Al Gore proposed creation of a hemispheric FTA and called for a 1994 summit of the Western Hemisphere countries. At the Miami Summit of the Americas held in December 1994, the 34 participating countries agreed to begin the process of negotiating an FTAA, and "the United States played a key role in orchestrating" this commitment.[102] Most important, the declaration of intent at Miami resulted in a mechanism to implement the agreement. In June 1995, the trade ministers met in Denver and established 12 working groups to discuss the various topics of the agreement and prepare background information. In March 1998, the trade ministers met in Costa Rica and approved a consensus document on the format of an FTAA. This document formed the basis on which the heads of state at the second hemispheric summit in Santiago, Chile, in April 1998 announced a detailed plan of action to conclude FTAA negotiations no later than 2005. If the FTAA is formed, it could be the largest regional grouping in the world, with a population of about 730 million, a combined GDP of almost $10 trillion, (U.S.) and total exports of more than $1 trillion.[103]

One potential problem for an FTAA is that the Western Hemisphere is highly diverse in the geographical distribution of foreign trade; thus, it is not a single "natural" region for an RTA. The United States accounts for 76 percent of the Western hemisphere's total GDP, and it would seem to be the main focal point of trade in the region. However, countries vary greatly in terms of their dependence on trade with the United States. Whereas more than 80 percent of Canadian and Mexican trade and about 60 percent of Central American and Caribbean trade is with the United States, the southern cone of South America has only about 20 percent of its trade with the

United States. For the southern cone, trade agreements with the EU and South American and Asian countries could be as important as concluding an agreement with the United States. Nevertheless, changes in global, regional, and national conditions have contributed to growing interest in an FTAA.

With the end of the Cold War, the United States devoted less attention to security concerns in Latin America and more to dealing with foreign debt and stimulating trade and investment. The relative decline of U.S. economic hegemony was another factor pushing the United States toward greater acceptance of participation in hemispheric RTAs. After joining the CUSFTA and NAFTA, it was natural for the United States to turn to Latin America. Whereas the United States had chronic trade deficits with East Asia and its trade with Europe was stagnant, the United States had substantial trade surpluses with Latin America. Furthermore, a large percentage of U.S. exports to Latin America were high value-added goods. U.S. exports to Latin America (excluding Mexico) increased by about 52 percent from 1994 to 1999, almost twice as fast as exports to countries outside the Western Hemisphere. The moves toward an FTAA were also sparked by changes in other Western Hemisphere countries. Canada had previously been ambivalent about strengthening ties with Latin America, but in 1992 it joined the Organization of American States, and in 1993 it joined with Mexico and the United States in NAFTA. In Latin America, the shift from import-substitution to export-oriented policies and the consolidation of civilian rule and democracy were additional factors conducive to negotiations for an FTAA. Finally the revival of regionalism on a more open basis than previously in Latin America served as a possible stepping-stone to a broader FTAA.[104]

Despite the greater interest in an FTAA, a wide diversity of views among countries in the hemisphere seems to indicate that negotiations for an FTAA will be protracted and difficult. Only a brief discussion of some of the major disputes is possible here. First, there were disputes over the process of forming an FTAA. The United States wanted a gradual extension of NAFTA to include other countries, but some other states led by Brazil argued that a FTAA should be a wholly new initiative negotiated by equal partners. These countries were concerned about NAFTA's focus primarily on issues of interest to the United States and were reluctant to comply with the NAFTA requirement that they free substantially all trade with the United States. The approach advocated by Brazil eventually prevailed, partly because the U.S. Congress refused to grant President Clinton fast-track authority for expanding NAFTA! Second, the United States wanted the negotiations to be conducted by individual countries, but Brazil proposed that the negotiations be held through regional groups such as Mercosur, the Andean Community, and the CACM. Brazil has suspicions about an FTAA and prefers to deepen Mercosur integration before turning to the issue of hemispheric integration. The Mercosur members supported Brazil's position to negotiate as a bloc, and the decision was made that each country could choose how it wanted to be represented. Whereas some countries such as the United States, Canada, and Mexico are represented individually, others such as the Mercosur members are negotiating as a group.[105]

Third, the United States from the outset has pressured for a "maximalist" approach that would go well beyond removing tariffs and NTBs. The United States would like the FTAA to improve on WTO commitments in such areas as services, investment, government procurement, intellectual property, and competition policy. By going beyond the WTO, the U.S. hopes to provide an impetus to moving the MTN agenda forward. However, the Latin Americans have argued that WTO commitments were part of a balanced outcome that should not be altered, unless the United States is willing to make similar concessions such as phasing out it's restrictions on textile imports and limiting its use of ADDs and CVDs. It is most unlikely that Latin Americans as Third World countries would agree to the deepening of integration proposed by the United States. The decision at Doha to launch a new round of WTO multilateral negotiations will also stretch the negotiating resources of many Latin American states.

The United States is of course the major market in the hemisphere, accounting for about 75 percent of total economic output. Without U.S. support and leadership, negotiations for an FTAA will not succeed. Nevertheless, discussion of the issues in dispute has demonstrated that the United States is sometimes unable to induce others to accept its views. Of the 34 participants in the negotiations, the United States, Brazil, and Mexico together account for two-thirds of the hemisphere's population and for more than 85 percent of total output. Brazil and Mexico have been the least enthusiastic of the major Latin American states for rapid negotiation of an FTAA, and Brazil has at times been able to gain support from its Mercosur partners and other South American countries in conflicts with the United States. However, Brazil's ability to get other Latin Americans to "join it in foot-dragging over the FTAA" has declined "as its neighbors have become ever more enticed by the idea of improved access to the world's biggest consumer market."[106] The difficulties U.S. presidents have encountered in renewing fast-track authority to negotiate trade agreements indicates that the U.S. position on an FTAA is also somewhat ambivalent. As discussed in Chapter 8, the last Congressional grant of fast-track authority expired in 1994, and President Clinton was unable to renew this authority during his administration. The lack of fast-track authority did not prevent the U.S. administration from beginning negotiations for an FTAA, but it decreased U.S. credibility and influence in the negotiations. In December 2001, the U.S. House of Representatives finally passed legislation to give President George W. Bush a renewal of fast-track authority (more recently called "trade promotion authority"), and it seemed a certainty that the Senate would follow with its own legislative approval. However, the strikingly narrow 215–214 House vote on the issue indicated that fast track authority continues to be a highly contentious issue in the U.S. Congress.[107]

In sum, the FTAA talks have made impressive progress, but there is still "a long distance to traverse between where the negotiations stand now and where they need to be by 2005."[108] From an orthodox liberal perspective, an FTAA can be a second-best option in moving toward freer trade *if* it is more trade creating than trade diverting and preferably goes beyond what has been achieved in the WTO. As is the case for NAFTA and Mercosur, realists point to the importance of power relationships and expect the United States and to a lesser extent Brazil to achieve much of what they want from an FTAA in the longer term. Historical structuralists are at the opposite pole from orthodox liberals, arguing that an FTAA would perpetuate Latin American dependency relationships with the United States and to a lesser extent Canada. The thousands of protestors at the third Summit of the Americas in Quebec City in April 2001 demonstrate that regional as well as global gatherings are now targets for civil society demonstrations. It is impossible to "categorize" the Quebec City protestors in terms of a theoretical perspective. Whereas some protestors were protectionists such as U.S. steel workers who wanted limits on imports from Brazil, others viewed the FTAA as a vehicle for MNCs to extend their influence, and still others had environmental concerns. Despite their differences, most of the protestors had concerns that the proposed FTAA, like the IMF, World Bank, and WTO, would be a significant contributor to pressures for globalization.

EAST ASIA

In the 1980s East Asia emerged as a major center of world production and trade. The region's impact on trade and other aspects of the global economy has grown markedly in recent years. As Table 9.2 shows, East Asia accounted for only 10.8 percent of world trade in 1970, whereas North America accounted for almost twice that amount (20.7 percent) and Western Europe accounted for more than four times that amount (48.2 percent). By 1990, East Asia's share of world trade had almost doubled, reaching 19.4 percent, while the shares of North America and Western Europe declined slightly to 18.1 and 46.8 percent, respectively.[109]

East Asia was not involved in the first wave of regional integration among LDCs in the 1960s, and in the current wave of regionalism, FTAs involving East Asia are still only in the planning stages. Of the two major groupings in the region, one is subregional (Association of Southeast Asian Nations, ASEAN) and the other extends beyond East Asia to include countries on both sides of the Pacific Ocean the Asia-Pacific Economic Cooperation or (APEC). Although formal institutional initiatives to promote regional integration have been far less important in East Asia than in other regions, trade and investment among East Asian countries have demonstrated impressive growth rates. Thus, the East Asian case shows that countries can develop strong regional linkages even without formal institutions.[110] A major reason for the rise in intraregional trade is that dynamic, rapidly growing economies (like those found in East Asia in the 1970s to 1980s) are likely to trade with one another. Indeed, several neighboring provinces of East Asian countries have developed close trade and investment linkages even though the relations among the central governments involved are not particularly

TABLE 9.2

REGIONAL SHARES OF WORLD TRADE (PERCENT)

	1970	1990
East Asia	10.8	19.4
North America (United States, Canada, Mexico)	20.7	18.1
Western Europe (European Union and European Free Trade Association)	48.2	46.8
Other countries	20.5	15.7

Source: Derived from Soogil Young, "East Asia as a Regional Force for Globalism," in Kym Anderson and Richard Blackhurst, eds., *Regional Integration and the Global Trading System* (New York: Harvester Wheatsheaf, 1993), p. 128, Table 6.1.

friendly. Another stimulus for trade is the wide diversity of Asian economies in terms of size, per capita income, and natural resources, which provides opportunities for specialization.

In addition to being informal and market oriented, East Asian regional linkages are also designed to increase the competitiveness of the region's firms in global markets. Thus, the internationalization of the production process in East Asia has contributed to the region's ability to market high-quality goods at competitive prices. Whereas Japan has provided capital and high-technology goods, the East Asian newly industrializing economies have provided goods and services with increasing levels of sophistication, and low-wage countries such as China, Indonesia, and Vietnam have been involved with labor-intensive assembly operations. (Chapter 11 provides a detailed discussion of the Japan-led production system in East Asia.) East Asian economies are not overly concerned about their lack of RTAs, partly because of the advantages they see in the WTO: it plays an important role in decreasing trade barriers such as "voluntary" export restraints that have restricted the access of East Asian goods to developed country markets, it provides S&D treatment for East Asian LDCs (although the NIEs are in the process of "graduating" to more developed country status), and it offers smaller East Asian states some protection from the pressures of major regional powers such as Japan and China.[111]

Despite the declared intentions of ASEAN and APEC to develop FTAs, it is uncertain that East Asian regional relationships will ever become as institutionalized as those of Europe and the Western Hemisphere. Slow economic growth provided a major motivation for EC members to develop "Europe 1992" and induced the United States, Canada, and Mexico to establish NAFTA. Until recently, East Asian economic performance, by contrast, has been quite successful, and these countries therefore have felt less need for formal arrangements. Persistent hostility and suspicions among East Asian states pose an additional obstacle to formal integration, with a number of countries having memories of Japan's military conquest in the 1930s, as well as concerns about dominance by China. Yet another obstacle is posed by the protectionist and interventionist industrial policies in many Asian countries. Formal regional arrangements would require more policy changes than many of these countries are willing to make. Finally, the United States continues to have considerable military and economic influence in East Asia, and it strongly opposes the establishment of a region-wide RTA limited to East Asian countries. Despite these obstacles to the development of more formal institutions, the East Asian economies are concerned about the protectionist and exclusionary aspects of the EU and NAFTA. If the global trade regime is ever seriously threatened by regional trading blocs, East Asian economies might be more willing to accept formal regional arrangements.[112]

The ASEAN

Indonesia, Malaysia, the Philippines, Singapore, and Thailand agreed to establish ASEAN in 1967, with the stated goals of promoting peace, stability, and economic growth in the region. Today ASEAN has 10 members, with the admission of Brunei (1984), Vietnam (1995), Laos (1997), Mayanmar (1997), and Cambodia (1999). ASEAN was largely a political organization for many years, with only a few relatively small programs to promote economic linkages. It was not until 1977 that the ASEAN countries signed an Agreement on Preferential Trading Arrangements (PTA), which provided for preferential treatment in terms of tariffs and nontariff measures on certain exports. The agreement had only limited product coverage, and it had little effect on intra-ASEAN trade. In January 1991 the ASEAN countries agreed to establish an ASEAN Free Trade Area (AFTA) by the year 2008 (the target date was subsequently shortened to 2003). However, AFTA will exclude services, unprocessed agricultural products, and natural resources from the free trade rules, and it will do little to address the central issue of NTBs.[113]

Major obstacles to the successful implementation of AFTA include the divisions among ASEAN countries, and the financial crisis that struck Southeast Asia in 1997 (discussed in Chapter 11). ASEAN was enlarged from 5 to 10 countries for a combination of sentimental, political-security, and economic reasons. Economically, the decision to admit Vietnam, Laos, Myanmar, and Cambodia was designed to promote market growth in the region. The 10 ASEAN countries constitute a combined market of 487 million people and a GDP of $675 billion. However, the advantages from market expansion depend on ASEAN's ability to provide S&D treatment and assistance to promote economic reform for the newer less developed members. When Vietnam, Laos, Myanmar, and Cambodia joined ASEAN, the founding members gave them more time to adjust to trade liberalization in AFTA, and assistance to move toward market reform at a faster pace. Nevertheless, the 1997 financial crisis has created major problems for ASEAN by intensifying competition among the members for investments and markets. The financial crisis has also exacerbated the problems of ASEAN as a two-tiered organization, because the founding members have become less willing and less able to provide the newer members with S&D treatment and assistance to promote their economic reform and development. As a result of the current problems, ASEAN members have discussed a variety of possibilities for reform. For example, the Chinese prime minister has proposed that China and ASEAN explore a free trade relationship, and ASEAN has commissioned a task force to study this possibility. (China's proposal shocked the Japanese, who assumed that Southeast Asia was in their sphere of influence.) How ASEAN meets the challenges confronting it will have a major effect not only on its ability to establish an FTA, but on the future viability of the organization.[114]

APEC

The largest regional initiative involving East Asia is APEC, which was first proposed by Australian Prime Minister Bob Hawke in 1989. As Table 9.3 shows, APEC emphasizes open regionalism, with its broad range of 21 members from Asia, Australasia, and North and South America. In view of its broad geographic reach on both sides of the Pacific, one may even call APEC a transregional rather than a regional grouping. The potential importance of APEC stems from the influence of its members: they include the world's three largest national economies—the United States, China, and Japan; and three of the five permanent members of the UN Security Council—China, Russia, and the United States. Economically, the APEC members together account for almost one-half of total world trade. In 1993 APEC became more prominent when it established a permanent secretariat in Singapore and began to hold summit meetings of

TABLE 9.3

MEMBERS OF ASIA-PACIFIC ECONOMIC COOPERATION (APEC)

Year of Joining	Member
1989	Australia, Brunei, Canada, Indonesia, Japan, Republic of Korea, Malaysia, New Zealand, Philippines, Singapore, Thailand, United States
1991	China, Hong Kong, Taiwan
1993	Mexico, Papua New Guinea
1994	Chile
1998	Peru, Russia, Vietnam

heads of government and state. Currently, almost 300 projects to promote economic and technical cooperation are operating under APEC's auspices, and future APEC targets include an FTA for developed country members by 2010 and for LDC members by 2020.[115]

Despite the considerable promise of APEC, there is a notable lack of consensus among the members as to the main objectives of the grouping. Indeed, the lack of agreement is evident in the title of APEC, which does not even specify whether it is an organization, a forum, or other type of entity. APEC to this point has in fact served more as a forum for exchanging ideas than as an organization producing substantive outcomes. Most APEC members place value on a large open regional or transregional grouping in the Asia-Pacific, but for a range of different reasons. This is certainly true for the three largest economies in APEC. The United States wanted to secure political-security and economic access to the region and did not want to be excluded from an East Asian trading bloc (East Asia overtook the EC as North America's largest foreign market region in the early 1980s), Japan wanted to limit U.S. unilateralism and to prevent the Western Hemisphere and Europe from erecting protectionist barriers toward Asia, and China as an emerging power viewed APEC as a useful forum for cooperation with other Asia-Pacific economies. Furthermore, China had not yet been accepted into the GATT/WTO, and APEC seemed to be one route to establishing its respectability. Smaller East Asian countries are also supportive of APEC because it prevents dominance by any one of the three largest economies and addresses some of the smaller countries' concerns regarding access to the large U.S. market.[116]

When the Australian prime minister first proposed that APEC be established, he wanted to model it after the OECD, which increases transparency by disseminating information about members' policies and promotes coordination of members' international and domestic economic policies. Thus, APEC was not originally intended to be a forum for trade negotiations. In 1993, however, trade liberalization became a central element in APEC's agenda at the group's summit meeting in Seattle because of the urging of the Western-oriented members—the United States, Canada, Australia, and New Zealand. Most Asian members by contrast were less committed to promoting trade liberalization and were more interested in emphasizing trade facilitation and economic and technical cooperation. The Asian countries' lack of enthusiasm for trade liberalization stemmed largely from concerns that the United States would use APEC as another forum for exerting pressure on them to open their markets.[117] Despite the ambivalence of most Asian countries, at the November 1994 APEC Summit in Bogor, Indonesia, the APEC members agreed to the goal of establishing a free and open trade and investment area for developed countries by 2010 and for LDCs by 2020. The November 1995 APEC Summit in Osaka, Japan, adopted an "action agenda" to begin implementing this free trade commitment by January 1997.

In view of the differing objectives of APEC members, it is not surprising that the agreement to establish an FTA is ambiguous in a number of respects. For example, the agreement does not clearly specify whether trade liberalization in such areas as services and agriculture are to be included and whether some APEC members are to categorized as developed countries or LDCs. China is reluctant to commit to free trade along with more developed countries by the year 2010, but most APEC members would be unwilling to classify the industrial parts of China along with the LDCs. The 1994 Bogor Summit declaration also does not specify how a free and open investment area is to be established, and it leaves the details for discussion at future meetings. The APEC in this respect "is very Asian with its broad consensus style, and very unlike North American and European regional pacts with their detailed liberalization schedules."[118] Because Asian members of APEC dislike the bargaining negotiations that take place in GATT/WTO, liberalization in APEC is to occur instead through concerted unilateral action. Under this process, each APEC country will independently develop its own plans for liberalization to reach the objective of free trade by the specified date. This type of liberalization depends on enlightened self-interest and peer pressure rather than the give-and-take of negotiations. The Asian states have also ensured that trade liberalization will take place through "open regionalism," because they are dependent on trade with Western Europe as well as North America. Thus, concessions to APEC members would be granted to *all* WTO members on an unconditional MFN basis.

Implementing such a proposal could of course prove difficult. Most APEC members other than Canada, Australia, Hong Kong, New Zealand, Singapore, and the United States have tariffs averaging above 10 percent, with levels for some products more than 30 percent, and it is highly uncertain that these countries would significantly lower their tariffs on a unilateral basis. Furthermore, U.S. policies could pose obstacles to APEC free trade plans for several reasons. First, the United States would be unwilling to extend its APEC concessions to Europe and other non-APEC areas on a nonreciprocal basis. Second, U.S. producer groups would argue strongly against having free trade with countries such as Japan, South Korea, and China without substantial domestic opening of their economies. In the U.S. view, its trade problems with these countries result not from border measures such as tariffs, but from domestic policies and societal factors that make it difficult for foreigners to compete. Phasing out tariffs in APEC will not result in reciprocal concessions unless domestic policy issues are also addressed.[119]

The size and diversity of the APEC membership could also interfere with plans for an FTA. Malaysia, in particular, has strongly criticized the size and regional scope of APEC and has argued instead for a regional grouping limited to Asian nations. In December 1990, Malaysian Prime Minister Mahathir Mohamad proposed that an East

Asian economic grouping be formed for this purpose. The Malaysian proposal was aimed not only at economic liberalism but also at countering the political power of the United States and Europe. In response to harsh criticism from the United States, an informal East Asian Economic Caucus was formed instead *within* APEC. If APEC's FTA objectives do not materialize, it is possible that the idea of a regional FTA limited to East Asian countries could reemerge in the future.[120]

The IPE Perspectives and East Asian Regionalism

Liberal economists tend to be highly supportive of APEC as an example of open regionalism that is likely to serve as a stepping-stone to global trade liberalization. APEC includes countries in a huge area spanning more than one continent, and liberals sometimes compare it favorably with the EU, which is more discriminatory. Liberals realize there are obstacles to promoting free trade in a forum as diverse as APEC, but they are hopeful that this brand of open regionalism will succeed in the long term. Indeed, one prominent liberal who was chair of APEC's eminent persons' group from 1992 to 1995 believes that APEC could become "the first big international institutional success of the post–Cold War era."[121]

Realists are more inclined to view APEC in political as well as economic terms as an effort by non-Asian countries such as Australia and the United States to prevent the formation of a regional trading bloc limited to Asians (as proposed by the Malaysian prime minister). From this perspective, the United States has used APEC "as a forum to maintain US power, [and] embrace the exclusionary East Asian identity within an inclusionary 'Asia-Pacific' identity."[122] Realists place less emphasis than liberals on the institutional aspects of Asian regionalism, and they point to the central role of Japan in establishing its own brand of regionalism. Indeed, Japanese MNCs, with the support of the government, have greatly increased their foreign direct investment throughout Asia, forging a regional production alliance. Instead of establishing an RTA, "Japan is using its Asian production alliance in part as a platform from which to continuing supplying high-technology products to Western markets."[123] Thus, realists place particular emphasis on the competitive challenge that Japan, China, and the East Asian NIEs pose to the West today.

Although APEC to this point has been a forum for discussion rather than an RTA, historical structuralists are concerned that APEC could eventually lead to "the erosion of social programs, downward harmonization of environmental, labour and health standards, and a permanent shift of political and economic power to large corporations."[124] Because some East Asian countries currently have policies that provide minimal protection for the environment, labor, and human rights, the freeing of trade and foreign investment in APEC could force other countries to sacrifice their own standards to remain competitive. As in the case of NAFTA, the member countries in APEC would be forced into a "competitive race to the bottom."[125] In line with this mode of thinking, civil society protestors at the November 1997 APEC summit in Vancouver, Canada, protested against what they viewed as the abuse of human rights in APEC countries and the globalizing effects of the APEC agenda.

Historical structuralists, like realists, also focus on the noninstitutional aspects of East Asian regionalism. In the view of historical structuralists, Japan and its MNCs have acted as the core economic power in the region, supplying the highest technology products and keeping most of the R&D at home. The East Asian NIEs (Hong Kong, South Korea, Singapore, and Taiwan) have acted as a semiperiphery supplying high- to medium-technology inputs, and the Southeast Asian countries and China have performed the role of a periphery, supplying the medium- to low-technology inputs. Because the other Asian countries depend on Japan for its high-technology inputs, they must maintain a trade surplus with the West to compensate for their growing trade deficit with Japan. Thus, Japanese capital is playing a dominant role in bringing about a large degree of informal integration in the East Asian region.[126]

CONCLUSION

In the postwar period there were two major waves of regionalism, the first in the 1950s and 1960s and the second since the mid-1980s. There is a fairly wide consensus that the second wave of regionalism is likely to be far more enduring than the first wave. Although there are some contradictions between the global and regional processes, globalization has clearly acted as a stimulus to the second phase of regionalism. Regional institutions are developing to deal with problems of global interdependence that nation-states are unable to deal with individually. States are also joining in regional groups to improve their competitiveness as the intensity and scope of global competition increase. Furthermore, internationalist firms within states that have expanded their exports and imports, multinational operations, and intrafirm trade have pressured for free market exchange at both the regional and global levels.

The revival of regionalism stems not only from globalization pressures but also from changes in North-North and North-South relations. Most significantly, the United States changed from a position of refusing to participate in RTAs to openly supporting them during the 1980s. One of the factors explaining the change in American policy was the decline in U.S. trade hegemony. As long as the United States was undisputed hegemon in the global trade regime, it was firmly committed to the multilateral route to trade liberalization. However, the United States was less willing to provide the public goods to maintain an open multilateral trade regime as its economic leverage declined, and it sought to regain some of its economic influence through joining in RTAs. The LDCs also turned to regionalism in the 1980s, but they generally supported a far more open regionalism than they had in the 1960s. The 1980s foreign debt crisis had a major effect in inducing LDCs to adopt orthodox liberal reforms, reflected in their new approach to regionalism. For example, Mexico engaged in unilateral liberalization of its trade policies, joined GATT in 1986, and formed NAFTA with the United States and Canada in the early 1990s.

The three IPE perspectives differ in their approach to RTAs. Liberals believe that multilateralism is the best possible route to trade liberalization, but they are generally supportive of open RTAs as a second-best option. Most liberals have a positive view of the current phase of regionalism because it seems to be serving as a stepping-stone rather than an obstacle to multilateral free trade. However, they are critical of some Third World RTAs, such as Mercosur, that are encountering problems in promoting trade liberalization. Liberals assume that all member countries will benefit from open RTAs, and they often argue that smaller countries will gain more benefits than larger countries in terms of expanded market shares and economies of scale.

Realists believe that the underlying power relationships between states will be evident in RTAs and that the more powerful states will gain no less, and probably more, from RTAs than the less powerful. Whereas RTAs give smaller member countries access to larger countries' markets, the larger countries will demand side payments in return. For example, in CUSFTA, the United States gained concessions from Canada in energy sharing, foreign investment, and trade in services, and in NAFTA, Mexico gave up any claim to the S&D treatment often accorded to LDCs in international trade agreements. In Mercosur, "Brazil's relative power has led it to adopt a modus operandi of . . . setting limits on imports or exports or erecting nontariff barriers without consulting other MERCOSUR countries, and negotiating only when those countries protest."[127]

Historical structuralists have a far more negative view than liberals of RTAs such as NAFTA. In the historical structuralist view, transnational capital is the main beneficiary of such agreements, and the working class and poorest people within member states are the main losers. Because RTAs often permit MNCs to locate their production facilities in the states with the lowest wages and environmental standards, they can have a detrimental effect on environmental, labor, health and safety, public service, and consumer protection standards in all member countries.

Chapters 8 and 9 have focused mainly on international trade issues. Trade and investment are closely related, and their relationship has intensified in recent years. Indeed, the director-general of the WTO has stated that "businesses now trade to invest and invest to trade—to the point where both activities are increasingly part of a single strategy to deliver products across borders."[128] Although the level of international trade has been increasing dramatically, foreign direct investment of MNCs has been increasing at an even faster rate. It is to the issue of MNCs that we now turn.

NOTES

1. Robert E. Hudec and James D. Southwick, "Regionalism and WTO Rules: Problems in the Fine Art of Discriminating Fairly," in Miguel Rodríguez Mendoza, Patrick Low, and Barbara Kotschwar, eds., *Trade Rules in the Making: Challenges in Regional and Multilateral Negotiations* (Washington, DC: Brookings Institution, 1999), p. 47.
2. World Trade Organization Secretariat, *Regionalism and the World Trading System* (Geneva: WTO, advance copy, April 1995), pp. 25–29; André Sapir, "EC Regionalism at the Turn of the Millennium: Toward a New Paradigm?," *World Economy* 23-9 (September 2000), p. 1135.
3. Gerald K. Helleiner, "Considering U.S.-Mexico Free Trade," in Ricardo Grinspun and Maxwell A. Cameron, eds., *The Political Economy of North American Free Trade* (Montreal: McGill-Queen's University Press, 1993), p. 50.
4. Helleiner, "Considering U.S.-Mexico Free Trade," pp. 50–51.
5. Vincent A. Mahler, "The Lomé Convention: Assessing a North-South Institutional Relationship," *Review of International Political Economy* 1–2 (Summer 1994), p. 246.

6. Andrew Hurrell, "Explaining the Resurgence of Regionalism in World Politics," *Review of International Studies* 21 (1995), p. 333. For a detailed study that demonstrates the diffi-culty in defining a "region" precisely, see Bruce M. Russett, *International Regions and the International System: A Study in Political Ecology* (Chicago: Rand McNally, 1967).

7. Even here there are exceptions. For example, the WTO categorizes the U.S.-Israel, Canada-Israel, and Canada-Chile free trade agreements as RTAs. The EU also has special agreements with a large number of ACP countries. However, the ACP countries are asso-ciate rather than full members of the EU.

8. Mancur Olson, *The Logic of Collective Action: Public Goods and the Theory of Groups* (Cambridge: Harvard University Press, 1965); Kenneth A. Oye, "Explaining Cooperation Under Anarchy: Hypotheses and Strategies," in Kenneth A. Oye, ed., *Cooperation Under Anarchy* (Princeton: Princeton University Press, 1986), pp. 18–20.

9. Hurrell, "Explaining the Resurgence of Regionalism in World Politics," pp. 345–347; Andrew Wyatt-Walter, "Regionalism, Globalization, and World Economic Order," in Louise Fawcett and Andrew Hurrell, eds., *Regionalism in World Politics: Regional Orga-nization and International Order* (Oxford: Oxford University Press, 1995), p. 77.

10. For a cataloging of the numerous early attempts to establish RTAs, see Fritz Machlup, *A History of Thought on Economic Integration* (New York: Columbia University Press, 1977), pp. 105–115.

11. See Michael Kaser, *Comecon: Integration Problems of the Planned Economies* (London: Oxford University Press, 1965).

12. The new integration agreement in 1957 was in fact called the European Economic Com-munity, but the name was later changed to European Community. The latter term is used in this book. Britain was the leading force behind the EFTA, which also included Austria, Denmark, Norway, Portugal, Sweden, and Switzerland.

13. Lia Valls Pereira, "Toward the Common Market of the South: Mercosur's Origins, Evolu-tion, and Challenges," in Riordan Roett, ed., *Mercosur: Regional Integration, World Mar-kets* (Boulder, CO: Lynne Rienner, 1999), p. 8.

14. Jagdish Bhagwati, "Regionalism and Multilateralism: An Overview," in Jaime de Melo and Arvind Panagariya, eds., *New Dimensions in Regional Integration* (Cambridge: Cam-bridge University Press, 1993), pp. 28–29.

15. Bhagwati, "Regionalism and Multilateralism: An Overview," pp. 29–31.

16. Kenneth N. Waltz, *Theory of International Politics* (Reading, MA: Addison-Wesley, 1979), p. 70.

17. In 1960, the OEEC was converted into the OECD, which also includes non-European in-dustrial countries as members. On the U.S. role in the formation of the OEEC, see Philip E. Jacob, Alexine L. Atherton, and Arthur M. Wallenstein, *The Dynamics of International Organization* rev. ed. (Homewood, IL: Dorsey Press, 1972), pp. 337–347.

18. See Joanne Gowa, "Bipolarity, Multipolarity, and Free Trade," *American Political Science Review* 83-4 (December 1989), pp. 1245–1256; Lawrence Krause, "Trade Policy in the 1990s I: Good-bye Bipolarity, Hello Regions," *The World Today* 46-5 (May 1990), pp. 83–86.

19. Hurrell, "Explaining the Resurgence of Regionalism in World Politics," pp. 341–342.

20. Mark A. Pollack, "International Relations Theory and European Integration," *Journal of Common Market Studies* 39-2 (June 2001), pp. 222–223; John J. Mearsheimer, "Back to the Future: Instability in Europe After the Cold War," *International Security* 15-1 (1990), pp. 47–48.

21. For one view of the troubles confronting GATT in the late 1980s and early 1990s, see Clyde V. Prestowitz, Jr., Alan Tonelson, and Robert W. Jerome, "The Last Gasp of GATTism," *Harvard Business Review* 69-2 (March–April 1991), pp. 130–138.

22. Bernard M. Hoekman and Michel M. Kostecki, *The Political Economy of the World Trad-ing System: From GATT to WTO* (Oxford: Oxford University Press, 1995), pp. 214–216.

23. Marc L. Busch and Helen V. Milner, "The Future of the International Trading System: International Firms, Regionalism, and Domestic Politics," in Richard Stubbs and Geoffrey R. D. Underhill, eds., *Political Economy and the Changing Global Order* (Toronto: McClelland & Stewart, 1994), p. 270.

24. Hudec and Southwick, "Regionalism and WTO Rules," pp. 47–48.

25. Duncan Cameron, "Introduction," in Duncan Cameron and Mel Watkins, eds., *Canada Under Free Trade* (Toronto: Lorimer, 1993), p. xxi.

26. Quoted in Dean Acheson, *Present at the Creation: My Years in the State Department* (New York: Norton, 1969), p. 30.

27. General Agreement on Tariffs and Trade, *Text of the General Agreement* (Geneva: GATT, July, 1986), Article 24; Richard Gibb and Wieslaw Michalak, eds., *Continental Trading Blocs: The Growth of Regionalism in the World Economy* (Chichester, UK: Wiley, 1994), pp. 7–9.

28. See R. G. Lipsey and Kelvin Lancaster, "The General Theory of Second Best," *The Review of Economic Studies* 24-1 (1956–57), pp. 11–32; and J. E. Meade, *Trade and Welfare* (London: Oxford University Press, 1955).

29. The terms *trade creation* and *trade diversion* were coined by Jacob Viner *after* GATT Article 24 was written. However, these terms clearly summarize the intent of Article 24. See Jacob Viner, *The Customs Union Issue* (New York: Carnegie Endowment for International Peace, 1950), pp. 41–55.

30. Hoekman and Kostecki, *The Political Economy of the World Trading System*, pp. 216–226.

31. Robert Z. Lawrence, *Regionalism, Multilateralism, and Deeper Integration* (Washington, DC: Brookings Institution, 1996), pp. 41–42.

32. Gardner Patterson, *Discrimination in International Trade, The Policy Issues: 1945–1965* (Princeton, NJ: Princeton University Press, 1966), pp. 146–147. See also C. Michael Aho, "More Bilateral Trade Agreements Would Be a Blunder: What the New President Should Do," *Cornell International Law Journal* 22-1 (Winter 1989), p. 25.

33. Bhagwati, "Regionalism and Multilateralism: An Overview," pp. 25–26.

34. Hoekman and Kostecki, *The Political Economy of the World Trading System*, p. 218; World Trade Organization Secretariat, *Regionalism and the World Trading System*, p. 7.

35. Robert E. Hudec, *The GATT Legal System and World Trade Diplomacy* (New York: Praeger, 1975), pp. 195–196; J. Michael Finger, "GATT's Influence on Regional Arrangements," in Melo and Panagariya, eds., *New Dimensions in Regional Integration*, pp. 136–37.

36. World Trade Organization Secretariat, *Regionalism and the World Trading System*, pp. 12–13.

37. Robert E. Hudec, "Discussion," in Melo and Panagariya, eds., *New Dimensions in Regional Integration*, p. 152.

38. Gary Clyde Hufbauer and Jeffrey J. Schott, *NAFTA: An Assessment*, rev. ed. (Washington, DC: Institute for International Economics, October 1993), p. 112.

39. The only two active agreements which GATT working parties approved are the Caribbean Community and Common Market (CARICOM) and the Czech and Slovak Republics Customs Union.

40. World Trade Organization Secretariat, *Regionalism and the World Trading System*, pp. 16–17; Jeffrey J. Schott, "More Free Trade Areas?" in Jeffrey J. Schott, ed., *Free Trade Areas and U.S. Trade Policy* (Washington, DC: Institute for International Economics, 1989), pp. 24–25.

41. See "Understanding on the Interpretation of Article XXIV of the General Agreement on Tariffs and Trade 1994," in WTO, *The Results of the Uruguay Round of Multilateral Trade Negotiations–The Legal Texts* (Geneva: WTO, 1994), pp. 31–34.

42. Hudec and Southwick, "Regionalism and WTO Rules," pp. 49–74; Sam Laird, "Regional Trade Agreements: Dangerous Liaisons?," *World Economy* 22-9 (1999), pp. 1192–1197.

43. Hudec, *The GATT Legal System and World Trade Diplomacy*, pp. 205–206; John H. Jackson, *World Trade and the Law of GATT* (Indianapolis, IN: Bobbs-Merrill, 1969), pp. 590–591. Jackson notes that the Havana Charter had a special article for RTAs among LDCs, which was not incorporated into the GATT.

44. Olivier Long, *Law and Its Limitations in the GATT Multilateral Trade System* (Dordrecht, Neths: Nijhoff, 1985), p. 101.

45. Laird, "Regional Trade Agreements," p. 1196; World Trade Organization Secretariat, *Regionalism and the World Trading System*, pp. 18–19; Hoekman and Kostecki, *The Political Economy of the World Trading System*, pp. 219–221.

46. For a detailed discussion of these regional preference schemes, see Bonapas Francis Onguglo, "Developing Countries and Trade Preferences," in Rodríguez Mendoza, Low, and Kotschwar, eds., *Trade Rules in the Making*, pp. 109–133.

47. Enzo R. Grilli, *The European Community and the Developing Countries* (Cambridge: Cambridge University Press, 1993), pp. 7–8.

48. Patterson, *Discrimination in International Trade*, p. 234; Desmond Dinan, *Ever Closer Union? An Introduction to the European Community* (Boulder, CO: Rienner, 1994), p. 457.

49. "European Economic Community—Association Agreements: Report of Working Party adopted on 4 April 1966," in General Agreement on Tariffs and Trade, *Basic Instruments and Selected Documents*, 14th supplement (Geneva: GATT, July 1966), pp. 105–106.

50. Matthew McQueen, "ACP-EU Trade Cooperation after 2000: An Assessment of Reciprocal Trade Preferences," *Journal of Modern African Studies* 36-4 (1998), p. 669.

51. Richard Gibb, "Post-Lomé: The European Union and the South," *Third World Quarterly* 21-3 (2000), pp. 457–467.

52. Onguglo, "Developing Countries and Trade Preferences," p. 119.

53. Francis A. S. T. Matambalya and Susanna Wolf, "The Cotonou Agreement and the Challenges of Making the New EU-ACP Trade Regime WTO Compatible," *Journal of World Trade* 35-1 (2001), pp. 123–144; Gibb, "Post-Lomé," pp. 465–478.

54. World Trade Organization Secretariat, *Regionalism and the World Trading System*, pp. 27–29; Sapir, "EC Regionalism at the Turn of the Millennium," p. 1135; Thomas C. Fischer, *The United States, the European Union, and the "Globalization" of World Trade* (Westport, CT: Quorum Books, 2000), p. 75.

55. See E. P. Wellenstein, "Unity, Community, Union—What's in a Name?," *Common Market Law Review* 29-2 (1992), pp. 205–212.

56. Stephen George and Ian Bache, *Politics in the European Union* (Oxford: Oxford University Press, 2001), pp. 87–104; Andrew Moravcsik, "Negotiating the Single European Act," in Robert O. Keohane and Stanley Hoffmann, eds., *The New European Community: Decisionmaking and Institutional Change* (Boulder, CO: Westview Press, 1991), p. 41.

57. Stephen George, "The European Union, 1992 and the Fear of 'Fortress Europe,'" in Andrew Gamble and Anthony Payne, eds., *Regionalism and World Order* (New York: St. Martin's Press, 1996), pp. 21–54.

58. Fischer, *The United States, the European Union, and the "Globalization" of World Trade*, p. 97.

59. Michael H. Abbey and Nicholas Bromfield, "A Practitioner's Guide to the Maastricht Treaty," *Michigan Journal of International Law* 15-4 (Summer 1994), pp. 1329–1357; George and Bache, *Politics in the European Union*, pp. 114–139; Fischer, *The United States, the European Union, and the "Globalization" of World Trade*, pp. 94–116; Robert Gilpin with Jean Millis Gilpin, *The Challenge of Global Capitalism: The World Economy in the 21st Century* (Princeton, NJ: Princeton University Press, 2000), pp. 200–202.

60. Fischer, *The United States, the European Union, and the "Globalization" of World Trade,* p. 136.

61. Grilli, *The European Community and the Developing Countries,* pp. 296–316.

62. Erik Faucompret and Jozef Konings, "The Integration of Central and Eastern Europe in the European Union," *Journal of World Trade* 33-6 (December 1999), pp. 121–127.

63. The 10 countries are Poland, Hungary, the Czech Republic, Slovakia, Bulgaria, Romania, Estonia, Latvia, Lithuania, and Slovenia.

64. Pier Carlo Padoan, "The Changing European Political Economy," in Stubbs and Underhill, eds., *Political Economy and the Changing Global Order,* pp. 340–342.

65. Quoted in "Arguments for Enlargement," *The Economist,* August 3, 1996, p. 41.

66. Fischer, *The United States, the European Union, and the "Globalization" of World Trade,* pp. 136–142; Haus, *Globalizing the GATT,* p. 66; "Arguments for Enlargement," pp. 41–42; "Slicing the EU's Shrinking Cake," *The Economist,* March 21, 1998, pp. 57–58.

67. John Agnew, "How Many Europes? The European Union, Eastward Enlargement and Uneven Development," *European Urban and Regional Studies* 8-1 (2001), pp. 29–38. For a discussion of three groups of CEECs in terms of their trade and foreign investment integration with the EU (the fast movers, the next tier, and the slow movers), see Panagiotis Liargovas and Dionysios Chionis, "Economic Integration between the European Union and the Transition Economies of Central European Initiative Countries," *Post-Communist Economies* 13-1 (2001), pp. 57–70.

68. "France and Enlargement: A Whiff of Veto in the Air?," *The Economist,* December 1, 2001, p. 49.

69. See J. J. Servan-Schreiber, *The American Challenge,* translated from the French by Ronald Steel (New York: Atheneum, 1979). The book was first published in 1967.

70. L. Alan Winters, "The European Community: A Case of Successful Integration?" in Melo and Panagariya, eds., *New Dimensions in Regional Integration,* p. 208.

71. J. M. C. Rollo, "The EC, European Integration and the World Trading System," in Vincent Cable and David Henderson, eds., *Trade Blocs? The Future of Regional Integration* (London: Royal Institute of International Affairs, 1994), pp. 57–58.

72. See Stephen R. Sleigh, "The Social Dimensions of Economic Integration," in Jo Marie Griesgraber and Bernhard G. Gunter, eds., *World Trade: Toward Fair and Free Trade in the Twenty-first Century* (London: Pluto Press, 1997), pp. 40–44.

73. Ralph I. Onwuka, "Beyond Lomé III: Prospects for Symmetrical EurAfrican Relations," in Ralph I. Onwuka and Timothy M. Shaw, eds., *Africa in World Politics: Into the 1990s* (London: Macmillan, 1989), pp. 83–84; Mahler, "The Lomé Convention," pp. 244–248.

74. Agnew, "How Many Europes?," p. 35.

75. Stephan Haggard, "The Political Economy of Regionalism in the Western Hemisphere," in Carol Wise, ed., *The Post-NAFTA Political Economy: Mexico and the Western Hemisphere* (University Park, PA: Pennsylvania State University Press, 1998), pp. 303–305.

76. J. L. Granatstein, "Free Trade Between Canada and the United States," in Dennis Stairs and Gilbert R. Winham, eds., *The Politics of Canada's Economic Relationship with the United States,* Royal Commission on the Economic Union and Development Prospect for Canada, (Toronto: University of Toronto Press, 1985) vol. 29, p. 11.

77. "U.S. Trade Act of 1974, as amended (Public Law 93-618)," Title VI, section 612, in *Legislation on Foreign Relations Through 1989* (Washington, DC: U.S. Government Printing Office, 1990), p. 456.

78. For a detailed discussion of the CUSFTA negotiations see G. Bruce Doern and Brian W. Tomlin, *Faith and Fear: The Free Trade Story* (Toronto: Stoddart, 1991); and Michael Hart with Bill Dymond and Colin Robertson, *Decision at Midnight: Inside the Canada-US Free-Trade Negotiations* (Vancouver: University of British Columbia Press, 1994). See

also Gilbert R. Winham, "Why Canada Acted," in William Diebold, Jr., ed., *Bilateralism, Multilateralism and Canada in U.S. Trade Policy* (Cambridge, MA: Ballinger, 1988), pp. 41–46.

79. See; Lawrence, *Regionalism, Multilateralism, and Deeper Integration,* pp. 67–68; and Helleiner, "Considering U.S.-Mexico Free Trade," pp. 47–48.

80. John Whalley, "Regional Trade Arrangements in North America: CUSTA and NAFTA," in Melo and Panagariya, eds., *New Dimensions in Regional Integration,* pp. 352–353.

81. See Theodore H. Cohn, "The Intersection of Domestic and Foreign Policy in the NAFTA Agricultural Negotiations," *Canadian-American Public Policy* no. 14 (Orono: University of Maine, September 1993).

82. Bernard Hoekman and Pierre Sauvé, "Liberalizing Trade in Services," *World Bank Discussion Papers* no. 243 (Washington, D.C.: World Bank, 1994); Hoekman and Kostecki, *The Political Economy of the World Trading System,* p. 131; Lawrence, *Regionalism, Multilateralism, and Deeper Integration,* pp. 69–72.

83. Rodney de C. Grey, *Trade Policy in the 1980s: An Agenda for Canadian-U.S. Relations* (Montreal: C.D. Howe Institute, 1981), pp. 56–57.

84. Some dispute-settlement panels in NAFTA can be trinational, but dispute settlement panels for CVD and ADD action are binational. If two countries complain about a third country's ADDs or CVDs, two binational panels are created. See Jon R. Johnson, *The North American Free Trade Agreement: A Comprehensive Guide* (Aurora, Ontario: Canada Law Book, 1994), p. 522.

85. Hudec and Southwick, "Regionalism and WTO Rules," p. 56.

86. Hufbauer and Schott, *NAFTA: An Assessment,* pp. 112–113.

87. Helleiner, "Considering U.S.-Mexico Free Trade," pp. 50–51.

88. Johnson, *The North American Free Trade Agreement,* p. 512; Mark MacKinnon, "NAFTA Members to Talk Reform," *Toronto Globe and Mail,* April 10, 2001, p. B1.

89. Robert W. Cox, *Production, Power, and World Order: Social Forces in the Making of History* (New York: Columbia University Press, 1987), p. 345; Ricardo Grinspun and Robert Kreklewich, "Consolidating Neoliberal Reforms: 'Free Trade' as a Conditioning Framework," *Studies in Political Economy* 43 (Spring 1994), p. 45.

90. Herman E. Daly, "Free Trade: The Perils of Deregulation," in Jerry Mander and Edward Goldsmith, eds., *The Case Against the Global Economy: For a Turn Toward the Local* (San Francisco: Sierra Club, 1996), p. 234.

91. Mark E. Rupert, "(Re) Politicizing the Global Economy: Liberal Common Sense and Ideological Struggle in the US NAFTA Debate," *Review of International Political Economy* 2-4 (Autumn 1995), pp. 679–681.

92. Mercosur is the acronym for Mercado Común del Sur (Spanish) or Mercado Común del Sul (Portuguese).

93. José Manuel Salazar-Xirinachs, Theresa Wetter, Karsten Steinfatt, and Danila Ivascanu, "Customs Unions," in José Manuel Salazar-Xirinachs and Maryse Robert, eds., *Toward Free Trade in the Americas* (Washington, D.C.: Brookings Institution, 2001), p. 76.

94. Jeffrey Cason, "On the Road to Southern Cone Economic Integration," *Journal of Interamerican Studies and World Affairs* 42-1 (2000), pp. 23–28; Heinz G. Preusse, "Mercosur—Another Failed Move Towards Regional Integration?," *World Economy* 24-7 (July 2001), pp. 911–914; Riordan Roett, "Introduction," in Riordan Roett, ed., *Mercosur: Regional Integration, World Markets* (Boulder, CO: Lynne Rienner, 1999), pp. 1–5.

95. Preusse, "Mercosur—Another Failed Move Towards Regional Integration?," pp. 915–916.

96. Preusse, "Mercosur—Another Failed Move Towards Regional Integration?," pp. 915–921; "Another Blow to Mercosur," *The Economist,* 31 March 2001, pp. 33–34; Cason, "On the Road to Southern Cone Economic Integration," p. 32.

97. Rafael A. Lecuona, "Economic Integration: NAFTA and Mercosur, a Comparative Analysis," *International Journal of World Peace* 16-4 (December 1999), pp. 41–42.

98. Cason, "On the Road to Southern Cone Economic Integration," p. 24. See also Salazar-Xirinachs, Wetter, Steinfatt, and Ivascanu, "Customs Unions," p. 76.

99. Lia Valls Pereira, "Toward the Common Market of the South: Mercosur's Origins, Evolution, and Challenges," in Roett, ed., *Mercosur: Regional Integration, World Markets,* pp. 7–13; Cason, "On the Road to Southern Cone Economic Integration," pp. 24–29; Preusse, "Mercosur—Another Failed Move Towards Regional Integration?," p. 914.

100. "Mercosur's Trial by Adversity," *The Economist,* 27 May, 2000, pp. 37–38.

101. Pedro da Motta Veiga, "Brazil in Mercosur: Reciprocal Influence," in Roett, ed. *Mercosur: Regional Integration, World Markets,* p. 30.

102. Haggard, "The Political Economy of Regionalism in the Western Hemisphere," p. 303.

103. Gary Clyde Hufbauer and Jeffrey J. Schott, with Diana Clark, *Western Hemisphere Economic Integration* (Washington, D.C.: Institute for International Economics, July 1994), p. 1; Jeffrey J. Schott and Gary C. Hufbauer, "Whither the Free Trade Area of the Americas?," *World Economy* 22-6 (August 1999), pp. 767–769; Paulo S. Wrobel, "A Free Trade Area of the Americas in 2005?," *International Affairs* 74-3 (July 1998), pp. 548–549.

104. Schott and Hufbauer, "Whither the Free Trade Area of the Americas?," pp. 774–776; Wrobel, "A Free Trade Area of the Americas in 2005?," pp. 550–554.

105. Haggard, "The Political Economy of Regionalism in the Western Hemisphere," pp. 310–314 and 334–335; Wrobel, "A Free Trade Area of the Americas in 2005?," pp. 555–556.

106. "Trade in the Americas," *The Economist,* 21 April 2001, p. 19.

107. Joseph Kahn, "House Supports Trading Powers Sought by Bush," *New York Times,* 7 December 2001, pp. A1 and A20.

108. José Manuel Salazar-Xirinachs, "The FTAA Process: From Miami 1994 to Quebec 2001," in Salazar-Xirinachs and Robert, eds., *Toward Free Trade in the Americas,* p. 300.

109. Soogil Young, "East Asia as a Regional Force for Globalism," in Anderson and Blackhurst, eds., *Regional Integration and the Global Trading System,* pp. 127–128.

110. Miles Kahler, *International Institutions and the Political Economy of Integration* (Washington, DC: Brookings Institution, 1995), pp. 107–108.

111. Lawrence, *Regionalism, Multilateralism, and Deeper Integration,* pp. 80–83.

112. Lawrence, *Regionalism, Multilateralism, and Deeper Integration,* pp. 83–86.

113. Young, "East Asia as a Regional Force for Globalism," p. 134; Lawrence, *Regionalism, Multilateralism, and Deeper Integration,* p. 79; Kahler, *International Institutions and the Political Economy of Integration,* p. 112.

114. Herman Joseph S. Kraft, "ASEAN and Intra-ASEAN Relations: Weathering the Storm?," *Pacific Review* 13-3 (2000), pp. 453–472; Joshua Kurlantzick, "Is East Asia Integrating?," *Washington Quarterly* 24-4 (Autumn 2001), pp. 19–28. For a detailed discussion of the AFTA plans see Emiko Fukase and Will Martin, "Free Trade Area Membership as a Stepping Stone to Development: The Case of ASEAN," *World Bank Discussion Paper* no. 421 (Washington, DC: World Bank, 2001).

115. John Ravenhill, "APEC Adrift: Implications for Economic Regionalism in Asia and the Pacific," *Pacific Review* 13-2 (2000), p. 320.

116. Johnny Chi-Chen Chiang, "Conceptualizing the APEC Way: International Cooperation in a Non-Insitutionalized Regime," *Issues & Studies* 36-6 (November/December 2000), pp. 183–187; Fred Bergsten, "The Case for APEC," *The Economist,* 6 January 1996, p. 62; Shuji Miyazaki, "APEC: The First Seven Years and the Road to Manila," *World Economic Affairs* 1-1 (Summer 1996), p. 20.

117. Ravenhill, "APEC Adrift," pp. 321–323.

118. Gary Hufbauer and Jeffrey J. Schott, "Toward Free Trade and Investment in the Asia-Pacific," in Brad Roberts, ed., *New Forces in the World Economy* (Cambridge, MA: MIT Press, 1996), pp. 217–218.

119. Hufbauer and Schott, "Toward Free Trade and Investment in the Asia-Pacific," pp. 219–220.

120. Richard Higgott and Richard Stubbs, "Competing Conceptions of Economic Regionalism: APEC Versus EAEC in the Asia Pacific," *Review of International Political Economy* 2-3 (Summer 1995), pp. 522–526. There is considerable variation in scholarly assessments of the degree to which APEC has been a successful grouping. For strikingly different perceptions see Chiang, "Conceptualizing the APEC Way"; Ravenhill, "APEC Adrift"; and Vinod Aggarwal, "Withering APEC? The Search for an Institutional Role," in Jörn Dosch and Manfred Mols, eds., *International Relations in the Asia-Pacific: New Patterns of Power, Interest, and Cooperation* (New York: St. Martin's Press, 2000), pp. 67–86.

121. Bergsten, "The Case for APEC," p. 63.

122. Glenn Hook, "Japan and the Construction of Asia-Pacific," in Gamble and Payne, eds., *Regionalism and World Order,* p. 193.

123. Walter Hatch and Kozo Yamamura, *Asia in Japan's Embrace: Building a Regional Production Alliance* (Cambridge: Cambridge University Press, 1996), p. 36.

124. Grinspun and Kreklewich, "Consolidating Neoliberal Reforms," p. 41.

125. Ralph Nader, "Introduction: Free Trade and the Decline of Democracy," in *The Case Against 'Free Trade': GATT, NAFTA, and the Globalization of Corporate Power* (San Francisco: Earth Island Press, 1993), p. 6.

126. Hatch and Yamamura, Asia in Japan's *Embrace,* chs. 1 and 2; Gary Gereffi, "Mexico's 'Old' and 'New' Maquiladora Industries: Contrasting Approaches to North American Integration," in Gerardo Otero, ed., *Neo-Liberalism Revisited: Economic Restructuring and Mexico's Political Future* (Boulder, CO: Westview Press, 1996), p. 96.

127. Cason, "On the Road to Southern Cone Economic Integration," p. 29.

128. Renato Ruggiero, Director General of the World Trade Organization, "Charting the Trade Routes of the Future: Towards a Borderless Economy," address delivered to the International Industrial Conference, San Francisco, 29 September 1997, *World Trade Organization Press Release* (Geneva; Press/77), p. 4.

Multinational Corporations and Global Production

The largest MNCs are in many respects the main agents of globalization. They produce and distribute goods and services across national boundaries; spread ideas, tastes, and technology throughout the world; and plan their operations on a global scale. MNCs are most commonly considered to be firms that control productive assets in more than one country. Parent firms in the home countries of MNCs acquire their foreign assets by investing in affiliate or subsidiary firms in host countries. This type of investment involves management rights and control and is referred to as *FDI. Portfolio investment,* by contrast, is investment without control; that is, it involves the purchase of bonds, money market instruments, or a small amount of equity securities or stocks of a firm, simply to realize a financial return.

The growing presence of MNCs in the world economy testifies to their role as agents of globalization. By 1998, there were about 63,000 parent firms with about 690,000 foreign affiliates. Although there are many MNCs, a large share of FDI is concentrated in a relatively small number of them. The world's 100 largest nonfinancial MNCs, based almost exclusively in developed countries, are the main drivers of international production. In 1998, these 100 MNCs held about $2 trillion in foreign assets, had total foreign sales of $2.1 trillion, and employed more than 6 million persons in their foreign affiliates. Despite variations in different years, FDI has generally increased more rapidly than trade. From 1973 to 1995, annual FDI outflows multiplied more than 12 times (from $25 billion to $315 billion), whereas the value of merchandise exports multiplied by 8.5 times. In 1999, world FDI outflows amounted to about $800 billion. Today, about a third of total world trade consists of intrafirm trade within MNCs, another third consists of MNC exports to nonaffiliates, and the remaining third consists of trade among national (that is, non-MNC) firms.[1]

The growing importance of MNCs has caused some analysts to argue that the critical problem in the study of IPE today "is the tension between states and multinationals, not states and markets."[2] Nevertheless, MNCs do not receive as much attention in

319

the IPE literature as one might expect; many international relations theorists continue to place primary emphasis on relations among governments. A major obstacle to the study of MNCs is the limited amount of reliable data. As private enterprises, MNCs are reluctant to provide information about themselves, and they are particularly adept at obscuring their activities. This problem is compounded by the fact that no international organization oversees foreign investment activities the way organizations monitor monetary relations, trade, and development assistance. Furthermore, the study of MNCs is highly controversial, and an analyst's view of "the facts" is often colored by his or her general perspective. Thus, it is not uncommon in public debates on MNCs for "anecdote to replace data" and for "the witty phrase to replace analysis."[3]

Liberals, realists, and historical structuralists have differing views regarding both the power of MNCs and their impact on states and societies. Liberal theorists often maintain that the mobility of MNCs gives them a major advantage over national governments, which are bound to specific territories. In the current age of interdependence, MNCs and private banks have therefore become "the major weavers of the world economy."[4] Historical structuralists also refer to the growing power of MNCs, but unlike liberals they argue that corporate managers constitute a transnational class that maintains and defends the capitalist system. Thus, writers from this perspective often assert that managers of major corporations have a predominant influence over the conduct of U.S. foreign policy.[5] Realists, by contrast, argue that the power of states over MNCs has not decreased and that MNCs retain close ties with their home governments. MNCs would not be able to expand their activities, according to realists, without the support of the most powerful states.[6]

Although liberals and historical structuralists agree that the influence of MNCs has increased, they strongly differ over the effects of this change. Many liberals believe that FDI contributes to increased efficiency in the use of the world's resources by stimulating innovation, competition, economic growth, and employment. MNCs also provide countries with numerous benefits, such as capital, technology, managerial skills, and marketing networks. Historical structuralists, by contrast, view MNCs as predatory monopolists that overcharge for their goods and services, limit the flow of technology, and create dependency relationships with host countries in the Third World.[7] MNCs can also have a negative impact on home countries, critics argue, by exporting jobs and imposing downward pressures on labor and on environmental standards.

DEFINITIONS AND TERMINOLOGY

Controversy exists not only over the importance and effects of MNCs but even over definitions and terminology.[8] MNCs are usually defined as firms that control assets in at least two countries, but some writers maintain that MNCs must have more of an international presence. For example, one of the classic studies on MNCs argues that only enterprises with manufacturing subsidiaries in at least six countries are "entitled to" the MNC label.[9] Those who favor more restrictive definitions of this type believe that the most important investment issues relate to the largest firms, which establish a number of foreign affiliates as part of a global strategy. However, restrictive definitions are often problematic because they exclude enterprises on a rather arbitrary basis.

This chapter therefore adopts the more expansive definition of MNCs as firms that operate in two or more countries. An enterprise is of course not an MNC simply because it does business in more than one country. To qualify as an MNC, a firm must possess at least one FDI project in which it has management rights or control. A firm can undertake FDI in a host country in one of two ways: *greenfield investment,* or the creation of new facilities and productive assets by foreigners; and *mergers and acquisitions (M&As),* or the purchase of stocks in an existing firm by foreigners with the purpose of participating in its management. In a cross-border merger, the assets and operations of two firms belonging to different countries are combined to establish a new legal entity. In a cross-border acquisition, a local company becomes an affiliate or subsidiary of a foreign company. During the past decade, most of the growth in international production has occurred through M&As rather than greenfield investment, and the data on M&As show that acquisitions are far more common than mergers.[10]

Although the definition of FDI may appear to be straightforward, there are differences of view over what constitutes "control." Until the 1960s, the U.S. Department of Commerce defined FDI as involving control over at least 25 percent of the equity of a foreign business, but the department subsequently lowered this figure to 10 percent. Japan also defines FDI as involving at least 10 percent equity ownership, but the minimum figures for Britain and Germany are 20 percent and 25 percent, respectively. In reality, the percentage of equity required for control varies in different circumstances. On the one hand, a foreign investor may gain managerial control of an enterprise by owning less than 10 percent of the stock if ownership is widely dispersed. On the other hand, 49 percent ownership may not confer control if a single individual or firm owns the other 51 percent. The important point is that a large shareholder may have considerable control over a company's operations even without holding a majority of shares.[11]

Differences exist not only over definitions but also over the use of the term MNC itself. The UN and a number of scholars prefer the term *transnational* to multinational because the ownership and control of most of these firms is not really multinational. Instead, a firm normally extends its operations from a single home country across national frontiers.[12] It is true that most MNCs have been *ethnocentric* or home country oriented, with directives and advice flowing from the headquarters to the affiliates and much of the MNCs' research and development being located in the home country. Nevertheless, a small but growing number of MNCs have become more *geocentric* or *stateless;* that is, they adopt a worldwide approach and are not as closely tied to any single state. Strategic alliances among MNCs from different states further complicate the task of associating an MNC with a specific home government. These alliances can take the form of production-sharing agreements, collaborative research and networking arrangements, and other types of cooperation. Finally, host states in some cases may induce an MNC to engage in activities attuned to the hosts' requirements. For example, MNCs can sometimes gain entry into a foreign country only by agreeing to form *joint ventures* with local firms. Joint ventures involving two or more firms are becoming increasingly common in Eastern European and Third World countries.[13]

The term transnational accurately reflects the fact that the home country continues to be significant for most international firms. Nevertheless, the existence of geocentric firms, strategic alliances, and joint ventures demonstrates that corporations differ in the degree to which their nationality has significance. This text uses the more common term MNC, simply to signify that a firm has ongoing managerial and productive activities in more than one country.[14]

WHY DO FIRMS BECOME MNCs?

To understand why firms become MNCs, it is important to distinguish between horizontal and vertical integration. A *horizontally integrated MNC* extends its operations abroad by producing the same product or product line in its affiliates in different countries. A *vertically integrated MNC* produces goods and services at different stages of the production process; that is, the outputs of some affiliates serve as inputs to other affiliates of the MNC.

Firms often engage in **horizontal integration** to defend or increase their market shares. Although a firm's exports from the home country may initially meet the demand for products and services in a foreign market, the firm may have to set up a subsidiary to compete with new local suppliers that enter the foreign market. By establishing a presence in the foreign market, the MNC can compete more effectively with local firms by lowering costs such as transportation and by becoming more attuned to the market's special characteristics. If the market is large enough, the firm may find it economically feasible to produce goods and services specifically attuned to the tastes of its consumers. If a firm is producing for LDC markets, producing directly in the LDCs may lower the labor costs of production.

Another reason firms engage in horizontal integration relates to the policies of foreign governments. When governments impose tariffs and NTBs that interfere with a firm's exports from its home country, the firm may respond by establishing foreign operations to "get behind" the external barriers. For example, Honda had the largest stake of the Japanese automakers in exports to the U.S. market in the early 1980s. When the United States imposed voluntary export restraints on Japanese auto imports from 1981 to 1985, Honda responded by becoming the first Japanese car manufacturer to produce automobiles in the United States. National and subnational governments also provide direct and indirect investment incentives to encourage firms to locate production facilities in their territories. The efforts of subnational governments to attract FDI have been especially notable since the early 1970s. Only 10 U.S. states had committed budgetary resources to attracting foreign investment before 1969, but 47 states had developed active investment programs by 1979.[15]

Firms often engage in **vertical integration** to avoid uncertainty and reduce transaction costs. Instead of depending on uncertain "arm's length transactions" with different owners at various stages of the production process, vertically integrated MNCs gain control of these transactions by *internalizing* them within the firm. Vertically integrated firms opt for *backward integration* when the raw materials and other inputs they require for production are not readily available or involve high transaction costs. Examples of such backward integration include steel firm investments in iron ore operations, oil company investments in the extraction of crude oil, and rubber manufacturer investments in natural rubber plantations. Backward integration may also enable MNCs to gain control over the quality of inputs. It is no accident that three vertically integrated MNCs accounted for 60 percent of the export trade in bananas in the 1980s; bananas are highly perishable and require specific handling and ripening conditions. When the growers, shippers, and distributors are not vertically integrated, the independent firms at each stage of the production process have more incentive to compromise quality control. The motivations for *forward vertical integration* are similar to those for backward integration: to reduce uncertainty and transaction costs and to ensure the quality of goods and services that reach the consumer.[16]

Another reason firms engage in vertical integration is to limit competition. When a small number of MNCs control the inputs such as raw materials for a particular industry, they can impose substantial barriers to the entry of new rival firms. As private firms, MNCs also engage in vertical integration to limit the scrutiny of their activities by nation-states. For example, MNCs sometimes manipulate their transfer prices without detection by governments. **Transfer prices** are the prices that affiliates of an MNC charge each other for the internal sales of goods and services. Transfer prices help the MNC to efficiently manage its internal operations and to monitor the performance of its affiliates. However, an MNC can shift its reported profits from high-tax to low-tax countries (and thus avoid paying some taxes) by artificially raising or lowering the prices each affiliate charges. In 1993, for example, the U.S. Internal Revenue Service ruled that Nissan Motor Company had used transfer prices to seriously underreport its U.S. income, and Nissan was required to pay the United States about $150 million.[17]

Firms that become MNCs must have the ability as well as the incentive to make this transition. Innovations in communications, transportation, and technology have enabled firms to internationalize their production more easily. Firms are also likely to multinationalize successfully if they are able to "think globally" and "act locally." On the one hand, large MNCs have numerous advantages resulting from their worldwide presence, such as economies of scale, access to global financing, special access to raw materials and other inputs, and the reputation of their brand names. On the other hand, MNCs operate in a world of nation-states in which they must cater to the demands and tastes of local consumers and adhere to national laws.[18]

THE HISTORICAL DEVELOPMENT OF FOREIGN DEBT INVESTMENT

Although the rapid expansion of MNCs is a post–World War II phenomenon, FDI and MNCs have a much longer history.[19] Some scholars trace the origins of the MNC to the transborder business operations of medieval banks such as the Medici bank in fifteenth-century Florence. In the sixteenth through eighteenth centuries, international trading companies such as the English, Dutch, and French East India Companies and the Hudson's Bay Company coordinated large amounts of cross-border business activity. In the nineteenth century, firms that we commonly consider to be MNCs became involved in more sustained, longer term investments in a wider array of activities and countries. Thousands of these MNCs existed by the time of World War II.

Despite the general growth of MNCs and FDI over time, a number of factors have affected the rapidity of growth—and sometimes the contraction—of MNC activity in different periods. First, MNC activity has increased more rapidly during periods of major advances in communications, transportation, and technology. These advances have facilitated the establishment and expansion of MNC control over foreign operations. Second, rapid economic growth has often stimulated the expansion of MNCs, whereas depressed economic conditions have had the opposite effect. Third, MNCs have expanded their operations more rapidly when national governments and the international system have been receptive to such activity. Internationally, for example, the development of rules governing private property encouraged FDI, whereas major wars had a depressing effect. Fourth, capital liberalization has prompted increased FDI, whereas capital and exchange controls have discouraged such activity. Finally, it is ironic that FDI has often expanded during periods of trade protectionism because MNCs have shifted production abroad to circumvent the trade barriers.[20] The historical discussion that follows is divided into three broad periods: before World War II, from the mid-1940s to the mid-1980s, and since the mid-1980s.

The Period Before World War II

Most economists traditionally maintained that long-term capital flows in the nineteenth and early twentieth centuries were composed mainly of portfolio investment rather than FDI. However, data on foreign investment flows for this early period were extremely limited, and there was confusion as to how investments should be categorized. As economists refined their definitions, they concluded that a greater share of total foreign investment was FDI than was earlier assumed. Indeed, some studies estimate that FDI accounted for as much as 45 percent of British foreign investment in 1913 to 1914.[21]

As the first country to industrialize and the global hegemon, Britain was the main force behind the dramatic growth of FDI in the nineteenth century. Although there were no government guarantees or international institutions to provide safeguards, investments were fairly secure for several reasons. First, economic risk was lower under the pre–World War I gold standard because currencies were convertible, dividends could be easily remitted, and exchange rates were reasonably stable. Second, political risk was lower because a large share of European investment was in colonial territories that operated under home country rules. Third, the lack of restrictions on capital flows facilitated the growth of FDI. And fourth, wars during this period were limited in scope. The nineteenth century was also a period of rapid advances in rail and sea transport and communications (for example, the telegraph), which facilitated the task of managing FDI over long distances.[22]

As Table 10.1 shows, British firms were clearly the leading source of FDI before World War II, accounting for 45 percent of the total in 1914 and 40 percent in 1938. Although the United States was an important host country for European FDI in the nineteenth century, it was also beginning to establish its own MNCs. The first major U.S. manufacturing MNC was the Singer Manufacturing Company, which had plants in four countries by the 1880s, and resource-based U.S. firms such as Standard Oil Company also established extensive offshore operations. Thus, Table 10.1 shows that the U.S. share of outward FDI increased dramatically from 14 percent in 1914 to 28 percent in 1938. Western Europe and the United States accounted for more than 90 percent of outward FDI before World War II.

TABLE 10.1

SHARE OF OUTWARD STOCK OF FOREIGN DIRECT INVESTMENT (PERCENTAGES)

	1914	1938
Britain	45	40
United States	14	28
Germany	14	1
France	11	9
Netherlands	5	10
Other Western Europe	5	3
Rest of world	6	9

Source: Geoffrey Jones, *The Evolution of International Business: An Introduction,* pp. 30, 42. Copyright © 1996 by Geoffrey Jones. First published 1996 by Routledge. By permission of International Thomas Publishing Services Ltd.

TABLE 10.2

SHARE OF INWARD STOCK OF FOREIGN DIRECT INVESTMENT (PERCENTAGES)

	1914	1938
Latin America	33	31
Asia	21	25
United States	10	7
Eastern Europe	10	2
Western Europe	8	7
Canada	6	10
Africa	6	7
Rest of world	6	11

Source: Geoffrey Jones, *The Evolution of International Business: An Introduction,* pp. 31, 43. Copyright © 1996 by Geoffrey Jones. First published 1996 by Routledge. By permission of International Thomas Publishing Services Ltd.

Table 10.2 shows that in marked contrast to the home countries for FDI, the largest recipients of FDI in 1914 and 1938 were LDCs in Latin America and Asia. Indeed, 63 percent of the world's FDI was directed to Latin America, Asia, and Africa in 1938. Other major recipients in 1938 were Canada (10 percent), the United States (7 percent), and Western Europe (7 percent). Whereas most of the FDI in manufacturing was concentrated in Western Europe and North America, the FDI in LDCs was mainly in natural resources and services (FDI in natural resources was also directed to Eastern Europe, Canada, and the United States).[23]

The rapid growth of FDI in the nineteenth century continued into the twentieth century and the interwar period. After World War I, however, foreign investment was hindered by the increase in global economic and political instability. For example, a number of host countries began to impose restrictions on inward FDI, the Soviet Union nationalized foreign property, and the gold exchange standard was suspended. As a result of the Great Depression and World War II, there was a severe contraction in MNC activities. Indeed, MNCs accounted for a much smaller share of world economic activity in 1949 than in 1929. It was not until after World War II that the vigorous growth of MNCs and FDI would resume.[24]

The Mid-1940s to the Mid-1980s

Britain was the leading source of FDI in the nineteenth and early twentieth centuries, but U.S. MNCs took over the mantle of leadership after World War II. As Table 10.3 shows, U.S. firms accounted for more than one-half (53.8 percent) of outward stocks of FDI in 1967. Under U.S. leadership, FDI entered a period of rapid expansion because of several changes in the postwar period. First, the developed countries experienced a sustained period of economic growth from 1950 to 1973, which was conducive to the expansion of MNC activity. Second, there were major improvements in international transportation and communications: faster jet and ocean transport, telex and satellite communications, and the fax machine all made contributions to the flow of capital. Third, most developed countries relaxed their controls over FDI after the return to convertibility of their currencies. (A notable exception was Japan, which continued to restrict foreign investment flows.)

Although U.S. MNCs accounted for the predominant share of FDI in the postwar period, their percentage of FDI has declined steadily since the late 1960s. A major reason for the declining U.S. percentage was the rapid economic growth in Japan, Germany, and other Western European countries as they recovered from the war. Thus, Table 10.3 shows that the U.S. share of total outward stocks of FDI fell from 53.8 percent in 1967 to 36.6 percent in 1985, whereas Japan's share rose from 1.4 percent to 6.5 percent and West Germany's share rose from 2.8 percent to 8.7 percent. Table 10.3 also shows that almost all the outward FDI flows in the postwar period have come from the developed market economies: 99 percent in 1960 and 96.9 percent in 1985. Nevertheless, MNCs based in Third World countries increased their share of outward FDI from only 1 percent in 1960 to about 3 percent in 1985. Most of this FDI came from OPEC states and from more prosperous LDCs in Asia and Latin America.

Table 10.4 shows that although the U.S. share of outward FDI was declining, the U.S. share of inward stocks of FDI was increasing from 11.2 percent in 1975 to 25.1 percent in 1985. Of the developed countries, only Japan maintained an extremely low share of inward FDI, which remained at 0.6 percent in 1985, largely because of governmental, societal, and cultural factors that limited investment flows. Thus, the developed market economies were the largest recipients as well as providers of FDI, accounting for about 75 percent of inward stocks from 1975 to 1985. Although Third World countries had received well over 60 percent of total FDI before World War II, this figure fell to about 30 percent in the immediate postwar period as FDI activities shifted from primary products to manufacturing. From the mid-1970s, the LDC share of inward FDI declined even further to about 25 percent because of LDC demands for more control over their natural resources, growing LDC external debts, and an increase in technology-related investment in the developed market economies.

TABLE 10.3

OUTWARD STOCKS OF FOREIGN DIRECT INVESTMENT, THE GROUP OF SEVEN (BILLIONS OF U.S. DOLLARS)

	1960		1967		1975		1980		1985		1990		1998	
	Value	%	Value	%	Value	%	Value	%	Value	%	Value	%	Value	%
United States	31.9	47.1	56.6	53.8	124.2	44.0	220.2	42.9	251.0	36.6	435.2	25.8	980.6	24.1
Japan	0.5	0.7	1.5	1.4	15.9	5.7	18.8	3.7	44.3	6.5	204.7	12.2	270.0	6.6
Germany (Federal Republic)	0.8	1.2	3.0	2.8	18.4	6.5	43.1	8.4	59.9	8.7	151.6	9.0	370.3	9.1
Britain	12.4	18.3	17.5	16.6	37.0	13.1	80.4	15.7	100.3	14.6	230.8	13.7	498.7	12.3
France	4.1	6.1	6.0	5.7	10.6	3.8	23.6	4.6	37.1	5.4	110.1	6.5	227.8	5.6
Italy	1.1	1.6	2.1	2.0	3.3	1.2	7.3	1.4	16.3	2.4	56.1	3.3	165.4	4.1
Canada	2.5	3.7	3.7	3.5	10.4	3.7	22.6	4.4	40.9	6.0	78.9	4.7	160.9	4.0
Total G-7[a]	53.3	78.7	90.4	85.8	219.8	77.9	416.0	81.0	549.8	81.0	1267.4	75.3	2673.7	65.8
Total DMEs[b]	67.0	99.0	—		275.4	97.7	507.5	98.8	664.2	96.9	1614.6	95.9	3650.0	89.8
Total	67.7	100.0	105.3	100.0	282.0	100.0	513.7	100.0	685.6	100.0	1684.1	100.0	4065.8	100.0

[a]G-7 = Group of Seven

[b]DMEs= developed market economies

Source: Centre on Transnational Corporations, *Transnational Corporations in World Development: Trends and Propects* (New York: United Nations, 1988), Table 1.2, p. 24 (1960 and 1975 figures); UN Economic and Social Council, Commission on International Corporations, *International Corporations in World Development: A Re-Examination,* E/C. 10/38 (New York: United Nations 1978), Table III-32, p. 236 (1967 figures); UNCTAD, *World Investment Report—1996* (New York: United Nations, 1996), Annex Table 4, pp. 245–247 (1980–90 figures); UNCTAD, *World Investment Report—2000,* (New York: United Nations 2000), p. 300 (1998 figures).

TABLE 10.4
INWARD STOCKS OF FOREIGN DIRECT INVESTMENT (BILLIONS OF U.S. DOLLARS)

	1975		1980		1985		1990		1998	
	Value	%	Value	%	Value	%	Value	%	Value	%
DMES[a]	185.3	75.1	373.5	77.5	538.0	73.2	1373.3	80.0	2690.1	67.0
Western Europe	100.6	40.8	200.3	41.6	244.8	33.3	758.7	44.2	1546.0	38.5
United States	27.7	11.2	83.0	17.2	184.6	25.1	394.9	23.0	811.8	20.2
Japan	1.5	0.6	3.3	0.7	4.7	0.6	9.9	0.6	26.1	0.7
Other	57.0	23.1	86.9	18.0	103.9	14.1	209.8	12.2	306.2	7.6
LDCs[b]	61.5	24.9	108.3	22.5	196.8	26.8	341.7	19.9	1241.0	30.9
Africa	16.5	6.7	20.8	4.3	27.0	3.7	41.6	2.4	84.4	2.1
Asia	13.0	5.3	38.0	7.9	91.8	12.5	175.9	10.2	741.3	18.5
Latin America and Caribbean	29.7	12.0	48.0	10.0	76.3	10.4	121.3	7.1	404.6	10.1
Other	2.3	0.0	1.5	0.3	1.7	0.2	2.9	0.2	10.7	0.3
Central and Eastern Europe	—		0.09	0.0	0.2	0.0	1.8	0.1	84.2	2.0
Total	246.8	100.0	481.9	100.0	734.9	100.0	1716.9	100.0	4015.3	100.0

[a]DMEs = developed market economies; [b]LDCs = less developed countries

Source: Centre on Transnational Corporations, *Transnational Corporations in World Development: Trends and Prospects* (New York: United Nations, 1988), Table 1.3, p. 25 (1975 figures); UNCTAD, *World Investment Report 1996* (New York: United Nations, 1996), Annex Table 3, pp. 239–243 (1980–90 figures); UNCTAD, *World Investment Report 2000* (New York: United Nations, 2000), pp. 294–299 (1998 figures).

Among the Third World countries, the most prosperous and resource-rich states received by far the most FDI. Thus, Table 10.4 shows that the share of FDI directed to Africa, which contains many of the LLDCs, declined from 6.7 percent in 1975 to only 3.7 percent in 1985. Asian and Latin American LDCs, by contrast, were receiving 12.5 and 10.4 percent of total inward FDI stocks in 1985 (the decline of the Latin American share from 12 percent in 1975 was partly due to the foreign debt crisis). Almost no FDI was directed to the Central and Eastern European socialist states (including the Soviet Union) from 1975 to 1985. By the mid-1980s most FDI was occurring among the developed market economies, and the LDCs had become increasingly marginalized.

The 1980s to the Present

The average annual growth rate of FDI rose in the 1980s to about 14 percent, the fastest growth rate since the late nineteenth century. Thus, Table 10.5 shows that inward and outward FDI as a share of the GDPs of the developed market economies increased dramatically, from 4.7 percent and 6.4 percent in 1980 to 12.1 percent and 16.4 percent in 1998. A number of factors account for the rapid growth of FDI since the early 1980s. Most important, with the reemergence of orthodox liberalism, many of the restrictions on international business were phased out. An end to restrictions on capital flows, along with deregulation and privatization in many developed countries and LDCs, gave MNCs more freedom to expand their activities. Furthermore, the shift of the emerging countries to market-oriented reforms after the breakup of the Soviet bloc opened up large new areas for FDI. Another factor in the expansion of FDI was the problems with international trade. The protracted GATT Uruguay round negotiations, combined with the use of nontariff measures, caused many MNCs to extend their activities abroad to circumvent these trade barriers. Finally, significant advances in information and transportation technologies enabled MNCs to extend their global network.[25]

A remarkable feature of FDI today is the degree to which the "Big Three"—the United States, the EU, and Japan—are directing their FDI to each other. U.S. firms have shown a strong preference for investing in Europe, intra-European investment has accelerated, and Japan and Western European countries have invested heavily in the United States. Until the late 1970s, Western European integration occurred largely through the expansion of trade, but in the 1980s the growth of intra-European FDI was more significant than the growth of trade. Table 10.6 shows that the nine largest host countries for FDI from 1985 to 1995 were also included among the largest home countries for FDI, and all but one of these nine (China) is an advanced industrial state.[26] The only important home country for FDI that is not also an important host country is Japan. Although Japan has eased some of its formal impediments to inward FDI, a number of informal barriers remain. As shown in Table 10.4, Japan accounted for only 0.7 percent of the total inward stocks of FDI in 1998—a strikingly small figure compared with the percentages for other G-7 countries.

Despite the continued predominance of developed countries in the outward and inward flows of FDI, several changes in the 1980s and 1990s are especially noteworthy. First, the United States lost its dominant position as a source of FDI. As

TABLE 10.5

SHARE OF INWARD AND OUTWARD FOREIGN DIRECT INVESTMENT STOCK AS A PERCENTAGE OF GROSS DOMESTIC PRODUCT

	1980	1985	1990	1995	1998
DMEs[a]					
Inward	4.7	6.1	8.3	8.8	12.1
Outward	6.4	7.5	9.8	11.7	16.4
United States					
Inward	3.1	4.6	7.1	7.6	9.5
Outward	8.1	6.2	7.8	9.9	11.5
Japan					
Inward	0.3	0.4	0.3	0.7	0.7
Outward	1.9	3.3	6.8	4.6	7.1
Germany					
Inward	4.0	5.3	6.8	6.9	9.3
Outward	4.7	8.6	9.2	11.1	17.3
Britain					
Inward	11.7	14.0	20.8	18.0	23.3
Outward	15.0	21.9	23.4	27.4	35.9
France					
Inward	3.4	6.4	7.2	9.4	11.7
Outward	3.6	7.1	9.2	12.0	15.9
Italy					
Inward	2.0	4.5	5.3	5.8	8.8
Outward	1.6	3.9	5.2	10.0	14.1
Canada					
Inward	20.6	18.6	19.7	21.5	23.9
Outward	9.0	12.4	14.8	20.6	26.9

[a]DMEs = developed market economies
Source: UNCTAD, *World investment Report 2000,* Annex Table B.6, pp. 319–320.

Table 10.3 shows, the U.S. share of outward stocks of FDI fell from 42.9 percent in 1980 to 24.1 percent in 1998. Second, there were erratic changes in Japan's share of FDI outflows. As Table 10.3 shows, Japan's share of outward FDI rose dramatically from 6.5 percent in 1985 to 12.2 percent in 1990. A strong Japanese yen as a result of the 1985 Plaza accord, combined with rising trade barriers such as voluntary export restraints on Japanese goods, forced Japanese corporations to invest and produce more abroad.[27] However, Table 10.3 shows that Japan's share of outward FDI returned to a lower level of 6.6 percent in 1998. The fall of Japan's FDI outflows resulted from persistent economic recession and the financial problems of major Japanese banks (see Chapter 11). These problems "led to changes in the corporate strategies of a number of Japanese . . . [MNCs] faced with a reduced ability to expand abroad."[28] Table 10.5 shows that Japan's outward FDI stock accounted for only 7.1 percent of its GDP in 1998, the lowest percentage of any country in the G-7.

TABLE 10.6

LEADING HOST ECONOMIES FOR FOREIGN DIRECT INVESTMENT (CUMULATIVE INFLOWS, 1985–95)[a]

Rank	Country	FDI (billions of dollars)
1	**United States**	477.5
2	**United Kingdom**	199.6
3	**France**	138.0
4	**China**	130.2
5	**Spain**	90.9
6	**Belgium-Luxembourg**	72.4
7	**Netherlands**	68.1
8	**Australia**	62.6
9	**Canada**	60.9
10	Mexico	44.1
11	**Singapore**	40.8
12	**Sweden**	37.7
13	**Italy**	36.3
14	Malaysia	30.7
15	**Germany**	25.9
16	**Switzerland**	25.2
17	Argentina	23.5
18	Brazil	20.3
19	**Hong Kong**	17.9
20	**Denmark**	15.7

[a]Economies in bold are also among the 20 leading home economies for FDI.
Source: World Trade Organization Annual Report 1996, Vol. 1, *Trade and Foreign Direct Investment*, p. 47, Table 4.1. Copyright © World Trade Organization 1996. By permission of the World Trade Organization.

A third significant change is that the developed market economy share of inward FDI has declined, and the LDC share has increased in recent years. Table 10.4 shows that the developed market economy share of inward FDI fell from 80 percent in 1990 to 67 percent in 1998, whereas the LDC share rose from 19.9 percent to 30.9 percent during the same period. Some Third World countries have emerged as important actors. Thus, Table 10.6 shows that a small group of rapidly growing Third World countries, including China, Mexico, Singapore, Malaysia, Argentina, Brazil, and Hong Kong, were included among the 20 leading host economies for FDI between 1985 and 1995. China's position is especially notable, because it now accounts for more than one-third of all FDI directed to the LDCs.[29] In contrast to the more prosperous LDCs, the LDCs in sub-Saharan Africa are becoming increasingly marginalized. Table 10.4 reveals that Africa accounted for only 2.1 percent of the inward stocks of FDI in 1998, compared with 18.5 percent for Asia and 10.1 percent for Latin America and the Caribbean.

A fourth development is the proliferation of firms engaging in FDI and the new forms of investment activity. Indeed, the number of MNCs headquartered in 15 major developed countries almost quadrupled between 1968 and 1993, from about 7,000 to 27,000. There has also been a marked shift in FDI from manufacturing and petroleum to service industries. Deregulation of the financial and telecommunications sectors in developed countries and privatization in some LDCs have stimulated this shift to services. New forms of FDI involving nonequity arrangements such as joint ventures, management contracts, technology licensing, and turnkey projects have also become more important. With these nonequity investments, firms provide certain benefits such as management skills or access to technology in return for royalties, fees, or revenue from sales.[30]

Although MNCs are having a growing impact on all states, they have a qualitatively different relationship with home and host states. The sections that follow therefore examine the interactions between home and host states separately. LDCs are normally host rather than home states for MNCs, so considerable discussion of host state-MNC relations is devoted to the LDCs. The discussion of home state-MNC relations is, by contrast, devoted mainly to the advanced industrial states.

MNCs AND HOST COUNTRY RELATIONS: THEORETICAL APPROACHES

Orthodox liberals had a highly positive view of foreign investment, which stemmed largely from liberal theories of trade. In accordance with the Heckscher-Ohlin theory (see Chapter 8), liberals assumed that countries have different factor endowments and that foreign investment flows to areas where it is most needed or in shortest supply. Thus, inward FDI provides external financing to compensate for inadequate amounts of local savings, export earnings, and foreign aid; tax revenues from MNC profits supplement local taxes; and managerial skills and technology are transferred. Orthodox liberals also viewed MNCs as performing an important role in altering traditional social attitudes and values, a change that was essential for modernization and development. Finally, some orthodox liberals posited the highly questionable assumption that MNCs operate in a perfectly competitive environment.[31]

The first major challenge to these orthodox liberal views came from two economists, Stephen Hymer and Charles Kindleberger. Hymer and Kindleberger argued that FDI cannot simply be equated with the movement of capital from the home to the host country. Instead, MNCs often get financing for FDI from other sources, including the borrowing of funds in the host country. Although FDI supporters espoused the benefits of free markets, Hymer and Kindleberger (and other writers such as Raymond Vernon) also argued that MNCs are oligopolistic by nature. An MNC lacks certain advantages that local firms possess, but it can gain competitiveness by creating an oligopolistic environment. This can be done by raising barriers to the entry of firms through the new technologies it uses, through its economies of scale, and through its privileged access to global finance. Thus, Hymer wrote that "the industries in which there is much foreign investment tend to be concentrated industries, while the industries in which there is little or no foreign investment tend to be unconcentrated."[32]

The strongest critics of the orthodox liberal perspective have been Marxists and dependency theorists. According to dependency theorists, MNCs prevent Third World states from achieving genuine autonomous development. For example, MNCs prevent local firms and entrepreneurs from participating in the most dynamic sectors of the economy, appropriate local capital rather than bringing in new capital from the outside, increase income inequalities in the host country, and use inappropriate capital-intensive technologies that contribute to unemployment. MNCs also undermine the host country's government, culture, and society by co-opting local business and government elites, imposing political and economic pressures on the host country (often with the help of the MNC's home country), and altering consumer tastes and attitudes.[33] Although the NIEs in Latin America and East Asia have moved along the path to industrialization, dependency theorists believe that MNCs prevent these states from achieving autonomous development. Thus, one study claims that MNCs in Brazil keep "the innovative side of their businesses as close to home as possible" and ensure that "the industrialization of the periphery will remain partial."[34]

Research over the years indicates that the effects of MNCs on host states are neither as positive nor as negative as orthodox liberal and dependency theorists maintain and that host countries often have more options than one would assume from dependency analysis. For example, one factor affecting a host state's options is the amount of competition among investors. If a host state has more investors to choose from, it has greater leverage vis-à-vis each investor. Although countries have become more dependent on investment in recent years, the sources of investment have become more diverse and numerous. As discussed, American MNCs are no longer as dominant as they were, and there are growing numbers of European, Japanese, and even Third World MNCs. Another factor affecting a host country's options is the "obsolescing bargain," which causes host state–MNC relations to change over time. Before an MNC enters a country, the host government is in a weak bargaining position because the MNC can pursue other options and the host state must provide significant incentives to attract the initial investment. The MNC's bargaining power stems from such factors as its sophisticated technology, brand name identification, access to capital, product diversity, and ability to promote exports. Thus, the initial investment agreement strongly favors the MNC. After the investment is made, however, the bargaining leverage shifts toward the host state because the MNC commits itself to immobile resources. The host state can treat these resources as a "hostage," and it gains bargaining, technological, and managerial skills through spinoffs from the foreign investment. As a result, the host state is likely to demand a renegotiation of the original bargain with the MNC and thereby gain more favorable terms.[35]

A number of studies indicate that the obsolescing bargain is more applicable in some cases than in others. For example, it is more likely to apply in projects that require large fixed investments. Such projects give foreign investors considerable leverage initially, but the large fixed investments can become hostage to the host government several years later. MNCs with smaller fixed investments, by contrast, can more easily threaten to withdraw from the host state. Another factor to consider is the type of technology an MNC uses for a project. Foreign investors using new and sophisticated technologies that are unavailable to the host state may be less vulnerable to aggressive host state policies at a later date. Yet another factor to consider is the importance of marketing, or product differentiation through advertising. When a firm's sales are determined to a large degree by brand identification and consumer loyalty, the firm is in a stronger position vis-à-vis the host authorities.[36]

These three factors—fixed investments, new technologies, and brand identification—have helped us predict whether a particular industry will be subject to the obsolescing bargain. For example, the obsolescing bargain is less applicable to more sophisticated manufacturing industries that are less dependent on resources in specific host states, rely on more advanced technologies, and manufacture differentiated products with brand names familiar to consumers. In contrast, the obsolescing bargain is more applicable to natural resource industries that involve large fixed investments and familiar technologies. LDCs can more easily demand a new bargain in these cases, and it is not surprising that LDC nationalizations in the past have been more common in natural resource industries. Studies of natural resource projects confirm that host states have often been successful in their demands for higher taxes, more processing of goods, joint marketing, and the employment of local people in management.[37]

Although an MNC's investment in a host state may be subject to uncertainties resulting from the obsolescing bargain, political unrest in the host state, and other factors, the MNC can follow a variety of strategies to offset these risks. One of the most important strategies open to large MNCs is vertical integration. By placing the various stages of production in different host states and maintaining control over the different stages, the MNC can decrease its vulnerability to the actions of particular host states. Another strategy is selecting local private partners for joint ventures or other types of arrangements. Evidence indicates that MNCs can often avoid strong pressures from a host state by establishing alliances with the local private sector. When an MNC becomes more firmly established in a host state, it can also build a political and economic base of support for itself by creating linkages with local suppliers, distributors, and consumers. One indication that MNCs have been successful in countering the risks of operating in host states is the fact that host country actions are often more circumscribed today than they were in the past. For example, there have been virtually no nationalizations of MNC affiliates in host states since the mid-1980s.

It is important to note that state-to-state interactions can have a significant effect on the bargaining relationship between host states and MNCs. Indeed, one analyst argues that "the traditional bargaining model of MNC-host developing country relations has become obsolete," and should be replaced with "a two-tier, multi-party bargaining process."[38] The first-tier bargaining occurs between governments of the host and home states bilaterally or through multilateral institutions. This tier has a major effect on the second-tier bargaining between MNCs and host states. For example, in recent years developed countries as home states have induced LDC host states to liberalize their policies toward FDI through bilateral investment agreements (discussed later in this chapter) and through conditions attached to IMF and World Bank structural adjustment loans. As a result of the first-tier bargaining, host states have been more amenable to MNC pressures and demands in the second-tier bargaining. In assessing the bargaining relationship between MNCs and host states, one must therefore also consider the role of other actors such as home states, international organizations, and NGOs.

CHANGES IN HOST COUNTRY POLICIES TOWARD MNCS

Host country policies toward MNCs have varied widely, ranging from nationalization of foreign investment operations on the one hand to efforts to attract MNCs through concessions and incentives on the other. Many governments welcome FDI in some sectors while limiting or blocking it in others (for example, in defense industries). Furthermore, governments often impose obligations such as performance requirements on MNCs to ensure that the host country benefits are maximized. Whereas some federal governments follow restrictive policies toward foreign investment, their subnational governments (for example, states or provinces) may at the same time be competing with one another to attract FDI.[39] Because there are extensive differences between host government policies in the South and the North, the following sections discuss these two groups separately.

The South

Before World War I, there were very few restrictions on MNCs in LDCs in the South. Colonial territories were of course open to foreign investment from the imperial powers, and countries that had gained their independence—for example, in Latin America—generally accepted the liberal view that foreign investment was necessary for their economic modernization and development. In the interwar period, some LDCs shifted to more nationalist policies. Russia's nationalization of its oil industry after the Russian Revolution in 1917 was an event that had a major impact on Third World attitudes. (*Nationalization* or *expropriation* refers to the forced takeover of FDI, with or without compensation.) Although confrontations with foreign oil companies followed in Iran, Argentina, Venezuela, and Bolivia, very few LDCs actually expropriated foreign assets. Nevertheless, Mexico nationalized most of its foreign oil industry in 1938 and avoided Western retaliation, partly because of the outbreak of World War II.

After World War II, the change to restrictive policies in the South was far more notable. In the most extreme instances, the spread of communism to China, North Korea, North Vietnam, and Cuba resulted in the nationalization of Western assets. In other parts of the South, many newly independent countries viewed limits on FDI as essential to their establishment of sovereignty. FDI often bred hostility because it involved foreign control over the LDCs' natural resources and public utilities and was often associated with the former colonial powers. Nevertheless, the ability of LDCs to pressure for a greater share of the benefits from FDI was limited because they lacked experience in dealing with MNCs, their sources of external finance were limited, and they were often preoccupied with security concerns. From 1946 to 1959, U.S. MNCs accounted for well over two-thirds of all new foreign-owned subsidiaries in the South, and LDCs had few alternative sources of FDI.[40]

In the 1960s and 1970s, several factors contributed to an increase in LDC leverage and activism vis-à-vis MNCs. The development of more non-U.S. MNCs gave the LDCs alternatives in seeking outside finance; LDCs gained more confidence and began to pressure MNCs to increase the benefits and reduce the costs of FDI; and

LDCs developed more managerial, administrative, and technical capabilities for regulating MNC behavior. As a result of increased LDC assertiveness, nationalization of foreign firms became widespread in the petroleum and mining industries in the late 1960s and early 1970s.[41] After OPEC succeeded in raising oil prices in 1973, LDCs also posed a major challenge to liberal-economic views of FDI in the UN. In the 1950s and 1960s, the liberal regime for FDI had emphasized national treatment, adequate compensation to MNCs for infringement of their rights and privileges, and the right of MNCs to seek support from their home countries. The LDCs instead pressured for agreements that would restrict the rights of MNCs, permit discrimination between national and multinational firms, and give host countries' legal institutions the authority to resolve investment disputes.

In the UN General Assembly, LDC views regarding MNCs were embodied in resolutions that the G-77 majority passed over the objections of many industrial states. For example, the 1974 Declaration on the Establishment of a New International Economic Order indicated that host states should unilaterally determine what rules to apply to MNCs operating in their territories. Although the G-77 was successful in winning approval for symbolic resolutions of this nature, it was unable to reach authoritative agreements acceptable to the advanced industrial states. For example, the G-77 failed in its efforts to reach a UN agreement on a comprehensive code of behavior for MNCs (see discussion later in this chapter).[42]

By the late 1970s, the LDCs shifted to more a conciliatory position toward MNCs, and the number of nationalizations declined for a number of reasons. First, the nationalization of large-scale petroleum and mining industries was largely completed by 1976. Second, the experience of many LDCs with nationalization of their natural resource industries was disappointing. Problems included declining productivity, failure to introduce new technologies, and continued dependence on MNCs for marketing their products. Third, the militancy of LDCs on foreign investment issues in the 1970s caused many MNCs to be reticent about investing in the Third World. MNCs often preferred to invest in more developed countries with natural resources, such as Australia, Canada, South Africa, and the United States. Finally, the 1979 oil price increase, followed by the world recession and the 1980s foreign debt crisis, led to severe cutbacks in commercial bank lending to LDCs. Third World fears about exploitation by MNCs were therefore largely replaced by concerns that their share of inward FDI was declining.[43]

A number of LDCs significantly liberalized their policies toward MNCs in the 1980s. Mexico, for example, unilaterally liberalized its policies toward FDI and participated in drafting the NAFTA provisions to free foreign investment activities. A number of other Latin American states, such as Argentina, Chile, Colombia, and Venezuela, also took unilateral steps to liberalize their investment policies. The most significant turnaround, however, was in the policies of the emerging CPEs, especially China. Although China was largely closed to FDI in the 1950s to 1970s, it passed laws in 1979, 1986, and 1988 that were more welcoming to FDI in some sectors, and it even granted foreign investors special treatment not available to domestic firms. MNCs that transfer advanced technology to China or export a substantial share of their output have received especially favorable treatment. Thus, China soon became the largest LDC host country for FDI.[44]

Although LDCs generally shifted to policies of welcoming FDI, some governments have imposed performance requirements on MNCs, such as local content and export requirements, and have pressured MNCs to enter into joint ventures with local firms. The East Asian NIEs, for example, have welcomed investment, but they have also attached a number of conditions to inward FDI. Nevertheless, even the East Asians are liberalizing their foreign investment policies as a result of the TRIMs agreement in the GATT Uruguay round and because of concerns that the industrial states may impose trade restrictions on host countries with performance requirements for foreign investors.

In the 1990s, LDC host government policies became even more open to FDI. Indeed, most governments including LDCs, developed countries, and emerging economies are seeking to attract FDI and to make their policies more favorable to investors in recognition of the fact that FDI is playing a larger and more important role in the global economy. Of the 1,035 changes in FDI laws of countries from 1991 to 1999, 974 were more favorable to FDI, and only 61 were less favorable to FDI. Most new measures by LDCs and emerging economies reduced sectoral restrictions to foreign entry or liberalized operations in industries that were previously closed or restricted to FDI. LDCs also offered additional incentives—mainly tax incentives—to promote investment in priority industries. Thus, Table 10.4 shows that the the LDC share of inward stocks of FDI rose from 19.9 percent in 1990 to 30.9 percent in 1998. FDI has become the largest source of external finance for LDCs, and during financial crises in recent years (see Chapter 11), LDCs have found FDI inflows to be more stable than bank lending and portfolio investment. Whereas access to bank lending and portfolio investment is influenced by investment ratings and short-term financial considerations, FDI responds more to underlying economic fundamentals.[45]

It is important to note that some of the poorest LDCs are finding it difficult to attract FDI even when they liberalize their investment policies. For example, most sub-Saharan African LDCs adopted policies to encourage FDI, partly under pressure from IMF and World Bank SAL programs. Nevertheless, low economic growth rates, civil conflicts, political crises, and high levels of indebtedness have had a depressing effect on their FDI inflows. As Table 10.4 shows, Africa's share of inward stocks of FDI declined from 6.7 percent in 1975 to 2.1 percent in 1998.[46]

The North

Developed country host states in the North are generally in a different position vis-à-vis MNCs than LDC host states in the South. Whereas MNCs in Third World countries have historically been involved in natural resource extraction and in lower technology manufacturing, investment in industrial states is usually based on higher technology production. MNCs also loom larger in LDC economies and create more dependence among LDCs than is the case for most industrial states. Furthermore, developed countries are often major home and well as host countries for FDI, so they are reluctant to restrict incoming foreign investment. Despite these differences, the policies toward incoming FDI have shifted over time in developed countries as well as LDCs.

In the nineteenth century, Western European countries, the United States, and Canada imposed very few controls over foreign-owned firms. This general openness to

MNCs resulted from the liberalism of the period, which was largely fostered by British hegemony. After World War I, Western European countries followed more open policies toward inward FDI than the United States, which restricted foreign ownership in a number of sectors, including banking, shipping, and petroleum. However, countries in Western Europe followed a "national champions" strategy in which they promoted the development of local enterprises in key sectors of the economy. At the end of World War II, the United States as the new global hegemon adopted more liberal policies toward FDI than Western Europe. The shift of European countries toward more restrictionist policies toward FDI was especially noticeable in the 1960s. At this time, Europeans were becoming more concerned that U.S. MNCs were contributing to the Americanization of the developed world. A French writer, Jean-Jacques Servan-Schreiber, expressed these concerns forcefully in his book *The American Challenge.*[47]

Servan-Schreiber attributed the American challenge to the dynamism of American society, and he called on Europe to respond by reforming its educational system, industrial policy, and social structure and by establishing its own MNCs. European governments responded partly by upgrading their policies of promoting national champions in key industries through subsidizing research, encouraging mergers, and increasing preferential procurement from national firms. However, European countries also responded to the American challenge by imposing specific requirements on foreign MNCs in such areas as job creation and export promotion. France in particular screened inward FDI carefully, and its rejection rate for FDI proposals in the late 1970s was much higher than elsewhere in Europe. When takeovers were proposed—even from other EC countries—the French government often tried to find a French buyer instead.

Canada also adopted a screening process in the 1970s because about 50 percent of its manufacturing output and about 70 percent of its oil production was foreign (that is, largely U.S.) controlled. As Table 10.5 shows, inward FDI accounted for 20.6 percent of Canada's GDP in 1980, compared with only 11.7 percent for Britain, 3.4 percent for France, 3.1 percent for the United States, and 0.3 percent for Japan. As early as the late 1950s, concerns about FDI contributed to increased Canadian nationalism, and a number of special commissions and task forces during the 1960s and early 1970s produced studies on the issue. The main concern was the high degree of Canadian dependence as a result of the extensive amount of U.S. foreign investment in the Canadian economy. In 1974 the Canadian government established the Foreign Investment Review Agency (FIRA) to determine whether foreign takeovers were of "significant benefit" to the country, and in 1980, Canada developed an interventionist National Energy Program (NEP) that was partly designed to increase Canadian ownership in the oil and gas industry. These policies produced significant tensions with the United States.[48]

Japan, however, had the most interventionist policy of the developed countries, and Table 10.4 shows that Japan's inward FDI accounted for only 0.7 percent of total inward FDI stocks in 1980, compared with 41.6 percent for Western Europe and 17.2 percent for the United States. Although this low level of inward investment resulted partly from the fact that Western MNCs were not prepared to adapt to the cultural and linguistic differences in Japan, there is no doubt that Japanese investment restrictions also played a critical role. Dating back to at least the sixteenth century, Japan's controls on international economic interactions resulted from its fear of foreign intervention and from national pride in its distinct economy, polity, and society. In the 1930s, Japan developed strategies aimed at extracting the benefits of foreign investment, such as access to capital and technology, while avoiding the drawbacks of foreign control. In the postwar period, Japan enacted its restrictive 1950 Foreign Investment Law, and it continued to impose restrictions on FDI inflows in the 1960s and 1970s.[49]

Although many developed countries restricted or imposed conditions on FDI in the 1970s, most of those countries liberalized their policies and shifted emphasis toward attracting FDI in the mid-to-late 1980s. Several major factors accounted for this change in policy. First, the phasing out of controls on global capital flows and the reemergence of orthodox liberalism under the leadership of U.S. President Ronald Reagan and British Prime Minister Margaret Thatcher caused countries to question the legitimacy of imposing FDI restrictions. Second, the increase in global competitiveness, along with economic problems such as unemployment in the developed countries, generated pressures on states to seek rather than restrict incoming FDI. The average unemployment rate in OECD countries rose from 3.3 percent in 1973 to 8.6 percent in 1983; thus, these countries placed considerable value on the jobs FDI could provide. Industrial states began to view inward FDI as an opportunity to enhance their international competitiveness, and they provided a range of financial incentives and tax concessions to attract MNCs.[50]

A third factor in the shift toward more open FDI policies was the changing position of the Western European states and Japan. As the position of these countries in the global economy became stronger vis-à-vis the United States, they felt pressures to ease their restrictions on incoming FDI. Traditionally, the EC was unwilling to support international rules on investment, and it was ambivalent about a 1981 U.S. proposal that GATT should compile an inventory of trade-related investment measures in host countries. However, the EC shifted to a position favoring greater discipline over host countries and supported the U.S. position at the TRIMs negotiations in the GATT Uruguay round. This change resulted largely from the fact that European MNCs greatly increased their outward investment in the 1980s. Because much of this investment was directed to the United States, European firms wanted to encourage the United States to retain its liberal policy on incoming FDI.[51]

As the disparity between Japan's growing outward investment and its restrictions on inward investment became increasingly evident, it also felt pressured to ease its inward restrictions on FDI, and Japan had removed most of its legal obstacles to inward FDI by the 1980s. Intangible barriers to entry, however, continue to limit the role of foreign firms in the Japanese economy. Foreign M&As are less common in Japan because a large percentage of the stock of Japanese firms is held either by shareholders that have close linkages with the firms' management or by members of *keiretsus* (groups with extensive cross-shareholdings). For example, of the 584 M&As involving Japan in 1992, 165 were Japanese firms acquiring other Japanese firms, 165 were Japanese firms acquiring foreign firms, and only 32 were foreign firms acquiring Japanese firms. Because M&As are so difficult, inward FDI in Japan has usually occurred through greenfield investments or joint ventures. However, it is difficult to develop new FDI production projects because of the high cost and complexities of doing business in Japan, the exclusionary business practices of the *keiretsu,* the complex distribution systems, the bureaucratic practices that discriminate against foreign firms, and the high cost of land. There is some evidence that the situation is changing, because the Japanese government is adopting policies to encourage greater openness, and foreign takeovers of Japanese firms are increasing. Nevertheless, Table 10.5 shows that inward FDI accounted for only 0.7 percent of Japan's GDP in 1998.[52]

A fourth reason for the shift toward more open investment policies is related to the pressures imposed on others by the United States. These pressures were felt most strongly in the United States' two neighboring countries, Canada and Mexico. For example, strong U.S. protests and a U.S. challenge in GATT were major factors explaining the Canadian Liberal government's decision to loosen the controls on inward FDI it had instituted through the FIRA and NEP. (Canada was also concerned about a decline in inward foreign investment at the time.) The Progressive Conservative government of Brian Mulroney, which was elected in 1984, then rescinded the NEP and replaced the FIRA with a new institution called Investment Canada. Unlike the FIRA, Investment Canada was far more involved with encouraging inward FDI than with reviewing it. Subsequently, the CUSFTA and NAFTA led to a further liberalization of Canadian (and Mexican) foreign investment regulations. It is important to note that Canada's position on inward FDI changed, not only because of U.S. pressure, but also because Canada (like the EC and Japan) was becoming a more important *source* of FDI. A growing segment of Canadian business interests believed that investment rules were necessary to protect their FDI abroad and that opening Canada to inward FDI was a necessary trade-off. As Table 10.5 shows, in 1998 outward FDI accounted for a higher percentage of Canada's GDP (26.9 percent) than inward FDI (23.9 percent).[53]

The United States was the main advocate of liberalized foreign investment policies and was highly critical of host government interventionism in the 1970s and the early 1980s. It is therefore ironic that the United States was the only major developed country that shifted somewhat toward more restrictive policies in the 1980s. This policy shift resulted largely from the relative decline of U.S. economic hegemony and from the increased U.S. role as a host as well as a home country for FDI. Table 10.5 shows that inward FDI accounted for only 3.1 percent of U.S. GDP in 1980, and 4.6 percent in 1985. However, FDI into the United States surged after 1986, and Table 10.5 shows that by 1990 inward FDI accounted for 7.1 percent of U.S. GDP. Some congressional leaders were concerned that foreign investors (especially Japanese investors) were acquiring U.S.-owned high technology firms and that the U.S. military was becoming too dependent on foreign-controlled suppliers. As a result, U.S. policies began to shift toward greater interventionism.

The more interventionist approach in the U.S. Congress was evident in a number of proposed and actual legislative changes. The most important was the Exon-Florio Amendment to the 1988 Omnibus Trade and Competitiveness Act, sponsored by Senator James Exon (D–Nebraska) and Representative James Florio (D–New Jersey). This amendment enables the president to block foreign mergers or acquisitions of U.S. firms when there is a possible danger to national security. The authority for implementing Exon-Florio rests with an interagency Committee on Foreign Investment in the United States (CFIUS), which was created as an oversight body in 1975. Some more extreme proposed measures were not actually passed in the U.S. Congress, and the Exon-Florio amendment represents a compromise between internationalist interests of the executive branch and more nationalist pressures in the Congress. The

CFIUS and U.S. presidents to this point have implemented the Exon-Florio amendment with considerable moderation. For example, during an active period of inward FDI from 1988 to 1992, CFIUS received 700 cases it judged worthy of review. However, it subjected only 13 of these cases to a 45-day extended review and referred only 9 of them to the president for a final decision. The president took action on only 1 of these 9 cases. Nevertheless, an administration wishing to limit inward FDI in the future could do so by liberally interpreting the national security clause in Exon-Florio. Despite the Exon-Florio amendment, the United States continues to strongly support a liberalized foreign investment regime in international forums. For example, the United States was the main force behind the TRIMs negotiations in the GATT Uruguay round, and behind negotiations for a MAI in the OECD.[54]

THE RELATIONSHIP BETWEEN HOME COUNTRIES AND THEIR MNCs

The number of major home countries for MNCs has always been surprisingly small. At least 80 percent of FDI before World War I originated in Western Europe, and Britain accounted for by far the largest share. Between World War I and 1980, only three developed countries accounted for 65 percent to 75 percent of the outward FDI stock—the United States, Britain, and the Netherlands. Although the sources of FDI became more diverse after 1980, six developed countries accounted for about 75 percent of the total in the early 1990s—the United States, Britain, Germany, France, Japan, and the Netherlands. Some LDCs, such as the East Asian and Latin American NIEs, have become more important as sources of FDI. Thus, outward FDI from LDCs increased from $4.8 billion in 1980 to $108.4 billion in 1993, and from about 3 percent of total outward FDI in the early 1980s to 9 percent in 1999. Nevertheless, Table 10.3 shows that the developed countries still accounted for 89.8 percent of outward FDI stock in 1998.[55] This discussion of FDI–home country relations therefore focuses mainly on the advanced industrial states.

The effects of FDI on the home country depend on both the characteristics of the home country and the characteristics of its MNCs. Realists often focus on the home country's characteristics, differentiating between rising and declining hegemons. When Britain and the United States first emerged as hegemons in the nineteenth and twentieth centuries, outward FDI seemed to have numerous benefits and virtually no costs to the home country because no powerful domestic groups viewed it as hurting their interests. As a hegemonic state declines, however, some important domestic groups begin to perceive outward FDI as having detrimental effects. In the United States, for example, domestic labor groups experienced rising unemployment in the 1970s, and they began to argue that U.S. FDI was exporting jobs and adversely affecting their interests.[56]

Whereas some theorists focus on the home state's characteristics, others devote more attention to the MNC's characteristics as the source of changing MNC–home state relations. Those who focus on the MNC often present evidence that a growing number of MNCs are becoming "denationalized" or "stateless" and are developing interests that increasingly diverge from the interests of their home countries. American oil companies, for example, became less closely identified with the U.S. national interest after the 1973 energy crisis, when they were accused of aiding the Arab oil embargo, and European oil companies refused to give their home markets preferential deliveries during the embargo, despite the requests of the home governments. In recent years, studies indicate that increasingly mobile capital is limiting the ability of home as well as host states to affect the behavior and activities of MNCs.

Whether policymakers focus primarily on the characteristics of the nation-state or the MNC as a causal factor, the fact remains that questions about the costs as well as benefits of FDI to home countries have increased in recent years. In this section we begin with a discussion of home country policies toward their MNCs. We then examine two contentious questions in regard to home country–MNC relations: (1) What are the costs and benefits of FDI for labor groups in the home country? and (2) What is the relationship between the competitiveness of a home country and the competitiveness of its MNCs?

Home Country Policies Toward Their MNCs

Although government policies toward outward FDI have been less extensive than those toward inward FDI, it is possible to identify a range of home country policies. Home governments normally view outward FDI as an indication of economic and political strength, and as beneficial to their competitiveness. Thus, home governments usually give their MNCs favored treatment and try to protect them from hostile actions by foreigners, particularly when the MNCs operate in strategic industries. On some occasions, however, home governments attempt to monitor, control, or even restrain outward FDI in the interests of the home economy. For example, home governments sometimes view their MNCs as tools of foreign policy and are willing to coerce them if necessary to affect their behavior. Furthermore, home governments sometimes associate outward FDI with a decrease in home country exports, a decline in the country's industrial base, and losses in domestic employment. In such circumstances, home countries may attempt to stem the flow of outward FDI.

The Pre–World War II Period   In the nineteenth and early twentieth centuries, home countries adopted policies to support their corporations and protect them when they encountered difficulties abroad. For example, European states sometimes intervened militarily in the colonial period to ensure that their trading and producing companies could develop and prosper. Furthermore, home governments in Europe provided subsidies and other types of assistance in the interwar years to support airlines, shipping firms, and oil companies, which they viewed as being closely tied to their strategic interests. In the 1930s, the Japanese army occupied Chinese plants and gave Japanese companies control over their management. The United States was also willing to support the interests of its companies in Latin America with military force, but the use of military force was not automatic. On certain occasions, governments took actions to limit outward FDI. For example, after the Nazis came to power the German government had to approve all new FDI, and it was willing to approve investments only in exceptional cases. Although U.S. officials expressed concerns as early as the 1920s that outward FDI could transfer technology and export employment to foreign countries, the U.S. government adopted no policies to restrict FDI outflows in the pre–World War II period.[57]

The Early Postwar Period   In the 1950s to 1970s, the United States as hegemonic power followed assertive policies in protecting its MNCs and in pressuring them for political and economic reasons. For example, the U.S. Congress responded to corporate lobbying by passing the Hickenlooper Amendment in 1962, which threatened to withhold development assistance from LDCs that nationalized affiliates of U.S. MNCs without providing adequate compensation. The United States also considered its MNCs to be tools of foreign policy vis-à-vis certain communist countries. For example, the U.S. government used its Trading with the Enemy Act and Foreign Assets Control Legislation in the 1960s and 1970s to limit the trade of U.S. subsidiaries with China, Cuba, North Vietnam, and North Korea. Host governments for U.S. subsidiaries in Canada, Europe, and Latin America viewed these policies as an infringement on their sovereignty, and they often adopted laws to counter the U.S. legislation.[58] The United States also took actions to control corporate behavior in response to its growing balance-of-payments deficit. In the 1960s, for example, the U.S. government called on its MNCs to limit the outflow of capital to their foreign affiliates, and in the 1970s, the government created the Domestic International Sales Corporation (DISC) program, which provided tax incentives to MNCs to encourage them to export from the United States rather than from abroad.

Most European governments recovering from World War II were concerned that outward FDI would adversely affect their balance of payments. However, they did little to either encourage or restrict outward FDI in the 1950s and 1960s. Japan was the only major economy that systematically restricted outward FDI for about two decades after World War II. In its efforts to keep scarce capital at home for postwar reconstruction, the Japanese government scrutinized every possible FDI project and approved only those that would increase exports, provide access to necessary raw materials, and pose no threat to Japanese producers. Thus, Table 10.3 shows that Japan accounted for only 0.7 percent outward stocks of FDI in 1960 and 1.4 percent in 1967. Japan did not begin to liberalize its controls on outward FDI until the late 1960s, when its balance-of-trade surpluses were rapidly increasing.[59]

The 1980s and 1990s   Although U.S. actions to limit dealings with communist countries became less frequent with the decline of the Cold War, they sometimes resurfaced in response to international events and domestic political pressures. In the early 1980s, for example, Western Europe and the Soviet Union agreed to construct a natural gas pipeline, in which Western European firms were to provide equipment needed for the pipeline's construction in return for future deliveries of Soviet natural gas. After Poland declared martial law in December 1981, the United States retaliated against the Soviet Union by imposing an embargo on materials produced by U.S. companies that were destined for use in constructing the pipeline. The United States not only prohibited subsidiaries of U.S. MNCs from exporting foreign-produced equipment and technology to the Soviet Union but also ordered foreign companies not to export goods produced with technology acquired under licensing agreements with U.S. companies. The Reagan administration's opposition to the pipeline stemmed from concerns that Western Europe would become overly dependent on Soviet gas supplies, and that the gas exports would provide the Soviet Union with hard currency receipts needed to strengthen its economy.

However, planning for the pipeline was already at an advanced stage when the Reagan administration tried to impede the project, and Europeans argued that the U.S. actions represented a new level of extraterritorial interference. Britain, France, West Germany, and Italy reacted harshly by ordering their resident companies to ignore the U.S. restrictions and provide the needed goods and technology to the Soviet Union. A number of companies, such as Dresser-France (a U.S. subsidiary) and licensees of General Electric in Britain, Italy, and West Germany, complied with the European counterorders. Initially, the United States retaliated by imposing penalties against these companies. However, when it became evident that the Europeans would not back down, the Reagan administration decided to remove most of its sanctions on the supply of equipment for the Siberian gas pipeline in November 1982, and the European sales proceeded.[60] Since the breakup of the Soviet Union, U.S. extraterritorial actions of this nature have been aimed mainly at Cuba. The controversial 1996 Helms-Burton Act is a prime example. This legislation penalizes *foreign* companies for doing business in Cuba if they use assets or property of U.S. MNCs (or individuals) that was nationalized after the 1959 Cuban Revolution. Affected foreign governments reacted angrily to this legislation and indicated that their resident companies would not abide by it.[61]

Other home countries have been far less inclined (and less able) than the United States to take such blatant political actions to control the behavior of their MNCs. In *economic* areas, however, Japan and the Western European countries have been more willing than the United States to establish close linkages with their MNCs to achieve common purposes. Indeed, the United States has been more inclined than other industrial states to maintain an arm's length relationship between business and the government (the U.S. defense and oil industries have been exceptions).[62] A number of realists have argued that the United States should develop its own industrial policy to support its MNCs and counter the policies of Japan and Europe, especially in high-technology areas. Such a policy would involve the establishment of institutional mechanisms to assess competitive trends in high-technology industries, along with a shift of federal R&D funds from military uses to dual-use and economic areas.[63] The United States has pursued some limited industrial policy initiatives, but certainly not to the same extent as Japan and some European countries. The adoption of industrial policy measures poses a realist challenge to liberal support for dependence on the market and on firms that are the lowest cost suppliers, regardless of their nationality.

The Effects of MNCs on Labor Groups in Home Countries

The effects of MNCs on labor groups is one of the most contentious issues in home countries. Liberal supporters of multinational activity often argue that the impact on labor groups is generally positive. Thus, they present evidence to demonstrate that MNCs have a better record than domestic firms with regard to job creation, export performance, and technological innovations in the home country. Liberals can also point to some studies showing that MNCs pay higher wages than domestic firms, although the results of these studies are inconclusive if other factors (such as size of the firm and training of the workers) are controlled.[64] Many labor groups, however, are unconvinced by this evidence, and labor dissatisfaction with outward FDI has taken a variety of forms in different countries. For example, labor groups in the United States have been especially concerned about the employment effects of outward FDI, whereas British trade unions have focused more on the possible weakening of labor's position in industrial relations.

In the view of many labor groups (and historical structuralists), the mobility of capital and MNCs puts immobile workers at a distinct disadvantage. Whereas MNCs can increase their flexibility and competitiveness by extending production to many countries, labor unions are largely limited to organizing themselves on a national or even local basis. Labor groups are particularly concerned that the transfer of MNC activities to subsidiaries in LDCs with lower wages and standards will produce a deterioration of working conditions in the home country. The geographical fragmentation of production by MNCs in different industrial states can also put labor at a disadvantage because of labor's difficulty in organizing on a multicountry basis.[65]

In the 1970s, when the United States was largely a home country for MNCs, organized labor began to strongly oppose outward FDI. U.S. union leaders called for restraints on outward investment, tax incentives to encourage U.S. MNCs to produce at home for export rather than producing abroad, and adjustment assistance for workers.[66] In 1971, for example, the AFL-CIO supported the ill-fated Burke-Hartke Bill, which would have ended the tax credit MNCs received for foreign income taxes and given the president authority to block new outward FDI. American labor's opposition to NAFTA is also based largely on concerns that U.S. MNCs will shift their operations to Mexico. Although NAFTA includes side agreements to deal with concerns about the lowering of labor and environmental standards, it is generally conceded that the side agreements provide little enforcement capability. Thus, organized labor in the United States has strongly opposed any moves to extend NAFTA to other countries.[67]

Beyond the national level, labor unions have been interested in developing a system of multinational collective bargaining since the early 1970s. The goal is to increase the ability of unions from different countries to bargain together with MNCs. Some of the initiatives international unions are taking to achieve this objective include holding world congresses of workers from the same MNC and putting all of an MNC's collective agreements into a single database to increase awareness of arrangements in different plants. It is evident, however, that multilateral collective bargaining has definite limitations. Even in the EU region, unions continue to be dominated by national structures. Furthermore, the NAFTA experience demonstrates that labor in developed country home states such as the United States, may have very different perspectives from labor in LDC host states such as Mexico.[68]

Competitiveness and Home Country–MNC Relations

As a growing number of MNCs have organized their operations on a global level, questions have arisen as to whether MNCs have worldwide interests that differ fundamentally from the interests of their home countries. Robert Reich has suggested that residents of a nation-state today must ask, "Who is *us*?" Does *us* include our MNCs?[69]

Phrased another way, is the competitiveness of a nation-state today closely linked with the competitiveness of its MNCs? This question has pitted a number of realists against liberals. Realists argue that the nationality of a state's firms and the amount of foreign ownership can have a major impact on the state's competitiveness. From this perspective, "a nation's standard of living in the long term depends on its ability to attain a high and rising level of productivity in the industries in which its firms compete."[70] Thus, some realists argue that a country such as Canada has a good standard of living but can never have the best because of the high degree of foreign ownership in its manufacturing industry. The best jobs, and most of the R&D, are usually located in the home country rather than in the host country.[71]

Liberals, by contrast, often argue that MNCs now seek profitable opportunities around the world and that "they are becoming disconnected from their home nations."[72] The competitiveness of a nation-state, from this perspective, is no longer closely linked with the competitiveness of its MNCs. Thus, liberals maintain that the economic future of the United States depends more on the education and skills of American workers than it does on U.S. corporate ownership. If Americans have the requisite technical training, foreign as well as U.S.-owned corporations will employ American workers in growing numbers. Some liberals go even further and assert that we are entering a "borderless world" in which the nationality of most corporations will no longer make a difference.[73] The position an analyst takes on either side of this competitiveness debate obviously affects his or her prescriptions for policymaking. Thus, realists argue that governments should pursue active industrial policies to promote their own MNCs in high-technology areas. Interventionist liberals, by contrast, believe that a government's policy should focus more on upgrading the technological skills and sophistication of the working population than on helping its own MNCs. In other words, governments must make their countries attractive so that global firms—regardless of their nationality—will want to do business, invest, and pay taxes there.[74]

Some evidence indicates that large MNCs are in fact becoming more global in their operations and outlook and less closely tied to their home countries. For example, the sales of foreign affiliates of U.S. firms were about four times greater than the total exports of goods from the United States between 1988 and 1990; foreign affiliates of U.S. MNCs accounted for 43 percent of their parent companies' total profits in 1990; and U.S. firms increased their foreign R&D spending by 33 percent from 1986 to 1988, whereas their R&D spending in the United States increased by only 6 percent. Furthermore, national boundaries are becoming blurred as some MNCs have spread their head office functions and listed their shares in stock exchanges in several countries. For example, Shell and Unilever have headquarters in different countries (Britain and the Netherlands), and Astra-Zeneca has its corporate headquarters in one country and conducts most of its R&D in another country. Another example of an MNC that has blurred national boundaries is Asea Brown Boveri (ABB), which was formed from a merger of Sweden's ASEA with Switzerland's Brown Boveri. ABB moved its headquarters from Stockholm to Zurich, which is more centrally located vis-à-vis major European markets. Although the managers of ABB are Swiss, German, and Swedish, the company does its business in English, and keeps its books in dollars.

The increase of cross-border M&As and conglomerate cross-holding of shares are additional complications in defining the nationality of MNCs today. Furthermore, the growth of integrated production systems makes it more difficult to determine where a product comes from. MNCs can insulate themselves from national policies and conditions by sourcing inputs, information, and personnel from around the world. Thus, an automobile manufactured by Ford may be assembled in Britain from inputs coming from all over Europe or elsewhere, from designs produced in the United States and Europe, and from stages of processing in many different locations. Thus, liberals argue that policies of home governments must change as the national origins, loyalties, and culture of some MNCs become increasingly blurred. In this age of globalization, the highest priority should be "to provide competitive conditions for businesses in general in the country rather than only for the country's firms in particular."[75]

Despite the blurring of nationalities, realists are correct when they argue that *most* MNCs continue to be home-country based and that the competitiveness of an MNC can affect the competitiveness of its home state. A major factor in promoting competitiveness is R&D, and there is evidence that MNCs in industrial countries keep much of their basic R&D activity at home. In 1984, for example, the ratio of R&D to sales for industrial machinery and equipment firms in Canada was only about 40 percent of the ratio in the United States, and much of this difference resulted from the high degree of foreign ownership in the Canadian industry. Although American MNCs are more willing than Japanese MNCs to invest in R&D abroad, even U.S. companies spent only 8.6 percent of their R&D funding in foreign countries in 1988.[76] R&D funding is also essential for the development of new technologies, and ownership and control of technologically sophisticated industries can have significance for a country's long-term national security. Another factor in a country's competitiveness is its ability to maintain a favorable trade balance, and there is evidence that U.S. affiliates of Japanese firms have a higher propensity than American firms to import goods and services into the United States.[77]

Although the competitiveness of a state can be tied to the competitiveness of its firms, it is important to note that there are important national differences in the operation of MNCs headquartered in different countries. For example, there is some evidence that U.S. MNCs favor their home country less than Japanese and German MNCs. Studies have shown that U.S. MNCs are more interested in the financial returns on investments, whereas Japanese MNCs place more emphasis on market share; U.S. MNCs are more willing to invest in overseas R&D activities than their Japanese counterparts; and German and Japanese MNCs place more emphasis on exporting from the home country than U.S. MNCs. Thus, Reich's question as to whether "our MNCs" look after "our national interests" may be more relevant for U.S. MNCs than for Japanese and German MNCs.[78]

Some liberal theorists argue that the term *competitiveness* has more meaning when applied to MNCs than to nation-states. A corporation may go out of business if it is not competitive, but countries normally continue to exist. Furthermore, companies such as Coca-Cola and Pepsi Co. are rivals involved in a zero-sum game, whereas the advanced industrial countries are each other's major trading partners even when they are in competition. International trade is not a zero-sum game; a prosperous European economy provides U.S. exporters with larger markets and offers U.S. consumers higher quality goods at lower prices than a weaker economy would.[79] A number of economists, however, present counterarguments to demonstrate that in an age of globalization, competitiveness is as much of a concern for states as it is for MNCs.[80]

A Regime for FDI: What Is to Be Regulated?

Although MNCs have an increasingly important role in the global economy, the principles, norms, and rules regulating MNCs and FDI are far more rudimentary than those regulating many other areas, such as global trade and monetary relations. Furthermore, no international organization has a role in a "foreign investment regime" comparable with that of the WTO in the global trade regime. Most government policies related to MNCs are formulated at the national level, but the transnational nature of MNCs makes these policies inadequate. Nevertheless, there has been little consensus regarding what a foreign investment regime should be regulating—the MNC, the host state, or the home state. The prominent role of private actors (MNCs, multinational banks, etc.) as sources of investment capital also makes international regulation a difficult and contentious issue.

According to orthodox liberals, investment agreements should be mainly concerned with regulating host state behavior so the investors can function freely in the global marketplace. Thus, there should be maximum protection for MNCs and FDI against nationalization, performance requirements, and other impediments. Home countries should have the right to intervene on behalf of their MNCs, in the orthodox liberal view, if the purpose is to counter host government actions that inhibit free investment flows. Realists and historical structuralists, by contrast, see some government limitations on foreign investment as legitimate. From a realist perspective, states will understandably want to ensure that MNC activity does not conflict with their national interest or national security. From a historical structuralist perspective, investment agreements should be mainly concerned with regulating MNCs and with protecting host governments. Because investors can easily move their assets across international borders, labor in both host and home countries is at a distinct disadvantage. Third World host countries are also in a particularly dependent position vis-à-vis MNCs, and they require special protection. Thus, international rules are required to limit the power of MNCs and the major home governments that provide them with support.

In the 1950s and 1960s, the United States as global hegemon provided much of the regulatory activity in the foreign investment area. American policy during this period was mainly aimed at protecting FDI flows against hostile actions of host states (such as nationalization) and ensuring that MNC behavior did not conflict with U.S. and Western objectives in the Cold War. European countries also began concluding *bilateral investment treaties* (BITs) in the 1960s, which provided some protection for their investments in LDCs (BITs are discussed later in this chapter). In the 1970s, attention shifted to developing an international regulatory framework for FDI, and several economists proposed that "a General Agreement for the International Corporation" be established, similar to GATT.[81] A number of developments in the 1970s contributed to sentiments that an international framework was needed primarily to regulate the behavior of MNCs. For example, MNCs engaged in currency speculation when the Bretton Woods pegged exchange rate regime was faltering; some industrial states such as France and Canada became concerned about the influence of U.S. MNCs and established mechanisms to screen foreign investment; and LDCs pressured for the international regulation of MNCs as part of their demands for a

NIEO.[82] A number of scholars supported these policy changes and expressed anti-MNC sentiments in the 1970s. For example, one noted writer on foreign investment argued that the MNC is "not accountable to any public authority that matches it in geographical reach" and that "global corporations must be regulated to restore sovereignty to government."[83]

Despite the widespread sentiments in the 1970s to exert some control over MNC behavior, the main initiatives in this direction came from the LDCs. Arguing that the customary rules of international law regarding foreign investment did not take sufficient account of Third World needs and interests, the G-77 pressured for UN resolutions aimed at regulating MNCs rather than host states. As a result of this LDC activism, the UN Economic and Social Committee set up a Commission on Transnational Corporations in 1974 with a mandate to develop a binding Code of Conduct for MNCs. Third World countries also engaged in a series of nationalizations in the 1960s and early 1970s, and the LDCs in OPEC posed a threat to the international oil companies when they sought to gain greater control over oil pricing and production. To counter these developments, the OECD ministers at the urging of the U.S. government decided to develop their own policy on MNCs, which sought to achieve a greater balance than the UN in recognizing the responsibilities of host states as well as MNCs.[84] Thus, the OECD adopted a Declaration and Decisions on International Investment and Multinational Enterprises in 1976 that included some guidelines for MNC behavior, but also sought to improve the foreign investment climate in host states.[85]

By the late 1970s, it was evident that the OECD states would not agree to LDC demands for a UN Code of Conduct for MNCs, and several factors contributed to a shift of the pendulum back to emphasis on controlling the behavior of host states. Most significantly, the LDC share of inward FDI was declining because of the foreign debt crisis, concerns about LDC political and economic stability, and the emphasis on high-technology investment in the developed countries. As the needs of LDCs for capital inflows increased, they gradually abandoned their interventionist policies toward MNCs. The increased bargaining power of the developed countries enabled them to begin forging a "consensus" in the 1980s that a stronger regime was necessary to facilitate increased flows of FDI and that the behavior of host countries—not MNCs—was in need of regulation. Although BITs had been the predominant source of foreign investment rules, the feeling grew stronger in the 1980s that multilateral rules were required.

BILATERAL INVESTMENT TREATIES

Countries have been concluding bilateral treaties specifically to promote and protect foreign investment for more than 40 years. Known generically as BITs, these treaties impose obligations on the contracting parties with regard to the treatment of foreign investment and provide dispute resolution mechanisms to enforce these obligations. It is important to note, however, that BITs were not the first bilateral treaties to provide protection for foreign investment. As early as the late eighteenth century, the United

States, and to a lesser extent Japan and a few Western European countries, concluded a series of Friendship, Commerce, and Navigation (FCN) treaties; Treaties of Establishment; and Treaties of Amity and Commerce. Unlike the BITs in the post–World War II period, these treaties dealt with many issues such as trade, maritime, and consular relations. However, these treaties also included property protection provisions related to investment, such as restrictions on a host country's right of expropriation. Another difference is that the postwar BITs have been concluded mainly between developed countries and LDCs, whereas the FCN treaties were also concluded between developed countries. A significant number of these FCN treaties remain in force today.[86]

After World War II, bilateral trade agreements became less significant because of the establishment of the multilateral trade regime under the GATT. Thus, investment protection became the main purpose of the BITs. In 1959 the Federal Republic of Germany negotiated the first two BITs, with Pakistan and the Dominican Republic. However, most of the BITs in the 1960s were concluded between Western European and African countries. Other major developed countries, including the United States and Japan, soon joined Western Europe in concluding BITs with the LDCs. It is interesting that the negotiation of BITs increased dramatically during the 1970s. Although LDCs were actively calling for an NIEO in the 1970s, this did not prevent them from concluding BITs that contained provisions they were actively opposing in the UN. The LDCs wanted to alter various international principles and legal norms as they applied to foreign investment, but they were prepared to participate in BITs for pragmatic reasons to attract FDI. Some CEECs, such as Romania and Yugoslavia, also signed their first BITs with the industrial states during the 1970s.

As discussed in Chapter 7, LDCs depended heavily on external loan financing by private banks for their development needs in the 1970s. However, the onset of the foreign debt crisis in 1982 resulted in a sharp reduction in commercial bank exposure, and the LDC debtor countries therefore became highly dependent on foreign investment for development finance. As a result, many LDCs and emerging CPEs concluded their first BITs in the 1980s. For example, China joined in a BIT for the first time in 1982; by the end of the 1980s China had concluded 25 BITs. The total number of BITs signed increased from 167 at the end of the 1970s to 386 at the end of the 1980s. The number of BITs increased even more rapidly in the 1990s, partly because LDC requirements for foreign investment increased as a result of a steady decline in developed country foreign aid. Thus, by the end of 1996 there were 1,332 BITs in existence. Although the predominant number of these BITs continue to be between developed countries and LDCs, there was also a rapid increase in the 1990s of BITs concluded between LDCs, usually from within the same region; this pointed to a change in status of some LDCs from being exclusively host countries to being home as well as host countries for FDI.

The BITs generally uphold the MFN treatment and national treatment principles, under which an MNC is assured of treatment at least as favorable as that granted to domestic firms or to MNCs from Third World countries. These treaties also often prohibit host country performance requirements that commit MNCs to export goods produced in the host country or to purchase goods and services locally. Furthermore, the BITs require payment of prompt and adequate compensation in the event of nationalization. From a Third World perspective, these BITs are very one-sided because they impose "obligations on the host state for the protection of foreign investment, without any corresponding obligations on the part of the home country or the foreign investor."[87] The industrial states also view the BITs as inadequate, but for very different reasons. They are particularly concerned that variation in their terms seriously limits the effectiveness of these bilateral agreements in international law.

Because LDCs and developed countries are both dissatisfied with BITs, the question arises as to why they have been, and continue to be, so important. From a developed country perspective, BITs have provided a "second best solution in the absence of a universal investment agreement."[88] Other than certain RTAs such as NAFTA, BITs continue to be the best means for regulating the treatment of foreign investors by LDC host countries. From an LDC host country perspective, joining in BITs with developed countries is necessary if they want to attract FDI. With the foreign debt crisis and the decline in foreign aid, LDC ideological views against BITs gave way to a more pragmatic approach. Thus, "whether BITs are one-sided agreements in favour of the capital-exporting country became less relevant than in past decades, as developing countries made special efforts to create conditions favourable to attracting FDI."[89]

Despite the rapid increase in the number of BITs in recent years, most developed countries, LDCs, and emerging economies would agree that they are an inadequate substitute for a stronger multilateral regime on foreign investment. However, wide differences among these groups on the issue of what is to be regulated—the MNC, the home state, or the host state—have to this point precluded the development of such a regime. A number of international and regional organizations have provisions dealing with foreign investment issues. The sections that follow focus on five efforts to develop a regime for foreign investment at the multilateral and regional levels.

1. The UN tried unsuccessfully to develop a code of conduct for MNCs; today it has little influence over FDI issues.
2. GATT/WTO has some provisions dealing with FDI and could play a much greater role in this area in the future.
3. RTAs such as the EU and NAFTA have stronger investment provisions than GATT/WTO and could serve as stepping-stones to a multilateral investment regime.
4. The OECD was negotiating a controversial MAI, but the MAI talks were suspended.
5. Private actors such as NGOs and business groups have become more influential because of the failure of governments to establish a multilateral foreign investment regime.

THE UN

As discussed earlier in this chapter, the late 1960s to 1970s was a period when LDCs, and some developed countries such as France and Canada, raised serious concerns about the effects of MNCs on the national sovereignty of host states. A high-profile case in the early 1970s that heightened LDC criticisms and brought the issue of regulating MNCs to UN attention was the involvement of the International Telephone and Telegraph Corporation (ITT) in the political affairs of Chile. The importance of this case stemmed from the fact that ITT was one of the world's largest and most successful MNCs. ITT was concerned that the Marxist candidate in the 1970 Chilean presidential election, Salvador Allende, would nationalize its Chilean affiliate without compensation. As a result, ITT engaged in a series of actions from 1970 to 1972 in attempts to prevent Allende's election, and then after Allende was elected to try to have him removed from power. ITT also attempted to involve the U.S. Central Intelligence Agency (CIA) and the U.S. Information Agency (USIA) in its clandestine activities.

ITT's actions became public in March 1972 when a syndicated columnist, Jack Anderson, published a series of documents on the issue, and there were serious repercussions. In the United States, a subcommittee of the U.S. Senate Committee on Foreign Relations conducted an investigation and released a well-documented report entitled *The International Telephone and Telegraph Company and Chile*.[90] Internationally, on Chilean initiative "the subject of multinational corporations was for the first time placed on the agenda of the United Nations."[91] Thus, the UN Secretary-General appointed a Group of Eminent Persons in 1972 to examine the impact of MNCs, particularly on LDCs. In 1974 the group issued a report strongly condemning "subversive political intervention on the part of" MNCs, such as ITT's actions in Chile, and recommending that a commission be established to develop a code of conduct "addressed to both Governments and multinational corporations."[92] In response, the UN established a *Commission on Transnational Corporations* to provide a forum to exchange views on MNCs, develop a comprehensive information system on MNC activities, and help establish a code of conduct. However, the commission met only on an annual basis, and a *UN Center on Transnational Corporations (UNCTC)* served as its secretariat.

The development of a comprehensive code of conduct for MNCs was a priority objective of the UN commission and UNCTC, and the Third World countries pressuring for an NIEO in the 1970s strongly supported this objective. An intergovernmental working group began preparing a draft text of the code and submitted its report to the commission in 1982. However, a long period of negotiations on the report followed because of fundamental disagreements among member states. For example, there was no consensus on whether the code should have the force of law or simply provide a set of voluntary guidelines. Most LDCs and socialist states supported the draft code because it focused on MNC behavior and sought to prevent MNC tax evasion, restrictive business practices, and transfer pricing. The developed countries as leading home states for MNCs, by contrast, strongly opposed the draft UN code because they believed it did not adequately address the issue of host-state treatment of MNCs. After years of sporadic negotiations, the UN finally abandoned its efforts to form a consensus on a code of conduct for MNCs in 1992. The UNCTC was dissolved in 1993 and replaced by a less proactive Division on Transnational Corporations and Investment located within UNCTAD.[93]

Since 1993, the UN's efforts have been directed to promoting purely voluntary standards of behavior for MNCs. For example, in January 1999 the UN Secretary-General Kofi Annan proposed that a "Global Compact" be established. The compact comprises nine principles drawn from human rights, labor standards, and the environment, and it urges business firms to act on those principles in their corporate affairs. Participating companies are asked to work with the UN in partnership projects and to provide notification at least once a year of concrete steps they have taken to act on the compact's principles. Unlike a regulatory instrument or code of conduct, the compact is voluntary, and serious questions can be raised about its ability to alter MNC behavior.[94]

GATT/WTO

The WTO is a natural institution to deal with FDI issues because of the close interaction between foreign investment and trade. A growing percentage of trade is intrafirm trade, and a number of regional as well as multilateral trade agreements today contain investment provisions. FDI has nevertheless been referred to as the *"neglected* twin" of trade; trade rather than investment was the focus of multilateral negotiations and institution building in the postwar period.[95] Indeed, investment was virtually "a forbidden subject in the context of the GATT" for many years because a number of governments were reluctant to accept limits on their rights to control FDI within their territorial boundaries.[96]

Although the United States for years had wanted GATT to regulate host country controls on foreign investment, GATT members did not seriously consider negotiating investment issues until the preparations for the Uruguay round in the 1980s. The decision was eventually made to hold negotiations on trade-related investment measures in the Uruguay round, but Brazil, India, and most other LDCs strongly opposed the TRIMs talks. As a result, TRIMs were very narrowly defined to accommodate governments that opposed any discipline over such issues, and the final TRIMs agreement deals with only the most obvious violations of existing GATT articles.[97] The TRIMs agreement does prohibit host countries from imposing "local content requirements" on FDI—that is, requirements that a certain percentage of an investor's inputs or value added must be of domestic origin. However, the agreement does not address many other issues, such as a host country's export performance requirements (requirements that a certain share of an investor's output be exported from the host country). In addition to TRIMs, the TRIPs and the GATS have provisions related to FDI because intellectual property and services issues involve foreign investment as well as trade. Thus, the provisions on foreign investment are scattered throughout the agreement, and they do not constitute a *comprehensive* body of rules for foreign investment.[98]

The view of most trade analysts is that TRIMs and other investment provisions in GATT/WTO are only "a tentative first step toward a multilateral investment regime."[99] Nevertheless, both the TRIMs and the NAFTA agreements created a precedent for the conduct of far more extensive multilateral negotiations on investment in the OECD (see the following discussion).[100]

REGIONAL APPROACHES: THE EUROPEAN UNION AND NORTH AMERICA FREE TRADE AGREEMENT

Liberal economists have viewed RTAs such as the EU and NAFTA as a "second-best" approach to dealing with FDI, because multilateral institutions such as the GATT/WTO have failed to develop a strong foreign investment regime. The EU is at a further stage of economic integration, and this is reflected in its system for regulation of foreign investment. The EU as a common market provides for the free movement of capital and the protection of FDI among the member states on a plurilateral basis. Thus, the European Commission has legal authority to monitor and regulate the activities of MNCs, with the ultimate goal of developing a "level playing field." The EU has been concerned—particularly in the 1970s and 1980s—that European MNCs have not been large enough to compete with American and Japanese MNCs. Thus, the EU's policy toward MNCs "is two-edged, encouraging multinational activity in a transnational European market, while seeking to remedy the concerns caused by this activity by specific binding measures of containment."[101] In view of the high level of integration of the EU, its method of dealing with foreign investment is less likely than the NAFTA's to serve as a model for future efforts to develop a multilateral foreign investment regime. This section therefore devotes more attention to the NAFTA.

The investment provisions in Chapter 11 of NAFTA "carry forward on a trilateral basis all of the key provisions of U.S. bilateral investment treaties."[102] For example, NAFTA commits the three member countries to provide MFN treatment and national treatment to foreign investors; to ban all new export performance, local content, and technology transfer requirements of foreign investors; and to phase out most existing performance requirements within 10 years. NAFTA also establishes a precedent that provides for binding arbitration of investment disputes in an international forum rather than in national courts. Most significant, private investors who are not represented by their government may submit their complaints against a NAFTA government directly to a three-member tribunal that has the authority to make final decisions and award damages. Although many BITs have investor-state dispute settlement provisions, most BITs are between a developed country and an LDC. The inclusion of such provisions in NAFTA (with two developed countries and one LDC as members) is significant because NAFTA goes beyond the bilateral level and may lead to the development of similar provisions in a multilateral investment agreement. In other international agreements such as GATT/WTO, only governments have "standing," and investors must be represented by governments in settling their claims. As discussed later, the investment dispute settlement provisions have been a source of considerable controversy.

Despite the groundbreaking nature of the NAFTA provisions, member states may claim numerous exceptions to the Chapter 11 obligations. For example, the United States has excluded its maritime industry from the investment provisions, whereas Canada has exempted its cultural industries and Mexico has shielded its energy and rail sectors. The rules of origin in NAFTA also include complex procedures for determining local content, which may disadvantage outside firms wishing to enter North America. Nevertheless, NAFTA establishes major precedents in the area of foreign investment, and in many respects it served as a model for OECD negotiations on a multilateral investment agreement.[103]

Because the NAFTA provisions go much further than those of multilateral agreements in liberalizing investment flows, they have been a source of considerable controversy. Most liberal economists today believe that "open investment policies should be the norm, with limited . . . exceptions allowed only when justified in the name of national security or some other overriding principle."[104] Liberals therefore generally applaud NAFTA for its significant advances in the liberalization of investment flows. Liberal criticisms of the NAFTA investment provisions stem from the fact that they contain sectoral exceptions and therefore have "not succeeded in completely liberalizing the North American investment regime."[105] Realists and historical structuralists, by contrast, view the NAFTA investment provisions as a serious threat to national sovereignty and to the ability of labor groups in all three countries to protect their interests. In the view of historical structuralists, the NAFTA investment rules increase capital mobility and give the capitalist class even greater advantages vis-à-vis labor. Thus, MNCs can now more easily transfer their operations from the United States and Canada to Mexico to benefit from lower labor costs and environmental standards, contributing to a competitive "race to the bottom."[106] Realists argue that NAFTA severely limits the ability of host countries to use performance requirements, preventing them from gaining positive spinoffs from foreign investment. Canada and Mexico in particular have imposed performance requirements to encourage investment in depressed regions and in certain sectors of the economy, such as manufacturing, and to ensure that foreign investment contributes to local employment and the growth of exports. By preventing these measures, NAFTA makes it difficult for host countries to channel foreign investment so that it promotes their regional and development objectives.

Liberals and realists have differing views of NAFTA's Chapter 11 investment-dispute-resolution provisions, which permit private investors to obtain relief directly against governments for alleged NAFTA violations. In the liberal view, "these procedures have the merit of distancing investment disputes from the political arena. An investor who feels that it has suffered damage by reason of a measure taken by a NAFTA country can pursue its claim without having to involve its government." Realists by contrast believe the investment dispute resolution provisions "provide a vehicle for investors to harass governments whose policies they dislike."[107] By giving MNCs legal standing in investment dispute settlement cases with governments, realists argue that the NAFTA provisions pose a direct threat to national sovereignty.

THE ORGANIZATION FOR ECONOMIC CORPORATION AND DEVELOPMENT

In September 1995, the members of the OECD began negotiations to establish an MAI. The OECD seemed to be a natural venue for extending rules for foreign investment beyond the bilateral and regional levels, because OECD countries account for about 85 percent of the outflows and 65 percent of the inflows of FDI. Furthermore, the OECD has had considerable experience in dealing with foreign investment issues. In 1961 the OECD adopted two codes on the liberalization of capital flows, and in 1976 it adopted a declaration on international investment that included voluntary Guidelines for Multinational Enterprises. The OECD developed these guidelines to provide an alternative to the draft UN code of conduct that would have imposed many more constraints on MNCs. Unlike the UN code, the OECD guidelines were approved by the membership, but there are mixed reviews regarding their effectiveness. Critics point out that the guidelines are limited to OECD members and that they have had little effect on MNC activities in most areas other than employment and industrial relations. For example, the guidelines call on MNCs to refrain from using facilities such as transfer pricing to avoid paying taxes. However, the guidelines are voluntary, and the U.S. Internal Revenue Service maintains that this admonition has *not* induced MNCs to pay their "fair share of taxes in the United States."[108]

Despite the limited effectiveness of the OECD guidelines, some influential practitioners and scholars believed that the OECD's "like-minded" developed country members were more likely to reach a strong foreign investment agreement than the larger and more diverse membership in the WTO. However, there was in fact no consensus among the developed countries that the OECD was the best venue for the negotiations. The United States wanted a comprehensive and binding MAI, and it had been frustrated by LDC opposition even to the limited TRIMs agreement negotiated in the GATT Uruguay round. Because OECD members are mainly developed countries, the United States believed the OECD would be the best forum for negotiating an MAI. The EU and Canada, by contrast, argued that their business communities had many more complaints about the treatment of FDI in LDCs than in other OECD countries. Thus, they believed MAI negotiations should be conducted in the wider WTO forum that included LDCs, even if the negotiations would be more protracted. Despite these differences of view, the decision was made to negotiate an MAI in the OECD for several reasons. First, there was no WTO consensus to address the investment issue because of opposition from many LDCs. Second, the European Commission negotiates on behalf of all EU members in the WTO, but EU members negotiate for themselves in the OECD. Some EU members were reluctant to expand the commission's mandate by going to the WTO. To allay concerns about the exclusivity of the MAI negotiations, the OECD ministers indicated that non-OECD countries would be consulted.[109]

In January 1997 the OECD secretariat produced the first draft text of an MAI. The basic purposes of the agreement were to dismantle foreign investment barriers and harmonize international investment rules. More specifically, the emerging MAI provisions were to focus on three aspects of rule making: protection for foreign investors, liberalization of investment, and dispute-settlement procedures. The investment-protection provisions would deal with such issues as compensation for expropriation of property, freedom of investors to transfer profits and dividends out of the host country, and fair and equitable treatment for foreign investors. The investment-liberalization provisions would impose various obligations on host countries, such as providing MFN and national treatment for foreign investors and limiting performance requirements. The dispute-settlement procedures would permit investors as well as states to submit complaints for binding settlement decisions at the international level. A number of these provisions were already included in BITs and in NAFTA; the significance of the MAI is that it would be multilateral in scope and more comprehensive in coverage than previous agreements.

The original deadline for concluding an MAI was May 1997, but differences among OECD members prevented negotiators from reaching an agreement. For example, the EU and Canada resented the Helms-Burton law that the United States used to sanction foreign companies for investing in Cuba, Iran, and Libya; France and Canada wanted to exempt culture from the agreement to protect their arts and media sectors; and OECD members had differing views regarding the extent to which environmental and labor measures should be included. The prolongation of negotiations because of the differences within the OECD gave outside critics such as the LDCs and a wide range of civil society groups the opportunity to organize opposition to an agreement.

LDCs led by India, Egypt, Pakistan, and Malaysia expressed strong hostility to an MAI because it was being negotiated in the OECD without their participation. Although most LDCs had become more open to foreign investment after the 1982 foreign debt crisis, they were concerned that the MAI would impose more obligations on host governments than on MNCs. Indeed, most OECD members seemed "to agree that an MAI should not impose any obligations on firms but that it should be binding on governments."[110] This consensus among OECD members resulted partly from the negative experiences of developed countries in the 1970s and 1980s with LDC efforts to develop a UN code of conduct for MNCs. Even more important was the revival of orthodox liberalism, which was most evident in changing attitudes toward the freeing of foreign investment and capital flows. In the LDC view, the financial crisis in East and Southeast Asia in the late 1990s (discussed in Chapter 11) indicated that capital and foreign investment should be regulated rather than given free reign, and that the MAI threatened the autonomous development of LDCs.[111]

The most effective opposition to the MAI was launched by a wide-ranging coalition of civil society NGOs. These NGOs argued that the MAI would threaten protection of human rights, labor and environmental standards, and LDCs. A particular concern was that the MAI would result in a race to the bottom among countries willing to lower their labor and environmental standards to attract foreign investment. A crucial turning point occurred when Ralph Nader and his consumer advocacy group acquired a copy of an OECD draft MAI agreement and put it on the Internet. Using a variety of Web sites, NGOs mobilized a strong and diverse opposition composed of human rights groups, labor and environmental groups, and consumer advocates. Gramscian theorists would argue that the NGOs representing disaffected groups organized a counter-hegemony, which used an electronic information tool—the Internet—"with incredible effectiveness to derail a planned trade pact designed to increase globalization."[112] By the time the OECD members decided to suspend their negotiations in October 1998, about 600 groups in 70 countries had expressed their opposition to the draft agreement, mainly through the Internet. The Internet helped to usher "civil society groups into the negotiating room, ending the days when negotiations were the province of expert officials working solely under political guidance from their governments."[113]

The unsuccessful efforts to negotiate an MAI demonstrate that the OECD is better placed to provide policy advice and analysis than to serve as a forum for negotiating binding and enforceable agreements on sensitive issues. A number of analysts have viewed the WTO as a better venue for negotiating and implementing an agreement on foreign investment. As discussed, the WTO already has agreements (TRIMs, TRIPs, and GATS) that deal with some aspects of foreign investment. The WTO would be a good forum for implementing a more comprehensive international investment accord because of its almost universal membership and because of the close linkages between trade and investment issues. However, a major obstacle to the future negotiation of an MAI under the WTO is the wide divergence of views on the issue among those with different theoretical perspecives. Liberal economists praise the idea of an MAI regulating host state behavior, arguing that the "extension of the rules governing the multilateral trading system to include investment-related issues would be a very positive step."[114] According to liberals, an MAI would establish a "level playing field" for foreign investors, with uniform and equitable rules for market access. An MAI would also facilitate the more efficient use of scarce economic resources and would eliminate distortions in investment flows. Realists and historical structuralists, by contrast, strongly oppose an MAI regulating host states for many of the same reasons that they oppose the NAFTA investment provisions. According to these critics, an MAI would enable MNCs to move operations to countries with lower environmental, labor, and consumer safety standards; ban performance requirements that countries use to promote their welfare and development; prevent restrictions on repatriation of profits and the removal of capital from the host country; and generally restrict the ability of host countries to sanction irresponsible behavior by MNCs. In view of these divergent perspectives, governments to this point have been unable to establish a strong, effective foreign investment regime. As a result, private actors have begun to play a greater role in asserting their influence on foreign investment issues.

PRIVATE ACTORS

The globalization process has contributed to increased capital mobility and the internationalization of production, which has given business firms greater freedom to choose where to locate their activities. National governments seeking FDI have therefore been less willing and able to impose regulations on MNCs. In view of the lack of multilateral mechanisms to regulate MNCs, NGOs have adopted a wide range of strategies in efforts to alter their behavior. For example, environmental and labor activists have joined with IOs and national regulatory agencies in pressuring MNCs to implement voluntary "certification" arrangements such as codes of conduct, monitoring standards, and production guidelines. The opportunity for cooperation has resulted from the desire of some NGOs to move beyond raising awareness to promoting reform, sometimes in collaboration with MNCs. As discussed with regard to the MAI, advances in communications, transportation, and technology have enabled NGOs to organize quickly and effectively and to broaden their surveillance activities. Thus, MNCs have had to deal with simultaneous, coordinated international actions by NGOs.

NGOs have employed a variety of strategies to target MNCs. Whereas some of these strategies such as consumer boycotts and exposure of corporate misconduct have been used for many years, other strategies such as shareholder activism and the creation of stewardship councils are of more recent origin. The important point is that both the older and newer strategies are now being used more frequently than in the past. NGOs can be categorized as conformers, reformers, and radicals in terms of their goals and strategies.[115] Conformers largely endorse MNC behavior and do not favor restrictions on their activities; reformers call for some regulation of MNCs and believe MNCs can be reformed; and radicals follow highly confrontational strategies toward MNCs, because they believe MNCs are not reformable. In some respects, conformers are similar to orthodox liberals, reformers are similar to interventionist liberals and realists, and radicals are similar to historical structuralists. Of particular interest to us here are NGOs that pressure for some regulation of MNCs: the reformist liberals, and the more critical radicals or historical structuralists.

NGOs pursuing liberal strategies prefer to promote responsible MNC behavior rather than engaging in ideological confrontation, because they believe MNCs can be reformed. For example, liberal strategies in the environmental area include ecoconsumerism, project collaboration, codes of conduct, and the development of private regimes. Ecoconsumerism refers to NGO campaigns to reward ecologically minded firms by purchasing products that have a less damaging effect on the environment. Project collaboration refers to environmental partnerships between NGOs and business firms to make production methods more environmentally responsible. Codes of conduct call on business firms to voluntarily decrease the release of pollutants, use sustainable energy sources, and appoint people with a commitment to the environment to their boards of directors. Private regimes bring companies and environmental groups together to develop accreditation procedures for good corporate conduct. They are more institutionalized than codes of conduct and provide ongoing opportunities for dialogue and review.[116]

Critical NGO strategies are more oppositional than liberal strategies and provide less scope for compromise and dialogue. Unlike liberal strategies, the primary purpose of critical strategies is to expose and punish allegedly irresponsible corporate behavior. Examples of critical NGO strategies include consumer boycotts, MNC monitors, counterinformation, and shareholder activism. Consumer boycotts tend to be more extreme than ecoconsumerism because they are designed to expose and punish alleged environmental abuses in the public arena. MNC monitors include groups such as the Multinationals Resource Center in the United States and Corporate Watch in Britain that monitor MNCs and disseminate information about their allegedly destructive activities. Counterinformation aims at refuting the claims a company makes about itself and encouraging consumers to boycott the company's products. NGOs engaging in shareholder activism encourage their supporters to purchase a small number of shares in a corporation in attempts to influence decision making in the shareholders' annual meetings. In the extreme, NGOs following critical or historical structuralist strategies aim to develop a counterhegemony to "confront the hegemonic formation of globalization," which includes MNCs.[117]

It is important to note that some NGOs employ liberal and critical strategies simultaneously. For example, Greenpeace has worked with companies to develop ozone-friendly refrigerators at the same time as it has encouraged consumers to boycott Shell over its alleged involvement with state suppression in Nigeria. In efforts to avoid negative NGO campaigns and government regulations, many MNCs have become more proactive in responding to environmental and other concerns with their own regulatory frameworks. Companies often benefit from collaboration with liberal NGOs. For example, MNCs that engage in project collaboration with environmental groups may gain a reputation for being environmentally responsible and may be able to employ the expertise of environmental NGOs in reforming their practices. Instead of binding commitments at the international level, business firms and associations have supported voluntary agreements as an alternative. For example, the International Chamber of Commerce endorsed 16 principles on the environment known as the *Business Charter on Sustainable Development* before the 1992 UN Conference on Environment and Development in Rio de Janeiro, Brazil.

Despite the numerous examples one can cite of liberal and critical NGO activities to alter the behavior of MNCs, one must question how effective these activities have been in practice. MNCs clearly have different levels of vulnerability to NGO strategies. Oil companies, for example, are less vulnerable to NGO pressures because governments depend on the MNCs' access to oil technology, expertise, and distribution networks. Furthermore, NGOs have limited monitoring capabilities. Although NGOs direct their campaigns and protests at certain high-profile companies, they permit other companies to be free riders and thus undermine the efforts to reform MNC behavior. Overall, it is likely that MNCs have not changed significantly as a result of NGO activities and that NGOs do not substitute for adequate multilateral regulation.[118] One can also question how realistic it is to expect MNCs to regulate themselves through voluntary codes of conduct. Governments "are at least formally accountable to their citizens . . when setting and enforcing standards," whereas "companies are primarily accountable to their own shareholders."[119] MNC self-regulation can supplement but not substitute for the responsibility of governments to set and maintain standards of behavior for business and other groups.

It is important to note that reformist and radical NGOs are themselves the target of numerous criticisms. For example, critics maintain that NGOs are not elected by the public and are not in fact representative of societal attitudes toward MNCs. Furthermore, NGOs are criticized for focusing almost exclusively on the regulation of MNC behavior, whereas the MAI was criticized for attempting to regulate only the behavior of host states. As discussed, no consensus has developed to this point on the need to achieve a balanced approach to regulation of MNCs, host states, and home states.

CONCLUSION

The postwar economy has been marked by increasing global interdependence among states. Initially, the liberalization of trade under GATT was the main factor contributing to globalization. However, since the 1980s, FDI has become even more important than trade as a force behind the growth of interdependence. Technological advances in communications and transportation enabled firms to extend their operations abroad, and MNCs increased their FDI to gain access to foreign markets, benefit from economies of scale, and gain control over all stages of the production process. Fewer than 200 American corporations and a small number of European firms were global in their operations in 1970, but in the 1980s there was a dramatic increase in both the number of global firms and the number of states that served as home countries. Thus, by the early 1990s, at least 1,000 firms could be categorized as global, and the home nations included the United States, most European countries, Japan, East Asian and Latin American NIEs, and some other Third World countries.[120]

Despite the extent of globalization of foreign investment, its growth across countries has been very uneven. As Tables 10.3 and 10.4 show, the developed market economies accounted for 89.8 percent of the outward stocks of FDI and 67 percent of the inward stocks of FDI in 1998. Thus, a triad including the EU, North America, and Japan are the main sources of FDI, and these areas direct most of their FDI to each other. From the 1950s to the early 1970s, the United States as the main source of FDI was highly critical of restrictions other developed countries were imposing on inward FDI. Nevertheless, Western Europe and Japan liberalized their inward FDI policies as they became more competitive with the United States and their outward FDI increased. The United States, by contrast, became more sensitive about incoming FDI as its economic hegemony declined. In 1988, for example, the U.S. Congress enacted the Exon-Florio Amendment, which enables the president to block foreign takeovers of U.S. firms that present a possible danger to national security. Despite Exon-Florio, the United States, like other developed countries, is basically committed to an open foreign investment regime. As major home countries for MNCs, the developed countries have a vested interest in removing obstacles to incoming FDI. Thus, it was the OECD countries that attempted to negotiate an MAI.

Unlike the developed countries, LDCs are primarily host countries rather than home countries for foreign investment. As host countries, LDCs have often been sensitive to the effects of MNCs on their ability to achieve autonomous economic development. In the 1970s, LDCs reacted strongly to the growing impact of MNCs, demanding greater control over their natural resources and the ability to nationalize MNCs as part of their demands for a NIEO. Nevertheless, the oil price increase of 1979, followed by world recession and the 1980s foreign debt crisis led to severe cutbacks in commercial bank lending to LDCs. Third World fears about exploitation by MNCs were largely replaced by concerns that their share of inward FDI was declining. Today, many LDCs are unilaterally liberalizing their foreign investment policies and competing for incoming investment.

As discussed throughout this chapter, liberals, realists, and historical structuralists have widely divergent views regarding MNCs. Liberals view MNCs as positive agents of global change, which contribute to increased efficiency and stimulate innovation, economic growth, and employment. Liberals also tend to downgrade the importance of an MNC's nationality, and they advise states to upgrade the skills of their populations to attract investment, regardless of the source. Realists, by contrast, believe that an MNC's nationality does make a difference and that the competitiveness of a nation-state and the competitiveness of its MNCs are closely interlinked. Realists also believe that host states should be able to impose performance requirements and other policies on MNCs to promote industrial development and protect their national interest. Historical structuralists argue that MNCs overcharge for their goods and services, create dependency relationships with LDC host states, and pose a major threat to labor groups in home as well as host states. Whereas MNCs can extend their operations to many countries, labor is largely limited to working and organizing itself on a national basis. Thus, MNCs often contribute to a deterioration of working conditions and a competitive race to the bottom by transferring operations to affiliates in countries with lower wages and environmental standards.

Most liberals, realists, and historical structuralists believe that some sort of foreign investment regime is necessary, but they have markedly different views as to what is to be regulated—the MNC, the host state, or the home state. The UN tried to develop a comprehensive code of conduct for MNCs in the 1970s and 1980s, but it abandoned these efforts in 1992 because of strong opposition from the major developed countries. In the 1990s, the OECD tried to conclude an MAI. Unlike the UN efforts to develop a code of conduct, the MAI was designed to regulate the behavior of host states rather than MNCs. However, divisions within the OECD, and strong opposition from LDCs and civil society groups, resulted in a suspension of OECD talks to establish an MAI.

In the absence of a multilateral regime limiting host state restrictions on FDI, liberals in the developed countries have pursued second-best options at the bilateral and regional levels. Important examples include the BITs and the investment provisions in the EU and the NAFTA. In the absence of a multilateral regime regulating MNCs, NGO civil society groups have pressured MNCs to alter their behavior through voluntary agreements and codes of conduct. Whereas liberal NGOs have emphasized reform of MNCs, critical NGOs have emphasized ideological confrontation.

In sum, regulation of FDI is a "patchwork quilt" because there is no effective multilateral regime for foreign investment as there is for trade and monetary relations. This situation is unlikely to change until a consensus develops as to *what* is to be regulated: the MNC, the host state, the home state, or all three.

NOTES

1. United Nations Conference on Trade and Development, *World Investment Report 2000: Cross-border Mergers and Acquisitions and Development* (New York: United Nations, 2000), pp. 4–28; John H. Dunning, *Multinational Enterprises and the Global Economy* (Wokingham, UK: Addison Wesley, 1993), pp. 14–15; World Trade Organization, *Annual Report 1996, Vol. 1, Trade and Foreign Direct Investment* (Geneva: WTO, 1996), p. 44.
2. Lorraine Eden, "Bringing the Firm Back In: Multinationals in International Political Economy," in Lorraine Eden and Evan H. Potter, eds., *Multinationals in the Global Political Economy* (New York: St. Martin's Press, 1993), p. 26.
3. Ethan B. Kapstein, "We Are US: The Myth of the Multinational," *The National Interest* (Winter 1991–92), p. 55.
4. DeAnne Julius, "International Direct Investment: Strengthening the Policy Regime," in Peter B. Kenen, ed., *Managing the World Economy: Fifty Years After Bretton Woods* (Washington, DC: Institute of International Economics, September 1994), p. 269.
5. Robert W. Cox, *Production, Power, and World Order: Social Forces in the Making of History* (New York: Columbia University Press, 1987), pp. 358–359; G. William Domhoff, "Who Made American Foreign Policy 1945–1963?" pp. 25–69, and William Appleman Williams, "The Large Corporation and American Foreign Policy," pp. 71–104, in David Horowitz, ed., *Corporations and the Cold War* (New York: Monthly Review Press, 1969).
6. See Stephen D. Krasner, "Power Politics, Institutions, and Transnational Relations," in Thomas Risse-Kappen, ed., *Bringing Transational Relations Back In: Non-State Actors, Domestic Structures and International Institutions* (Cambridge: Cambridge University Press, 1995), p. 279.

7. Stephen Hymer, "The Multinational Corporation and the Law of Uneven Development," in George Modelski, ed., *Transnational Corporations and World Order* (San Francisco: Freeman, 1979), p. 398.

8. See Yair Aharoni, "On the Definition of a Multinational Corporation," *Quarterly Review of Economics and Business* 11-3 (Autumn 1971), pp. 27–37; Grazia Ietto-Gillies, *International Production: Trends, Theories, Effects* (Cambridge, MA: Polity Press, 1992), pp. 17–20.

9. Raymond Vernon, *Sovereignty at Bay: The Multinational Spread of U.S. Enterprises* (New York: Basic Books, 1971), p. 11.

10. UNCTAD, *World Investment Report 2000*, pp. 99–136.

11. Edward M. Graham and Paul R. Krugman, *Foreign Direct Investment in the United States* 3rd ed. (Washington, DC: Institute for International Economics, January 1995), pp. 9–11; Geoffrey Jones, *The Evolution of International Business: An Introduction* (London: Routledge, 1996), pp. 4–6.

12. See, for example, United Nations Centre on Transnational Corporations (UNCTC), *Transnational Corporations in World Development: Third Survey* (New York: United Nations, 1985).

13. Howard V. Perlmutter, "The Tortuous Evolution of the Multinational Corporation," *Columbia Journal of World Business* 4-1 (January–February 1969), p. 11; Wyn Grant, "Perspectives on Globalizational and Economic Coordination," in J. Rogers Hollingsworth and Robert Boyer, eds., *Contemporary Capitalism: The Embeddedness of Institutions* (Cambridge: Cambridge University Press, 1997), pp. 322–325; Susan Strange, "Global Government and Global Opposition," in Geraint Parry, ed., *Politics in an Interdependent World: Essays Presented to Ghita Ionescu* (Aldershot, UK: Edward Elgar, 1994), pp. 26–27.

14. Although most political scientists and American scholars prefer the term *MNC*, economists, business professors, and British scholars often opt instead for the term *multinational enterprise (MNE)*. MNE is a more accurate term in their view because an "enterprise" includes "a network of corporate and non-corporate entities in different countries joined together by ties of ownership." See United Nations Department of Economic and Social Affairs, *Multinational Corporations in World Development* (New York: United Nations, 1973), p. 4; Eden, "Bringing the Firm Back In," p. 55.

15. Laura D'Andrea Tyson, "They Are Not Us: Why American Ownership Still Matters," *The American Prospect* 4 (Winter 1991), p. 42; John M. Kline, *State Government Influence in U.S. International Economic Policy* (Lexington, MA: Heath, 1983), p. 63.

16. Jean-François Hennart, "The Transaction Cost Theory of the Multinational Enterprise," in Christos N. Pitelis and Roger Sugden, eds., *The Nature of the Transnational Firm* (London: Routledge, 1991), pp. 143–151; Mark Casson, *Alternatives to the Multinational Enterprise* (London: Macmillan, 1979), p. 45.

17. Graham and Krugman, *Foreign Direct Investment in the United States*, p. 83. For a discussion of transfer pricing, see Lorraine Eden, *Multinational Enterprise and Economic Analysis* (Toronto: University of Toronto Press, 1997); Alan M. Rugman and Lorraine Eden, eds., *Multinationals and Transfer Pricing* (London: Croom Helm, 1985); and Wagdy M. Abdallah, *International Transfer Pricing Policies: Decision-Making Guidelines for Multinational Companies* (New York: Quorum Books, 1989).

18. See Lorraine Eden, "Thinking Globally—Acting Locally: Multinationals in the Global Political Economy," in Lorraine Eden and Evan H. Potter, eds., *Multinationals in the Global Political Economy* (New York: St. Martin's Press, 1993), pp. 1–2; Michael E. Porter, *The Competitive Advantage of Nations* (New York: Free Press, 1990), p. 53.

19. See Charles Wilson, "The Multinational in Historical Perspective," in Keiichiro Naka-gawa, ed., *Strategy and Structure of Big Business,* Proceedings of the First Fuji Confer-ence (Tokyo: University of Tokyo Press, 1974), p. 265; Peter Hertner and Geoffrey Jones, "Multinationals: Theory and History," in Peter Hertner and Geoffrey Jones, eds., *Multina-tionals. Theory and History* (Aldershot, UK: Gower, 1986), p. 1.

20. Jones, *The Evolution of International Business,* pp. 23–25.

21. See Peter Svedberg, "The Portfolio-Direct Composition of Private Foreign Investment in 1914 Revisited," *The Economic Journal* 88 (December 1978), pp. 763–777; and T. A. B. Corley, "Britain's Overseas Investments in 1914 Revisited," *Business History* 36-1 (Janu-ary 1994), pp. 71–88.

22. Julius, "International Direct Investment," pp. 272–273.

23. Jones, *The Evolution of International Business,* pp. 28–32.

24. Edward M. Graham, *Global Corporations and National Governments* (Washington, DC: Institute for International Economics, May 1996), pp. 25–26, 136–140; John H. Dunning, "Changes in the Level and Structure of International Production: The Last One Hundred Years," in Mark Casson, ed., *The Growth of International Business* (London: Allen and Unwin, 1983), p. 88.

25. Jones, *The Evolution of International Business,* pp. 52–59.

26. Peter J. Buckley and Mark Casson, *The Future of the Multinational Enterprise,* 2nd ed. (London: Macmillan, 1991), p. 11. See also United Nations Centre on Transnational Cor-porations (UNCTC), *World Investment Report 1991: The Triad in Foreign Direct Invest-ment* (New York: United Nations, 1991).

27. Dennis J. Encarnation, *Rivals Beyond Trade: America Versus Japan in Global Competi-tion* (Ithaca, NY: Cornell University Press, 1992), p. 5; Kiyoshi Kojima, *Direct Foreign In-vestment: A Japanese Model of Multinational Business Operations* (New York: Praeger, 1978), pp. 1–18.

28. United Nations Conference on Trade and Development, *World Investment Report 1999: Foreign Direct Investment and the Challenge of Development* (New York: United Nations, 1999), p. 42.

29. World Trade Organization, *Annual Report—1996, Vol. 1,* p. 47.

30. Graham, *Global Corporations and National Governments,* pp. 22–24; Julius, "Interna-tional Direct Investment," pp. 276–277; Ietto-Gillies, *International Production,* pp. 25–32.

31. Ietto-Gillies, *International Production,* pp. 78–84.

32. Stephen Herbert Hymer, *The International Operations of National Firms: A Study of Di-rect Foreign Investment* (Cambridge, MA: MIT Press, 1976), p. 100; Ietto-Gillies, *Inter-national Production,* pp. 86–90.

33. Theodore H. Moran, "Multinational Corporations and Dependency: A Dialogue for De-pendentistas and Non-Dependentistas," *International Organization* 32-1 (Winter 1978), pp. 79–100.

34. Peter Evans, *Dependent Development: The Alliance of Multinational, State, and Local Capital in Brazil* (Princeton, NJ: Princeton University Press, 1979), p. 37.

35. Vernon, *Sovereignty at Bay,* pp. 46–59; Raymond Vernon, "Sovereignty at Bay Ten Years After," *International Organization* 35-3 (Summer 1981), pp. 521–523; Ravi Ramamurti, "The Obsolescing `Bargaining Model'? MNC–Host Developing Country Relations Revis-ited," *Journal of International Business Studies* 32-1 (2001), p. 25.

36. Theodore H. Moran, "Multinational Corporations and the Developing Countries: An Overview," in Theodore H. Moran, ed., *Multinational Corporations: The Political Econ-omy of Foreign Direct Investment* (Lexington, MA: Heath, 1985), pp. 3–24.

37. See Stephen J. Kobrin, "Testing the Bargaining Hypothesis in the Manufacturing Sector in Developing Countries," *International Organization* 41-4 (Autumn 1987), pp. 609–638.

38. Ramamurti, "The Obsolescing `Bargaining Model'?," p. 23.
39. On the policies of subnational governments toward FDI, see, for example, Kline, *State Government Influence in U.S. International Economic Policy;* Douglas M. Brown and Earl H. Fry, eds., *States and Provinces in the International Economy* (Berkeley, CA: Institute of Governmental Studies Press, University of California, 1993); and Peter Karl Kresl and Gary Gappert, eds., *North American Cities and the Global Economy: Challenges and Opportunities,* Urban Affairs Annual Review 44 (Thousand Oaks, CA: Sage, 1995).
40. Jones, *The Evolution of International Business,* pp. 288–291.
41. Stephen J. Kobrin, "Expropriation as an Attempt to Control Foreign Firms in LDCs: Trends from 1960 to 1979," *International Studies Quarterly* 28-3 (September 1984), pp. 337–342.
42. Stephen D. Krasner, *Structural Conflict: The Third World Against Global Liberalism* (Berkeley, CA: University of California Press, 1985), pp. 176–195; Horst Heininger, "Transnational Corporations and the Struggle for the Establishment of a New International Economic Order," in Alice Teichova, Maurice Lévy-Leboyer, and Helga Nussbaum, eds., *Multinational Enterprise in Historical Perspective,* pp. 351–361.
43. Kobrin, "Expropriation as an Attempt to Control Foreign Firms in LDCs," p. 338; Jones, *The Evolution of International Business,* pp. 294–295.
44. Graham, *Global Corporations and National Governments,* pp. 17–20.
45. UNCTAD, *World Investment Report 2000,* pp. 6, 7, 17–18.
46. United Nations Conference on Trade and Development, *World Investment Report 1994: Transnational Corporations, Employment, and the Workplace* (New York: United Nations, 1994), pp. 91–97; Graham, *Global Corporations and National Governments,* pp. 97–100.
47. J. J. Servan-Schreiber, *The American Challenge,* translated from French by Ronald Steel (New York: Atheneum, 1979). The book was first published in 1967. See also Jones, *The Evolution of International Business,* pp. 274–277.
48. Stephen Clarkson, *Canada and the Reagan Challenge: Crisis and Adjustment, 1981–85* updated ed. (Toronto, Ontario: James Lorimer & Company, 1985), pp. 3–113; Tom Keating, *Canada and World Order: The Multilateralist Tradition in Canadian Foreign Policy.* 2nd ed. (Don Mills, Ontario: Oxford University Press, 2002), p. 195; C. Fred Bergsten, "Coming Investment Wars? Multinational Corporations in World Politics," *Foreign Affairs* 53-1 (October 1974), pp. 136–139; Barbara Jenkins, *The Paradox of Continental Production: National Investment Policies in North America* (Ithaca, NY: Cornell University Press, 1992), pp. 113–117.
49. Mark Mason, *American Multinationals and Japan: The Political Economy of Japanese Capital Controls, 1899–1980* (Cambridge, MA: Council on East Asian Studies, Harvard University, 1992), pp. 243–247.
50. Jones, *The Evolution of International Business,* pp. 280–281.
51. Graham, *Global Corporations and National Governments,* pp. 96–97.
52. Paul N. Doremus, William W. Keller, Louis W. Pauly, and Simon Reich, *The Myth of the Global Corporation* (Princeton, NJ: Princeton University Press, 1998), pp. 77–78; Robert Z. Lawrence, "Japan's Low Levels of Inward Investment: The Role of Inhibitions on Acquisitions," in Kenneth Froot, ed., *Foreign Direct Investment* (Chicago: University of Chicago Press, 1993), pp. 85–107; C. Fred Bergsten and Marcus Noland, *Reconcilable Differences? United States–Japan Economic Conflict* (Washington, DC: Institute for International Economics, 1993), pp. 79–82; and Encarnation, *Rivals Beyond Trade,* pp. 36–41.
53. Jenkins, *The Paradox of Continental Production,* pp. 117–121; Clarkson, *Canada and the Reagan Challenge,* pp. 83–113; Keating, *Canada and World Order,* pp. 195–196.
54. Edward M. Graham and Michael E. Ebert, "Foreign Direct Investment and US National Security: Fixing Exon-Florio," *The World Economy* 14-3 (September 1991), pp. 245–268;

Edward M. Graham and Paul R. Krugman, *Foreign Direct Investment in the United States* (Washington, DC: Institute for International Economics, January 1995), pp. 126–132; Doremus, Keller, Pauly, and Reich, *The Myth of the Global Corporation*, pp. 76–77.

55. John H. Dunning, Roger van Hoesel, and Rajneesh Narula, "Third World Multinationals Revisited: New Developments and Theoretical Implications," in John H. Dunning, ed., *Globalization, Trade and Foreign Direct Investment* (Amsterdam: Elsevier, 1998), p. 257; Jones, *The Evolution of International Business*, pp. 194–195; UNCTAD, *World Investment Report 2000*, p. 71.

56. Robert Gilpin, *U.S. Power and the Multinational Corporation: The Political Economy of Foreign Direct Investment* (New York: Basic Books, 1975), p. 62.

57. UNCTC, *Transnational Corporations in World Development—Trends and Prospects* (New York: United Nations, 1988), p. 240; Jones, *The Evolution of International Business*, pp. 219–220.

58. Robert T. Kudrle, "The Several Faces of the Multinational Corporation: Political Reaction and Policy Response," in W. Ladd Hollist and F. LaMond Tullis, eds., *An International Political Economy, International Political Economy Yearbook* (Boulder, CO: Westview Press, 1985), vol. 1, pp. 176–177; Jack N. Behrman and Robert E. Grosse, *International Business and Governments: Issues and Institutions* (Columbia: University of South Carolina Press, 1990), pp. 82–85; Gilpin, *U.S. Power and the Multinational Corporation*, pp. 142–144.

59. Jones, *The Evolution of International Business*, pp. 221–222.

60. Gary Clyde Hufbauer and Jeffrey J. Schott, "The Soviet-European Gas Pipeline: A Case of Failed Sanctions," in Moran, ed. *Multinational Corporations: The Political Economy of Foreign Direct Investment*, pp. 219–245.

61. Paul Lewis, "Cuba Trade Law: Export of U.S. Ire and Politics," *New York Times*, 15 March, 1996, pp. C1, C3; "Biter Bitten: The Helms-Burton Law," *The Economist*, 8 June, 1996, p. 45.

62. Robert B. Reich, "Who Is Us?" *Harvard Business Review* 90–1 (January–February 1990), pp. 59–60; Vernon, *Sovereignty at Bay*, pp. 214–215.

63. Laura D'Andrea Tyson, *Who's Bashing Whom? Trade Conflict in High-Technology Industries* (Washington, DC: Institute for International Economics, November 1992), pp. 289–295.

64. See Peter Enderwick, *Multinational Business and Labour* (London: Croom Helm, 1985); Richard E. Caves, *Multinational Enterprise and Economic Analysis* (Cambridge: Cambridge University Press, 1962), pp. 131–159; Theodore H. Moran, "Multinational Corporations and the Developed World: An Analytical Overview," in Moran, ed. *Multinational Corporations: The Political Economy of Foreign Direct Investment*, pp. 139–146.

65. Gordon Betcherman, "Globalization, Labour Markets and Public Policy," in Robert Boyer and Daniel Drache, eds., *States Against Markets: The Limits of Globalization* (London: Routledge, 1996), p. 258; Ietto-Gillies, *International Production*, pp. 136–143.

66. See, for example, Sol C. Chaikin, "Trade, Investment, and Deindustrialization: Myth and Reality," in Moran, ed., *Multinational Corporations: The Political Economy of Foreign Direct Investment*, pp. 159–172.

67. Gary Clyde Hufbauer and Jeffrey J. Schott, *NAFTA: An Assessment, rev. ed.* (Washington, DC: Institute for International Economics, October 1993), p. 159.

68. Robert O'Brien, "The Agency of Labour in a Changing Global Order," in Richard Stubbs and Geoffrey R.D. Underhill, eds., *Political Economy and the Changing Global Order*, 2nd ed. (Don Mills, Ontario: Oxford University Press, 2000), pp. 42–44.

69. Reich, "Who Is Us?" pp. 53–64; Robert B. Reich, *The Work of Nations: Preparing Ourselves for 21st-Century Capitalism* (New York: Vintage Books, 1991), chap. 25.

70. Porter, *The Competitive Advantage of Nations*, p. 2; Tyson, "They Are Not Us," pp. 37–49.

71. Lester Thurow, *Head to Head: The Coming Economic Battle Among Japan, Europe, and America* (New York: Morrow, 1992), p. 201.

72. Reich, *The Work of Nations*, p. 8.

73. Kenichi Ohmae, *The Borderless World: Power and Strategy in the Interlinked Economy* (New York: HarperPerennial, 1991), p. 10.

74. Reich, *The Work of Nations*, p. 163; Ohmae, *The Borderless World*, p. 194.

75. UNCTAD, *World Investment Report 2000*, pp. 20–21; Robert B. Reich, "Who Do We Think They Are?" *The American Prospect* 4 (Winter 1991), p. 51; Grant, "Perspectives on Globalization and Economic Coordination," pp. 323–324.

76. Fred Lazar, "Corporate Strategies: The Costs and Benefits of Going Global," in Boyer and Drache, eds., *States Against Markets*, p. 285; Louis W. Pauly and Simon Reich, "National Structures and Multinational Corporate Behavior: Enduring Differences in the Age of Globalization," *International Organization* 51-1 (Winter 1997), p. 13.

77. See Richard G. Harris and William G. Watson, "Three Visions of Competitiveness: Porter, Reich and Thurow on Economic Growth and Policy," in Thomas J. Courchene and Douglas D. Purvis, eds., *Productivity, Growth and Canada's International Competitiveness*, Proceedings of a Conference at Queen's University (Kingston, Ontario: John Deutsch Institute for the Study of Economic Policy, 1993), pp. 254–256; Graham and Krugman, *Foreign Direct Investment in the United States*, p. 84.

78. See Pauly and Reich, "National Structures and Multinational Corporate Behavior," pp. 1–30; and Doremus, Keller, Pauly, and Reich, *The Myth of the Global Corporation*, chaps. 3–5.

79. Paul Krugman, "Competitiveness: A Dangerous Obsession," *Foreign Affairs* (March/April 1994), pp. 31–33. See also Paul Krugman, "Competitiveness: Does It Matter?" *Fortune* (March 7, 1994), pp. 109–115.

80. Clyde V. Prestowitz, Jr., "The Fight over Competitiveness: A Zero-Sum Debate?" *Foreign Affairs* (July/August 1994), p. 189.

81. Paul M. Goldberg and Charles P. Kindleberger, "Toward a GATT for Investment: A Proposal for Supervision of the International Corporation," *Law and Policy in International Business* 2 (Summer 1970), pp. 295–325.

82. Christopher J. Maule and Andrew Vanderwal, "International Regulation of Foreign Investment," *International Perspectives*, (November/December 1985), p. 22.

83. Vernon, *Sovereignty at Bay*, p. 249; Richard J. Barnet and Ronald E. Müller, *Global Reach: The Power of the Multinational Corporations* (New York: Simon & Schuster, 1974), p. 375.

84. Peter Muchlinski, *Multinational Enterprises and the Law* (Oxford: Blackwell, 1995), pp. 578–592; Oswaldo de Rivero B., *New Economic Order and International Development Law* (Oxford: Pergamon Press, 1980), pp. 88–92.

85. See Organisation for Economic Co-operation and Development, *International Investment and Multinational Enterprises: Review of the 1976 Declaration and Decisions* (Paris: OECD, 1979).

86. This section on BITs relies on United Nations Conference on Trade and Development, *Bilateral Investment Treaties in the Mid-1990s* (New York and Geneva: United Nations, 1998), pp. 1–19; Paul Bryan Christy, III. "Negotiating Investment in the GATT: A Call for Functionalism," *Michigan Journal of International Law* 12-4 (Summer 1991), pp. 754–763; World Trade Organization, *Annual Report 1996*, vol. 1, p. 62; and Jon R. Johnson, *The North American Free Trade Agreement—A Comprehensive Guide* (Aurora, Ontario: Canada Law Book, 1994), p. 277. For a discussion of private international legal efforts to regulate MNCs, see A. Claire Cutler, "Public Meets Private: The International

Harmonization and Unification of Private International Law," *Global Society* 13-1 (January 1999), pp. 25–48.

87. UNCTC, *Transnational Corporations in World Development: Trends and Prospects*, p. 337.

88. UNCTAD, *Bilateral Investment Treaties in the Mid-1990s*, p. 4.

89. UNCTAD, *Bilateral Investment Treaties in the Mid-1990s*, p. 16.

90. Reproduced in United States Senate, "The International Telephone and Telegraph Company and Chile, 1970–1971," in George Modelski, ed., *Transnational Corporations and World Order* (San Francisco: W.H. Freeman, 1979), pp. 226–244.

91. Modelski, ed., *Transnational Corporations and World Order*, p. 177.

92. United Nations, "Report of the Group of Eminent Persons to Study the Impact of Multinational Corporations on Development and on International Relations," in Modelski, ed., *Transnational Corporations and World Order*, pp. 323, 330.

93. UNCTC, *The United Nations Code of Conduct on Transnational Corporations* (New York: United Nations, September 1986), pp. 1–6; R. Alan Hedley, "Transnational Corporations and Their Regulation: Issues and Strategies," *International Journal of Comparative Sociology* 40-2 (May 1999), pp. 218–221; "Target Practice," *New Internationalist*, (August 1993) p. 15; Leslie Sklair, *Sociology of the Global System*, 2nd ed. (Hertfordshire, UK: Prentice Hall/Harvester Wheatsheaf, 1995), p. 53.

94. "The Global Compact—What It Is and Isn't," <http://www.unglobalcompact.org>.

95. See De Anne Julius, *Foreign Investment: The Neglected Twin of Trade*, Occasional Papers no. 33 (Washington, DC: Group of Thirty, 1991).

96. Christy, "Negotiating Investment in the GATT," p. 746.

97. John Croome, *Reshaping the World Trading System: A History of the Uruguay Round* (Geneva: World Trade Organization, 1995), p. 138.

98. Graham, *Global Corporations and National Governments*, pp. 71–76; Julius, "International Direct Investment," p. 281.

99. Jeffrey J. Schott, with Johanna W. Buurman, *The Uruguay Round: An Assessment* (Washington, DC: Institute for International Economics, November 1994), p. 112.

100. Ernest H. Preeg, *Traders in a Brave New World: The Uruguay Round and the Future of the International Trading System* (Chicago: University of Chicago Press, 1995), pp. 195–196.

101. John Robinson, *Multinationals and Political Control* (New York, NY: St. Martin's Press), p. 44. See also Hedley, "Transnational Corporations and Their Regulation," p. 223.

102. Johnson, *The North American Free Trade Agreement*, p. 275.

103. Edward M. Graham and Christopher Wilkie, "Multinationals and the Investment Provisions of the NAFTA," *International Trade Journal* 8-1 (Spring 1994), pp. 9–38; Schott, with Buurman, *The Uruguay Round: An Assessment*, pp. 112–114.

104. Graham, *Global Corporations and National Governments*, p. 47.

105. Alan M. Rugman and Michael Gestrin, "A Conceptual Framework for a Multilateral Agreement on Investment: Learning from the NAFTA," in Sauvé and Schwanen, eds., *Investment Rules for the Global Economy*, p. 170.

106. Fred Lazar, "Investment in the NAFTA: Just Cause for Walking Away," *Journal of World Trade* 27-5 (October 1993), pp. 28–29; Jim Stanford, "Investment," in Duncan Cameron and Mel Watkins, eds., *Canada Under Free Trade* (Toronto: Lorimer, 1993), pp. 164–166.

107. Johnson, *The North American Free Trade Agreement*, p. 512.

108. Quoted in Hedley, "Transnational Corporations and Their Regulation," p. 222. See also Robinson, *Multinationals and Political Control*, pp. 150–157.

109. Elizabeth Smythe, "The Multilateral Agreement on Investment: A Charter of Rights for Global Investors or Just Another Agreement?," in Fen Osler Hampson and Maureen Appel Molot, eds., *Canada Among Nations 1998: Leadership and Dialogue* (Toronto, On-

tario: Oxford University Press, 1998), pp. 241–245; William A. Dymond, "The MAI: A Sad and Melancholy Tale," in *Canada Among Nations 1999: A Big League Player?* (Toronto, Ontario: Oxford University Press, 1999), p. 26.

110. Edward M. Graham and Pierre Sauvé "Toward a Rules-Based Regime for Investment: Issues and Challenges," in Sauvé and Schwanen, eds., *Investment Rules for the Global Economy,* p. 135.

111. Elizabeth Smythe, "The Multilateral Agreement on Investment: A Charter of Rights for Global Investors or Just Another Agreement?," in Fen Osler Hampson and Maureen Appel Molot, eds., *Canada Among Nations 1998: Leadership and Dialogue* (Toronto, Ontario: Oxford University Press, 1998), pp. 239–277; "MAI on Six-Month Hold," *Bridges Weekly Trade News Digest* 2-16 (4 May 1998), pp. 3–4; "MAI in Doubt After France Withdraws from Talks," *Bridges Weekly Trade News Digest* 2-40 (19 October 1998), pp. 3–5.

112. Peter Morton, "MAI Gets Tangled in Web," *The Financial Post,* 22 October 1998, p. 3.

113. Dymond, "The MAI," p. 50.

114. Graham and Sauvé, "Toward a Rules-Based Regime for Investment," p. 101.

115. Jan Aart Scholte with Robert O'Brien and Marc Williams, "The WTO and Civil Society, *Journal of World Trade* 33-1 (1999), pp. 112–116.

116. The discussion of environmental NGOs in this section draws heavily on Peter Newell, "Environmental NGOs, TNCs, and the Question of Governance," in Dimitris Stevis and Valerie J. Assetto, eds., *The International Political Economy of the Environment: Critical Perspectives* (Boulder, CO: Lynne Rienner, 2001), pp. 85–107. On corporate codes of conduct see Raymond J. Waldmann, *Regulating International Business through Codes of Conduct* (Washington, DC: American Enterprise Institute for Public Policy Research, 1980); Neil Kearney, "Corporate Codes of Conduct: The Privatized Application of Labour Standards," and Petrina Fridd and Jessica Sainsbury, "The Role of Voluntary Codes of Conduct and Regulation—A Retailer's View," in Sol Picciotto and Ruth Mayne, eds., *Regulating International Business: Beyond Liberalization* (London: Macmillan, 1999), pp. 205–234; and Gary Gereffi, Ronie Garcia-Johnson, and Erika Sasser, "The NGO-Indus," *Foreign Policy,* 125 (July/August 2001), pp. 56–65.

117. Robert W. Cox, "Civil Society at the Turn of the Millennium: Prospects for an Alternative World Order," *Review of International Studies* 25 (1999), p. 26.

118. Newell, "Environmental NGOs, TNCs, and the Question of Governance," pp. 100–104.

119. Ruth Mayne, "Regulating TNCs: The Role of Voluntary and Governmental Approaches," in Picciotto and Mayne, eds., *Regulating International Business,* p. 246.

120. Schwanen, "Investment and the Global Economy," pp. 2–3; Graham, *Global Corporations and National Governments,* p. 27.

CHAPTER 11

International Development

The Bretton Woods system and its institutions have often been credited with contributing "to almost unprecedented global economic growth and change over the past five decades."[1] However, a substantial majority of the world's people living in the South have received little benefit from this growth. Poverty, hunger, and disease are prevalent in much of the world, and the gap between the rich states of the North and most of the poor states of the South is persistent and growing. According to the World Bank, the average income in the world's richest 20 countries is 37 times higher than the average income in the poorest 20 countries—a gap that has doubled in the last 40 years. About 2.8 billion of the world's 6 billion people live on less than $2 a day, and 1.2 billion people live on less than $1 a day. Almost 44 percent of those living on less than $1 a day live in South Asia.[2] As discussed in Chapter 2, LDCs generally have low levels of economic development, marked by low per capita incomes, inadequate infrastructure facilities (such as communications and transportation), and limited access to modern technology. The economic development problems of LDCs in turn often prevent them from fostering social and political development. Thus, many LDCs have inadequate health and educational facilities, low literacy rates, and high infant mortality rates. Politically, many LDCs have difficulty maintaining stable governments that also allow for some degree of democratic participation.[3]

Although severe economic and social problems confront a substantial majority of people in the South, there are major differences in economic development among the Third World economies. As Table 11.1 shows, the NIEs of East Asia and Latin America have per capita GNPs in the middle- to high-income range, reaching $29,610 in Singapore and $23,520 in Hong Kong, China. Some OPEC states such as Kuwait and Saudi Arabia also have per capita GNPs in the high-income and upper middle-income range. Indeed, countries such as Singapore, Kuwait, and Saudi Arabia are not eligible to borrow World Bank funds.[4] In stark contrast, the poorest African and Asian states, such as Mozambique, Malawi, Ethiopia, Cambodia, and Nepal, have per capita GNPs in the $100 to $260 range. In addition to their higher incomes, Table 2.2 in Chapter 2 shows that East Asia (excluding China) ranks higher than other Third World regions

TABLE 11.1

Per Capita GNP of Southern Economies, 1999

HIGHER AND MIDDLE-INCOME ECONOMIES

East Asian NIEs		Latin American NIEs	
Singapore	$29,610	Argentina	$7,600
Hong Kong, China	23,520	Brazil	4,420
South Korea	8,490	Mexico	4,400

LOW INCOME ECONOMIES

Africa		Asia	
Nigeria	$310	Bangladesh	$370
Mozambique	230	Vietnam	370
Malawi	190	Cambodia	260
Ethiopia	100	Nepal	220

Source: World Bank, *World Development Report 2000–2001: Attacking Poverty,* (Washington, D.C.: World Bank, 2001), Table 1, pp. 274–275.

TABLE 11.2

Growth of Real GDP per Capita (Average Annual Percentage Change)

Group	1965–73	1973–80	1980–89
Industrial countries	3.7	2.3	2.3
Less developed countries			
Sub-Saharan Africa	2.1	0.4	−1.2
East Asia	5.3	4.9	6.2
South Asia	1.2	1.7	3.0
Europe, Middle East, and North Africa	5.8	1.9	0.4
Latin America and the Caribbean	3.8	2.5	−0.4

Source: World Bank, *World Development Report 1991,* Table 1, p. 3. Copyright © 1991 by The International Bank for Reconstruction and Development/The World Bank. By permission of Oxford University Press.

on a wide range of human development indicators such as infant mortality rates, adult literacy rates, and access to safe water.

The East Asian NIEs were also the most rapidly growing Third World economies during the critical periods of the oil and foreign debt crises from 1973 to 1989. Indeed, Table 11.2 shows that East Asia managed to increase its average annual economic growth rate to 6.2 percent during 1980–89, a period marked by a global recession and the foreign debt crisis. Sub-Saharan Africa and Latin America and the Caribbean, by contrast, had *negative* economic growth rates (of −1.2 percent and −0.4 percent) during the 1980–89 period. Many scholars therefore refer to the 1980s as a lost decade for much of the South, which experienced a serious debt crisis, declining prices for raw material exports, declining foreign investment, and capital flight. In 1991, the World

Bank reported that the real income gap between the North and all Third World regions except East Asia was widening.[5]

During the 1990s, many Third World countries continued to experience problems with economic growth. As in the 1980s, there were major differences among Third World regions. In East Asia, the number of people living on less than $1 a day fell from about 420 million in 1987 to 280 million in 1998. In contrast, the number of poor people have been increasing in South Asia, Latin America, sub-Saharan Africa, and the transition countries of Europe and Central Asia.[6] Table 2.3 in Chapter 2 shows that 19 of the 43 LLDCs for which statistics are available had negative GDP per capita growth rates from 1990 to 1998. As discussed in this chapter, even the higher income East and Southeast Asian economies experienced a serious financial crisis in the late 1990s that raised questions about the sustainability of rapid economic development in the region.

In view of their vulnerabilities, LDCs have traditionally been ambivalent about their relations with the developed states. Although they have looked to the North for trade, foreign investment, development assistance, and technology transfers, the LDCs are fearful that these linkages contribute to their dependence on the North and to threats to their autonomy. Third World countries have also been ambivalent about the IMF, World Bank, and GATT/WTO. Although the KIEOs have helped LDCs gain access to external finance and foreign markets for their exports, LDCs resent the fact that the developed countries are the dominant actors in the KIEOs. Furthermore, LDC debtor countries believe that the conditions attached to IMF and World Bank SALs often inhibit rather than further their development efforts.[7]

Despite the South's ambivalence about its relations with the North, a series of developments have induced LDCs to increase their Northern linkages, adopt liberal-economic policies prescribed by developed countries, and participate more fully in the global economy. First, a major turning point was the 1980s foreign debt crisis, when a number of LDCs were unable to meet their debt repayment obligations. As discussed in Chapter 7, the debtor LDCs were forced to turn to the IMF, the World Bank, and the developed states for assistance. The failure of inward-looking ISI policies, combined with the conditions of IMF and World Bank SALs, induced LDCs to shift to more open economic policies with an emphasis on trade liberalization, deregulation, and privatization. A second factor inducing Third World countries to open their economies has been the revival of orthodox liberalism. For example, Chapter 8 discussed the growing Northern opposition to S&D treatment for LDCs in trade and Northern pressure on LDCs to liberalize their trade policies. Most LDCs refused to become signatories to the NTB codes concluded at the GATT Tokyo round in the late 1970s, but the Uruguay round negotiations were organized as a single undertaking in which the LDCs were expected to be full participants in all the agreements.

A third factor causing LDCs to participate more fully in the global economy has been the growing fear that most of the South is becoming increasingly marginalized. Major reasons for this marginalization include the decline of the Cold War and the breakup of the Soviet bloc and Soviet Union. Consistent with realist predictions, the decline of the Cold War has deprived the LDCs of a traditional source of leverage they had in extracting concessions from both the East and the West. Thus, Western developed countries have been less willing to provide foreign aid.

Table 11.5 shows that net ODA fell from 0.52 percent of the GNP of OECD donor countries at the height of the Cold War in 1960 to 0.37 percent in 1980 and to only 0.24 percent in 1999.[8]

In addition to the steady decline of aid, the number of aid recipients increased dramatically in the 1990s as a result of the breakup of the Soviet bloc and Soviet Union. Eastern Europe and the former Soviet Union were foreign aid donors until the end of the 1980s. In the 1990s, by contrast, these countries turned to the West for assistance and became competitors with the LDCs for export markets, development finance, and inward foreign investment. At the 1991 OECD Council meeting, the OECD ministers provided assurances that "their co-operation with developing countries will not be diminished because of their support for central and eastern Europe,"[9] but the statistics on development assistance indicate otherwise. To interpret these statistics, it is necessary to discuss the OECD's terminology for aid giving. *ODA* refers to grants or loans provided by the official (or public) sector of OECD countries to LDCs for development purposes. To qualify as ODA, loans must be concessional rather than commercial; that is, they must have a "grant element" of at least 25 percent. (The "grant element" is zero for a loan at an interest rate of 10 percent. As the interest rate declines below 10 percent, the grant element of the loan increases, and a grant with zero interest rate has a grant element of 100 percent.) The OECD categorizes aid to Russia, the Ukraine, and most Eastern European states as *official aid (OA)* rather than ODA, because the recipients are transition economies rather than LDCs. OA meets all the requirements for ODA in terms of concessionality, except that the recipients are classified as transition economies. (China and many of the smaller and poorer FSU countries are categorized as LDCs and receive ODA. FSU countries that are LDCs include Armenia, Azerbaijan, Kyrgyz Republic, Tajikistan, Kazakstan, Turkmenistan, and Uzbekistan.)[10]

The important point is that ODA to the South has declined since the end of the Cold War, partly because a considerable amount of OA and ODA is now being directed to the former CPEs in Eastern Europe, the FSU countries, and China. As Table 11.3 shows, in 1995–96 three former CPEs (China, Poland, and Russia), and in 1998–99 two former CPEs (China and Russia) were among the 10 largest recipients of ODA and OA from the OECD countries.

This chapter assesses the various strategies LDCs have pursued in efforts to promote their economic development, such as import substitution, socialist strategies, and export-led growth. In accordance with the revival of orthodox liberalism, LDCs in recent years have shifted to more open economic policies. Current development policies fall short, however, in meeting the needs of the poorest and most disadvantaged in society (such as Third World women and children) and in looking after the needs of the future as well as the present (for example, in preserving the environment). As background for examining the LDC economic development strategies, it is first necessary to briefly discuss the three major IPE perspectives and to describe the functions of the World Bank, which "enjoys a unique position as a generator of ideas about economic development."[11] In the postwar period, the World Bank and the United States in particular have had considerable influence over the ideological and operational models used to promote development in the South.

TABLE 11.3

TEN LARGEST RECIPIENTS OF ODA^a OR OA^b
FROM THE OECD COUNTRIES

1995–96		1998–99	
Country	Amount[c]	Country	Amount
1. China	2,412	1. Indonesia	2,426
2. Indonesia	2,118	2. China	2,249
3. Poland	2,018	3. India	1,558
4. Egypt	1,937	4. Egypt	1,554
5. India	1,708	5. Russia	1,239
6. Israel	1,484	6. Israel	1,143
7. Russia	1,228	7. Thailand	1,098
8. Philippines	1,195	8. Philippines	955
9. Thailand	1,059	9. Vietnam	887
10. Bangladesh	849	10. Bangladesh	795

[a]ODA = Official Development Assistance
[b]OA = Official Aid
[c]Millions of Dollars
Source: OECD, *Development Co-operation Report 1997,* (Paris: OECD, 1998), p. 79; OECD, *Development Co-operation Report 2000,* (Paris: OECD, 2001), p. 101.

THE IPE PERSPECTIVES AND NORTH-SOUTH RELATIONS

This section briefly summarizes some of the main tenets of the three IPE perspectives as they relate to North-South relations. For a more detailed discussion of these perspectives, see Chapters 3 to 5.

Realist writers in the developed states, preoccupied with the issues of power and influence, tend to ignore the economic interests of the poorer countries of the South. In the realist view, "Third World states want power and control as much as wealth,"[12] and it is only when Third World states pose a challenge to the economic predominance of the North that most realists take notice. In the 1970s, for example, realists looked at the increased leverage of OPEC in raising oil prices and at the attempts of Third World countries to gain more power and wealth through their calls for an NIEO. In the 1980s and 1990s, realists became interested in the challenge the East Asian developmental state model posed to the North. Despite the lack of realist attention to poverty in the South, realist ideas have had considerable influence on LDC policies. For example, Alexander Hamilton and Friedrich List emphasized state building and argued that the late industrializers of their time (the United States and Germany) required a large degree of government involvement if they were to "catch up" with Britain—the leading state. Major Third World development strategies such as import substitution and export-oriented industrialization draw on Hamilton and List's ideas calling for a larger role for the state in promoting economic development.

Liberals believe that the growth of interdependence has widespread benefits, and they often argue that North-South linkages provide even more benefits to LDCs than to the developed states. The economic problems of LDCs, from the liberal perspective, stem more from their inefficient domestic policies than from their dependent position in the global economy. Thus, LDCs that follow open economic policies and increase their linkages with the developed states are most likely to achieve successful development. Although all liberals encourage LDCs to follow open, market-oriented policies, interventionist liberals (also called reformist liberals) recognize that inequalities between the North and South can put the Third World states at a distinct disadvantage. Unlike orthodox liberals, who emphasize equal treatment and reciprocity, interventionist liberals call on Northern states to give more consideration to the special needs of the South. Nevertheless, interventionist liberals believe that the necessary changes can occur within the existing capitalist order, and they share the faith of other liberals in private enterprise and the market.

The historical structuralist views of most interest in this chapter are those of dependency and world-system theorists. (For a discussion of the classical Marxist view of development, see Chapter 5.) Dependency theorists reject both the optimism of liberals and the liberal view that Third World economic problems result primarily from inefficient domestic policies. From the dependency view, structural factors related to the global capitalist economy are responsible for constraining LDC development possibilities. Thus, dependency theorists argue that the advanced capitalist states in the core of the global economy either "underdevelop" Third World countries in the periphery or prevent them from attaining genuine, autonomous development. Dependency theorists are also interested in class linkages, and they maintain that elites in the South (the "comprador" class) collaborate with foreign capitalists in the North to reinforce the pattern of Third World dependency. Because some Third World states such as the East Asian and Latin American NIEs were successfully industrializing, world-system theorists modified the classical dependency argument by introducing a third category of countries, the semiperiphery. Countries may move upward (or downward) from the periphery to the semiperiphery and even to the core, but world-system theorists believe that this only rarely occurs. Whereas some historical structuralists call for a redistribution of resources from the core to the periphery, the more extreme theorists believe that the core will never willingly agree to such a transfer of resources. Thus, they call for a domestic social revolution in the South and/or a severing of contacts with the developed states. The solution for disadvantaged groups, according to Gramscian theorists, is the development of a "counterhegemony."

THE WORLD BANK GROUP

It is important to provide some background discussion of the World Bank before examining LDC economic development strategies. The World Bank's policies have been subject to numerous criticisms, and it currently faces some major stresses and uncertainties as an institution. Nevertheless, the World Bank has had a major effect on LDC development strategies, because of its dominant role "as a non-private lender, as a research and idea-generating unit, and as a provider of advice to the Third World."[13] Developed countries traditionally have preferred to give most of their ODA bilaterally, or directly to recipient countries. However, the share of ODA extended multilaterally through IOs has increased from only about 5 percent in 1960–64 to 20 percent in 1970–74, 29 percent in 1980–84, and 33 percent in 1995–97.[14] The World Bank has benefited from this shift toward multilateral aid because it is the largest lender of multilateral funds for international development.

The World Bank's considerable influence on the lending side stems not only from the amount of funding it provides, but even more importantly from "its role as a rating agency for others."[15] The World Bank's lending decisions, data collection, and country analysis have a powerful influence on bilateral donors, regional development banks, and those providing private portfolio and direct investment. The World Bank also has an influential role in the ongoing debates over economic development; indeed, global "debates on development issues" are often "framed in terms of 'pro or anti' World Bank positions."[16] Several factors account for the World Bank's influence in generating ideas on development: the World Bank affects the terms under which LDCs gain access to development financing and international capital markets, it has the largest group of development economists and the largest research and policy analysis budget of any development organization, and the global media pay considerable attention to the World Bank's major studies and reports. In view of the World Bank's influence, it is necessary to describe its organizational characteristics and to briefly discuss the views of proponents and critics of World Bank policies.

Located in Washington, D.C., the World Bank is actually a World Bank group composed of five institutions (see Figure 2.1 in Chapter 2). The first of these institutions, the IBRD, was planned at the Bretton Woods conference. Foreign aid was *not* a central concern of the Western developed states at Bretton Woods. They were mainly interested in establishing the IMF to deal with monetary and balance of payments issues, and the decision to establish the IBRD was "something of an afterthought."[17] The Western developed countries also expected the IBRD to give priority to European reconstruction over Third World development, and Harry Dexter White of the U.S. Treasury Department in fact suggested that the new institution should be called the "Bank for Reconstruction."[18] Because of LDC protests, the negotiators decided that the IBRD would devote equitable consideration to reconstruction and development; but the first IBRD loans in 1947 in fact went to France, the Netherlands, and Denmark for European reconstruction. It was not until the United States established the European Recovery Program or Marshall Plan for Western Europe in 1948 that the IBRD shifted its focus from reconstruction to Third World development.[19]

As is the case for the IMF, the World Bank is a weighted voting institution. Each member state has a capital subscription (or quota) based on its economic strength, which determines its financial contribution to the World Bank and the number of votes it has in the policymaking bodies (see Chapter 6). The G-5 countries have the largest subscriptions and the largest number of votes. In June 2001, the G-5 had 37.4 percent of the votes in the IBRD Board of Governors; the United States led with

16.4 percent, followed by Japan, Germany, France, and Britain, with 7.9 percent, 4.5 percent, 4.3 percent, and 4.3 percent of the votes, respectively.[20] Member states in fact pay only 10 percent of their subscriptions to the IBRD and hold the remaining 90 percent as callable capital if needed to meet the IBRD's financial obligations. The IBRD receives by far the greatest share of its funds for development loans, not from these subscriptions, but from its borrowing on world capital markets. It has been able to depend on the capital markets for funding because of its good record in LDC repayment of loans and because of its large reserves of members' callable capital. Thus, the principal U.S. bond-rating services have given IBRD bonds a triple-A credit rating.

To make its bonds attractive to purchasers, the IBRD must pay market interest rates on its financial borrowing, and it must therefore in turn charge near-conventional interest rates on loans to LDC borrowers. For example, the interest rate on IBRD loans in 1997 was about 6.8 percent, the grace period was 3 to 5 years, and the maturity period ranged from 15 to 20 years.[21] IBRD loans are not concessional enough (i.e., they have too low a grant element) to qualify as ODA. Thus, the OECD introduced the concept of *Official Development Finance (ODF)* to recognize the developmental value of hard loans from multilateral institutions such as the IBRD. ("Hard loans" have higher interest rates and shorter repayment periods, whereas "soft loans" are more concessional with lower interest rates and longer repayment periods.) The IBRD's quasi-commercial loans are considered to be ODF because the IBRD extends them for development purposes, it accompanies the loans with economic and technical advice, which is often in short supply in the South, and LDCs receive the IBRD loans on better terms than they could obtain from borrowing directly on capital markets.

To be a World Bank member, a country must also be a member of the IMF. This requirement deterred most Communist countries from joining the World Bank for many years—even though they would have liked to receive World Bank loans—because members must provide the IMF with detailed information about their economies (see Table 2.4 in Chapter 2). The Western developed states were willing to give the World Bank and its staff considerable discretion in loan giving because of the lack of Communist members, the World Bank's weighted voting system, and the dominant position of Western countries on the professional staff. As in the IMF, the *board of governors* is theoretically the main policymaking body in the World Bank. Although every member state has one governor, the governors have different numbers of votes based on the weighted voting system. The governors meet only once a year to review the bank's operations and policies, admit new members, and amend the Articles of Agreement; they delegate most of their functions to the *board of executive directors.* The executive board, which also has weighted voting, is responsible for approving all World Bank loan proposals and for developing the general policies of the bank. Whereas the G-5 countries are each assured of always appointing their own executive directors because of their large number of votes, coalitions of member countries elect the other executive directors every two years. (Normally China, Saudi Arabia, and Russia each have enough votes to elect their own executive directors, but they have fewer votes than the G-5 countries.) Elected executive directors cannot split their votes; that is, they must cast the votes of their entire coalition group as a unit.

The United States is the most important member of the World Bank, and there are a number of indicators of its influence. As mentioned, the United States has more votes than any other member country. Furthermore, English is the World Bank's only working language, reflecting U.S. influence and the World Bank's location in Washington, D.C. The American view that a single working language contributes to efficiency contrasts with the view of many other countries that cultural and ethnic diversity dictates the need for more than one working language in IOs.[22] In addition, the executive directors regularly accept the U.S. government's nominee for World Bank president, even though the directors are theoretically responsible for selecting the president. Whereas the U.S. Treasury Department handles most matters related to U.S. involvement in the World Bank, the White House nominates the World Bank presidents and "invariably chooses candidates with connections to the U.S. political establishment."[23]

Despite the continued influence of the United States, its predominance has clearly declined. In the early years, the IBRD was extremely dependent on the U.S. capital market as a source of funds; markets in other countries were extremely limited. Over time, however, the share of the World Bank's outstanding securities held in the United States has steadily declined. U.S. voting power in the IBRD has also fallen from about 40 percent of the total to less than 17 percent, and this decline is reflected in voting outcomes. Whereas the United States virtually had a blocking veto on loan decisions during the 1940s and 1950s, some World Bank loans have been approved in recent years even when the U.S. executive director has abstained or voted against them. Nevertheless, the World Bank would not approve loans on a regular basis that the United States strongly opposed.[24]

The IBRD was the only World Bank group institution until the International Finance Corporation (IFC) was established in 1956 (see Figure 2.1 in Chapter 2). Reflecting the World Bank group's liberal-economic orientation, the IFC encourages private business and investment in LDCs, and today it is the largest multilateral source of loans and equity financing for private-sector projects in the Third World. To promote private enterprise, the IFC is active in areas where the IBRD cannot operate. IBRD loans are directed only to governments, or with a government guarantee. The IFC by contrast can make loans to private ventures in LDCs without a government guarantee; indeed, it may not even accept a government guarantee. The IFC also invests in equity shares of corporations and acts as a broker bringing foreign and domestic partners together in joint ventures. Furthermore, the IFC has persuaded commercial banks to lend more to LDCs, partly through joint financing deals with banks as co-lenders. Like the IBRD, the IFC charges near-commercial rates on its loans. In the 1980s, the U.S. Reagan administration's emphasis on the private sector elevated the IFC's importance in the World Bank group, and the IFC reported net profits of $142 million in the 1992–93 fiscal year. These profits, combined with the high interest rate on IFC loans, raise questions among critics as to whether the IFC is primarily a money-making or a philanthropic institution. Nevertheless, the IFC maintains that it promotes development by providing technical, financial, and environmental advice for Third World development projects.[25]

In 1960, the IDA became the third World Bank group institution (see Figure 2.1 in Chapter 2). The IDA was formed largely in response to Third World complaints that the poorer LDCs could not pay the high interest rates on the IBRD's hard loans. Even major LDCs such as India and Pakistan were reaching the limits of their borrowing ability on conventional terms in the late 1950s. Third World countries also opposed the World Bank's weighted voting system, and throughout the 1950s they demanded a soft-loan agency in which they would have greater control. The industrial states finally agreed to create the IDA as a soft-loan agency in 1960, but they insisted that the agency be under World Bank auspices with its weighted voting system. Although the IDA and IBRD are legally and financially distinct, they share the same staff and their projects must meet the same criteria.[26]

The IDA provides soft loans or "credits" to Third World governments with no interest rate, 10-year grace periods, and 35- to 40-year maturities. Unlike IBRD and IFC loans, IDA credits are concessional enough to be categorized as "ODA." IDA credits are extended only to the poorest or neediest countries. A number of LDCs and transition economies with somewhat stronger economies are eligible for IBRD loans but not for IDA credits; examples of these countries are Argentina, Brazil, Mexico, Malaysia, Thailand, Iran, Egypt, the Czech Republic, Hungary, Russia, the Ukraine, and China. A small middle range group of countries with somewhat weaker economies are eligible for a blend of IBRD and IDA funds; examples include India, Pakistan, Indonesia, Nigeria, Bolivia, the Federal Republic of Yugoslavia, Azerbaijan, and Uzbekistan. Countries with the weakest economies are eligible for IDA credits, but not for IBRD loans. In 2001, 64 World Bank group members were in this category; examples include Bangladesh, Nepal, Vietnam, Honduras, Tanzania, Republic of the Congo, Kenya, Ethiopia, Albania, Georgia, Armenia, and Mongolia.[27] Unlike the IBRD and IFC, the interest-free terms of IDA credits give it no basis for borrowing on capital markets. IDA funds therefore depend primarily on the willingness of the developed country member governments to provide "negotiated replenishments." The negotiations are often protracted and difficult; other donors often wait for the United States to pledge funds before making their own pledges, and the U.S. Congress has regularly delayed its approval of IDA contributions. Orthodox liberal views that LDCs should rely more on private capital and less on World Bank "handouts" pose a constant threat to IDA's financial viability.[28]

The fourth and fifth institutions of the World Bank group—the *International Centre for Settlement of Investment Disputes (ICSID)* and the *MIGA*—were established to encourage the flow of private foreign investment to LDCs and transition economies (see Figure 2.1 in Chapter 2). The ICSID was established in 1966 to provide international facilities for conciliation and arbitration of disputes over FDI. The need for a neutral international forum arose because foreign investors were concerned that the courts in host countries would not be impartial, and issues of sovereignty and national dignity prevented host countries from submitting disputes to foreign courts. The MIGA was established in 1988 to provide guarantees to foreign investors against losses caused by noncommercial risks such as currency inconvertibility, expropriation, war, and civil disturbances. The MIGA also provides technical assistance to help LDCs and transition economies disseminate information on investment opportunities.[29]

It is important to note that the World Bank has considerable influence over bilateral as well as multilateral aid giving. The World Bank is a key source of data and analysis on development issues, and its reports, publications, and activities play a central role in debates among development experts and government officials. The World Bank also chairs a large number of aid consortia and **consultative groups.** These groups bring together donor states that provide development assistance to a particular recipient and enable them to coordinate their bilateral aid giving and avoid needless duplication. From the view of Third World countries, however, consultative groups often permit donors to exert collective pressures on a recipient government because only one recipient and many donors attend each meeting.[30]

As the most important multilateral development institution, the World Bank has also provided a model for the formation of regional development banks, including the Inter-American Development Bank (established in 1960), the African Development Bank (1964), the Asian Development Bank (1966), and the European Bank for Reconstruction and Development (1991). Like the World Bank, the regional development banks usually raise money on international capital markets and lend this money at near-commercial rates of interest. Because the regional banks' credit ratings are backed by member countries' subscriptions (most of which are callable rather than paid in), they can borrow and lend money at favorable rates of interest. These banks also have IDA-type soft-loan affiliates, which must raise their funds from government subscriptions. The regional banks perform an important role in supporting smaller development projects at the regional level, whereas the World Bank directs most of its funding to larger projects and programs.[31]

It is impossible to detail the numerous arguments here in favor of, and against, World Bank policies and activities. Instead, we provide a brief outline of some of the most salient issues raised by critics and supporters. In general terms, critics of the World Bank have ranged from historical structuralists on the left to orthodox liberals on the right. Historical structuralists accuse the World Bank of "prying state control of its Third World member countries out of the hands of nationalists and socialists who would regulate international capital's inroads."[32] Historical structuralists also argue that World Bank loans enrich developed country exporters and MNCs at the expense of the poorest people and LDCs. Some orthodox liberals, by contrast, charge that IOs such as the World Bank "have an evident interest in ever-increasing multinational aid" and suggest that the World Bank should "impose a greater check on the staff's tendency to be 'state enthusiasts.' "[33] Defenders often view the World Bank as adopting interventionist or reformist liberal policies as a development institution and consider it inevitable "that the Bank should be subjected to severe criticism from the ideologues of both left and right."[34]

As this chapter discusses, the World Bank has in fact often been too ready to disregard challenges to its liberal free market approach to development problems, and it has been more willing to accept studies emphasizing government failure than studies emphasizing market failure.[35] In the 1980s and 1990s, the World Bank became a stronger supporter of orthodox liberal policies and pressured LDCs to adopt these policies through its SALs. Only recently has the World Bank become more aware of the problems resulting if measures are not taken to cushion vulnerable groups and countries from unrestrained market pressures. Other criticisms of the World Bank range from its dismissive and patronizing attitude toward other institutions such as the United Nations Development Program (UNDP), UNICEF, and the regional development banks; its highly centralized structure in Washington, D.C., with too little staff time spent in the field; and its practice of giving priority to large-project commitments with fast-disbursing loans over project supervision, implementation, and evaluation.

In fairness to the World Bank, one should note that as the largest multilateral development institution it is sometimes a target of criticism regardless of the policies it adopts. For example, some critics charge that the World Bank is too slow to alter its approach to development in response to civil society pressures and the changing requirements of LDCs. However, when the World Bank alters its policies, others charge that "under pressure from NGOs and other interest groups" the World Bank rushes "to embrace the latest fads in development thinking regardless of their substantive merits."[36] Furthermore, the World Bank, like all IOs, is to a large degree a creature of its most important member states. Thus, the World Bank's ability to provide increased IDA funds for the poorest LDCs in Asia and sub-Saharan Africa ultimately depends on the willingness of the developed countries to provide IDA replenishments.

Having provided some background on the World Bank group, we now turn to a discussion of Third World development strategies.

IMPORT-SUBSTITUTING INDUSTRIALIZATION

In the early postwar period, the ideas of several major economists had a significant influence on development strategies of LDCs. First, Third World development strategies drew on the interventionist liberal ideas of John Maynard Keynes. Although Keynes called for a greater role for the government in welfare and job creation in developed states, his ideas contributed to the view that LDC governments should also have a major role in promoting economic development. Second, Third World development strategies drew on the ideas of Raúl Prebisch and Hans Singer. In 1950, Prebisch and Singer separately published studies arguing that there was a growing gap in the incomes of developed countries and LDCs because of a long-term decline in the prices of primary products (raw materials and agricultural goods). To close the income gap with the developed countries, LDCs would have to alter the structures of their economies, decreasing their emphasis on the production of primary products and focusing first and foremost on industrialization.[37]

In arguing that LDCs were disadvantaged because of their role as primary product exporters, Prebisch and Singer directly contradicted the views of liberal economists that free trade based on comparative advantage benefits all states. According to the Prebisch-Singer thesis, the demand of individuals for industrial goods such as automobiles and televisions rises as their incomes go up, but the same does not apply to the demand for raw materials and agricultural products. Indeed, the demand for raw materials may even decline in developed countries as technological advances lead to the discovery of substitute products (such as synthetic rubber as a replacement for natural rubber). Thus, Third World countries that depend on the export of primary products suffer from declining terms of trade. When LDCs raise their production of primary products in attempts to garner more revenue, they are simply faced with lower prices and more abject levels of poverty as surplus stocks accumulate. Prebisch therefore argued that an ISI strategy would permit LDCs to produce manufactured goods at home that they had previously imported. As discussed in Chapter 5, Prebisch began to use the terms "center" and "periphery" as early as the 1950s, and his classic work formed the core of Latin American structuralist policies in the 1950s and 1960s. Although Prebisch's structuralism was a precursor (along with Marxism) of dependency theory, it was *not* dependency theory. Latin American structuralism was not based on class analysis and was much more optimistic than dependency theory that LDCs could catch up with developed countries through a combination of protectionism and state-promoted industrialization.[38]

Realists such as Hamilton and List had supported policies similar to ISI for late industrializers in the eighteenth and nineteenth centuries, and some LDCs in Latin America and the Middle East had developed ISI policies as a short-term response to the Great Depression in the interwar period. However, it was not until after World War II that the South adopted ISI as a long-term development strategy. Central to ISI was the argument that LDCs should protect and support their infant industries through tariff and nontariff barriers to industrial imports and through subsidies and other incentives to promote industrial growth. Only through an emphasis on industrial development (and a deemphasis on agriculture) would LDCs be able to compete on a more equal footing with the developed states.

In the 1950s and 1960s, LDCs in Latin America, South and Southeast Asia, and Africa followed ISI policies, and import subtitution "emerged as the new gospel for Third World industrialization."[39] Although ISI is considered to be a realist development strategy with strong nationalist overtones, it is interesting that the World Bank was generally supportive of Third World ISI policies in the 1950s. The World Bank has always been interested in promoting private enterprise in LDCs, but it was affected by postwar interventionist liberal views that the state had an important role to play in the development process. The World Bank's approach to development placed considerable emphasis on industrialization, which normally meant ISI in the 1950s. Because of the infant industry problem for LDCs, the World Bank accepted the fact that ISI would involve some degree of trade protectionism. Furthermore, the World Bank provided funding for major infrastructure projects such as transportation and communications facilities, power projects, and port developments, which Third World countries required to promote industrialization.[40]

Initially, ISI policies seemed to provide major gains for LDCs. For example, Latin America registered healthy industrial growth rates in the 1940s to 1950s, and the Mexican economy grew at annual average rates of 6.5 percent until 1970. India's steel production increased by six times during its first three 5-year plans from 1951 to 1966, and some African countries such as Ghana also registered major industrial gains. International economic conditions were highly favorable to the success of ISI strategies in the 1950s and early 1960s, and LDCs benefited from a period of prosperity and growth in North America and Western Europe. Furthermore, the South's output of agricultural products generally did not suffer in the 1960s even though ISI policies downgraded the role of agriculture because the Rockefeller Foundation–supported "green revolution" led to the development of new dwarf strains of high-yielding grains. The green revolution exacerbated differences between rich and poor farmers in the South because only the rich could afford the large amounts of irrigation, fertilizer, and other inputs required to grow the new high-yielding grains. Nevertheless, increased agricultural output in India and other Asian countries masked the fact that ISI policies were promoting industrialization at the expense of agriculture.[41]

Despite the initial successes of ISI policies, external problems and internal distortions started to become evident in LDCs employing ISI in the 1960s and 1970s. International economic changes such as the food and oil crises of the 1970s were especially important in exposing the weaknesses of the ISI strategy. Inclement weather, Soviet crop shortfalls, and other unexpected events in the early 1970s led to greatly increased demand for food imports, and global food stocks in 1972–73 fell to their lowest levels in 20 years. Many LDCs lacked *effective demand,* or demand backed by purchasing power, so they had less ability than countries such as the Soviet Union and Japan to purchase foodstuffs on global markets at inflated prices. Thus, the global food crisis in the early 1970s had its severest effects on the South.[42] When OPEC managed to limit supplies and drastically raise oil prices in 1973, a number of LDC oil importers such as India were doubly hit by the food and energy crises. These new external stresses exposed a number of weaknesses in ISI as a development strategy.

First, the global food crisis in the early 1970s pointed to the pitfalls for LDCs in overemphasizing industrialization at the expense of agriculture. The neglect of agriculture under ISI eventually led to poverty in the countryside, the need for foodgrain imports, and the stagnation of agricultural exports. Indeed, the LDC share of world agricultural exports fell from 44 percent in 1955 to 32 percent in 1970. The decline in revenue from agricultural exports simply exacerbated problems of balance-of-payments deficits and lack of funding for investment in the South. Second, despite the emphasis of the ISI strategy on promoting self-sufficiency, ISI ironically increased LDC dependence on the developed countries and their MNCs. In view of their shortages of capital and foreign exchange, LDCs considered foreign investment to be "a necessary evil" if they were to succeed in industrializing, and they therefore encouraged inward FDI as part of their ISI policies. As a result, MNCs were able to set up subsidiaries behind the trade barriers of LDCs. This fact helps to explain why the U.S. government supported ISI as part of "its vigorous efforts to secure favorable conditions for U.S. foreign direct investment."[43] American policies were less consistently pro–free trade in the postwar period than many hegemonic stability theorists have indicated.

The most serious weakness of the ISI strategy was its inability to accomplish what it was supposed to be best at: promoting industrial competitiveness. Industrialization seemed to proceed well under an "easy" first stage of ISI, but the second stage of ISI was far more difficult. In the first stage, LDCs replaced imports of nondurable consumer products such as shoes, household goods, and clothing, with domestic production. LDCs are better able to produce labor-intensive goods that do not require the use of advanced technology, large amounts of capital investment, or a network of component suppliers. There is also a sizable domestic market in LDCs for the purchase of nondurable consumer goods. However, LDCs had to move on to a second stage of ISI to maintain high industrial growth rates, replacing imports of intermediate goods (e.g., petrochemicals and steel) and producer and consumer durables (e.g., refrigerators and automobiles) with domestic production. These second-stage products were more difficult for LDCs to produce, because they are capital intensive and depend on economies of scale and higher levels of technology. LDC producers had to import much of the technology and inputs required to produce these goods, and the cost of the imported inputs outweighed any savings from producing the final goods locally. Finally, the emphasis on increasing capital-intensive production under ISI concentrated development gains in a small percentage of the population in industrial enclaves, and unemployment emerged as a major problem for most people outside these enclaves. ISI policies therefore simply exacerbated the inequalities of income among individuals within Third World countries.[44]

Those LDCs pursuing the second stage of ISI suffered from a slowdown in the growth of primary product exports, dependence on imports for the production of second-stage goods, and a failure to increase manufactured exports. In response to their balance-of-payments problems, these LDCs sought external loans, aid, and investment and turned increasingly to trade protectionism. By the 1960s, therefore, some liberal economists were arguing that "an import substitution policy tends to be less and less successful the longer it continues,"[45] and the World Bank was changing its views and beginning to oppose ISI policies. For example, the World Bank began to sponsor a series of studies in 1965 that demonstrated the high cost of ISI in LDC automotive industries and in the production of heavy electrical and manufacturing equipment. By the late 1960s, "the financing of profitable import-substituting industry by IFC and [World] Bank-financed development finance companies, without much regard for the relation of domestic to international prices" was giving way "to a more discriminating policy of industrial financing."[46] Even Prebisch, who had initially encouraged Latin American LDCs to follow ISI policies, began to question these policies, arguing that "the proliferation of industries of every kind in a closed market has deprived the Latin American countries of the advantages of specialization and economies of scale."[47]

Despite the problems with second-stage ISI, many Latin American and South Asian countries continued following an ISI strategy because domestic interest groups with vested interests in trade protectionism limited the ability of governments to institute policy change.[48] It was not until the foreign debt crisis of the 1980s that most LDCs finally dispensed with ISI as a development strategy and shifted to a more outward-oriented strategy (see the following discussion). Although many LDCs persisted with ISI policies in the 1960s and 1970s, some sought other alternatives. A second group of LDCs adopted a more extreme inward-looking strategy than ISI, turning to socialist central planning based on the Soviet Union model. However, LDC experiments with socialism also encountered a number of problems. A third group of LDCs, the East Asian NIEs, changed from ISI to export-led growth strategies at a fairly early stage, and they experienced far more impressive economic growth rates than other LDCs. As a result, the economic development community began to look positively at export-led growth as an alternative strategy to promote economic development.

SOCIALIST DEVELOPMENT STRATEGIES

By the 1960s, there was already growing disillusionment with ISI policies, which contributed to uncompetitive industries and balance-of-payments problems. Scholars challenged the ISI approach from both the right and the left, and many left-leaning scholars turned to dependency theory (see the discussion of dependency theory in Chapter 4).[49] According to dependency theorists, the ISI strategy did not adequately restructure the peripheral Third World economies or increase their leverage vis-à-vis the core. LDCs could promote autonomous development, dependency theorists argued, only by turning to socialism and severing their linkages with the North. Although most LDCs continued with ISI, a small number of LDCs such as China, North

Korea, Cuba, Ethiopia, Mozambique, Vietnam, Laos, Cambodia, and Burma eventually opted for socialist central planning strategies. China was the only one of these LDCs with the size and resources to be able to reap major economic benefits from socialist central planning.[50]

The socialist development strategies were generally patterned after the Soviet model, which involved the abolition of the capitalist market economy and private ownership and the establishment of state control over the economy and its resources. Thus, state central planning largely replaced market signals in economic decisions concerning the allocation of resources and investment and the setting of production targets, wages, and prices. Third World countries opting for the socialist route were more concerned than nonsocialist LDCs about the redistributional aspects of economic development. Thus, they often registered more gains than nonsocialist LDCs in reducing economic and social inequities by providing better access to health care and education, improving the status of women, and opening parks and other facilities for use of the public. Despite the advances of some socialist LDCs in social areas such as health and education, these countries encountered a number of economic problems.

A major problem with the socialist strategy was that LDCs other than China were simply too small and lacking in resources to engage in central planning on the Soviet/Eastern European model. For example, LDCs lacked the communications and transportation infrastructure essential for central planning and a well-trained technocratic bureaucracy necessary to design and monitor the plans. Third World countries also encountered many of the same problems that plagued the Soviet Union and Eastern Europe. Thus, central planners were more successful in setting production targets and increasing the quantity of output than they were in ensuring the quality of output and the efficient use of resources. Although LDCs were generally ill equipped to employ socialist central planning, Western aid and investment policies did not make their task easier. For example, World Bank and U.S. Agency for International Development (AID) officials believed that foreign aid should be designed at least partly to promote private enterprise. Thus, most LDCs that followed a socialist development model were not major beneficiaries of Western development assistance programs.

A prime example of the problems facing LDCs that pursued a socialist economic development model was Mozambique. Shortly after gaining independence in 1975, a Marxist government in Mozambique sought to loosen its linkages with South Africa's apartheid government and to follow a path of socialist development. However, the state had to intervene massively in the economy to achieve its egalitarian and socialist objectives, and this was beyond the capacity of the Mozambique government. In agriculture, for example, Mozambique established communal villages and about 2,000 state farms that were intended to be the main source of the country's food supplies. Nevertheless, total agricultural production fell drastically after 1975 because farmers continued to prefer family plots over farming on a communal basis, and the government could devote only limited resources to the state farms and communal villages. Although Mozambique sought to promote cooperative ties with the West as well as with socialist countries, the U.S. Congress maintained a ban on U.S. foreign aid to Mozambique (often over the objections of the U.S. executive branch) from 1975 to 1984. Partly in response to its support for refugees and liberation movements in southern Africa, Mozambique was also the target of a major destabilization campaign launched by the South African government. By the end of 1983, Mozambique was facing a severe economic crisis, marked by a lack of foodstuffs for the population, a shortage of foreign exchange, and a serious decline in local production. As a result, the Mozambique government had to default on its debts, and it became a major recipient of international aid. In response to assistance and debt-rescheduling negotiations with the IMF, World Bank, and the Paris and London Clubs, Mozambique introduced a series of orthodox liberal reforms.[51]

Mozambique's experiences were repeated with some variations in a number of other LDCs seeking to pursue socialist economic objectives, and when the Soviet bloc collapsed in the late 1980s and early 1990s, the socialist LDCs could no longer look to the "Second World" for economic and military support. Thus, very few LDCs are persisting with socialist strategies today, and even the few holdouts such as Cuba are seeking to establish closer ties with the capitalist world.[52]

EXPORT-LED GROWTH

The experience of the East Asian NIEs—South Korea, Taiwan, Singapore, and Hong Kong—was very different from that of most other Third World countries. The East Asian NIEs all adopted export-led growth strategies, and they registered impressive growth rates and improvement in their economic performance. Export-led growth strategies were far more successful than either the socialist or ISI strategies in the 1970s and 1980s. In examining the effects of export-led growth on economic development, it is more useful to discuss the experience of South Korea and Taiwan because Singapore and Hong Kong have a unique status in the South. Both are so small geographically that they are more akin to city-states than countries, and Hong Kong was a British crown colony before it was incorporated into mainland China. Hong Kong was also the only East Asian NIE that never followed ISI policies.

Taiwan and South Korea adopted ISI policies in the 1950s, and they experienced serious economic problems. Both countries had large balance-of-payments deficits, which were covered mainly by foreign aid, and their exports consisted almost entirely of primary commodities. In the 1960s, Taiwan and South Korea followed the example of Japan and shifted from ISI to a policy that encouraged the growth of manufactured exports. While maintaining a moderate degree of trade protection of the domestic market, these governments encouraged exports with tax incentives, export credits, export targets, and duty-free imports of inputs required by exporters and their suppliers. Taiwan and South Korea also abandoned minimum wage legislation and imposed only minimal taxes on the employment of labor so that employment in export-oriented industries could increase rapidly. In the early 1980s, Southeast Asian economies such as Malaysia, Indonesia, and Thailand followed the path taken by Japan and the East Asian NIEs and switched to export-led growth strategies. Thus, analysts sometimes refer to Hong Kong, Singapore, South Korea, and Taiwan as the "first-tier" East Asian NIEs, and to Malaysia, Indonesia, and Thailand as the "second-tier" Southeast Asian NIEs.

The change from ISI to export-led growth strategies had a dramatic effect on the economic performance of the East Asian NIEs. For example, South Korea's GDP

TABLE 11.4

GDP[a] PER CAPITA AND EXPORT/GDP RATIOS

	GDP PER CAPITA		EXPORT/GDP RATIOS	
	1963	1988	1963	1988
East Asian NIEs[b]				
Hong Kong	$2247	$11,952	39.0	51.1
South Korea	747	4094	2.3	35.4
Singapore	1777	11,693	124.5	164.2
Taiwan	980	4607	15.3	51.8
Latin American NIEs				
Argentina	$2949	$3474	10.0	10.2
Brazil	1400	3424	6.0	9.5
Chile	3231	3933	11.6	31.9
Mexico	2312	3649	5.1	11.9

[a]GDP = Gross Domestic Product
[b]NIEs = Newly Industrializing Economics
Source: Bela Balassa, *Policy Choices for the 1990s* (London: Macmillan, 1993), pp. 57 and 59.

grew at an average annual rate of more than 8 percent throughout the 1960s, and its exports rose from about $31 million in 1960 to $882 million in 1970. Of significance was not only the dramatic growth of South Korean and Taiwanese exports but also the change in their composition. In the 1960s and early 1970s, the majority of the rapidly growing exports were industrial products that required large amounts of unskilled labor and relatively little capital. Over time, industrial wages increased, and there was a structural transformation in the two economies as they began to produce more sophisticated industrial goods that required more highly skilled labor. Thus, by the late 1980s Taiwan and South Korea were the tenth and thirteenth largest exporters of manufactures in the world.[53]

The economic successes of the East Asian NIEs from the 1960s to the 1980s were often compared with the less favorable economic fortunes of the Latin American NIEs—Argentina, Brazil, Chile, and Mexico.[54] Although the Latin American NIEs instituted some reforms to provide more incentives for exports in the 1960s, their policies continued to be based primarily on ISI. Thus, the first two columns of Table 11.4 show that per capita GDP growth rates were much higher for the East Asian NIEs than for the Latin American NIEs. For example, whereas South Korea's GDP per capita of $747 was well *below* the per capita GDPs of all four Latin American NIEs in 1963, by 1988 South Korea's per capita GDP of $4,094 was *above* the figures for all the Latin American NIEs. The change was even more dramatic for Hong Kong and Singapore: their GDPs soared to more than $11,000 by 1988. The last two columns of Table 11.4 show that the export-to-GDP ratios were also higher for the East Asian NIEs than for the Latin American NIEs. South Korea again provides a striking example. Whereas the South Korean export-to-GDP ratio of 2.3 was well below the figures for the Latin American NIEs in 1963, its export-led growth policies resulted in an export-to-GDP ratio of 35.4 in 1988, exceeding the ratios of all the Latin American NIEs. The export-to-GDP ratios in 1988 for Singapore (164.2), Taiwan (51.8), and Hong Kong (51.1) were much higher than the ratios for the Latin American NIEs. Finally, there were striking differences in the composition as well as the level of exports. By the late 1980s, Taiwan, South Korea, and Hong Kong were *each* producing more manufactured exports than all of Latin America.[55]

The East Asian NIEs had a few years of reduced growth during the debt crisis in the 1980s, but they did not have to seek debt rescheduling, and they soon adjusted their economics and returned to a pattern of rapid growth. Although the East Asian NIEs had about the same ratios of debt obligations to GDP as other oil importers, their ratios of debt obligations to exports were much lower. Their relatively healthy export positions, combined with large infusions of foreign investment (especially from Japan), enabled them to garner sufficient revenue to continue their debt payments without depending on IMF and World Bank SALs. The Latin American NIEs following ISI strategies, by contrast, were more severely affected by the debt crisis and had to seek substantial funding from the IMF and the World Bank.[56]

As we discuss later, the East Asian NIEs, and the Southeast Asian countries that followed in their footsteps, began to encounter some economic problems in the late 1980s. These problems became starkly evident in the late 1990s. Nevertheless, just as ISI had been viewed as the "gospel for Third World industrialization" in the 1950s,[57] so the East Asian export-led growth strategy emerged as the new gospel for many development specialists from the 1970s to the early 1990s. Although there was a general consensus that the East Asian export-led growth policies were more successful than the Latin American ISI policies, there was a wide divergence of views as to the reasons for the East Asians' success.

The IPE Perspectives and the East Asian Experience

Liberals, realists, and historical structuralists offered widely differing explanations for the success of the East Asian NIEs' export-led growth strategy from the 1960s to the 1980s. According to liberal economists, the strong East Asian economic performance resulted from the fact that the export-led growth strategy was "outward-oriented," as opposed to the "inward-oriented" ISI strategy of the Latin American NIEs.[58] From this perspective, the East Asians were successful because they did not have "the mistrust of markets and private entrepreneurship that motivates large-scale doctoring in other Asian countries and in African and South American countries."[59] Thus, the East Asian NIEs encouraged the growth of free markets, competition, and private entrepreneurship through the liberalization of policies on trade, foreign investment, and exchange rates. In sum, liberals generally attributed the success of the East Asian NIEs to their willingness to follow the example of the Western developed states, which had reaped major benefits from open market policies.

In contrast to the liberals, realists argued that the key to East Asian economic growth (with the possible exception of Hong Kong) was the existence of a strong *developmental state*, which had "a fundamental role in engineering economic growth, development and success in these countries."[60] As early as the eighteenth and nineteenth centuries, Hamilton and List had argued that late industrializers required state intervention if they were to catch up with more advanced nations (see Chapter 3). However, it was not until the early 1980s that Chalmers Johnson first used the phrase *developmental state* in his seminal works on Japan and the East Asian NIEs.[61]

According to realists, the developmental states of East Asia had several common characteristics. First, the state provided extensive guidance to the market, strictly controlling investment flows, promoting the development of technology, and protecting selected infant industries. Second, the state identified development as its top objective, encouraging citizens to increase investment rather than current consumption and using repression if necessary to enforce its priorities. Third, the state invested heavily in education to ensure that the population had the skills to meet the standards of global competitiveness. And fourth, the state depended on a highly skilled, technocratic bureaucracy that was committed to instituting economic reforms. Although the ISI and export-led growth models both depended on a large degree of government intervention, realists argued that the policies differed in two critical respects: First, the East Asian developmental state focused primarily on developing the country's export industries, whereas the ISI strategy sought to build an industrial base mainly to meet domestic demand. Second, the ISI strategy generally protected all local industries, whereas the East Asian developmental state supported a small number of key industries that were considered to be "winners."[62]

In marked contrast to the liberals and realists, dependency and world-system theorists argued that the NIEs were not in fact achieving genuine economic development. Although the Latin American and East Asian NIEs had ascended to a semiperiphery, which was somewhere above the level of the peripheral Third World states, they were simply "more advanced exemplars of dependent development," still dependent on the industrial states in the core.[63] Thus, André Gunder Frank argued that when "the NICs [newly industrializing countries] produce end products such as shirts, radios or even cars they are simply increasing their dependent integration into a worldwide division of labor . . . in which they are allocated the least remunerative and technologically obsolete contribution."[64]

In addition to the three main IPE perspectives, a fourth perspective explained the success of the East Asian NIEs in terms of domestic social factors, which are often referred to collectively as *political culture*. Political culture can be defined as widely shared social values that affect a state's political economy. Those who emphasized political culture as the key to the East Asians' success argued that the realist focus on the role and strength of the state was insufficient because "the nature of . . . society is important in determining whether or not state policies are effective."[65] The four East Asian NIEs (Hong Kong, South Korea, Taiwan, and Singapore) and China and Japan all have political cultures that are strongly influenced by Confucianism.[66] Confucianism is a secular philosophy that emphasizes respect for authority, the role of the government in promoting and protecting the public good, the importance of education, and the value of strong kinship ties in creating incentives for family-based entrepreneurship. Thus, Confucian philosophy is highly supportive of an economic development model based on collective values, hard work and enterprise, and a benevolent state staffed by the most educated individuals. According to some theorists focusing on political culture, Confucianism was a major factor explaining the success of Japan and the East Asian NIEs in promoting economic development. (Political culture theorists generally differentiate Southeast Asia from East Asia because the Southeast Asians lack "a unifying cultural force comparable to Confucianism in East Asia."[67])

Most analysts argued that of the four perspectives, the realist model of the strong developmental state provided the best explanation for the rapid economic growth of the East Asian and Southeast Asian states. However, a financial crisis that beset East and Southeast Asia in the late 1990s raised serious questions about the realist and other models and demonstrated "how rapidly an informed consensus can change."[68]

The Financial Crisis in East and Southeast Asia

In 1993 the World Bank issued a research report entitled *The East Asian Miracle* in which it examined the region's "remarkable record of high and sustained economic growth" from 1965 to 1990 (the report is discussed later in this chapter), and a number of policymakers and academics began to refer to the East Asians as "miracle economies."[69] The widely divergent perspectives discussed earlier indicated that economists could not provide a fully satisfactory explanation for the East Asian successes, and the choice of the term "miracle" implied that "the phenomenon was beyond purely scientific explanation."[70] Although rapid growth continued in East Asia during the first half of the 1990s, questions arose about the vigor of these economies in 1996 when export growth slowed, earnings declined, and surplus capacity developed in many industries. Analysts expressed increasing concerns in 1997 when problems emerged in Thailand's real estate and financial sector, several large South Korean enterprises or *chaebol* failed, and the Japanese economy continued to stagnate. Then a full-blown financial crisis started in July 1997 when Thailand allowed its *baht* currency to float. Subsequently, a number of Southeast and East Asian economies permitted their currencies to float, and they depreciated sharply. The four countries affected most by the crisis were Thailand, Indonesia, Malaysia, and South Korea. Foreign investors lost confidence in the currencies of these countries, and eventually the most severely affected countries had to seek large IMF and World Bank loans to bolster their currencies and economies.[71]

The 1990s East Asian financial crisis was different from the 1980s foreign debt crisis in two major respects. First, in the 1980s foreign debt crisis governments in Latin America, sub-Saharan Africa, and Eastern Europe held a significant share of the debt, even though the lenders were mainly banks and other private institutions. The East Asian NIEs affected by the 1990s financial crisis in contrast had relatively small states, and their debts were held largely by the private sector. Second, the main concerns in the debt crisis related to the overall indebtedness and high debt-service ratios of the debtor states, whereas the main concerns in the East Asian financial crisis related to short-term debt levels and outflows of portfolio investment. Despite these differences, both the debt and financial crises were preceded by large volumes of private capital inflows and resulted in a sudden reversal of these flows.[72]

By early 1999, the worst part of the East Asian financial crisis was over, and although the Japanese economy remained weak, other East Asian economies began to recover as U.S. and European demand for their exports increased. Recovery continued during the rest of 1999, and by 2000 there was growing confidence in the future of

East Asian economic growth. Nevertheless, the East Asian economies have been slow to institute some needed economic reforms, and they continue to be vulnerable to changing economic conditions.[73] It is therefore important to examine how East Asia could have shifted so abruptly from "miracle" to "meltdown" status, and how such changes can be avoided in the future.

The emergence of serious economic problems in East Asia in 1997 caused some analysts to question whether the "miracle" was over or even whether it had ever occurred, and "just as economics had struggled to find a fully convincing explanation of" the rapid East Asian growth, "it now struggled to explain the 'meltdown.'"[74] Among theorists, historical structuralists had questioned whether the East and Southeast Asian states were achieving genuine, autonomous development, and they believed the financial crisis added weight to their arguments. The East Asian NIEs grew far more rapidly than LDCs in other regions for most of the 1970s and 1980s, but their development was more fragile and "dependent" in some respects than was earlier assumed. Although the existence of strong developmental states contributed to economic growth in East and Southeast Asia, this growth was highly dependent on the policies of the United States and Japan. Countries such as Taiwan and South Korea, with strategic geographic positions vis-à-vis the Soviet Union and China, had special linkages with the United States, extending back to the 1950s. Thus, the United States provided South Korea and Taiwan with large sums of military and economic aid and opened its market to their exports while permitting them to follow protectionist policies. East and Southeast Asian economic growth also stemmed from special linkages with Japan. Japanese colonialism had created the social foundations for industrialization in East Asia, but also the foundations for dependency relations. When the Japanese yen increased greatly in value as a result of the Plaza Agreement in 1985 (see Chapter 6), Japanese companies made huge investments in subsidiary plants throughout East Asia to take advantage of cheaper costs of production. These Japanese investments helped the East Asians avoid some the worst effects of the debt crisis that ravaged Latin American and African countries in the 1980s.

Beginning in the late 1980s, however, it became evident that the dependence of East Asia on the United States and Japan could have major costs as well as benefits. For example, the United States responded to its growing balance-of-payments deficits by becoming more protectionist and by accusing some East Asian economies of being unfair traders. After the passage of new U.S. trade legislation in 1988, South Korea and Taiwan offered trade concessions they had previously resisted because the United States threatened to retaliate against their "unfair" trade practices. With the breakup of the Soviet Union and the decline of the Cold War, the United States was also less willing to continue supplying large amounts of aid and other support to South Korea and Taiwan. In sum, changes in the United States' economic and strategic position made it less willing to provide the East Asian NIEs with the economic and military support it had given them from the 1950s to the mid-1980s.[75]

East and Southeast Asian economic development was also fragile because of the region's dependent relationship with Japan. Although East Asian economies were exporting increasing amounts of industrial goods to the West, these goods often were produced by Japanese subsidiaries, were designed in Japan, included imported Japanese components, and depended on Japanese technology. For example, South Korea seems to have successfully developed an automobile industry, but the industry is highly dependent on Japanese auto parts and advanced technology. When a large Korean industrial conglomerate (called Samsung) received government approval to enter the auto industry in 1994, it indicated that it would "import all of the advanced technology it needs from Nissan" in Japan.[76] The dependence of East and Southeast Asia on Japan had negative effects on these countries' balance of trade and payments. Whereas the East Asians generally had large trade surpluses with the West, their trade deficits with Japan were growing steadily. The depreciation of the Japanese yen relative to the U.S. dollar from 1995 put growing downward pressure on East Asian currencies, many of which were pegged (at least in part) to the U.S. dollar. As Japanese exports became more competitive and Japanese markets absorbed a declining share of East Asian exports, problems of indebtedness and lack of competitiveness in the region increased. The financial crisis began when Thailand had to begin floating its *baht* currency in July 1997 (the *baht* had previously been pegged to a basket of currencies, with the U.S. dollar having predominant weight).[77]

Although historical structuralists were correct in pointing to East Asian dependence on the United States and Japan as one source of the financial crisis, realists and liberals consider the historical structuralists to be unduly negative. As discussed, by 2000 East Asia had largely recovered from the financial crisis and there was renewed confidence in economic growth in the region. Even if the East Asian NIEs had not been "miracle economies," they *had* developed rapidly for several decades, and many expected their economic development to resume. It is therefore important to discuss the liberal and realist perspectives on the crisis. As early as 1968, a prominent U.S. political scientist had argued that authoritarian governments provided needed stability and order in developing societies and that democratic practices were a luxury that should be introduced only later.[78] For a number of years, the authoritarian governments of East Asia strictly limited individual freedoms and assumed a strong role in providing guidance to the developmental state. Although individual freedoms were strictly limited, realists pointed out that these governments oversaw some marked improvements in economic growth and prosperity. However, liberals by contrast attributed the East Asian financial crisis to the pervasive role of governments and government-business linkages in the region.

In the liberal view, the currency crisis in the late 1990s revealed that the authoritarian developmental states were not as efficient and immune to political pressures as realist writers on the East Asian "miracle" often implied. For example, the one-party authoritarian states and close government-business linkages in these countries contributed to widespread nepotism, and the operation of banks and access to credit depended more on political connections than on market forces. With weak financial regulation, lenders and foreign investors rapidly expanded credit to risky borrowers. Huge sums were spent for questionable building and real estate projects, without regard for their necessity or how they would be financed.[79] These inefficiencies challenged the contention of realists that East Asian authoritarian states facilitated the development process.

Whereas liberals questioned realist interpretations of the benefits of authoritarian developmental states, realists questioned liberal claims that the East Asians benefited from increased global economic interdependence. Indeed, realists maintained that "the process of deeper financial integration constituted a necessary condition" for the East Asian financial crisis to occur.[80] Most of the East Asian economies had opened their capital accounts, and the region experienced a dramatic increase in international capital inflows in the early 1990s. According to this interpretation, the financial crisis resulted because these countries were highly vulnerable to the massive reversal of capital flows resulting from the loss of confidence in East Asian currencies. Furthermore, realists argued that deeper financial integration contributed to a contagion effect in which creditors engaged in speculative attacks on currencies, not because of economic fundamentals, but because of the actions of other creditors.[81]

Realists, historical structuralists, and some liberals also charged that the liberal-economic measures of economic development, which emphasize composite statistics such as the growth in GDP and per capita GDP, led to an overestimation of East and Southeast Asian development. As early as the mid-1990s some economists were already maintaining that East Asian economic growth resulted largely from physical and human capital accumulation rather than from major increases in total factor productivity. In other words, increased inputs of labor and capital rather than increased efficiency explained much of the rapid East Asian economic growth in the 1980s and early 1990s. Thus, the noted economist Paul Krugman has argued in reference to the East Asian countries that

> Sustained growth in a nation's per capita income can only occur if there is a rise in output *per unit of input.* Mere increases in inputs, without an increase in the efficiency with which those inputs are used—investing in more machinery and infrastructure—must run into diminishing returns; input-driven growth is inevitably limited.[82]

Environmentalists have also maintained that the East and Southeast Asian recipe for rapid economic growth is not sustainable in the long term. In Indonesia, for example, logging practices are contributing to a deforestation rate of 2.4 million hectares per year; in the Malaysian state of Sarawak, loggers have removed 30 percent of the forest area in 23 years; and in Vietnam, resources are being exported with little concern for the social and environmental consequences.[83] Of particular importance in this regard is the concept of *sustainable development,* which was popularized by NGOs in the early 1980s and received multilateral approval in the 1987 report of the World Commission on Environment and Development (the Brundtland Report). The Brundtland Report describes sustainable development as a policy that "meets the needs of the present without compromising the ability of future generations to meet their own needs."[84] Sustainable development is a controversial concept because LDCs have argued that they cannot afford to divert resources from their immediate development to pay the costs of following environmentally friendly policies. The LDCs also point out that developed states did not adopt sustainable policies when they were developing and that the North today produces more global pollutants than the South. Nevertheless, East Asians will not be able to sustain their economic growth rates in the long term if they disregard the effects of environmental degradation.

There is no doubt that the export-led growth model has a number of strengths and that the East Asian developmental state outperformed other Third World countries according to most economic indicators in the 1970s and 1980s. However, the financial crisis demonstrated some serious weaknesses in their export-led growth strategy. Another development strategy was strongly supported by the IMF, the World Bank, and most industrial states in response to the 1980s foreign debt crisis, and more recently in response to the 1990s East Asian financial crisis: the orthodox liberal model.

THE REVIVAL OF ORTHODOX LIBERALISM

Development specialists have discussed a number of factors that are likely to prevent other LDCs from adopting the positive aspects of the East Asian developmental state model. For example, two characteristics of the developmental state are critical to its effective functioning: a highly skilled technocratic bureaucracy and close cooperation between major economic groupings such as agriculture, business, and labor. Most LDCs "still lack the highly professional merit-based bureaucracies and the tradition of cooperation between key economic actors that would permit them to replicate the East Asian model."[85] Successful developmental states have also generally been authoritarian or semiauthoritarian, which has enabled them to guide the economy and control labor, business, and other private groups. However, current globalization pressures are causing democracy (in a political sense) to spread around the world, and this raises questions as to whether other LDCs could replicate the rapid economic growth rates of the East Asians. The most important constraint on replicating the East Asian developmental state model in other Third World states was evident much earlier—in the late 1970s to early 1980s—with the return of orthodox liberalism. In line with the new orthodoxy the IMF and World Bank adopted the view that "the market rational/market ideological approach is the only correct course for development."[86]

When British Prime Minister Margaret Thatcher and U.S. President Ronald Reagan led a shift to the right with the revival of orthodox liberalism in the late 1970s and early 1980s, the IMF, World Bank, and others launched a strong attack on realist or statist development strategies in the South. In response to the 1980s debt crisis, the IMF and World Bank were powerful advocates of what later became known as the *Washington consensus*. Strongly endorsed by the Reagan administration, the U.S. Treasury, the Federal Reserve, and the international financial institutions in the 1980s, the Washington consensus refers to the orthodox liberal belief that "the combination of democratic government, free markets, a dominant private sector and openness to trade is the recipe for prosperity and growth."[87] (Ironically, this is not what John Williamson meant by the term when he coined it in 1989.[88]) In applying the Washington consensus to the 1980s debt crisis, the IMF and World Bank imposed a range of conditions on their SALs, including requirements that recipient LDCs control inflation, decrease government spending, balance their budgets, privatize state-owned enterprises, deregulate financial and labor markets, and liberalize their policies toward trade and investment.[89] As discussed in Chapter 7, the IMF and World Bank ruled out cross-conditionality in a formal, legal sense, but there is no doubt that they sometimes engaged in this practice on an informal basis to jointly impose the Washington consensus on LDC borrowers.[90]

Structural Adjustment and the Theoretical Perspectives

In the 1980s, a large number of LDC debtor countries implemented World Bank and IMF-financed structural adjustment programs (SAPs), and the Third World became "a laboratory for a huge experiment" in promoting economic development through orthodox liberalism.[91] Perceptions of SAPs varied widely in accordance with the competing theoretical perspectives. For example, three studies of the effects of SAPs in sub-Saharan Africa presented strikingly different conclusions. The first study concluded that "the performance of poor compliers deteriorates over time and is significantly worse than the performance of countries that comply" with the structural adjustment policy conditions;[92] the second study found that countries that followed World Bank structural adjustment policy conditions most closely "failed to grow as quickly as several less compliant African economies during the same period";[93] and the third study argued that structural adjustment policies "followed over the past decade are leading to the destruction of the [African] continent . . . with the failure of the state being an immediate outcome and environmental deterioration being devastating in the long run."[94] In view of these starkly different perceptions, it is important to briefly discuss SAPs and the three major theoretical perspectives.

Historical structuralists believe SAPs are not "simply an innocuous remedial package for sustained growth and development." Instead, they are "an almost deliberate scheme for the perpetuation of export dependency . . . and reproduction of existing conditions of global inequality."[95] Furthermore, SAPs subordinate peripheral governments to MNCs, international banks, and core area governments, and increase the inequalities of income between classes.[96] The World Bank, the IMF, and other Northern-dominated institutions caused the problems of Third World indebtedness in the first place; it is therefore unrealistic to expect that they will ever design SAPs to alleviate Third World problems.

Whereas historical structuralists are the harshest critics, orthodox liberals are the strongest supporters of structural adjustment. They believe that SAPs provide the necessary prescriptions and discipline based on the Washington consensus for the problems of LDC debtors. Interventionist liberals would agree with orthodox liberals that SAPs are often necessary to combat domestic inefficiencies and corruption in Third World debtor economies. However, they are more receptive than orthodox liberals to state interventionism, and they argue that the World Bank and the IMF should be doing more to focus on the human development aspects of adjustment. From this perspective, the World Bank should be more sensitive to the implications of its adjustment policies for the poorest groups and states in the Third World.[97] From a realist perspective, the World Bank and the IMF are not following the correct policies in emphasizing the downsizing of government through privatization, deregulation, and trade liberalization. Realists argue that late industrializers, whether they be the United States and Germany in the nineteenth century, the East Asian NIEs from the 1950s to the 1980s, or other LDCs today, *require* a large degree of government interventionism to catch up with the leading powers. A strong state in the realist view is an essential prerequisite for Third World economic development.

Despite these differing perceptions, most analysts today would agree that there were some serious problems with SAPs in the 1980s and 1990s. After referring to some strengths of the SAPs, we turn to a discussion of the problems.

Structural Adjustment and Questions About Orthodox Liberalism

The World Bank's SALs were generally most effective in middle-income LDCs that were exporters of manufactures, such as Brazil, Morocco, the Philippines, South Korea, Thailand, Uruguay, and Yugoslavia. These countries had more developed institutions for bringing about policy reforms, and better resilience in dealing with the disruptions and sacrifices resulting from structural adjustment policies. Thus, liberal studies indicate that SAPs in middle-income countries often reduced government budget deficits, increased export earnings, increased financing available for private investment, and enhanced economic efficiency and growth. However, the effect of SAPs on the poorest and most highly indebted LDCs, and on the poorest groups *within* LDCs, was a far more contentious issue.

In the early 1980s, many World Bank officials believed that SAPs would not hurt the poor. Although these programs were not designed to deal with poverty or to promote equity, the World Bank endorsed liberal-economic views holding that benefits from the efficient allocation of resources under freer markets would naturally "trickle down" to the poor. However, a number of critics rejected this trickle-down theory and argued that the poorest groups were having to bear a disproportionate share of the adjustment burdens. The persistence or exacerbation of poverty in low-income LDCs and in vulnerable groups within LDCs gave credence to these criticisms and eventually forced the World Bank to rethink its approach.[98] In addition to the effects of SALs on the poor, critics also charged that the emphasis of SAPs on privatization, deregulation, and openness gave inadequate attention to the need for effective LDC governments, and that the World Bank's "top-down" approach to structural adjustment did not give sufficient attention to the need for local participation in "owning" policies and implementing reforms. Furthermore, critics argued that SAPs were designed in the 1980s for LDCs with large public sectors and substantial public debts, and that they were inappropriate for the East Asian NIEs, whose problems were substantially different in the 1990s.

The sections that follow examine these criticisms by focusing on one Third World region, and one group within Third World states, in which the effects of SAPs have been most controversial: the sub-Saharan African states and Third World women. We then turn to a discussion of World Bank attempts to address the problems with its structural adjustment policies.

Structural Adjustment and Sub-Saharan Africa

Some of the strongest criticisms of SAPs have related to their effects on sub-Saharan Africa. (In this section, the term *Africa* refers to sub-Saharan Africa.) The decade of the 1980s, when more than two-thirds of African states were receiving World Bank and IMF SALs, is generally considered to be a lost decade for Africa. During this period, economic growth and industrial production stagnated, agricultural output lagged behind population growth, per capita incomes and investment declined, and unemployment increased. Each year the United Nations Development Program ranks countries according to a "human development index," which includes such factors as per capita incomes, adult literacy rates, education, and life expectancy. In 1996, 14 of the 15 lowest ranked countries in terms of the human development index were African. In 1997, 19 of the 26 poorest countries in the world in terms of per capita GNP were African.[99] A comprehensive 1988 study by the United Nations Program of Action for African Recovery and Development concluded that although SAPs had registered a few gains, "for the majority of African states, there has not been even a hint of recovery."[100]

Liberal-economic supporters of structural adjustment argue that these programs are often blamed for problems caused by general economic deterioration. Thus, the World Bank and IMF were simply reacting to the Third World debt crisis, which had resulted from both inefficient LDC economic policies and a series of unfavorable global economic changes stemming from the 1970s oil crisis. Furthermore, liberals maintain that many problems in Africa, such as political instability, civil wars, and famine, have been unusually resistant to solution and that African economic conditions would be even worse without IMF and World Bank SAPs. Liberals maintain that because state-led strategies such as ISI were clearly unsuccessful, the World Bank and IMF market-led prescriptions are the best possible strategies for bringing about adjustment and growth.[101]

Critics, by contrast, argue that IMF and World Bank SAPs in Africa are defective in several major respects: they place too much emphasis on market-oriented policies, they do not contribute to economic growth, and their costs fall most heavily on the poorest groups and countries. The strongest criticisms relate to IMF and World Bank demands that Third World debtors downgrade the role of the government and emphasize privatization so that market forces can operate. Because the public sector provides a critical source of employment for Africans, a downgrading of the government's role increases unemployment and underemployment. As governmental capacity declines, crucial infrastructure such as transportation and communications, and services such as health care and education also suffer. Furthermore, the emphasis on privatization does not take account of the fact that private firms are often unwilling or unable to supply essential public goods required for development. Third World countries must therefore rely heavily on their governments to provide the resources for technical and scientific education of the populace and for other aspects of human capital necessary for industrialization and competitiveness.

Critics also oppose the emphasis IMF and World Bank SAPs place on trade liberalization. Middle-income Latin American and East and Southeast Asian countries may reap some major benefits from freer trade, but the benefits are far more dubious for lower income African and Asian LDCs. Because many Latin American and East and Southeast Asian countries have had lengthy periods of sheltering their domestic industries, these industries may now be better able to compete with growing imports. Most African LDCs, by contrast, are only beginning to embark on the path to industrialization, and they require continued protection for their infant industries. Critics charge that World Bank and IMF market-based prescriptions have been ineffective and have harmed the economic development process in Africa. This is especially true because most African LDCs are at an early stage of economic development and continue to require a substantial role for the government.[102]

Structural Adjustment and Third World Women

A major criticism of IMF and World Bank SAPs is that they have disregarded gender issues. Almost all societies (economically developed as well as less developed) are characterized in varying degrees by gender inequality and the exploitation of women, critics argue that it is therefore not possible for SAPs to be "gender neutral." By disregarding the subsidiary role of women, these programs often reinforce male bias and exacerbate the economic and social problems confronting Third World women.

The positions of Third World women vary widely as a result of diverse cultural values, historical factors, levels of economic development, and types of government in different LDCs. Women in the same society may also occupy vastly different positions depending on such factors as social class and ethnicity. Nevertheless, it is possible to generalize about some characteristics of women's positions in Third World societies:

- In the household, women spend much more time than men, on the average, on unpaid subsistence work involving child care, food production and preparation, health care, and education.
- In work outside the home, women are overrepresented relative to men in the "informal" sector of the economy. Unlike formal-sector employment, work in the informal sector is largely unaffected by government regulations and standards. About three-fourths of those in the informal sector are service providers such as roadside food stall operators, market traders, messengers, and shoe shiners. Informal-sector earnings on the average are well below those of the formal sector.
- In the formal sector, women are more concentrated in the lower skilled, lower wage occupations, and they are often paid less than men for doing the same work.
- Compared with men, women are more important in agricultural labor and less important in industry. In Africa, for example, women produce about 90 percent of the food, but they are less important in the production of export crops.
- If one combines women's lower wages in the formal sector with their overrepresentation in agriculture, the informal sector, and work in the household, women's incomes are normally significantly less than those of men. Thus, households in which women are the sole breadwinners are among the poorest groups in Third World societies.[103]

The position of women in Third World societies as outlined here should be considered in any SAPs. However, World Bank policy prescriptions are based on macroeconomic concepts, which view the economy as a whole rather than looking at individual firms or households. Because much of women's time is spent doing unpaid subsistence work in the household, which does not appear in production statistics, the World Bank gives little attention to the effect of its structural adjustment policies on women's work time. For example, SAPs usually call for cutbacks in government spending, leading to decreases in the provision of public goods in areas such as health, education, and water and sanitation facilities. As a result of these cutbacks, much of the burden of health care and education shifts to the community and household, where women have most of the responsibilities.

World Bank and IMF policy prescriptions that raise the cost of basic foodstuffs simply add to the problems of Third World women. SAPs usually require that LDCs lower government deficits by phasing out food subsidies and provide incentives to farmers by raising the prices they receive for their tradeable goods. Because of the higher food costs, women must use cheaper foods that take longer to prepare, such as coarse grain and root crops rather than wheat products, and they must rely on home baking rather than the purchase of bread. Hospitals, too, may succeed in cutting their costs per patient largely by shifting many of the costs of care to the unpaid economy of the household.[104] The World Bank views cutbacks in government spending and subsidies as an indication of increased efficiency, but costs are in fact simply being shifted from the paid to the unpaid economy, where women do most of the work.

Even if women worked only in the household, the off-loading of government services and subsidies would place unreasonable new burdens on them. The need for income, however, "has forced women into the labour force to protect their families' survival."[105] Thus, women as a proportion of the total labor force rose in Asia from 29 percent in 1950 to 33.8 percent in 1985, and in Latin America from 18 percent to 24.2 percent. Women have often fared poorly as members of the formal and informal labor force under SAPs. In sub-Saharan Africa, for example, farmers were paid higher prices to encourage them to produce more crops for the export market. Cash crops, however, tend to be men's crops, whereas subsistence food crops are more often women's crops. Men also tend to market most of the crops produced by both women and men, and women do not benefit from the increased prices because men often keep a high proportion of the revenue for their own use.[106]

Critics thus argue that SAPs affect Third World women adversely in their multiple roles as mothers, managers of the household, community leaders, and workers in the formal and informal sectors. Only when the World Bank and IMF dispense with the myth that structural adjustment is gender neutral will they be able to confront the problems that their SAPs pose for Third World women.

ANOTHER SHIFT IN DEVELOPMENT STRATEGY?

In the late 1980s and the 1990s, the World Bank became more responsive to criticisms of its structural adjustment policies and began to take a second look at its orthodox liberal approach to development. The question therefore arises as to whether the World Bank's reassessment of its SALs is an indication of another shift in development strategy. To answer this question, we discuss three areas of particular concern to the World Bank: its approach to the role of the state in development, to the poorest LDCs and the most vulnerable groups in LDCs, and to the "top-down" imposition of conditionality based on the Washington consensus. The World Bank's reassessment can be divided into two major periods: from the late 1980s to 1994, and from 1995 to early 2002.

The Late 1980s to 1994

In the late 1980s to 1994, the World Bank began to reassess its approach to the role of the state in development, and to the poorest LDCs and most vulnerable groups. Protracted economic and political problems in the least developed states in Africa and Asia led to a gradual recognition by the World Bank that the state had a significant role to play in economic development. At the same time, however, the bank did not wish to veer too far from orthodox liberal views favoring the unfettered market. The evolution in World Bank thinking was evident throughout the 1990s. In its 1991 *World Development Report,* the World Bank acknowledged that "governments need to do more in those areas where markets cannot be relied upon" such as health, education, nutrition, family planning, and poverty alleviation. Nevertheless, the 1991 report basically adhered to the orthodox liberal position and reiterated World Bank views that "governments need to do less in those areas where markets work, or can be made to work."[107]

The Japanese government reacted negatively to the 1991 report and expressed frustration with the liberal orthodoxy that had come to dominate World Bank thinking in the 1980s. Japan insisted that the World Bank give more recognition to the value of the Japanese and East Asian developmental state model, and it called on the World Bank to commission a study of the issue. As a result, the World Bank published a policy research report in September 1993 entitled *The East Asian Miracle: Economic Growth and Public Policy* (henceforth, "the report"), which sought to determine why East Asia had such "a remarkable record of high and sustained economic growth."[108] The report made some concessions to the possible value of government intervention in specific circumstances, noting that Japanese, Korean, and Taiwanese government policies of allocating credit to high-priority activities "may have been beneficial."[109] (Some observers claim that this was a necessary concession to Japan's Ministry of Finance, which financed the report.[110]) Most of the report, however, questioned the value of government-directed industrial policy in East Asia, indicated that the East Asian model would not necessarily be successful elsewhere, and cautioned that the East Asian successes should not "be taken as an excuse to postpone needed market-oriented reform."[111] Furthermore, the report claimed that the Southeast Asian economies of Malaysia, Thailand, and Indonesia (unlike the Northeast Asian economies) achieved rapid growth without industrial policy, and that other Third World countries would be better off emulating the Southeast Asians. In sum, the World Bank's approach to the role of the state in development did not change significantly in the early 1990s. Although the report gave more recognition than previous World Bank studies to governmental involvement in East Asian development, it attributed the East Asians' success primarily to their liberal market-friendly approach.[112]

The World Bank also began to address the issue of the poorest LDCs and most vulnerable groups in the late 1980s to 1990s. To understand the World Bank's view on poverty in the 1980s and 1990s, it is necessary to provide some historical background. It is possible to identify four major phases in World Bank thinking (and in the thinking of the foreign aid community in general) on poverty reduction.[113] In the first phase from 1945 to the late 1960s, the World Bank focused on large economic infrastructure projects to provide LDCs with transportation and communication facilities, port development, power projects, and other public utilities. World Bank officials believed that large transfers of capital and technology would contribute to industrial development, employment, and a reduction of poverty. This is the "trickle-down" approach to development aid, which assumes that prosperity will "eventually trickle down from the top, alleviating the problem of poverty at the bottom."[114] Although LDCs achieved rapid economic growth rates in the 1960s, the large capital-intensive projects bypassed the neediest and contributed to a worsening of income distribution within LDCs. Thus, World Bank President Robert McNamara ushered in the second phase in the 1970s, in which the World Bank began to give more explicit attention to poverty production. It developed more "basic human needs" projects, which provided basic health, educational, and family-planning services to the poor; increased the involvement of women; and gave special attention to the poorest LDCs.[115] Although these declared intentions to focus on basic needs were only partly fulfilled in practice, the World Bank did increase its lending in the 1970s for agricultural and rural development, low-cost urban housing and slum rehabilitation, and primary and nonformal education.[116]

Alleviating poverty by directly targetting the poorest, however, was a far more difficult and complex task than had been anticipated, and orthodox liberals argued that the basic needs approach distracted attention from the need to promote economic growth. Thus, disillusionment with the basic needs approach along with significant global changes in the 1980s—the foreign debt crisis and the return of orthodox liberalism—ushered in the third phase of the World Bank's approach to poverty. In some respects, the third phase in the 1980s was similar to the first phase in the 1950s–1960s when the World Bank relied on trickle-down theories of poverty reduction. World Bank SALs in the 1980s were conditioned on the implementation of orthodox liberal policies, and the basic needs of vulnerable groups were in fact largely forgotten. Indeed, the previous discussion of sub-Saharan Africa and Third World women shows that the poorest and most vulnerable groups in Third World countries often bore a disproportionate share of the burden of World Bank and IMF structural adjustment policies.

Throughout the 1980s, there were growing pressures on the World Bank as the main multilateral development agency to devote some attention to the distributional effects of structural adjustment. For example, in a 1987–88 two-volume study entitled *Adjustment with a Human Face*, UNICEF indicated that it was necessary to include a "poverty alleviation dimension" in adjustment programs.[117] These pressures eventually resulted in a fourth phase of World Bank thinking on poverty, which began in the late 1980s and continues today. The fourth phase has similarities to the second phase in which the World Bank devoted more explicit attention to basic human needs and poverty production. For example, in 1989 the World Bank shifted its position somewhat when it acknowledged that "sub-Saharan Africa has now witnessed almost a decade of falling per capita incomes and accelerating ecological degradation" and that there was a need for "special measures . . . to alleviate poverty and protect the vulnerable."[118] Most significantly, the World Bank devoted the 1990 issue of its *World Development Report* to poverty and began to redesign its SAPs to decrease adverse effects on the poor.[119]

Despite the World Bank moves in the late 1980s and early 1990s to devote more attention to poverty reduction and the role of the state in development, a tension continued to exist between pressures for orthodox liberal reforms on the one hand and concerns with the state and poverty on the other. Thus, the World Bank's strategies for poverty reduction and for promoting state effectiveness continued to have major limitations. In December 1994 the World Bank had to confront the shortcomings of its development approach more directly when Mexico—a country the Western policy establishment had viewed as a model of economic management—encountered serious economic problems and had to again appeal for emergency loans. Mexico had implemented an economic strategy based largely on the World Bank model and had lowered its trade barriers and had even signed the NAFTA with the United States and Canada. By early 1995, the "Asian miracle," the failure to promote satisfactory levels of growth in the LLDCs, and the 1994–95 Mexican crisis raised serious questions about the World Bank's approach to development. On its fiftieth anniversary, NGOs launched a "Fifty Years is Enough" campaign aimed at the World Bank and IMF, and it was evident that the World Bank "had no option but to modify its approach to development" if it was to continue to be an effective development institution.[120] The new World Bank President James Wolfensohn was appointed in June 1995 with the task of rebuilding the World Bank's confidence and legitimacy.

1995 to Early 2002

Wolfensohn immediately instituted a process designed to alter the World Bank's policy outlook and mode of operation. A highly significant development was the appointment of Joseph Stiglitz in February 1997 as the new World Bank chief economist. Stiglitz had written earlier about the limits of privatization and the need for a stronger role for the state in development, and his appointment signified a shift away from the World Bank's adherence to the Washington consensus.[121] Policy statements and decisions indicated that the World Bank's approach was changing in regard to the role of the state in development, poverty reduction, and the top-down imposition of conditionality based on the Washington consensus.

Regarding the role of the state in development, the World Bank focused its 1997 *World Development Report* on "The State in a Changing World." The report rejected orthodox liberal preferences for a minimalist state and argued that state minimalism "is at odds with evidence of the world's development success stories."[122] Although the report opposed state-dominated development, it also warned against the dangers of stateless development. Thus, the report maintained that "development requires an effective state, one that plays a catalytic, facilitating role, encouraging and complementing the activities of private businesses and individuals."[123] More specifically, the report attributed sub-Saharan Africa's severe development problems to a deterioration in the effectiveness and legitimacy of the state. Stiglitz as the World Bank's chief economist went beyond the 1997 *World Development Report,* and expressed support for a strong state role in creating a robust financial system and establishing a focused industrial policy.

Regarding poverty, Wolfensohn's October 1988 annual address to the World Bank board of governors described poverty as the "other crisis" along with the 1987 financial crisis, and he signaled that the World Bank would devote increased attention in development policy to the poorest individuals in society. There was strong support "to make poverty reduction the core issue in the Bank's agenda at the beginning of the new century," and an important World Bank initiative was its *Voices of the Poor* study in which it consulted about 60,000 poor people in more than 50 countries. Furthermore, the main theme of the World Bank's 2000–2001 *World Development Report* was "Attacking Poverty."[124] The report proposed a three-pronged strategy for attacking poverty that involved promoting opportunity, facilitating empowerment, and enhancing security. The World Bank's discussion of facilitating empowerment departed from its traditional focus on economic issues and emphasized the need to strengthen the participation of poor people in political processes.

Potentially most significant was Wolfensohn's introduction of a *Comprehensive Development Framework (CDF)* in January 1999. The CDF is designed to take a much broader holistic approach to development than structural adjustment, emphasizing the linkages among the financial, social, and institutional aspects of development. Furthermore, the CDF is a major attempt to alter World Bank lending practices. Unlike the coercive conditionality of structural adjustment policy, the CDF emphasizes partnership between donors and the government, and between the government and civil society. Thus, the CDF is designed to substitute a consultative rather than a top-down framework for providing development finance.[125]

Despite the World Bank's expressed intentions to move away from the Washington consensus and alter its approach to development, there are reasons to question whether the World Bank is in fact shifting to a new development strategy. First, it is easier for officials of the World Bank (and other institutions) to verbally support objectives such as meeting basic human needs and supporting poverty reduction than it is to convert these objectives into practice. Second, international events have constrained the World Bank's ability to alter its development strategies. For example, the World Bank's 1997 *World Development Report* on the need for an effective state was released only several months before the East Asian financial crisis. Orthodox liberals could argue that the financial crisis demonstrated the weaknesses in East Asia's strong developmental state model, and Japan's continued economic problems add weight to their arguments (as discussed, realists of course interpret these events differently).

A third reason for constraints on the World Bank relates to the reaction of its major members, especially the United States. The World Bank's chief economist Stiglitz was the strongest advocate of the proposed changes, and he was often critical of the IMF, World Bank, and U.S. policies toward the Third World. Stiglitz's relations with some officials in the U.S. Treasury Department were already strained when a draft copy of the 2000–2001 *World Development Report* on attacking poverty was produced by one of Stiglitz's appointees. The draft report was highly controversial in the IMF and World Bank as well as the United States. For example, the report's empowerment section "attracted immediate criticism," and some of the World Bank's own leading economists charged that the draft devoted too little emphasis to economic growth.[126] Furthermore, critics charged that the World Bank's CDF that Stiglitz strongly supported represented "a capitulation to NGOs."[127] In response to pressures, Stiglitz and the director of the draft 2000–2001 *World Development Report* left the World Bank "in controversial circumstances."[128]

In sum, it is uncertain today that the World Bank is significantly altering its approach to development, because the strongest supporter of a new approach—the World Bank's chief economist—was retired from his position. As realists would point out, ultimately the World Bank and other international economic organizations cannot

TABLE 11.5

NET ODA[A] TO THE THIRD WORLD COUNTRIES AS A PERCENTAGE OF GNP (OECD MEMBERS)

	1960	1970	1980	1990	1999
Australia	0.38	0.59	0.48	0.34	0.26
Austria	—	0.13	0.23	0.25	0.26
Belgium	0.88	0.48	0.50	0.46	0.30
Canada	0.10	0.43	0.43	0.44	0.28
Denmark	0.09	0.38	0.74	0.94	1.01
Finland	0	0	0.22	0.63	0.33
France	1.38	0.65	0.63	0.60	0.39
Germany	0.31	0.32	0.44	0.42	0.26
Ireland	0	0	0.16	0.16	0.31
Italy	0.22	0.16	0.17	0.31	0.15
Japan	0.24	0.23	0.32	0.31	0.35
Luxembourg	0	0	0	0.21	0.66
Netherlands	0.31	0.63	0.97	0.92	0.79
New Zealand	0	0	0.33	0.23	0.27
Norway	0.11	0.33	0.87	1.17	0.91
Portugal	1.45	0.45	0	0.25	0.26
Spain	0	0	0	0.20	0.23
Sweden	0.05	0.37	0.78	0.91	0.70
Switzerland	0.04	0.14	0.24	0.32	0.35
United Kingdom	0.56	0.37	0.35	0.27	0.23
United States	0.53	0.31	0.27	0.21	0.10
Total	**0.52**	**0.34**	**0.37**	**0.33**	**0.24**

[a]ODA = Official Development Assistance
Source: OECD, *Development Co-operation,* (Paris: OECD, various years).

diverge too far from the policy preferences of their most important members. For example, the World Bank's stated objectives in its 2000–2001 *World Development Report* on attacking poverty can only be realized if its member countries are willing to support this objective with meaningful policy changes. As discussed, the pressures of globalization and the end of the Cold War diminished the concern of the developed states about poverty and discontent in the Third World.

A prime example of the growing marginalization of the poorest states and individuals is the extent to which foreign aid has declined in recent years. In 1969, a Commission on International Development (the Pearson Commission), which had been formed at the suggestion of the World Bank to study foreign aid, recommended that every advanced industrial state should devote at least 0.7 percent of its GNP to development assistance.[129] Table 11.5 shows that despite this recommendation, the members of the OECD have *decreased* rather than increased the percentage of their GNP devoted to ODA countries in recent years. The OECD countries' net ODA as a share of GNP declined from 0.52 percent in 1960 to 0.37 percent in 1980 and to 0.24 percent in 1999. Table 11.5 shows that the ODA of the two largest bilateral aid donors,

Japan and the United States, amounted to only 0.35 percent and 0.10 percent of their GNPs in 1999. The World Bank and the developed states have become more aware of the need to adopt SAPs and development programs that recognize the important role of Third World states and are attuned to the needs of the poorest and most vulnerable groups. Nevertheless, in the current environment of global competitiveness and orthodox liberalism, the commitment to these objectives is inevitably limited.

CONCLUSION

The postwar period has generally been marked by prosperity and economic growth for the developed states of the North, but this has not been the case for the poorer countries and peoples in the South. Indeed, other than a small number of NIEs and the OPEC states, the income gap between the North and the South has been growing. This chapter examines some of the strategies LDCs have used in attempts to promote their economic development and discusses the important role the World Bank group has played as the largest multilateral development organization in framing the debates on these strategies. The discussion of ISI, socialist, export-led growth, and orthodox liberal models provides some basis for drawing preliminary conclusions about the most appropriate development strategies for Third World states.

First, all of the development strategies followed over the years have shortcomings, and we are unlikely to find the "perfect" development strategy. Development is clearly a more difficult and complex process than Walt Rostow had indicated in his widely read 1960 book on *The Stages of Economic Growth*.[130] Rostow claimed that societies move through five stages on their way to modernity, and his predictions regarding LDC growth were overly optimistic. For example, Rostow argued that an LDC reaching the takeoff stage would be transformed in such a way that its growth would be self-sustaining thereafter. Such predictions raised false hopes that Third World economic development was a readily achievable and irreversible process. Whereas Rostow's liberal prescriptions for economic growth placed major emphasis on the need for domestic changes (i.e., modernization), historical structuralists place primary emphasis on the need for altering international relations (e.g., relations of dependency). The reality is that economic development is an extremely complex process that requires *both* domestic and international changes. Only a small number of LDCs such as the East Asian NIEs have been fortunate enough to meet both the domestic and international requirements for rapid economic development. However, even the East Asian economies had to confront a financial crisis in the late 1990s, which demonstrated just how difficult it is today to avoid serious setbacks on the path to development.

Second, the same development strategy is not necessarily feasible or desirable for all Third World states. Although a number of East and Southeast Asian LDCs achieved impressive economic growth rates through an export-led growth strategy, it is unlikely that many other LDCs could emulate their experience. The East Asian NIEs' success resulted from a confluence of favorable external and domestic circumstances, such as U.S. and Japanese support and the presence of highly skilled, technocratic government bureaucracies in East Asia. These characteristics are often lacking in poorer African and Asian LDCs. Indeed, many sub-Saharan African countries with ongoing economic and political crises today would find it impossible to follow the developmental state model of the East Asian NIEs. The return to liberal orthodoxy in the 1980s has also precluded many LDCs from following state-led growth policies. Instead, IMF and World Bank SAPs have pressured LDC debtors to engage in deregulation, privatization, and other measures to downsize the role of the state.[131]

Third, negative experiences with IMF and World Bank SAPs have pointed to the pitfalls of focusing on the economic aspects of development without looking sufficiently at the social and human aspects. Thus, the United Nations Development Program began to publish an annual *Human Development Report* in 1990 to emphasize the fact that "there was no automatic link between growth and human development."[132] The human development approach assesses development not only in terms of a country's per capita GDP growth but also in terms of such factors as life expectancy, health and sanitation facilities, education, employment, the income gap between rich and poor, the gender gap, and the rural-urban gap. In thinking about human development, for example, it is necessary to understand how women's unpaid subsistence work in the household puts them at a disadvantage in markets.[133] Only by taking such human factors into consideration can we understand that the main purpose of economic development should be to improve human well-being.

Fourth, an economic development strategy should strike a realistic balance "between the state and the market so as to stimulate a positive and dynamic interaction between them."[134] Whereas ISI policies emphasize state intervention and give too little consideration to market signals, orthodox liberal approaches disregard the fact that late industrializers often require an active role for the state. Governments in East and Southeast Asia were particularly adept at using market interactions to their advantage, and this enabled them to register some striking economic gains, even during the 1980s foreign debt crisis. However, the East and Southeast Asians have also too often substituted "political whim . . . for proper risk assessment for commercial activities," and their failure to provide sufficient banking regulations was a major factor contributing to their 1990s financial crisis.[135] The mixed record of the East Asian governments indicates that it is not government regulation per se that should concern us but finding the amount and type of regulation that will ensure economic stability, confidence, and the proper functioning of market signals.

Finally, an economic development strategy should take account of the difference in wealth and power between the North and the South. Except in a small number of East Asian NIEs, the North-South income gap has continued to widen, and the 1980s foreign debt crisis was a reminder of the degree to which the South is still dependent on the North. Although Northern linkages in trade, foreign investment, and other economic areas are critical to the South, development strategies should also aim at permitting the South to act somewhat independently (within the limits of global interdependence today). One possible route to greater self-sufficiency is through establishing more South-South economic linkages. South-South trade linkages can enable LDCs to foster new comparative advantages and can contribute to their production and export of industrial goods. Indeed, about 60 percent of the goods traded among Third World countries are manufactures.[136]

All three theoretical perspectives—realism, liberalism, and historical structuralism—have had something important to say regarding the most appropriate strategies for promoting economic development. Furthermore, there seems to be no single "best" development strategy for all Third World states, because of major differences among these states and their positions in the world. A variety of development strategies therefore will be, and should be, pursued in the future, as they have been in the past.

NOTES

1. Bretton Woods Commission, *Bretton Woods: Looking to the Future*, Commission Report, Staff Review, Background Papers (Washington, DC: Bretton Woods Committee, July 1994), p. B3.
2. World Bank, *World Development Report 2000/2001: Attacking Poverty* (New York: Oxford University Press, 2001), p. 3.
3. See Howard Handelman, *The Challenge of Third World Development* (Upper Saddle River, NJ: Prentice Hall, 1996), pp. 3–10.
4. World Bank, *Annual Report 2001* (Washington, DC: World Bank, 2001), vol. 1, pp. 139–140.
5. World Bank, *World Development Report 1991: The Challenge of Development* (New York: Oxford University Press, 1991), p. 2.
6. World Bank, *World Development Report 2000/2001*, p. 3.
7. Stephan Haggard, *Developing Nations and the Politics of Global Integration* (Washington, DC: Brookings Institution, 1995), p. 1.
8. See Tomohisa Hattori, "Reconceptualizing Foreign Aid," *Review of International Political Economy* 8-4 (Winter 2001), p. 646.
9. Organisation for Economic Co-operation and Development, *Development Co-operation—1994 Report* (Paris: OECD, 1995), p. 86.
10. For a list of all LDCs qualifying for ODA, and of all transition economies qualifying for OA, see OECD, *Development Co-operation Report 1998* (Paris: OECD, 1999), p. A98.
11. Robert Wade, "Japan, the World Bank, and the Art of Paradigm Maintenance: The East Asian Miracle in Political Perspective," *New Left Review* 217 (May/June 1996), p. 5.
12. Stephen D. Krasner, *Structural Conflict: The Third World Against Global Liberalism* (Berkeley, CA: University of California Press, 1985), p. 3.
13. Gustav Ranis, "The World Bank Near the Turn of the Century," in Roy Culpeper, Albert Berry, and Frances Stewart, eds., *Global Development Fifty Years After Bretton Woods* (New York: St. Martin's Press, 1997), p. 73.
14. Hattori, "Reconceptualizing Foreign Aid," p. 644.
15. Ranis, "The World Bank Near the Turn of the Century," p. 73.
16. Wade, "Japan, the World Bank, and the Art of Paradigm Maintenance," p. 5. See also Guy Gran, *Development by People: Citizen Construction of a Just World* (New York: Praeger, 1983), p. 28.
17. Barry Eichengreen and Peter B. Kenen, "Managing the World Economy under the Bretton Woods System: An Overview," in Peter B. Kenen, ed., *Managing the World Economy: Fifty Years After Bretton Woods* (Washington, D.C.: Institute for International Economics, 1994), p. 6.
18. Victor L. Urquidi, "Reconstruction vs. Development: The IMF and the World Bank," paper presented to "Bretton Woods Revisited: An International Conference," Bretton Woods, New Hampshire, October 15–17, 1994, revised text, November 11, 1994, p. 11.

19. Edward S. Mason and Robert E. Asher, *The World Bank Since Bretton Woods* (Washington, DC: Brookings Institution, 1973), pp. 52–53; Robert E. Wood, *From Marshall Plan to Debt Crisis: Foreign Aid and Development Choices in the World Economy* (Berkeley, CA: University of California Press, 1986), p. 29. Chile was the first LDC to receive an IBRD loan in March 1948, and Mexico and Brazil received loans in early 1949.

20. *The World Bank Annual Report—2001* (Washington, DC: World Bank, 2001), vol. 2, pp. 44–46.

21. *The World Bank Annual Report—1997* (Washington, DC: World Bank, 1997), pp. 134–137.

22. See Theodore Cohn, "Developing Countries in the International Civil Service: The Case of the World Bank Group," *International Review of Administrative Sciences* 41-1 (1975), pp. 47–56.

23. Stephen Fidler, "Who's Minding the Bank?," *Foreign Policy* 126 (September/October 2001), p. 41.

24. See Krasner, *Structural Conflict*, pp. 146–150; Cheryl Payer, *The World Bank: A Critical Analysis* (New York: Monthly Review Press, 1982), pp. 43–48.

25. *International Financial Corporation Annual Report—1995* (Washington, DC: IFC, 1995), pp. 5–6; "Hey, Big Lender," *The Economist*, April 23, 1994, pp. 81–82.

26. See Ronald T. Libby, "International Development Association: A Legal Fiction Designed to Secure an LDC Constituency," *International Organization* 29-4 (Autumn 1975), pp. 1065–1072.

27. For a complete listing of the countries in these three categories, see *The World Bank Annual Report—2001*, vol. 1, pp. 139–140.

28. Paul Lewis, "Clinton Backs Funds for World Bank Agency," *New York Times*, October 12, 1995, p. C4; "Aid for the World's Poorest," *New York Times*, October 18, 1995, p. A18; *The World Bank Annual Report—1998*, p. xii.

29. The idea of establishing a MIGA emerged as early as the 1950s (*Convention Establishing the Multilateral Investment Guarantee Agency and Commentary on the Convention* [Washington, DC: IBRD, October 11, 1985], p. 47). For a detailed discussion of the MIGA, see Ibrahim F. I. Shihata, *MIGA and Foreign Investment: Origins, Operations, Policies and Basic Documents of the Multilateral Investment Guarantee Agency* (Dordrecht: Nijhoff, 1988).

30. See Anne O. Krueger, Constantine Michalopoulos, and Vernon W. Ruttan, with Keith Jay, *Aid and Development* (Baltimore, MD: Johns Hopkins University Press, 1989), pp. 106–108; and John White, *Pledged to Development: A Study of International Consortia and the Strategy of Aid* (London: Overseas Development Institute, 1967).

31. See John White, *Regional Development Banks: A Study of Institutional Style* (London: Overseas Development Institute, 1970). The most comprehensive recent studies of the multilateral development banks are contained in a five-volume series published in association with the North-South Institute in Ottawa, Canada: E. Phillip English and Harris M. Mule, *The African Development Bank;* Nihal Kappagoda, *The Asian Development Bank;* Chandra Hardy, *The Caribbean Development Bank;* Diana Tussie, *The Inter-American Development Bank;* and Roy Culpeper, *Titans or Behemoths?* (Boulder, CO: Rienner, 1995–97).

32. Payer, *The World Bank: A Critical Analysis*, p. 20.

33. P. T. Bauer, *Reality and Rhetoric: Studies in the Economics of Development* (London: Weidenfeld and Nicolson, 1984), p. 70; Kalman Mizsei, "The Role of the Bretton Woods Institutions in the Transforming Economies," in *Bretton Woods: Looking to the Future,* p. C-103.

34. Robert L. Ayres, *Banking on the Poor: The World Bank and World Poverty* (Cambridge, MA: MIT Press, 1983), p. 15.

35. Ranis, "The World Bank Near the Turn of the Century," p. 76.

36. Fidler, "Who's Minding the Bank?," p. 45. See also Ranis, "The World Bank Near the Turn of the Century," p. 84.

37. See Raúl Prebisch, *The Economic Development of Latin America and Its Principal Problems* (New York: United Nations Economic Commission for Latin America, 1950) 7-1, pp. 1–59; H. W. Singer, "The Distribution of Gains Between Investing and Borrowing Countries," *American Economic Review* 40-2 (May 1950), pp. 473–485.

38. For a detailed discussion of Latin American structuralism see Anil Hira, *Ideas and Economic Policy in Latin America: Regional, National, and Organizational Case Studies* (Westport, CT: Praeger, 1998), ch. 3.

39. Ozay Mehmet, *Westernizing the Third World: The Eurocentricity of Economic Development Theories* (London: Routledge, 1995), p. 78; John Rapley, *Understanding Development: Theory and Practice* (Boulder, CO: Rienner, 1996), pp. 27–34.

40. Luiz Carlos Bresser Pereira, "Development Economics and the World Bank's Identity Crisis," *Review of International Political Economy* 2-2 (Spring 1995), pp. 215–217; Devesh Kapur, John P. Lewis, and Richard Webb, *The World Bank: Its First Half Century, Volume 1:* History (Washington, DC: Brookings Institution Press, 1997), p. 451; Mason and Asher, *The World Bank Since Bretton Woods,* pp. 150–153.

41. See Rapley, *Understanding Development,* pp. 27–36.

42. Theodore Cohn, *Canadian Food Aid: Domestic and Foreign Policy Implications* (Denver, CO: University of Denver, Graduate School in International Studies, 1979), pp. 25–27.

43. Sylvia Maxfield and James N. Nolt, "Protectionism and the Internationalization of Capital: U.S. Sponsorship of Import Substitution Industrialization in the Philippines, Turkey and Argentina," *International Studies Quarterly* 34-1 (March 1990), p. 50.

44. Anne O. Krueger, *Trade Policies and Developing Nations* (Washington, DC: Brookings Institution, 1995), pp. 3–10, 33–44; Rapley, *Understanding Development,* pp. 33–44; Stephan Haggard, *Pathways from the Periphery: The Politics of Growth in the Newly Industrializing Countries* (Ithaca, NY: Cornell University Press, 1990), pp. 9–14.

45. Anne O. Krueger, "The Effects of Trade Strategies on Growth," *Finance and Development* 20-2 (June 1983), p. 8.

46. Mason and Asher, "The World Bank Since Bretton Woods," pp. 378–379; Bresser Pereira, "Development Economics and the World Bank's Identity Crisis," p. 216.

47. Raúl Prebisch, *Towards a Dynamic Development Policy for Latin America* (New York: United Nations, 1963), p. 71. See also Raúl Prebisch, "Five Stages in My Thinking on Development," in Gerald M. Meier and Dudley Seers, eds., *Pioneers in Development* (New York: Oxford University Press, 1984), p. 181.

48. See Bela Balassa, "The Process of Industrial Development and Alternative Development Strategies," in Bela Balassa, ed., *The Newly Industrializing Countries in the World Economy* (New York: Pergamon Press, 1981), pp. 5–16.

49. Joseph L. Love, "The Origins of Dependency Analysis," *Journal of Latin American Studies* 22 (February 1990), pp. 143–160.

50. This section draws partly on Rapley, *Understanding Development,* pp. 44–47.

51. James H. Mittelman and Mustapha Kamal Pasha, *Out from Underdevelopment Revisited: Changing Global Structures and the Remaking of the Third World,* 2nd ed. (London: Macmillan, 1997), pp. 181–214.

52. David Slater, "The Political Meanings of Development: In Search of New Horizons," in Frans J. Schuurman, ed., *Beyond the Impasse: New Direction in Development Theory* (London: Zed Books, 1993), pp. 101–105.

53. John M. Page, "The East Asian Miracle: An Introduction," *World Development* 22-4 (1994), p. 619; Robert Wade, *Governing the Market: Economic Theory and the Role of Government in East Asian Industrialization* (Princeton, NJ: Princeton University Press, 1990), p. 34.

54. See, for example, Arnold C. Harberger, "Growth, Industrialization and Economic Structure: Latin America and East Asia Compared," in Helen Hughes, ed., *Achieving Industrialization in East Asia* (Cambridge: Cambridge University Press, 1988), pp. 164–194; Haggard, *Pathways from the Periphery*, chs. 3–7; and Bela Balassa, *Policy Choices for the 1990s* (London: Macmillan, 1993), pp. 56–67.

55. Wade, *Governing the Market*, p. 34.

56. Krueger, *Trade Policies and Developing Nations*, pp. 20–23.

57. Mehmet, *Westernizing the Third World*, p. 78.

58. On inward- versus outward-oriented development strategies, see Bela Balassa, *The Newly Industrializing Countries in the World Economy* (New York: Pergamon Press, 1981), pp. 6–24.

59. Staffan Burenstam Linder, *The Pacific Century: Economic and Political Consequences of Asian-Pacific Dynamism* (Stanford, CA: Stanford University Press, 1986), p. 31.

60. Ronen Palan and Jason Abbott, with Phil Deans, *State Strategies in the Global Political Economy* (London: Pinter, 1996), p. 78.

61. See Chalmers Johnson, "Introduction—The Taiwan Model," in James C. Hsiung et al., eds., *Contemporary Republic of China: The Taiwan Experience 1950–1980* (New York: Praeger, 1981), pp. 9–18; and Chalmers Johnson, *MITI and the Japanese Miracle: The Growth of Industrial Policy, 1925–1975* (Stanford, CA: Stanford University Press, 1982).

62. Rapley, *Understanding Development*, pp. 124–127; Adrian Leftwich, "Bringing Politics Back In: Towards a Model of the Developmental State," *Journal of Development Studies* 31-3 (February 1995), pp. 401–403.

63. Peter Evans, *Dependent Development: The Alliance of Multinational, State, and Local Capital in Brazil* (Princeton, NJ: Princeton University Press, 1979), p. 33.

64. Quoted in William Nester, "The Development of Japan, Taiwan and South Korea: Ends and Means, Free Trade, Dependency, or Neomercantilism?", *Journal of Developing Societies* 6 (1990), p. 206.

65. Cal Clark and Steve Chan, "MNCs and Developmentalism: Domestic Structure as an Explanation for East Asian Dynamism," in Thomas Risse-Kappen, ed., *Bringing Transnational Relations Back In: Non-State Actors, Domestic Structures and International Institutions* (Cambridge: Cambridge University Press, 1995), p. 125.

66. For a detailed discussion of Confucian political culture in East Asia, see Lucian W. Pye with Mary W. Pye, *Asian Power and Politics: The Cultural Dimensions of Authority* (Cambridge, MA: Belknap Press of Harvard University Press, 1985), ch. 3.

67. Pye, *Asian Power and Politics*, p. 90; Clark and Chan, "MNCs and Developmentalism," pp. 120–123.

68. Christopher Lingle, "What Ever Happened to the 'Asian Century'?", *World Economic Affairs* 2-2 (Spring 1998), p. 32.

69. World Bank, *The East Asian Miracle: Economic Growth and Public Policy*, Policy Research Report (Oxford: Oxford University Press, 1993), p. 1.

70. Graham Bird and Alistair Milne, "Miracle to Meltdown: A Pathology of the East Asian Financial Crisis," *Third World Quarterly* 20-2 (1999), p. 421.

71. Stephan Haggard, *The Political Economy of the Asian Financial Crisis* (Washington, DC: Institute for International Economics, August 2000), p. 3.

72. James Busumtwi-Sam, "International Financial Institutions, International Capital Flows and Financial Liberalization in Developing Countries," in Stephen McBride and John Wiseman, eds., *Globalization and Its Discontents* (London, UK: Macmillan, 2000), pp. 88–90; Glassman and Carmody, "Structural Adjustment in East and Southeast Asia," p. 77.

73. Shahid Yusuf, "The East Asian Miracle at the Millennium," in Joseph E. Stiglitz and Shahid Yusuf, eds., *Rethinking the East Asian Miracle* (Oxford, UK: Oxford University Press and the World Bank, 2001), pp. 1–4.

74. Bird and Milne, "Miracle to Meltdown: A Pathology of the East Asian Financial Crisis," p. 422. See also Seth Mydans, "An 'Asian Miracle' Now Seems Like a Mirage," *New York Times,* October 22, 1997, pp. A1, A8.

75. Walden Bello and Stephanie Rosenfeld, *Dragons in Distress: Asia's Miracle Economies in Crisis* (San Francisco: Institute for Food and Development Policy, 1990), pp. 3–10; I. M. Destler, *American Trade Politics,* 2nd ed. (Washington, DC: Institute for International Economics, 1992), pp. 131–133.

76. Walter Hatch and Kozo Yamamura, *Asia in Japan's Embrace: Building a Regional Production Alliance* (Cambridge: Cambridge University Press, 1996), p. 37.

77. Jim Glassman and Pádraig Carmody, "Structural Adjustment in East and Southeast Asia: Lessons from Latin America," *Geoforum* 32-1 (February 2001), pp. 79–80.

78. See Samuel P. Huntington, *Political Order in Changing Societies* (New Haven, CT: Yale University Press, 1968).

79. Edward A. Gargan, "Currency Assault Unnerves Asians," *New York Times,* July 29, 1997, pp. A1, C15; Joseph Stiglitz, "How to Fix Asian Economies," *New York Times,* October 31, 1997, p. A19.

80. Haggard, *The Political Economy of the Asian Financial Crisis,* p. 4.

81. Stephan Haggard and Andrew MacIntyre, "The Political Economy of the Asian Economic Crisis," *Review of International Political Economy* 5-3 (Autumn 1998), p. 405; Haggard, *The Political Economy of the Asian Financial Crisis,* pp. 5–6.

82. Paul Krugman, "The Myth of Asia's Miracle," *Foreign Affairs* 73-6 (November/December 1994), p. 67. See also Alwyn Young, "The Tyranny of Numbers: Confronting the Statistical Realities of the East Asian Growth Experience," *Quarterly Journal of Economics* 110-3 (August 1995), pp. 641–680.

83. Walden Bello, "Overview of Current Economic, Strategic and Political Developments in Southeast and South Asia," *Focus Files* (Bangkok, Thailand, October 1997), p. 3.

84. World Commission on Environment and Development, *Our Common Future* (Oxford: Oxford University Press, 1987), p. 8.

85. Handelman, *The Challenge of Third World Development,* p. 228.

86. Palan and Abbott, *State Strategies in the Global Political Economy,* p. 99.

87. Christopher L. Gilbert and David Vines, "The World Bank: An Overview of Some Major Issues," in Christopher L. Gilbert and David Vines, eds., *The World Bank: Structures and Policies* (Cambridge, UK: Cambridge University Press, 2000), p. 16.

88. See John Williamson, "Democracy and the 'Washington Consensus,' " *World Development* 21-8 (August 1993), pp. 1329–1336.

89. Ngaire Woods, "The Challenges of Multilateralism and Governance," in Gilbert and Vines, eds., *The World Bank: Structures and Policies,* p. 141.

90. Richard E. Feinberg, "The Changing Relationship Between the World Bank and the International Monetary Fund," *International Organization* 42-3 (Summer 1988), pp. 552–556; Jacques J. Polak, *The World Bank and the International Monetary Fund: A Changing Relationship,* Brookings Occasional Papers (Washington, DC: Brookings Institution, 1994), pp. 16–17.

91. Rapley, *Understanding Development,* p. 76.

92. Farhad Noorbakhsh and Alberto Paloni, "Structural Adjustment and Growth in Sub-Saharan Africa: The Importance of Complying with Conditionality," *Economic Development and Cultural Change* 49-3 (April 2000), pp. 479–509.

93. Cited in Bob Milward, "The Heavily Indebted Poor Countries and the Role of Structural Adjustment Policies," in *Developments in Economics: An Annual Review* (Lancashire, UK: Causeway Books, 2001), p. 38.

94. J. Barry Riddell, "Things Fall Apart Again: Structural Adjustment Programmes in Sub-Saharan Africa," *Journal of Modern African Studies* 30-1 (1992), p. 67.

95. Gloria Thomas-Emeagwali, "Introductory Perspectives: Monetarists, Liberals and Radicals: Contrasting Perspectives on Gender and Structural Adjustment," in Thomas-Emeagwali, ed., *Women Pay the Price*, p. 5.

96. Glassman and Carmody, "Structural Adjustment in East and Southeast Asia," p. 82.

97. Thomas-Emeagwali, "Introductory Perspectives," pp. 3–4.

98. James H. Weaver, "What Is Structural Adjustment?," in Daniel M. Schydlowsky, ed., *Structural Adjustment: Retrospect and Prospect* (Westport, CT: Praeger, 1995), pp. 12–13; Barend A. de Vries, "The World Bank's Focus on Poverty," in Jo Marie Griesgraber and Berhard G. Gunter, eds,, *The World Bank: Lending on a Global Scale* (London: Pluto Press, 1996), pp. 68–69.

99. United Nations Development Program, *Human Development Report 1996* (New York: Oxford University Press, 1996), pp. 136–137; World Bank, *World Development Report 1997: The State in a Changing World* (New York: Oxford University Press, 1997), p. 214.

100. Quoted in Julius O. Ihonvbere, "Economic Crisis, Structural Adjustment and Africa's Future," in Gloria Thomas-Emeagwali, ed., *Women Pay the Price: Structural Adjustment in Africa and the Caribbean* (Trenton, NJ: Africa World Press, 1995), p. 137.

101. For a strong defense of World Bank SAPs in Africa, see Elliot Berg, "African Adjustment Programs: False Attacks and True Dilemmas," in Schydlowsky, ed., *Structural Adjustment*, pp. 89–107.

102. Rapley, *Understanding Development*, pp. 83–92; Riddell, "Things Fall Apart Again: Structural Adjustment Programmes in Sub-Saharan Africa," pp. 53–68.

103. Frances Stewart, "Can Adjustment Programmes Incorporate the Interests of Women?," in Haleh Afshar and Carolyne Dennis, eds., *Women and Adjustment Policies in the Third World* (New York: St. Martin's Press, 1992), pp. 22–24.

104. Diane Elson, "Male Bias in Macro-Economics: The Case of Structural Adjustment," in Diane Elson, ed., *Male Bias in the Development Process* (Manchester, UK: Manchester University Press, 1991), pp. 175–178.

105. Stewart, "Can Adjustment Programmes Incorporate the Interests of Women?," p. 27.

106. Elson, "Male Bias in Macro-Economics," p. 173; Stewart, "Can Adjustment Programmes Incorporate the Interests of Women?," p. 22.

107. World Bank, *World Development Report 1991*, p. 9.

108. World Bank, *The East Asian Miracle: Economic Growth and Public Policy* (New York: Oxford University Press, 1993), p. 1.

109. World Bank, *The East Asian Miracle*, p. 274.

110. K. S. Jomo, "Rethinking the Role of Government Policy in Southeast Asia," in Stiglitz and Yusuf, eds., *Rethinking the East Asian Miracle*, p. 462.

111. World Bank, *The East Asian Miracle*, p. 26.

112. See Jomo, "Rethinking the Role of Government Policy in Southeast Asia," pp. 461–463; and Wade, "Japan, the World Bank, and the Art of Paradigm Maintenance," pp. 3–36.

113. On the four major phases, see Ravi Kanbur and David Vines, "The World Bank and Poverty Reduction: Past, Present and Future," in Gilbert and Vines, eds., *The World Bank: Structures and Policies*, pp. 87–107; and Kapur, Lewis, and Webb, *The World Bank: Its First Half Century*.

114. Mohammed H. Malek, "Towards an Integrated Aid and Development Programme for Europe," in Mohammed H. Malek, ed., *Contemporary Issues in European Development Aid* (Aldershot, UK: Avebury, 1991), p. 142.

115. Organisation for Economic Co-operation and Development, *Twenty-five Years of Development Co-operation: A Review—1985 Report* (Paris: OECD, November 1985), p. 49. The basic human needs approach was not in fact "new" in the 1970s, because the August 1961 Charter of the U.S.-Latin American Alliance for Progress had also emphasized basic needs.

116. Ayres, *Banking on the Poor,* pp. 4–6; Anthony Bottrall, "The McNamara Strategy: Putting Precept into Practice," *ODI Review* 1 (1974), pp. 70–80; Paul Dickson, "A Fresh Look at the World Bank," *Vista* 8-6 (June 1973), pp. 24–49.

117. Giovannia Andrea Cornia, Richard Jolly, and Frances Stewart, eds., *Adjustment with a Human Face, Vol. 1: Protecting the Vulnerable and Promoting Growth* (Oxford, UK: Clarendon Press, 1987), p. 7.

118. World Bank, *Sub-Saharan Africa: From Crisis to Sustainable Growth, a Long-Term Perspective Study* (Washington DC: World Bank, 1989), pp. 17, xi. See also Ihonvbere, "Economic Crisis, Structural Adjustment and Africa's Future," pp. 138–147.

119. See World Bank, *World Development Report 1990, "Poverty"* (New York: Oxford University Press, 1990).

120. John Pender, "From 'Structural Adjustment' to Comprehensive Development Framework: Conditionality Transformed?," *Third World Quarterly* 22-3 (2001), p. 402. See also Kevin Danaher, ed., *50 Years is Enough: The Case Against the World Bank and the International Monetary Fund* (Boston: South End Press, 1994).

121. Pender, "From 'Structural Adjustment' to Comprehensive Development Framework," pp. 402–403.

122. World Bank, *World Development Report 1997,* Foreword, p. iii. The bank's views on state minimalism reflected views of others at the time that it was necessary to take a "second look" at the role of the state in development. See for example, Paul Streeten, "Markets and States: Against Minimalism," *World Development* 21-8 (August 1993), pp. 1281–1298; and the articles from a symposium on "The State and Economic Development" in *Journal of Economic Perspectives* 4-3 (Summer 1990).

123. World Bank, *World Development Report 1997,* p. iii.

124. Kanbur and Vines, "The World Bank and Poverty Reduction," p. 88. See also World Bank, *World Development Report 2000/2001;* and Pender, "From 'Structural Adjustment' to Comprehensive Development Framework," pp. 404–406.

125. World Bank, *World Development Report 1999/2000* (New York: 2000), pp. 21–23; Paul Collier, "Conditionality, Dependence and Coordination: Three Current Debates in Aid Policy," in Gilbert and Vines, eds., *The World Bank: Structures and Policies,* p. 323.

126. Robert Wade, "Showdown at the World Bank," *New Left Review* 7 (January/February 2001), p. 132.

127. Fidler, "Who's Minding the Bank?," p. 46.

128. Pender, "From 'Structural Adjustment' to Comprehensive Development Framework," p. 407.

129. *Partners in Development,* Report of the Commission on International Development, chaired by Lester B. Pearson (New York: Praeger, 1969), p. 152.

130. W. W. Rostow, *The Stages of Economic Growth: A Non-Communist Manifesto* (Cambridge: Cambridge University Press, 1960).

131. Rapley, *Understanding Development,* pp. 135–154.

132. United Nations Development Program, *Human Development Report 1996,* p. 1.

133. Diane Elson, "Economic Paradigms Old and New: The Case of Human Development," in Culpeper, Berry, and Stewart, eds., *Global Development Fifty Years After Bretton Woods,* p. 60.

134. Cristóbal Kay, "For a Renewal of Development Studies: Latin American Theories and Neoliberalism in the Era of Structural Adjustment," *Third World Quarterly* 14-4 (1993), p. 695.

135. Lingle, "What Ever Happened to the 'Asian Century'?," p. 33.

136. Rapley, *Understanding Development,* pp. 155–157. See also Elizabeth Parsan, *South-South Trade in Global Development* (Aldershot, UK: Avebury, 1993).

Concluding Comments

The last three decades of the twentieth century have been marked by a series of unexpected and disruptive developments in global politics and economics. Most notable of these developments were the food and oil crises in the 1970s, the foreign debt crisis in the 1980s, the breakup of the Soviet bloc and Soviet Union in the 1980s–1990s, and the financial crisis in East and Southeast Asia in the late 1990s. As globalization has increased, events in one part of the world have also had a greater impact on distant areas, and predictions about the future of the global political economy have become more hazardous. Nevertheless, the historical discussion in this book enables us to speculate about current and possible future changes in the twenty-first century. Relying on the major themes of this book, Chapter 12 examines contemporary trends in the global political economy.

Current Trends in the Global Political Economy

This book provides a comprehensive approach to the study of IPE, introducing the student to the major theoretical perspectives and substantive issue areas. The three perspectives of realism, liberalism, and historical structuralism have evolved and influenced each other over time, and some theoretical approaches such as hegemonic stability theory, regime theory, and the business conflict model draw on more than one of the major perspectives. Approaches that focus on domestic-international linkages and establish connections between comparative political economy and IPE are becoming more common and contributing to further changes in the study of IPE.

To help in linking theory and practice, this book focuses on three themes central to the study of IPE: globalization, North-North relations, and North-South relations. Issues surrounding the emerging states of Eastern Europe and the FSU are subsumed under these three themes, because the Cold War has virtually ended and the former CPEs are becoming increasingly integrated in the capitalist global economy. Whereas the more developed former Eastern bloc states such as the Czech Republic and Hungary have levels of development almost comparable with some of the industrial states of the North, the poorer countries of the former Second World face severe economic problems more comparable with those of LDCs in the South. It is useful in this concluding chapter to examine where we are today with these three themes of globalization, North-North relations, and North-South relations and to speculate about the future.

GLOBALIZATION

Globalization is a process that involves both the broadening and deepening of interdependence among societies and states throughout the world. *Broadening* refers to the geographic extension of linkages to encompass virtually all major societies and states, and *deepening* refers to an increase in the frequency and intensity of interactions. This book has *not* adopted an extreme view of globalization that argues that we are entering a "borderless world" where MNCs are losing their national identities and nation-states are losing their distinctiveness.[1] In fact, globalization is a process that affects some states and regions more than others, that threatens the state's autonomy in some respects but does not prevent it from making policy choices, and that contributes to fragmentation and conflict as well as unity and cooperation. Although there was a high degree of economic interdependence among states and societies in the nineteenth and early twentieth centuries, globalization is more encompassing today than it was at any time in the past. Advances in technology, communications, and transportation are facilitating the globalization process as never before; the role of the MNC in generating FDI, trade, and technology is unprecedented; and with the breakup of the Soviet bloc, the capitalist economic system is spreading throughout the globe, and international economic organizations are becoming truly universal in membership.

Realists, liberals, and historical structuralists have widely divergent views of globalization. Realists emphasize the continuing importance of the nation-state and often question whether there is in fact a significant increase in globalization. Although realists may acknowledge that global interdependence is increasing in some areas, they believe this occurs only with the permission or encouragement of the most powerful states and that these states continue to dictate the terms and limits of such transactions. Liberals, by contrast, believe there is a significant level of globalization that is eroding state control, and they view the growth of global interdependence as a positive development. Whereas realists believe that globalization occurs at the whim of the state, liberals attach far more importance to such factors as technological change and advances in communications and transportation that are beyond state control. Liberals also argue that globalization is increasing as a result of the demands of domestic and transnational societal actors such as internationalist firms.[2]

Historical structuralists, like liberals, believe that globalization is having a significant impact, but unlike liberals, they believe globalization has extremely negative consequences for the poorer states and classes in the periphery of the global economy. Some Gramscian theorists argue that globalization is leading to the development of a "transnational historic bloc" composed of the largest MNCs, international banks, international economic organizations, and international business groups in the most powerful capitalist states. A crucial element of this transnational historic bloc is the power and mobility of transnational capital, which is putting national groups such as labor unions on the defensive. The only way to counter such a transnational historic bloc, according to Gramscians, is to develop a counterhegemonic bloc composed of the disadvantaged and disaffected such as labor, human rights, environmental, consumer, development, and women's groups. A counterhegemonic bloc of this nature would be committed to replacing the current corporate view of liberalization with a more democratic, participatory model based on socialism.[3]

Globalization and Triadization

Globalization today is in many respects more akin to "triadization." The integrative processes are most intense among three major regions that contain most of the world's developed market economies: Western Europe, North America, and Japan/East Asia.[4] Countries in these three regions are the main sources of foreign direct investment, and they direct most of their FDI to each other. In 1995, for example, the developed market economies accounted for 92.1 percent of the outward stocks of FDI and for 72.1 percent of the inward stocks of FDI. Western Europe, North America, and Asia also dominate international trade flows, and they trade much more with each other than with other parts of the world. In 1993, North America, Western Europe, and Asia accounted for 84.2 percent of global merchandise exports and for 90.2 percent of world exports of manufactures.[5]

Although some LDCs have increased their share of inward FDI, the distribution of this investment has been very uneven. On the one hand, 10 LDCs located mainly in East Asia and Latin America (Singapore, Brazil, Mexico, China, Hong Kong, Malaysia, Egypt, Argentina, Thailand, and Colombia) received about three-fourths of total FDI inflows to Third World countries in the 1980s. On the other hand, the LLDCs—most of which are in sub-Saharan Africa—received only 1.5 percent of the FDI inflows to the Third World during 1980–84, and their share fell to 0.7 percent in 1985–89. (The United Nations has designated 48 LDCs as "least developed."[6]) Many of the poorest Third World countries have also received little benefit from the expansion of world trade. Although the Asian countries' share of world trade grew from 4.6 percent to 12.5 percent between 1970 and 1991, the share for other LDC regions declined. The LLDCs, with about 10 percent of the world's people, accounted for only 0.3 percent of world trade in 1997—which was about half of their share two decades earlier.[7]

Although historical structuralists have warned against Southern dependence on the North, an even greater problem for most of the poorer Third World countries today is the threat of marginalization. The breakup of the Soviet bloc and the decline of the Cold War decreased the leverage of LDCs in gaining economic concessions from both East and West. This marginalization of the poorer Southern countries is likely to continue because the triad of the EU, North America, and Japan will be primarily interested in increasing their economic linkages with the more prosperous Third World countries and with the emerging states of Eastern Europe and the FSU.[8]

Globalization and the Nation-State

Globalization has constrained the ability of developed states to continue providing the social welfare benefits that citizens came to expect in the 1950s to 1970s, and the revival of orthodox liberalism has made such social expenditures seem less legitimate. Globalization has also limited the ability of the state to regulate the national economy. For example, the massive growth of international capital flows has contributed to volatility and misalignment in currency exchange rates. Major fluctuations in exchange rates interfere with the state's ability to promote economic regulation and stability.

Liberal economists generally view the increase in capital flows as a favorable development because financial markets impose necessary discipline on states, and global savings and resources move to their most productive locations. Historical structuralists, by contrast, view increased capital mobility as a highly negative development because the fear of capital outflows can force governments to adopt policies that adversely affect the poorest and weakest in society. If governments do not adopt "capital-friendly" policies, MNCs and international banks can readily shift their funds to more welcoming locations. Thus, MNCs tend to locate their production facilities in the states with the lowest wages, environmental standards, and taxes. Realists believe that the increase in global financial flows in recent years has occurred with the permission or even encouragement of the most powerful states and that these states continue to dictate the terms for such transactions. Although the United States, Britain, and others adopted policies that contributed to the globalization of finance, this globalization "has had unintended consequences for those who promoted it," and realists overlook the fact that it may be extremely difficult for states to regain control over the global market forces they have unleashed.[9]

Southern states are especially vulnerable to the freeing of capital flows, as the financial crisis in the late 1990s demonstrated. East and Southeast Asian countries had opened their economies to freer capital flows in the years leading up to the crisis, and a surge of bank lending and portfolio investment contributed to risky and ill-advised investments in the region. When serious weaknesses in the economies of these countries became evident, there was a "rush of international capital out of the region in 1997—a movement that was more frenzied than its mad rush to get into the area in earlier years."[10] Although domestic political and economic factors in the Asian economies contributed to the financial crisis, a major external factor was the volatility of capital flows or contagion. "Contagion" refers to "the spread of currency and asset market problems from one market to another."[11] As investor concern spreads from country to country, even sound financial institutions can be adversely affected. Thus, one currency after another in East and Southeast Asia was depreciated sharply, countries experienced severe liquidity crises, and the IMF became deeply involved in providing finance.

Even the first deputy managing director of the IMF has acknowledged that the "factors contributing to contagion suggest it has been excessive—and that a way should be found to moderate it."[12] There is also a consensus developing that Third World and emerging countries should not open their capital markets too rapidly, because it may be difficult for them to make adequate adjustments. In 1993, the G-7 released a study that examined possible multilateral approaches to dealing with the negative effects of international capital mobility, but policy coordination among the G-7 countries may be difficult for several reasons. First, states often give priority to their own national concerns over the need for coordination. Second, it is questionable whether governments have the will to regain control over capital and foreign investment movements in the present climate of orthodox liberalism. Third, although there is general agreement that LDCs must be more careful in liberalizing capital flows, that is about all the experts agree on. Many analysts blame the IMF for mishandling the financial crisis in East and Southeast Asia, but there is a notable lack of consensus on proposals for reform.[13] Nevertheless, civil society groups are becoming more activist and demanding that the state reestablish some controls. Chapter 10, for example, discusses the role that disaffected labor and environmental groups, human rights groups, and consumer advocates in industrial states played in organizing opposition to the OECD's negotiation of a MAI. Societal groups of course do not have the capability to develop regulations over global financial markets, but they may play a role in eventually pressuring the developed states to cooperate in establishing such global regulatory capabilities.

Globalization and Inequality

Many liberals recognize that globalization may contribute to inequalities among and within states in the short term. However, they believe that the efficiency gains from globalization will reduce these inequalities in the long term. As discussed in Chapter 11, orthodox liberals argue that benefits from the efficient allocation of resources under freer markets "eventually trickle down from the top, alleviating the problem of poverty at the bottom."[14] Realists and historical structuralists, by contrast, believe there will be long-term losers as well as winners from globalization. From the realist perspective, the most powerful states have considerable control over the pace and direction of globalization, and they can use the globalization process "to reinforce their position and their relative power." For less powerful states, by contrast, globalization "is a process which is happening to them and to which they must respond."[15] Historical structuralists also believe that globalization benefits the most powerful capitalist states and nonstate actors such as MNCs in the core at the expense of peripheral states and vulnerable societal groups.

Although the statistics are sometimes conflicting, it does seem that globalization and liberalization in combination have contributed to greater inequalities both among and within states. As discussed in Chapter 11, the World Bank reports that the average income in the richest 20 countries is 37 times higher than the average income in the poorest 20 countries—a gap that has doubled in the last 40 years. The growing inequalities among countries are of course most evident between the North and the South. About 1.2 billion of the world's 6 billion people live on less than $1 a day, and almost 44 percent of these people live in South Asia. Although the number of people living on less than $1 a day declined in East Asia between 1987 and 1998, the numbers of poor people in South Asia, Latin America, sub-Saharan Africa, and the transition countries of Europe and Central Asia increased during this period.[16]

In many developed states, globalization has resulted in an increase in *overall* income, but also in a rise in unemployment. In 1995, 7.5 percent of the work force or 34 million people in the OECD countries were unemployed, and from 1979 to 1997, unemployment in the EU more than doubled, to 11 percent. In the United States, the employment picture was healthier in the late 1990s, but there is evidence that the income gap between the rich and poor was widening. Globalization has also contributed to greater inequalities within a number of LDCs and former Soviet bloc countries. For example, the United Nations Development Program reported in 1997 that a falling share of national income was going to the poorest 20 percent of the people in several Latin American countries (Argentina, Chile, the Dominican Republic, Ecuador, Mexico, and Uruguay) and that in 16 of 18 countries in Eastern Europe and the Commonwealth of Independent States (the FSU countries other than Estonia, Latvia, and Lithuania) income distribution had worsened and poverty had increased.[17]

Mexico, a Third World country that has been something of a pacesetter in liberalizing its economic policies since the mid–1980s, provides a prime example of the fact that there are both winners and losers from globalization. On the one hand, policies such as the privatization of state industries and the 1992 land reform permitting investors to purchase land from smallholders were highly beneficial to owners of capital and to large commercial farms. On the other hand, the share of Mexicans living in absolute poverty rose from 19 percent in 1984 to 24 percent in 1989, and in rural areas the number of poor people increased from 6.7 million to 8.8 million. Although large commercial fruit and vegetable producers in Mexico are benefiting from free trade in agriculture under NAFTA, many Mexican corn and bean subsistence farmers who must compete with U.S. producers (by far the largest group engaged in agricultural production) could lose what little they have.[18]

It is important to note that there are variations among countries, indicating that the domestic policies of governments (and their positions in the global economy) can make a difference. For example, there is evidence that some Asian LDCs, such as China, India, Bangladesh, and Vietnam, have liberalized their trade and investment policies while also reducing poverty to some extent. Variations among LDCs in the concentration of land ownership, the degree to which production is labor intensive, and other factors can influence the way in which globalization affects the distribution of wealth in society. In the developed world, some Scandinavian countries have liberalized while still maintaining a substantial social safety net. In the short to medium term, then, globalization contributes to inequalities within and among a number of states, but the policies of states can ameliorate these effects. As for the long term, it is difficult to either prove or disprove the orthodox liberal claim that globalization will eventually contribute to a decrease in inequalities.

Globalization and Democracy

Many liberals believe that globalization is helping to promote stable democratic governments throughout the world. Indeed, they can point to the spread of liberal democratic practices in southern Europe in the 1970s, in Africa and Latin America in the 1980s, and in the emerging states of Eastern Europe and the FSU in the late 1980s and 1990s. Historical structuralists, by contrast, argue that globalization is transferring control from democratically accountable governments to MNCs, international banks, and IOs. For example, the investment chapter of NAFTA prohibits a range of performance requirements that governments have traditionally imposed on foreign investment to ensure that it serves the interests of the national economy. Historical structuralists also argue that income inequalities resulting from globalization contribute to growing disparities in political influence. These inequalities in the economic and political arenas inevitably decrease the opportunities for democratic policymaking.[19]

The liberal and historical structuralist perspectives are in fact both important for understanding the relationship between globalization and democracy. As liberals have noted, globalization has forced a number of governments to open their societies both economically and politically. Thus, liberal democratic practices such as constitutional guarantees, freedom of speech, open elections, and a multiparty system have spread to a number of countries throughout the world. Nevertheless, historical structuralists point out that the poorest individuals in LDCs often lack employment, education, sanitation and health facilities, and even enough food to eat. To these people, the economic right to an adequate standard of living is of far more relevance than Western-oriented political rights such as free speech and democratic elections. Because socioeconomic inequalities have increased with globalization, it is difficult to argue that globalization has genuinely contributed to democracy in the Third World. Even in the developed states, democratically accountable governments have lost some of their authority over social and economic policymaking to MNCs and international bureaucracies. If governments lose too much authority, one must question whether liberal democratic practices such as open elections in fact provide the citizenry with meaningful choices. Real decision-making power under these circumstances may shift away from the majority of the populace "even if political struggles, which give the illusion that genuine power struggles are occurring, persist."[20]

Globalization and Civil Society

As discussed throughout this book, globalization has contributed to the growth of civil society groups committed to social change. There are in fact three major types of civil society groups in terms of their objectives and strategies: conformers, reformers, and radicals (also called critical groups).[21] Conformers largely endorse the current behavior of liberal-economic IOs such as the KIEOs, and private actors such as MNCs. Reformers accept the existence of, and sometimes the need for the KIEOs and MNCs, but believe that they *should* be and *can* be reformed. Radical or critical groups believe that the KIEOs and MNCs are not reformable, and they seek to decrease their influence or even to abolish them.[22] Reformers are more inclined to rely on cooperative strategies to alter the behavior of the KIEOs and MNCs, whereas radical or critical groups prefer to engage in ideological—and sometimes physical—confrontation. Conformers and reformers are similar to liberals, with reformers committed to a reintroduction of embedded liberalism that takes account of the social effects of the market. Radical or critical groups are similar to historical structuralists because they are committed to a transformation of the capitalist system. Whereas the conformer, reformer, and critical groups are pure models, some NGOs in fact employ reformer and critical strategies simultaneously. For example, Greenpeace has worked with companies to develop ozone-friendly refrigerators at the same time as it has encouraged consumers to boycott Shell over its alleged involvement with state suppression in Nigeria.

Reformer and critical groups have been increasingly vocal in recent years. Many of their protests are directed at international institutions and MNCs that are viewed as promoting globalization. For example, this book has discussed civil society protests against the OECD's (unsuccessful) attempt to establish a MAI and against the WTO, APEC, the proposed FTAA, and MNCs as purveyors of globalization. In opposing globalization, civil society groups ironically are able to benefit from some of the effects of globalization such as the World Wide Web. As discussed in Chapter 11, the Web was particularly useful to NGO protestors against the MAI. The Web has been helpful to NGO protestors because it "facilitates networked sociopolitical relationships in important new ways, it (potentially) increases NGOs' organizational effectiveness and political significance, and it helps to foster more broadly participatory (transnational) political processes."[23]

The question arises as to whether a "global civil society" is likely to develop a counterhegemony in opposition to the forces of globalization in Gramscian terms.[24]

Civil society groups clearly have had some influence in particular cases such as their opposition to attempts to establish a MAI, and a number of international institutions and MNCs have responded to civil society pressures by establishing communication channels and procedures with NGOs. Nevertheless, it is highly unlikely that a global civil society will establish a counterhegemony for several reasons. First, it is important to note that most civil society groups are conformers; that is, a "silent majority." Although conformer groups may be dissatisfied with some features of the global economic order, they are not sufficiently dissatisfied to attempt to institute major changes. Many conformer groups are also net beneficiaries of the current global order.

Second, civil society groups in fact have a strikingly diverse range of objectives, and it is often easier for them to agree on what they are against than on what type of world order they favor as an alternative. For example, labor and environmental groups tend to be closely linked with developed country interests that are often quite different from the perceived interests of LDCs. Thus, civil society groups committed to LDC debt forgiveness such as Jubilee 2000 (discussed in Chapter 7) generally have very little in common with developed country–based labor and environmental groups. Even more importantly, right-wing as well as left-wing groups are part of civil society, and the changes they pressure for are sometimes directly in conflict. A third obstacle to the development of a counterhegemony relates to the differences in strategies and tactics discussed earlier. Thus, reformer and critical groups may have widely divergent views regarding the legitimacy of violent protests. In sum, civil society groups have had some influence in inducing international institutions and MNCs to adopt bottom-up as well as top-down modes of decision making, but one should not overestimate the effect civil society groups are likely to have on the global political economy.

Globalization and Migration

It is quite common for individuals, societal groups, and states to support some aspects of globalization from which they benefit and at the same time to oppose other aspects of globalization that pose a real or presumed threat to them. The cross-border movement of people is one area in which there is often a more generalized negative societal reaction to globalization. Whereas many states and societal groups have supported the freeing of trade and capital flows, they have been far more resistant to the cross-border movement of people. In the area of migration, societies and governments have demonstrated particular resistance to the forces of globalization, and there are growing signs of anti-immigrant sentiment in a number of industrial states. For example, a public opinion survey conducted by the EU in 1993 found that 52 percent of respondents felt there were too many immigrants, and a 1993 New York Times/CBS national telephone survey reported that 61 percent of Americans favored a decrease in the number of immigrants, compared with 42 percent in a 1977 Gallup poll.[25] The September 11, 2001 terrorist attacks on the World Trade Center in New York and the Pentagon in Washington, D.C. added greatly to public and governmental concerns about migration.

Despite these negative societal attitudes, the politics of immigration is complex and there are also countervailing tendencies. For example, the market demand for certain types of foreign workers sometimes makes it difficult for political leaders to limit immigration. Newly naturalized immigrants can also form an important voting constituency, and the Clinton administration adopted a "Citizenship USA" plan in 1996 under which more than 1 million people were sworn in, often in citizenship ceremonies with up to 12,000 to 15,000 individuals. These new citizens provided Clinton with an important source of votes for his reelection.[26]

The migration issue demonstrates that globalization can produce a highly defensive societal reaction in certain areas. Although citizens and states may wish to regulate cross-border migration because of valid concerns with such issues as illegal immigration and terrorism, societal groups may also seek to impose limits for more questionable reasons. For example, labor groups are often sensitive about the immigration issue because there has been a gradual shift in demand away from less skilled workers in the developed states. There is no conclusive empirical evidence of a linkage between increased unemployment among semi-skilled and unskilled workers in the developed states on the one hand, and immigration from Third World countries on the other. Indeed, some analysts argue that migrants often enter low-wage occupations that do not attract the local population, that many migrants are self-employed and create their own jobs, and that migration can stimulate growth and thus in fact reduce unemployment.[27] Nevertheless, concerns about the effects of migration on employment remain. Hostility to immigrants is also often heightened by groups with less legitimate objectives linked with extreme nationalism, racism, and suspicion of those who are different. For example, some extremist groups such as the Federation for American Immigration Reform (FAIR) have called for "a temporary moratorium on all immigration except spouses and minor children of U.S. citizens."[28]

Most IPE scholars who write about globalization focus on issues such as trade, foreign investment, and capital flows. They often do not even discuss migration because "no other issue remains so much under the thrall of states and so resistant to globalizing effects."[29] Nevertheless, as globalization increases the pressures for migration will grow along with the pressures for other types of international interactions, and it is important that migration becomes a more integral part of the study of IPE.

NORTH-NORTH RELATIONS

The second theme examined in this book relates to the interactions among the developed countries of the North. The issue of international economic management is primarily a North-North issue because the Northern states in the OECD are the only countries with the wealth and power to look after the management of the global economy. This book has discussed two factors that contribute to international economic management: hegemony and international institutions.

The Current State of U.S. Hegemony

Part III of this book provides a mixed picture of the current state of U.S. economic hegemony. On the one hand, the United States continues to demonstrate a number of strengths as a global hegemon. With the breakup of the Soviet bloc and Soviet Union, the United States has emerged as the unchallenged military power in the world. As long as the threat of violent conflict persists, a state with hegemony in security matters will also be able to exercise a degree of power over economic and other nonsecurity areas.[30] The U.S. dollar continues to serve as the main international currency, and in the weighted-voting Bretton Woods institutions (the IMF and the World Bank), the United States continues to have the most votes. Even more important, the United States has a considerable amount of co-optive power (also referred to as structural or soft power): it is often successful in getting "other countries to *want* what it wants."[31] For example, Part III shows that the United States played a critical role in setting the agenda for the GATT Uruguay round negotiations and in guiding the policies of industrial states on a range of issues extending from liberalized capital flows to the foreign debt crisis and international development.

On the other hand, Part III also provides a number of indications of U.S. hegemonic decline. The U.S. dollar shifted from top-currency to negotiated-currency status in the 1960s, the United States has had chronic balance-of-trade deficits since 1971, the United States has become more dependent on FDI inflows in recent years and has accounted for a declining share of outward FDI, and Japan surpassed the United States for the first time in 1989 as the largest single-country donor of ODA.

Despite the conflicting signals about the status of U.S. hegemony, almost all analysts agree that American economic power has declined *in a relative sense* since 1945. Its predominance at the end of World War II was so great that the relative position of the United States was bound to decline as a result of economic reconstruction in Europe and Japan. It is therefore useful to examine whether there is a country or group of countries that could replace the United States as global hegemon.

Is There a Candidate to Replace the United States as Global Hegemon?

An extensive body of literature exists on the question of whether Japan could be the next global hegemon.[32] In the late 1980s, some academics and policymakers took a rather positive view of Japan's hegemonic prospects. For example, one scholar wrote that "if any country surpasses the United States as the world's leading economic power, it will be Japan."[33] By the early to mid-1990s, however, most analysts were highly skeptical about Japan's ability and willingness to lead. Arguments against Japan's possible rise to hegemonic status stemmed from the views that Japan lacks both military power and ideological appeal and that it would be unwilling to assume the global responsibility of leadership. In the late 1990s, further questions were raised about Japan's hegemonic potential when a financial crisis hit many countries in East and Southeast Asia. Many hoped that Japan would set an example of reform because it shared some economic problems with other East and Southeast Asian states such as failing banks, questionable bookkeeping methods, and corrupt interlocking corporate relationships.[34] Political indecisiveness and inflexible economic and social practices, however, have prevented Japanese leaders from adopting bold policies to reform the economy. Despite Japan's economic strengths, it is highly unlikely that Japan will replace the United States as a global hegemon.

Some writers speculate that the EU could become the top power, and one economist has even predicted that "future historians will record that the 21st century belonged to the House of Europe."[35] However, the EU will not have the ability and willingness to lead unless it becomes a more cohesive unit. In May 1997, the EU heads of government agreed that 11 EU members would form an economic and monetary union and replace their national currencies, and Greece later joined this group as the twelfth EU member. In view of the combined strength of these countries' economies, the euro will be the world's second most important currency and could eventually supplant the U.S. dollar as the key currency in the global monetary regime. Nevertheless, continued divisions among EU countries over a wide range of economic and political issues could prevent the EU from assuming hegemonic responsibilities.

A third possibility is that global leadership is becoming more collective in nature and that the United States is best placed to lead this collectivity because its strength is so multidimensional; that is, it encompasses military, political, economic, scientific, cultural, and ideological power resources.[36] To lead the collectivity, however, the United States must accept the reality that its ability to act unilaterally is declining. The U.S. capacity for unilateral action is decreasing both because of its relative decline in economic power and because economic management must be collective if it is to deal adequately with capital flows and other economic transactions in this age of globalization.

The most obvious candidates for collective leadership in the core would be the triad: the United States, the EU, and Japan. However, the possibilities that such a collective leadership will succeed is questionable in view of ongoing disputes among these three actors and the difficulties the EU has in reaching agreements internally among its own member states. Even if the states in the triad reached agreement on major issues, it is uncertain that they could achieve hegemony. A number of NIEs, along with major powers such as China and India, are gaining economic influence, so it may become less feasible to leave global management to the countries within the triad.[37] A final possibility is that because globalization is upgrading the importance of transnational actors such as MNCs and international banks, no state—or collectivity of states—can become hegemonic. In other words, MNCs and internationally mobile capital may be vying with the nation-state today for global hegemony.[38]

The Role of International Institutions

International institutions—both international regimes and IOs—are discussed under "North-North relations" because the rich Northern countries have clearly assumed the largest role in setting the principles, norms, and rules for these institutions. Three KIEOs have performed major functions in overseeing economic management: the IMF, the World Bank, and GATT/WTO. As discussed, the three main IPE perspectives present widely differing views of these organizations. Whereas liberals believe that the KIEOs are beneficial organizations that seek to promote economic efficiency and openness, realists view the KIEOs as rather passive creatures of their most powerful member states, and historical structuralists consider the KIEOs to be a mechanism by which the capitalist core countries exploit weaker countries in the periphery. Instead of attempting to decide which of these views of the KIEOs is most accurate (all three perspectives in fact have some validity), this section provides an assessment of the current and possible future influence of these organizations.

The KIEOs have all been quite adaptable in altering their functions to meet changing economic circumstances, and it is likely they will continue to have important roles in global economic management. As discussed in Chapter 6, the IMF lost one of its two main functions—looking after the pegged exchange rate system—when the major economic powers shifted to floating exchange rates in 1973. The IMF also became a less essential source of loans for more creditworthy LDCs in the 1970s when international private banks recycled large sums of petrodollars to the South. In the 1980s, however, the IMF regained its stature when it took the lead role (along with the United States) in managing the Third World foreign debt crisis. With the breakup of the Soviet Union, the IMF also became an essential source of funding for Russia and other emerging economies. When a financial crisis affected East and Southeast Asian countries in the late 1990s, the IMF again was given the lead responsibility for dealing with the crisis. Furthermore, the IMF is currently seeking to establish a role for itself in promoting the orderly liberalization of capital movements.[39]

The conditionality the IMF places on its loans has long created resentment in Third World countries, and this resentment increased as the IMF attached more intrusive conditions to its SALs to highly indebted countries in the 1980s and 1990s (see discussion of this issue in Chapter 7). Nevertheless, because the IMF retained the confidence of the advanced industrial states, it was able to maintain its important and influential position. The financial crisis of the late 1990s marked somewhat of a turning point because economists and policymakers in the developed states began to attack the IMF's stabilization programs in countries such as South Korea, Indonesia, and Russia. For example, critics charged that the IMF imposed the same conditions on loans to South Korea that it had imposed on foreign debtors in the 1980s, even though South Korea had fundamentally different economic problems. South Korea's foreign debt and current account deficit were both low, and its problems were related to a temporary lack of liquidity resulting from short-term debts rather than from insolvency. In Indonesia and Russia, serious economic problems persisted despite the IMF's involvement, and the IMF was accused of simply bailing out governments and foreign investors without bringing about longer term economic solutions. Thus, one noted economist strongly criticized the IMF programs as being "too flawed to be a standard of good or bad performance."[40]

Despite the strong criticisms of the IMF, most analysts in the developed states believe that abolishing the organization is not the answer, and that emphasis should be placed instead on "refocusing the IMF."[41] The IMF serves an important function for both the North and the South as a lender of last resort, and if it were dismantled another organization like it would most likely be reinvented. The IMF also performs a useful function in deflecting the anger of Third World countries over the conditionality on loans; without the IMF, this anger would be aimed more directly at the United States, Germany, Japan, and other developed states. Furthermore, the IMF may seem uncertain about the proper macroeconomic solutions today, but it is certainly not alone in lacking definitive answers. Most analysts who referred to the East and Southeast Asian countries as miracle economies did not predict that the fortunes of these countries would change so drastically, and the policy prescriptions of different experts for dealing with the current problems are often contradictory. It is therefore likely that the IMF will continue to play a central role as a lender of last resort and will adapt its functions to meet changing circumstances as it has in the past. In view of the East Asian financial crisis, the G-7 leaders and their finance ministers have begun to address the IMF's shortcomings and to discuss proposals for creating a more stable international monetary and financial regime. Their views were expressed succinctly by the U.S. Secretary of the Treasury in April 1998, when he stated that the global community's task was to construct a "new international financial architecture."[42] This statement gave impetus to a number of studies proposing changes in the IMF and the global monetary and financial regime.[43] It is too early to state which of these proposals will eventually be adopted.

Of the three KIEOs, the World Bank group is probably in the most uncertain position. The IBRD or World Bank initially provided long-term loans for European reconstruction and Third World development. When the World Bank lost its reconstruction function, it shifted its attention almost solely to the Third World. The World Bank's importance has stemmed partly from the fact that it is the largest source of multilateral financing for Third World development. In recent years, however, "public support and public resources for official development assistance have declined."[44] The decline in development assistance has resulted from a variety of factors: aid agencies have not succeeded in promoting economic development, the end of the Cold War removed the security rationale for providing aid, and states want to cut spending in an increasingly competitive global environment. "Aid fatigue" in the advanced industrial states has of course had adverse effects on the World Bank's functioning. For example, the United States and other donors have often been reluctant to replenish funding for the World Bank group's soft-loan affiliate, the IDA (see Chapter 11).

The foreign debt crisis in the early 1980s gave the World Bank as well as the IMF new functions to perform. However, both the World Bank and the IMF began to provide SALs to Third World debtors, and the IMF rather than the World Bank was given responsibility for coordinating the response to the foreign debt crisis. As IMF and World Bank functions increasingly overlapped, questions were raised about whether the World Bank was "redundant." Still another problem confronting bank officials has been the high degree of controversy surrounding the current World Bank president's efforts to alter the institution's policy outlook and mode of operation (see Chapter 11). The World Bank, however, has been highly adaptable, and it will probably continue to function as a separate institution. As discussed in Chapter 11, sub-Saharan Africa is currently facing a development crisis, and the World Bank is the only multilateral organization with the economic resources and technical expertise to deal with the crisis. The World Bank has also managed to carve out for itself "a unique position as a generator of ideas about economic development."[45] Indeed, in its 1997 *Annual Report* the World Bank indicated that it was placing greater emphasis on "building a sound knowledge base to support nonlending (as well as lending) activities."[46] The World Bank's influence as a disseminator of ideas depends on the expertise of its operating staff as well as on its important position as a source of development finance. Thus, it seems likely that the World Bank will continue to operate as a KIEO.

Of the three KIEOs, the WTO is likely to become the most important. Unlike the IMF and the World Bank, which impose conditions only on Third World and emerging country borrowers, the WTO establishes rules for almost all of the world's major trading nations. The WTO moved much closer to becoming a universal membership organization recently when China became a new member, and Russia is certain to become a member in the future. The WTO's importance is ironic because its predecessor, the GATT, became a permanent organization only by default when the Havana Charter and the proposed ITO did not receive final approval. Nevertheless, the informal nature of GATT permitted it to be highly adaptable.

Although GATT negotiations were initially designed to lower tariff barriers, the trade organization also began to negotiate reductions in NTBs at the Kennedy round in the 1960s, and it expanded these negotiations on NTBs at the Tokyo round in the 1970s. The Uruguay round in the 1980s and 1990s was by far the most complex and ambitious GATT negotiation. Thus, the new WTO oversees regulations not only for trade in goods but also for trade in services, intellectual property, and trade-related investment measures. It is also possible that the WTO will eventually oversee the implementation of an MAI. Some analysts warn that the expansion of regional integration is threatening the global trade regime, but RTAs today are generally more open than they were in the 1960s. Thus, regional agreements such as the EU, NAFTA, Mercosur, and APEC are more likely to serve as stepping-stones than as obstacles to global free trade. In sum, the WTO is likely to emerge as the most important of the KIEOs.

NORTH-SOUTH RELATIONS

The population of the South accounted for almost 65 percent of the total world population in 1950, and by 1996 the population of the South had climbed to almost 80 percent of the world total. A number of emerging economies that were formerly part of the Second World are now receiving foreign debt and development finance from the advanced industrial states and thus have some characteristics in common with the South. Most of the "world" is therefore the Third World. Nevertheless, as this book has shown, Southern countries have had relatively little influence in setting the agenda and making decisions regarding the global political economy.

In addition to the weak economic and political positions of most LDCs, there are major divisions within the South that prevent it from taking unified actions. For example, poverty is spread very unevenly among LDC geographic regions. The United Nations has identified 48 LDCs as "least developed" because they have extremely low per capita incomes and literacy rates and are poorly endowed with natural resources. Almost all of these LLDCs are in sub-Saharan Africa and South Asia. Poverty also has a differential impact on societal groups in the South, with women and children most severely affected. Furthermore, there are indications that globalization is marginalizing the weakest states and societal groups, even as it has contributed to growth in many of the stronger states. For example, the poorest LDCs, which have 20 percent of the world's population, saw their share of world trade fall from about 4 percent in 1960 to less than 1 percent in 1990. Private investment flows to LDCs increased from $5 billion in 1970 to $173 billion in 1994, but about 75 percent of this investment went to only 10 countries, mainly in East and Southeast Asia and Latin America.[47]

The statistics on the poorest LDCs and societal groups indicate that development strategies over the years have had only limited success—especially if one believes that a certain degree of equity is necessary for development to be considered successful. The sections that follow examine how the concept of "development" is changing and consider whether there is a demonstrated best path to development.

Changing Concepts of Development

In the 1950s and 1960s, economic development was usually equated with material economic growth, and the essential indicators of development were a country's GDP and per capita income. In the orthodox liberal view, Western industrial states with high per capita incomes had achieved successful development, and LDCs could acquire similar wealth if they simply followed the same path set by the already developed states. Orthodox liberals were not concerned about redistributing wealth to the poorest groups in LDCs because they believed that the prosperity of Third World countries that followed liberal-economic policies would "eventually trickle down from the top, alleviating the problem of poverty at the bottom."[48]

Although the South experienced unprecedented economic growth in the 1960s, there were indications that unemployment, poverty, and the gap between the rich and the poor were increasing. Thus, a number of development specialists rejected the orthodox liberal view that growth would naturally trickle down to the poor, and they proposed that conscious efforts should be made to redistribute income to the poor and meet their basic human needs for health, education, food and clean water, and family planning services. From this perspective, GDP and per capita income are not the only important indicators of economic development, and human development indicators must also be considered. These human development indicators include such measures as life expectancy, health and sanitation, literacy rates, education, employment, malnourishment, the position of women and children, and rural-urban disparities. The human development approach demonstrates that development must be measured "through investment in people and not just in machinery, buildings, and other physical assets."[49]

Another change in the concept of development came from those who are concerned about environmental degradation. Of particular importance in this regard was the concept of sustainable development, which was popularized by some NGOs in the early 1980s and received multilateral approval in the 1987 report of the World Commission on Environment and Development (the Brundtland Report). The Brundtland Report describes sustainable development as a policy that "meets the needs of the present without compromising the ability of future generations to meet their own needs."[50] Sustainable development is a controversial concept because LDCs often argue that they cannot afford to divert resources from their immediate development needs to pay the costs of following environmentally friendly policies. The LDCs also point out that the advanced industrial states did not adopt sustainable policies when they were developing and that the North today produces more pollutants than the South. If the North expects the South to follow more environmentally friendly policies, from this perspective, it must be willing to compensate the South with financial resources.[51]

The prevailing concepts of development have a major effect on policymaking, so it is essential that we opt for a broad rather than narrow concept of development, for two reasons. First, recent decades of experience have shown that rapid economic growth does not necessarily enrich people's lives and may even enhance income gaps and poverty under some circumstances. A broader concept of development includes not only economic growth but also human development, poverty reduction, and environmental protection. Second, as interdependence increases, the form that development takes can have major implications for the entire globe. For example, the World Bank estimates that more than 2 million people in China die each year from the effects of air and water pollution and that the effects of this pollution may extend far beyond the boundaries of China. Aside from the United States, China is now the largest source of greenhouse gases that are linked to global warming, and China and India are the two fastest growing sources of these gases.[52] In an age of globalization, we can no longer afford to adopt a narrow concept of development that is limited to economic growth. Thus, the developed countries must provide assistance to Third World countries that lack the capacity to transfer scarce resources from economic growth to other critical development objectives such as sustainability and the reduction of poverty.

Is There a "Best" Development Strategy?

Chapter 11 discussed several major development strategies, including import substitution, socialist development models, export-led growth, and orthodox liberalism. Liberals, realists, and historical structuralists disagree as to which strategy is best to follow, and they even sometimes disagree as to the type of strategy a state is actually following. For example, when the East Asian export-led growth model was experiencing its greatest success in the 1970s and 1980s, liberals attributed the success of these countries to their outward, market orientation. Realists, by contrast, attributed the East Asians' success to the existence of a strong developmental state that promoted an effective industrial policy, and historical structuralists argued that the East Asians were following a strategy based on dependency, which was not as successful as the realists and liberals assumed. The experience with different development strategies indicates that *none* of these strategies is necessarily "the best" and that each strategy has both strengths and weaknesses. Furthermore, in view of the diverse nature of the South today, a strategy that may be best for one LDC may not be best or even feasible for another. A brief recounting of the strengths and weaknesses of the major development strategies will help to reinforce these points.

As discussed in Chapter 11, ISI was a commonly used development strategy among LDCs in the 1950s and 1960s. The easier first stage of ISI resulted in economic growth and industrialization in a number of LDCs. However, those countries in Latin America and elsewhere that continued onto a second stage of ISI encountered increasing problems with balance-of-payments deficits, uncompetitive industries, and increased dependence on external finance. When problems arose with ISI, some Southern countries adopted more extreme inward-looking policies and attempted to follow the socialist planning model of the Soviet Union. Central planning contributed to increases in industrial production in some countries, but even larger LDCs such as China were plagued by inefficiencies, low-quality production, and lack of competitiveness. For smaller Third World countries such as North Korea, Cuba, Ethiopia, Mozambique, Vietnam, and Burma, which lacked resources, the attempts at central planning were even more ineffective. Nevertheless, these countries did register some gains in social areas, such as providing better access to health care and education, improving the status of women, and adopting measures to reduce social and economic inequalities.[53]

The East Asian NIEs, which followed the Japanese model and turned from import substitution to export-led growth policies in the 1960s, were by far the most successful group of LDCs in increasing their economic growth from the 1960s to the 1980s. Although liberals and realists often agreed that other Southern countries should learn from the example of the East Asian miracle, they had widely differing interpretations of the reasons for these countries' success. The realists in fact were probably more accurate in their interpretations: the East Asian NIEs (other than Hong Kong) had strong developmental states that provided extensive guidance to the market, controlled investment flows, promoted the development of technology, and protected selected infant industries.

A financial crisis in the 1990s, however, demonstrated that the developmental state in East and Southeast Asia was not as efficient and immune to political pressures as was earlier assumed. Thus, the crisis stemmed partly from the failure of governments to develop adequate regulations for banking and other financial institutions. It also became evident that the East Asians had benefited from a unique set of circumstances in which the United States and Japan gave them favored treatment in terms of military and economic aid, trade, and foreign investment. The cost of this special treatment was the development of dependent linkages, and when U.S. and Japanese policies changed in the 1990s, the East and Southeast Asian states were highly vulnerable. In addition, environmentalists raised questions about the sustainability of rapid economic growth in East and Southeast Asia, where little action was being taken to prevent environmental degradation. By the late 1990s, few analysts were still claiming that the export-led growth model was the answer to Third World development problems.

In the 1980s, the debt crisis and IMF and World Bank SALs ushered in yet another Southern development strategy, based on orthodox liberalism. In marked contrast to import substitution and export-led growth, the orthodox liberal strategy emphasized decreased government spending, privatization, deregulation, and liberal policies toward trade and foreign investment. In middle-income LDCs the SAPs had some positive effects in reducing government budget deficits, increasing export earnings, and enhancing economic efficiency and growth. However, IMF and World Bank SALs also had some negative effects on the poorest LDCs in sub-Saharan Africa and Asia and on vulnerable groups in LDCs, such as women and children. Critics argued that the SAPs underestimated the need for involving the state in development and for maintaining social, health, and educational programs for vulnerable groups, despite their financial costs. Supporters of orthodox liberalism, however, asserted that Southern countries would benefit most from liberalizing their economies and from following in the path of Western Europe and North America.[54]

In view of the global spread of orthodox liberalism, the question arises as to whether we have reached the "end of history" for Southern development strategies and whether liberalism has become the only acceptable path to follow.[55] This is not likely to be the case. As discussed, even the World Bank has now acknowledged that SAPs will succeed only if they take account of the need for strong, stable Third World governments in promoting development and include some distributional goals vis-à-vis the poorest and most vulnerable groups. The problems with SAPs also serve as a reminder that development strategies for the future should avoid the "northern ethnocentrism which permeated much of orthodox development thinking" with its "false claim of universality."[56] As realists have noted, strategies that provide an active role for the government, such as import substitution and export-led growth, may be necessary for Southern countries at various stages in their development if they are to catch up with the leading states. Both import substitution and export-led growth strategies have encountered some problems, but this could mean that we need to find the correct regulatory regime rather than simply opting for deregulation and privatization. As for historical structuralists, they have pointed out correctly that we must be concerned with the distributional effects of development strategies and with overdependence on the North as a possible hindrance to Southern development.

We have *not* reached the end of history in terms of development strategies. The "best" development strategy is likely to include realist and historical structuralist as well as liberal components, and again, the best strategy for some Third World states may not necessarily be the best strategy for others.

A Final Word on Theory and Practice

This book has tried to join together theory and practice in the study of IPE. This introduction to IPE has focused on the three major theoretical perspectives: realism, liberalism, and historical structuralism. Significant changes have occurred in recent years, including the breakup of the Soviet Union and the end of the Cold War, the pressures of globalization, and the emergence of common threats to humanity such as environmental degradation. These changes have revealed a need for "new theoretical categorizations."[57] One approach to the shortcomings of the three main IPE perspectives is to develop new theories and models that draw on more than one theoretical perspective. This book has focused on several of these "hybrid" theories, particularly hegemonic stability theory and regime theory. Another approach is to develop new theoretical perspectives in IPE that focus on approaches (e.g., constructivism) and issues (e.g., feminism and environmentalism) that the three traditional perspectives largely ignore.[58]

The globalization phenomenon points to yet another direction theorists should follow: the development of theories that explore domestic-international interactions in the global political economy. With globalization, the sensitivity of national economies to changes in capital, foreign investment, and trade flows has dramatically increased, as the 1990s financial crisis in East and Southeast Asia clearly demonstrates. As states become more interdependent, policies that were traditionally considered to be domestic (e.g., government subsidies) can also have a major impact on outsiders. This book has focused on a number of issues that involve domestic and international interactions, but a more systematic examination of such issues is essential to increasing our understanding of IPE. Although no country today can escape the fact of growing international interdependence, a country's openness to outside influences also depends on domestic factors. A country's policies result from a variety of domestic factors such as the position and influence of socioeconomic groups and the nature of the country's political institutions. As a country becomes more involved in foreign trade and investment, domestic political conflict may increase between societal groups that benefit from greater international openness and groups that depend on protectionism and economic closure. The extent to which the government adopts more open economic policies depends not only on the relative influence of these societal groups but also on the country's domestic political institutions. Existing institutions can exert strong pressures on governments either to accede to the forces of globalization or to resist these forces with more protectionist economic policies. The reluctance of the U.S. Congress to give Clinton fast-track approval to expand the NAFTA and to negotiate other trade liberalization agreements is one example of the important role of domestic institutions. All three of the traditional IPE perspectives have devoted too little attention to domestic variables, and the study of IPE will benefit from the increased attention that is currently being given to domestic-international interactions.[59]

Students have been introduced to a range of theoretical approaches in this book and have seen how these theories are applied to substantive IPE issue areas. As one noted international relations theorist has stated, "to think theoretically one must be constantly ready to be proven wrong,"[60] and this book has shown that all theoretical perspectives have been partially correct and partially incorrect in their assessments of a wide range of IPE issues. It is only through formulating and reformulating our theories that we will be able to address anomalies and increase our understanding of the global political economy.

NOTES

1. The "borderless world" terminology derives from Kenichi Ohmae's *The Borderless World: Power and Strategy in the Interlinked Economy* (New York: HarperPerennial, 1990).

2. See Helen V. Milner, *Resisting Protectionism: Global Industries and the Politics of International Trade* (Princeton, NJ: Princeton University Press, 1988).

3. See Stephen Gill and David Law, "Global Hegemony and the Structural Power of Capital," in Stephen Gill, ed., *Gramsci, Historical Materialism and International Relations* (Cambridge: Cambridge University Press, 1993), pp. 93–124; and Mark E. Rupert, "(Re) Politicizing the Global Economy: Liberal Common Sense and Ideological Struggle in the US NAFTA Debate," *Review of International Political Economy* 2-4 (Autumn 1995), pp. 679–681.

4. Riccardo Petrella, "Globalization and Internationalization: The Dynamics of the Emerging World Order," in Richard Boyer and Daniel Drache, eds., *States, Against Markets: The Limits of Globalization* (London: Routledge, 1996), pp. 77–78.

5. United Nations Conference on Trade and Development, *World Investment Report 1996* (New York: United Nations, 1996), pp. 239–247; General Agreement on Tariffs and Trade, *International Trade: Trends and Statistics 1994* (Geneva: GATT, 1994), pp. 22, 58.

6. For the United Nations list of 48 LLDCs, see United Nations Conference on Trade and Development, *The Least Developed Countries—1997 Report* (New York: United Nations, 1997), p. 152.

7. United Nations Development Programme, *Human Development Report—1997* (New York: Oxford University Press, 1997), pp. 83–84.

8. United Nations Centre on Transnational Corporations, *World Investment Report 1991: The Triad in Foreign Direct Investment* (New York: United Nations, 1991), pp. 9–15.

9. Ethan B. Kapstein, *Governing the Global Economy: International Finance and the State* (Cambridge, MA: Harvard University Press, 1994), p. 6. See also Eric Helleiner, *States and the Reemergence of Global Finance: From Bretton Woods to the 1990s* (Ithaca, NY: Cornell University Press, 1994).

10. Walden Bello, "East Asia: On the Eve of the Great Transformation?," *Review of International Political Economy* 5-3 (Autumn 1998), p. 426.

11. Stephan Haggard and Andrew MacIntyre, "The Political Economy of the Asian Economic Crisis," *Review of International Political Economy* 5-3 (Autumn 1998), p. 383.

12. Stanley Fischer, "Lessons from a Crisis," *The Economist,* October 3, 1998, p. 27.

13. John B. Goodman and Louis W. Pauly, "The Obsolescence of Capital Controls? Economic Management in an Age of Global Markets," *World Politics* 46-1 (October 1993), p. 81; Tony Porter, "Capital Mobility and Currency Markets: Can They Be Tamed?," *International Journal* 51-4 (Autumn 1996), p. 676; "Global Finance: Don't Wait Up," *The Economist,* October 3, 1998, pp. 83–84.

14. Mohammed H. Malek, "Towards an Integrated Aid and Development Programme for Europe," in Mohammed H. Malek, ed., *Contemporary Issues in European Development Aid* (Aldershot, UK: Avebury, 1991), p. 142.

15. Andrew Hurrell and Ngaire Woods, "Globalisation and Inequality," *Millennium* 24-3 (1995), p. 458.

16. World Bank, *World Development Report 2000/2001: Attacking Poverty* (New York: Oxford University Press, 2001), p. 3.

17. United Nations Development Programme, *Human Development Report—1997,* pp. 88–89.

18. United Nations Development Programme, *Human Development Report—1997,* p. 88. For a discussion of the effects of NAFTA on Mexican agriculture, see Theodore H. Cohn, "The Intersection of Domestic and Foreign Policy in the NAFTA Agricultureal Negotiations," *Canadian-American Public Policy,* no. 14 (Orono, ME: University of Maine, September 1993), pp. 24–33.

19. Ian Robinson, "Globalization and Democracy," *Dissent* (Summer 1995), pp. 374–377. For a detailed examination of globalization and democracy, see David Held, *Democracy and the Global Order: From the Modern State to Cosmopolitan Governance* (Cambridge: Polity Press, 1995).

20. Marjorie Griffin Cohen, "Democracy and the Future of Nations: Challenges for Disadvantaged Women and Minorities," in Boyer and Drache, eds., *States Against Markets,* p. 407; Stephen Gill, "Globalization, Democratization, and the Politics of Indifference," in James H. Mittleman, ed., *Globalization: Critical Reflections* (Boulder, CO: Rienner, 1996), pp. 213–218.

21. The terms conformers, reformers, and radicals are used in Jan Aart Scholte with Robert O'Brien and Marc Williams, "The WTO and Civil Society," *Journal of World Trade* 33-1 (1999), pp. 107–123. Civil society is divided into liberal and critical groups in Peter Newell, "Environmental NGOs, TNCs, and the Question of Governance," in Dimitris Stevis and Valerie J. Assetto, eds., *The International Political Economy of the Environment: Critical Perspectives* (Boulder, CO: Lynne Rienner, 2001), pp. 85–107.

22. On civil society and the KIEOs see Robert O'Brien, Anne Marie Goetz, Jan Aart Scholte, and Marc Williams, *Contesting Global Governance: Multilateral Economic Institutions and Global Social Movements* (Cambridge, UK: Cambridge University Press, 2000).

23. Craig Warkentin and Karen Mingst, "International Institutions, the State, and Global Society in the Age of the World Wide Web," *Global Governance* 6-2 (April-June, 2000), p. 240.

24. Robert W. Cox, "Civil Society at the Turn of the Millennium: Prospects for an Alternative World Order," *Review of International Studies* 25 (1999), pp. 3–28.

25. Myron Weiner, *The Global Migration Crisis: Challenge to States and to Human Rights* (New York: HarperCollins, 1996), p. 3.

26. "Immigration: Suspicious Minds," *The Economist,* July 4, 1998, p. 25.

27. Keith Griffin, "Nine Good Reasons to Love Labor Migration," *UC Mexus News,* of California Institute for Mexico and the United States, p. 2.

28. "What Is the Federation for American Immigration Reform?," http://www.fairus.org, p. 1.

29. Malcolm Waters, *Globalization* (London: Routledge, 1995), p. 89.

30. Susan Strange, *States and Markets* 2nd ed. (London: Pinter, 1994), p. 29.

31. Joseph S. Nye, Jr., "Soft Power," *Foreign Policy* 80 (Fall 1990), p. 166. See also Joseph S. Nye, Jr., *Bound to Lead: The Changing Nature of American Power* (New York: Basic Books, 1990); and Susan Strange, "The Persistent Myth of Lost Hegemony," *International Organization* 41-4 (Autumn 1987), pp. 551–574.

32. Good overall surveys of this leterature include Alan Rix, "Japan and the Region: Leading from Behind," in R. Higgott, R. Leaver, and J. Ravenhill, eds., *Pacific Economic Relations in the 1990s* (Boulder, CO: Rienner, 1993), pp. 62–82; and Philip J. Meeks, "Japan and Global Economic Hegemony" (pp. 41–67), and Koji Taira, "Japan as Number Two: New Thoughts on the Hegemonic Theory of World Governance" (pp. 251–263) in Tsuneo Akaha and Frank Langdon, eds., *Japan in the Posthegemonic World* (Boulder, CO: Rienner, 1993).

33. See Ronald A. Morse, "Japan's Drive to Pre-Eminence," *Foreign Policy* no. 69 (Winter 1987–88), pp. 3–21.

34. "Dangerous Inertia in Japan," *New York Times,* December 23, 1997, p. A12; "Japan on the Brink," *The Economist,* April 11, 1998, pp. 15–17. See also Ron Bevacqua, "Whither the Japanese Model? The Asian Economic Crisis and the Continuation of Cold War Politics in the Pacific Rim," *Review of International Political Economy* 5-3 (Autumn 1998), pp. 410–423.

35. Lester Thurow, *Head to Head: The Coming Economic Battle Among Japan, Europe, and America* (New York: Morrow, 1992), p. 258.

36. Nye, "Soft Power," pp. 154–155; Samuel Huntington, "The U.S.—Decline or Renewal?," *Foreign Affairs* 67-2 (Winter 1988–89), p. 90.

37. Aaron Segal, "Managing the World Economy," *International Political Science Review* 11-3 (1990), p. 362.

38. Stephen Gill, "Global Finance, Monetary Policy and Cooperation among the Group of Seven, 1944–92," in Philip G. Cerny, ed., *Finance and World Politics: Markets, Regimes and States in the Post-hegemonic Era* (London: Elgar, 1993), p. 105.

39. See Stanley Fischer, "Capital Account Liberalization and the Role of the IMF," paper released by the International Monetary Fund, September 1997, p. 12.

40. Jeffrey Sachs, "Global Capitalism: Making it Work," *The Economist,* September 12, 1998, p. 25. See also David E. Sanger, "I.M.F.'s Bearer of Bad Tidings," *New York Times,* October 30, 1998, pp. C1 and C3.

41. See Martin Feldstein, "Refocusing the IMF," *Foreign Affairs* 77-2 (March/April 1998), pp. 20–33; Jagdish Bhagwati, "The Capital Myth: The Difference between Trade in Widgets and Dollars," *Foreign Affairs* 77-3 (May/June 1998), p. 11.

42. U.S. Treasury Secretary Robert Rubin quoted in Shalendra D. Sharna, "Constructing the New International Financial Architecture: What Role for the IMF?," *Journal of World Trade* 34-3 (2000), pp. 47–70.

43. See, for example, Barry Eichengreen, *Toward A New International Financial Architecture: A Practical Post-Asia Agenda* (Washington, DC: Institute for International Economics,

February 1999); and Michele Fratianni, Paolo Savona, and John J. Kirton, eds., *Governing Global Finance: New Challenges, G7 and IMF Contributions* (forthcoming).

44. Organisation for Economic Co-operation and Development, *Development Co-operation: Efforts and Policies of the Members of the Development Assistance Committee—1996* (Paris: OECD, 1997), p. 1.

45. Robert Wade, "Japan, the World Bank and the Art of Paradigm Maintenance: The East Asian Miracle in Political Perspective," *New Left Review* 217 (May/June 1996), p. 5.

46. World Bank, *Annual Report 1997* (Washington, DC: World Bank, 1997), p. 7.

47. World Bank, *World Development Report 1990: Poverty* (New York: Oxford University Press, 1990), pp. 1–2; United Nations Development Programme, *Human Development Report 1996* (New York: Oxford University Press, 1996), pp. 8–9.

48. Mohammed H. Malek, "Towards an Integrated Aid and Development Programme for Europe," in Mohammed H. Malek, ed., *Contemporary Issues in European Development Aid* (Aldershot, UK: Avebury, 1991), p. 142.

49. Wilfred L. David, *The Conversation of Economic Development: Historical Voices, Interpretations, and Reality* (Armonk, NY: Sharpe, 1997), p. 177.

50. World Commission on Environment and Development, *Our Common Future* (Oxford: Oxford University Press, 1987), p. 8.

51. See Maurice F. Strong, "Achieving Sustainable Global Development," in the South Centre, *Facing the Challenge: Responses to the Report of the South Commission* (London: Zed Books, 1993), pp. 305–313.

52. Nicholas D. Kristof, "Across Asia, a Pollution Disaster Hovers," *New York Times,* November 28, 1997, pp. A1, A10.

53. John Rapley, *Understanding Development: Theory and Practice in the Third World* (Boulder, CO: Rienner, 1996), pp. 44–47.

54. See Walter Russell Mead, "Asia Devalued," *New York Times Magazine,* May 31, 1998, pp. 38–39.

55. See Francis Fukuyama, "The End of History?," *The National Interest* 16 (Summer 1989), pp. 3–18.

56. Kay, "For a Renewal of Development Studies," p. 697.

57. Thomas J. Biersteker, "Evolving Perspectives on International Political Economy: Twentieth-Century Contexts and Discontinuities," *International Political Science Review* 14-1 (January 1993), p. 27.

58. On constructivism see Kurt Burch and Robert A. Denemark, eds., *Constituting International Political Economy* (Boulder, CO: Lynne Rienner, 1997).

59. See Robert O. Keohane and Helen V. Milner, eds. *Internationalization and Domestic Politics* (Cambridge: Cambridge University Press, 1996); and Helen V. Milner, *Interests, Institutions, and Information: Domestic Politics and International Relations* (Princeton: Princeton University Press, 1997).

60. James N. Rosenau, "Thinking Theory Thoroughly," in James N. Rosenau, *The Scientific Study of Foreign Policy* rev. ed. (London: Pinter, 1980), p. 30.

APPENDIX

Acronyms and Abbreviations

AASM: Associated African States and Madagascar

ABB: Asea Brown Boveri

ACP: African, Caribbean, and Pacific

ADDs: antidumping duties

AFTA: ASEAN Free Trade Area

AID: Agency for International Development

AMF: Asian Monetary Fund

APEC: Asia-Pacific Economic Cooperation

ASEAN: Association of Southeast Asian Nations

BIS: Bank for International Settlements

BITs: bilateral investment treaties

C-20: Committee of Twenty

CACM: Central American Common Market

CAP: Common Agricultural Policy

CARIBCAN: Canadian Trade, Investment, and Industrial Cooperation program

CARICOM: Caribbean Community and Common Market

CDF: Comprehensive Development Framework

CEECs: Central and Eastern European countries

CFIUS: Committee on Foreign Investment in the United States

CIA: Central Intelligence Agency

CMEA: Council for Mutual Economic Assistance

COCOM: Coordinating Committee

CPE: centrally planned economy

CRTA: Committee on Regional Trade Agreements

CU: customs union

CUSFTA: Canada-U.S. Free Trade Agreement

CVDs:: countervailing duties

DISC: Domestic International Sales Corporation

EAI: Enterprise for the Americas Initiative

EC: European Community

ECB: European Central Bank

ECLA: Economic Commission for Latin America

ECSC: European Coal and Steel Community

ECU: European currency unit

EFTA: European Free Trade Association

EMS: European Monetary System

EMU: European Economic and Monetary Union

ERM: Exchange rate mechanism

EU: European Union

FAIR: Federation for American Immigration Reform

FCN: Friendship, Commerce, and Navigation

FDI: foreign direct investment

FIRA: Foreign Investment Review Agency

FSU: former Soviet Union

FTA: free trade area

FTAA: Free Trade Area of the Americas

G-5: Group of Five
G-7: Group of Seven
G-8: Group of Eight
G-10: Group of Ten
G-24: Group of 24
G-77: Group of 77
GAB: General Arrangements to Borrow
GATS: General Agreement on Trade in Services
GATT: General Agreement on Tariffs and Trade
GDP: gross domestic product
GNP: gross national product
GSP: generalized system of preference
HIPC: Heavily Indebted Poor Countries (initiative)
IBRD: International Bank for Reconstruction and Development
ICSID: International Centre for Settlement of Investment Disputes
IDA: International Development Association
IDB: Inter-American Development Bank
IFC: International Finance Corporation
IMF: International Monetary Fund
IO: international organization
IPC: Integrated Program for Commodities
IPE: international political economy
ISI: import-substituting industrialization
ITO: International Trade Organization
ITT: International Telephone and Telegraph Corporation
KIEOs: keystone international economic organizations
LAFTA: Latin American Free Trade Association
LDC: less developed country
LIC: low-income country
LLDC: least developed country
M&As: mergers and acquisitions
MAI: Multilateral Agreement on Investment
MFA: Multi-Fiber Arrangement
MFN: most favored nation
MIC: middle-income country
MIGA: Multilateral Investment Guarantee Agency
MNC: multinational corporation
MTNs: multilateral trade negotiations
NAB: New Arrangements to Borrow
NAFTA: North American Free Trade Agreement
NEM: New Economic Mechanism

NEP: National Energy Program
NGO: nongovernmental organization
NIE: newly industrializing economy
NIEO: New International Economic Order
NTB: nontariff barrier
OA: official aid
ODA: official development assistance
ODF: official development finance
OECD: Organization for Economic Cooperation and Development
OEEC: Organization for European Economic Cooperation
OPEC: Organization of Petroleum Exporting Countries
PRC: People's Republic of China
PTA: preferential trading arrangement
Quad: Quadrilateral Group
R&D: research and development
RTA: regional trade agreement
RTAA: Reciprocal Trade Agreements Act
S&D: special and differential (treatment)
SAL: structural adjustment loan
SAP: structural adjustment program
SDRs: special drawing rights
SEA: Single European Act
SPARTECA: South Pacific Regional Trade and Economic Cooperation Agreement
TOA: Treaty of Asunción
TRIMs: Trade-Related Investment Measures
TRIPs: Trade-Related Intellectual Property Rights
UN: United Nations
UNCTAD: United Nations Conference on Trade and Development
UNCTC: United Nations Center on Transnational Corporations
UNDP: United Nations Development Program
UNFPA: United Nations Fund for Population Activities
UNHCR: United Nations High Commissioner for Refugees
UNICEF: United Nations Children's Fund
UNIFEM: United Nations Development Fund for Women
UR Understanding: Uruguay Round Understanding on the Interpretation of GATT Article 24
USIA: United States Information Agency
WTO: World Trade Organization

G L O S S A R Y

absolute advantage A condition in which a country is able to produce a good more efficiently and at a lower cost than another country (or countries). Liberal-economic trade theorists maintain that countries benefit by specializing in the production of goods for which they have an absolute advantage. See *comparative advantage.*

antidumping duties (ADDs) Duties a country may impose on imported goods if it determines that the goods are being dumped and that this is causing or threatening material injury to its domestic producers. See *dumping.*

Asia-Pacific Economic Cooperation (APEC) An "open" regional initiative that includes the three largest national economies (the United States, Japan, and China) and has members from Asia, Australasia, and North and South America. Initially, foreign and economic ministers attended APEC meetings, but in 1993, the forum began to hold annual summit meetings of heads of state. Although APEC's economic activities to this point have been rather limited, the goal has been established to form a free trade area, and there are possibilities for agreements on competition policies, product standards, dispute settlement, and private investment.

Association of Southeast Asian Nations (ASEAN) Established in 1967 with the objectives of promoting peace, stability, and economic growth in the region, ASEAN today has 10 Southeast Asian countries as members. ASEAN was largely a political organization for many years, but in 1977 the members signed a preferential trade agreement, and the members have a stated goal of establishing an ASEAN Free Trade Area (AFTA).

Baker Plan A plan proposed by U.S. Secretary of the Treasury James A. Baker III in 1985, to deal with the LDC foreign debt crisis. The plan emphasized the postponement of some debt payments, the provision of new IMF and World Bank loans as an incentive for continued lending by private banks, and structural changes in debtor country policies.

balance of payments A summary record of all international economic transactions that a country has, normally over a one-year period. The most important components of the balance of payments are the *current account* and the *capital account.*

Bank for International Settlements (BIS) The oldest of the international financial institutions, formed in 1930 to oversee German war reparations. The BIS is located in Basel, Switzerland, and is the main forum for cooperation and consultation among central bankers in the OECD countries. It helps to deal with exchange rate problems and provides credit to central banks that lack liquidity. In response to the 1980s debt crisis, the BIS provided "bridging" finance until IMF and World Bank loans were available and adopted measures to increase confidence in the international banking system.

basic human needs A foreign aid approach focused on the poorest among and within LDCs. The basic human needs (or basic needs) approach was prominent in the 1970s and marked a shift from the emphasis on GNP growth in the 1960s. Aid programs, according to this approach, should emphasize basic health, education, family planning, rural development, and services to the poor; the increased involvement of women in development programs; and special attention to the problems of the least developed countries.

bilateral aid   A type of foreign assistance that flows directly from a donor to a recipient government. The largest percentage of official development assistance is given bilaterally. See *foreign aid, multilateral aid,* and *official development assistance.*

bilateral investment treaties (BITs)   Bilateral treaties that developed countries have been negotiating with LDCs to promote and protect foreign investment. The BITs generally uphold the MFN and national treatment principles, often prohibit host country performance requirements, and require prompt and adequate compensation in the event of nationalization.

Brady Plan   A plan proposed by U.S. Secretary of the Treasury Nicholas Brady in 1988, after it became evident that the Baker Plan was insufficient to deal with the foreign debt crisis. The Brady Plan introduced the idea that debt relief or reduction was necessary for some LDCs with severe and protracted debt problems, in exchange for structural adjustment of the debtors' economies.

Bretton Woods system   Bretton Woods, New Hampshire, was the location of meetings in July 1944 that culminated in the creation of the postwar economic order. The IMF and International Bank for Reconstruction and Development (or World Bank) were established at Bretton Woods, as was the monetary regime of pegged exchange rates. This monetary regime ended in 1973, when major countries shifted to flexible exchange rates.

Canada-U.S. Free Trade Agreement (CUSFTA)   Concluded in 1988, the CUSFTA resulted from a change in U.S. policy in which it agreed to participate in RTAs, and from Canada's desire to gain more assured access to the U.S. market. The NAFTA replaced the CUSFTA in 1994. See *North American Free Trade Agreement.*

capital   A factor of production, along with land and labor. Capital consists of physical assets such as equipment, tools, buildings, and other manufactured goods, which are capable of generating income, and it consists of financial assets such as stocks, which presumably reflect a firm's physical assets. Marxists view capital in social and political as well as economic terms and emphasize capital's exploitation of labor in the capitalist system.

capital account   A major item in the balance of payments, which records the amounts a country lends to and borrows from nonresidents. Countries often finance their current account deficits with a net inflow of capital, or a surplus in their capital accounts. The transactions in the capital account include *foreign direct investment* and *portfolio investment.*

capital market   A capital market consists of all those institutions in a country (e.g., the stock exchange, banks, and insurance companies) that match supply with demand for long-term capital. Unlike a capital market, a money market deals with shorter term loanable funding. The World Bank floats bonds on the capital markets of the developed states to acquire much of its funding for lending purposes.

central bank   The public authority responsible for managing a country's money supply and for regulating and controlling its monetary and financial institutions and markets. All developed countries and most LDCs rely on a central bank for such regulatory activities. ˙

civil society   A wide range of nongovernmental, noncommercial organizations outside of official circles that seek to reinforce or alter existing norms, rules, and social structures.

Committee of Twenty (C-20)   A forum composed of representatives of both developed countries and LDCs, which attempted to reform the international monetary regime after the 1971 devaluation of the U.S. dollar. After two years of deliberations, the C-20 proposal failed to receive approval.

common market   The third stage of regional integration, which has the characteristics of a customs union *plus* the free mobility of factors of production (i.e., capital and labor). See *customs union, economic union,* and *free trade area.*

comparative advantage   A country has a comparative advantage in producing good A if it can produce A at a *relatively* lower cost than other goods, even if it does not have an absolute advantage in producing any good. Comparative advantage is a powerful liberal-economic theory justifying specialization and free trade.

competitiveness   A frequently cited definition of competitiveness, developed by the U.S. President's Commission on Industrial Competitiveness, is "the degree to which . . . [a nation] can, under free and fair market conditions, produce goods and services that meet the tests of international markets while simultaneously expanding the real income of its citizens." Wide disagreement exists, however, over the most important factors determining competitiveness and over the relationship between the competitiveness of states and firms.

concessional loans   (or *soft loans*) Loans that have lower interest rates, longer grace periods, and longer repayment periods than *commercial* or *hard loans.*

conditionality   A concept that is most closely associated with the IMF but is also associated with World Bank SALs. As a condition for receiving IMF loans above a certain level, borrowers must explicitly commit themselves to follow a prescribed set of policies. These policies typically include decreased government spending, increased government revenues, devaluation, deregulation, and privatization.

consultative group   A group that brings together donor states that provide development assistance to a particular recipient. In using consultative groups, donors seek to coordinate their bilateral aid giving and to exert collective pressure on recipient states.

countervailing duties (CVDs)   Duties a country may impose on imported goods if it determines that the goods are benefiting from trade-distorting subsidies in the exporting country and that this is causing or threatening material injury to domestic producers.

current account   A major item in the balance of payments, which records a country's trade in goods and services with foreigners, investment income and payments, and gifts and other transfers paid to and received from foreigners.

customs union (CU)   The second stage of regional integration, in which the member countries eliminate tariffs on all (or substantially all) their trade with each other and develop a common external tariff toward outside countries.

debt service ratio   (or debt-to-export ratio) The ratio of a country's interest and principal payments on its debt to its export income; often used to assess a country's ability to repay its foreign debt. The East Asian NIEs had stronger export positions than the Latin American NIEs and were better able to service their foreign debts in the 1980s.

dependency theory   A historical structuralist development theory that argues that the world is hierarchically organized, with the leading capitalist states in the core of the global economy dominating and exploiting the poorer states in the periphery.

devaluation   A reduction in the official rate or value at which one currency is exchanged for another. When a country devalues its currency, the prices of its imported goods and services increase, while its exports become less expensive to foreigners. A country can therefore gain certain trade advantages through devaluation of its currency.

developmental state   A term first used by Chalmers Johnson in the early 1980s to describe Japan and the East Asian NIEs. According to realists, the East Asian developmental state provided extensive guidance to the market, identified development as its primary objective, invested heavily in education, and depended on a highly skilled technocratic bureaucracy. Questions about the efficacy of the developmental state have become more common since the East Asian financial crisis of the late 1990s.

dollarization   The likelihood that a country will replace its own currency with the currency of another country, usually within the same region.

dumping   Selling a product in an export market at a lower price than charged in the home market, or below the cost of production.

economic union   The fourth stage of regional integration, which has the characteristics of a common market and harmonizes the industrial, regional, fiscal, monetary, and other economic policies of member countries. A full economic union also involves the adoption of a common currency by the members.

economism   An overemphasis on the importance of the economic sphere, and a corresponding underemphasis on the autonomy of the political sphere.

endogenous growth theory   Posits that technological change is not simply the result of fortunate breakthroughs in the quest for new knowledge that are exogenous to the basic factors of production determining economic growth. Instead, technological knowledge is an important endogenous factor of production along with labor and capital that provides developed countries and their firms major advantages over LDCs.

Eurocurrencies   National currencies traded and deposited in banks outside the home country, frequently (but not necessarily) in Europe. The most common form of Eurocurrencies are U.S. dollars or Eurodollars. International firms and national governments often prefer to use the Eurocurrency market for deposits and loans because the transactions in this market are free of most government regulations.

European Coal and Steel Community (ECSC)   Six Western European countries (Belgium, France, West Germany, Italy, Luxembourg, and the Netherlands) formed the ECSC in 1951. Although the ECSC integrated the member countries' coal and steel resources, it was created primarily to prevent France and Germany from renewing their age-old rivalries. Seven years later, the six ECSC member countries expanded the integration process by forming the *European Community*.

European Community (EC)   A regional integration agreement formed in 1957 among 6 Western European countries for political as well as economic reasons. In economic terms, the EC goals were to establish a customs union and a common market. The EC also established a complex institutional structure, including a Commission, Council of Ministers, European Court of Justice, and European Parliament. Membership in the EC increased to 12 countries by 1986, and in 1993 the EC was superseded by the *European Union*.

European Union (EU)   The EU became the successor organization to the EC in 1993, largely as a result of the "Europe 92" program. Europe 92 was designed to complete the establishment of a single market by the removal of remaining fiscal, nontariff, technical, and other barriers to trade. The EU has moved to both widen and deepen the integration process in Europe. As for widening, EU membership increased from 12 to 15 countries in 1995, and future membership of East European countries was under consideration. As for deepening, 12 members of the EU have joined in an economic and monetary union (EMU) with a common currency (the euro).

exchange rate   The number of units of one currency that can be exchanged for a unit of another currency. See *fixed exchange rates* and *floating exchange rates*.

export-led growth   An outward-looking economic development strategy that emphasizes the production of industrial goods for export to developed countries. Export-led growth is commonly associated with the economic success of the NIEs in East Asia. See *import-substituting industrialization*.

fast-track authority   Measures first introduced in the 1974 U.S. Trade Act to expedite congressional approval of trade agreements negotiated by the U.S. executive. Under the fast track, the president can assure U.S. trading partners that Congress will vote for or against negotiated agreements without amendments within a fixed period. Such authority is often necessary because other countries are reluctant to negotiate trade agreements with the United States that the U.S. Congress can later seek to amend.

fiscal policy   Fiscal policy affects the economy through changes in government spending, taxes, or both. When a government uses fiscal policy to deal with a balance-of-payments deficit, it lowers government expenditures, raises taxes, or both to withdraw purchasing power from the public. See *monetary policy*.

fixed exchange rates   In a fixed exchange rate system, currencies are given official exchange rates, and governments regularly take actions to keep the market rates of their currencies close to the official rates.

floating exchange rates or **flexible exchange rates**   In a floating exchange rate system, the supply of and demand for each currency in the foreign exchange market determine its exchange rate. With *free-floating exchange rates,* governments do not intervene and the market alone determines currency valuations. With *managed floating,* central banks intervene to deal with disruptive conditions such as excessive fluctuations in exchange rates. Although managed floating is considered to be legitimate, the IMF calls on central banks to avoid *dirty floating,* which refers to a government's manipulation of exchange rates to prevent effective balance-of-payments adjustment or to give that country an unfair competitive advantage.

foreign aid   The administered transfer of resources to recipient countries for the stated purpose of promoting their welfare and economic development. The greatest share of foreign aid is official development assistance, but aid is also provided by private or nongovernmental organizations. According to the Development Assistance Committee of the OECD, only grants that do not require repayment and concessional loans with a grant element of at least 25 percent should qualify as foreign aid. See *concessional loans, bilateral aid, multilateral aid,* and *official development assistance.*

foreign direct investment (FDI)   Investment involving the ownership and control of assets in one country by residents of another country. The foreign residents are usually MNCs that have management rights or control in a branch plant or subsidiary. FDI may occur through the creation of new productive assets by foreigners (i.e., greenfield investment) or through the purchase of stock in an existing firm. See *portfolio investment.*

free trade area (FTA)   The first stage of regional integration, in which the member countries are to eliminate tariffs on all (or substantially all) trade with one another. However, each member country can continue to levy its own tariffs and follow its own trade policies toward nonmembers.

General Agreement on Tariffs and Trade (GATT)   A provisional treaty that became the main global trade organization in 1948 by default when a planned International Trade Organization did not receive final approval. As an organization, GATT provided a written code of behavior, a forum for multilateral negotiations, and a venue for dispute settlement on trade issues. When the more formal WTO was formed in 1995, GATT reverted to its original status as a treaty regulating trade in goods.

General Agreement on Trade in Services (GATS)   A set of concepts, principles, rules, and commitments by members that apply to measures affecting trade in services. The GATS was established as a result of the GATT Uruguay Round agreement, and is a treaty under the WTO.

generalized system of preferences (GSP)   In the 1970s, the developed countries agreed to establish a GSP in response to LDC demands. Under the GSP, individual developed countries can waive MFN treatment and give preferential treatment to imports of specific goods from LDCs. Thus, the import duties for some LDC products are lower than those levied on developed countries' products.

gold standard   A monetary system in which central banks fix the value of their currencies in terms of gold and hold official international reserves in gold. A regime based on the gold standard existed from the 1870s to 1914, and many countries unsuccessfully tried to restore it after World War I. In a *gold exchange standard* (e.g., the Bretton Woods regime), central banks hold their international reserves in two forms—gold and foreign exchange—in any proportion they choose.

gross domestic product (GDP)   The total value of production of goods and services in a country, including those produced by foreigners as well as nationals. See *gross national product.*

gross national product (GNP)   The GNP is similar to the gross domestic product, except that the GNP includes the income domestic residents earn in foreign countries and excludes the income foreigners accumulate in the domestic market.

Group of Five (G-5)   The G-5 includes the finance ministers and central bank governors of the largest developed economies: the United States, Japan, Germany, France, and Britain. It has played a major role at times in coordinating monetary and other economic policies.

Group of Seven (G-7)   The G-5 plus Italy and Canada. The G-7 includes the seven largest industrial democracies, which account for about two-thirds of global output. G-7 heads of state and government hold annual summit meetings in efforts to provide leadership in international economic policy.

Group of Eight (G-8)   The G-8 includes the G-7 members plus Russia. Although Russia is theoretically a full member, serious economic problems prevent it from participating fully in the G-7's economic deliberations.

Group of Ten (G-10)   The G-10 includes the 10 developed countries that established the General Arrangements to Borrow with the IMF in 1962. Eleven countries are in fact members of the G-10 today—the G-7 plus the Netherlands, Belgium, Sweden, and Switzerland. In addition to providing supplementary finance, the G-10 regularly meets to discuss important matters related to the international monetary regime.

Group of 24 (G-24)   The G-24 was formed by the G-77 in 1972 to represent the interests of LDCs on international monetary issues. The G-24 is composed of eight finance ministers or central bank governors from each of the three main LDC regions—Africa, Asia, and Latin America.

Group of 77 (G-77)   The principal group representing Third World economic interests in negotiations with developed countries. The G-77 derives its name from the 77 LDCs that formed the group in 1964, but well over 100 LDCs are in fact members of the group today.

Heavily Indebted Poor Countries (HIPC) initiative   An initiative proposed in 1996 to provide debt relief for the HIPC. Unlike early plans (e.g., the Baker and Brady plans), the HIPC initiative was designed to permit rescheduling of debts of low-income LDCs to the IMF and World Bank. An enhanced HIPC initiative was established in 1999. See *Baker Plan* and *Brady Plan.*

Heckscher-Ohlin theorem   A theory named after two Swedish economists that postulates that comparative advantage is determined by the relative abundance and scarcity of factors of production (land, labor, and capital). Thus, capital-rich countries (usually the more advanced nations) should specialize in capital-intensive production, whereas countries with an abundance of cheap labor (many LDCs) should specialize in labor-intensive production.

hegemonic stability theory   A theory asserting that a relatively open and stable international economic system is most likely to exist when a hegemonic state is willing and able to provide leadership. The hegemonic state may manage the global economic system through coercive tactics, the provision of public goods, or both. See *hegemony* and *public goods.*

hegemony   Leadership, preponderant influence, or dominance in the international system, usually (but not always) associated with a particular nation-state. Gramscian theorists use the term hegemony in a cultural sense to connote not only the dominance of a single world power but also the complex of "ideas" that social groups use to legitimize their authority.

horizontal integration   A horizontally integrated MNC extends its operations abroad by producing the same product or product line in plants located in different countries. Firms often engage in horizontal integration to defend or increase their market share. See *multinational corporation* and *vertical integration.*

import-substituting industrialization (ISI)   A Third World strategy to promote economic development by replacing industrial imports with domestic production through trade protectionism and government assistance to domestic firms. Import substitution is most commonly associated with the economic problems of a number of Latin American LDCs.

infrastructure   The underlying framework of basic facilities, equipment, institutions, and installations that are crucial for the growth and functioning of an economy. Examples of infrastructure include transportation systems, public utilities, finance systems, laws and law enforcement, education, and research.

instrumental Marxism   A form of Marxism that perceives formal government institutions as responding in a passive manner to the interests and pressures of the capitalist class. See *structural Marxism.*

International Monetary Fund (IMF)   An international financial organization formed in 1944 to uphold the Bretton Woods system of pegged exchange rates (until the move to floating rates in 1973) and to provide countries with short-term loans for balance-of-payments problems. The IMF has had a leading role in dealing with the 1980s foreign debt crisis and the 1990s financial crisis.

liquidity   The ease with which an asset can be used at a known price in making payments. Cash is the most liquid form of an asset.

Lomé Conventions   Trade and aid agreements between the EU and 71 African, Caribbean, and Pacific (ACP) countries. The Lomé Conventions replaced the earlier Yaoundé Conventions, and provide the ACP countries with associate status in the EU.

London Club   An informal group of large private commercial banks that have provided credit to Third World countries encountering debt repayment problems. The London Club has no formal structure or specific location for its meetings. Meetings often occur in "creditor committees," in which the largest creditor banks coordinate their positions in debt rescheduling negotiations with individual LDC debtor countries. See *Paris Club.*

macroeconomics   The branch of economics that deals with the behavior of the economy as a whole. For example, macroeconomics is concerned with overall levels of employment, growth, production, and consumption. It examines such issues as monetary and fiscal policy, the banking system, trade, and the balance of payments.

market   An arrangement in which goods, services, and factors of production are bought and sold in response to relative prices, which are determined by the interaction of supply and demand.

market economy   An economy in which the market coordinates individual choices to determine the types of goods and services produced and sold and the methods of production.

mercantilism   A policy of states from the sixteenth to eighteenth centuries to build up their power and wealth relative to other states, largely by maintaining a balance-of-trade surplus. States that rely on government involvement and trade protectionism to increase their power and wealth today are often considered to be *neomercantilist.*

Mercosur   Mercosur was formed in March 1991, when Argentina, Brazil, Paraguay, and Uruguay signed the Treaty of Asunción to establish a common market according to an agreed timetable. The significance of Mercosur as a Third World RTA stems from the importance of its two largest members, Brazil and Argentina.

monetary policy   Monetary policy influences the economy through changes in the money supply. When a government uses monetary policy to deal with a balance-of-payments deficit, its central bank limits public access to funds for spending purposes and makes such funds more expensive.

most-favored-nation (MFN) treatment   A principle stipulating that every trade advantage, favor, privilege, or immunity a GATT/WTO member gives to any country must be extended to all other member states. A major exception to MFN treatment is provided for regional integration agreements.

multilateral aid   A type of foreign assistance in which donor governments provide funding through international organizations (such as the World Bank) whose policies are collectively determined. See *bilateral aid, foreign aid,* and *official development assistance.*

multinational corporation (MNC)   An enterprise that owns and controls facilities for production, distribution, and marketing in at least two countries. Also referred to as a transnational corporation or multinational enterprise.

national treatment   A principle stating that all GATT/WTO members should treat foreign products—after they have been imported—as favorably as domestic products with regard to internal taxes and other internal charges and regulations.

New International Economic Order (NIEO)   A set of proposals for extensive international economic reform and concessions from the developed countries of the North, which Third World countries presented to the United Nations in the 1970s. These included LDC demands for control over their economies and natural resources, control over foreign investment, greater assistance for economic development, greater access to markets in developed countries, and increased prices for LDC commodity exports. The Northern states ultimately rejected most of these demands for change.

nontariff barriers (NTBs)   An incredibly large array of measures other than tariffs that restrict imports, assist domestic production, and promote exports. As tariffs declined because of successive rounds of GATT negotiations, nontariff barriers became relatively more important. NTBs are often more restrictive, ill defined, and inequitable than tariffs.

North American Free Trade Agreement (NAFTA)   An FTA joining the United States, Canada, and Mexico, which entered into force in January 1994. The importance of NAFTA stems from the inclusion of the United States, the comprehensive nature of the agreement, and the fact that it is the first reciprocal free trade accord among developed countries and an LDC. Unlike the WTO, NAFTA does not give special and differential treatment to the LDC member (Mexico).

official aid (OA)   Flows of foreign aid that meet the same criteria of eligibility as *official development assistance.* The only difference is that recipients of official aid are the more advanced emerging countries (e.g., Russia, Hungary, and Poland) and a small number of advanced Third World countries (e.g., Kuwait and Singapore).

official development assistance (ODA)   Flows of foreign aid to LDCs and multilateral institutions from official government agencies. See *bilateral aid, foreign aid,* and *multilateral aid.*

official development finance (ODF)   Nonconcessional or "hard" loans that the IBRD provides to LDCs and transition economies. Although the IBRD's quasi-commercial loans are not concessional enough to be classified as ODA or OA, they are classified as ODF because the IBRD extends them for development purposes, it accompanies the loans with economic and technical advice, and LDCs receive the IBRD loans on better terms than they could obtain from borrowing directly on capital markets.

optimum currency area   A concept first developed by Robert Mundell, an optimum currency area is an area that maximizes the benefits minus the costs of using a common currency. Regions that are optimum currency areas are subject to common economic shocks, have a high degree of labor mobility, and have a tax-transfer system that transfers resources from economically strong to weak areas.

Organization for Economic Cooperation and Development (OECD)   An organization of 30 mainly developed countries located in Paris, France. The OECD conducts policy studies on economic and social issues, serves as a forum for the developed countries to discuss members' economic policies and promote cooperation and policy coordination, and sometimes serves as a forum for negotiation or prenegotiation.

Organization for European Economic Cooperation (OEEC)   An organization of Western European countries formed in 1948, which was responsible for developing a program for distribution of Marshall Plan funds and for facilitating moves toward convertibility of European currencies and the liberalization of trade in Western Europe. In 1960 the OEEC was replaced by the OECD, which also includes non-European developed countries as full members.

Pareto-optimal outcome   A condition of equilibrium in which no one actor can be made better off without making someone else worse off. A Pareto-suboptimal outcome, by contrast, is one in which all actors prefer another outcome to the equilibrium outcome. See *prisoners' dilemma.*

Paris Club   An informal grouping of creditor governments (members of the OECD) that meets with individual LDC debtor governments to negotiate debt-rescheduling agreements. The Paris Club normally meets in the French Ministry of Finance, but it has no legal status or written rules, no voting procedure, and no formal organizational structure.

portfolio investment   The purchase of stocks, bonds, and money market instruments by foreigners for the purpose of realizing a financial return, which does not result in foreign management, ownership, or legal control.

prisoners' dilemma   A game used by theorists (often in international relations) to examine situations in which individual rationality induces each state to "cheat" regardless of the actions taken by others. Such individually rational actions, however, can produce a Pareto-suboptimal outcome; hence the "dilemma" in the prisoners' dilemma. See *Pareto-optimal outcome*.

public goods   Also called *collective goods*, these are goods that are *nonexcludable* (i.e., all states have access to them) and *nonrival* (i.e., any state's use of the good will not decrease the amount available for others). Hegemons often provide public goods, according to the liberal interpretation of hegemonic stability theory. A major problem associated with public goods is the existence of *free riders* because even noncontributing states (or individuals) can benefit from the provision of public goods.

Quadrilateral Group of Trade Ministers or **Quad**   An informal grouping of trade ministers and trade officials from the United States, the European Commission, Japan, and Canada, which helps to resolve differences among the major traders and to help set the agenda for meetings and negotiations in the global trade regime.

reciprocity   The GATT/WTO principle that a country benefiting from another country's trade concessions should provide roughly equal benefits in return. *Specific reciprocity*, the more demanding type, requires concessions of equivalent value between two actors within a strict period. *Diffuse reciprocity* is less demanding, with more flexibility in terms of equivalence of value and the time period for granting reciprocal concessions.

regime   A form of institution dealing with a specific issue area in international relations, in which principles, norms, rules, and decision-making procedures affect actors' expectations and behavior. *International organizations* are more concrete and formal institutions than regimes and are often embedded within regimes. For example, the WTO is embedded within the global trade regime.

rules of origin   Regulations designed to prevent importers from bringing goods into a free trade area through member countries with the lowest duties and then shipping them to partner countries that have higher duties. Rules of origin often provide an excuse for protectionism.

safeguards   Term usually applied to Article 19 of GATT (the general escape clause). This article permits countries to take emergency protection measures to counter unexpected import surges that cause, or are likely to cause, serious injury to domestic industry. Safeguard actions are to be applied on a nondiscriminatory basis, and affected countries can request compensation.

seignorage   The profit and advantages accruing to a "seigneur" or sovereign power from issuing money. The term usually refers to the influence and power a hegemon acquires as a result of its position as the top-currency state.

single undertaking   A single undertaking indicates that acceptance of an agreement requires acceptance of all its parts. The GATT Uruguay round agreement was a single undertaking because it required LDCs to accept all parts of the agreement; this was in marked contrast to the NTB Tokyo Round codes, in which most LDCs did not participate.

special drawing rights (SDRs)   Artificial international reserves created and managed by the G-10 and used among central banks. SDRs have been issued only two times, and efforts to have them supplement (or replace) the U.S. dollar as the main international monetary reserve have been unsuccessful.

Stolper-Samuelson theory   According to the Stolper-Samuelson theory, trade liberalization benefits abundantly endowed factors of production and hurts poorly endowed factors of production in a state. Building on the Heckscher-Ohlin theorem, this theory helps explain why some domestic groups in a state are free-trade oriented and why other groups are protectionist.

strategic trade theory   A realist theory indicating that a state can successfully intervene through industrial targeting to alter its comparative or "competitive" advantage vis-à-vis other states. In deciding on its intervention strategies, a state tends to favor industries with presumed advantages in research and development, technology, economies of scale, and market power.

structural adjustment loans (SALs)   Medium-term balance-of-payments financing provided by the World Bank and IMF to LDCs. To receive such loans, borrowing countries must agree to institute structural reforms prescribed by the IMF, World Bank, or both.

structural Marxism   Structural Marxists view the state as relatively autonomous of direct political pressure from particular capitalists, but they believe that the state acts in the long-term interests of the capitalist class.

sustainable development   A policy that recognizes the complementarity between economic development and environmental conservation. Sustainable development was popularized by nongovernmental organizations in the early 1980s and received multilateral approval in 1987 by the Brundtland Commission. According to the Brundtland Commission, sustainable development "meets the needs of the present without compromising the ability of future generations to meet their own needs."

tariffs   Taxes levied on products that pass through a customs border. Although tariffs are usually imposed on imports, they may also be applied to exports. Import tariffs are most commonly used as a means of protectionism, but they may also be valued as a source of revenue for the state.

terms of trade   The relationship between the prices of a country's exports and the prices of its imports. In the late 1940s and early 1950s, structuralists such as Raúl Prebisch argued that relations between the core and periphery were marked by unequal exchange, in which there were deteriorating terms of trade for LDCs in the periphery. LDCs were therefore advised to follow ISI policies.

Trade-Related Intellectual Property Rights (TRIPs)   An agreement that establishes minimum standards of protection for copyrights, patents, and other types of "intellectual property"; provides for remedies available to members to protect these rights; and extends some basic GATT principles to intellectual property. The TRIPs agreement was concluded during the GATT Uruguay round and is part of the WTO.

Trade-Related Investment Measures (TRIMs)   The TRIMs is a rather weak and narrowly defined agreement to impose some discipline over trade-related investment issues. The TRIMs agreement prohibits host countries from imposing local content requirements on FDI, but the agreement does not address many other issues such as a host country's export performance requirements.

transfer prices   Prices used by a business firm for the internal sale of goods and services among its divisions (i.e., for intrafirm trade). Although transfer prices help an MNC to efficiently manage its internal operations, an MNC may artificially raise or lower its transfer prices to shift its reported profits from high-tax to low-tax countries.

Triffin dilemma   Named after Robert Triffin, the Triffin dilemma described the position of the United States as the top-currency state. Continued balance-of-payments deficits would create a "confidence" problem in the U.S. dollar, but if the United States moved to reduce its payments deficit, there would be a shortage of U.S. dollars for liquidity purposes. The Triffin dilemma therefore refers to the conflict between the liquidity and confidence functions of a top-currency state.

United Nations Conference on Trade and Development (UNCTAD)   A permanent organ of the United Nations General Assembly, created in 1964 as a result of Third World dissatisfaction with existing international economic organizations such as GATT. UNCTAD is primarily concerned with promoting international trade, economic development, and the interests of LDCs.

vertical integration   A vertically integrated MNC controls and coordinates production of goods and services at different stages of the production process. When an MNC is vertically integrated, the outputs of some of its affiliates serve as inputs to other affiliates. Firms often engage in vertical integration to avoid uncertainty, reduce transaction costs, and limit competition. See *horizontal integration.*

voluntary export restraints   A practice by which countries have circumvented the GATT Article 11 ban on import quotas by pressuring other countries to "voluntarily" decrease their exports of specific products.

Washington consensus   A term referring to the orthodox liberal belief that countries can best achieve economic growth through free markets, a dominant private sector, democratic government, and trade liberalization. (Ironically, this is not what John Williamson meant by the term when he coined it in 1989.)

World Bank group   The largest multilateral group of institutions providing international development financing for Third World countries and emerging centrally planned economies. The group consists of five institutions, including the International Bank for Reconstruction and Development (formed at Bretton Woods in the 1940s), the International Finance Corporation (formed in 1956), the International Development Association (created in 1960), the International Centre for the Settlement of Investment Disputes (established in 1966), and the Multilateral Investment Guarantee Agency (established in 1988).

world-system theory   Like dependency theory, world-system theory rejects the view of modernization theorists that countries in the periphery have problems because they follow traditional practices. World-system theorists argue that problems in the periphery stem from capitalism, a global system for organizing economic activities that has existed since the "long sixteenth century." To explain the fact that some countries in the periphery have experienced some development, world-system theorists introduced the concept of the semiperiphery.

World Trade Organization (WTO)   The main global trade organization, established as the successor to GATT in 1995 by the signatories to the GATT Uruguay round agreement. Under the WTO are various agreements, including the General Agreement on Tariffs and Trade (GATT), the General Agreement on Trade in Services (GATS), the Agreement on Trade-Related Intellectual Property Rights (TRIPs), and the Agreement on Trade-Related Investment Measures (TRIMs).

SELECTED BIBLIOGRAPY

TOPICS

I. General Studies—International Political Economy

Ashley, Richard K. "Three Modes of Economism." *International Studies Quarterly* 27-4 (December 1983): 463–496.

Baldwin, David A., ed. *Neorealism and Neoliberalism: The Contemporary Debate*. New York: Columbia University Press, 1993.

Biersteker, Thomas J. "Evolving Perspectives on International Political Economy: Twentieth-Century Contexts and Discontinuities." *International Political Science Review* 14-1 (January 1993): 7–33.

Boyer, Robert, and Daniel Drache, eds. *States Against Markets: The Limits of Globalization*. London: Routledge, 1996.

Burch, Kurt, and Robert A. Denemark, eds. *Constituting International Political Economy*. Boulder, CO: Rienner, 1997.

Caporaso, James A. "Global Political Economy." In *Political Science: The State of the Discipline II*, ed. Ada Finifter, 451–481. Washington, DC: American Political Science Association, 1993.

Cerny, Philip G., ed. *World Politics: Markets, Regimes and States in the Post-Hegemonic Era*. London: Elgar, 1993.

Cox, Robert W. *Production, Power, and World Order: Social Forces in the Making of History*. New York: Columbia University Press, 1987.

Crane, George T., and Abla Amawi, eds. *The Theoretical Evolution of International Political Economy: A Reader.* New York: Oxford University Press, 2nd edition, 1997.

Doyle, Michael W., and G. John Ikenberry. *New Thinking in International Relations Theory.* Boulder, CO: Westview Press, 1997.

Fieleke, Norman S. *The International Economy Under Stress.* Cambridge, MA: Ballinger, 1988.

Frieden, Jeffry A., and David A. Lake, eds. *International Political Economy: Perspectives on Global Power and Wealth.* New York: St. Martin's Press, 3rd edition, 1995.

Gerschenkron, Alexander. *Economic Backwardness in Historical Perspective.* Cambridge, MA.: Harvard University Press, 1962.

Gilpin, Robert, with Jean Gilpin. *The Political Economy of International Relations.* Princeton, NJ: Princeton University Press, 1987.

———. *The Challenge of Global Capitalism: The World Economy in the 21st Century.* Princeton, NJ: Princeton University Press, 2000.

Howlett, Michael, and M. Ramesh. *The Political Economy of Canada: An Introduction.* Toronto, Canada: McClelland & Stewart, 1992.

Jones, R. J. Barry. *Perspectives on Political Economy.* London: Pinter, 1983.

Kegley, Charles W., Jr., ed. *Controversies in International Relations Theory: Realism and the Neoliberal Challenge.* New York: St. Martin's Press, 1995.

Kenen, Peter B., ed. *Managing the World Economy: Fifty Years After Bretton Woods.* Washington, DC: Institute for International Economics, 1994.

Kindleberger, Charles P. *Power and Money: The Economics of International Politics and the Politics of International Economics.* New York: Basic Books, 1970.

Knorr, Klaus. "Economics and International Relations: A Problem in Teaching." *Political Science Quarterly* 62-4 (December 1947): 552–568.

Kresl, Peter Karl, and Gary Gappert, eds. *North American Cities and the Global Economy: Challenges and Opportunities.* Urban Affairs Annual Review 44. Thousand Oaks, CA: Sage, 1995.

Lindblom, Charles E. *Politics and Markets: The World's Political-Economic Systems.* New York: Basic Books, 1977.

Mander, Jerry, and Edward Goldsmith, eds. *The Case Against the Global Economy: For a Turn Toward the Local.* San Francisco, CA: Sierra Club, 1996.

McKinlay, R. D., and R. Little. *Global Problems and World Order.* London: Pinter, 1986.

Murphy, Craig N., and Roger Tooze, eds. *The New International Political Economy.* Boulder, CO: Rienner, 1991.

O'Hara, Phillip Anthony, ed. *Encyclopedia of Political Economy,* vols. 1 and 2. London: Routledge, 1999.

Olson, Mancur. *The Logic of Collective Action: Public Goods and the Theory of Groups.* Cambridge, MA: Harvard University Press, 1965.

Peterson, V. Spike, and Anne Sisson Runyan. *Global Gender Issues.* Boulder, CO: Westview Press, 2nd edition, 1999.

Polanyi, Karl. *The Great Transformation.* Boston, MA: Beacon Press, 1965.

Schwartz, Herman M. *States versus Markets: History, Geography, and the Development of the International Political Economy.* New York: St. Martin's Press, 2nd edition, 2000.

Staniland, Martin. *What Is Political Economy? A Study of Social Theory and Underdevelopment.* New Haven, CT: Yale University Press, 1985.

Stevis, Dimitris, and Valerie J. Assetto, eds. *The International Political Economy of the Environment: Critical Perspectives.* Boulder, CO: Rienner, 2001.

Strange, Susan. "International Economics and International Relations: A Case of Mutual Neglect." *International Affairs* 46 (April 1970): 304–315.

———, ed. *Paths to International Political Economy.* London: Allen & Unwin, 1984.

———. *States and Markets.* London: Pinter, 1988.

Strange, Susan, and Roger Tooze, eds. *The International Politics of Surplus Capacity*. London: Allen & Unwin, 1981.

Stubbs, Richard, and Geoffrey R. D. Underhill, eds. *Political Economy and the Changing Global Order*. Toronto, Canada: Oxford University Press, 2nd edition, 2000.

Tickner, J. Ann. *Gender in International Relations: Feminist Perspectives on Achieving Global Security*. New York: Columbia University Press, 1992.

Webb, Michael C. *The Political Economy of Policy Coordination: International Adjustment Since 1945*. Ithaca, NY: Cornell University Press, 1995.

Whitworth, Sandra. *Feminism and International Relations: Towards a Political Economy of Gender in Interstate and Non-Governmental Institutions*. London: Macmillan, 1994.

Yarbrough, Beth V., and Robert M. Yarbrough. *The World Economy: Trade and Finance*. Fort Worth, TX: Harcourt Brace, 3rd edition, 1994.

II. Globalization

Amin, Samir. "The Challenge of Globalization." *Review of International Political Economy* 3-2 (Summer 1996): 216–259.

Burback, Roger, Orlando Núñez, and Boris Kagarlitsky. *Globalization and Its Discontents: The Rise of Postmodern Socialisms*. London: Pluto Press, 1997.

Carnoy, Martin, Manuel Castells, Stephen S. Cohen, and Fernando Henrique Cardoso. *The New Global Economy in the Information Age: Reflections on Our Changing World*. University Park, PA: Pennsylvania State University Press, 1993.

Cerny, Philip G. "Globalization and the Changing Logic of Collective Action." *International Organization* 49-4 (Autumn 1995): 595–625.

Cohn, Theodore H., Stephen McBride, and John Wiseman, eds. *Power in the Global Era: Grounding Globalization*. London: Macmillan, 2000.

"Globalization." Special issue of *International Journal* 51-4 (Autumn 1996).

Held, David. *Democracy and the Global Order: From the Modern State to Cosmopolitan Governance*. Cambridge, MA: Polity Press, 1995.

Hirst, Paul, and Grahame Thompson. *Globalization in Question*. Cambridge, MA: Polity Press, 1996.

Holm, Hans-Henrik, and Georg Sorensen, eds. *Whose World Order? Uneven Globalization and the End of the Cold War*. Boulder, CO: Westview Press, 1995.

Hurrell, Anthony, and Ngaire Woods. "Globalisation and Inequality." *Millennium* 24-3 (1995): 447–470.

Jones, R. J. Barry. *Globalisation and Interdependence in the International Political Economy: Rhetoric and Reality*. London: Pinter, 1995.

Kapstein, Ethan B. *Governing the Global Market: International Finance and the State*. Cambridge, MA: Harvard University Press, 1994.

Mander, Jerry, and Edward Goldsmith, eds. *The Case Against the Global Economy: For a Turn Toward the Local*. San Francisco, CA: Sierra Club, 1996.

McBride, Stephen, and John Wiseman, eds. *Globalization and Its Discontents*. London: Macmillan, 2000.

McGrew, Anthony G., et al. *Global Politics: Globalization and the Nation-State*. Cambridge, MA: Polity Press, 1992.

Mittelman, James H. *Globalization: Critical Reflections*. Boulder, CO: Rienner, 1996.

Ohmae, Kenichi. *The Borderless World: Power and Strategy in the Interlinked Economy*. New York: Harper Perennial, 1990.

Robertson, Roland. *Globalization: Social Theory and Global Culture*. London: Sage, 1992.

Sklair, Leslie. *Sociology of the Global System.* Hertfordshire, UK: Prentice Hall/Harvester Wheatsheaf, 2nd edition, 1995.

Waters, Malcolm. *Globalization.* London: Routledge, 1995.

III. Institutional Framework for Managing the Postwar World Economy

Acheson, A. L. K., J. F. Chant, and M. F. J. Prochowny, eds. *Bretton Woods Revisited.* Toronto, Canada: University of Toronto Press, 1972.

Assetto, Valerie J. *The Soviet Bloc in the IMF and the IBRD.* Boulder, CO: Westview Press, 1988.

Bakker, Age F. P. *International Financial Institutions.* New York: Longman, 1996.

Bayne, Nicholas. *Hanging in There: The G7 and G8 Summit in Maturity and Renewal.* Aldershot, UK: Ashgate, 2000.

Bergsten, C. Fred, and C. Randall Henning. *Global Economic Leadership and the Group of Seven.* Washington, DC: Institute for International Economics, June 1996.

Blair, David J. *Trade Negotiations in the OECD: Structures, Institutions and States.* London: Kegan Paul, 1993.

Bleicher, Samuel A. "UN v. IBRD: A Dilemma of Functionalism." *International Organization* 42-1 (Winter 1970): 31–47.

Brabant, Jozef M. van. *The Planned Economies and International Economic Organizations.* Cambridge, UK: Cambridge University Press, 1991.

Bretton Woods Commission. *Bretton Woods: Looking to the Future.* Commission Report, Staff Review, Background Papers. Washington, DC: Bretton Woods Committee, July 1994.

Camps, Miriam, with C. Gwin. *Collective Management: The Reform of Global Economic Organizations.* New York: McGraw-Hill, 1980.

Cavanagh, John, Daphne Wysham, and Marcos Arruda, eds. *Beyond Bretton Woods: Alternatives to the Global Economic Order.* London: Pluto Press, 1994.

Cutajar, Michael Zammit, ed. *UNCTAD and the North-South Dialogue: The First Twenty Years.* Oxford, UK: Pergamon Press, 1985.

Danaher, Kevin, ed. *50 Years Is Enough: The Case Against the World Bank and the International Monetary Fund.* Boston, MA: South End Press, 1994.

Feeney, William. "Chinese Policy in Multilateral Financial Institutions." In *China and the World: Chinese Foreign Policy in the Post-Mao Era,* ed. Samuel S. Kim, 266–292. Boulder, CO: Westview Press, 1984.

Feinberg, Richard E. "The Changing Relationship Between the World Bank and the International Monetary Fund." *International Organization* 42–3 (Summer 1988): 545–560.

Ferguson, Tyrone. *The Third World and Decision Making in the International Monetary Fund: The Quest for Full and Effective Participation.* London: Pinter, 1988.

Gilbert, Christopher L., and David Vines, eds. *The World Bank: Structures and Policies.* Cambridge, UK: Cambridge University Press, 2000.

Gold, Joseph. "The Relationship Between the International Monetary Fund and the World Bank." *Creighton Law Review* 15 (1982): 499–521.

Hajnal, Peter I., ed. *The Seven Power Summit: Documents from the Summits of Industrialized Countries 1975–1989.* New York: Kraus International Publications, 1989.

———. *The G7/G8 System: Evolution, Role and Documentation.* Aldershot, UK: Ashgate, 1999.

Hart, Jeffrey A. *The New International Economic Order: Conflict and Cooperation in North-South Economic Relations, 1974–77.* London: Macmillan, 1983.

Higgott, Richard A., Geoffrey R. D. Underhill, and Andreas Bieler, eds. *Non-State Actors and Authority in the Global System.* London: Routledge, 2000.

Jacobson, Harold K. *Networks of Interdependence: International Organizations and the Global Political System.* New York: Knopf, 1979.

Jacobson, Harold K., and Michel Oksenberg. *China's Participation in the IMF, the World Bank, and GATT: Toward a Global Economic Order.* Ann Arbor, MI: University of Michigan Press, 1990.

Johnson, Hazel J. *Global Financial Institutions and Markets.* Oxford, UK: Blackwell, 2000.

Kapur, Devesh, John P. Lewis, and Richard Webb. *The World Bank: Its First Half Century, Volume 1: History.* Washington, DC: Brookings Institution Press, 1997.

Karns, Margaret P., and Karen A. Mingst. *The United States and Multilateral Institutions: Patterns of Changing Instrumentality and Influence.* Boston, MA: Unwin Hyman, 1990.

Kirshner, Orin, ed. *The Bretton Woods–GATT System: Retrospect and Prospect After Fifty Years.* Armonk, NY: M. E. Sharpe, 1996.

Kirton, John J., and George M. von Furstenberg, eds. *New Directions in Global Economic Governance: Managing Globalisation in the Twenty-first Century.* Aldershot, UK: Ashgate, 2001.

Lang, Laszlo. "International Regimes and the Political Economy of East-West Relations." *Occasional Paper Series* no. 13. New York: Institute for East-West Security Studies, 1989, 19–22.

Laszlo, Ervin, et al. *The Obstacles to the New International Economic Order.* New York: Pergamon Press, 1980.

Mason, Edward S., and Robert E. Asher. *The World Bank Since Bretton Woods.* Washington, DC: Brookings Institution, 1973.

Morgenthau, Henry, Jr. "Bretton Woods and International Cooperation." *Foreign Affairs* 23-2 (January 1945): 182–194.

O'Brien, Robert, Anne Marie Goetz, Jan Aart Scholte, and Marc Williams. *Contesting Global Governance: Multilateral Economic Institutions and Global Social Movements.* Cambridge, UK: Cambridge University Press, 2000.

Polak, Jacques J. *The World Bank and the International Monetary Fund: A Changing Relationship.* Brookings Occasional Papers. Washington, DC: Brookings Institution, 1994.

Prügl, Elisabeth. "Gender in International Organization and Global Governance: A Critical Review of the Literature." *International Studies Notes* 21-1 (Winter 1996): 15–24.

Putnam, Robert D., and Nicholas Bayne. *Hanging Together: Cooperation and Conflict in the Seven-Power Summits.* London: Sage, revised edition, 1987.

Risse-Kappen, Thomas, ed. *Bringing Transnational Relations Back In: Non-State Actors, Domestic Structures and International Institutions.* Cambridge, UK: Cambridge University Press, 1995.

Rochester, J. Martin. "The Rise and Fall of International Organization as a Field of Study." *International Organization* 40-4 (Autumn 1986): 777–813.

Ruggie, John Gerard., ed. *Multilateralism Matters: The Theory and Praxis of an Institutional Form.* New York: Columbia University Press, 1993.

Sauvant, Karl P. *The Group of 77: Evolution, Structure, Organization.* New York: Oceana Publications, 1981.

Shihata, Ibrahim F. I. *MIGA and Foreign Investment: Origins, Operations, Policies and Basic Documents of the Multilateral Investment Guarantee Agency.* Dordrecht, The Netherlands: Nijhoff, 1988.

Van Dormael, Armand. *Bretton Woods: Birth of a Monetary System.* London: Macmillan, 1978.

Williams, Marc. *Third World Cooperation: The Group of 77 in UNCTAD.* London: Pinter Publishers, 1991.

———. *International Economic Organisations and the Third World.* New York, NY: Harvester Wheatsheaf, 1994.

World Commission on Environment and Development. *Our Common Future* (The Brundtland Report). Oxford, UK: Oxford University Press, 1987.

IV. The Realist Perspective

Baldwin, David A. *Economic Statecraft.* Princeton, NJ: Princeton University Press, 1985.

Evans, Peter B., Dietrich Rueschemeyer, and Theda Skocpol, eds. *Bringing the State Back In.* Cambridge, UK: Cambridge University Press, 1985.

Gilpin, Robert. *War and Change in World Politics.* Cambridge, UK: Cambridge University Press, 1981.

———. "The Richness of the Tradition of Political Realism." *International Organization* 38-2 (Spring 1984), pp. 287–304.

Grieco, Joseph. *Cooperation Among Nations: Europe, America, and Non-Tariff Barriers to Trade.* Ithaca, NY: Cornell University Press, 1990.

Hart, Jeffrey A. *The New International Economic Order: Conflict and Cooperation in North-South Economic Relations, 1974–77.* London: Macmillan, 1983.

Heckscher, Eli F. *Mercantilism,* vol. 2. London: Allen & Unwin, 1934.

Hirschman, Albert O. *National Power and the Structure of Foreign Trade.* Berkeley, CA: University of California Press, expanded edition, 1980.

Johnson, Chalmers. *MITI and the Japanese Miracle: The Growth of Industrial Policy, 1925–1975.* Stanford, CA: Stanford University Press, 1982.

Keohane, Robert O., ed. *Neorealism and Its Critics.* New York: Columbia University Press, 1986.

Kirshner, Jonathan. "Political Economy in Security Studies After the Cold War." *Review of International Political Economy* 5-1 (Spring 1998): 64–91.

Krasner, Stephen D. *Defending the National Interest: Raw Materials Investments and U.S. Foreign Policy.* Princeton, NJ: Princeton University Press, 1978.

———. *Structural Conflict: The Third World Against Global Liberalism.* Berkeley, CA: University of California Press, 1985.

Lake, David A. "Power and the Third World: Toward a Realist Political Economy of North-South Relations." *International Studies Quarterly* 31-2 (June 1987): 217–234.

Levi-Faur, David. "Friedrich List and the Political Economy of the Nation-State." *Review of International Political Economy* 4-1 (Spring, 1997): 154–178.

List, Friedrich. *The National System of Political Economy.* Translated by Sampson S. Lloyd. London: Longmans, Green, 1916.

Machiavelli, Niccolò. *The Prince and the Discourses.* New York: Modern Library, 1940.

Mastanduno, Michael. "Economics and Security in Statecraft and Scholarship." *International Organization* 52-4 (Autumn 1998): 825–854.

Mastanduno, Michael, David A. Lake, and G. John Ikenberry, "Toward a Realist Theory of State Action." *International Studies Quarterly* 33-4 (December 1989): 457–474.

Morgenthau, Hans. J., revised by Kenneth W. Thompson. *Politics Among Nations: The Struggle for Power and Peace.* New York: Knopf, 6th edition, 1985.

Rothstein, Robert L. *The Weak in the World of the Strong: The Developing Countries in the International System.* New York: Columbia University Press, 1977.

Syrett, Harold C., ed. *The Papers of Alexander Hamilton,* vol. 10. New York: Columbia University Press, 1966.

Thucydides. *The History of the Peloponnesian War.* Translated by Richard Crawley. London: Dent, Everyman's Library, 1963.

Viner, Jacob. "Power versus Plenty as Objectives of Foreign Policy in the Seventeenth and Eighteenth Centuries." *World Politics* 1 (October 1948): 1–29.

Waltz, Kenneth N. *Theory of International Politics.* Reading, MA: Addison Wesley, 1979.

V. Hegemonic Stability Theory

Akaha, Tsuneo, and Frank Langdon, eds. *Japan in the Posthegemonic World*. Boulder, CO: Rienner, 1993.

Calleo, David P. *Beyond American Hegemony: The Future of the Western Alliance*. New York: Basic Books, 1987.

Cowhey, Peter F., and Edward Long. "Testing Theories of Regime Change: Hegemonic Decline or Surplus Capacity?" *International Organization* 37-2 (Spring 1983): 157–188.

Gill, Stephen. "American Hegemony: Its Limits and Prospects in the Reagan Era." *Millennium* 15-3 (Winter 1986): 311–336.

Huntington, Samuel P. "Transnational Organizations in World Politics." *World Politics* 25-3 (April 1973): 333–368.

Kennedy, Paul. *The Rise and Fall of the Great Powers: Economic Change and Military Conflict from 1500 to 2000*. New York: Random House, 1987.

Keohane, Robert O. "The Theory of Hegemonic Stability and Changes in International Economic Regimes, 1967–1977." In *Change in the International System*, eds. Ole R. Holsti, Randolph M. Siverson, and Alexander L. George, 131–162. Boulder, CO: Westview Press, 1980.

———. *After Hegemony: Cooperation and Discord in the World Political Economy*. Princeton, NJ: Princeton University Press, 1984.

Kindleberger, Charles P. *The World in Depression, 1929–1939*. Berkeley, CO: University of California Press, 1973.

———. "Dominance and Leadership in the International Economy: Exploitation, Public Goods, and Free Rides." *International Studies Quarterly* 25-2 (June 1981): 242–254.

Mead, Walter Russell. *Mortal Splendor: The American Empire in Transition*. Boston, MA: Houghton Mifflin, 1987.

Morse, Ronald A. "Japan's Drive to Pre-Eminence." *Foreign Policy* 69 (Winter 1987–88): 3–21.

Nau, Henry R. *The Myth of America's Decline: Leading the World Economy into the 1990s*. New York: Oxford University Press, 1990.

Nye, Joseph S., Jr. "U.S. Power and Reagan Policy." *Orbis* 26-2 (Summer 1982): 391–411.

———. "Understating U.S. Strength." *Foreign Policy* 72 (Fall 1988): 105–129.

———. *Bound to Lead: The Changing Nature of American Power*. New York: Basic Books, 1990.

———. "Soft Power." *Foreign Policy* 80 (Fall 1990): 153–171.

———. "The Changing Nature of World Power." *Political Science Quarterly* 105-2 (Summer 1990): 177–192.

Olson, Mancur. *The Logic of Collective Action: Public Goods and the Theory of Groups*. Cambridge, MA: Harvard University Press, 1965.

Russett, Bruce. "The Mysterious Case of Vanishing Hegemony; or, Is Mark Twain Really Dead?" *International Organization* 39-2 (Spring 1985): 207–231.

Snidal, Duncan. "The Limits of Hegemonic Stability Theory." *International Organization* 39-4 (Autumn 1985): 579–614.

Stein, Arthur A. "The Hegemon's Dilemma: Great Britain, the United States and the International Economic Order." *International Organization* 38-2 (Spring 1984): 355–386.

Strange, Susan. "The Persistent Myth of Lost Hegemony." *International Organization* 41-4 (Autumn 1987): 551–574.

———. "The Future of the American Empire." *Journal of International Affairs* 42 (Fall 1988): 1–17.

———. "Finance, Information, and Power." *Review of International Studies* 16-3 (July 1990): 259–274.

Thurow, Lester. *Head to Head: The Coming Economic Battle Among Japan, Europe, and America.* New York: Morrow, 1992.

Webb, Michael C., and Stephen D. Krasner. "Hegemonic Stability Theory: An Empirical Assessment." *Review of International Studies* 15 (Spring 1989): 183–198.

Zuckerman, Mortimer B. "A Second American Century." *Foreign Affairs* 77-3 (May/June, 1998): 18–31.

VI. The Liberal Perspective

Arblaster, Anthony. *The Rise and Decline of Western Liberalism.* New York: Basil Blackwell, 1984.

Axelrod, Robert. *The Evolution of Cooperation.* New York: Basic Books, 1984.

Balassa, Bela, ed. *The Newly Industrializing Countries in the World Economy.* New York: Pergamon Press, 1981.

Bauer, P. T., and B. S. Yamey. "Against the New Economic Order." *Commentary* 63-4 (April 1977): 25–31.

Black, C. E. *The Dynamics of Modernization: A Study in Comparative History.* New York: Harper & Row, 1966.

Cooper, Richard N. *The Economics of Interdependence: Economic Policy in the Atlantic Community.* New York: McGraw-Hill, 1968.

Cutler, A. Claire. "The 'Grotian Tradition' in International Relations." *Review of International Studies* 17 (1991): 41–65.

Eichner, Alfred S. *A Guide to Post-Keynesian Economics.* White Plains, NY: M. E. Sharpe, 1979.

Fox, Annette Baker, Alfred O. Hero Jr., and Joseph S. Nye Jr., eds. *Canada and the United States: Transnational and Transgovernmental Relations.* New York: Columbia University Press, 1976.

Friedman, Milton, ed. *Essays in Positive Economics.* Chicago, IL: University of Chicago Press, 1953.

Friedman, Milton, and Rose Friedman. *Free to Choose: A Personal Statement.* New York: Harcourt Brace Jovanovich, 1980.

Fukuyama, Francis. "The End of History?" *The National Interest* 16 (Summer 1989): 3–18.

Hall, Peter A., ed. *The Political Power of Economic Ideas: Keynesianism across Nations.* Princeton, NJ: Princeton University Press, 1989.

Hayek, F. A. *New Studies in Philosophy, Politics, Economics and the History of Ideas.* Chicago, IL: University of Chicago Press, 1978.

Jones, R. J. Barry, and Peter Willetts, eds. *Interdependence on Trial: Studies in the Theory and Reality of Contemporary Interdependence.* London: Pinter, 1984.

Keohane, Robert O., and Joseph S. Nye Jr., eds. *Transnational Relations and World Politics.* Cambridge, MA: Harvard University Press, 1972.

———. *Power and Interdependence: World Politics in Transition.* Boston, MA: Little, Brown, 1977.

Keynes, John Maynard. *The General Theory of Employment, Interest, and Money.* New York: Harcourt, Brace and World, 1935.

Krasner, Stephen D., ed. *International Regimes.* Ithaca, NY: Cornell University Press, 1983.

Lerner, Daniel. *The Passing of Traditional Society: Modernizing the Middle East.* New York: Free Press, 1964.

Moggridge, D. E. *Keynes.* London: Macmillan, 1976.

Moravcsik, Andrew. "Taking Preferences Seriously: A Liberal Theory of International Politics." *International Organization* 51-4 (Autumn 1997): 513–553.

Oye, Kenneth A., ed. *Cooperation Under Anarchy.* Princeton, NJ: Princeton University Press, 1986.

Ricardo, David. *The Principles of Political Economy and Taxation.* Homewood, IL: Irwin, 1963.

Risse-Kappen, Thomas, ed. *Bringing Transnational Relations Back In: Non-State Actors, Domestic Structures and International Institutions.* Cambridge, UK: Cambridge University Press, 1995.

Rostow, W. W. *The Stages of Economic Growth: A Non-Communist Manifesto.* Cambridge, UK: Cambridge University Press, 1960.

————. *Why the Poor Get Richer and the Rich Slow Down.* Austin, TX: University of Texas Press, 1980.

Schattschneider, E. E. *Politics, Pressures and the Tariff: A Study of Free Enterprise in Pressure Politics, as Shown in the 1929–1939 Revision of the Tariff.* Hamden, CT: Archon Books, 1935. Reprint, 1963.

Smith, Adam. *The Wealth of Nations.* London: Dent & Sons, Everyman's Library, 1910.

von Mises, Ludwig. *Planning For Freedom.* South Holland, IL: Libertarian Press, 1974.

VII. International Institutions and Regime Theory

Cohn, Theodore H. "The Changing Role of the United States in the Global Agricultural Trade Regime." In *World Agriculture and the GATT,* International Political Economy Yearbook, vol. 7, ed. William P. Avery, 17–38. Boulder, CO: Rienner, 1993.

Cutler, A. Claire, and Mark W. Zacher, eds. *Canadian Foreign Policy and International Economic Regimes.* Vancouver, BC Canada: University of British Columbia Press, 1992.

de Senarclens, Pierre. "Regime Theory and the Study of International Organizations." *International Social Science Journal* (November 1993): 45–138.

Haggard, Stephan, and Beth A. Simmons. "Theories of International Regimes." *International Organization* 41-3 (Summer 1987): 491–517.

Hollingsworth, J. Rogers and Robert Boyer, eds. *Contemporary Capitalism: The Embeddedness of Institutions.* Cambridge, UK: Cambridge University Press, 1997.

Jacobson, Harold K. *Networks of Interdependence: International Organizations and the Global Political System.* New York: Knopf, 1979.

Kahler, Miles. *International Institutions and the Political Economy of Integration.* Washington, DC: Brookings Institution, 1995.

Keohane, Robert O. *After Hegemony: Cooperation and Discord in the World Political Economy.* Princeton, NJ: Princeton University Press, 1984.

————. *International Institutions and State Power: Essays in International Relations Theory.* Boulder, CO: Westview Press, 1989.

Krasner, Stephen D., ed. *International Regimes.* Ithaca, NY: Cornell University Press, 1983.

Lang, Laszlo. "International Regimes and the Political Economy of East-West Relations." *Occasional Paper Series* no. 13. New York: Institute for East-West Security Studies, 1989.

Levy, Marc A., Oran R. Young, and Michael Zürn. "The Study of International Regimes." *European Journal of International Relations* 1-3 (1995): 267–330.

Martin, Lisa and Beth Simmons. "Theories and Empirical Studies of International Institutions." *International Organization* 52-4 (Autumn 1998): 729–757.

Mearsheimer, John J. "The False Promise of International Institutions." *International Security* 19-3 (Winter 1994–95): 5–49.

Rittberger, Volker, ed. *International Regimes in East-West Politics.* London: Pinter, 1990.

Rittberger, Volker, with Peter Mayer, eds. *Regime Theory and International Relations.* Oxford, UK: Clarendon Press, 1993.

Rochester, J. Martin. "The Rise and Fall of International Organization as a Field of Study." *International Organization* 40-4 (Autumn 1986): 777–813.

Rosenau, James N., and Ernst-Otto Czempiel, eds. *Governance Without Government: Order and Change in World Politics.* Cambridge, UK: Cambridge University Press, 1992.

Snidal, Duncan, "International Political Economy Approaches to International Institutions." In *Economic Dimensions in International Law,* eds. Jagdeep S. Bhandari and Alan O. Sykes, 477–512. Cambridge, UK: Cambridge University Press, 1997.

Taylor, Phillip. *Nonstate Actors in International Politics: From Transregional to Substate Organizations.* Boulder, CO: Westview Press, 1984.

Zacher, Mark W., with Brent A. Sutton. *Governing Global Networks: International Regimes for Transportation and Communications.* Cambridge, UK: Cambridge University Press, 1996.

VIII. The Historical Structuralist Perspective

Aglietta, Michel. *A Theory of Capitalist Regulation: The US Experience.* Translated by David Fernbach. London: New Left Books, 1979.

Avineri, Shlomo, ed. *Karl Marx on Colonialism and Modernization: His Dispatches and Other Writings on China, India, Mexico, the Middle East and North Africa.* Garden City, NY: Doubleday, 1968.

Baran, Paul A. *The Political Economy of Growth.* New York: Monthly Review Press, 1962.

Blaney, David L. "Reconceptualizing Autonomy: The Difference Dependency Theory Makes." *Review of International Political Economy* 3-3 (Autumn 1996): 459–497.

Brewer, Anthony. *Marxist Theories of Imperialism: A Critical Survey.* London: Routledge, 2nd edition, 1990.

Caporaso, James. "Dependency Theory: Continuities and Discontinuities in Development Studies." *International Organization* 34-4 (Autumn 1980): 605–628.

Cardoso, Fernando Henrique. "The Consumption of Dependency Theory in the United States." *Latin American Research Review* 12-3 (1977): 7–24.

Cardoso, Fernando Henrique, and Enzo Faletto. *Dependency and Development in Latin America.* Translated by Marjory Mattingly Urquidi. Berkeley, CA: University of California Press, 1979.

Chase-Dunn, Christopher. "International Economic Policy in a Declining Core State." In *America in a Changing World Political Economy*, eds. William P. Avery and David Rapkin, 77–96. London: Longman, 1982.

————. "Comparing World-Systems: Toward a Theory of Semiperipheral Development." *Comparative Civilizations Review* 19 (Fall 1988): 29–66.

Clark, Cal, and Donna Bahry. "Dependent Development: A Socialist Variant." *International Studies Quarterly* 27-3 (September 1983): 271–293.

Cox, Robert W. *Production, Power, and World Order: Social Forces in the Making of History.* New York, NY: Columbia University Press, 1987.

————. "Civil Society at the Turn of the Millennium: Prospects for an Alternative World Order." *Review of International Studies* 25 (1999): 3–28.

De Vroey, Michel. "A Regulation Approach Interpretation of Contemporary Crisis." *Capital & Class* 23 (Summer 1984): 45–66.

dos Santos, Theotonio. "The Structure of Dependence." *American Economic Review* 60-2 (May 1970): 231–236.

Evans, Peter. *Dependent Development: The Alliance of Multinational, State, and Local Capital in Brazil.* Princeton, NJ: Princeton University Press, 1979.

————. "After Dependency: Recent Studies of Class, State, and Industrialization." *Latin American Research Review* 20-2 (1985): 149–160.

Foster-Carter, Aidan. "From Rostow to Gunder Frank: Conflicting Paradigms in the Analysis of Underdevelopment." *World Development* 4-3 (March 1976): 167–180.

Frank, André Gunder. *Capitalism and Underdevelopment in Latin America: Historical Studies of Chile and Brazil.* New York: Monthly Review Press, 1967.

Galtung, Johan. "A Structural Theory of Imperialism." *Journal of Peace Research* 8-2 (1971): 81–117.

Gereffi, Gary. *The Pharmaceutical Industry and Dependency in the Third World.* Princeton, NJ: Princeton University Press, 1983.

Gill, Stephen, ed. *Gramsci, Historical Materialism, and International Relations.* Cambridge, UK: Cambridge University Press, 1993.

Gramsci, Antonio. *Selections from the Prison Notebooks of Antonio Gramsci.* Edited and translated by Quintin Hoare and Geoffrey Nowell Smith. New York: International Publishers, 1971.

Hobson, J. A. *Imperialism: A Study.* Ann Arbor, MI: University of Michigan Press, 1965.

Jessop, Bob. *The Capitalist State: Marxist Theories and Methods.* Oxford, UK: Martin Robertson, 1982.

Krader, Lawrence. *The Asiatic Mode of Production: Sources, Development and Critique in the Writings of Karl Marx.* Assen, The Netherlands: Van Grocum, 1975.

Laclau, Ernesto. "Feudalism and Capitalism in Latin America." *New Left Review* 67 (May/June 1971): 19–38.

Lenin, V. I. *Imperialism: The Highest Stage of Capitalism.* Revised translation. New York: International Publishers, 1939.

Lipietz, Alain. *Towards a New Economic Order: Postfordism, Ecology and Democracy.* Translated by Malcolm Slater. New York: Oxford University Press, 1992.

Love, Joseph L. "The Origins of Dependency Analysis." *Journal of Latin American Studies* 22 (February 1990): 143–168.

Marx, Karl, and Frederick Engels. *Selected Works.* New York: International Publishers, 1968.

McGowan, Pat, and Stephen G. Walker. "Radical and Conventional Models of U.S. Foreign Economic Policy Making." *World Politics* 33-3 (April 1981): 347–382.

Miliband, Ralph. *The State in Capitalist Society.* New York: Basic Books, 1969.

O'Leary, Brendan. *The Asiatic Mode of Production: Oriental Despotism, Historical Materialism and Indian History.* Oxford, UK: Basil Blackwell, 1989.

Owen, Roger, and Bob Sutcliffe, eds. *Studies in the Theory of Imperialism.* Burnt Mill, Harlow Essex, UK: Longman, 1981.

Palma, Gabriel. "Dependency: A Formal Theory of Underdevelopment or a Methodology for the Analysis of Concrete Situations of Underdevelopment?" *World Development* 6-7/8 (July/August 1978): 881–924.

Parkin, Frank. *Marxism and Class Theory: A Bourgeois Critique.* London: Tavistock, 1979.

Prebisch, Raúl. *Towards a Dynamic Development Policy for Latin America.* New York: United Nations, 1963.

Sassoon, Anne Showstack, ed. *Approaches to Gramsci.* London, UK: Writers and Readers Publishing Cooperative Society, 1982.

Shannon, Thomas Richard. *An Introduction to the World System Perspective.* Boulder, CO: Westview Press, 2nd edition, 1996.

Skocpol, Theda. "Wallerstein's World Capitalist System: A Theoretical and Historical Critique." *American Journal of Sociology* 82-5 (March 1977): 1075–1090.

Smith, Tony. "The Underdevelopment of Development Literature: The Case of Dependency Theory." *World Politics* 31-2 (January 1979): 247–288.

Valenzuela, J. Samuel, and Arturo Valenzuela. "Modernization and Dependency: Alternative Perspectives in the Study of Latin American Development." *Comparative Politics* 10 (July 1978): 535–557.

Wallerstein, Immanuel. *The Modern World System: Capitalist Agriculture and the Origins of the European World-Economy in the Sixteenth Century.* New York: Academic Press, 1974.

———. *The Capitalist World-Economy.* New York: Cambridge University Press, 1979.

———. *The Politics of the World-Economy: The States, the Movements and the Civilizations.* London: Cambridge University Press, 1984.

Warren, Bill. *Imperialism: Pioneer of Capitalism.* London: New Left Books, 1980.

Williams, Glen. "On Determining Canada's Location Within the International Political Economy." *Studies in Political Economy* 25 (Spring 1988): 107–140.

IX. Domestic-International Interactions

Avery, William P. *World Agriculture and the GATT.* Boulder, CO: Rienner, 1993.

——. "American Agricultural and Trade Policymaking: Two-Level Bargaining in the North American Free Trade Agreement." *Policy Sciences* 29 (1996): 113–136.

Busch, Marc L., and Helen V. Milner. "The Future of the International Trading System: International Firms, Regionalism, and Domestic Politics." In *Political Economy and the Changing Global Order*, eds. Richard Stubbs and Geoffrey R. D. Underhill. Toronto, Canada: McClelland & Stewart, 1994.

Cohn, Theodore H. "The Intersection of Domestic and Foreign Policy in the NAFTA Agricultural Negotiations." *Canadian-American Public Policy no. 14.* Orono, ME: University of Maine, September 1993.

Cohn, Theodore H., and Patrick J. Smith. "Subnational Governments as International Actors: Constituent Diplomacy in the Pacific Northwest." *BC Studies* 110 (Summer 1996): 25–59.

Coleman, William D., and Grace Skogstad. *Policy Communities and Public Policy in Canada: A Structural Approach.* Mississauga, Canada: Copp Clark Pitman, 1990.

Comisso, Ellen, and Laura D'Andrea Tyson, eds. *Power, Purpose, and Collective Choice: Economic Strategy in Socialist States.* Special issue of *International Organization* 40-2 (Spring 1986).

Cox, Ronald W. *Power and Profits: U.S. Policy in Central America.* Lexington, KY: University Press of Kentucky, 1994.

Eichengreen, Barry. *The Gold Standard and the Great Depression, 1919–1939.* New York: Oxford University Press, 1992.

Evangelista, Matthew. "Domestic Structure and International Change." In *New Thinking in International Relations*, eds. Michael W. Doyle and G. John Ikenberry. Boulder, CO: Westview Press, 1997.

Evans, Peter B., Harold K. Jacobson, and Robert D. Putnam, eds. *Double-Edged Diplomacy: International Bargaining and Domestic Politics.* Berkeley, CA: University of California Press, 1993.

Friman, H. Richard. "Side-Payments versus Security Cards: Domestic Bargaining Tactics in International Economic Negotiations." *International Organization* 47-3 (Summer 1993): 387–410.

Gibbs, David N. *The Political Economy of Third World Intervention: Mines, Money, and U.S. Policy in the Congo Crisis.* Chicago, IL: University of Chicago Press, 1991.

Gourevitch, Peter. "The Second Image Reversed: The International Sources of Domestic Politics." *International Organization* 32-4 (Autumn 1978): 881–912.

——. *Politics in Hard Times: Comparative Responses to International Economic Crises.* Ithaca, NY: Cornell University Press, 1986.

——. "Squaring the Circle: The Domestic Sources of International Cooperation." *International Organization* 50-2 (Spring 1996): 349–373.

Ikenberry, G. John. "The Irony of State Strength: Comparative Responses to the Oil Shocks in the 1970s." *International Organization* 40-1 (Winter 1986): 105–137.

Ikenberry, G. John, David A. Lake, and Michael Mastanduno, eds. *The State and American Foreign Economic Policy.* Special issue of *International Organization* 42-1 (Winter 1988).

Katzenstein, Peter J. "International Relations and Domestic Structures: Foreign Economic Policies of Advanced Industrial States." *International Organization* 30-1 (Winter 1976): 1–45.

——, ed. *Between Power and Plenty: Foreign Economic Policies of Advanced Industrial States.* Special issue of *International Organization* 31-4 (Autumn 1977).

Keohane, Robert O., and Helen V. Milner, eds. *Internationalization and Domestic Politics.* Cambridge, UK: Cambridge University Press, 1996.

Kresl, Peter, Karl Kresl, and Gary Gappert. *North American Cities and the Global Economy: Challenges and Opportunities.* Thousand Oaks, CA: Sage, 1995.

Milner, Helen V. *Resisting Protectionism: Global Industries and the Politics of International Trade.* Princeton, NJ: Princeton University Press, 1988.

————. "Resisting the Protectionist Temptation: Industry and the Making of Trade Policy in France and the United States During the 1970s." *International Organization* 41-4 (Autumn 1987): 639–665.

Nowell, Gregory P. *Mercantile States and the World Oil Cartel, 1900–1939.* Ithaca, NY: Cornell University Press, 1994.

Putnam, Robert D. "Diplomacy and Domestic Politics: The Logic of Two-Level Games." *International Organization* 42 (Summer 1988): 427–460.

Risse-Kappen, Thomas, ed. *Bringing Transnational Relations Back In: Non-State Actors, Domestic Structures and International Institutions.* Cambridge, UK: Cambridge University Press, 1995.

Rogowski, Ronald. *Commerce and Coalitions: How Trade Affects Domestic Political Alignments.* Princeton, NJ: Princeton University Press, 1989.

Simmons, Beth A. *Who Adjusts? Domestic Sources of Foreign Economic Policy During the Interwar Years.* Princeton, NJ: Princeton University Press, 1994.

Stolper, Wolfgang F., and Paul A. Samuelson. "Protection and Real Wages." *Review of Economic Studies* 9-1 (November 1941): 58–73.

X. International Monetary and Financial Relations

Bird, Graham. *The International Monetary System and the Less Developed Countries.* London: Macmillan, 2nd edition, 1982.

————. "The Political Economy of the SDR: The Rise and Fall of an International Reserve Asset." *Global Governance* 4-3 (1998): 355–379.

Britton, Andrew, and David Mayes. *Achieving Monetary Union in Europe.* London: Sage, 1992.

Cerny, Philip G., ed. *Finance and World Politics: Markets, Regimes and States in the Post-hegemonic Era.* London: Elgar, 1993.

Cohen, Benjamin J. *Organizing the World's Money: The Political Economy of International Monetary Relations.* New York: Basic Books, 1977.

————, ed. *The International Political Economy of Monetary Relations.* Aldershot, UK: Elgar, 1993.

————. *The Geography of Money.* Ithaca, NY: Cornell University Press, 1998.

Cooper, Richard N. "Prolegomena to the Choice of an International Monetary System." *International Organization* 29-1 (Winter 1975): 63–97.

Dam, Kenneth W. *The Rules of the Game: Reform and Evolution in the International Monetary System.* Chicago, IL: University of Chicago Press, 1982.

De Grauwe, Paul. *The Economics of Monetary Union.* Oxford, UK: Oxford University Press, 2nd edition, 1994.

Dell, Sidney. "On Being Grandmotherly: The Evolution of IMF Conditionality." *Essays in International Finance no. 144.* Princeton, NJ: Princeton University, October 1981.

Eichengreen, Barry. *International Monetary Arrangements for the 21st Century.* Washington, DC: Brookings Institution, 1994.

————. *Toward a New International Financial Architecture: A Practical Post-Asia Agenda.* Washington, DC: Institute for International Economics, February 1999.

Eichengreen, Barry, and Jeffry Frieden, eds. *The Political Economy of European Monetary Unification.* Boulder, CO: Westview Press, 1994.

Eijffinger, Sylvester C.W., and Jakob de Haan. *European Monetary and Fiscal Policy.* Oxford, UK: Oxford University Press, 2000.

Feldstein, Martin. "Refocusing the IMF." *Foreign Affairs* 77-2 (March/April 1998): 20–33.

Ferguson, Tyrone. *The Third World and Decision Making in the International Monetary Fund: The Quest for Full and Effective Participation.* London: Pinter, 1988.

Frankel, Jeffrey A., and Shang-Jun Wei. "Is a Yen Bloc Emerging?" in Symposium on "Economic Cooperation and Challenges in the Pacific." *Joint U.S.-Korea Academic Studies* 5 (1995): 145–175.

Fratianni, Michele, and Jürgen von Hagen. *The European Monetary System and European Monetary Union.* Boulder, CO: Westview Press, 1992.

Gardner, Richard N. *Sterling-Dollar Diplomacy in Current Perspective: The Origins and Prospects of Our International Economic Order.* New York: Columbia University Press, expanded edition, 1980.

Gold, Joseph. *Membership and Nonmembership in the International Monetary Fund: A Study in International Law and Organization.* Washington, DC: International Monetary Fund, 1974.

Gowa, Joanne. *Closing of the Gold Window: Domestic Politics and the End of Bretton Woods.* Ithaca, NY: Cornell University Press, 1983.

Hamouda, Omar F., Robin Rowley, and Bernard M. Wolf, eds. *The Future of the International Monetary System: Change, Coordination or Instability?* Aldershot, UK: Elgar, 1989.

Helleiner, Eric. *States and the Reemergence of Global Finance: From Bretton Woods to the 1990s.* Ithaca, NY: Cornell University Press, 1994.

Horsefield, Keith J. *The International Monetary Fund, 1945–65: Twenty Years of Monetary Cooperation. Vols. I–III.* Washington, DC: International Monetary Fund, 1969.

James, Harold. *International Monetary Cooperation Since Bretton Woods.* Washington, DC: International Monetary Fund, 1996.

Kapstein, Ethan B. *Governing the Global Economy: International Finance and the State.* Cambridge, MA: Harvard University Press, 1994.

Lavigne, Marie. "Eastern European Countries and the IMF." In *East-West Economic Relations in the Changing Global Environment,* eds. Béla Csikós-Nagy and David G. Young, 298–311. London: Macmillan, 1986.

Levitt, Malcolm, and Christopher Lord. *The Political Economy of Monetary Union.* London: Macmillan, 2000.

McKinnon, Ronald I. "The Rules of the Game: International Money in Historical Perspective." *Journal of Economic Literature* 31-1 (March 1993): 1–44.

Mundell, Robert A. "A Theory of Optimum Currency Areas." *American Economic Review* 51-4 (September 1961): 657–665.

Odell, John S. *U.S. International Monetary Policy: Markets, Power, and Ideas as Sources of Change.* Princeton, NJ: Princeton University Press, 1982.

Plumptre, A. F. W. *Three Decades of Decision: Canada and the World Monetary System, 1944–75.* Toronto, Canada: McClelland & Stewart, 1977.

Schweitzer, Pierre-Paul. "Political Aspects of Managing the International Monetary System." *International Affairs* 52-2 (April 1976): 208–218.

Sharma, Shalenda D. "Constructing the New International Financial Architecture: What Role for the IMF?" *Journal of World Trade* 34-3 (2000): 47–70.

Solomon, Robert. *The International Monetary System, 1945–1981.* New York: Harper & Row, 2nd edition, 1982.

Strange, Susan. *Sterling and British Policy: A Political Study of an International Currency in Decline.* London: Oxford University Press, 1971.

———. *Casino Capitalism.* Oxford, UK: Basil Blackwell, 1986.

Triffin, Robert. *Gold and the Dollar Crisis: The Future of Convertibility.* New Haven, CT: Yale University Press, revised edition, 1961.

Webb, Michael C. *The Political Economy of Policy Coordination: International Adjustment Since 1945.* Ithaca, NY: Cornell University Press, 1995.

Williamson, John. *The Failure of World Monetary Reform, 1971–74.* Sunbury-on-Thames, UK: Nelson, 1977.

———. *The Exchange Rate System.* Washington, DC: Institute for International Economics, revised edition, June 1985.

XI. Foreign Debt

Biersteker, Thomas J., ed. *Dealing with Debt: International Financial Negotiations and Adjustment Bargaining.* Boulder, CO: Westview Press, 1993.

Bouchet, Michel Henri. *The Political Economy of International Debt.* New York: Quorum Books, 1987.

Busumtwi-Sam, James. "The Role of the IMF and the World Bank in International Development." In *United Nations Reform,* eds. Hanna Newcombe and Eric Fawcett, 248–266. Toronto, Canada: Dundurn Press, 1995.

Cline, William R. *International Debt and the Stability of the World Economy.* Policy Analyses in International Economics 4. Washington, DC: Institute for International Economics, 1983.

———. *International Debt Reexamined.* Washington, DC: Institute for International Economics, 1995.

Cohen, Benjamin J. "Balance-of-Payments Financing: Evolution of a Regime." In *International Regimes,* ed. Stephen D. Krasner, 315–336. Ithaca, NY: Cornell University Press, 1983.

Corbridge, Stuart. *Debt and Development.* Oxford, UK: Blackwell Publishers, 1993.

D'Andrea Tyson, Laura. "The Debt Crisis and Adjustment Responses in Eastern Europe: A Comparative Perspective." *International Organization* 40-2 (Spring 1986): 239–285.

Eichengreen, Barry, and Peter H. Lindert, eds. *The International Debt Crisis in Historical Perspective.* Cambridge, MA: MIT Press, 1989.

Elson, Diane. "How Is Structural Adjustment Affecting Women?" *Development* (1989-1): 67–74.

———. "From Survival Strategies to Transformation Strategies: Women's Needs and Structural Adjustment." In *Unequal Burden: Crises, Persistent Poverty, and Women's Work,* eds. Lourdes Beneria and Shelley Feldman, 26–48. Boulder, CO: Westview Press, 1992.

Feinberg, Richard E., and Ricardo Ffrench-Davis, eds., *Development and External Debt in Latin America: Bases for a New Consensus.* Notre Dame, IN: University of Notre Dame Press, 1988.

Feinberg, Richard E., and Valeriana Kallab, eds. *Adjustment Crisis in the Third World.* New Brunswick, NJ: Transaction Books, 1984.

Fishlow, Albert. "Lessons from the Past: Capital Markets During the Nineteenth Century and the Interwar Period." *International Organization* 39-3 (Summer 1985): 383–439.

Frieden, Jeff. "Third World Indebted Industrialization: International Finance and State Capitalism in Mexico, Brazil, Algeria, and South Korea." *International Organization* 35-3 (Summer 1981): 407–431.

Honeywell, Martin, ed. *The Poverty Brokers: The IMF and Latin America.* London: Latin America Bureau, 1983.

Husain, Ishrat, and Ishac Diwan, eds. *Dealing with the Debt Crisis: A World Bank Symposium.* Washington, DC: World Bank, 1989.

Kahler, Miles. "Politics and International Debt: Explaining the Crisis." *International Organization* 39-3 (Summer 1985): 357–382.

———, ed. *The Politics of International Debt.* Ithaca, NY: Cornell University Press, 1986.

Körner, Peter, Gero Maass, Thomas Siebold, and Ranier Tetzlaff. *The IMF and the Debt Crisis: A Guide to the Third World's Dilemma.* Translated by Paul Knight. London: Zed Books, 1986.

Krugman, Paul. "LDC Debt Policy." In *American Economic Policy in the 1980s*, ed. Martin Feldstein, 691–739. Chicago, IL: University of Chicago Press, 1994.

Kuhn, Michael G., with Jorge P. Guzman. *Multilateral Official Debt Rescheduling: Recent Experience, World Economic and Financial Surveys*. Washington, DC: International Monetary Fund, November 1990.

Lipson, Charles. "The International Organization of Third World Debt." *International Organization* 35-4 (Autumn 1981): 603–631.

———. "Bankers' Dilemmas: Private Cooperation in Rescheduling Sovereign Debts." In *Cooperation Under Anarchy*, ed. Kenneth A. Oye, 200–225. Princeton, NJ: Princeton University Press, 1986.

Pastor, Robert A., ed. *Latin America's Debt Crisis: Adjusting to the Past or Planning for the Future?* Boulder, CO: Rienner, 1987.

Payer, Cheryl. *The Debt Trap: The IMF and the Third World*. Middlesex, UK: Penguin, 1974.

———. *Lent and Lost: Foreign Credit and Third World Development*. London: Zed Books, 1991.

Rieffel, Alexis. "The Paris Club, 1978–1983." *Columbia Journal of Transnational Law* 23-1 (1984): 63–110.

———. "The Role of the Paris Club in Managing Debt Problems." No. 161, *Essays in International Finance*. Princeton, NJ: Princeton University, December 1985.

Sachs, Jeffrey. "External Debt and Macroeconomic Performance in Latin America and East Asia." In *Brookings Papers on Economic Activity 2*, eds. William C. Brainard and George L. Perry, 523–574. Washington, DC: Brookings Institution, 1985.

———, ed. *Developing Country Debt and Economic Performance, Vol. 1: The International Financial System*. Chicago, IL: University of Chicago Press, 1989.

———. "Making the Brady Plan Work." *Foreign Affairs* 68-3 (Summer 1989): 87–104.

Smith, Gordon W., and John T. Cuddington, eds. *International Debt and the Developing Countries: A World Bank Symposium*. Washington, DC: World Bank, 1985.

Stallings, Barbara. *Banker to the Third World: U.S. Portfolio Investment in Latin America, 1900–1986*. Berkeley, CA: University of California Press, 1987.

XII. Global Trade Relations

Aggarwal, V. K. *Liberal Protectionism: The International Politics of Organized Textile Trade*. Berkeley, CA: University of California Press, 1985.

Bhagwati, Jagdish. *The World Trading System at Risk*. New York: Harvester Wheatsheaf, 1991.

Brown, William Adams, Jr. *The United States and the Restoration of World Trade: An Analysis and Appraisal of the ITO Charter and the General Agreement on Tariffs and Trade*. Washington, DC: Brookings Institution, 1950.

Cameron, James, and Karen Campbell, eds. *Dispute Resolution in the World Trade Organisation*. London: Cameron, 1998.

Cline, William R., ed. *Trade Policy in the 1980s*. Washington, DC: Institute for International Economics, 1983.

Cohn, Theodore H. *The International Politics of Agricultural Trade: Canadian-American Relations in a Global Agricultural Context*. Vancouver, Canada: University of British Columbia Press, 1990.

Conybeare, John A. C. *Trade Wars: The Theory and Practice of International Commercial Rivalry*. New York: Columbia University Press, 1987.

Cortney, Philip. *The Economic Munich: The I.T.O. Charter, Inflation or Liberty, The 1929 Lesson*. New York: Philosophical Library, 1949.

Croome, John. *Reshaping the World Trading System: A History of the Uruguay Round*. Geneva, Switzerland: World Trade Organization, 1995.

Curzon, Gerard. *Multilateral Commercial Diplomacy: The General Agreement on Tariffs and Trade and Its Impact on National Commercial Policies and Techniques.* London: Michael Joseph, 1965.

Dam, Kenneth W. *The GATT: Law and International Economic Organization.* Chicago, IL: University of Chicago Press, 1970.

Destler, I. M. *American Trade Politics.* Washington, DC: Institute for International Economics and The Twentieth Century Fund, 2nd edition, June 1992.

Diebold, William, Jr. *The End of the I.T.O. Essays in International Finance.* No. 16. Princeton, NJ: International Finance Section, Department of Economics and Social Institutions, Princeton University, October 1952.

Dunoff, Jeffrey L. "Institutional Misfits: The GATT, the ICJ and Trade-Environment Disputes." *Michigan Journal of International Law* 15-4 (Summer 1994): 1043–1128.

Evans, John W. *The Kennedy Round in American Trade Policy: The Twilight of the GATT?* Cambridge, MA: Harvard University Press, 1971.

Finlayson, Jock A., and Mark W. Zacher. "The GATT and the Regulation of Trade Barriers: Regime Dynamics and Functions." In *International Regimes,* ed. Stephen D. Krasner, 273–314. Ithaca, NY: Cornell University Press, 1983.

———. *Managing International Markets: Developing Countries and the Commodity Trade Regime.* New York: Columbia University Press, 1988.

Goldman, Patti A. "Resolving the Trade and Environment Debate: In Search of a Neutral Forum and Neutral Principles." *Washington and Lee Law Review* 49-4 (Fall 1992): 1279–1298.

Greenaway, David, Robert C. Hine, Anthony P. O'Brien, and Robert J. Thornton, eds. *Global Protectionism.* London: Macmillan, 1991.

Griesgraber, Jo Marie, and Bernhard G. Gunter, eds. *World Trade: Toward Fair and Free Trade in the Twenty-first Century.* London: Pluto Press, 1997.

Haus, Leah A. *Globalizing the GATT: The Soviet Union's Successor States, Eastern Europe, and the International Trading System.* Washington, DC: Brookings Institution, 1992.

Higgott, Richard A., and Andrew Fenton Cooper. "Middle Power Leadership and Coalition Building: Australia, the Cairns Group, and the Uruguay Round of Trade Negotiations." *International Organization* 44-4 (Autumn 1990): 589–632.

Hirschman, Albert O. *National Power and the Structure of Foreign Trade.* Berkeley, CA: University of California Press, 1945.

Hoekman, Bernard M., and Michel M. Kostecki. *The Political Economy of the World Trading System: From GATT to WTO.* Oxford, UK: Oxford University Press, 1995.

Hudec, Robert E. *The GATT Legal System and World Trade Diplomacy.* New York: Praeger, 1975.

———. *Developing Countries in the GATT Legal System.* Thames Essay no. 50. Aldershot, UK: Gower, for the Trade Policy Research Institute, 1987.

———. *Enforcing International Trade Law: The Evolution of the Modern GATT Legal System.* Salem, NH: Butterworth Legal Publishers, 1993.

Jackson, John H. *World Trade and the Law of GATT.* Indianapolis, IN: Bobbs-Merrill, 1969.

———. "World Trade Rules and Environmental Policies: Congruence or Conflict?" *Washington and Lee Law Review* 49-4 (Fall 1992): 1227–1278.

———. *The World Trading System: Law and Policy of International Economic Relations.* Cambridge, MA: MIT Press, 2nd edition, 1997.

Kock, Karin. *International Trade Policy and the GATT, 1947–1967.* Stockholm, Switzerland: Almqvist & Wiksell, 1969.

Kostecki, M. M. *East-West Trade and the GATT System.* London: Macmillan, for the Trade Policy Research Centre, 1979.

Krasner, Stephen D. "State Power and the Structure of International Trade." *World Politics* 28 (April 1976): 317–347.

Krueger, Anne O. *Trade Policies and Developing Nations.* Washington, DC: Brookings Institution, 1995.

———, ed. *The WTO as an International Organization.* Chicago, IL: University of Chicago Press, 1998.

Lake, David A., *Power, Protection, and Free Trade: International Sources of U.S. Commercial Strategy, 1887–1939.* Ithaca, NY: Cornell University Press, 1988.

Long, Olivier. *Law and Its Limitations in the GATT Multilateral Trade System.* Dordrecht, The Netherlands: Nijhoff, 1985.

Mason, Edward S., and Robert E. Asher. *The World Bank Since Bretton Woods.* Washington, DC: Brookings Institution, 1973.

McGovern, Edmond. *International Trade Regulation: GATT, The United States and the European Community.* Exeter, UK: Globefield Press, 1982.

Odell, John S., and Thomas D. Willett. *International Trade Policies: Gains from Exchange Between Economics and Political Science.* Ann Arbor, MI: University of Michigan Press, 1990.

Organisation for Economic Co-operation and Development. *Integration of Developing Countries into the International Trading System.* Paris: OECD, 1992.

Preeg, Ernest. *Traders and Diplomats: An Analysis of the Kennedy Round of Negotiations Under the General Agreement on Tariffs and Trade.* Washington, DC: Brookings Institution, 1970.

———. *Traders in a Brave New World: The Uruguay Round and the Future of the International Trading System.* Chicago, IL: University of Chicago Press, 1995.

Raghavan, Chakravarthi. *Recolonization: GATT, the Uruguay Round and The Third World.* London: Zed Books, 1990.

Runge, C. Ford, with François Ortalo-Magné and Philip Vande Kamp. *Freer Trade, Protected Environment: Balancing Trade Liberalization and Environmental Interests.* New York: Council on Foreign Relations Press, 1994.

Schattschneider, E. E. *Politics, Pressures and the Tariff: A Study of Free Private Enterprise in Pressure Politics, as Shown in the 1929–1939 Revision of the Tariff.* Hamden, CT: Archon Books, 1963, unaltered from the 1935 edition.

Scherer, F. M., and Richard S. Belous. *Unfinished Tasks: The New International Trade Theory and the Post-Uruguay Round Challenges.* Issues Paper no. 3. Washington, DC: British–North American Committee, May 1994.

Schott, Jeffrey J., assisted by Johanna W. Buurman. *The Uruguay Round: An Assessment.* Washington, DC: Institute for International Economics, November 1994.

———, ed. *The WTO after Seattle.* Washington, DC: Institute for International Economics, July 2000.

Stegemann, Klaus. "Policy Rivalry Among Industrial States: What Can We Learn from Models of Strategic Trade Policy?" *International Organization* 43-1 (Winter 1989): 73–100.

Thomas, Jeffrey S., and Michael A. Meyer. *The New Rules of Global Trade: A Guide to the World Trade Organization.* Toronto, Canada: Carswell, 1997.

Tyson, Laura D'Andrea. *Who's Bashing Whom? Trade Conflict in High-Technology Industries.* Washington, DC: Institute for International Economics, November 1992.

Viner, Jacob. *Studies in the Theory of International Trade.* New York: Augustus M. Kelly, Reprint of Economic Classics, 1965.

Whalley, John, ed. *Developing Countries and the Global Trading System,* vol. 1. Ann Arbor, MI: University of Michigan Press, 1989.

Whalley, John, and Colleen Hamilton. *The Trading System After the Uruguay Round.* Washington, DC: Institute for International Economics, July 1996.

Wilcox, Clair. *A Charter for World Trade.* New York: Macmillan, 1949.

Winham, Gilbert. *International Trade and the Tokyo Round Negotiations.* Princeton, NJ: Princeton University Press, 1986.

————. *The Evolution of International Trade Agreements.* Toronto, Canada: University of Toronto Press, 1992.

Wolfe, Robert. "Global Trade as a Single Undertaking: The Role of Ministers in the WTO." *International Journal* 51-4 (Autumn 1996): 690–709.

————. *Farm Wars: The Political Economy of Agriculture and the International Trade Regime.* London: Macmillan, 1998.

XIII. Regionalism and Globalism

Abbey, Michael H., and Nicholas Bromfield. "A Practitioner's Guide to the Maastricht Treaty." *Michigan Journal of International Law* 15-4 (Summer 1994): 1329–1357.

Anderson, Kym, and Richard Blackhurst, eds. *Regional Integration and the Global Trading System.* Hertfordshire, UK: Harvester Wheatsheaf, 1993.

Appleton, Barry. *Navigating NAFTA.* Scarborough, Canada: Carswell, 1994.

Balassa, Bela. *The Theory of Economic Integration.* London: Allen and Unwin, 1962.

Cable, Vincent, and David Henderson, eds. *Trade Blocs? The Future of Regional Integration.* London: Royal Institute of International Affairs, 1994.

Cameron, Duncan, and Mel Watkins, eds. *Canada Under Free Trade.* Toronto, Canada: Lorimer, 1993.

Cohn, Theodore H. "Emerging Issues in Canada-U.S. Agricultural Trade Under the GATT and FTA." *Canadian-American Public Policy no. 10.* Orono, ME: University of Maine, Canadian-American Center, June 1992.

————. "NAFTA, GATT and Canadian-U.S. Agricultural Trade Relations." *The North-South Agenda Papers 10.* Coral Gables, FL: North-South Center, University of Miami, November 1994.

Diebold, William, Jr., ed. *Bilateralism, Multilateralism and Canada in U.S. Trade Policy.* Cambridge, MA: Ballinger, 1988.

Dinan, Desmond. *Ever Closer Union? An Introduction to the European Community.* Boulder, CO: Rienner, 1994.

Doern, G. Bruce, and Brian W. Tomlin. *Faith and Fear: The Free Trade Story.* Toronto, Canada: Stoddart, 1991.

Dosch, Jörn, and Manfred Mols, eds. *International Relations in the Asia-Pacific: New Patterns of Power, Interest, and Cooperation.* New York: St. Martin's Press, 2000.

Edwards, Sebastian. "Latin American Economic Integration: A New Perspective on an Old Dream." *The World Economy* 16-3 (May 1993): 317–324.

Fawcett, Louise, and Andrew Hurrell. *Regionalism in World Politics: Regional Organization and International Order.* New York: Oxford University Press, 1995.

Fischer, Thomas C. *The United States, the European Union, and the "Globalization" of World Trade.* Westport, CT: Quorum Books, 2000.

Gamble, Andrew, and Anthony Payne, eds. *Regionalism and World Order.* London: Macmillan, 1996.

George, Stephen, and Ian Bache. *Politics in the European Union.* Oxford, UK: Oxford University Press, 2001.

Ghosh, B. N. *Dependency Theory Revisited.* Aldershot, UK: Ashgate, 2001.

Gibb, Richard, and Wieslaw Michalak, eds. *Continental Trading Blocs: The Growth of Regionalism in the World Economy.* Chichester, UK: Wiley, 1994.

Globerman, Steven, and Michael Walker, eds. *Assessing NAFTA: A Trinational Assessment.* Vancouver, Canada: Fraser Institute, 1993.

Grilli, Enzo R. *The European Community and the Developing Countries.* Cambridge, UK: Cambridge University Press, 1993.

Grinspun, Ricardo, and Maxwell A. Cameron, eds.. *The Political Economy of North American Free Trade*. Montreal, Canada: McGill-Queen's University Press, 1993.

Haas, Ernst B. *The Obsolescence of Regional Integration Theory*. Berkeley, CA: University of California, Institute of International Studies, Research Series no. 25, 1975.

Hart, Michael, with Bill Dymond and Colin Robertson. *Decision at Midnight: Inside the Canada-US Free-Trade Negotiations*. Vancouver, Canada: University of British Columbia Press, 1994.

Hatch, Walter, and Kozo Yamamura. *Asia in Japan's Embrace: Building a Regional Production Alliance*. Cambridge, UK: Cambridge University Press, 1996.

Higgott, Richard, Richard Leaver, and John Ravenhill, eds. *Pacific Economic Relations in the 1990s: Cooperation or Conflict?* Boulder, CO: Rienner, 1993.

Hufbauer, Gary Clyde, and Jeffrey J. Schott. *NAFTA: An Assessment*. Washington, DC: Institute for International Economics, revised edition, October 1993.

———. *Western Hemisphere Economic Integration*. Washington, DC: Institute for International Economics, July 1994.

Johnson, Jon R. *The North American Free Trade Agreement: A Comprehensive Guide*. Aurora, Canada: Canada Law Book, 1994.

Jovanovic, Miroslav N. *International Economic Integration*. London: Routledge, 1992.

Kahler, Miles. *Regional Futures and Transatlantic Economic Relations*. New York: Council on Foreign Relations, 1995.

Kaser, Michael. *Comecon: Integration Problems of the Planned Economies*. London: Oxford University Press, 1965.

Keohane, Robert O., and Stanley Hoffmann. *The New European Community: Decisionmaking and Institutional Change*. Boulder, CO: Westview Press, 1991.

Kirschner, Heinrich. "The Framework of the European Union Under the Treaty of Maastricht." *Journal of Law and Commerce* 13-2 (Spring 1994): 233–245.

Lawrence, Robert Z. *Regionalism, Multilateralism and Deeper Integration*. Washington, DC: Brookings Institution, 1996.

Lipsey, R. G., and Kelvin Lancaster. "The General Theory of Second Best." *The Review of Economic Studies* 24-1 (1956–57): 11–32.

Lister, Marjorie. *The European Community and the Developing World: The Role of the Lomé Convention*. Aldershot, UK: Avebury, 1988.

Ludlow, Peter. "The Maastricht Treaty and the Future of Europe." *Washington Quarterly* (Autumn 1992): 119–137.

Machlup, F. *A History of Thought on Economic Integration*. London: Macmillan, 1977.

Melo, Jaime de, and Arvind Panagariya, eds. *New Dimensions in Regional Integration*. Cambridge, UK: Cambridge University Press, 1993.

Mendoza, Miguel Rodriguez, Patrick Low, and Barbara Kotschwar, eds. *Trade Rules in the Making: Challenges in Regional and Multilateral Negotiations*. Washington, DC: Brookings Institution, 1999.

Nader, Ralph. *The Case Against 'Free Trade': GATT, NAFTA, and the Globalization of Corporate Power*. San Francisco, CA: Earth Island Press, 1993.

Patterson, Gardner. *Discrimination in International Trade. The Policy Issues: 1945–1965*. Princeton, NJ: Princeton University Press, 1966.

Robson, Peter. *The Economics of International Integration*. London, UK: Allen and Unwin, 3rd edition, 1987.

Roett, Riordan, ed. *Mercosur: Regional Integration. World Markets*. Boulder, CO: Rienner, 1999.

Rupert, Mark E. "(Re) Politicizing the Global Economy: Liberal Common Sense and Ideological Struggle in the US NAFTA Debate." *Review of International Political Economy* 2-4 (Autumn 1995): 658–692.

Salazar-Xirinachs, José Manuel, and Maryse Robert, eds. *Toward Free Trade in the Americas*. Washington, DC: Brookings Institution, 2001.

Schott, Jeffrey J., ed. *Free Trade Areas and U.S. Trade Policy.* Washington, DC: Institute for International Economics, 1989.

Smith, Murray G., with C. Michael Aho and Gary N. Horlick. *Bridging the Gap: Trade Laws in the Canadian-U.S. Negotiations.* Toronto, Canada: Canadian-American Committee, 1987.

Stairs, Dennis, and Gilbert R. Winham, eds. *The Politics of Canada's Economic Relationship with the United States,* vol. 29, Royal Commission on the Economic Union and Development Prospect for Canada. Toronto, Canada: University of Toronto Press, 1985.

Steger, Debra P. *A Concise Guide to the Canada–United States Free Trade Agreement.* Toronto, Canada: Carswell, 1988.

Stone, Frank. *The Canada–United States Free Trade Agreement and the GATT.* Ottawa, Canada: Institute for Research for Public Policy, November 1988.

Viner, Jacob. *The Customs Union Issue.* New York: Carnegie Endowment for International Peace, 1950.

Wilcox, Clair. *A Charter for World Trade.* New York: Macmillan, 1949.

Wise, Carol, ed. *The Post-NAFTA Political Economy: Mexico and the Western Hemisphere.* University Park, PA: Pennsylvania State University Press, 1998.

Wise, Mark, and Richard Gibb. *Single Market to Social Europe: The European Community in the 1990s.* Essex, UK: Longman, 1993.

World Trade Organization. *Regionalism and the World Trading System.* Geneva, Switzerland: World Trade Organization, April 1995.

XIV. Multinational Corporations and Global Production

Barnet, Richard J., and Ronald E. Müller. *Global Reach: The Power of the Multinational Corporations.* New York: Simon & Schuster, 1974.

Behrman, Jack N., and Robert E. Grosse. *International Business and Governments: Issues and Institutions.* Columbia, NY: University of South Carolina Press, 1990.

Bergsten, C. Fred, and Marcus Noland. *Reconcilable Differences? United States–Japan Economic Conflict.* Washington, DC: Institute for International Economics, 1993.

Buckley, Peter J., and Mark C. Casson. *The Future of the Multinational Enterprise.* London: Macmillan, 2nd edition, 1991.

Casson, Mark, ed. *The Growth of International Business.* London: Allen and Unwin, 1983.

Caves, Richard E. *Multinational Enterprise and Economic Analysis.* Cambridge, UK: Cambridge University Press, 2nd edition, 1996.

Cutler, A. Claire. "Public Meets Private: The International Harmonization and Unification of Private International Law." *Global Society* 13-1 (January 1999): 25–48.

Dunning, John H. *Multinational Enterprises and the Global Economy.* Wokingham, UK: Addison-Wesley, 1993.

———, ed. *Globalization, Trade and Foreign Direct Investment.* Amsterdam, The Netherlands: Elsevier, 1998.

Eden, Lorraine. *Taxing Multinationals.* Toronto, Canada: University of Toronto, 1997.

Eden, Lorraine, and Evan H. Potter, eds. *Multinationals in the Global Political Economy.* New York: St. Martin's Press, 1993.

Encarnation, Dennis S. *Rivals Beyond Trade: America versus Japan in Global Competition.* Ithaca, NY: Cornell University Press, 1992.

Enderwick, Peter. *Multinational Business and Labour.* London: Croom Helm, 1985.

Froot, Kenneth, ed. *Foreign Direct Investment.* Chicago, IL: University of Chicago Press, 1993.

Gilpin, Robert. *U.S. Power and the Multinational Corporation: The Political Economy of Foreign Direct Investment.* New York: Basic Books, 1975.

Graham, Edward M. *Global Corporations and National Governments.* Washington, DC: Institute for International Economics, May 1996.

Graham, Edward M., and Paul R. Krugman. *Foreign Direct Investment in the United States.* Washington, DC: Institute for International Economics, 3rd edition, January 1995.

Hennart, Jean-Francois. "The Transaction Cost Theory of the Multinational Enterprise." In *The Nature of the Transnational Firm*, eds. Christos N. Pitelis and Roger Sugden, pp. 143–151. London: Routledge, 1991.

Hertner, Peter, and Geoffrey Jones. *Multinationals: Theory and History.* Aldershot, UK: Gower, 1986.

Hymer, Stephen Herbert. *The International Operations of National Firms: A Study of Direct Foreign Investment.* Cambridge, MA: MIT Press, 1976.

Ietto-Gillies, Grazia. *International Production: Trends, Theories, Effects.* Cambridge, MA: Polity Press, 1992.

Jenkins, Barbara. *The Paradox of Continental Production: National Investment Policies in North America.* Ithaca, NY: Cornell University Press, 1992.

Jones, Geoffrey. *The Evolution of International Business: An Introduction.* London: Routledge, 1996.

Julius, De Anne. *Foreign Investment: The Neglected Twin of Trade.* Occasional Papers no. 33. Washington, DC: Group of Thirty, 1991.

Kindleberger, Charles P. *American Business Abroad: Six Lectures on Direct Investment.* New Haven, CT: Yale University Press, 1969.

Kindleberger, Charles P., and David B. Audretsch, eds. *The Multinational Corporation in the 1980s.* Cambridge, MA: MIT Press, 1983.

Kojima, Kiyoshi. *Direct Foreign Investment: A Japanese Model of Multinational Business Operations.* London: Croom Helm, 1978.

Krugman, Paul. "Competitiveness: A Dangerous Obsession." *Foreign Affairs* (March/April 1994): 28–44.

———. "Competitiveness: Does It Matter?" *Fortune* (March 7, 1994): 109–115.

Mason, Mark. *American Multinationals and Japan: The Political Economy of Japanese Capital Controls, 1899–1980.* Cambridge, MA: Council on East Asian Studies, Harvard University, 1992.

Mason, Mark, and Dennis Encarnation, eds. *Does Ownership Matter? Japanese Multinationals in Europe.* Oxford, UK: Clarendon Press, 1994.

Modelski, George, ed. *Transnational Corporations and World Order: Readings in International Political Economy.* San Francisco, CA: Freeman, 1979.

Moran, Theodore H., ed. *Multinational Corporations: The Political Economy of Foreign Direct Investment.* Lexington, MA: Heath, 1985.

Muchlinski, Peter. *Multinational Enterprises and the Law.* Oxford, UK: Blackwell, 1995.

Ohmae, Kenichi. *The Borderless World: Power and Strategy in the Interlinked Economy.* New York: HarperPerennial, 1991.

Pauly, Louis W., and Simon Reich. "National Structures and Multinational Corporate Behavior: Enduring Differences in the Age of Globalization." *International Organization* 51-1 (Winter 1997): 1–30.

Pitelis, Christos N., and Roger Sugden, eds. *The Nature of the Transnational Firm.* London: Routledge, 1991.

Porter, Michael E. *The Competitive Advantage of Nations.* New York: Free Press, 1990.

Reich, Robert B. *The Work of Nations: Preparing Ourselves for Twenty-first Century Capitalism.* New York: Vintage Books, 1991.

Robinson, John. *Multinationals and Political Control.* New York: St. Martin's Press, 1983.

Rugman, Alan M., and Lorraine Eden, eds. *Multinationals and Transfer Pricing.* London: Croom Helm, 1985.

Sauvé, Pierre, and Daniel Schwanen. *Investment Rules for the Global Economy: Enhancing Access to Markets.* Policy Study 28. Toronto, Canada: Howe Institute, 1996.

Servan-Schreiber, J. J. *The American Challenge.* Translated by Ronald Steel. New York: Atheneum, 1979.

Smythe, Elizabeth. "The Multilateral Agreement on Investment: A Charter of Rights for Global Investors or Just Another Agreement." In *Canada Among Nations—1998: Leadership and Dialogue.*, eds. Fen Osler Hampson and Maureen Appel Molot, 239–277. Toronto, Canada: Oxford University Press, 1998.

Stopford, John M., and Susan Strange, with John S. Henley. *Rival States, Rival Firms: Competition for World Market Shares.* Cambridge, UK: Cambridge University Press, 1991.

Teichova, Alica, Maurice Lévy-Leboyer, and Helga Nussbaum. *Multinational Enterprise in Historical Perspective.* Cambridge, UK: Cambridge University Press, 1986.

Trinational Institute on Innovation, Competitiveness and Sustainability. Papers presented at Whistler, Canada, August 14–21, 1994. Vancouver, Canada: Simon Fraser University, Harbour Centre, 1994.

Tyson, Laura D'Andrea. *Who's Bashing Whom? Trade Conflict in High-Technology Industries.* Washington, DC: Institute for International Economics, November 1992.

Vernon, Raymond. *Sovereignty at Bay: The Multinational Spread of U.S. Enterprises.* New York: Basic Books, 1971.

Waldmann, Raymond J. *Regulating International Business through Codes of Conduct.* Washington, DC: American Enterprise Institute for Public Policy Research, 1980.

XV. International Development

Afshar, Haleh, and Carolyne Dennis, eds. *Women and Adjustment Policies in the Third World.* New York: St. Martin's Press, 1992.

Amsden, Alice H. "Why Isn't the Whole World Experimenting with the East Asian Model to Develop? Review of the East Asian Miracle." *World Development* 22-4 (1994): 627–633.

Ayres, Robert L. *Banking on the Poor: The World Bank and World Poverty.* Cambridge, MA: MIT Press, 1983.

Balassa, Bela, ed. *The Newly Industrializing Countries in the World Economy.* New York: Pergamon Press, 1981.

Baldwin, David A. "The International Bank in Political Perspective." *World Politics* 18-1 (October 1965): 68–81.

Bauer, P. T. *Reality and Rhetoric: Studies in the Economics of Development.* London: Weidenfeld and Nicolson, 1984.

Bello, Walden. "East Asia: On the Eve of the Great Transformation?" *Review of International Political Economy* 5-3 (Autumn 1998): 424–444.

Bello, Walden, and Stephanie Rosenfeld. *Dragons in Distress: Asia's Miracle Economies in Crisis.* San Francisco, CA: Institute for Food and Development Policy, 1990.

Benería, Lourdes, and Shelley Feldman. *Unequal Burden: Economic Crises, Persistent Poverty, and Women's Work.* Boulder, CO: Westview Press, 1992.

Bhagwati, Jagdish N., and John Gerard Ruggie. *Power, Passions, and Purpose: Prospects for North-South Negotiations.* Cambridge, MA: MIT Press, 1984.

Chilcote, Ronald H., and Dale L. Johnson, eds. *Theories of Development: Mode of Production or Dependency?* Beverly Hills, CA: Sage, 1983.

Cohn, Theodore H. "Politics in the World Bank Group: The Question of Loans to the Asian Giants." *International Organization* 28-3 (Summer 1974): 561–571.

———. "Developing Countries in the International Civil Service: The Case of the World Bank Group." *International Review of Administrative Sciences* 41-1 (1975): 47–56.

———. *Canadian Food Aid: Domestic and Foreign Policy Implications.* Denver, CO: Graduate School of International Studies, 1979.

Cornia, Giovannia Andrea, Richard Jolly, and Frances Stewart, eds. *Adjustment with a Human Face. Vol. 1: Protecting the Vulnerable and Promoting Growth.* Oxford, UK: Clarendon Press, 1987.

Culpeper, Roy. *The Multilateral Development Banks. Vol. 5: Titans or Behemoths?* Boulder, CO: Rienner, 1997.

Culpeper, Roy, Albert Berry, and Frances Stewart, eds. *Global Development Fifty Years After Bretton Woods.* New York: St. Martin's Press, 1997.

Dorraj, Manochehr, ed. *The Changing Political Economy of the Third World.* Boulder, CO: Rienner, 1995.

Elson, Diane, ed. *Male Bias in the Development Process.* Manchester, UK: Manchester University Press, 1991.

English, E. Philip, and Harris M. Mule. *The Multilateral Development Banks. Vol. 1: The African Development Bank.* Boulder, CO: Rienner, 1996.

Evans, Peter. *Dependent Development: The Alliance of Multinational, State, and Local Capital in Brazil.* Princeton, NJ: Princeton University Press, 1979.

Gold, Thomas B. *State and Society in the Taiwan Miracle.* Armonk, NY: M. E. Sharpe, 1986.

Gran, Guy. *Development by People: Citizen Construction of a Just World.* New York: Praeger, 1983.

Griesgraber, Jo Marie, and Bernhard G. Gunter, eds. *The World Bank: Lending on a Global Scale.* London: Pluto Press, 1996.

Haggard, Stephan. *Pathways from the Periphery: The Politics of Growth in the Newly Industrializing Countries.* Ithaca, NY: Cornell University Press, 1990.

———. *Developing Nations and the Politics of Global Integration.* Washington, DC: Brookings Institution, 1995.

———. *The Political Economy of the Asian Financial Crisis.* Washington, DC: Institute for International Economics, August 2000.

Haggard, Stephan, and Andrew MacIntyre. "The Political Economy of the Asian Economic Crisis." *Review of International Political Economy* 5-3 (Autumn 1998): 381–392.

Handelman, Howard. *The Challenge of Third World Development.* Upper Saddle River, NJ: Prentice-Hall, 1996.

Hardt, John P., and Richard F. Kaufman, eds. *East-Central European Economies in Transition.* Armonk, NY: M. E. Sharpe, for the Joint Economic Committee, U.S. Congress, 1995.

Hatch, Walter, and Kozo Yamamura. *Asia in Japan's Embrace: Building a Regional Production Alliance.* Cambridge, UK: Cambridge University Press, 1996.

Hira, Anil. *Ideas and Economic Policy in Latin America: Regional, National, and Organizational Case Studies.* Westport, CT: Praeger, 1998.

Hsiung, James. C., et al., eds. *Contemporary Republic of China: The Taiwan Experience 1950–1980.* New York: Praeger, 1981.

Hughes, Helen, ed. *Achieving Industrialization in East Asia.* Cambridge, UK Cambridge University Press, 1988.

Johnson, Chalmers. *MITI and the Japanese Miracle: The Growth of Industrial Policy, 1925–1975.* Stanford, CA: Stanford University Press, 1982.

Kappagoda, Nihal. *The Multilateral Development Banks. Vol. 2: The Asian Development Bank.* Boulder, CO: Rienner, 1995.

Krasner, Stephen D. *Structural Conflict: The Third World Against Global Liberalism.* Berkeley, CA: University of California Press, 1985.

Krueger, Anne O. *Trade Policies and Developing Nations.* Washington, DC: Brookings Institution, 1995.

Krueger, Anne O., Constantine Michalopoulos, and Vernon W. Ruttan, with Keith Jay. *Aid and Development.* Baltimore, MD: Johns Hopkins University Press, 1989.

Mason, Edward S., and Robert E. Asher. *The World Bank Since Bretton Woods.* Washington, DC: Brookings Institution, 1973.

Mason, Mike. *Development and Disorder: A History of the Third World Since 1945.* Toronto, Canada: Between the Lines, 1997.

Mehmet, Ozay. *Westernizing the Third World: The Eurocentricity of Economic Development Theories.* London: Routledge, 1995.

Mittelman, James H., and Mustapha Kamal Pasha. *Out from Underdevelopment Revisited: Changing Global Structures and the Remaking of the Third World.* London: Macmillan, 2nd edition, 1997.

Mosley, Paul, Jane Harrigan, and John Toye. *Aid and Power: The World Bank and Policy-based Lending,* vol. 1. London: Routledge, 1991.

Otero, Gerardo, ed. *Neoliberalism Revisited: Economic Restructuring and Mexico's Political Future.* Boulder, CO: Westview Press, 1996.

Payer, Cheryl. *The World Bank: A Critical Analysis.* New York: Monthly Review Press, 1982.

Pereira, Luiz Carlos Bresser. "Development Economics and the World Bank's Identity Crisis." *Review of International Political Economy* 2-2 (Spring 1995): 211–247.

Prebisch, Raúl. *The Economic Development of Latin America and Its Principal Problems.* New York: United Nations Economic Commission for Latin America, 1950.

———. *Towards a Dynamic Development Policy for Latin America.* New York: United Nations, 1963.

Pye, Lucian W., with Mary W. Pye. *Asian Power and Politics: The Cultural Dimensions of Authority.* Cambridge, MA: Belknap Press, 1985.

Rapley, John. *Understanding Development: Theory and Practice.* Boulder, CO: Rienner, 1996

Reynolds, Lloyd G. *Economic Growth in the Third World, 1850–1980.* New Haven, CT: Yale University Press, 1985.

Schuurman, Frans J. *Beyond the Impasse: New Direction in Development Theory.* London: Zed Books, 1993.

Schydlowsky, Daniel M., ed. *Structural Adjustment: Retrospect and Prospect.* Westport, CT: Praeger, 1995.

Sen, Gita, and Caren Grown. *Development, Crises, and Alternative Visions: Third World Women's Perspectives.* New York: Monthly Review, 1987.

Shonfield, Andrew. *The Attack on World Poverty.* New York: Random House, 1960.

Singer, H. W. "The Distribution of Gains Between Investing and Borrowing Countries." *American Economic Review* 40-2 (May 1950): 473–485.

Stiglitz, Joseph E., and Shahid Yusuf, eds. *Rethinking the East Asian Miracle.* Oxford, UK: Oxford University Press and the World Bank, 2001.

Thomas-Eneagwali, Gloria, ed. *Women Pay the Price: Structural Adjustment in Africa and the Caribbean.* Trenton, NJ: Africa World Press, 1995.

Tussie, Diana. *The Multilateral Development Banks. Vol. 4: The Inter-American Development Bank.* Boulder, CO: Rienner, 1995.

Wade, Robert. *Governing the Market: Economic Theory and the Role of Government in East Asian Industrialization.* Princeton, NJ: Princeton University Press, 1990.

———. "Japan, the World Bank, and the Art of Paradigm Maintenance: The East Asian Miracle in Political Perspective." *New Left Review* 217 (May/June 1996): 3–36.

White, John. *Pledged to Development: A Study of International Consortia and the Strategy of Aid.* London: Overseas Development Institute, 1967.

Wood, Robert E. *From Marshall Plan to Debt Crisis: Foreign Aid and Development Choices in the World Economy.* Berkeley, CA: University of California Press, 1986.

World Bank. *Sub-Saharan Africa: From Crisis to Sustainable Growth,* a Long-Term Perspective Study. Washington, DC: World Bank, 1989.

————. *The East Asian Miracle: Economic Growth and Public Policy.* Policy Research Report. Oxford, UK: Oxford University Press, 1993.

XVI. Documentary Sources

A number of international and regional organizations and national government agencies provide valuable information and data on issues related to international political economy. Below is a selected list of some useful sources from international organizations. (Unless a date is mentioned, most of these sources are serial publications.)

International Finance Corporation (IFC)
   Annual Reports
   Articles of Agreement

International Monetary Fund (IMF)
   Annual Reports
   Articles of Agreement
   Balance of Payments Statistics Yearbook
   Direction of Trade Statistics
   Finance and Development Journal
   Government Finance Statistics Yearbook
   International Financial Statistics
   IMF Survey newsletter
   IMF Working Papers
   IMF Papers on Policy Analysis and Assessment
   Summary Proceedings of the Board of Governors
   World Economic Outlook (a survey of global economic developments)

Multilateral Investment Guarantee Agency (MIGA)
   Annual Reports
   Convention Establishing the MIGA

Organization for Economic Cooperation and Development (OECD)
   Development Co-operation: Efforts and Policies of the Members of the Development Assistance Committee
   Economic Surveys
   Financing and External Debt of Developing Countries (was called *External Debt of Developing Countries* until 1984)
   International Direct Investment Statistics Yearbook
   Main Economic Indicators: Sources and Methods
   Twenty-five Years of Development Co-operation: A Review—1985 Report

United Nations Centre on Transnational Corporations (no longer exists)
   Transnational Corporations
   Transnational Corporations in World Development: Trends and Prospects, 1988
   The United Nations Code of Conduct on Transnational Corporations, 1986

United Nations Conference on Trade and Development
    Bilateral Investment Treaties in the Mid-1990s. New York and Geneva: United Nations, 1998.
    Handbook of International Trade and Development Statistics
    International Monetary and Financial Issues for the 1990s
    Report of the Trade and Development Board
    The Least Developed Countries—Annual Report
    Trade and Development Report
    Transnational Corporations
    UNCTAD Bulletin
    UNCTAD Review
    World Investment Report

United Nations Department for Economic and Social Information and Policy Analysis
    International Trade Statistics Yearbook
    Monthly Bulletin of Statistics
    World Economic and Social Survey (*World Economic Survey* before 1995)

United Nations Development Program
    Human Development Report

United Nations Industrial Development Organization (UNIDO)
    Industry and Development: Global Report

World Bank
    Annual Reports
    Annual World Bank Conference on Development Economics
    Articles of Agreement
    Summary Proceedings of the Board of Governors
    World Debt Tables
    World Development Report

World Trade Organization (WTO) and General Agreement on Tariffs and Trade (GATT)
    Basic Instruments and Selected Documents
    GATT Activities
    GATT Focus newsletter
    WTO Focus newsletter
    International Trade: Trends and Statistics
    Results of the Uruguay Round of Multilateral Trade Negotiations: The Legal Texts
    Text of the General Agreement on Tariffs and Trade
    Texts of the Tokyo Round Agreements
    Trade Policy Reviews
    WTO Annual Reports
    WTO Press Releases

I N D E X